B×T
W9-BTE-751

The Year's Work in English Studies

VOLUME 58

1977

Edited by
JAMES REDMOND

and

LAUREL BRAKE
DAVID DANIELL
ROBIN ROBBINS
A. V. C. SCHMIDT
(associate editors)

Published for

THE ENGLISH ASSOCIATION
by
JOHN MURRAY ALBEMARLE STREET LONDON

Wingate College Library

© The English Association 1979

Typeset by Reproduction Drawings Ltd, Sutton, Surrey
Printed in Great Britain by
Redwood Burn Limited
Trowbridge and Esher
0 7195 3724 X

083309

Preface

It may help the user of this work to remember that books are sometimes published a year later in the U.S.A. than they are in the U.K. (and vice versa), that the year of publication is not always that which appears on the title-page of the book, and that the inevitable omissions of one year are made good in the next; thus the search for a notice of a book or article may have to extend to the volume after the expected one and sometimes to that which precedes it. Reports of important omissions will earn our gratitude.

Offprints of articles are always welcomed, and editors of journals that are not easily available in the U.K. are urged to join the many who already send us complete sets. These should be addressed to The Editor, *The Year's Work in English Studies,* The English Association, 1, Priory Gardens, Bedford Park, London W4 ITT. We are grateful to the authors and publishers who have made our task easier by supplying books and articles for volume 58. The editors of the *M.L.A. International Bibliography, Anglo-Saxon England, The Chaucer Review, English Language Notes, Philological Quarterly,* and *Restoration and Eighteenth Century Theatre Research* have put us deeply in their debt by providing advance proofs of their bibliographies. In drawing the reader's attention at the beginning of chapters to the main bibliographical aids, we presuppose in each case a reference to the *M.L.A. International Bibliography,* and to the *Annual Bibliography of English Language and Literature* published by the Modern Humanities Research Association.

James Redmond
Westfield College
London University*

*For the academic year 1979–80, at Dept. of English, University of California, Riverside, Calif. 92521, U.S.A.

Abbreviations

ABC	*American Book Collector*
ABELL	*Annual Bibliography of English Language and Literature*
ABR	*American Benedictine Review*
AEB	*Analytical and Enumerative Bibliography*
AI	*American Imago*
AKML	*Abhandlungen zur Kunst-, Musik-, und Literaturwissenschaft*
AL	*American Literature*
ALASH	*Acta Linguistica Academiae Scientiarum Hungaricae*
AN	*Acta Neophilologica*
AMon	*Atlantic Monthly*
AnL	*Anthropological Linguistics*
AnM	*Annuale Medievale*
AN&Q	*American Notes and Queries*
AQ	*American Quarterly*
AR	*Antioch Review*
Archiv	*Archiv für das Studium der Neueren Sprachen und Literaturen*
ArchL	*Archivum Linguisticum*
ArielE	*Ariel: A Review of International English Literature*
ArL	*Archivum Linguisticum*
ArlQ	*Arlington Quarterly*
ArP	*Aryan Path*
ArQ	*Arizona Quarterly*
A.R.S.	Augustan Reprint Society
AS	*American Speech*
ASch	*American Scholar*
ASE	*Anglo-Saxon England*
ASoc	*Arts in Society*
ASPR	*Anglo-Saxon Poetic Records*
ATQ	*American Transcendental Quarterly: Journal of New England Writers*
AUMLA	*Journal of Australasian U. Language and Literature Ass.*
AUPG	American University Publishers Group Ltd.
AWR	*The Anglo-Welsh Review*
BAASB	*British Association for American Studies Bulletin*
BB	*Bulletin of Bibliography*
BBSIA	*Bulletin Bibliographique de la Société Internationale Arthurienne*
BC	*Book Collector*
BDEC	*Bulletin of the Department of English* (Calcutta)
BFLS	*Bulletin de la Faculté des Lettres de Strasbourg*
BGDSL	*Beiträge zur Geschichte der deutschen Sprache?*
BHR	*Bibliothèque d'Humanisme et Renaissance*

BI	*Books at Iowa*
BJA	*British Journal of Aesthetics*
BJDC	*British Journal of Disorders of Communication*
BJR	*Bulletin des Jeunes Romanistes*
BJRL	*Bulletin of the John Rylands Library*
BLJ	*British Library Journal*
BLR	*Bodleian Library Record*
B.M.	British Museum
BMQ	*British Museum Quarterly*
BNL	*Blake Newsletter*
BNYPL	*Bulletin of the New York Public Library*
BP	*Banasthali Patrika*
BRMMLA	*Bulletin of the Rocky Mountain Modern Language Association*
BS	*Blake Studies*
BSE	*Brno Studies in English*
BSLP	*Bulletin de la Société de Linguistique de Paris*
BSNotes	*Browning Society Notes*
BST	*Brontë Society Transactions*
BSUF	*Ball State University Forum*
BuR	*Bucknell Review*
CahiersE	*Cahiers Élisabéthains*
C&L	*Christianity and Literature*
Carrell	*The Carrell: Journal of the Friends of the Univ. of Miami Library*
C.B.E.L.	*Cambridge Bibliography of English Literature*
CE	*College English*
CEA	*CEA Critic*
CEAAN	*Center for Editions of American Authors Newsletter*
CentR	*The Centennial Review*
CERVE	*Cahiers d'Études et de Recherches Victoriennes et Edouardiennes*
ChauR	*The Chaucer Review*
ChiR	*Chicago Review*
ChLB	*Charles Lamb Bulletin*
CHum	*Computers and the Humanities*
CJ	*Classical Journal*
CJIS	*Canadian Journal of Irish Studies*
CJL	*Canadian Journal of Linguistics*
CLAJ	*College Language Association Journal*
CLC	*Columbia Library Columns*
ClioW	*Clio: An Interdisciplinary Journal*
CLJ	*Cornell Library Journal*
CLQ	*Colby Library Quarterly*
CLS	*Comparative Literature Studies*
C&M	*Classica et Medievalia*
ColF	*Columbia Forum*
CollG	*Colloquia Germanica*
CollL	*College Literature*
ColQ	*Colorado Quarterly*
CompD	*Comparative Drama*

CompL	*Comparative Literature*
ConL	*Contemporary Literature*
ConnR	*Connecticut Review*
ContempR	*Contemporary Review*
CP	*Concerning Poetry*
CQ	*The Cambridge Quarterly*
CR	*The Critical Review*
Crit	*Critique: Studies in Modern Fiction*
CritI	*Critical Inquiry*
Critique	*Critique* (Paris)
CritQ	*Critical Quarterly*
CSHVB	*Computer Studies in the Humanities and Verbal Behavior*
CSR	*Christian Scholar's Review*
C.U.P.	Cambridge University Press
D.A.	*Dictionary of Americanisms*
D.A.E.	*Dictionary of American English*
DAI	*Dissertation Abstracts International*
DHLR	*The D.H. Lawrence Review*
DiS	*Dickens Studies*
DM	*The Dublin Magazine*
D.N.B.	*Dictionary of National Biography*
DownR	*Downside Review*
DQR	*Dutch Quarterly Review*
DR	*Dalhousie Review*
DramS	*Drama Survey* (Minneapolis)
DSN	*Dickens Studies Newsletter*
DubR	*Dublin Review*
DUJ	*Durham University Journal*
DVLG	*Deutsche Vierteljahrsschrift für Literaturwissenschaft und Geistesgeschichte*
EA	*Études Anglaises*
EAL	*Early American Literature*
E&S	*Essays and Studies*
ECLife	*Eighteenth-Century Life*
ECS	*Eighteenth-Century Studies*
EDH	*Essays by Divers Hands*
E.E.T.S.	Early English Text Society
EHR	*English Historical Review*
EI	*Études Irlandaises (Lille)*
EIC	*Essays in Criticism*
EJ	*English Journal*
ELangT	*English Language Teaching*
ELH	*Journal of English Literary History*
ELN	*English Language Notes*
ELR	*English Literary Renaissance*
ELT	*English Literature in Transition*
ELWIU	*Essays in Literature* (Western Illinois U.)
EM	*English Miscellany*
E.P.N.S.	English Place-Name Society
EPS	*English Philological Studies*
ES	*English Studies*

ESA	*English Studies in Africa*
ESC	*English Studies in Canada*
ESQ	*Emerson Society Quarterly*
ESRS	*Emporia State Research Studies*
ETJ	*Educational Theatre Journal*
EWN	*Evelyn Waugh Newsletter*
Expl	*Explicator*
FCEMN	*Fourteenth-Century English Mystics Newsletter*
FDS	Fountainwell Drama Series
FH	*Frankfurter Hefte*
FLang	*Foundations of Language*
FMLS	*Forum of Modern Language Studies*
ForumH	*Forum* (Houston)
GaR	*Georgia Review*
GL	*General Linguistics*
GR	*Germanic Review*
GRM	*Germanisch-romanische Monatsschrift*
HAB	*Humanities Association Bulletin*
HAR	*Humanities Association Review*
HC	*The Hollins Critic*
HJ	*Hibbert Journal*
HLB	*Harvard Library Bulletin*
HLQ	*Huntington Library Quarterly*
HOPE	*History of Political Economy*
HQ	*Hopkins Quarterly*
HRB	*Hopkins Research Bulletin*
HSE	*Hungarian Studies in English*
HSL	*Hartford Studies in Literature*
HTR	*Harvard Theological Review*
HudR	*Hudson Review*
IJES	*Indian Journal of English Studies*
IJSL	*International Journal of the Sociology of Language*
IndL	*Indian Literature*
IowaR	*Iowa Review*
IRAL	*International Review of Applied Linguistics*
IShav	*Independent Shavian*
IUR	*Irish University Review*
JA	*Jahrbuch für Amerikastudien*
JAAC	*Journal of Aesthetics and Art Criticism*
JAF	*Journal of American Folklore*
JAmS	*Journal of American Studies*
JBS	*Journal of British Studies*
JChL	*Journal of Child Language*
JCSA	*Journal of the Catch Society of America*
JEGP	*Journal of English and Germanic Philology*
JFI	*Journal of the Folklore Institute*
JGE	*Journal of General Education*
JHI	*Journal of the History of Ideas*
JIL	*Journal of Irish Literature*

JJQ	James Joyce Quarterly
JL	Journal of Linguistics
JML	Journal of Modern Literature
JMRS	Journal of Medieval and Renaissance Studies
JNT	Journal of Narrative Technique
JRUL	Journal of the Rutgers University Library
JVLB	Journal of Verbal Learning and Verbal Behavior
JWCI	Journal of the Warburg and Courtauld Institutes
JWMS	Journal of the William Morris Society
KanQ	Kansas Quarterly
KN	Kwartalnik Neofilologiczny (Warsaw)
KR	Kenyon Review
KSJ	Keats-Shelley Journal
KSMB	Keats-Shelley Memorial Bulletin
L&H	Literature and History
L&P	Literature and Psychology
L&S	Language and Speech
Lang&S	Language and Style
LanM	Les Langues Modernes
LaS	Louisiana Studies
LB	Leuvense Bijdragen
LC	Library Chronicle
LCP	Library Chronicle (U. of Pennsylvania)
LCUT	Library Chronicle of the University of Texas
LeedsSE	Leeds Studies in English
Lg	Language
LHR	Lock Haven Review
LHY	Literary Half-Yearly
Lib	Library
LMag	London Magazine
LWU	Literatur in Wissenschaft und Unterricht
MÆ	Medium Ævum
McNR	McNeese Review
M&H	Medievalia et Humanistica
M&L	Music and Letters
MarkhamR	Markham Review
MASJ	Midcontinent American Studies Journal
MBL	Modern British Literature
MD	Modern Drama
M.E.D.	Middle English Dictionary
MFS	Modern Fiction Studies
MHRev	Malahat Review
MichA	Michigan Academician
MiltonN	Milton Newsletter
MiltonQ	Milton Quarterly
MiltonS	Milton Studies
MinnR	Minnesota Review
MissQ	Mississippi Quarterly
M.L.A.	Modern Language Association of America

MLJ	*Modern Language Journal*
MLN	*Modern Language Notes*
MLQ	*Modern Language Quarterly*
MLR	*Modern Language Review*
MLS	*Modern Language Studies* (a publication of the Northeast Modern Language Association)
ModA	*Modern Age*
ModSp	*Moderne Sprachen*
MP	*Modern Philology*
MQ	*Midwest Quarterly*
MQR	*Michigan Quarterly Review*
MR	*Massachusetts Review*
MS	*Mediaeval Studies*
MSE	*Massachusetts Studies in English*
MSpr	*Moderna Språk*
MW	*The Muslim World* (Hartford, Conn.)
NA	*Nuova Antologia*
N&Q	*Notes and Queries*
NCF	*Nineteenth-Century Fiction*
NCTR	*Nineteenth Century Theatre Research*
NDQ	*North Dakota Quarterly*
NegroD	*Negro Digest*
NEQ	*New England Quarterly*
NH	*Northern History*
NL	*Nouvelles Littéraires*
NLB	*Newberry Library Bulletin*
NLH	*New Literary History*
NM	*Neuphilologische Mitteilungen*
NMAL	*Notes on Modern American Literature*
NMQ	*New Mexico Quarterly*
NMS	*Nottingham Medieval Studies*
Novel	*Novel: A Forum on Fiction*
NRF	*Nouvelle Revue Française*
NS	*Die Neuren Sprachen*
N.T.	New Testament
NTM	*New Theatre Magazine*
NWR	*Northwest Review*
NYH	*New York History*
N.Y.P.L.	New York Public Library
OB	*Ord och Bild*
OBSP	*Oxford Bibliographical Society Proceedings*
O.E.D.	*Oxford English Dictionary*
OEN	*Old English Newsletter*
OL	*Orbis Litterarum*
OR	*Oxford Review*
O.T.	Old Testament
O.U.P.	Oxford University Press
OUR	*Ohio University Review*
PAAS	*Proceedings of the American Antiquarian Society*

PAPA	*Publications of the Arkansas Philological Association*
PAPS	*Proceedings of the American Philosophical Society*
PBA	*Proceedings of the British Academy*
PBSA	*Papers of the Bibliographical Society of America*
PCLAC	*Proceedings of the California Linguistics Association Conference*
PCP	*Pacific Coast Philology*
P.E.N.	Poets, playwrights, editors, essayists, novelists
PLL	*Papers on Language and Literature*
PLPLS	*Proceedings of the Leeds Philosophical and Literary Society*
PMLA	*[Publications of the Modern Language Association of America]*
PN	*Poe Newsletter*
PP	*Philologica Pragensia*
PQ	*Philological Quarterly*
PR	*Partisan Review*
PRMCLS	*Papers from the Regional Meeting of the Chicago Linguistics Society*
P.R.O.	Public Record Office
PTL	*PTL: A Journal for Descriptive Poetics and Theory*
PULC	*Princeton University Library Chronicle*
QJS	*Quarterly Journal of Speech*
QQ	*Queen's Quarterly*
QR	*Quarterly Review*
RECTR	*Restoration and Eighteenth-Century Theatre Research*
REEDN	*Records of Early English Drama Newsletter*
RenD	*Renaissance Drama*
RenP	*Renaissance Papers*
RenQ	*Renaissance Quarterly*
Ren&Ref	*Renaissance and Reformation*
RES	*Review of English Studies*
RHL	*Revue d'Histoire Littéraire de la France*
RHT	*Revue d'Histoire du Théâtre*
RLC	*Revue de Littérature Comparee*
RLMC	*Rivista di Letterature Moderne e Comparate*
RLV	*Revue des Langues Vivantes*
RMS	*Renaissance and Modern Studies*
RN	*Renaissance News*
RORD	*Research Opportunities in Renaissance Drama*
RQ	*Riverside Quarterly*
RRDS	Regents Renaissance Drama Series
RRestDS	Regents Restoration Drama Series
RS	*Research Studies*
R.S.L.	Royal Society of Literature
RUO	*Revue de l'Université d'Ottawa*
SAB	*South Atlantic Bulletin*
SAQ	*South Atlantic Quarterly*
SatR	*Saturday Review*
SB	*Studies in Bibliography*

SBC	*Studies in Browning and His Circle*
SBHT	*Studies in Burke and His Time*
SBL	*Studies in Black Literature*
SCB	*South Central Bulletin*
SCN	*Seventeenth-Century News*
SCR	*South Carolina Review*
SDR	*South Dakota Review*
SED	*Survey of English Dialects*
SEL	*Studies in English Literature 1500–1900* (Rice University)
SELit	*Studies in English Literature* (Japan)
SF&R	Scholars' Facsimiles and Reprints
SFQ	*Southern Folklore Quarterly*
SH	*Studia Hibernica* (Dublin)
ShakS	*Shakespeare Studies* (Tennessee)
ShawR	*Shaw Review*
ShN	*Shakespeare Newsletter*
SHR	*Southern Humanities Review*
ShS	*Shakespeare Survey*
ShStud	*Shakespeare Studies* (Tokyo)
SIR	*Studies in Romanticism*
SJH	*Shakespeare-Jahrbuch* (Heidelberg)
SJW	*Shakespeare-Jahrbuch* (Weimar)
SL	*Studia Linguistica*
SLitI	*Studies in the Literary Imagination*
SLJ	*Southern Literary Journal*
SM	*Speech Monographs*
SMC	*Studies in Medieval Culture*
SN	*Studia Neophilologica*
SNL	*Satire Newsletter*
SNNTS	*Studies in the Novel* (North Texas State U.)
SoQ	*The Southern Quarterly*
SoR	*Southern Review* (Louisiana)
SoRA	*Southern Review* (Adelaide)
SP	*Studies in Philology*
SQ	*Shakespeare Quarterly*
SR	*Sewanee Review*
SRen	*Studies in the Renaissance*
SRO	*Shakespearean Research Opportunities*
SSF	*Studies in Short Fiction*
SSL	*Studies in Scottish Literature*
SSMP	*Stockholm Studies in Modern Philology*
S.T.C.	*Short-Title Catalogue*
SWR	*Southwest Review*
TC	*The Twentieth Century*
TCBS	*Transactions of the Cambridge Bibliographical Society*
TCL	*Twentieth Century Literature*
TDR	*The Drama Review*
TEAS	Twayne's English Authors Series
ThQ	*Theatre Quarterly*
ThRI	*Theatre Research International*
ThS	*Theatre Survey*

THY	*The Thomas Hardy Yearbook*
TkR	*Tamkang Review*
TLS	*Times Literary Supplement*
TN	*Theatre Notebook*
TP	*Terzo Programma*
TPS	*Transactions of the Philological Society*
TQ	*Texas Quarterly*
TRB	*Tennyson Research Bulletin*
TriQ	*Tri-Quarterly*
TSE	*Tulane Studies in English*
TSL	*Tennessee Studies in Literature*
TSLL	*Texas Studies in Literature and Language*
TUSAS	Twayne's United States Authors Series
TWC	*The Wordsworth Circle*
TYDS	*Transactions of the Yorkshire Dialect Society*
UCTSE	*University of Cape Town Studies in English*
UDQ	*University of Denver Quarterly*
UES	*Unisa English Studies*
UMSE	*University of Mississippi Studies in English*
UR	*University Review* (Kansas City)
URev	*University Review* (Dublin)
USSE	*University of Saga Studies in English*
UTQ	*University of Toronto Quarterly*
UWR	*University of Windsor Review*
VN	*Victorian Newsletter*
VP	*Victorian Poetry*
VPN	*Victorian Periodicals Newsletter*
VQR	*Virginia Quarterly Review*
VS	*Victorian Studies*
VSB	*Victorian Studies Bulletin*
VWQ	*Virginia Woolf Quarterly*
WAL	*Western American Literature*
WascanaR	*Wascana Review*
WCR	*West Coast Review*
WF	*Western Folklore*
WHR	*Western Humanities Review*
WLT	*World Literature Today* (Formerly *Books Abroad*)
WSCL	*Wisconsin Studies in Contemporary Literature*
WTW	Writers and their Work
WVUPP	*West Virginia University Bulletin: Philological Papers*
WWR	*Walt Whitman Review*
XUS	*Xavier University Studies*
YES	*Yearbook of English Studies*
YPL	*York Papers in Linguistics*
YR	*Yale Review*
YULG	*Yale University Library Gazette*
YW	*The Year's Work in English Studies*
ZAA	*Zeitschrift für Anglistik und Amerikanistik*
ZCP	*Zeitschrift für Celtische Philologie*
ZDL	*Zeitschrift für Dialektologie und Linguistik*

Contents

Note: Notices of books published in German, identified by the
initials H.C.C., have been contributed by H. C. Castein Dr.phil.
Lecturer in Modern Languages in the University of London
(Goldsmiths' College)

Literary History and Criticism: General Works

T. S. DORSCH

1. Reference Works

J. A. Cuddon's *Dictionary of Literary Terms*[1] is probably the most complete work of its kind that has appeared. It defines some thousands of terms, not merely those in regular use in European literary criticism, but a great many as well that relate specifically to non-European languages and literatures. Many terms require only a four- or five-line description, but the more important forms and genres are given several pages, which usually include a history of their development. There is much quotation or close reference. This is a very useful work.

Another helpful reference work, in a different field of interest, is *Who's Who in the Theatre,* of which the sixteenth edition now appears[2], following a gap of five years since the previous edition was published. This stout volume prints playbills from 1971 to 1975 for the theatres of London, New York, Stratford-upon-Avon, Chichester, and Stratford, Ontario. These are followed by the long biographical section of nearly 1000 pages outlining the careers of leading figures of the English-speaking stage—actors, actresses, designers, playwrights, directors, and producers. The final sections list such interesting subsidiary items as long runs (headed by *The Mousetrap*), the working dimensions of London theatres, names in previous editions, and deaths in the world of the theatre over the past five years. The book will be of special value to theatre-historians; but it contains much that will be of interest to other readers of *YW*.

From a group of German scholars, led by Heinz Kosok and Horst Priessnitz, comes a collection of papers on the literature in English produced in a number of countries other than England[3]. Five papers are devoted to various aspects of American literature. Australia, Canada, New Zealand, India, the West Indies, and 'black' Africa are other countries whose literatures are treated, and Irish and 'Anglo-Scottish' literature is also included. Necessarily within the scope of a single volume of no great length, only surveys of these various literatures can be provided. Chinua Achebe and Wole Soyinka, for example, are given about three pages

---

[1] *A Dictionary of Literary Terms*, compiled by J. A. Cuddon. André Deutsch. pp. xii + 745. £11.50.
[2] *Who's Who in the Theatre: A Biographical Record of the Contemporary Stage,* ed. by Ian Herbert, with Christine Baxter and Robert E. Finley. Sixteenth edition. London: Pitman, and Detroit: Gale Research. pp. xxvi + 1389. $50.
[3] *Literaturen in englischer Sprache: Ein Überblick über englischsprachige Nationalliteraturen ausserhalb Englands,* ed. Heinz Kosok and Horst Priessnitz. Bonn: Bouvier Verlag Herbert Grundmann. pp. v + 261. DM 48.

between them, and Patrick White fares even worse. However, as a mere outline the volume has its value for those who read German. It is a pity that it has no index.

The Oxford Literary Guide to the British Isles[4], edited by Dorothy Eagle and Hilary Carnell, is a book which will give a great deal of pleasure to a great many readers. It is divided into two main sections. The first and larger is an alphabetical register of place-names, from Abberley, known to Dryden, Addison, and Pope, to Zennor, the home for a couple of years during the first world war of D. H. Lawrence and his wife Frieda. No doubt many borderline decisions had to be taken, and perhaps every reader will find some omissions; nevertheless the compilers have been very thorough in their search for places of even comparatively minor literary interest: Levens Hall, where Mrs. Humphry Ward wrote Helbeck of Bannisdale, Seaham Hall, the home of Byron's wife Anne Isabella Milbanke, Uppingham School, at which Norman Douglas, James Elroy Flecker, and Ronald Firbank were educated—the list could be greatly prolonged. Much space is naturally devoted to London, the Lake District, and other places with numerous literary associations. The second section of the volume lists several hundred authors, together with the localities with which they were at various times connected. Cross-reference between the two sections yields much fascinating matter about the lives of English authors.

The nature of The English Association Handbook of Societies and Collections[5], edited by Alicia C. Percival, is to some degree indicated by its title. The aim of this useful work is to list and describe 'the many societies and associations, national and local, which are concerned with the study and creation of English literature and with the English language, and major libraries and book collections, publicly and privately owned, which specialise in any aspect of these subjects'. It includes much helpful information about the activities of the various societies and qualifications for membership, and about the scope of the special libraries and access to them. There are nearly 400 entries, and the book provides some agreeable browsing as well as practical help.

2. Collections of Essays

This year's volume of Essays and Studies[6], collected by W. Moelwyn Merchant, departs somewhat from the normal pattern in that several of the papers are not purely 'literary', but aim at showing that literary insights may be intensified 'by invoking the methods and techniques of other disciplines'. Thus in 'Heroes, Heroism and Heroic Literature' Michael Swanton illustrates ways in which our understanding of the literature of the European Heroic Age may be deepened, not only by reassessment of critical documentary sources, but also by calling in aid such cognate

---

[4] The Oxford Literary Guide to the British Isles, compiled and ed. by Dorothy Eagle and Hilary Carnell. O.U.P. pp. xiv + 416 + 13 pp. maps. £3.95.

[5] The English Association Handbook of Societies and Collections, ed. by Alicia C. Percival. The Library Assn. for the English Assn. pp. xii + 139.

[6] Essays and Studies 1977, N. S. Vol. 31. Collected for the English Assn. by W. Moelwyn Merchant. John Murray. pp. viii + 109. $4.

disciplines as archaeology, philology, and the history of ideas. In '"That Shakespeherian Rag"' Terence Hawkes exemplifies Shakespeare's technique of inviting his audience to 'note' certain 'oral, non-discursive, *performed* dimensions of the play that lie beyond the words'. Terence Spencer writes interestingly on Shakespeare's use of Julio Romano's name as that of the sculptor who executed the supposed statue of Hermione in *The Winter's Tale*. Eluned Brown, in 'Henry Vaughan's Biblical Landscape', sets out to show that the Bible 'is not only the starting-point for many of Vaughan's lesser poems, but also shapes in a profound way many of the major ones'. G. Ingli James puts forward the view that Blake's mixed media often proved a mixed blessing, as for example in his illustrated edition of Gray, 'whose two components pull in opposite directions'. Josef Herman writes of ways in which literature can awaken the creative energies of the painter. Mike Weaver brings out the interest of the film versions of Poe's *The Fall of the House of Usher* made by Jean Epstein (1928) and James Sibley Watson (1929) as examples of early avant-garde film. Christopher Fry contributes a note on 'Theatre and History'. 'In the theatre history means people rather than events. What they do is less important than what they feel and suffer while doing it.' Richard Luckett describes some twentieth-century writings which owe much of their inspiration to Renaissance music. Finally, in 'Criticism and the Religious Prospect' Nathan A. Scott, Jr, makes a case for the study of theology as part of the equipment of the literary critic.

In *Contemporary Approaches to English Studies*[7] Hilda Schiff brings together a number of papers delivered at an English Association symposium. The volume opens with George Steiner's 'Why English?', in which Steiner, drawing attention to the world-wide diffusion of the English language and of literature in English written in many countries, urges that the contents of English syllabuses in our schools and universities should be extended and strengthened. Raymond Williams, ranging over the work of a number of critics from Matthew Arnold to the present day, discusses ways in which we should study the place of literature in the society which produces it. The title of Leon Edel's paper is 'The Poetics of Biography'. In an entertaining dialogue on the steps of the British Museum between 'Plutarchus', 'Poeticus', and 'Criticus', Edel, rejecting a number of current literary 'ideologies', asserts strong claims for a central place for subjectivity in the interpretation of literature. The main purpose of Jonathan Culler's paper is to demonstrate that a structuralist approach to literature 'is directly relevant to the practical study and teaching of literature'. In 'Tragedy and Moral Education' Christopher Butler sets out to show 'how literature in general and tragedy in particular have profound moral effects, provided we accept that literature throws light on the way we see the world and the beliefs we entertain about it'. In the final paper Terry Eagleton argues that the Marxist literary critics provide 'a truly dialectical criticism, conscious of its historical roots and relations, and so capable of interrogating the limits of other critical methods which substitute their own *synthetic* totalities. . . for the founding totality of history itself'.

[7]*Contemporary Approaches to English Studies*, ed. by Hilda Schiff. London: Heinemann, for the English Assn. N.Y.: Barnes & Noble. pp. vi + 105. £3.80.

The Literature of Fact[8] is a collection of papers from the English Institute. The opening paper, 'History and Myth in the Bible', is by Northrop Frye. Frye believes that the Bible speaks the 'primary language' of literature, yet Biblical scholars have on the whole failed to see it as a literary work; but 'no book could have had the Bible's literary influence without itself possessing a literary form, however many other things it may also possess'. In 'The Fictions of Factual Representation' Hayden White argues, with special reference to *The Origin of Species*, that historical discourse and narrative must always to some degree rely for their effect on the preponderance in them of particular figures of speech—in Darwin's case the figure of metonymy. Victor Turner, writing as an anthropologist, provides a comparative analysis of certain central African rituals of affliction and 'the highly sophisticated literary mixture of myth and history constituted by the *Purgatorio* of Dante'. In 'The Fact of Beatrice in *The Vita Nuova*' Jerome Mazzaro relates Dante's work to that of other 'autobiographic poets' such as Petrarch, Sidney, and Wordsworth. David Hackett Fischer urges historians to write what he calls a 'braided narrative', one which develops new forms of narration and new techniques of characterisation for the presentation of his leading figures, and which 'refines' the fact-finding apparatus of scholarship. In a paper entitled 'On Repetition' Edward W. Said draws a distinction 'between history as the narrative of essentially biological descent ("filiation") and history as the narrative of non-natural descent ("affiliation")'. This he does with analysis of the historical myth of the paternity of Louis Napoleon.

3. Forms, Genres, Themes

This year has produced fewer books than usual on poetic theory and poetic techniques. Among the more ambitious comes Harold Bloom's *Poetry and Repression*[9]. Bloom takes exception to a number of current approaches to the criticism of poetry—among others to Freudian interpretations, to the 'deconstructions' of Jacques Derrida and Paul de Man, to the American New Criticism, to a variety of structuralist and archetypal critical systems. In their stead he places a close analysis of poems 'not just as linguistic entities, but as intentions of their shapers' will to power—power over history, over other poems, and over the poets' own selves'. Blake, Wordsworth, Shelley, Keats, Tennyson, Browning, Yeats, Emerson, Whitman, and Wallace Stevens are the poets to whom he devotes most of his attention; he aims at showing how poetic tradition 'emerges from the process of revisionism and canon-formation'. Bloom's book is disfigured by its all too frequent use of a characteristically American critical jargon. (Of Tennyson's *Mariana*: 'The catachresis here is the hothouse-forcing of the crisis-situation, since it would be difficult to imagine a more extreme state of self-consciousness than the one that Mariana so dialectically enjoys.') However, it is possible to draw from it some insights which might lead to a closer understanding of Romantic poetry.

[8] *The Literature of Fact: Selected Papers from the English Institute*, ed. with a Foreword by Angus Fletcher. New York: Columbia U. P., 1976. pp. xxviii + 172. $10.60.
[9] *Poetry and Repression: Revisionism from Blake to Stevens*, by Harold Bloom. New Haven, Conn: Yale U. P. pp. viii + 293. $11.95, £7.20.

In a volume entitled *Homer to Brecht*[10], Michael Seidel and Edward Mendelson have gathered together sixteen essays devoted to the study of the European epic and dramatic traditions. Of special interest in the epic section are James Nohrnberg's papers on the *Iliad* and the *Inferno;* but Traugott Lawler and Maria DiBattista also contribute sensible discussions, on the *Æneid* and *Don Quixote* respectively. There are sound papers also in the dramatic section. Perhaps the most helpful way of indicating the scope of the volume is a listing of its subjects that have not hitherto been mentioned. Michael Holahan provides a paper on the *Oresteia;* Paul H. Fry on *Oedipus the King* and *Phaedra;* Charles Balestri on *The Bacchae;* Clifford Earl Ramsey on *A Midsummer Night's Dream;* Mark Rose on *Hamlet;* Maria DiBattista on *The Misanthrope;* Fred J. Nichols on *Faust;* Walter Reed on *The Cherry Orchard* and *Hedda Gabler;* and Edward Mendelson on *The Caucasian Chalk Circle* and *Endgame.* The volume as a whole is a helpful addition to the criticism of the fields of literature that it covers.

For some four decades Dame Muriel Bradbrook has held a leading place among critics of European drama, particularly Elizabethan drama. Now ten of her Cambridge colleagues have joined forces to produce in her honour a volume entitled *English Drama*[11]. Richard Axton shows how powerfully the Tudor interludes were influenced by mediaeval folk drama; he goes on to demonstrate in some detail that the author of *Calisto and Melebea* was guided by native traditions in this adaptation of the Spanish novel *La Celestina.* Marie Axton argues, with copious illustration, that Tudor masques for the most part incorporated political matter, differing in this respect from the flattering Jacobean masques. In 'Comic Form in Ben Jonson' Leo Salingar brings out the extent of Jonson's interest in alchemy. Alchemy, he suggests, is the latent theme of *Volpone,* and he shows how this theme is here adapted to the comic techniques of Aristophanes and Lucian. Anne Barton discusses the decline of the history play during the Stuart period, and brings out relationships between Ford's *Perkin Warbeck* and other post-Shakespearian plays about heroic pretenders. Mary Ann Radzinowicz analyses *Samson Agonistes,* and shows how Milton's treatment of his hero results in '"medicinable tragedy", a psycho-aesthetic theory of tragedy made functional in one of the great tragic poems of our culture'. In 'Exotick but Rational Entertainments' Richard Luckett describes the origins and development of English 'dramatic opera', differentiating it from the Italian lyrical opera which eventually superseded it. Howard Erskine-Hill offers a study of John Gay's drama; he emphasises its wealth of dramatic experiment, and draws comparisons between it and the drama both of the seventeenth and of the twentieth centuries. Gillian Beer writes on 'uses of theatre' in the Victorian novel, drawing her examples from, among others, Dickens and Charlotte Brontë. In 'Waiting for Prospero' John Northam makes a case for regarding *The Tempest* as a 'touchstone' for such modern playwrights as Strindberg, Ibsen, and Beckett. Raymond Williams describes the composition of English theatre audiences in the nineteenth century, and notes their preference for

[10] *Homer to Brecht: The European Epic and Dramatic Traditions,* ed. by Michael Seidel and Edward Mendelson. New Haven, Conn: Yale U. P. pp. viii + 352. $17.50.
[11] *English Drama: Forms and Development. Essays in Honour of Muriel Clara Bradbrook,* ed. by Marie Axton and Raymond Williams, C.U.P. pp x + 263. £7.50.

traditional English forms of drama. The volume closes with a list, compiled by Patricia Rignold, of Dame Muriel's numerous publications.

A playwright intends his words to be spoken and acted, but many people read plays, whether because they cannot attend performances, or for other reasons. In *How to Read a Play*[12] Ronald Hayman sets out to show the reader how he may, by careful reading, see through the written word to the playwright's intentions. He must learn to use an inner eye and an inner ear, to translate stage directions into the appropriate actions, to interpret characters without the help of players—in a word, to provide for himself everything that is provided for him in the theatre. Hayman illustrates his book with helpful analyses of passages from a number of plays.

First published in 1972, *The Uses of Drama* is now made available as a paperback[13]. Readers of *YW* may wish to be reminded that this volume, edited by John Hodgson, is an anthology of passages on various aspects of drama from writers ranging in time from Aristotle to the present day, and including both scholars and men of the theatre. It covers such things as the purpose and nature of drama, the 'elements' of drama, the value of drama in education, and the search for a new drama in the theatre.

Michael Black's *Poetic Drama as Mirror of the Will*[14] is in the main a study of English and French drama, with a glance also at the Spanish theatre. The greater part of the book is devoted to poetic drama in Renaissance England, with Shakespeare as the central figure, and in 'classical' France, where Racine is given the fullest treatment. The two differ greatly. The English drama is essentially popular, the French is not. Both, however, 'give direct access to the inner nature, the will or basic self, of the main characters', as Black illustrates in analyses of such plays as *Othello* and *Phèdre*. He goes on to discuss attempts to revive poetic drama in the Romantic period, and gives reasons for their failure in competition with opera and the novel.

From Richard Bjornson comes an extremely interesting book on *The Picaresque Hero in European Fiction*[15]. This is both a comprehensive historical survey of the genre and an excellent work of criticism which analyses in some detail the most important Spanish, French, German, and English works in the tradition, touching also upon a number of less well-known novels and upon some translations. The picaresque novel was brought to birth in the anonymous *Lazarillo de Tormes,* and reached its golden age in Spain in the late sixteenth and the seventeenth centuries with such works as Mateo Alemán's *Guzman de Alfarache* and Francisco de Quevedo's *El Buscon*. The best example in Germany is Hans von Grimmelshausen's *Simplicissimus* (1668), and in France Alain René Lesage's *Gil Blas;* from English examples Bjornson selects Defoe's *Moll Flanders* and Smollett's *Roderick Random*. He brings out inter-relationships between these novels, and subjects them to judicious criticism. It is hoped that he will continue the work that he has begun in this admirable book.

[12] *How to Read a Play,* by Ronald Hayman. Eyre Methuen. pp. 96. £3.50, pb £1.50.

[13] *The Uses of Drama: Acting as a Social and Educational Force.* An anthology ed. by John Hodgson. Eyre Methuen. pp. 223. pb £2.25.

[14] *Poetic Drama as Mirror of the Will,* by Michael Black. Vision. pp. 199. £5.40.

[15] *The Picaresque Hero in European Fiction,* by Richard Bjornson. Wisconsin U. P. pp. x + 308. $10.50.

Working in the same field, Harry Sieber has written for the Critical Idiom series a short book entitled *The Picaresque*[16]. In so slim a volume Sieber cannot deal at length with individual novels, but he covers, often of necessity only in summary, more ground than Bjornson, dealing with the *picaro* as he appears in America as well as in Europe, and coming down to the twentieth century. This book is an intelligent and helpful brief treatment of a large subject.

Alan Shelston contributes to the same series a volume entitled *Biography*[17]. Though confined, like Sieber, to an outline study, he manages to bring out the essential qualities of, for example, Plutarch, or of the founders of English biography, as we understand the term today—George Cavendish and William Roper, the chroniclers of the lives respectively of Cardinal Wolsey and Sir Thomas More. He goes on to trace the course of English biography down to present times. His book ought, perhaps, to have borne the title *English Biography*, for, apart from Plutarch, he cannot find room for any but English biographers; but his work on these deserves to be commended.

Sir Victor Pritchett's Presidential Address to the English Association, *Autobiography*[18], provides, as one would expect, some sensible and lively comments on the autobiographical writings of such figures as St Augustine, Benvenuto Cellini, John Bunyan, Boswell, and Gibbon. Sir Victor glances also at some less well-known authors, and then turns to one of 'the minor sinners', himself, whose chief aim in his writings about his family and himself 'was to stop memory sliding into respectable consistency'. No great depth can be expected in a short address, but Sir Victor is always readable, and always worth reading for his views on literature.

Victor E. Neuburg's book, *Popular Literature*[19], covers, as its title no doubt suggests, a very wide field of reading matter. At its simplest popular literature 'can be defined as what the unsophisticated reader has chosen for pleasure', whatever his social background; but of course Neuburg spreads his net more widely than such a definition might imply. He begins with the introduction of printing into England, which led to the publication of many ballads and broadsides, and comes down to the end of the nineteenth century, when the circulation of such journals as *Pearson's Weekly* reached figures well beyond a million. He pays regard also to the readers for whom literature of this kind was written and the publishers by whom it was disseminated. This is an interesting book which contributes judiciously to the study of a not insignificant area of English writing. It is well illustrated.

That strange creature the incubus, and his female counterpart the succubus, have a long ancestry in literature. In his book *The Incubus in English Literature*[20], Nicolas Kiessling traces the existence of such a

---

[16] *The Picaresque*, by Harry Sieber. Methuen. (The Critical Idiom) pp. viii + 85. £2.35, pb £1.20.
   [17] *Biography*, by Alan Shelston. Methuen. (The Critical Idiom) pp. x + 82. £2.35, pb £1.20.
   [18] *Autobiography*, by V. S. Pritchett. The English Association. pp. 10.
   [19] *Popular Literature: A History and a Guide*. From the beginning of printing to the year 1897. By Victor E. Neuburg. Harmondsworth: Penguin Books. pp. 302. pb £1.25.
   [20] *The Incubus in English Literature: Provenance and Progeny*, by Nicolas Kiessling. Seattle: Washington State U. P. pp. vii + 104. $6.

creature in Herodotus, and the widespread belief in antiquity in lustful incubi is suggested by the large number of names coined for them. Kiessling is chiefly interested in their appearance in English literature from mediaeval times, through the Elizabethan period (they are frequently used in Elizabethan drama), down to the preoccupation of the Romantic poets with demon lovers, and, more recently the writings of Yeats. Kiessling's book will interest students both of literature and of folklore.

In *The Language of Adam*[21] Russell Fraser explores mankind's 'enduring desire to overcome linguistic barriers and so to make a more nearly homogeneous society'. Men search for a language in which a word carries a single meaning without the possibility of confusion. Fraser considers the influence of such philosophers as Plato, Aristotle, St Thomas Aquinas, St Augustine, and Duns Scotus; with a very wide range of reference, especially to writers of the sixteenth and seventeenth centuries, in particular Bacon, he demonstrates the belief that was widely diffused in those centuries that a universal or common language could be brought into being. The modern science of linguistics, Fraser suggests, takes its rise from the realisation of past centuries that such beliefs were illusionary.

4. Bibliographical Studies

This year's volume of *Studies in Bibliography*[22] opens with a paper, by G. Thomas Tanselle, on 'Descriptive Bibliography and Library Cataloguing'. Tanselle brings out clearly the differences between the two processes, but they are both parts of a larger undertaking, and 'anything which produces greater communication between bibliographers and cataloguers is a move in the right direction'. John S. O'Connor carries further his work on the Shakespeare First Folio compositors in 'A Qualitative Analysis of Compositors C and D in the Shakespeare First Folio'. William P. Williams sets out, in 'Chetwin, Crooke, and the Jonson Folios', to clear up some of the muddle and confusion surrounding the publication of the 1640 folio edition of Ben Jonson's *Works*. Isobel Grundy marshals much new information about the *Verses Addressed to the Imitator of the First Satire of the Second Book of Horace* (1733), an attack on Pope made by Lord Hervey and Lady Mary Wortley Montague. In 'The Dating of the Two *Hyperions*' Leonidas M. Jones among other things adds fresh support to the argument that Keats wrote the Induction to *The Fall of Hyperion* in September and October 1817. From his study of some 170 *incunabula* printed in Florence, A. J. Dunston is able to identify some sets of Venetian woodcut capitals used by a number of printers of the period. R. H. Miller provides information about the composition and the text of Sir John Harington's *A Supplie or Addicion to the Catalogue of Bishops, to the Yeare 1608*. Nicholas Temperley furnishes a probable identification of the 'Middleburg Psalms', to which reference is frequently made in the seventeenth century, in a volume of metrical and prose psalms printed at Middleburg in 1600.

[21] *The Language of Adam: On the Limits and Systems of Discourse*, by Russell Fraser. New York: Columbia U. P. pp. xvi + 288. $8.75.

[22] *Studies in Bibliography: Papers of the Bibliographical Society of the University of Virginia*, Vol. 30. Ed. by Fredson Bowers. Charlottesville: Virginia U. P. pp. iv + 283. $20.

This volume contains also the following shorter papers: 'Marginal Rules as Evidence', by Ernest W. Sullivan II; 'New Texts of Marvell's Satires', by A. S. G. Edwards and R. M. Schuler; 'The Text of Colley Cibber's *The Double Gallant*', by John W. Bruton; 'The Motives of Puffing: John Newbery's Advertisements, 1742-1767', by John Dawson Carl Buck; 'The Writing and Printing of Joseph Warton's *Essay on Pope*', by David Fairer; 'A Compositional History of the *Biographia Literaria*', by Daniel Mark Fogel; 'Printer's Copy for Part of Volume Seven of the W. B. Yeats *Collected Works in Verse and Prose* (1908)', by J. R. Mulryne; 'Robert Frost's "Kitty Hawk"', by John St. C. Crane; 'Graham Green's Second Thoughts: The Text of *The Heart of the Matter*', by David Leon Higdon; 'Towards a New Chronology for the Dramatic Eclogues of Juan del Encina', by Henry W. Sullivan; and 'Additions and Corrections to the Second Edition of Donald Wing's *Short-Title Catalogue*', by Clinton Sisson and Jeri S. Smith.

The one important disadvantage of Pollard and Redgrave's *Short-title Catalogue* is that room could not be found in it for a title index, and this disadvantage is shared by Donald Wing's *Short-Title Catalogue*, which carries on the work of Pollard and Redgrave by listing books printed in England from 1641 to 1700. Last year a tribute was paid in this chapter of *YW* to A. F. Allison and V. F. Goldsmith for their production of the first volume of a work which fills the gap left by Pollard and Redgrave. An equally warm welcome must now be given to the second (and final) volume, by the same authors, *Titles of English Books. . . 1641-1700*[23], which does the same for Wing. This volume lists the short-titles, and many sub-titles, of English books, wherever printed, and of foreign books printed in England, which appeared in the period covered by Wing. It supplies also the name of the author, the pseudonym, or the initials under which they are listed by Wing. The only books excluded are those of unknown authorship and those which come under official and class headings.

Anthony Petti's *English Literary Hands from Chaucer to Dryden*[24] will be of great interest to all students of the earlier periods of English literature, and of especial interest to palaeographers. Petti opens with general sections on such matters as the survival of mediaeval and Renaissance manuscripts, the materials on which and with the help of which they were produced, and the terminology and the techniques of early English writing. He goes on to describe and analyse more than two dozen scripts which were used at various times in the period covered by his study, from Roman cursive and Roman uncial down to the English round hand of the second half of the seventeenth century. After introductory matter of these and other kinds, he reproduces in photo-facsimile examples of the handwriting of about fifty English writers—Chaucer (?), Spenser, Shakespeare, Ben Jonson, Donne, Milton, and Dryden among them—supplies versions

[23] *Titles of English Books (And of Foreign Books Printed in England): An Alphabetical Finding-List by Title of Books Published under the Author's Name, Pseudonym, or Inititals*. Vol. II, 1641-1700. By A. F. Allison and V. F. Goldsmith. Dawson. pp. iv + 318. £17.

[24] *English Literary Hands from Chaucer to Dryden*, by Anthony G. Petti. Arnold. pp x + 133. £14.50.

of them in print, and analyses them with careful notes. This is a fine work of scholarship, and it also provides agreeable reading.

A number of librarians have contributed to the preparation of *National Library and Information Services*[25], which aims at providing guidance for those who are responsible for the planning of such services. Every aspect of the planning is covered: policy and financial control, manpower, buildings, costs and revenues, the classification and cataloguing of books and papers, abstracting and indexing services—all the numerous factors which must be taken into account when a new library is to be built or an old one adapted to modern circumstances.

George Jefferson's *Library Co-operation* was first published in 1946. Since then many important developments have taken place in his field, some of them resulting from the Local Government Act and the British Library Act, both of 1972. The computer and the microfilm have also come to play a very significant part in the storage and transfer of information. In his new edition[26] Jefferson has incorporated a great deal of new information which takes cognisance of all the innovations of recent years, and which illustrates the ever-increasing need for international co-operation and for planning ahead.

From Robert B. White, Jr, comes an annotated bibliography entitled *The English Literary Journal to 1900*[27]. A great part of the book consists of a list of English literary journals, and where a title is not self-explanatory a brief description is supplied. Two further sections cover persons and places concerned with such journals; for authors whose contributions form only a minor part of their literary activities (Swift, or Coleridge, or Dickens), only their relationship to literary periodicals is considered relevant to the bibliography. There is extensive cross-reference, and there are four helpful indexes.

5. Translations and Anthologies

Of the translations that have appeared during the year, perhaps the most interesting is the version of Petrarch's *Africa*[28] produced by Thomas G. Bergin and Alice S. Wilson. In this comparatively little-known poem Petrarch aimed at reviving the classical epic for his own times. Moreover, rejecting mediaeval notions of history as fantasy, and of literature as something essentially didactic, he strove to recreate true historical events and figures. The poem, written in Latin, has as its hero Scipio Africanus the Elder, and celebrates his victory over Hannibal in the Second Punic War. The translation, in blank verse, has moments of flatness, but on the whole it runs easily, and the modern reader can gain from it some sense of the grandeur of Petrarch's design and of his skill in establishing character and situation. The translators have provided an interesting introduction and helpful annotations.

[25] *National Library and Information Services: A Handbook for Planners,* ed. by C. V. Penna, D. J. Foskett, and P. H. Sewell. Butterworth. pp. xxiv + 231. £8.

[26] *Library Co-operation,* by George Jefferson. André Deutsch. pp. 189. £4.95.

[27] *The English Literary Journal to 1900: A Guide to Information Scources,* by Robert B. White, Jr. Detroit: Gale Research Co. pp. xiv + 311. $18.

[28] *Petrarch's 'Africa',* translated and annotated by Thomas G. Bergin and Alice S. Wilson. New Haven, Conn: Yale U. P. pp. xxii + 289. £12.60.

With the publication of the eighth and final volume of the Oxford Ibsen[29] J. W. McFarlane has brought to completion his monumental task of producing translations of all the plays of Ibsen. He has himself been responsible for most of the translations, and has written all the critical introductions and commentaries. The present volume contains *Little Eyolf, John Gabriel Borkman,* and *When We Dead Awaken.* The translations are no less readable than those that have appeared in the earlier volumes, and once again McFarlane has provided an introduction which discusses the plays interestingly in the context of Ibsen's dramatic output as a whole and in the light of modern scholarship.

The latest addition to the Oxford Books of Verse is *The Oxford Book of Welsh Verse in English*[30], which has been collected by Gwyn Jones, and which supplants Thomas Parry's *Oxford Book of Welsh Verse* of 1962. Jones has aimed at covering the whole span of Welsh verse, from that of Taliesin in the sixth century, here translated by Anthony Conran, down to that of Gwyn Thomas, who was born in 1936. In all there are 238 poems, and the authors represented include poets of the standing of George Herbert, Henry Vaughan, Christopher Smart, and Wilfred Owen, to choose a few almost at random. Jones introduces the volume with an interesting historical survey.

In *The Faber Book of Epigrams and Epitaphs*[31] Geoffrey Grigson has brought together more than 700 short poems in English which conform to one or other of the generally accepted definitions of the term epigram— either a very short poem with a witty or satirical sting in the tail, or a eulogistic poem of up to twenty lines or so, such as some of the epigrams of Martial (who also, of course, excelled in satirical epigram), or Milton's fine 'Epitaph on the Admirable Dramatic Poet, W. Shakespeare'. Both types are well represented in this collection. The reader will not be greatly helped by the naming or quotation of particular examples; he may be assured that he will find all his favourites here, together probably with many dozens of verses that are new to him. He can hardly fail to enjoy the volume.

[29] The Oxford Ibsen, Vol. VIII: *Little Eyolf, John Gabriel Borkman, When We Dead Awaken,* ed. and translated by John Walter McFarlane. O.U.P. pp. xiv + 390. £10.50.

[30] *The Oxford Book of Welsh Verse in English,* chosen by Gwyn Jones. O.U.P. pp. xxxviii + 313. £3.95.

[31] *The Faber Book of Epigrams and Epitaphs,* ed. with an introduction by Geoffrey Grigson. Faber. pp. xii + 291. £6.95, pb £2.95.

II

English Language

RICHARD M. HOGG and MARY BRENNAN

This chapter is divided into two. The first section, by Richard Hogg, deals with historical studies, including the history of linguistics, and all lexicographical material, whether historical or not, as well as linguistic studies bearing upon the literary use of English. In the second section, Mary Brennan deals with descriptive studies, general bibliographical material, and publications in cognate fields of enquiry relevant to the English scholar.

Section I

(a) *Introductory*

Some of the areas covered in this section are very clearly in a healthy condition, as can be seen by the continuing flow of material on onomastics and the history of linguistics, together with a lively burst of interest in stylistics. Nevertheless there must be some concern over the paucity of new work on syntax and, to a lesser extent, phonology. Particularly disturbing is the lack of new work being published on the Middle English period.

In the present economic circumstances where, as Barbara Strang pointed out last year, it is becoming more and more difficult to gain access to what is known to exist, and where in some particular areas it is difficult even to know what exists, the availability of useful bibliographical material is becoming ever more essential. Therefore a new bibliography by Markey, Kyes and Roberge[1] of materials on the origin and development of Germanic and its dialects is especially to be welcomed. This bibliography is valuably comprehensive, with 8298 separate entries, and even more useful is the inclusion of both an *Index Verborum* and a Subject Index. The latter is impressively detailed and the work as a whole is a most welcome research tool. The same publisher has also issued a bibliography on analogy, edited by Anttila and Brewer[2]. This, however, is a rather less useful work, containing only just over 400 entries and being without the useful indexes of its companion volume. It may best be viewed as a supplement to the monograph by Anttila discussed in (b) below.

---

[1] *Germanic and its Dialects: A Grammar of Proto-Germanic. III: Bibliography and Indices*, ed. by T. L. Markey, R. L. Kyes and P. T. Roberge. Amsterdam: John Benjamins. pp. xlviii + 504. £26.
[2] *Analogy: a Basic Bibliography*, ed. by Raimo Anttila and W. A. Brewer. Amsterdam: John Benjamins. pp. xiv + 50.

For a general indication of the amount of work being done in the fields of Old and Middle English, we may turn as usual to the annual research in progress lists in *NM*. Rather encouragingly, this year Carl T. Berkhout, in 'Old English Research in Progress 1976–1977' (Vol. 78, pp. 268–276) is able to report six items under *Language Studies* and four items under *Word Studies*, half of these ten being dissertations. On the other hand, it is quite disconcerting to find that R. H. Robbins has nothing at all to report in 'Middle English Research in Progress 1976–1977' (Vol. 78, pp. 277–279) and that Thomas A. Kirkby can report only two articles, under *Prosody and Language*, in 'Chaucer Research in Progress 1976–1977' (Vol. 78, pp. 280–286). Admittedly, these compilers must rely on researchers to keep them informed of work in progress, but these figures do reinforce the impression that work on Middle English language is in a perilously weak condition. As an indication of the rather restricted nature of these research lists, it is instructive to compare the bibliography of materials published on Old English language in *ASE*, which is also compiled by Carl T. Berkhout ('Bibliography for 1976, §2. Old English Language' *ASE*, Vol. 6, pp. 271-276), where there are 100 entries, supplemented by many entries in other sections. Perhaps the current enthusiasm for O'd English will overflow into the later periods of the language.

In what follows the material is divided under the following heads: (b) general; (c) phonology/orthography; (d) syntax/morphology; (e) vocabulary; (f) onomastics; (g) stylistics; (h) history of linguistics. Within each division general works come first, followed by chronologically restricted works in historical sequence.

(b) *General*

This year I have not noticed any useful introductions to the history of the language for the general reader, but it is perhaps appropriate to mention here a new edition of Harold B. Allen's *Linguistics and English Language*, which I have seen reported[3]. Presumably Theodora Bynon's *Historical Linguistics*[4], in the Cambridge Textbooks in Linguistics series, is intended for the undergraduate specialist or postgraduate, but it is a textbook which it is difficult to recommend whole-heartedly. In the first part of the book Dr Bynon examines the status of neogrammarian, structuralist and transformationalist theories of language change, and in the second part she discusses problems of language contact, leaning heavily on the work of sociolinguists such as Labov. As a textbook it suffers from an over-concentration on theory at the expense of a full consideration of practical problems (such as internal reconstruction), which the student will have to look at elsewhere, but which need to be understood first of all. Theory is fine, as long as one has a clear idea about the topic on which one is theorising. There is, too, an air of uncertainty about some of the English examples which Dr Bynon discusses. A collection of papers by J. Peter Maher[5] unfortunately cloaks what appears to be a trenchant attack on

---

[3] *Linguistics and English Language*, Second Edition, by Harold B. Allen. Arlington Heights, Ill.: Goldentree Bibliographies.
[4] *Historical Linguistics*, by Theodora Bynon. Cambridge Textbooks in Linguistics. Cambridge: C.U.P. pp. x + 301. £12.50, pb £4.50.
[5] *Papers on Language Theory and History*, by J. Peter Maher. Amsterdam: John Benjamins. pp. xx + 171. £12.80.

Wingate College Library

generative theories of language change in almost impenetrable language. A similar approach is to be found in Raimo Anttila's monograph on analogy[6], where the style of argument is likely to alienate even the most sympathetic reader.

Three interesting collections of papers have appeared during the year. Robert Di Pietro and Edward Blansitt have edited the proceedings of the third *LACUS* Forum[7], which is fast approaching the status of an annual periodical. Included in this collection are papers by Bolinger, Jankowsky, Markey, Pike, Householder and Toon, some of which I refer to in more detail in the appropriate divisions below. Paul J. Hopper has edited a *Festschrift* for Winfred P. Lehmann[8], and below I refer to papers in this collection by Moulton and Malkiel. Makkai, Makkai and Heilmann edit a collection of papers stemming from the International Congress at Bologna in 1972[9]. The most interesting papers for the anglicist here are those by Labov, Lockwood and McIntosh, and again these are discussed separately below. New to me at least are the *Proceedings* of the California Linguistics Association Conference[10], which appear largely to contain papers by graduate students.

Among individual articles on general topics we should note E. Seebold's plea for a greater use of internal reconstruction in any consideration of language change ('Internal Reconstruction of Proto-Languages', *TPS* 1976–77, pp. 51–65) and also L. M. Davis's 'Dialectology and Linguistics' (*Orbis*, Vol. 26, pp. 24–30).

It is not every day that a new Old English manuscript is found. The paper by Bella Schauman and Angus Cameron ('A Newly-Found Leaf of Old English from Louvain', *Anglia*, Vol. 95, pp. 298–312) is especially interesting in that the manuscript presented there supplements our meagre knowledge of the Anglian dialects. A full text, translation and commentary are provided. A paper by Eric Stanley ('How the Elbing deprives the Vistula of its Name and converts it to the Elbing's Own Use in "Vistula-Mouth"', *NQ*, Vol. 222, pp. 2–11) is an elegant demonstration of how much can be teased out of an apparently innocuous short passage of prose by learning and scholarship. In 'Three Old English Texts' (*NM*, Vol. 78, pp. 328–338) J. L. Mitchell makes good use of a review of three recent introductory books on Old English to reflect interestingly on changing tastes and approaches in Old English scholarship.

For later periods of English by far the most important work is a new introduction to and survey of Early Modern English by Charles Barber[11]. Dr Barber pays special attention to such areas as attitudes to language and

[6] *Analogy*, by Raimo Anttila. State-of-the Art Reports, 10. The Hague: Mouton. pp. viii + 152. £10.90.

[7] *The Third LACUS Forum 1976*, ed. by Robert J. Di Pietro and Edward L. Blansitt Jr. Columbia S.C.: Hornbeam Press Inc. pp. ix + 630.

[8] *Studies in Descriptive and Historical Linguistics: Festschrift for Winfred P. Lehmann*, ed. by Paul J. Hopper. Amsterdam: John Benjamins. pp. x + 502. £28.80.

[9] *Linguistics at the Crossroads*, ed. by Adam Makkai, Valerie Becker Makkai and Luigi Heilmann. Padua/Lake Bluff, Ill.: Liviana Editrice/Jupiter Press. pp. vii + 502. L. 18000.

[10] *Sixth California Linguistics Association Conference: Proceedings* [= *PCLAC*, Vol. 6]. San Diego, Cal.: Campanile Press.

[11] *Early Modern English*, by Charles Barber. The Language Library. André Deutsch. pp. 360. £7.50.

the development of vocabulary, which are clearly of most interest to the general reader, and matters of more specialised interest, such as phonology, receive much less, although still adequate, space. The book can safely be recommended to the general reader and also to the undergraduate approaching Early Modern English for the first time, although some may be put off by the rather conservative attitudes which Dr Barber sometimes displays, most clearly reflected in the rather stiff style in which the book is written. Apart from this book, we must also take note of George B. Jack's 'The Date of *Havelok*' (*Anglia*, Vol. 95, pp. 20–33) in which he cogently argues for the regrettably negative conclusion that the available evidence does not allow us to be nearly as precise about the date of composition of the poem as has been previously suggested. Finally here, although slightly outside the range of this section, it is pleasant to report the publication of the second volume of the *Linguistic Atlas of Scotland*[12]. As well as providing a further 80 lexical maps, this volume contains an extremely useful index of words listed in the two volumes so far.

(c) *Phonology/Orthography*

The basic argument of a new work by John Anderson and Charles Jones[13] is that many apparently diverse changes in the history of English share a common 'impulse'. However true this may be, such an argument may not be quite as illuminating as the authors believe. Certainly it is disappointing to see these scholars consistently understating the often difficult but surely revealing differences between the sound changes they discuss. The book is, however, interesting for its introduction of 'dependency phonology', which is closely related to the dependency grammar which Anderson has made familiar through his several syntactic studies, and also for the two authors' discussion of syllable structure; see the report in 1976 (*YW* 57.18). For hesitant readers the two authors have conveniently supplied samples of their work in John Anderson's 'Noch einmal AE. *samcucu*' (*YPL*, Vol. 7, pp. 67–75), which is written in English, despite the (regrettable) title, and Charles Jones' 'Segment Gemination and Syllable Shape' (*YPL*, Vol. 7, pp. 47–66). If Anderson and Jones seem on occasion to pay insufficient attention to the minutiae of linguistic detail, they appear as angels beside James Foley, whose new book[14], in its idiosyncratic search for a universal phonology completely independent of phonetics, pays alarmingly little attention to the available data. Amongst the articles on general phonological topics, we may note especially a rather lengthy plea by Bo Ralph ('Rule Extension in Historical Phonology', *SL*, Vol. 30, pp. 164–191) for a more sophisticated analysis of the concept of rule simplification, and also a demonstration of the application of stratificational linguistics to an analysis of Grimm's Law by David Lockwood in 'A Stratificational Interpretation of Phonological Change' (Makkai, Makkai and Heilmann[9], pp. 301–314).

[12] *The Linguistic Atlas of Scotland*, Vol. 2, by J. Y. Mather and H. H. Speitel. Croom Helm. pp. 292.
[13] *Phonological Structure and the History of English*, by John M. Anderson and Charles Jones. North-Holland Linguistic Series, 33. Amsterdam: North-Holland Publishing Co. pp. viii + 189.
[14] *Foundations of Theoretical Phonology*, by James Foley. Cambridge Studies in Linguistics, 20. Cambridge: C.U.P. pp. xiii + 151. £7.75.

The Old English period appears to have received considerable attention from phonologists. I have not yet seen S.-S. Kim's book[15], but I hope to report on this next year, especially in the light of its South Korean provenance. In 'The Actuation and Implementation of an Old English Sound Change' (Di Pietro and Blansitt[7], pp. 614–622) Thomas E. Toon has much interesting evidence on the loss of *h* in *hn, hl, hr, hw* clusters, and Kurt Rydland's 'Old Northumbrian æw-Spellings for Original /eo/+ lwl: Scribal Error or Vowel Change? Some Evidence from Modern Northern Dialects' (*ES*, Vol. 58, pp. 289–295) is symptomatic of the increasing and welcome use of modern dialect work to further our knowledge of the earlier stages of the language. There are two papers by Richard M. Hogg on rather different topics. 'The Chronology and Status of Second Fronting' (*ArchL*, Vol. 8, pp. 70–81) resurrects the old question of the relative chronology of that sound change, whereas 'Old English *r*-Metathesis and Generative Phonology' (*JL*, Vol. 13, pp. 165–176) utilises the evidence surrounding Old English metathesis to point out some weaknesses in generative theories of sound change. The question of secondary stress in Anglo-Saxon poetry has always been a difficult one, and William G. Moulton in 'Secondary Stress in Germanic Alliterative Verse' (Hopper[8], pp. 393–404) tackles the question once more in an interesting attempt to show that such stress must have existed. Finally, although J. D. Woods in 'Gemination in Old Saxon Nouns' (*Orbis*, Vol. 26, pp. 94–111) does not deal with Old English, his article provides a useful basis for a comparison of the synchronic phonologies of the two languages.

This year the burden of carrying on research in Middle English phonology seems to have fallen exclusively on the shoulders of Gillis Kristensson — where have our native scholars gone? Kristensson's work is, nonetheless, most welcome indeed. The topic of a brief pamphlet by this scholar is the distribution of Old English /a:/ in the Lincolnshire dialects of Middle English[16]. Using the evidence of Lay Subsidy Rolls, Kristensson is able to show that the pattern of dialect isoglosses with respect to this phonological feature is closely correlated with patterns of immigration and hence, presumably, general lines of communication. The approach is closely reminiscent of Samuels' work on the rise of Standard English. In 'A Case of the Role of Functional Load' (*Anglia*, Vol. 95, pp. 450–453), Kristensson suggests that the differential unrounding of [ɸ] and [ɸ:] in some Middle English dialects may have been partly motivated by their different status within the vowel system. There is slightly more to report for the Early Modern English period. Monica Bjurman has written a workmanlike commentary to Bellot's *Le Maistre d'Escole Anglois*[17], although the reader will early notice a distinct Scandinavian bias in her discussion (but that is not to be taken as a value judgement).

William Labov's 'On the Use of the Present to Explain the Past'

---

[15] *A History of the Vowels of Early (West Saxon) Old English*, by Suk-San Kim. Seoul: Pan Korea Book Corp. pp. 272, US $4.58.

[16] *Studies on the Early 14th-Century Population of Lindsey (Lincolnshire)*, by Gillis Kristensson. *Scripta Minora Regiae Societatis Humaniorum Litterarum Lundensis*, (1976–1977), 2. Lund: CWK Gleerup.

[17] *The Phonology of Jacques Bellot's Le Maistre d'Escole Anglois (1580)*, by Monica Bjurman. Stockholm Studies in English, XL. Stockholm: Almqvist and Wiksell. pp. 166.

(Makkai, Makkai and Heilmann[9], pp. 226–261) is especially interesting in that he uses his well-known methods to investigate the '*meat – mate* problem' in English, and his comments are worthy of the attention of even the 'purest' of historical linguists. The same can hardly be said for Morris Halle's 'Tenseness, Vowel Shift and the Phonology of the Back Vowels in Modern English' (*LingI*, Vol. 8, pp. 611–625). Despite the title, Andrew L. Sihler's 'Morphologically Conditioned Sound Change and O.E. Past Participles in *-en*' (*GL*, Vol. 17, pp. 76–91) has most relevance to later periods of the language. Although the topic is inherently interesting, Sihler is unfortunately less than convincing.

On orthographical matters the most important work to note is Angus McIntosh's 'Scribal Profiles from Middle English Texts' (Makkai, Makkai and Heilmann[9], pp. 262–275), which constitutes a further plea for the necessity of investigating individual scribal practice in any detailed study of the earlier periods of the language. Joshua A. Fishman has edited a new collection of papers[18] dealing with problems in the creation of new, and revision of existing, writing systems, which is more probably of interest to the language planner or social historian than to the historical linguist, although there are some fine papers within its covers. There is, however, very little direct discussion of English, and this is partly compensated for by Axel Wijk's impassioned survey of and arguments for Modern English spelling reform[19], especially in the teaching of children to read. But a major difficulty here is that everyone, Wijk included, seems to have settled behind well-fortified defences.

(d) *Syntax/Morphology*

There has been surprisingly little work completed on syntax this year, and even what has been produced seems to fall more naturally into the class of promises rather than the class of actualities. Perhaps the most important general paper is David Lightfoot's 'Syntactic Change and the Autonomy Thesis' (*JL*, Vol. 13, pp. 191–216), in which he argues that syntactic change can proceed independently of semantic and phonetic change, all of this argument being conducted within one particular transformational theory of syntactic change. But it would be premature to judge the adequacy of Lightfoot's thesis now, since he promises a longer monograph on the topic which we look forward to. In the meantime it is to be hoped that he will correct a number of unfortunate factual errors. Despite the scarcity of new syntactic work, a further collection of papers edited by Li[20] suggests that the study of syntactic change has not yet gone out of fashion. The paper in this collection of most interest to students of the history of English will be Robert P. Stockwell's look at the ways in which Old English gradually changed from SvOV to SvVO word order ('Motivations for Exbraciation in Old English', pp. 291–314). On the other hand, Jorge Hankamer's 'Multiple Analyses' (pp. 583–607) shows, *inter alia*, the dangers of doing diachronic analysis without investigating

[18] *Advances in the Creation and Revision of Writing Systems*, ed. by Joshua A. Fishman. The Hague: Mouton. pp. xxviii + 495. £25.40.
[19] *Regularized English/Regularized Inglish*, by Axel Wijk. Stockholm: Almqvist and Wiksell. pp. 112. Sw.kr. 52.25.
[20] *Mechanisms of Syntactic Change*, ed. by Charles N. Li. Austin, Tx.: U. of Texas P. pp. xix + 620.

the history of the language concerned (you might not have believed that anyone could be so foolish). One other paper of general interest must be mentioned, for L. E. Breivik, in 'A Note on the Genesis of Existential There' (*ES*, Vol. 58, pp. 334–358), is totally convincing in a demonstration that existential *there* existed alongside locative *there* in both Old and Middle English.

It is rather distressing to report that there appear to be only four papers worthy of mention on the syntax of individual periods of the language, three of which are merely short notes and the fourth of which, Marla Yoshida's 'Syntactic Change in Old English: the Anglo-Saxon Chronicle' (*PCLAC*, Vol. 6, pp. 91–98), is decidedly anti-climactic. The only other paper on Old English is by Bruce Mitchell ('Old English *ac* as an Interrogative Particle', *NM*, Vol. 78, pp. 98–100), in which he demonstrates, by a careful sifting of the evidence, that it is most unlikely that *ac* was used as an interrogative particle in Old English. The haul from Middle English is no more encouraging. In *Luste* in *Ancrene Wisse*' (*NM*, Vol. 78, pp. 24–26) George B. Jack neatly argues that the present subjunctive of *lusten* can also be used with indicative meaning in that work, and N. F. Blake, in 'Another Northernism in *The Reeve's Tale*' (*N&Q* Vol. 222, pp. 400–401) indicates two examples of a Northern uninflected genitive which are probably original readings. These notes by Mitchell, Jack and Blake are all scholarly and convincing, but the issues are ones of minor importance.

There is very little more to report for morphology, although Stepen R. Anderson's 'On the Formal Description of Inflation' (*PRMCLS*, Vol. 13, pp. 15–44) seems to be a welcome sign that generativists have, not without some embarrassed blushes, discovered that morphology exists, although it is somewhat worrying to discover that Anderson cannot, apparently, spell the name of such a prominent morphologist as Peter Matthews correctly. On the other hand, a rather interesting paper by Ellen Broselow ('Language Change and Theories of the Lexicon', *PRMCLS*, Vol. 13, pp. 58–68), which deals with the morphology of some Old English feminine abstract nouns, still displays the generativist tendency to treat morphology as phonology (as well as an idiosyncratic use of the classification 'weak feminine'). On much more traditional lines, A. S. C. Ross complements his study of Rushworth 1, reported in *YW* 57, p. 16, with 'Notes on the Accidence of Rushworth 2' (*NM*, Vol. 78, pp. 300–308), in which he points out that the Old English gender system is much more fully preserved in Rushworth 2 than in the Lindisfarne gloss from which it was partially copied. It is a considerable jump, both chronologically and topically, to the final paper on morphological matters, which is Yakov Malkiel's 'Why Ap-*ish* but Worm-*y*?' (Hopper[8], pp. 341–364). The paper is a characteristically wide-ranging and fascinating study of the competition in English between these rival derivational affixes.

(e) *Vocabulary*

After the gap reported last year (*YW* 57.18), it is pleasant to report the publication of two further fascicles of the *Middle English Dictionary*[21],

[21] *Middle English Dictionary*, Fascicles M4 and M5, ed. by Sherman M. Kuhn. Ann Arbor, Mich.: U. of Michigan P. pp. 385–512, 513–640. £3.75 each fascicle.

namely *M4* and *M5*, which together take us as far as *molein*. As far as I can tell, however, the distribution of the *M.E.D.* in Great Britain is still rather unsatisfactory, and private subscribers at least continue to experience difficulty in obtaining timely receipt of the issues as they appear. It is overwhelmingly tempting to discern friendly rivalry between the *M.E.D.* and the *Dictionary of the Older Scottish Tongue,* and the latter keeps its hat firmly in the ring with the publication of the first part of the letter *P*, taking us as far as *Pavil(1)ion*[22]. Another publication of interest to specialists in mediaeval language will be the first fascicle of a new *Anglo-Norman Dictionary*, covering the letters *A–C*[23]. This has just arrived on my desk, so I have been unable to inspect it in detail, but it is clear that its primary aim is glossarial. Naturally, there is no new volume of the O.E.D. Second Supplement this year, but this gap in the lexicographical year is to a small extent filled by Barbara Strang's review of the second volume ('A Supplement to O.E.D.: H–N', *N&Q*, Vol. 222, pp. 388–399), which dwells usefully on matters of general lexicographical principle as well as giving a number of additions and amendments to the entries in the Supplement. There are two other works best classed as dictionaries to report this year. Firstly there is an introduction to Old English vocabulary by Stephen A. Barney[24]. Although this book is designed to help introductory students to learn Old English vocabulary, the whole purpose seems vitiated by the false assumption that such vocabulary learning is more easily done by going to a work such as this rather than by reading the actual texts. The lay-out of the book, too, is obfuscating rather than clarifying, with a much too heavy emphasis on etymology. Finally, a supercilious approach, as in the use of 'Old Anguish' for 'Old English', does nothing to endear the work to this reader at least. Secondly, James A. Ruffner has edited a reference guide to eponyms, which no doubt will find a place on some library shelves[25]. The work, however, is primarily designed for indexers, and it will be of rather less use to the anglicist.

Turning now to etymological topics, we may firstly mention two further notes by Alfred Bammesberger, the fruits, doubtless, of his projected Old English etymological dictionary. The first of these ('Two Old English Glosses', *ES*, Vol. 58, pp. 1–3) dismisses *blefla* from the vocabulary and reinterprets *unfligge* as from **-flug-ja-*. Despite the evidence he produces, I remain slightly unconvinced by the first. I have not been able to see the second paper by Bammesberger ('Zur Herkunft von AE. ondrædan und andrysne', *BGDSL*, Vol. 99, pp. 206–212). In 'Old English *lēod-*' (*ES*, Vol. 58, pp. 97–100) Eric P. Hamp addresses himself to the difficult problem of the interrelations between the various nouns formed from that base, and even if he cannot give a fully definitive answer, he clarifies the issues with his customary erudition. Finally under etymology we might note a somewhat speculative discussion by Martyn F. Wakelin

---

[22] *A Dictionary of the Older Scottish Tongue,* Part XXIX, *PA-Pavil(l)ion.* Chicago, Ill.: U. of Chicago P. pp. 245–364. £10.90.

[23] *Anglo-Norman Dictionary,* Fascicle 1: *A-Cyvere,* ed. by Louise W. Stone and William Rothwell, prepared by T. B. W. Reid. pp. xv + 1–138. The Modern Humanities Research Association.

[24] *Word-Hoard,* by Stephen A. Barney. New Haven, Conn.: Yale U. P. pp. xv + 108. £7.20, pb £2.15.

[25] *Eponyms Dictionaries Index,* ed. by James A. Ruffner. Detroit, Mich.: Gale Research Co. pp. xxx + 730. $45.

of the origin of *churm* 'churn' ('OED *churm, churming'*, *NM*, Vol. 78, pp. 386–388).

There seems little to report in the field of word-formation purely and simply, but James L. Rosier, in 'Generative Composition in *Beowulf'* (*ES*, Vol. 58, pp. 193–203), interestingly demonstrates how various methods of word-formation, but especially compounding, cluster together in *Beowulf* in order, as he says, 'to give meaning variety and order through symmetry, to create meaning'.

As last year there are a number of studies in the area of semantic interpretation. In 'The Meaning of **Motan'* (*NM*, Vol. 78, pp. 215–232) Harry Jay Solo argues that **motan* did not develop the meaning of 'necessity' until late in the Old English period and that in Old English poetry it has always the meaning of 'permission'. In making such a rigid distinction as he does between the meanings, he risks being accused of trying too hard. Unlike the situation elsewhere, Middle English comes off quite well in comparison with Old English. W. A. Davenport, in 'The Word *norne* and the Temptation of Sir Gawain' (*NM*, Vol. 78, pp. 256–263), is wholly convincing in his discussion of the various meanings of the verb *norne* in the Gawain group of poems, especially in his insistence that the central meaning of the word was 'say', 'declare' or 'reveal'. Nicholas Jacobs suggests, although not without reservation, that *Porte* may have had the sense 'Ottoman Government' in the *Morte Arthure,* despite the chronological difficulties involved ('The Ottoman *Porte* in Middle English', *N&Q*, Vol. 222, pp. 306–307). Next we find Francis P. Magoun Jr attempting a closer definition of two Chaucerian phrases in 'Two Chaucer Items' (*NM*, Vol. 78, p. 46). For the Modern English period Martin Fido takes an interesting snapshot of a semantic change in progress in 'A Note on Jane Austen's Use of *Cross'* (*ES*, Vol. 58, pp. 230–231).

Two works provide additional material (one, albeit, in a negative form) for the *Dictionary of Old English*, about which there has been no information this year. A short monograph by W. J. P. Boyd[26] has useful information and comments on 71 hard glosses in the *Lindisfarne Gospels,* while D. G. Scragg re-analyses *forhtleasness* as a compound in 'Old English *forhtleasness, unforhtleasness'* (*N&Q*, Vol. 222, pp. 399–400). A bridging-point to the supplementary material for the *O.E.D.* is supplied by Vincent DiMarco and Leslie Perelman in 'Noteworthy Lexical Evidence in the Middle English *Letter of Alexander to Aristotle'* (*Neophil*, Vol. 61, pp. 297–303), which also contains some material of a more purely Middle English relevance. Collections of supplementary material for *O.E.D.* are: Wayne H. Siek, 'Sir Thomas Wyatt: Some Additions to and Corrections of O. E. D.' (*ES*, Vol. 58, pp. 399–407); C. W. Whitworth Jr, 'Some Words in Two Thomas Lodge Romances (1591-2)' (*N&Q*, Vol. 222, p. 516). Notes on individual items are: D. S. Herrstrom, *'Commatic'* (*N&Q*, Vol. 222, pp. 307–308); R. V. Holdsworth, *'A Clean Sheet'* (*N&Q*, Vol. 222, p. 205); Jürgen Schäfer, *'Genitival'* (*N&Q*), Vol. 222,

[26] *Aldred's Marginalia:Explanatory Comments in the Lindisfarne Gospels,* by W. J. P. Boyd. Exeter Mediaeval English Texts and Studies, 4. Exeter: U. of Exeter pp. x + 62. £5.

p. 123) and 'Licebane' (*N&Q*, Vol. 222, p. 555). In these last two cases readers should note that the author is the same, although spelt differently on the second occasion by *N&Q*.

(f) *Onomastics*

Despite the somewhat pessimistic tone of Margaret Gelling's review (*N&Q*, Vol. 222, pp. 172–173) of the proceedings of the 1975 conference on personal names held at Erlangen, reported in *YW* 57.20–21, the study of onomastics has seemed in 1977 to be in a healthy condition. True, there is a heavy reliance on a small band of highly dedicated onomasticians, but the work they produce is of an impressive quality, and no one could fail to observe the lively interest which they bring to their study. Some evidence of this can be seen in the production of a newsletter-cum-periodical entitled *Nomina,* edited by Peter McClure and published by English Name Studies[27]. The first issue contains, *inter alia,* useful information on available courses in name studies, reports on work in progress, and information on recently completed theses. The second issue adds to this information as well as containing brief articles by John Field, Klaus Forster, George Broderick and Ian Fraser. A further indication of the increasing interest of and in place-name studies is to be found in the reprinting, within two years, of a collection of previously published keynote papers edited by Kenneth Cameron under the general title *Place-Name Evidence for the Anglo-Saxon Invasion and Scandinavian Settlements*[28], not previously reported in *YW*. This collection contains four papers by the editor himself, two by Margaret Gelling and one each by John McNeile Dodgson and Barrie Cox, all of which are extremely important, despite not always being easy to find, and all of which show how revolutionary a field of study the investigation of place-names has become in the last fifteen years or so. The availability of these papers in such an accessible form is greatly to be welcomed.

No new major general study has been published this year, but this gap is very clearly compensated for by the publication of a new edition of Professor Cameron's *English Place-Names*[29]. It is unfortunate that many libraries, so heavily squeezed financially, may feel that they can get along with earlier editions. But given the rapidity with which new views have entered this area, this new edition of an authoritative general survey is quite indispensable. One book on a more particular topic must be reported. This, of course, is the thoroughly welcome publication of the first volume in the *EPNS* series on the place-names of Dorset, by A. D. Mills[30]. This volume deals with the south-eastern part of the county, and we are promised a further four volumes in the complete survey of the county. It would be premature as yet, therefore, to discuss the work in any detail.

[27] *Nomina,* ed. by Peter McClure. Hull: English Name Studies. £1. for both issues.
[28] *Place-Name Evidence for the Anglo-Saxon Invasion and Scandinavian Settlements,* collected by Kenneth Cameron. Nottingham: English Place-Name Society. 1975, repr. 1977. pp. v + 171.
[29] *English Place-Names,* by Kenneth Cameron. Third Edition with supplement. Batsford. £5.95.
[30] *The Place-Names of Dorset,* Part I, by A. D. Mills. E.P.N.S., Vol. LII. pp. xxxvii + 384. £8.50.

Also of relevance here is Gillian Fellows Jensen's review (*N&Q*, Vol. 222, pp. 55–57) of Margaret Gelling's study of the place-names of Berkshire in the same series (reported in *YW* 57.21).

There are a number of articles on place-names which are of general or theoretical interest, but pride of place must unquestionably go to Kenneth Cameron's 1976 Sir Israel Gollancz Memorial Lecture to the British Academy, entitled 'The Significance of English Place-Names' (*PBA*, Vol. 62 (1976), pp. 135–155). Although very clearly a *Forschungsbericht* on place-name studies as they have developed since Hugh Smith gave a similar lecture to the British Academy twenty years previously, it is no reflection on the members of the Academy to say that this paper can be unhesitatingly recommended to any undergraduate who shows the least sign of interest in the field; rather, it is a tribute to Professor Cameron's lightness and clarity of exposition. Gillian Fellows Jensen's 'Place-Names and Settlement History: A Review' (*NH*, Vol. 13, pp. 1–26) gives a more detailed account of the same topic which is perhaps slightly less accessible to the novitiate, but compensates for this by a bibliography of recent work on place-name studies.

Of work on more individual aspects of place-name studies, the most important paper would appear to be Margaret Gelling's 'Latin Loan-Words in Old English Place-Names' (*ASE*, Vol. 6, pp. 1–13), in which she both reconsiders her earlier work on the element *wīchām* and draws our attention to other elements, most notably *camp* and *funta*, which seem to provide more evidence for some contact between the Germanic settlers and a Latin-speaking administration before the collapse of Roman rule in England. I have not been able to see a further paper by the same author entitled 'Topographical Settlement Names' (*The Local Historian*, Vol. 12, pp. 273–277). Christer Johansson has a short note re-presenting some of Ekwall's views in 'The Place-Names in a Herefordshire Charter' (*SN*, Vol. 49, pp. 185–187). A curiosity is 'Hungarian Place-Names in the United States' (Di Pietro and Blansitt[7], pp. 219–227) by Isabella H. Janda.

The study of personal names has produced rather less work this year, but we should note that a new edition of E. G. Withycombe's dictionary of Christian names has been published[31], containing about forty additional entries. Erik Tengstrand, in 'The Middle English Surname *atte Bewe*' (*SN*, Vol. 49, pp. 131–134), deals with the two difficult problems of the source of the personal name *Bewe* (suggesting a possible etymon in O.E. *bēow* 'barley') and its relationship to the place-names *Beauxfield* and *Bewsborough*.

(g) *Stylistics*

Given the amount of work on stylistics which seems to be being published at present, it is perhaps just as well that a new introduction to part of the field has been written by Roger Fowler[32]. As one has come to expect from this author, the style is clear and simple, and many readers will find this work a useful guide to the complexities of transformational

---

[31] *The Oxford Dictionary of English Christian Names*, by E. G. Withycombe. Oxford: Clarendon Press. pp. xlvii + 310. £4.50.

[32] *Linguistics and the Novel*, by Roger Fowler. Methuen. pp. xiii + 145. £4.25, pb £2.

grammar and (even more complex) text linguistics, as both theories are applied to a stylistic analysis of the novel. One's only *caveat* must be that the book is a little dull, and I doubt very much that Fowler's arguments will convert the unconvinced. On the other hand, Fowler's book will provide a gentle run-in to the much more difficult, but extremely provoking, book by Mary Louise Pratt[33]. Here Ms Pratt argues that the opposition between 'poetic' and 'ordinary' language is false and that, rather, we should construct a unified theory of discourse, applicable to all types of language use. In proposing such a theory she relies heavily on the sociolinguistic work of William Labov and the speech act theories most closely associated with John Searle. Ms Pratt's arguments against the traditional opposition of two types of language seem wholly convincing, although her own proposals seem a trifle skimpy. Nevertheless, all those seriously interested in stylistic theory will have to read and respond to this book. Another general work, edited by M. Peter, will, despite its English title[34], unfortunately be accessible only to those fluent in the Slavic languages, only two papers in the collection being in English. I have been unable to assess the relevance or interest of the remainder to anglicists, although to judge by the titles of individual papers, most would appear to be somewhat peripheral.

The relatively new periodical *PTL* is a mine of information on new developments in stylistic theory. To read all the articles therein would be a heady experience indeed, but papers by Christine Brooke-Rose ('Surface Structure in Narrative: the Squirm of the True, III', PTL, Vol. 2, pp. 517–562), John M. Lipski ('Poetic Deviance and Generative Grammars', *PTL*, Vol. 2, pp. 241–256) and Janos Petöfi ('Semantics – Pragmatics – Text Theory', *PTL*, Vol. 2, pp. 119–149) should give most readers a good general appreciation of recent developments.

Turning away from the most theoretical works, we find a most impressive bridge to particular studies in Norman Blake's *The English Language in Medieval Literature*[35], which is partly an outgrowth from his inaugural lecture at Sheffield and the article reported in *YW* 57.13. Professor Blake argues cogently that in order to understand medieval literature we must rid ourselves of our twentieth-century assumptions, especially about language, and proceed from a detailed study of mediaeval attitudes to language. The work will not be easy, but Professor Blake shows that it can be profitable. This book cannot be given to undergraduate students without their first having a solid grounding in Old and Middle English language, requiring, as it does, considerable powers of linguistic analysis and sophistication, but students beyond their first year should find this an exciting work. Another book on the language of non-contemporary literature has just arrived on my desk. This is *Graces of Harmony*, by Percy G. Adams[36].

[33] *Towards a Speech Act Theory of Literary Discourse*, by Mary Louise Pratt. Bloomington, Ind. and London: Indiana U. P. pp. xix + 236. £8.75.

[34] *The Structure and Semantics of the Literary Text*, ed. by M. Peter. Budapest: Akademiai Kiado. pp. 144. $9.

[35] *The English Language in Medieval Literature*, by Norman F. Blake. Dent. pp. 190. £7.95.

[36] *Graces of Harmony: Alliteration, Assonance and Consonance in Eighteenth-Century British Poetry*, by Percy G. Adams. Athens, Ga.: U. of Georgia P. pp. xiii + 253. $12.

I have not had time to read this work, but the blurb promises us a study of the use of 'phonal devices' such as alliteration, assonance and consonance in British poetry, especially between 1660 and 1800.

There are a number of papers on more detailed topics. In chronological order we may mention firstly Harvey Minkoff's 'An Example of Latin Influence on Ælfric's Translation Style' (*Neophil*, Vol. 61, pp. 127–142), where the author shows how painstakingly Ælfric adhered to Latin syntax in his translation of Genesis. In 'Linguistic Factors Underlying Style Levels in Four Homilies of Wulfstan' (*Neophil*, Vol. 61, pp. 287–296), Ida Masters Hollowell presents some statistical analysis of High and Low Style in Homilies II, IV, V and XX. Susan Wittig, in 'Formulaic Style in the Middle English Romances' (*NM*, Vol. 78, pp. 250–255) presents some introductory statistics which should be helpful in any reassessment of the method of composition of these poems, but much more work will need to be done, and not merely in the area of statistical analysis. Two papers on literature of the post-mediaeval period share both a community of approach and a commendably literate style. Carey McIntosh ('A Matter of Style: Stative and Dynamic Predicates', *PMLA*, Vol. 92, 110–121) analyses predicate types in four seventeenth-century plays and relates this analysis to the concept of 'nominal' and 'verbal' style, while Zelda and Julian Boyd ('To Lose the Name of Action', *PTL*, Vol. 2, pp. 21–32) consider durative and punctual descriptions of events in some poems of Tennyson.

Finally we may note two articles on metrics, both of which attempt to remove some of the more obvious crudities and rigidities of generative metrics. Of these, Paul Kiparsky's 'the Rhythmic Structure of English Verse' (LingI, Vol. 8, pp. 189–247) seems rather more successful than D. Gary Miller's 'Language Change and Poetic Options' (*Lg*, Vol. 53, pp. 21–38), although even Kiparsky's paper will seem too mechanical for many readers.

(h) *History of Linguistic Thought*

The most impressive and enjoyable work published this year in English Language studies is far from wholly linguistic. But K. M. Elisabeth Murray's biography of her grandfather, Sir James A. H. Murray, must surely be read by everyone interested in the English Language, and not merely by the specialist[37]. The book is beautifully written and the reader is drawn into the late Victorian world, enthralled and entranced. With a wealth of fascinating characters – 'Grandfather Dictionary' himself, Frederick Furnivall, Benjamin Jowett, and many, many others – this biography is as unputdownable as a Dickens novel (I well remember devouring it eagerly on Boxing Day). Not the least remarkable feature are the splendid photographs. One's only complaint must be that Miss Murray was obliged to publish it under the imprint of an American University press. Further comment on this would be superfluous.

Returning to earth, we may note a number of useful books which have been published this year. André Joly and Jean Stéfani have edited

[37] *Caught in the Web of Words: James Murray and the Oxford English Dictionary*, by K. M. Elisabeth Murray. New Haven, Conn. and London: Yale U. P. pp. xiv + 386. £6.95.

a collection of papers with the general theme of contextualising the Port Royal grammar, both in terms of its predecessors and later grammars[38]. Amongst the contributors, apart from the editors themselves, are Louis G. Kelly, Ulrich Ricken and Hans Aarsleff. All the articles are in French, some being translated from English originals. Terence H. Wilbur, in *The Lautgesetz Controversy*[39], edits a reprinting of some of the crucial papers in the controversy over the alleged exceptionless nature of sound change, including papers by Curtius, Delbrück, Brugmann, Schuchardt, Collitz and Jespersen. The papers are usefully drawn together in a long introduction by the editor. Then we find two books concerned with the English grammatical tradition. In *Sensible Words*[40] Murray Cohen is interested in the relation between English grammatical practice and the history of ideas in the seventeenth and eighteenth centuries. As such, this work will appeal to those not primarily interested in the history of linguistics as well as those whose main interest is such. The book is, however, somewhat heavy going. The same can hardly be said of a rather lightweight monograph by Glendon F. Drake[41], which provides a brief survey of prescriptivism in the United States. Despite its claim to cover the last 150 years, there is a very heavy concentration on the past two decades, with special reference to reactions to *Webster's Third New International Dictionary* and the rise to quasi-autonomous status of Black English. The book is scarcely intellectually demanding and may best be viewed as an elementary guide to some of the issues which prescriptivism raises.

In conclusion I may briefly mention three articles. In 'The European Engagement of William D. Whitney' (Di Pietro and Blansitt[7], pp. 29–38), Kurt R. Jankowsky contributes some biographical notes on the career of the famous Sanskritist. James L. Rosier, in 'A New Old English Glossary: Nowell upon Huloet' (*SN*, Vol. 49, pp. 189–194), presents some hitherto unrecognised contributions to Old English lexicography by the sixteenth-century student of Anglo-Saxon, Laurence Nowell, which demonstrates considerable fluency in historical lexicography on Nowell's part. S. W. Reid presents us with 'An Index to Robert Lowth's *Short Introduction to English Grammar*' (*SN*, Vol. 49, pp. 135–137).

Section II

Although work on many aspects of English Grammar continues to flourish, this year (unlike 1976) has not seen the publication of major works dealing solely with English. It does not seem appropriate, therefore, to treat English Grammar under a separate heading. Items relating to syntactic, semantic and phonological theory are treated, in that order, under *Linguistic Theory*. It should be noted that the English language is

[38] *La Grammaire Générale: des Modistes aux Idéologues,* ed. by André Joly and Jean Stéfani. Villeneuve-d'Ascq: Publications de l'Université de Lille III. pp. ix + 255.

[39] *The Lautgesetz Controversy: A Documentation (1885–86),* ed. by Terence H. Wilbur. Amsterdam: John Benjamins. pp. xcv + ca. 500.

[40] *Sensible Words: Linguistic Practice in England 1640–1785,* by Murray Cohen. Baltimore, Md. and London: Johns Hopkins U. P. pp. xxv + 188. £8.75.

[41] *The Role of Prescriptivism in American Linguistics, 1820–1970,* by Glendon F. Drake. Amsterdam: John Benjamins. pp. x + 130. £10.65.

closely examined in many of these works, and with a few exceptions, I have largely ignored items which focus exclusively on languages other than English. As indicated in Section I of this chapter it continues to be difficult to gain access to works which should be included in this review. In some cases there is also confusion about the precise date of publication, either due to the non-simultaneous publication of items in two countries, or to the publication of 'corrected editions' of volumes. A further major source of difficulty to the reviewer is the vast number of publications relating to English Language teaching, and, indeed, the wealth of material in Applied Linguistics generally. As in previous years, such material is largely excluded from this survey, except where individual items include original theoretical contributions. For those whose interest lies within this area, *Language Teaching and Linguistics: Abstracts*[42] contains useful material while *Language and Language Behaviour: Abstracts*[43] covers the wide field of theoretical and applied linguistics.

(a) *Linguistic Theory*

Formal Syntax[44] is an account of the proceedings of a conference on the *Formal Syntax of Natural Language* held in June 1976. The speed with which this volume has been brought to press gives some encouragement, as access to current linguistic developments has been difficult for some years. The volume is important, not only because of the eminence of the contributors, but also because it represents an effort by some of the founders of TG Grammar to provide a detailed and largely non-polemical answer to some of their critics. The short, clear, introduction focuses on what the editors call 'perhaps the most fundamental problem facing linguistic theory, namely, accounting for the possibility of language acquisition. Several of the early exponents of TG Grammar, including Ross, Chomsky and Emonds, attempted to characterise a fairly narrow class of grammars available to the language learner. The book reflects what is termed by one of the contributors 'the autonomous systems view' according to which the grammar of a language is described in terms of a number of distinct components, each of which can be described independently of the others, and each of which may make use of quite distinct types of organisation. The editors reject the criticism that such a division has not been proved by use of empirical evidence, by denying the possibility of 'proof' one way or the other. The division of grammar into components can be inferred only in complex and indirect ways from the confused mass of data of natural language. The contributors include Peter Culicover, Thomas Wasow, Adrian Akamajian, Noam Chomsky, Joan Bresnan, Emmon Bach, Barbara Hall Partee, Stephen Anderson and Ray Jackendoff. The presentation reflects that of the original conference, with formal papers followed by formal prepared comments.

Two items which belong here, and which are clearly important, have unfortunately not been available for consultation: they are *Conjectures*

---

[42] *Language Teaching and Linguistics: Abstracts.* Cambridge: C.U.P. Vol. II.

[43] *Language and Language Behaviour: Abstracts.* Cambridge: C.U.P. Vol II.

[44] *Formal Syntax: Proceedings of the MSSB-UC, Irvine Conference on the Formal Syntax of Natural Language,* ed. by Peter W. Culicover, Thomas Wasow and Adrian Akmajian. New York and London: Academic Press. pp. 500. £12.90.

and Refutations in Syntax and Semantics[45] by Michael K. Brame, and
Essays on Form and Interpretation[46] by Noam Chomsky. Both volumes
are in the North-Holland Studies in Linguistic Analysis Series edited by
Noam Chomsky, Joan Bresnan and Michael K. Brame.

This year I have discovered only one introductory work on TG
grammar. While one can acknowledge the need for clear and comprehensive accounts of this major theory, too many attempts in the past
have concentrated on old and all-too-familiar ground, and have failed to
make any genuinely new contribution to the field. There were several
exceptions last year, and these are gaining in popularity. Bent Jacobsen's
Transformational Generative Grammar[47] is, as its subtitle says, an account
of the genesis and development of TG theory. It is in part, then, a historical survey of linguistics prior to *Syntactic Structures,* with the first
section devoted to 'American Structuralism'. In the second section, 'From
Taxonomic to Generative Grammar', the author examines the new assumption incorporated in a TG approach, and these assumptions are further
discussed in the third section where TG is compared with traditional
grammar. The fourth and by far the longest section in the book (374
pages) provides a detailed account of the major transformational rules.
The final section deals with later modifications and adaptations and
includes sections on case grammar and generative semantics. This is a
sound example of its kind: for those who already have some acquaintance
with the theory the final section is rather too short and limited, but for
the genuine beginner the notes and bibliographical material at the end of
each chapter provide a helpful guide to an undoubtedly complex area. A
more general introductory work is Stockwell's *Foundations of Syntactic
Theory*[48] which despite its title also takes a closer look at semantic and
functional analyses. Much of the account reflects Stockwell's own views
on current theory, including his suggestion of the need to de-emphasise
formalism in modern linguistic theory.

Dissatisfaction with existing TG theories has led to the development
of so-called 'relational grammar'. A further volume in the *Syntax and
Semantics* series is devoted solely to papers on this topic, and is edited
by Peter Cole and Jerrold Sadock[49]. The notion of relational grammar
incorporates a number of theoretical variations. However, central to most
of these is the view that relational terms such as 'subject' and 'object' are
primitives within the system, rather than derivable from structure in the
narrow sense. The editors suggest that this notion is intuitively attractive,
accords well with the insights of traditional grammar and, more import-

[45] *Conjectures and Refutations in Syntax and Semantics,* by Michael K. Brame.
(Studies in Linguistic Analysis). Amsterdam and New York: North-Holland Pub. Co.
pp. 180. $18.95.
[46] *Essays on Form and Interpretation,* by Noam Chomsky. (Studies in Linguistic
Analysis). Amsterdam and New York: North-Holland Pub. Co. pp. 216. $13.95.
[47] *Transformational-Generative Grammar – An Introductory Survey of its Genesis
and Development,* by Bent Jacobsen. (North-Holland Linguistic Series, 17). Amsterdam and New York: North-Holland Pub. Co. pp. xv + 525. £10.
[48] *Foundations of Syntactic Theory,* by Robert P. Stockwell. (Foundations of
Modern Linguistics Series). Englewood Cliffs, N.J.: Prentice-Hall. £8.35 and £4.85.
[49] *Grammatical Relations,* ed. by Peter Cole and Jerrold M. Sadock. Syntax
and Semantics. Vol. 8. London and New York: Academic Press.

antly, allows a direct statement of cross-linguistic generalisations. Thus passivisation can be stated in terms of subject-object movements without reference to the particular word-order and morphological patterns involved in individual languages. Several papers discuss problems in the recognition and identification of the central notions of subject and object. Fillmore's chapter, 'The Case for Case Reopened' provides a most useful account of the history and development of his own theory of case grammar, and attempts to elucidate the links between the notion of deep case and grammatical relations. The author suggest that a 'saliency hierarchy' determines what gets foregrounded within a sentence, and a 'case hierarchy' determines how the foregrounded nominals are assigned grammatical function. Geoffrey Pullum's chapter 'Word-Order Universals and Grammatical Relations' suggests that our understanding of basic word-order in the languages of the world must now be revised. Pullum and other authors cite the work of Perlmutter and Postal as of inspirational importance in the development of relational grammar, and it is a matter of regret that the 1974 papers quoted in this volume remain unpublished. Illustrative material from many languages both exotic and familiar is cited, and as with other titles on the syntax and semantics series this is a well-produced and informative work.

On Case Grammar[50] discusses many of the same problems as the above volume. John Anderson provides an account of the links between his own development of case grammar and the work of Fillmore and others. The volume aims to provide a definition of the role of case and grammatical relations within grammatical theory and attempts to tackle what Anderson calls the fundamental problem in case grammar, namely identifying the empirical correlates of case relations. Despite the deceptively simple introduction this is a tightly packed and often difficult book but worthy of some effort in interpretation.

Two items which focus primarily on languages other than English are worth noting here. Andrew Radford's *Italian Syntax*[51] examines what the author sees as inadequacies in the traditional TG framework and attempts to use a relational approach to overcome these problems while Linda Waugh[52] uses French as the focus for her discussion of the nature of word-order.

A far more radical answer to the inadequacies of prevailing theories of grammar is provided in S. K. Shaumyan's *Application Grammar as a Semantic Theory of Natural Language*[53]. Shaumyan distinguishes a genotype language, which he characterises as a universal semiotic system that models semantic processes, and a phenotype grammar which provides correspondence rules connecting the genotype language and natural language. If this seems all too familiar as the deep/surface structure distinc-

[50] *On Case Grammar: Prolegomena to a Theory of Grammatical Relations*, by John Anderson. Croom Helm. pp. 313. £9.95.

[51] *Italian Syntax: Transformational and Relational Grammar*, by Andrew Radford. (Cambridge Studies in Linguistics, al). Cambridge:. C.U.P. pp. 271.

[52] *A Semantic Analysis of Word-Order*, by Linda R. Waugh. (Cornell Linguistic Contributions, 1). Leiden: E. J. Brill. pp. xii + 231.

[53] *Applicational Grammar as a Semantic Theory of Natural Language*, by S. K. Shaumyan. Edinburgh: Edinburgh U.P. pp. viii + 184.

tion and the role of transformational rules, beware! The author insists that there is no such link and that the genotype language is 'a fundamentally new concept and has no counterpart in transformational grammar'. The problem is that, left without the support of concepts from traditional and transformational grammar, the reader has to interpret the nature of the theory and concepts proposed simply from the text itself. This is not an easy task and one suspects that the fact that this is a translation is only part of the problem. If 'applicational grammar' has a future, a more gentle introduction to its theoretical basis is probably required.

While it is usual to mention here only works written in English, it is worth noting the useful 'Anglistische Arbeitschefte' series written in German, which this year produces three volumes. Konig's *Form and Funktion*[54] discusses speech act theory with particular reference to the analysis of tag questions. Rudiger Schreyer[55] provides an introduction to stratificational grammar which, although it is as old as TG, has never achieved the same popularity. This work, incidentally, must have been a nightmare to the printers in that it contains numerous extremely complex diagrams not all of which are easily understandable. A third volume[56] in this series concerns test methods, and includes chapters on testing in phonology, syntax, morphology and semantics.

This year sees the publication of two useful and important volumes on 'Discourse Analysis'. Malcolm Coulthard offers a readable and concise introduction[57] to the field. Attention is drawn to some of the major problems in establishing a theory of discourse, including the identification of units of discourse and the types of rule involved in the creation of 'coherent text'. While agreeing with other authors that everyday conversation reveals a high degree of structuring, Coulthard maintains that the descriptive categories so far put forward have not been adequately defined. The chapter on classroom interaction provides a short critique of work in this area, much of it non-linguistic in orientation; the rest of the chapter deals with the analytic model developed by the author and John Sinclair at Birmingham. The inclusion of a chapter on the acquisition of discourse reflects a growth area in child language studies. (See below, Section b). This is a useful book which should make discourse analysis accessible to a much wider range of readers: it should be particularly useful in undergraduate courses and in Colleges of Education. Teun A. van Dijk's *Text and Context*[58] is much more theoretically oriented and much more demanding. The author makes use of many concepts from formal and logical semantics and provides an explanatory chapter aimed at helping

---

[54] *Form und Funktion*, by Ekkehard König. (Anglistische Arbeitshefte, 13). Tübingen: Niemeyer. pp. 98. DM 11.80.
[55] *Stratifikationsgrammatik: Eine Einführung*, by Rudigen Schreyer. (Anglistische Arbeitshefte). Tübingen: Neimeyer. pp. 118.
[56] *Testmethoden und Linguistische Theorie*, by Wolf-Dietrich Bald. (Anglistische Arbeitshefte, 15). Tübingen: Neimeyer. pp. 105, DM 10.80.
[57] *An Introduction to Discourse Analysis*, by Malcolm Coulthard. (Applied Linguistics and Language Study Series). Longman. pp. xv + 195. £2.50.
[58] *Text and Context: Explorations in the Semantics and Pragmatics of Discourse*, by Teun A van Dijk. (Longmans Linguistics Library, 21). Longman. pp. xvii + 261.

the reader come to grips with formal semantic methodology. In the first section van Dijk argues that a semantic characterisation of discourse structure should also be given on a more global level of macro-structures, in that conditions of semantic coherence can be related to such notions as topic of conversation or topic of discourse. In Part II, 'Pragmatics', the author provides an analysis of discourse in terms of the sequencing of speech acts and the systematic relations between structures of text and context.

Van Dijk's discussion of formal semantics and pragmatics reflects the increasing work on these areas in current linguistics. The introduction of new kinds of formalism into the study of semantics has caused some difficulty in making recent semantic theories available to a wider audience. George Dillon's *Introduction to Contemporary Linguistic Semantics*[59] attempts a fairly gentle introduction to semantic theories developed over the last fifteen years. While the early chapters are fairly traditional in their approach ('The meaning of a Word', 'Semantic Roles', etc), later chapters reflect the influence of logical theories in the discussion of negatives, quantifiers and connectives, as well as the impact of speech act theory and pragmatics. The book has a refreshingly descriptive bias. Each chapter ends with a section of exercises and problems to which answers are given at the back of the book. A more thorough and admirably clear introduction to formal logic and its relevance for modern linguistics is provided in *Logic in Linguistics*[60]. The authors provide an account of set theory, propositional logic, modal logic, intensional logic and categorial grammar. An attempt is made in the final chapter to point to ways in which formal languages can be and are being exploited in the study of natural languages. This chapter, which draws together several threads of argument from earlier in the book, could have been greatly extended, thus giving the student who has mastered the information in the earlier pages more substantial evidence of the relevance of logic in linguistics. Useful exercises and a key are provided.

Janet Dean Foder[61], in one of the most illuminating and fascinating books on linguistics in recent years, provides an account of theories of meaning in generative grammar. While fulfilling her aim of bringing together the different theories within generative grammar, clarifying them and indicating their relations to each other, she also succeeds in moving beyond generative semantics to an informative and fascinating account of the links between philosophical theories and current linguistic theories. In the preface it is suggested that there would be no point to an undigested summary of contradicting claims, and the author comments that she has tried to restrict her evaluative comments to specific points and not to prejudge major issues. In fact it is the balance achieved between exposition

---

[59] *Introduction to Contemporary Linguistic Semantics*, by George L. Dillon. (Foundations of Modern Linguistics Series). Englewood Cliffs, N.J.: Prentice-Hall. pp. xvii + 150.

[60] *Logic in Linguistics*, by Jens Allwood, Lars-Gunnar Anderson and Östen Dahl. (Cambridge Textbooks in Linguistics). Cambridge: C.U.P. pp. x + 185. £2.95.

[61] *Semantics: Theories of Meaning in Generative Grammar*, by Janet Dean Foder. (The Language and Thought Series). Hassocks, Sussex: The Harvester Press pp. xi + 225. £12.95.

and evaluation in terms of both content and style which makes this book outstanding. Moreover, it is worth noting that this book takes up the challenge where most introductory accounts of TG theory leave off: how very many textbooks have been produced which relegate generative semantics to a few paragraphs in the final chapter! The volume contains a useful bibliography. My only regret is that the cost will be prohibitive for many students of linguistics: let us hope that the publishers may consider producing a soft cover version so that this book can be widely used in colleges and universities.

The publication of several important items on semantics no doubt reflects the renewed attention given to this field over the last few years. One author whose interest goes back many years is John Lyons, and his two-volume *Semantics* seems set to become a classic in its own right. Lyons set out to write 'a fairly short' introduction which would be of interest to students from several disciplines: the resulting work is in fact 897 pages long. Volume 1[62] is the more general of the two volumes, and sets semantics within a wider semiotics context, with chapters on semiotics, behaviourist semantics and reference, sense and denotation. The final two chapters are concerned more specifically with the structuralist approach to semantics, which Lyons regards as by no means dead and buried. Volume 2[63] is more directly linguistic in focus, with three successive chapters devoted to 'Semantics and Grammar': topics include general areas such as 'Generative Grammar', 'Grammatical Ambiguity' and specific aspects such as 'Locative Subject', 'Causativity and Transitivity'. Other chapters deal with 'Context Style and Culture', 'Mood and Illocutionary Force' and 'Modality'. John Lyons is well known to students of linguistics for his clarity of style, fairness of presentation and originality of perspective. This work is no exception: while fairly expounding the theories of fellow linguists, Lyons makes numerous original contributions. These volumes demand much closer attention and more detailed analysis than can be provided here.

Lyons' account of 'speech act theory' and the notion of 'illocutionary force' provides a useful background to *Prepositional Structure and Illocutionary Force*[64] by Jerrold J. Katz. This is a fascinating attempt to weld together two quite distinct linguistic theories, or, more accurately, traditions, as both strands contain a wide variety of approaches. The two traditions are those of 'speech act theory' and 'generative grammar'. Given that the origins of these theories lie in two quite different disciplines, philosophy (albeit linguistic philosophy) and linguistics, the author's task is not an easy one. Speech act adherents will no doubt be somewhat dismayed by the radical solution proposed by Katz, given that the performance-slant Austin gave to speech act theory has had to be 'eliminated': 'it was even necessary to reject speech act theory itself insofar as it is taken as an account of a *uniform* type of knowledge speakers exercise in performing and identifying speech acts'. The author's aim is

[62] *Semantics, Vol. 1*, by John Lyons. Cambridge: C.U.P. pp. 372.
[63] *Semantics, Vol. 2*, by John Lyons. Cambridge: C.U.P. pp. xiv + 525. £4.95.
[64] *Propositional Structure and Illocutionary Force*, by Jerrold J. Katz. Hassocks, Sussex: The Harvester Press. pp. xv + 249. £13.50.

to produce a theory within the framework of generative grammar to represent formally the illocutionary force. To do this Katz has two sub-theories, one of which is part of the theory of competence, concerned with the kind of knowledge the speaker-hearer has about the type of illocutionary information contained within the grammatical structure of sentences: the other is part of the theory of performance, and is concerned with the way in which grammatical information and information about a speech context interact so that we can 'assign an utterance meaning to the use of a sentence'. Whatever one's view of the radical refinements of speech act theory suggested by Katz, the volume must be welcomed as a serious attempt to integrate the notion of illocutionary force within a coherent linguistic theory.

One of the classical topics in semantics is discussed by Samuel Levin for *The Semantics of Metaphor*[65]. The author examines the notion of metaphor from both a linguistic and a philosophical point of view and attempts to establish a consistent theory to account for deviant sentences.

An important volume which contains articles relevant to both syntactic and semantic studies is noted here but has not been available for examination. *Linguistics at the Crossroads*[66] includes sections on 'The Search for Relevance' (with articles by M. Halliday, R. J. Di Pietro and J. W. Oller), 'The Changing Face of TG Grammar' (M. Halle, J. D. McCawley and A. Koutsoudas), 'Recent Issues in Tagmemics' (K. L. Pike and others), 'The Interrelationship of Dialectology and Historical Change' (R. Nash, W. Labov, A. McIntosh), 'New European View' (S. K. Shaumyan and others) and 'Attainments in Cognitive and Stratificational Linguistics' (S. M. Lamb, V. Becker Makkai, E. M. Hemick).

Volume 5[67] of the North-Holland Series 'Fundamental Studies in Computer Science' examines some of the problems in constructing adequate models to represent the meaning and structure of natural language. Several articles of wider relevance include 'John is easy to please' by Barbara Hall Partee, 'Questions and Commands' by John Lyons and 'Scenes and Frames Semantics' by Charles Fillmore.

We now turn to several items relating to phonological theory. Probably the most important is Alan Sommerstein's *Modern Phonology*[68] which attempts to provide a survey of phonological theory over the last fifty years. Attention is given to the different types of phonemic analysis – prosodic and stratificational approaches and generative phonology. In a most useful and clear introduction on 'Aims and Principles', Sommerstein distinguishes the major different approaches to phonological theory as characterised by different accounts of the *goals* of phonological theory. 'Classical phonology' was, and is, concerned to establish which phonetic

[65] *The Semantics of Metaphor*, by Samuel R. Levin. Baltimore, Md.: Johns Hopkins U.P. pp. xi + 150. $12.

[66] *Linguistics at the Crossroads*, ed. by Adam Makkai, Valerie Becker Makkai and Luigi Heilmann. Lake Bluff, Ill.: Jupiter Press. pp. vii + 520.

[67] *Linguistics Structures Processing: Studies in Linguistics, Computational Linguistics and Artificial Intelligence*, ed. by Antonio Zampolli. (Fundamental Studies in Computer Science, Vol 5). Amsterdam and New York: North-Holland Pub. Co. pp. xvi + 586.

[68] *Modern Phonology*, by Alan H. Sommerstein. Edward Arnold. pp. x + 282. £5.95.

features do or can serve to distinguish one utterance from another: generative phonology is concerned to locate the 'principles' determining the pronunciation of the words, phrases and sentences of a language, and the extent to which these principles are derivable from more general principles determining the organisation of all human language. Sommerstein's account and, in particular, his exposition and critique of generative phonology, should make this difficult area more accessible to a wide range of linguistics students, including those whose main concerns are not primarily phonological.

George N. Clements has edited the first volume of *Harvard Studies in Phonology*[69] which includes studies of several languages (Kikuyu, Mohawk, Ewe) as well as articles of a more general theoretical interest.

Topics in Phonological Theory[70] presents the authors' views on several key areas in phonology, including the suggested 'non-phonetic' basis of phonology, the role of derivational history and the role of syntax and the lexicon in phonology. Kenstowicz and Lisseberth make use of their sometimes controversial analyses of aspects of particular phonological systems to explicate their theories.

Two items which are on the borderline for inclusion here, relate to phonetics rather than phonology. Lieberman's *Speech Physiology and Acoustic Phonetics*[71] is, however, an important introduction to phonetic theory and quantitative methodologies, and as such should be of interest to a fairly wide audience. Key topics include sound spectography, speech synthesis and speech perception. J. C. Catford's contribution is concerned with 'Fundamental Problems in Phonetics'[72].

I turn now to a brief indication of some of the most important items within the journals. *Linguistic Inquiry* continues as a source of important and detailed discussions of current topics in linguistic theory. Volume 8 includes an important article by Noam Chomsky and Howard Lasnik on 'Filters and Controls'[73]. The authors attempt to examine four related problems: restricting the options for transformational grammar; perceptual strategies and syntactic rules; problems of obligatory control and properties of the complementiser system. It is suggested that together with independent conditions on the syntax of logical form, an adequate theory of 'filters and controls' can impose a complex system of constraints on the well-formedness of surface structures. Other useful articles include Robert Fiengo's discussion of trace theory[74], and Edwin Williams's account of 'Discourse and Logical Form'[75]. As always with this periodical some of

[69] *Harvard Studies in Phonology, Vol 1*, ed. by George N. Clements. Cambridge, Mass.: Harvard University, Department of Linguistics. pp. 482. $7.50.

[70] *Topics in Phonological Theory*, by Michael Kenstowicz and Charles Kisseberth. New York and London: Academic Press. pp. 242. £11.10.

[71] *Speech Physiology and Acoustic Phonetics*, by Philip Lieberman. New York: Macmillan. pp. xiv + 206.

[72] *Fundamental Problems in Phonetics*, by J. C. Catford. Edinburgh: Edinburgh U.P.

[73] 'Filters and Controls', by Noam Chomksy and Howard Lasnik. *Linguistic Inquiry* Vol. 8 No. 3. pp. 425–504.

[74] 'On Trace Theory', by Robert Fiengo. *Linguistic Inquiry* Vol. 8 No. 1. pp. 35–61.

[75] 'Discourse and Logical Form', by Edwin S. Williams. *Linguistic Inquiry* Vol. 8 No. 1. pp. 101–139.

the most interesting material is to be found under 'Remarks and Replies' or 'Squibs and Discussion'.

As well as articles on specific aspects of particular languages Volume 53 of *Language* contains useful articles on many aspects of linguistic theory. Geoffrey Pullum and Deidre Wilson[76] argue that there is no principled basis for a separate category (M) 'Modal' and suggest that all modals as well as other auxiliaries should be generated in the same way as main verbs. While Shibatani's article[77] is mainly concerned with data from Japanese and Korean, his general suggestion that grammatical relations and cases must be clearly distinguished is worth noting as there has been much confusion of the two in recent literature. Paul Schachter[78] returns to the familiar problem of providing rules to account for the ungrammaticality of such items as 'John ate quickly and a grilled sandwich,' and 'It's odd for John to be busy and that Helen is idle now'.

Schachter proposes a Co-ordinate Constituent Constraint which refers to both the syntactic and semantic properties of such constructions, and postulates that one can expect there to be other universal constraints on grammars which depend on the interaction of syntactic and semantic properties. Alexander Grosu and Sandra A. Thompson[79] examine a different set of constraints which apply to the distribution of NP clauses.

Two items in *Journal of Linguistics* Vol. 13 discuss particular aspects of pragmatics. D. A. Cruse in 'The Pragmatics of Lexical Specifity'[80] tries to establish what factors determine which lexical items a speaker will choose in any given context. Thus given the items 'spaniel', 'dog' and 'animal', which can all refer to the same object, why does the speaker use one word rather than another? Cruse is also concerned to examine the semantic and pragmatic consequences of the speaker's choice. William Downes[81] discusses the account of imperatives within linguistic theory and suggests that the surface meaning hypothesis or pragmatic analysis provide a plausible account of the imperative construction. In other words, everything that is required for main clause infinitives to have the illocutionary potential of commanding is present in the surface structure.

(b) *Psycholinguistics*

It is interesting to note that as with TG introductions, (see above) introductory texts on psycholinguistics have not flooded the market as they did last year. I have noted only one such volume[82] and this stands out as an exceptional contribution in terms of both content and clarity.

[76] 'Autonomous Syntax and the Analysis of Auxiliaries', by Geoffrey Pullum and Deidre Wilson. *Language* Vol. 53. pp. 741–788.
[77] 'Grammatical Relations and Surface Cases', by Masayoshi Shibatani. *Language* Vol. 53. pp. 789–809.
[78] 'Constraints on Co-ordination', by Paul Schachter. *Language* Vol. 53. pp. 86–103.
[79] 'Constraints on the Distribution of NP Clause', by Alexander Grosu and Sandra A. Thompson. *Language* Vol. 53. pp. 104–151.
[80] 'The Pragmatics of Lexical Specificity', by D. A. Cruse. *Journal of Linguistics* Vol. 13. pp. 153–164.
[81] 'The Imperative and Pragmatics', by William Downes. *Journal of Linguistics* Vol. 13. pp. 77–97.
[82] *Psychology and Language,* by Herbert H. Clark and Eve V. Clark. New York: Harcourt Brace Jovanovich. pp. xvi + 608. £7.45.

The authors, Herbert and Eve Clark, are well known for their contributions to psycholinguistic research, especially in relation to the acquisition of semantics and the study of comprehension. They aim specifically 'to spell out the aims and organising principles that give psycholinguistics integrity'. This is not an easy task, but one which they carry out admirably. They suggest that one of the principles which provides for coherence within psycholinguistics is that its subject matter can be summed up in relation to three mental processes: the study of listening, of speaking, and of the acquisition of these two skills by children. The Clarks, therefore, organise their discussion around these three principles, and present sections on comprehension, production and acquisition. Much of their account may already be familiar, especially within the area of language acquisition. However, their discussion gives some space to functional as well as structural accounts of language development, thus reflecting the increase of interest in this area in recent years. The book is well planned, with a summary and suggestions for further reading at the end of each chapter, a glossary of terminology and an extensive and up-to-date bibliography. This volume is surely likely to become a standard textbook for students in linguistics, psychology and other related fields, since the soft cover edition is very reasonably priced, by current standards.

Eve Clark is also one of the contributors to *Language Learning and Thought*[83], a collection of articles edited by John MacNamara. This is specifically not intended as an introductory textbook for undergraduates, but is directed at 'all serious scholars and students interested in language learning'. MacNamara suggests that if language and 'thought' are distinct and autonomous, linguists are led to the conclusion that in developing language, the child must develop not only these two separate domains, but also some apparently abstract representation of the relation between the two. This volume is mainly concerned with eight major facets of the relationship between thought and language: the contribution of non-verbal signs to the understanding of language; the learning of phonology; the learning of morphology; strategies of vocabulary learning; concepts and words; the learning of syntax in natural language; the learning of syntax in artificial language, and propositional operations involved in the understanding of sentences. The eight major contributions on these topics are each followed by a chapter of commentary and discussion. The contribution on phonology by Paul Kiparsky and Lise Menn suggests that the child is faced with two distinct problems in learning phonology: the quasi-physiological problem of his own limited phonetic abilities, and the cognitive problem of learning the abstract regularities of the phonological system. The authors suggest that the child's solution to both problems takes the same form, in that the child devises a set of underlying representations and general rules which allow lexical exceptions and which may operate in extrinsic order. Bruce Derwing's comments on the Kiparsky-Menn chapter are summed up in his title 'Is the child really a "Little Linguist"?'. For Derwing the 'learning principles' posited by Kiparsky and Menn fall into the category of other operating principles attributed

[83] *Language Learning and Thought,* ed. by John MacNamara. (Perspectives in Neurolinguistics and Psycholinguistics). New York and London: Academic Press. pp. xii + 296.

to children developing language; that is, they are merely hypothetical
linguistic notions which have no psychological reality. This objection is
closely linked to Derwing's oft-repeated claim that 'innateness' as an
explanation of phenomenon is 'tantamount to an admission of a failure
to explain it' since innateness is a purely negative notion. Much of the
dispute here seems to rest as much on disagreement as to appropriate
criteria for the establishment of adequate explanatory theories of language
development. The notion of 'operating principles' in language development
is closely associated with the name of Dan Slobin, and in this volume
Slobin examines language change within the development of language in
childhood. In doing so he is attempting to clarify the psycholinguistic
processes which make language possible. Four language imperatives are
suggested as the source of change within the child's linguistic system:
be clear; be humanly processible in ongoing time; be quick and easy;
be expressive. Slobin illustrates the results of these instructions in terms of
a series of 'diachronic stories'. Eve Clark's contribution presents a general
account of how the child establishes the correspondence between an
utterance he hears and the context in which it occurs. She attempts to
identify the child's strategies in dealing with different conceptual domains,
and like Slobin suggests that by examining the changes made by the child
and pin-pointing the properties and relations that he appears to find
salient we may be able to establish an initial theory of the acquisition of
meaning. Other useful articles in this worthwhile collection are by
Katherine Nelson, I. M. Schlesinger, Seymour Papest, Shannon Dawn
Moeser and Gillian Sankoff.

Another volume in the Perspectives in Neurolinguistics and Psycholinguistics series is *Mind, Brain and Consciousness*[84] by Jason Brown. This
book is concerned with producing a brain model of cognition in the areas
of language, action, perception, thought and memory, affect, consciousness and volition and creativity. It is clearly directed at a more specialised
audience than another volume in the same series, *Genie*[85]. This provides
a psycholinguistic study of 'one of the most appalling cases of child abuse,
isolation and neglect' ever discovered. After a life of completely inhuman
treatment, tied to a chair and locked in a room, Genie was faced with the
task of learning language (and learning to cope with life outside her prison)
at the age of thirteen years seven months. It is of course one of the ironies
of this tragic situation that Genie's background has given linguists, psychologists and others a chance to examine some of the fundamental
questions concerning the process of language acquisition. One of the most
important of these relates to whether it is possible to establish a 'critical
period' of language development and, if so, what kind of language learning
is possible after the critical period. Susan Curtiss developed a series of
comprehension and production tests to evaluate Genie's learning in the
areas of phonology, morphology, syntax and semantics. While Genie's

[84] *Mind, Brain and Consciousness: The Neuropsychology of Cognition*, by Jason
Brown. (Perspectives in Neurolinguistics and Psycholinguistics). New York and
London: Academic Press. pp. 200. £9.80.
    [85] *Genie: A Psycholinguistic Study of a Modern Day 'Wild Child'*, by Susan
Curtiss. (Perspectives in Neurolinguistics and Psycholinguistics). New York and
London: Academic Press. pp. 288. £11.10.

acquisition of language has been slow and her productive ability is still very limited, Curtiss suggests that the evidence shows that her language behaviour is clearly rule-governed. Moreover, the information gleaned so far seems to provide overwhelming evidence for the critical period hypothesis: Genie has right-hemisphere language and this suggests that the left-hemisphere may no longer be able to function in acquisition after the critical period. This volume is a remarkable study and a tribute to the sensitivity of its author.

Haiganoosh and Harry Whitaker have produced the third volume of *Studies in Neurolinguistics*[86] (see *YW* 57.37) which includes articles by Michael Paradis on 'Bilingualism and Aphasia', John Marshall and Freda Newcombe on 'Variability and Constraint in Acquired Dyslexia' and John T. Lamendella on the 'Limbic System in Human Communication'.

Yet another volume in this same series is edited by Sidney J. Segalowitz and Frederick A. Gruber. *Language Development and Neurological Theory*[87] like the Whitaker volume is more geared to specialists than the general reader, and focuses on four main areas: cerebral specialisation for language in normals; cerebral specialisation for language in brain-damaged patients; the development of cerebral dominance; and speech perception.

Returning now to the more directly linguistic aspects of child language development, we have a volume devoted to the topic of '*Child Discourse*'[88]. As suggested by Coulthard, discourse acquisition is now itself in the course of development as a field of study in its own right. The editors of this volume sees it as a move towards establishing an inter-disciplinary study of child discourse. They suggest that this new work shares several central ideas: the view, taken from both a theoretical and methodological standpoint, that natural conversation should be the data source; the recognition that sentences are not the highest level of analysis and 'units' such as moves, turns, exchanges, stories, and conversations have been suggested which must be identifiable and analysable; social context is directly relevant to linguistic rules; variability is a normal and perhaps systematic aspect of linguistic production, and finally language is diverse in function, and functions cannot be directly mapped by structural features. The volume is divided into three sections, 'Speech Events', 'Function and Act', and 'Social Meaning' and there is a general introduction by the editors. One approach to the study of discourse is to examine certain identifiable categories of organised interaction as a starting point: such categories include play, arguments, narratives and teaching and these topics are examined in closer detail in Section I. The fundamental problem of the relationship between structure and function is further analysed in the section on speech acts. An important critique by Elinor

[86] *Studies in Neurolinguistics Vol. 3.* ed. by Haiganoosh Whitaker and Harry A. Whitaker. (Perspectives in Neurolinguistics and Psycholinguistics). New York and London: Academic Press. pp. 334. £14.45.

[87] *Language Development and Neurological Theory*, ed. by Sidney J. Segalowitz and Frederick A. Gruber. (Perspectives in Neurolinguistics and Psycholinguistics). New York and London: Academic Press. pp. 400. £13.85.

[88] *Child Discourse*, ed. by Susan Ervin-Tripp and Claudia Mitchell-Kernan. (Language Thought and Culture: Advances in the Study of Cognition). New York and London: Academic Press. pp. xii + 266. £6.75.

Ochs Keenan examines the notion of repetition. She suggests that investigations of child language have viewed as identical utterances those which were only superficially similar: the functions of these utterances and the roles they played within discourse varied considerably. The notion of 'repetition' in child language is one which deserves closer examination, and Keenan's discussion raises important issues. The final section on 'Social Meaning' includes a fascinating account of the acquisition of one aspect of communicative competence: 'Learning what it means to talk like a lady'. Although many of the major problems in discourse theory are reflected within these pages, the need for a further refinement of discourse categories and their relevance to child language is also clearly shown.

H. R. Schaffer[89] has edited the proceedings of a Symposium on 'Mother-Infant Interaction' held in Scotland in 1975. The contributions elaborate upon the suggestions already made in the literature that in studying the interactive behaviour between mother and child, from the very earliest stages, one can discover systematic modes of communication which precede specifically linguistic patterns. Moreover, such communicative abilities may prove to be essential prerequisites to the development of language. Contributors include R. A. Hinde, C. Trevarthen, J. S. Bruner and D. N. Stern. Also relevant here, but unavailable for review is *Interaction, Conversation and the Development of Language*[90] by M. Lewis and L. A. Rosenblum.

Catherine Snow[91] is also concerned with the mother-child interaction. She examined the speech of mothers to their infants at several points between three and eighteen months and she suggests that the mothers used a conversational model, and that changes in the mothers' speech reflected the children's growing ability to function as conversational partners. Blount and Padgug[92], examining parent-child speech in Spanish and English, suggest that two parental strategies are relevant to 'interactional development: 'affective-interactional', which promotes joint activity and shows that the child is valued, and 'semantic-interactional' which introduces lexical and referential information into the interaction. The latter is likely to develop as the child begins to respond to the lexical content of parental speech.

The child's early concepts are examined by J. M. Anglin in *Word, Object and Conceptual Development*[93]. Anglin looks in particular at what Cruse calls 'lexical specificity' and Anglin himself refers to as 'level of references'. He reports on a series of experiments using picture arrays demanding responses from the specific intermediate and general levels. While the adults consistently varied the terms, using the most specific

[89] *Studies in Mother-Infant Interaction*, ed. by H. R. Schaffer. New York and London: Academic Press. pp. x + 478. £15.60.

[90] *Interaction, Conversation and the Development of Language*, by M. Lewis and L. A. Rosenblum. New York: John Wiley. pp. 344. £15.50.

[91] 'The Development of Conversation Between Mothers and Babies', by Catherine Snow in *JChL* Vol. 4. pp. 1-22.

[92] 'Prosodic, Paralinguistic and Interactional Features in Parent-Child Speech: English and Spanish', by Ben G. Blount and Elsie J. Padgug in *JChL* Vol.4. pp. 67-86.

[93] *Word, Object and Conceptual Development*, by J. M. Anglin. New York: W. W. Norton and Company. pp. x + 302.

possible, the children generally avoided using specific terms and refused to choose when a general term was required. Anglin relates the children's deficiencies in these areas to referential behaviour on the part of the mothers. Semantic over-extension, which has been the object of much study in child language, is explained by Anglin in terms of the perceptual similarity of the objects as opposed to any functional relationship which may exist.

We move now from semantic acquisition to phonological development. T. M. S. Priestley[94] examines a particular strategy used by one child to cope with polysyllabic words. This strategy involved the child internalising the initial consonant and the first vowel and one other noticeable consonant, and the fact that the word was of more than one syllable. Priestly argues that this strategy gives strong support to the view that the syllable should be regarded as the basic unit in phonological acquisition if not also in adult phonology.

J. H. V. Gilbert and B. A. Purves examine 'Temporal Constraints on Consonant Clusters in Child Speech Production' (*JChL* Vol 4 pp 417–432) and suggest that the timing programme used by children to achieve cluster control is different from that of adults.

The acoustic features of early infant vocalisations are discussed in two separate articles: Murry *et al*[95] examined the fundamental frequencies of infant cries and found that there was a tendency for a male infant to have a higher fundamental frequency than a female. Other acoustic parameters may however prove to be more important in distinguishing cry types. The results of the study by Laufer and Horii[96] showed little developmental change in the fundamental frequency in the first four weeks of life. The directly linguistic relevance of these phonetic studies is not always clear.

The Sounds of Children[97] is a non-academic, popular account of language development with particular reference to specific varieties, eg 'Black English', and 'the native Spanish speaking child'; and is meant more as a guide to parents than as a serious contribution to the study of phonology.

I turn now to more general questions in child language study. Ruth Clark ('What's the use of imitation?' in *JChL* Vol 4 pp 341–358) puts forward examples which she suggests indicate that imitation should not be regarded as of only 'marginal significance' in the learning of syntax. She suggests that many idiosyncratic features of children's speech seem to be traceable to the interaction of imitation and other simple mechanisms. Examples such as 'That's mine jam' are explained as a type of 'coupling' which involves imitation of elliptical utterances: these imitated utterances are then coupled with other constituents to produce a longer utterance. Other utterances are described as 'amalgams' of two different utterances,

[94] 'One Idiosyncratic Strategy in the Acquisition of Phonology', by T. M. S. Priestley in *JChL* Vol. 4. pp. 45–65.

[95] 'Acoustical Characteristics of Infant Cries: Fundamental Frequency', by T. Murry, P. Amundson and H. Hollien in *JChL* Vol. 4. pp. 321–328.

[96] 'Fundamental Frequency Characteristics of Infant Non-Distress Vocalisation During the First Twenty-Four Weeks', by M. Z. Laufer and Y. Horii in *JChL* Vol. 4. pp. 171–184.

[97] *The Sounds of Children*, by F. Williams, R. Hopper and D. S. Natalicio. Englewood Cliffs, N.J.: Prentice-Hall. pp. vii + 136.

eg 'Why didn't you allowed to shut the door?'. That such utterances do occur in child speech is well known. The real question which remains is the extent to which productive development can be explained by reference to such devices as coupling and amalgamating. Clark may be right in suggesting that further evidence is needed to clarify the role of imitation, but her discussion, although interesting, does not wholly 'rehabilitate' imitation.

A. A. Abrahamsen[98] has produced a useful interdisciplinary guide to the ever-expanding field of child language. The book contains five sections: the first deals with general resources and describes introductory surveys, reviews and anthologies: Part Two deals with syntactic development and Part Three with semantic development. A fourth section under the title 'Beyond Grammar' covers theories of language development and pragmatics and the fifth section deals with phonological development.

Joan Tough's account of the *Development of Meaning*[99] provides an account of her language and environment project. She examines the language used by children from different social environments at the ages of three, five and seven and considers how the differences she finds affect general learning strategies. Joan Tough's work has been influential within educational circles, particularly within colleges of education and within primary schools. Despite the author's refreshing commonsense in matters linguistic, some problems still remain in providing a totally coherent functional framework for language development: in this respect Joan Tough is no different from the numerous other writers who find the functional viewpoint intuitively attractive, but have so far failed to give it the formalism demanded of a linguistic theory.

The Language Needs of Minority Group Children[100] are discussed by June Derrick in a short but lucid account of the complex problems faced by the teacher in helping children who come from widely divergent linguistic and cultural backgrounds. She describes clearly the kind of 'deceptive fluency' which allows children to 'get by' in English but does not allow them to produce a sustained piece of descriptive writing. Useful bibliographical material is provided.

Gillian Fenn's study[101] is concerned with educationally severely subnormal children while Michael Marland[102] examines the way in which it is possible to apply some of the insights of language development research to the school setting. Language, suggests Marland, should not be the concern of English teachers alone: he proposes the development of a language policy throughout the school affecting every aspect of the curriculum.

[98] *Child Language: An Interdisciplinary Guide to Theory and Research*, by A. A. Abrahamsen. Baltimore: University Park Press. pp. xxiv + 381.

[99] *The Development of Meaning: A Study of Children's Use of Language*, by Joan Tough. Allen & Unwin. pp. 198. £2.95.

[100] *Language Needs of Minority Group Children*, by June Derrick. Windsor, England: NFER Publishing Company. pp. 59.

[101] *The Development of Syntax in a Group of Educationally Severely Subnormal Children*, by Gillian Fenn. (Exeter Linguistic Studies, 2). Exeter: U. of Exeter P. pp. iv + 120.

[102] *Language Across the Curriculum*, by Michael Marland. Heinemann Educational Books. pp. x + 309. £2.95.

(c) *Sociolinguistics*

Dell Hymes[103] has produced a collection of previously unpublished papers aimed at showing the shortcomings of a linguistics theory which is deprived of a theory of speech acts and equally of the inadequacy of an anthropological approach which ignores such concepts as structure and function.

The notion of acceptability in language is examined in a volume containing twelve previously unpublished essays edited by Sidney Greenbaum[104]. One fascinating article provides an account of Israel as a country of language learners where linguistic 'authority' is the authority of the canonical texts not the speaker's own intuitions. Jan Svartvik and David Wright suggest that the auxiliary 'ought' is disappearing from the language in certain contexts and within certain groups including younger speakers. W. J. M. Levelt and colleagues attempt to examine the different psychological processes underlying judgements of acceptability and judgements of grammaticality.

Sidney Greenbaum also argues for the importance of acceptability judgements in 'Contextual Influence on Acceptability Judgements' (*Linguistics* 187 pp 5-11). Max Adler in *Welsh and Other Dying Languages in Europe*[105] describes the apparent death throes of a number of European languages: most space is given to the Welsh language. Those interested in the phenomenon of 'language death' will find Vol 191 of *Linguistics* particularly interesting. As the editors remark, the term language death has dramatic overtones, though, perhaps, not quite as dramatic as other terms which have been used including 'language decay' and the highly emotive 'language suicide'. All the contributions to the volume are concerned with cases of imminent language death. In developing an interdisciplinary approach to the problem, and examining political, social, psychological and linguistic aspects, the editors have to begin the process of developing a coherent theory of the processes which result in the extinction of once viable languages.

H. Giles has edited a large volume on *Language Ethnicity and Intergroup Relations*[106]. Contributors include Joshua Fishman ('Language and Ethnicity'), Peter Trudgill and George A. Tzavaras ('Why Albanian Greeks are not Albanians: Language Shift and Ethnicity in Attica and Biotia'), Charles Husband ('News Media, Language and Race Relations: A Case Study in Identity Maintenance'), and Howard Giles, Richard Y. Bourkis and Donald M. Taylor ('Towards a Theory of Language in Ethnic Group Relations').

R. K. S. Macaulay[107] has analysed sociolinguistic variation in Glasgow.

[103] *Foundations in Sociolinguistics: An Ethnographic Approach*, by Dell Hymes. Tavistock Press. pp. x + 248.

[104] *Acceptability in Language*, ed. by Sidney Greenbaum. (Contributions to the Sociology of Language, 17). The Hague: Mouton. pp. x + 123.

[105] *Welsh and Other Dying Languages in Europe*, by Max Adler. *Linguistics* 187.

[106] *Language Ethnicity and Intergroup Relations*, ed. by H. Giles. (European Monographs in Social Psychology). New York and London: Academic Press. pp. 370. £14.50.

[107] *Language, Social Class and Education: A Glasgow Study*, by R. K. S. Macaulay, with the assistance of S. D. Trevelyan. Edinburgh: Edinburgh U. P. pp. viii + 179. £4.50.

The analysis is based upon a sample of forty-eight informants divided into four classes. Macaulay also provides attitudinal data from educators and employers. While the study is fascinating and useful, the author would probably be the first to admit that it raises many more questions than it answers. Glasgow is a rich hunting ground for the keen sociolinguist, yet it is noticeable how little in the way of solid linguistic field-work has been carried out in this area. One problem raised by Macaulay's approach is the influence of the interviewer upon the speech of the informant: this is a recurring problem but an important one in this particular case at least. If the only interviewer used is one whose speech patterns are as alien to the informant as Southern English is to the 'typical' Glaswegian, then we cannot expect a 'true' sample to be obtained.

Scotland is also the location for Kenneth Mackinnon's study of language in a Gaelic Community[108]. The author, while recognising the existence of two languages, does not accept the view that there is a constant competition for dominance by one language over the other. It may appear that the Scottish Gaelic-speaking communities present a special case of 'diglossia', with English as the H variety and Gaelic as the L variety. Leaving aside the different interpretation of the notion 'diglossia', Mackinnon points out that an interesting aspect of linguistic usage within these communities is that a highly developed formal variety of Gaelic is used for Church services: in this case Gaelic is quite clearly the H variety. It is interesting to note that as with linguistic studies of urban Scotland, the whole complex area of Gaelic usage has been virtually ignored by linguists and sociolinguists. It is to be hoped that these contributions will initiate serious studies of these neglected but important areas.

Bilingualism is the subject of an interdisciplinary volume edited by Peter Hornby[109]. As well as recognising the elements of conflict frequently found in bilingual communities and resulting at times in explosive political situations, this volume also focuses on some of the more positive aspects of having access to more than one language. Topics examined include the effects of bilingualism on cognitive development; the social and personal identity of the bilingual; 'normal' language behaviour within the bilingual community, and the influence of bilingualism on social interaction.

Also relevant here is an item which properly belongs to *YW* 57; *The Bilingual Child*[110], edited by Antonio Simoes, includes details of research findings on bilingualism as they relate to the educational field in general and classroom practice in particular.

Bilingualism in Education is also the special topic of Vol. 198 of *Linguistics*. This again reflects an interdisciplinary and international approach widening out the scope of study to embrace languages and communities which have so far received very little attention in the literature. The editor of this special edition, E. Glyn Lewis, points out that

[108] *Language Education and Social Processes in a Gaelic Community*, by Kenneth Mackinnon. Routledge & Keegan Paul. pp. xi + 222.
[109] *Bilingualism: Psychological Social and Educational Implications*, ed. by Peter A. Hornby. New York and London: Academic Press. pp. 180. £6.75.
[110] *The Bilingual Child: Research and Analysis of Existing Educational Themes*, ed. by Antonio Simoes Jr. New York and London: Academic Press. pp. 292. £12.80. (1976).

'attitude' to languages and to ethnic groups associated with those languages emerges as a major concern and suggests that attitude studies should be extended to explore the varying approaches to the concept of bilingual education. Particular contributions include Kenneth Mackinnon on 'Gaelic', Bernard Spolsky on 'American Indian Bilingual Education', J. J. Smolicz and R. McL. Harris on 'Ethnic Languages in Australia' and George I. Za'rour and Rawdah Z. Nashif on 'Attitudes towards the Language of Science Teaching at the Secondary Level in Jordan'.

Yet another volume *The Bilingual Education Movement: Essays on its Progress*[111] reflects the explosion of work in this area. Much of this material looks at the question of bilingual education from the perspective of work in Canada and Texas. However, the volume also includes observations relating to a much wider context as indicated by Joshua Fishman's contribution 'Language and Culture in the Global Community'. William Mackey[112] has also co-edited another volume on bilingualism relating primarily to the North-American context.

A number of items have appeared this year on Pidgins and Creoles including volumes by Max Adler[113] and A. Valdman[114]. Unfortunately neither of these volumes has been available for consultation.

Papers in Language Variation[115] is a collection of papers dating back to 1953 and originally given at the South Atlantic section of the American Dialect Society. The papers are in the tradition of geographical dialect study and bear little relation to current models of sociolinguistic variation.

Language in Africa[116] is geared towards the intelligent layman and as well as describing the linguistic complexity of the continent of Africa raises some of the intrinsic problems in language collating.

(d) *General*

The problem with establishing a category simply entitled 'general' is that items of major importance which truly belong to the 'general' category and items that 'don't quite fit' elsewhere are thrown together with perhaps a certain loss of dignity to all concerned. I have not wholly avoided the problem here but begin the section with two books which are by highly respected authors whose work always demands attention, Dwight Bolinger and Charles F. Hockett. *Meaning and Form*[117] by Dwight Bolinger is a series of essays which examines exactly that, the relationship between form − or forms − and meaning. Bolinger 'reaffirms the old principle that the natural condition of a language is to preserve

[111] *The Bilingual Education Movement: Essays on its Progress*, ed. by William F. Mackey, Jacob Ornstein et al. El Paso, Tx. Texas Western Press. pp. 153. $10.
[112] *Bilingualism in Early Childhood*, ed. by William F. Mackey and Theodore Anderson. Rowley, Mass.: Newbury House. xi + 443. £11.20.
[113] *Pidgins, Creoles and Lingua Francas: A Sociolinguistic Study*, by Max Adler. Hamburg: Helmut Busch Vertag. pp. v + 46.
[114] *Pidgin and Creole Linguistics*, ed. by Albert Valdman. Bloomington Ind.: U. of Indiana P. pp. xvi + 399.
[115] *Papers in Linguistic Variation: SAMLA-ADS Collection*, ed. by David L. Shores and Carol P. Hines. University, Alabama: U. of Alabama P. pp xiv + 321. $10.
[116] *Language in Africa: An Introductory Survey*, ed. by Edgar Gregersen. New York: Gordon & Breach. pp. xvii.
[117] *Meaning and Form*, by Dwight Bolinger. (English Language Series, 11). Longman. pp. xii + 212.

one form for one meaning and one meaning for one form'. In the course of his essays Bolinger attempts to bring forward illustrative material from different areas of English grammar to support his theories.

In his preface to *A View from Language*[118] Hockett says that what the essays have in common is that none of them is a technical treatment of a technical linguistic topic: 'instead they look out from language at other things or back at language in the light of other things'. The essays range in date from 1948 to the present day. While some of these essays are classics in their own right, to the student nurtured on Chomskian or post-Chomskian linguistics, the volume as a whole has a rather historical ring to it. Hockett's own notes provide useful asides and pointers both to developments within linguistics generally and developments of his own ideas.

Soviet Semiotics[119] provides a reflection of work on semiotics within the U.S.S.R. Daniel P. Lucid comments in his introduction that semiotics as a science embodies the current preoccupation with procedure and methodology, while its central topic — meaning and communication — constitutes a central problem of our time. The volume contains sections on 'Modelling Systems', 'Communication Studies', 'Text Analysis', 'Art and Literature' and the 'Typology of Culture'.

Olga Akhmanova is one of the most prolific of Russian writers. Two volumes this year are *Linguistic Terminology*[120], which examines that specific branch of lexicography, metalanguage, while *The Principles of Linguistic Confrontation*[121] takes the notion of contrastiveness in linguistics and widens it into the notion of confrontation.

A more gentle introduction to the field of semiotics is *Structuralism and Semiotics*[122] by Terence Hawkes. The account moves through a historical discussion of the development of theories of signs to an examination of Culler's proposal for the development of 'poetics' which would stand to literature as linguistics does to language.

Turning now to signs within a linguistic system, and more specifically to the manual and gestural sign language, we have a further volume concerning the structure of ASL, the American Sign Language. Lynn Friedman[123] has collected together a series of articles which attempt to 'purge' sign language analyses of theories and assumptions based upon the study of oral languages. Friedman's own contribution examines the formational properties of ASL and presents refinements of Stokoe's original account of ASL 'phonology'. One of the most useful and interesting articles in the volume is Mark Mandel's 'Iconic Devices in American Sign Language'

[118] *The View from Language: Selected Essays 1948-1978*, by C. F. Hockett. Athens, Ga.: The U. of Georgia P. pp. 338.

[119] *Soviet Semiotics: An Anthology*, ed. by Daniel P. Lucid. Baltimore, Md. and London: The Johns Hopkins U. P. pp. 259.

[120] *Linguistic Terminology*, by Olga Akhmanova. Moscow: Moscow U.P. pp. 188.

[121] *The Principles of Linguistic Confrontation*, by Olga Akhmanova and Dmitrij Melencuk. Moscow: Moscow U. P. pp. 176.

[122] *Structuralism and Semiotics*, by Terence Hawkes. (New Accents). Methuen pp. 192. £2.10.

[123] *On the Other Hand: New Perspectives in American Sign Language*, ed. by Lynn A. Friedman. (Language Thought and Culture). New York and London: Academic Press. pp. xii + 245.

which examines the many different types of relationship which may exist between the manual sign and its referent. Now that sign language researchers have developed confidence in their own subject, they are free from the constraints of proving that sign languages really are languages and can get down to the business of explaining their unique features.

This year sees several more titles which properly belong under the heading 'Ape Linguistics' – Washoe has a lot to answer for. *Language Learning by a Chimpanzee*[124] is an account of the 'Lana' project aimed to develop a computer-based language training programme to investigate the linguistic ability of chimpanzees. The chimpanzee's 'conversations' are transcribed for evaluation by other researchers.

Progress in Ape Research[125] has a much wider perspective but includes a very useful section on 'Communication and Language on Great Apes', which includes articles by Roger S. Fouts, Gordon W. Hewes and Peter Marler.

Finally I note the publication of a new edition of Ferre's *Language Logic and God*[126]. I have been unable to obtain a copy of this review: it will be interesting to see how the author tackles the question of 'talking apes'.

[124] *Language Learning by a Chimpanzee – The Lana Project,* edited by Duane M. Rumbaugh. (Communication and Behavior). New York and London: Academic Press. pp. 304. £12.40.
[125] *Progress in Ape Research,* edited by Geoffrey H. Bourne. New York and London: Academic Press. pp. 320. £11.35.
[126] *Language Logic and God,* by F. Ferre. Westport, Conn.: Greenwood Publishing. pp. 184. $14.

III

Old English Literature

T. A. SHIPPEY

Comprehensive bibliographies of Anglo-Saxon studies appear annually in *ASE* and *OEN*, the former prepared by a team of scholars under the general editorship of Peter Clemoes, the latter currently by Carl T. Berkhout. *OEN* also publishes an annual account of 'The Year's Work in OE Studies', again as a co-operative effort co-ordinated by Rowland L. Collins; and abstracts of as yet unpublished papers delivered at some American conferences. The list of 'O.E. Research in Progress' published annually in *NM* is also at present compiled by Carl T. Berkhout.

1. Social, Cultural and Intellectual Background

Basil Clarke's *Exploratory Studies*[1] into mental disorder in fact cover fairly familiar ground as regards the Anglo-Saxons, weighing the barely ponderable evidence for elf-shot, faith-healing, social dynamics and miracles, with particular reference to the *Vita s. Guthlaci*. More material issues are considered in 'Sutton Hoo published: a review' (*ASE*), by Martin Biddle and others, an article which generally supports the evidence given in Volume 1 of the official account of that excavation (see *YW* 56,63), though not without suggestions for further work and a strong 'devil's advocate' argument from R. I. Page against the Rædwald identification. In 'Anglo-Saxon Lyre Tuning Pegs from Whitby, N. Yorks.' (*Medieval Archaeology*) D. K. Fry identifies four previously unremarked objects from excavations of 1924–5, concluding that their poor fit would necessitate frequent retuning of any lyre of which they were part. The appropriateness of the find to Cædmon's monastery is noted, though the date of the pegs cannot be fixed. A much larger find is described in Philip Rahtz and Donald Bullough's 'The parts of an Anglo-Saxon mill' (*ASE*). For the first time physical evidence has been unearthed to compare with Anglo-Saxon vocabulary: *mylentroh* can now for instance be interpreted as the hollowed or planked construction that connects the wheel to the head of water, while *ger* may not mean 'fish-weir' but often 'mill-dam'. More widely significant is the question of the dating of technological change. Charter evidence leads the authors to place the building of one mill at Woodstone as closely as 944–956. In the same journal Margaret Gelling's 'Latin loan-words in O.E. place-names' considers such words as *vicus* for a 'sub-Roman settlement which had not been taken over or obliterated', *campus* for 'stretches of uncultivated land', *fontana* for an artificially-

---

[1] *Mental Disorder in Earlier Britain: Exploratory Studies,* by Basil Clarke. Cardiff: U. of Wales P. 1977. pp. xii + 335. £10.

improved spring, etc. These, she thinks, are more likely to have been learnt by Anglo-Saxons from Latin speakers than from Welsh (at least in S.E. England), and point to a 'phase of overlap and controlled settlement'. The article is a sequel to the author's earlier piece in *Medieval Archaeology* (1967), itself reprinted along with seven other useful articles from 1966–1973 in *Place-Name Evidence for the Anglo-Saxon Invasion and Scandinavian Settlements*[2]. Much of the material from these is however subsumed in Professor Cameron's *PBA* lecture of last year (*YW* 57. 43–4).

On the historical side, Peter Hunter-Blair's *An Introduction to Anglo-Saxon England*[3] achieves a second edition, with new material on place-names, town-life, coins, the Feddersen Wierde excavations etc. The same author's *Northumbria in the Days of Bede*[4] claims not to be a regular history but a 'series of impressions' of such varied matters as Northumbrian geology, the cosmology of Jarrow, the effect of ships and the sea-shore on Northern monasteries, and schoolroom behaviour. Mr Hunter-Blair is not afraid to use literary material, to confess ignorance, or to speculate. His ideal reader is a traveller prepared to walk across country and peer at the stone cross-fragments yet embedded in the walls of mediaeval churches, and also to temper this concern with *materialia* with reflections on the fate of 'short-lived rheumaticky Anglo-Saxon man'. There are two important collections from English universities, *Mercian Studies*[5] from Leicester, and *Early Medieval Kingship*[6] from Leeds. In the former, Wendy Davies's 'Annals and the Origins of Mercia' argues from the evidence of post-Conquest chroniclers first, that these themselves go back to 'some mid- or East Anglian archive . . . not available when the Anglo-Saxon Chronicle was compiled'; second, that they indicate that Penda became king perhaps as early as 607; and third, that his dynasty began with Crida some quarter-century earlier. As for the invasion of Mercia by the Anglo-Saxons, the idea that this took place in 515 was at least an early one. Cyril Hart's 'The Kingdom of Mercia' in the same volume considers the Tribal Hidage and attempts to map its many names. His review of chronology, however, works on the premise that genealogies are facts, with such sentences as 'After Ecgfrith's death . . . there had to be the most extraordinary hark-back over eight generations before a suitable claimant could be found in the person of Cenwulf'. Exactly this sort of reasoning is rejected by David N. Dumville's 'Kingship, Genealogies and Regnal Lists', in the Leeds collection. He insists, with modern anthropological comparisons, that pre-literates only preserve 'versions of their history which explain current social groupings and institutions', and

---

[2] *Place-Name Evidence for the Anglo-Saxon Invasion and Scandinavian Settlements*, collected by Kenneth Cameron with intro. by Margaret Gelling. Nottingham: English Place-Name Society. 1975, repr. 1977. pp. 171. £2.25.

[3] *An Introduction to Anglo-Saxon England*, 2nd ed. by Peter Hunter-Blair. Cambridge: C.U.P. 1977. pp. xv + 380. £12.50, pb £4.50.

[4] *Northumbria in the Days of Bede*, by Peter Hunter-Blair, Victor Gollancz. 1976. pp. 254, 16 ill. £5.95.

[5] *Mercian Studies*, ed. by Ann Dornier. Leicester: Leicester U.P. (distributed in the U.S.A. by Humanities Press, N.J.) 1977. pp. 255, 68 figs. £6.95.

[6] *Early Medieval Kingship*, edited by P. H. Sawyer and I. N. Wood. Leeds: School of History, U. of Leeds. 1977. pp. viii + 194. £3.50.

has some penetrating remarks on genealogical corruptions and the political involvement of professionally learned classes.

Further use of modern anthropology is found in three more essays from the same Leeds volume: P. H. Sawyer's 'Kings and Merchants', which points to the 'essentially uncommercial' nature of Dark Age society; Janet L. Nelson's 'Inauguration Rituals', which considers *inter alia* the case of King Edgar, arguing that he was anointed as early as 960–961 but then recrowned in 975 to express a new 'hegemonial imperialism'; and Patrick Wormald's *'Lex Scripta* and *Verbum Regis:* Legislation and Germanic Kingship from Euric to Cnut'. This last, a most stimulating piece, denies the old distinction between *Lex/Volksrecht* and *Capitulare/Königsrecht,* but nevertheless argues that barbarian law-codes 'were not solely practical' but represented a part of the royal advisers' self-image (as heirs to Rome, counterparts of the Children of Israel, etc.). 'Pronouncement and enforcement of the law remained essentially an oral process', he suggests. This relatively subtle view of the interaction of speech and writing is further elaborated in the same author's 'The Uses of Literacy in Anglo-Saxon England and its Neighbours' (*TRHS*), which gives full weight to the stubborn aristocratic resistance to letters, at least among men, as also to a certain 'jealous restriction of literacy' among Irish *filid* and conceivably Anglo-Saxon monks. 'Vernacular literature', we are reminded, 'does not in itself imply a wide reading public'.

These opinions are not denied by M. A. Meyer's 'Women and the 10th Century English Monastic Reform' (*RB*), which considers the role in that movement of royal and noble widows, especially Edgiva, wife of Edward the Elder, and Ethelthryth, second wife of Edgar. Eric John's 'War and Society in the Tenth Century: The Maldon Campaign' (*TRHS*) is far more iconoclastic. Among other opinions unfamilar to literary scholars are his assertions that the Viking commander was certainly Olaf Tryggvason, that Byrhtnoth was earl of Northumbria not ealdorman of Essex, and that the monastic reform was the start of a rot that led to Maldon, Ethelred, and eventually Hastings. Mr John feels that monastic expropriations led to a legacy of secular disaffection amounting almost to civil war, while Byrhtnoth's death caused the collapse of the 'pro-monastic aristocracy'; all this explains the defeatism of the Abingdon Chronicler and his reluctance to admit that the 'epidemic of treachery' he described went straight back to the 'excesses' of Dunstan, Æthelwold and their followers. He also believes that Byrhtnoth won an earlier battle at Maldon in 988. The OE poem is given little weight in this article; but criticism of it is bound to be affected.

An evident monastic bias shows itself in the thousand lines of French verse whose discovery is announced in William Rothwell's 'The Life and Miracles of St Edmund: A Recently-Discovered MS' (*BJRL*), for they present a monk of Bury succeeding against bad king Swein where even the redoubtable Ulfketel had failed. Other eleventh-century apocrypha are considered in Christine Fell's 'English history and Norman legend in the Icelandic saga of Edward the Confessor' (*ASE*). D. P. Kirby's 'Welsh bards and the border' (*Mercian Studies*) looks at a group of Welsh poems on the exploits of Cadwallon and notes an early lack of Welsh interest in Mercia leavened by some possible resentment of the activities of British clerical 'quislings'. On the Anglo-Latin front, Michael Winterbottom,

'Aldhelm's Prose Style and its origins' (*ASE*), analyses five examples of Aldhelm's prose style to show that it is more probably derived from Continental than from Hisperic models. Michael Lapidge's 'L'Influence Stylistique de la Poésie de Jean Scot', in *Jean Scot Érigène et l'Histoire de la Philosophie*[7], concurs; studying the 'graecisms' of John the Scot, it argues that these were an original trait not derived from Ireland, but eventually disseminated to England via Fleury. The same author considers the migrations of 'The Medieval Hagiography of St. Ecgwine' (*Vale of Evesham Historical Society Research Papers*, 6), from Byrhtferth of Ramsey probably *c.*1014 to Dominic of Evesham and later redactors, one of them discernibly embroiled on the side of King Henry against Anselm *c.*1100. 'The Latin and OE glosses in the *ars Tatuini*' (*ASE*) are also traced by Vivien Law, the former to Breedon pre-731, the latter either to Canterbury or to Continental scribes using Canterbury material. In 'Two lost documents of king Athelstan' (*ASE*), Eric E. Barker perceives attestors or donators from Athelstan's retinue between 934 and 937 in two name-lists from the Durham *Liber Vitae*.

Besides other work on coins, buildings and archaeology, *Mercian Studies* contains Rosemary Cramp's 'Schools of Mercian Sculpture', a study in sudden changes, and Hazel Wheeler's 'Aspects of Mercian Art: the Book of Cerne', which tries to place Cambridge University Library MS LI.1.10 in Lichfield *c.*818-830, on the basis of similarity to the British Museum Bede and to Royal MS I.E.vi. Robert Deshman's 'The Leofric Missal and tenth-century English art' (*ASE*) argues that the Glastonbury drawings in the second part of Bodley MS 579 are under strong influence from Winchester, and that the criticised term 'Winchester style' is not a complete misnomer after all. Carl Nordenfalk's *Celtic and Anglo-Saxon Painting*[8] gives a selection of plates with a brief introduction defending the Irish origin of Northumbrian art.

2. Vocabulary

In 'A New OE Glossary: Nowell upon Huloet' (*SN*) James L. Rosier identifies Lawrence Nowell's hand in annotations to a sixteenth-century *Abcedarium;* they show Nowell introducing law-terms and place-names to the format of an English dictionary and with them 'a lexicographical method based on historical principles'. Peter Bierbaumer, 'Zu J. V. Goughs Ausgabe einiger altenglischer Glossen' (*Anglia)* makes a string of corrections to an earlier *Anglia* article (*YW* 55.41) on glosses in four manuscripts.

On single words, Alfred Bammesberger offers a series of etymologies and revisions: 'Two OE Glosses' (*ES*) eliminates *blefla* as a ghost-word and corrects *un-flycge* to *-flycg;* 'Zum Ansatz von ae. *bedæcc(e)an*' (*Münchener Studien zur Sprachwissenschaft*, 1976) again eliminates a ghost-word; 'AE. *sneowan/sniwan* und gotisch *sniwan*' (*Zeitschrift für*

[7] *Jean Scot Érigène et l'Histoire de la Philosophie* (Colloques Internationaux du Centre National de la Recherche Scientifique, no. 561). Paris: Edition du CNRS. 1977 245.00 Fr.

[8] *Celtic and Anglo-Saxon Painting: Book Illumination in the British Isles 600–800*, by Carl Nordenfalk. Chatto & Windus. 1977. pp. 128, 48 plates. £4.95.

Vergleichende Sprachforschung, 1976) argues for a short vowel in the O.E. verb; 'AE. *gamban* "Tribut"' (*Die Sprache*, 1976) gives this word an etymology from **gam-bann-a*, 'earth-offering' whence 'tribute'; 'Zur Herkunft von AE. *ondrædan* und *andrysne*' (*BDGSL*) argues that these two words were not originally connected, but have both suffered from morpheme boundary shift (**and-redan* to *on-drædan*, e.g.) as from complex semantic shifts. Eric P. Hamp exposes *inter alia* a calque from *bro/cymro* to *leod/geleod* in 'OE *-leod*' (*ES*). Ernst A. Ebbinghaus derives 'The Etymology of OE *mælsceafa*' (*General Linguistics*) not from 'meal-shaver' but from 'ornament-shaver', by way of allusion to the appearance of cabbages after caterpillars or 'coleworms' have been at them; in the same journal (1976) the same author takes 'OE *agu* "pica"' or 'magpie' back to an IE root meaning 'fast', cp. Gothic *ahaks* for the homing pigeon. W. B. Lockwood's 'Some British Bird-Names (II)' (*TPS* 1977 for 1975) derives *cyta* 'kite' and **tela* 'teal' from mere onomatopoeia, but the 'ruff' or 'reeve' both from its feathery frill and from OE *hreoh*, 'fierce'.

Nigel F. Barley considers gestures as well as words to make 'Two Emendations to *Iudicia Monasterialia* (Cotton Tiberius A III)' (*NM*), and though these merely confirm the old emendation of *wicelre* to *micelre*, and propose *beordræst* 'dregs of beer' for *beorhreste*, the method has its admirers, see section 3 below. More interesting from the literary point of view is Dieter Kartschoke's 'Selfsceaft' (*Zeitschrift für Deutsches Altertum*), which argues that the crux in *Genesis B* 523 should be *self-sceafte*, 'to the self-created', a reference to Satan not Adam, and borrowed from Avitus's idea that the devil proclaims himself *suus ipse creator*. Carola L. Gottzmann's study of 'Sippe' in *Sprachwissenschaft* shows that it is impossible to give this word a meaning equally valid for all ages; and that *Beowulf* in particular exhibits a fairly idiosyncratic confusion between ties of blood and ties of loyalty, as between peace and the community living in peace, the *sibbegedriht*. Heather Stuart sees a higher degree of precision in 'Some OE Medical Terms' (*Parergon*, 1975), for instance *lǣcecrǣft*, 'an approved medical fact or hypothesis' and *lǣcedom*, 'method of cure' or 'a particular incident', though this sort of distinction does not apply equally to all sources. Harry J. Solo feels that in spite of citations for the verb under its 'secondary' meaning of necessity, 'The Meaning of **Motan*' (*NM*) is just 'to be permitted', and that that applies even to the notorious crux of *Maldon* line 30. Bruce Mitchell does not think there is (yet) enough evidence, even from *Beowulf* 1990, for 'O.E. *Ac* as an Interrogative Particle' (*NM*). And D. G. Scragg 'O.E. *Forhtleasness, Unforhtleasness*' (*N&Q*) shows that the former word is correct in a Vercelli homily and need not be emended to the latter. It means 'cowardly lack of faith' not 'fearlessness'.

Three longer works complete this section. Stephen A. Barney's *Word-Hoard*[9] is avowedly pedagogic, a listing of the two thousand words most frequent in *Beowulf* and J. C. Pope's *Seven OE Poems* in 200 groups of etymologically related words. Compounds are listed at the bottom of each group, and common errors (like thinking *wine* means 'wine') receive special treatment. But the most useful feature of the book is its imagin-

---

[9] *Word-Hoard: an Introduction to O.E. Vocabulary*, by Stephen A. Barney. New Haven, Conn. and London: Yale U.P. 1977. pp. xvi + 108. £2.15.

ative presentation of cognates and etymologies; this running commentary on semantic change will arrest even the bored student, and keeps alive a branch of knowledge now sinking into the oblivion of scholarly glossaries. John Lindow's *Comitatus, Individual and Honor*[10] also moves on to a favourite stamping-ground of former *Germanisten*, the complex of words such as *gesiþ, gedryht, hired, ar* etc., together with their much more frequent O.N. and Germanic analogues. Many interesting conclusions are drawn, such as the increasing replacement of martial glory (*tir*) by the 'honor of social utility' expressed in such words as *sómi*; or the mutual influence of English and Scandinavian in such pairs as *hired/hirð* and *weorðung/verðung*. As with *'sippe'* (see Carola L. Gottzmann above), it is noted that 'in *Beowulf . . . gedryht* is closer to the *comitatus* than elsewhere in O.E.', though even in that poem the word is always qualified by some term such as *æþelinga*. These considerations of semantics will have to be weighed by those wishing to redate the poem, as some scholars apparently do. Klaus R. Ginda's *'Arbeit' und 'Mühe'*[11], finally, describes an entire semantic field with exemplary thoroughness. Eleven words are considered; *weorc* covers work and good deeds and military service indifferently, offering a measurement of 'social utility' or 'performance (with claim to value)'. Against it words like *gewinn* or *geswinc* measure the dimension of toil and trouble, with significant extensions in some texts towards monastic/ascetic ideas of the value of study and of labour as an end in itself. Once again this development of a grid enables texts to be placed. It is interesting that *bisgu, bisgung* has lost pejorative value in the translation of the Benedictine Rule, but not in line 88 of *The Seafarer*.

3. Old English: General

This is perhaps the place to mention two studies which grapple with the problem of an alien communication-system in its acutest form. Winfried Noth's 'Semiotics of the OE Charm' (*Semiotica*, 19) insists that it is important to consider not only words but also actions and signs for a proper understanding of these magical texts/events/messages. The author notes several difficulties in distinguishing charms from mere 'leechdoms', and sub-categorises agreed charms in several different ways. He observes however that these 'factors of the communicative process' were not always well-differentiated by users, while the main features of O.E. charms included also 'lack of differentiation between sign and object' and 'lack of differentiation between the stations of the communication process'. Charms, it seems, worked in a way like modern advertisements — the less alert you were to their semiotics the more likely you were to do what the wizard said. Drid Williams's 'The Arms and Hands, with Special Reference to an Anglo-Saxon Sign System' (*Semiotica*, 21) takes up a similar stance with reference to the text *De computo vel loquela*

[10] *Comitatus, Individual and Honor: Studies in North Germanic Institutional Vocabulary* (U. of California Publications in Linguistics 83), by John Lindow. Berkeley and Los Angeles, Calif. and London.: U. of California P. 1976. pp. xviii + 175. £6.40.
[11] *'Arbeit' und 'Mühe': Untersuchungen zur Bedeutungsgeschichte ae. Wörter*, by Klaus R. Grinda. München: Wilhelm Fink Verlag. 1975. pp. 320. DM68.

digitorum. A striking feature of her article is its reduction of movements to a system of notation which can record anything from *Swan Lake* to a High Mass! However little can be recovered with certainty of Anglo-Saxon finger codes, for illustrators did not understand them.

More familiar problems are confronted in N. F. Blake's *The English Language in Medieval Literature*[12], a book which sets out to defend the study of those two things from the encroachments of modernity. Professor Blake explains many ways in which mediaeval works are unlike these of post-print eras: they are usually 'clerical and anonymous', do not respond to biographical approaches, exploit denotation as much as connotation, etc. His examples are drawn from all periods between 700 and 1500, but among O.E. cruces considered are *meoduscerwen* in *Andreas* (mediaeval lack of response to verbal echoes), *dreorigne* in *Wanderer* 18 (modern expansiveness spoiling ancient gnomic brevity), *modþryðo wæg* in *Beowulf* (modern editors interpreting via punctuation). This is a useful and thoughtful book: though its utility is perhaps framed rather narrowly by the nature of dialogue within university departments of English. Malcolm Godden's chapter on 'OE' in *Editing Medieval Texts*[13] takes a wider historical perspective in tracing the history of O.E. editions from the sixteenth century to now and on into the future. Dr. Godden thinks there is little to be done editorially on O.E. verse, much on O.E. prose, and especially on single manuscripts. Detailed studies of these would help to explain how they were compiled, and also how texts were used by compilers; they would provide 'material for a fuller understanding of Anglo-Saxon culture as a whole', with the last phrase incidentally including much more attention to those Anglo-Latin texts often regarded as peripheral by full-time Latinists.

Two shorter contributions from the journal *In Geardagum*, no. 2, approach more tenuous distinctions between O.E. and modern culture. Dean Loganbill's 'Mind and Process in the Continuity of English Literature' discusses the alleged 'concrete thinking' of archaic or primitive societies, in which the distinction between 'I' and 'It', or Self and Nature, is not fully marked; but concludes that from this point of view Anglo-Saxon literature as we have it is not always so primitive or 'concrete' after all. Paul C. Bauschatz's 'O.E. Conjunctions: Some Semantic Considerations' tends to disagree, arguing that O.E., and O.E. poetry in particular, handles temporal and causal connections in a way quite different from ours. The point may be conceded, though on occasion one feels that some of Professor Bauschatz's conundrums over *þa* could be solved by a more peremptory style of translation. Thomas H. Bestul argues for a more limited continuity in 'St Anselm and the Continuity of Anglo-Saxon Devotional Tradition' (*Annuale Medievale*); the emotionalism thought by many to be an Anselmian invention is to be found in a whole body of private devotional prayers written in England between 950 and 1100 and

---

[12] *The English Language in Medieval Literature*, by N. F. Blake. London: Dent, and Totowa N.J.: Rowman & Littlefield. 1977. pp. 190. £7.95.

[13] *Editing Medieval Texts English French and Latin Written in England* (Papers given at the Twelfth Annual Conference on editorial problems, University of Toronto), ed. by A. G. Rigg. New York and London: Garland Publishing Inc. 1977. pp. viii + 128. $12.

preserved e.g. in the Athelstan, Leofric, Cambridge, Canterbury and Bury Psalters. Anselm could have read such things, for Anglo-Saxon manuscripts were known in Normandy; three twelfth-century manuscripts show his work mingled with and assimilated into the 'English devotional tradition'.

4. Poetry: General

Continuity is a major theme also of D. K. Pearsall's *O.E. and M.E. Poetry*[14]. Indeed there are hints that Professor Pearsall is in a way working backwards. Thus he does not believe that the 'Alliterative Revival' of the fourteenth century was a revival after all, rather the return to poetic dignity of a habit seen also in written prose, formal speech, and at several stations of an alliterative continuum. This opinion begins to be set out in chapter 3, 'Late OE Poetry and the Transition', but involves the author earlier on in such beliefs as: that most O.E. poetry was written before 850; that *Maldon* has 'little in common with the heroic lay'; that *Finnsburh* is 'untouched by Christianity or indeed by any humane or civilising impulse whatever'; that behind *Beowulf* there was 'a body of well-known heroic "lays"', and so on. These opinions could be defended, indeed form part of an old view of literary history, but they do not produce attractive readings of some texts, and entail a rather low view of *Exodus, Andreas* etc. Professor Pearsall is however very strong on the monastic educational system, and deals particularly well with minor O.E. and early M.E. verse; no other book covers this wide field anything like as well. Raymond P. Tripp Jr offers an avowedly subjective piece 'On the Continuity of English Poetry between *Beowulf* and Chaucer' (*Poetica* Tokyo 6, 1976). He shows unexpected similarities in the handling of great speeches, seasonal change, ignorance motifs etc., though they are held together only within 'the developing mentality . . . of the English nation'. Bernice W. Kliman's 'Women in Early English Literature, *Beowulf* to the *Ancrene Wisse*' (*NMS*) lacks even this framework, hopping from 'peaceweaver' to 'anchoress' with considerable agility and much scorn for rabbinical misogyny; it is fortunate that *Hali Meiðhad* lies outside the author's scope.

There are then several pieces which, by their contrast with each other, expose the radical uncertainty of much O.E. criticism. Norman Blake's 'The Dating of OE Poetry', in *An English Miscellany*[15], is highly iconoclastic, arguing in brief that most O.E. poetry is post-Alfredian, from such evidence as absence of classical reference in *The Phoenix,* absence of poetic phrases in Alfred's prose, the use of *Beowulf* in Blickling 17, the mixture of Mercian and West Saxon in poetic texts. Not all the arguments are convincing (especially the ones about the Beowulfian textual tradition), but the article as a whole provokes much thought. Against this the drift of W. F. Bolton's 'Alcuin and OE Poetry' (*YES*) is that there are many parallels between Alcuin and O.E. poems, of diction and of concept, which at least implies that the latter are eighth or early ninth century. Stanley

---

[14] *Old English and Middle English Poetry* (Routledge History of English Poetry Vol. 1), by Derek Pearsall. Routledge & Kegan Paul. 1977. pp. xiv + 352. £8.75.
[15] *An English Miscellany presented to W. S. Mackie,* ed. by Brian S. Lee. Cape Town, London and New York: O.U.P. (S. Africa). 1977. pp. 218. £6.50.

B. Greenfield, meanwhile, casts doubt on some Anglo-Latin linkings in 'OE Words and Patristic Exegesis – *hwyrftum scriþað*: A Caveat' (*MP*). T. D. Hill's argument of 1971 that the phrase quoted is a deliberate allusion to Psalms 11 : 9 and circling sinners is refuted by pointing out that *hwyrft* need not mean 'circle' while *scriþan* has strong associations of speed and directness. Loren C. Gruber, finally, keeps an old 'Germanic' orientation alive in 'The Agnostic Anglo-Saxon Gnomes: *Maxims I* and *II*, *Germania*, and the Boundaries of Northern Wisdom' (*Poetica* Tokyo 6, 1976). The *Maxims* poems are seen as 'archaic initiatory utterances' which have been in one way or another 'revalorized', like the relatively rational 'gnomes' chosen by Tacitus to fill his own sceptic or agnostic 'moral vacuum'. The same theme is considered again by Professor Gruber in 'The Rites of Passage: *Hávamál*, Stanzas 1–5' (*Scandinavian Studies*), which though concerned mostly with O.N. nevertheless makes points applicable to O.E., especially about the need for 'epistemological enterprise' in translation. The two articles embody an underlying disagreement with Professor Blake over date and with Professor Pearsall over monasticism; the views of Professors Blake and Pearsall are furthermore in several respects incompatible; no clear basis for a developing consensus emerges.

On the question of metre, David L. Hoover writes a perfect example of the 'Yes, but . . .' school of criticism in his rejoinder to T. C. Cable, 'O.E. Meter Again' (*JEGP*). Professor Cable's views on metre (for which see *YW* 55. 81–2) are largely accepted, but refined over the question of A verses with anacrusis, reasoned with over clashing stresses and the equation of types D2 and E, and queried over the 'inevitability' of the Sievers 5-type system. On the formulaic issue, Earl R. Anderson cites a scene from the *De Gestis Herwardi Saxonis* in 'Passing the Harp in Bede's Story of Cædmon: a Twelfth Century Analogue' (*ELN*); while Richard C. Payne rescrutinises scholarly debate and evidence for the 'literary habits of the mediaeval cloister' in 'Formulaic Poetry in OE and its Backgrounds' (*SMC*). Jeff Opland, 'On Anglo-Saxon Poetry and the Comparative Study of Oral Poetic Traditions' (*Acta Germanica*), continues to develop African parallels, making interesting points against the assumption that all Germanic poetic traditions were similar, that *scop* and *gleoman* must be equated. Oral poetry can be spontaneously eulogistic and also composedly narrative. Similar dissatisfaction with the history of formulaic debate emerges from the journal *Semeia*, whose issue no. 5 (1976) is devoted to orality and includes several articles by Robert C. Culley, Albert B. Lord and others which mention O.E. *en passant*. The most relevant of them is Susan Wittig's 'Theories of Formulaic Narrative', which argues that there is a tendency to confuse the presentation of a poem with its generation, while there are two latent but inconsistent theories of the latter in existence: one that of 'slots' waiting to be filled, the other that of a 'template' of which all formulas are variants. The latter is seen as the more powerful theory, analogous to Chomskian transformational-generative grammar as 'slots' are to Saussurian 'syntagmatic' grammar. It can be applied to scenes and plots as well as phrases.

Four studies offer variant approaches to the definition of heroic ethos. Michael Swanton, 'Heroes, Heroism and Heroic Literature' (*E&S*), begins with the late Roman Empire, and sees in it a rise of new men and of 'the strongly active Pelagian ethic of self-reliance'. This in its turn gave way to the 'feudal ideology of *auctoritas dei gratia'*, of which we see signs even in *Beowulf,* while the earlier ethical confrontation is reflected in stories of Germanus and Vortigern, in the debate between open and closed societies of Pelagius and Augustine, two adversaries with 'unusually deep personal respect' for each other. Close to seventy Pelagian tracts remain unexplored, notes Mr Swanton; they should not be dismissed lightly. In similar vein Frederick P. Pickering's 'Historical Thought and Moral Codes in Medieval Epic', one of several interesting articles in *The Epic in Medieval Society*[16], asserts that besides Augustine and Boethius the Dark Ages had a third history-teacher, the 'mistress' of history herself. Her teachings were less moral than those of the others; also less bogus than those of *Heilsgeschichte,* into whose follies Professor Pickering is grateful that secular (German) poets refused to be drawn. But this article is especially useful to Anglo-Saxonists for its interpretations of mediaeval response to Boethius. In the same volume Franz H. Bäuml's 'The Unmaking of the Hero: Some Critical Implications of the Transition from Oral to Written Epic' argues that in oral tradition poet = reciter = narrator = text; but as these are separated by literacy, commentary and irony become possible, as we see in such variably formulaic poems as *Kudrun* or the *Nibelungenlied.* Irony is similarly opposed to gnomicism in this reviewer's 'Maxims in OE Narrative: Literary Art or Traditional Wisdom?', in Odense University's *Oral Tradition/Literary Tradition*[17]. Critics such as Robert B. Burlin (*YW* 56.70) have made out a strong case for the literary art of Beowulfian maxims; but cases can also be made out for their widespread and non-literary utility, as for highly non-literary ineptness in the use of maxims in for instance *Genesis B.* This last feature may point to something 'compulsive' in poetic gnomicism; the *swa sceal* set of Beowulfian sayings is considered to show how 'maxims are like magic: they make propriety (*sceal*) equal reality (*bið*)'.

Robert R. Black also offers 'Some Notes and Queries on the Uses of Irony' (*In Geardagum*), with special reference to the *Guthlac* poems' temptation scenes and their possible awareness of Prudentius's *Psychomachia.* Eugene R. Kintgen, '*Lif, Lof, Leof, Lufu* and *Geleafa* in OE Poetry' (*NM*), takes passages from several poems which appear to play on these words and argues that their collocation is not random but strategic. G. Storms's 'Notes on OE Poetry' (*Neophilologus*) deals with *myne wisse* in *Beowulf* and *The Wanderer* (it means 'give a thought to'), and with the latter poem's *wyrmlicum* (moderating *fah* not *weal*).

5. Beowulf

It is a little surprising that a text with facing-page translation of *Beowulf* has not recently been available in English; now two have appeared. The first, though admirable in its confidence that poetry will get through any syntactic barrier to any audience, is perhaps only a curiosity. John

---

[16] *The Epic in Medieval Society: Aesthetic and Moral Values,* ed. by Harald Scholler. Tübingen: Max Niemeyer Verlag. 1977. pp. xii + 410. DM 26.45.

[17] *Oral Tradition/Literary Tradition: a symposium,* ed. by Hans Bekker-Nielsen *et al.* Odense: Odense U.P. 1977. pp. 121. £5.

Porter edits *Beowulf*[18] and then translates it half-line at a time with heavy archaism and no concessions to modern word-order: 'I my know/ gracious Hrothulf/that he the youths will/in honour hold . . . '. Howell D. Chickering's *Beowulf: A Dual-Language Edition*[19], is much more ambitious, indeed framed at every point by consciousness of scholarly debate. Sometimes one wonders whether a naive reader could follow the translation by itself, not because of any infelicities in the language (which aims at reproducing the 'craggy' sentence structure and the 'heroic restraint' of the original) but because of its embedded learned indecisions. Thus *aþum-swerian* in the text of line 84 is translated as 'his sworn son-in-law', a compromise surely between the (meaningless) MS reading *aþum swerian* and the (reconstructed) editorial *aþum-sweoran*. The latter may be wrong, but the former cannot be right. Why preserve it so vestigially? The point does serve as a reminder to a tutor reading through the poem in class; and this seems to be Professor Chickering's intended audience. His long Introduction is what the class needs, his long paragraph-by-paragraph Commentary throws up topics for the tutor, his Bibliography refers continually to current debates without choosing sides. The text is not free from errors (lines 176 and 275 have been replaced by repetitions of 178 and 276 respectively), but the volume as a whole meets a real need, economically.

Raymond P. Tripp Jr produces two articles dependent on a very sceptical approach to the received text of the poem. 'The Exemplary Role of Hrothgar and Heorot' (*PQ*) repunctuates and retranslates lines 67–70 to remove their hints of pride and arbitrariness, though in a way which depends on taking *ærn* as masculine not neuter. 'The Archetype Enters History and Goes to Sleep: What Beowulf does in Heorot' (*In Geardagum*) does the same to lines 703 ff. *Wið earm gesæt* refers to Grendel's hold, not the hero's; Beowulf was at that moment asleep, and previous references to watchers mean God or Grendel; *ealle buton anum* means 'all without exception'; and so on. In general the emendations make Beowulf less culpable, more evidently under divine protection. John F. Vickrey also offers major rereadings in 'The narrative structure of Hengest's revenge in *Beowulf*' (*ASE*). He repeats the convincing argument of D. K. Fry that *unhlitme* means 'of free will' not 'without choice', and hence that Hengest *could* go home; and goes on to argue that the whole sequence of lines 1127–41 is 'not literal' but 'symbolical', an 'extended metaphor' for Hengest's revenge in which winter is misery and spring solace; this involves retranslation of *eard gemunde, fundode, ohte* etc. Sherman M. Kuhn's 'Further Thoughts on *brand Healfdenes*' (*JEGP*) insists that *brand* in line 1020 need not be emended to *bearn* nor taken as periphrasis for Hrothgar. Ellen Spolsky's 'OE Kinship Terms and *Beowulf*' (*NM*) notes again the poem's confusions over *aþum* and *nefa* and suggests that the

[18] *Beowulf*, ed. and trans. by John Porter. Pirate Press. 1975. no pagination. £0.80.

[19] *Beowulf: A Dual-Language Edition*, trans. with introduction and commentary by Howell D. Chickering Jr. Garden City, N.Y.: Anchor P./Doubleday. 1977. pp. xiv + 390. $4.95.

intended audience was less interested in marking generations than in stressing 'comradeship in arms . . . mutual responsibility for welfare'.

Moralistic and patristic approaches to the poem continue to dominate orthodoxy. Joseph F. Tuso, *'Beowulf* and the Theological Virtues' (*In Geardagum*), believes first that the poem's author and audience 'would have been familiar with the Bible and St Paul', second that the poem has three movements dominated by faith, hope and charity, third that these virtues are evident from the funeral of Scyld the *god cyning* or 'god-king'. Lars Malmberg, 'Grendel and the Devil' (*NM*), repeats Klaeber's finding that *godes andsaca* is a well-known term for the devil and asserts that Grendel's defeat thus 'acquires a deeper significance'. J. B. Allen, 'God's Society and Grendel's Shoulder-Joint (*NM*), feels that the influence of Gregory's *Moralia in Job* on *Beowulf* is 'generally conceded' and furthermore that a Dijon MS of that work contains a 'plausible' illustration of the poem's final scene. In his comment on Job 31: 22 Gregory said the shoulder stands for *socialis vitae conjunctio;* since this is just what Grendel threatens, it is right that his own emblem of it should be destroyed. S. L. Dragland, 'Monster-Man in *Beowulf'* (*Neophilologus*), sees the poem as ironic and the hero as containing symbolically the 'human germ of failure' for himself as for heroes; the resemblances between heroes and monsters are detailed, and it is shown that Heorot, Beowulf and Denmark are all eroded from within. Patricia Silber turns to 'Gold and its Significance in *Beowulf'* (*Annuale Medievale*) but also insists that it becomes an image of evil after line 2200, 'carrying within it the seeds of doom and destruction'; she too believes that the fault lies not in men but in society. G. Hughes's 'Beowulf, Unferth and Hrunting: An Interpretation' (*ES*) sees Unferth as deeply involved in Scylding rottenness, but proclaims that the real clue to his behaviour lies in jealousy stemming from his underrated role as 'warrior and champion'. His speech of challenge might be no more than reasonable objection 'if Unferth's version of the contest with Breca was the only one current at the Scylding court'. But how are we to infer that? This is treating fiction as fact, in the old Bradleyan style. Willem Helder's 'Beowulf and the Plundered Hoard' (*NM*) connects the dragon with the fires of Doomsday, line 2419 with the garden of Gethsemane, the thief with II Peter 3: 10. A surprising conclusion is that treasure-robbing stems not from pride or cupidity but is 'an exemplary Christian act'. God too will plunder back his own, in time. Almost the culmination of this equation-seeking approach is, unexpectedly, the second part of James Smith's *'Beowulf* – II' (*English*). Here the late Professor Smith shakes off the carefully extractive style of his first part (*YW* 57. 52) to declare that 'it is antecedently probable that the religious life was the poet's ideal', and that the story is there to present a 'hierarchy of moral values'. Grendel is the devil; his mother is evil in the heart; the *niceras* are 'the smaller sins which a greater sin inevitably breeds'; Grendel's head is 'the gruesome memory of a sin'; the sword-hilt 'represents a copy of the Scriptures' (though in the possession of Grendel's mother); and much else.

Two studies from *The Epic in Medieval Society* (see Section 4) offer some resistance to prevailing ironies. Kenneth L. Schmitz's 'Shapes of Evil in Medieval Epics: a Philosophical Analysis' compares *Beowulf* with the *Cid, Roland,* the *Nibelungenlied,* introducing the concept of a poetic 'horizon' of presupposition and compatibility and suggesting that the Beowulfian one tends to equate monsters with human ignorance. Charles J. Donahue, 'Social Function and Literary Value in *Beowulf*', iterates his belief in a 'liberal' Christianity with room for both Christ and Ingeld, and asserts that 'a thorough-going Christian *Beowulf*' would be 'contorted'. F. H. Whitman, 'The Kingly Nature of *Beowulf*' (*Neophilologus*), also refuses to accept Beowulfian piety, and points out that the hero impresses not by caution and moderation but by pride, daring, *joie de vivre* — qualities often deprecated or excluded by early Christian authors. The same critic notes that 'Corrosive Blood in *Beowulf*' (*Neophilologus*) may be a memory of Pliny.

Probably the most interesting works on the poem this year are two studies concerned with technicalities of composition. H. Ward Tonsfeldt, 'Ring Structure in *Beowulf*' (*Neophilologus*), shows several cases of a sort of narrative chiasmus within the poem: the coastguard's 'who? who from? where from?' is answered by Beowulf in reverse order; lines 129–149 frame Grendel in the middle with retreating retainers round him and on the periphery a sorrowful king; the Finnsburh Episode can be read the same way. However the author resists the temptation to see annular structures everywhere, as also to draw firm inferences about orality; his point is to resist the old charges of 'lack of steady advance'. In a rather similar way James L. Rosier revives the idea of 'echo-words' in 'Generative Composition in *Beowulf*' (*ES*). In lines 2200-2208a, for instance, we have a little pattern of *heard-, hilde-, rice;* and Professor Rosier finds and categorises some 140 similar patterns within the poem, some of considerable length and complexity (e.g. lines 2602-31a). The author concludes very rightly that in a closed (if not fixed) poetic mode 'the essential pressure or tension or motion of the creative process is to work internally upon and within the language . . . and through that tension or motion to enrich perception itself'. It is rare to see scholarship move with such assurance from objective causes to subjective effects. Each of the articles just mentioned has a lesser counterpart elsewhere. C. Frey's 'Lyric in Epic: Hrothgar's Depiction of the Haunted Mere, *Beowulf* 1357-76a' (*ES*) investigates the 'sonic structure' of that passage verbally, syntactically and metrically, so that 'insets' can be identified; and Livia Polanyi's 'Lexical Coherence Phenomena in Beowulf's Debate with Unferth' (*Rackham Literary Studies*) ponders kinship, homes, lands, boasts, hands, arms etc., to show how words in speeches reveal character.

There are finally three minor comparative pieces: David M. Gaunt's 'The Creation-Theme in Epic Poetry' (*CL*) opposes lines 86-98 of the poem to passages from Virgil and elsewhere in which creation-singers act as poetic mouthpieces; John Turville-Petre's *Beowulf* and *Grettis saga:* an Excursion' (*SBVS*) reviews old similarities with some new ideas on *hepti-* and *hæft-;* William C. Johnson Jr's '*Beowulf* and *The Volsungasaga*' (*In Geardagum*) contrasts funerals and dragon-killings to show Beowulfian relish for 'the numinous unknown'.

6. The Junius Manuscript

Only two of the four poems in this receive attention this year, but both appear in new editions. Robert E. Finnegan's *Christ and Satan*[20] is a relatively modest work, which has reverted to the old and ugly printer's habit of justifying b half-lines on the left. It incorporates a number of rather fierce textual emendations, marked off in bold type, but at the same time keeps some of the manuscript's stranger readings (such as *heofene* in line 10, surely for *geofene*). One wonders whether a motive is not on occasion to pick quarrels with the 1925 edition of M. D. Clubb. However the introduction contains several interesting ideas, such as that the Junius MS was meant to be about the 'ages of man' (*Christ and Satan* being seventh leading to eighth), that the poem is responding to the Adoptionist heresy of *c.*800, that like many O.E. homilies it is at once dramatic and hortatory. Peter J. Lucas's new edition of *Exodus*[21] comes over as very much fuller and more ambitious. It takes 74 pages to print 590 lines, which means that all but eight lines per page is footnotes; its glossary is very complete, and its introduction aims at something like total coverage; naturally it is expensive. This is perhaps why the editor has felt bound to make such positive claims about the origin of the codex (at Malmesbury), which do not seem likely to stand. He has also allowed himself to emend the text boldly in places, at others to retain previously discarded MS readings. It is 'in principle unacceptable' to emend *onhwæl* at line 161, but *wolcne* for *wolcnum* at line 350 is 'necessary on grounds of sense' (and also to improve a moral parallel). Such decisions are of course an editor's duty, but the non-use of diacritics in the text means that readers have to be careful they are not unwittingly working from a modern critical construct, on occasion of some length. In the introduction the sections on style and on exegesis are particularly novel and suggestive.

Smaller works on these two poems are J. R. Hall's 'Pauline Influence on *Exodus*, 523-548' (*ELN*), which makes a series of parallels between the poem and II Corinthians 3: 6: and Hugh T. Keenan's '*Christ and Satan:* Some Vagaries of OE Poetic Composition' (*SMC*, 1975), which suggests that some of the difficulties in this poem over Adam's creation and Satan's son can be removed by the concept of 'figural time' and by the idea that the poem is typologically anticipating Judgement Day. Thomas D. Hill's 'The Fall of Satan in the OE *Christ and Satan*' (*JEGP*) considers similar questions. Why does the poem say that Satan rebelled against Christ specifically (a view 'neither commonplace nor wholly unparalleled' in OE literature), and that the devil had a son whom he claimed would usurp Christ's role? Professor Hill suggest that the source is Augustine's gloss on John 8: 44; the devil did not stand in 'truth' = Christ, he was the father of 'lies' = *mendax* personified. Ruth M. Ames, 'The Old Testament Christ and the OE Exodus' (*SMC*) notes that many exegetes took Christ to be present in the Old Testament as 'word' or 'wisdom'; though this seems to us mere anachronism *Exodus* could have been read the same

---

[20] *Christ and Satan: A Critical Edition*, ed. by Robert E. Finnegan. Waterloo, Ontario: Wilfred Laurier U.P. 1977. pp. xii + 169. $7, pb $4.50.
[21] *Exodus*, ed. by Peter J. Lucas. Methuen. pp. xvi + 198. £12.

way, and conceived 'not as an allegory but as a history of the Israelites from a Christological point of view'. Some corroboration of this opinion is offered by Milton McC. Gatch, see Section 10 below.

7. Poems of the Vercelli Book

Very little has appeared in this area this year. *The Dream of the Rood* is translated as far as line 89 by John Nist, 'Dream of the Cross' (*OEN*). Marie Michelle Walsh plumbs 'The Baptismal Flood in the OE *Andreas:* Liturgical and Typological Depths' (*Traditio*), and draws out a series of correspondences. Andreas's Christ-like passion makes the flood waters efficacious for baptism; the young men later indeed need to be baptised after having gone *through* the flood, but that is to refer to the post-missionary practice of infant baptism; the death of fourteen Merme-donians is there to remind us of 'judgemental selectivity'; the references to Joshua and Tobias can also be provided with patristic glosses. Even the angel with the fire has baptismal associations, and anyone who balks at this must remember that 'No Anglo-Saxon reader would have been bothered' by such discrepancies. Robert C. Rice traces 'The penitential motif in Cynewulf's *Fates of the Apostles* and in his epilogues' (*ASE*), suggesting that the poem is a 'penitential exemplum' in which the *siðgeo-mor* poet and readers contrast their sinful state with the glory of the apostles; the epilogues of the other three Cynewulf poems have peni-tential associations too. Warren Ginsberg, 'Cynewulf and his Sources: *The Fates of the Apostles*' (*NM*), sets the poem within an onomastic tradition. Thomas is identified by a resurrection story because his name means *Christo similis;* John, or *gratia dei,* is given a mention of Christ's birth. Cynewulf's 'signatures' gloss his own name so as to identify him with 'paradigm of the apostles'.

8. The Exeter Book

Very little has appeared on the longer poems in this codex this year. Barbara A. Mackenzie's 'The Happy Land' in *An English Miscellany* is a rhyming translation of *The Phoenix* 1–84. Thomas D. Hill finds 'A Litur-gical Source for Christ I, 164–213 (Advent Lyric VII)' (*MÆ*), in a York antiphon preserved in a text 'compiled by Alcuin about 790 AD'. This supports the *ASPR* division of speeches in which Joseph is troubled, not Mary, while the rest of Alcuin's text is in other respects closer to the O.E. poem than is the traditional Advent sequence.

A 'source' of another kind is offered by Tony Millns for '*The Wanderer* 98: *Weal wundrum heah wyrmlicum fah*' (*RES*), in 'herring-bone masonry' of the sort found at Leicester, Portchester, Stoke d'Abernon and other sites. Marijane Osborn sees the poem much less tangibly in 'Classical Meditation in *The Wanderer*' (*Comparison*, 1975), an article which moves from the contrast of 'reason' and 'understanding' to a 'holy calm' via a sequence of antiphonal voices. Neil Hultin, 'The External Soul in *The Seafarer* and *The Wanderer*' (*Folklore*), confronts the definite statement of Ælfric that 'if the soul leaves the body then the body dies', but brings in stories of soul-travel from Gregory's *Dialogues* to prove that alternatives to that view are not necessarily pagan. Joyce M. Hill, '*þis Deade Lif*: A Note on *The Seafarer*, lines 64-66' (*ELN*), finds parallels in Ælfric and other homilists to the poem's famous oxymoron — though all use the adjective *deadlic*, 'mortal', not quite the same as *dead*, 'dead'. In *An English Miscellany* Brian K. Green presents a companion piece, '*Spes Viva*: Structure and Meaning in *The Seafarer*', to last year's article on *The Wanderer* (*YW* 57. 55); the poem is seen as having a 'peculiar metaphoric unity', a 'meiotic pattern', and as working through alternations of hope and life, reality and ideal and harsher reality still.

Deor is explained twice this year. Jerome Mandel's 'Exemplum and Refrain: the Meaning of *Deor*' (*YES*) works on the premise that the poem was didactic not consolatory, and that it was aimed at an audience most of whom had themselves suffered maim, wound or exile. Very restrictive connections are invoked: in stanza 5 *þæs* cannot refer to Eormanric's warriors' suffering for that might imply (why?) that 'the members of [the poet's] audience are made miserable by their lord'. At the end possible referents of *þæs* and *þisses* are considered at length. Thomas T. Tuggle also analyses 'The Structure of *Deor*' (*SP*) to show how revenge is achieved, desired, transcended, but his translations are often questionable. Can *þæt mæð hilde* mean 'the harvest of battle', *monge* 'from many', *frige* 'passion', *sorglufu* 'sore love'? On *The Wife's Lament* Alain Renoir contributes two pieces, 'Christian Inversion in *The Wife's Lament*' (*SN*) — which refers the increasing passivity of the *geong mon* to the Lord putting down the mighty from their seat — and 'A Reading of *The Wife's Lament*' (*ES*) which concentrates on the poem's emotional words and its use of pronouns to avoid self-pity and enlist reader/listener participation. Joseph Harris injects a certain scepticism with 'A Note on *eorðscræf/eorðsele* and Current Interpretations of *The Wife's Lament*' (*ES*). A vital question about the poem is whether its speaker is alive or — as recent views based on *eorðsele* have claimed — dead. Clearly, says Professor Harris, she must be alive or the boasts about 'death alone' would be hollow. So what is the *eorðsele*? It could be one of the underground *Grubenhäuser* which have been excavated, which women appear to have used for weaving, which (insulated with dung) gave such words as *dyngja*, 'the house where the women weave', to O.N. Allegorical interpretations rely 'too much on imagery, ignoring its concatenation in narrative syntax', observes Professor Harris politely; he would prefer a more 'quotidian' setting for this poem than the grave. One might remark that it begins to sound like Gretchen's song in *Faust*. Harry E. Kavros offers 'A Note on *Wulf and Eadwacer*' in *ELN*, namely that *ungelic* and *ungelice* need different translations. And Karl P. Wentersdorf has many interesting 'Observations on *The Ruin*' in *MÆ*, agreeing with the identification of its scene as Bath, citing Giraldus Cambrensis's phrase about Bath's 'gilded gables', and comparing this with the poem's *heah horngestreon*. Lines 21a-32a are presented in the end as a close and accurate picture of specific ruins. Thoms H. Bestul, finally, treats a peripheral member of the 'elegy' group in 'The OE *Resignation* and the Benedictine Reform' (*NM*). He divides the poem at line 75a (see *YW* 57. 56), and argues that it was composed in the reign of Edgar from such informal penitential prayers as were collected by reformed monks in British Museum MS Arundel 155, etc.

Non-elegiac poems receive, as usual, scanty treatment. Loren C. Gruber's 'Of Holly, Vassalage and *Oþþæt:* Three Notes on *Maxims I'* (*In Geardagum*) returns to the theme of epistemological translation (see section 4 above), and argues that holly was burnt to free the soul, that lines 67–70 are not as greedy as they sound, that lines 46–7 refer to 'an initiatory process'. R. E. Kaske looks closely at 'The Conclusion of the OE *Descent into Hell'* in *Paradosis: Studies in Memory of Edwin A. Quain*[22]. He would solve the very vexed question of *git Iohannis* in line 135 by assuming that the speaker is still John, but that *Iohannis* is there genitive dependent on earlier *fullwihte,* while the other party in the dual pronoun is the water of Jordan itself, with reference to the idea of Christ's baptism reciprocally purifying water: a bold expedient syntactically, but not impossible. On the same poem Daniel Sheerin's 'St. John the Baptist in the Lower World' (*Vigiliae Christianae,* 1976) may be of indirect use to O.E. scholars. It suggests a 'Eusebian' source for Bede's hymn on the Beheading of John, and considers John's role in the Harrowing as seen by early commentators.

Minor riddle-scholarship continues to be for the most part wild. Karl Schneider's 'Zu vier ae. Rätseln', in the *Gedenkschrift für Jost Trier*[23], makes a solid point in observing that we cannot always find riddle-solutions because we cannot always recognise riddle-objects. So 70 might be not just 'harp' but also a corn-drying frame, still called in Austria a *Harpfe* but of course completely unfamiliar to urban readers. Riddle 92 may be both 'yew' and 'bow and arrow' with similar dual reference. However, peasant folklore is also introduced to justify seeing cultic may-trees in 30a and sacred fires made by need-drills in 50. For these there is little direct evidence in Old or indeed modern English. F. H. Whitman heads in a completely opposite direction in 'Significant Motifs in Riddle 53' (*MÆ*), claiming that the answer here, 'treachery' and all, is 'Cross'. Gregory K. Jember's 'Riddle 57: A New Proposal' (*In Geardagum*) replaces birds or midges by demons, and gives a sinister twist to *Nemnað hy sylfe,* 'Name them yourselves'. Geoffrey Russom, 'Exeter Riddle 47: A Moth Laid Waste to Fame' (*PQ*), replaces 'moth' by 'mutability' and feels that the moral is not to lay up treasure on earth, where moth and rust do corrupt, etc. In 'Riddles 53, 54 and 55: an Archetypal Symphony in Three Movements' (*SMC*), John Miles Foley keeps the old solutions of battering-ram, butter-churn, cross (and others), but insists that all three are only metaphors for the 'act of entry and impregnation', sc. 'the penetration of heaven's enclosure by the redemptive emblem of the cross and the impregnation of God's kingdom with the saved souls of men'. He seems already to have been affected by Gregory K. Jember's 'A Generative Method for the Study of Anglo-Saxon Riddles' in the same volume, for this casually equates *goma, guma* and *gomen* in Riddle 49, 'cross, cap, reed flute, reed pen, kelp weed' in Riddle 60, and says all these latter are subsumed in a 'generative' solution, 'Revenant or Spirit'. The methodology of all this is 'anything goes'.

[22] *Paradosis: Studies in Memory of Edwin A. Quain,* ed. by Harry G. Fletcher III and Mary B. Schulte. New York: Fordham U.P. 1976. pp. xiv + 220. $20.
[23] *Gedenkschrift für Jost Trier,* ed. by Hartmut Beckers and Hans Schwarz. Köln and Wien: Böhlau Verlag. 1975. pp. xii + 391. DM.98.

One can see that editing the Riddles requires a rare combination of qualities. A certain toughness of mind is essential to resist solutions which are intellectual vanity; on the other hand retreating into scholarly caution leaves one with no solutions at all, which is arguably worse. Craig Williamson's *The O.E. Riddles of the Exeter Book*[24] strikes just about the right balance, calling on all the resources of material archaeology and close textual study on the hard-headed side, but leaving room for flights of humour and fancy on the other, just to remind us of the Riddles' role as entertainment. Professor Williamson offers some twelve new solutions to riddles, some of them based on recent archaeological discoveries (such as 'ship's figurehead' for 72), and rehabilitates eight to ten old ones, including Franz Dietrich's 'nightingale' for no. 6 — a view based incidentally on one of the many close-up photos of marginalia, which in this case shows that the mark by no.6 cannot be a runic C and therefore gives no support to *cuscote, ceo,* etc. Witty solutions are accepted, but abstract ones on the whole are not, while piety and folklore are sifted with equal rigour. Riddle 73 indeed shows well the editor's brisk way with ancient fooleries, for its answer is all but given in the runes DNLH in the middle of it. 'Hand', suggest some, reading backward and emending; 'elk' or 'elk-hunter', proposes Professor Eliason, changing a couple of letters; *Hælend,* 'Saviour' is the new orthodox solution, sticking to the runes but forgetting the riddle-text itself. *Hland,* 'Urine', says Professor Williamson briefly — actually he uses a ruder word. One gladly forfeits archetypes and methodologies to have the answer right.

9. Other Poems

Problems with the Riddles are to some extent paralleled by work elsewhere. Nigel F. Barley's 'Structure in the Cotton Gnomes' (*NM*) brings an anthropological perspective to bear on that poem, not without a certain patronage of Anglo-Saxonists, whom he believes to be stuck in the opinions of Blanche Williams's edition of 1914. His oppositions, mediations and structural unities are then fairly commonplace, but he does make the point that poets could generate 'pseudo-maxims' on the model of real ones.

Something like that attitude is more clearly revealed in J. R. Hall's 'Perspective and Wordplay in the O.E. *Rune Poem'* (*Neophilologus*), which dwells on the use of 'double focus' in *rad, ac, æsc* and elsewhere; the definitions resemble riddles while also trying to say something true. Eric P. Hamp takes the thought even further in his deceptively-titled 'On the Importance of *os* in the structure of *The Runic Poem'* (*Studia Germanica Gandensia*, 1976). He too begins with *rad,* but notes that *os* goes further in playing on homophones, not on semantic shifts within a single word. Most of the poem's definitions are by contrast single-valued, but nevertheless form loose patterns of prosperity/affliction, or (in the runes for *sigel, tir, dæg, lagu*) of daylight set against the dangerous sea. One poet was responsible; but as *os* shows, his work was only the last stage of a whole 'history of reshapings', with homonyms and riddles grafted on

[24] *The Old English Riddles of the Exeter Book,* edited by Craig Williamson. Chapel Hill, N.C.: U. of North Carolina P. 1977. pp. xx + 484. $30.

to an original gnomic structure. Thomas D. Hill also considers both synchrony and diachrony in 'The *æcerbot* charm and its Christian user' (*ASE*), bringing out a system of 'quaternities' echoed in learned texts, but also noting possible practical utility – for *uncuþ sæd* spreads the farmer's bets.

Heather Stuart reminds us sharply of scholars' 'stubborn determination' to preserve old wrong traditions in dismissing '"Spider" in OE' (*Parergon*); the word in *Wið dweorh* is *spiden*, all the folkloristic chatter about spiders is irrelevant, she prefers *unspedig*, 'poverty', and compares *earmig* in the *Wenne* charm. John P. Hermann shows similar impatience with less reason in '*Solomon and Saturn (II)*, 339A: *Niehtes Wunde*' (*ELN*). Why have scholars balked at the thought that Christ 'rescued us from the wound of night'? Darkness is sin in the Bible, so the 'wound of night' is sin too, and *Nergend* must be a verb; the parallel with the previous line is merely fortuitous. One remembers Joseph Harris's sage remarks about imagery and (narrative) syntax in Section 8 above. Professor Harris indeed reappears with a cogent solution to '*Stemnettan: Battle of Maldon*, Line 122a' (*PQ*). Evidence from M.E., etymology and context shows it means neither 'stood firm' nor 'cried out' but 'fell silent' – a minor but distinct elucidation of the poem's progress. John P. Hermann's 'The Theme of Spiritual Warfare in the O.E. *Judith*' (*PQ*) also begins with a true observation, that the poem diverges from the Apocrypha in letting the Hebrews (implausibly) attack the Assyrians before the latter have started to panic. What this shows is that Judith and the Hebrews represent the Church, allegorically, which should not wait for sin to waver before advancing on it. Joseph B. Trahern Jr, finally, adds one more scrap to the O.E. verse corpus in 'An OE Verse Paraphrase of Matthew 25: 41' (*Medievalia*): a passage from Napier homily 49 can be read as six regular lines of verse. More striking is the fact that the same verse is paraphrased in *Christ III* 1519–23, *Christ and Satan* 625–6, *Guthlac* 624 ff. But this bit is neater, too neat for a homilist's impromptu. Does that not indicate another (good) lost poem?

10. Prose

Further lost texts are proved by Bella Schauman and Angus Cameron, 'A Newly-Found Leaf of O.E. from Louvain' (*Anglia*). The leaf, here thoroughly edited, comprises a series of 'leechdoms' against foot, thigh and loin troubles, and against paralysis. It appears to be Mercian, datable 850–900, thus pushing back the 'traditions of medical writing in English ... by at least a century', and forming one of 'the very oldest pieces of non-documentary O.E. prose yet known'. Where, one wonders, did M. Henri Omant buy it? A much more familiar piece of archaic prose is considered in James H. Wilson's 'Cynewulf and Cyneheard: The Falls of Princes' (*PLL*), which argues for meaningful patterns, moral involvement and morally justifiable ends, though by way of such quite unjustifiable translations as 'They lay upon Cyneheard's men and fought' (from *hie simle feohtende wæran oþ hie alle lægon?*) or 'their kinsmen with Cynewulf' (from *eowre geferan ... mid þam cyninge*). O. Arngart confesses honest doubt in 'Further Notes on the Durham Proverbs' (*ES*); no analogue solves 15, though the author thinks it might have the sense of 'As they brew, so let them drink'.

On Alfredian prose, David Yerkes has three small pieces: 'The text of the Canterbury fragments of Werferth's translation of Gregory's *Dialogues* and its relation to the other MSS' (*ASE*); 'An Unnoticed Omission in the modern critical editions of Gregory's *Dialogues'* (*RB*); and 'An Elementary Way to Illuminate Detail of Textual History' (*Manuscripta*). Respectively, these print some 250 largely incomplete lines of an O.E. fragment from Canterbury Cathedral Library MS Add. 25 and place it in a stemma; indicate a few Latin lines surviving in a Northumbrian MS *c.*700 now at Wroclaw; and show that the original of the two O.E. *Dialogues* translations used *in* and *on* indiscriminately and so cannot have been Wærferth's autograph. Audrey Meaney considers 'Alfred and his Secretariat' much more widely in *Parergon* 1975, looking at the connections between eight or ten O.E. MSS mostly from Winchester. Angelika Lutz, 'Zur Rekonstruktion der Version G der Angelsächsischen Chronik' (*Anglia*), shows how a judicious use of Lawrence Nowell's 1562 transcript and Abraham Wheloc's edition of the largely burnt 'G' Chronicle can recover much of their original, and make possible a contrast between that and *its* original, the Parker Chronicle. E. G. Stanley recovers a touch of humour from a familiar *Orosius* Passage in 'How the Elbing deprives the Vistula of its Name and Converts it to the Elbing's own use in "Vistula-Mouth"' (*N&Q*); it's the little river *Ilfing* that steals the name of the big river *Wisle,* not the other way round.

Ælfric's style and sources continue to receive attention. 'The Sources of Ælfric's Prayers in Cambridge U.L. MS Gg.3.28', according to Donald G. Bzdyl in *N&Q*, lie in such liturgical books as the Leofric Missal, the Durham Ritual, etc. J. E. Cross pushes the date of the Latin source of Ælfric's Life of St. George' (*N&Q*) back to the mid-eighth century, and offers a guide to variant versions recorded. Harvey Minkoff gives 'An Example of Latin Influence on Ælfric's Translation Style' (*Neophilologus*) by considering placement of participles and auxiliary verbs. In the *Hepta teuch* Ælfric followed the Latin much more closely than in the *Catholic Homilies;* he really meant *ne ða endebyrdnysse awendan.* Ida Masters Hollowell also gets down to basics. Her 'Linguistic Factors Underlying Style Levels in Four Homilies of Wulfstan' (*Neophilologus*) are words per clause, proportion of subordinate clauses, proportions of nouns and verbs, and clausal 'content level'. In all factors there are sharp differences between 'low style' homilies (Bethurum 2 and 4) and 'high style' ones (5 and 20). Stephanie Hollis's pursuit of 'The thematic structure of *Sermo Lupi'* (*ASE*) may however not appear successful to all. One can see there are tensions in it, e.g. between the 'this is all God's plan' theory and the 'this is all the result of sin' one, but whether these either were deliberate or are resolved remains arguable. Both Ælfric and Wulfstan are considered in much wider perspective by Milton McC. Gatch's *Preaching and Theology in Anglo-Saxon England*[25]. The main conclusions of this major study are, first, that much Ælfrician teaching must have been set within the Carol-

---

[25] *Preaching and Theology in Anglo-Saxon England: Ælfric and Wulfstan,* by Milton McC. Gatch. Toronto and Buffalo: U. of Toronto P. 1977. pp. xiv + 266. £10.50.

ingian 'Prone' — a service of translation and explanation not integrated within the Mass (like homilies of the patristic era) nor within other services like modern sermons. This conclusion however makes the *Catholic Homilies* appear much more original in design, for they retain traces of their monastic origins through their transfer to catechetical settings.Ælfric is also seen driving an original line through the chaos of eschatology, while Wulfstan too pursued individual aims through individual methods. It is wrong to treat them as mere copyists, though they were theologically 'conservative', or even as mere stylists. But were they successful? Professor Gatch feels some doubt as to whether their movement really succeeded in 'purifying the intellectual life of the church' — in view of the continuing carelessness of anonymous homilies — but thinks they have a historical place in the build-up to the Twelfth Century Renaissance. An edition of 'Ælfric's Excerpts from Julian of Toledo' is appended,with an invaluable bibliography and footnotes.

Michael Korhammer's *Die monastischen Cantica im Mittelalter*[26] is another major study, consisting of a hundred-page edition of the Latin monastic canticles and their O.E. interlinear renderings in Durham Cathedral Library MS B.III.32 and British Museum Cotton MS Vespasian D.XII, plus a much longer introduction. This latter defines canticles as texts from the Latin Old Testament chanted by Benedictines and kindred orders 'during the third nocturn of the Sunday and holiday office'; distinguishes an Anglo-Saxon type from a later Cluniac one; compares the five MSS of this Anglo-Saxon type with fifty other later or foreign MSS so as to bring out their internal relations; and finally discusses three or four hundred words in the glosses. The Durham tradition is thought to agree with the interlinear Benedictine Rule and also with Ælfric, the Vespasian one with Ælfric again, but even more with the Lambeth Psalter gloss. This latter tradition seems to have connections with Winchester but then, possibly, with East Anglia. Further enquiries are made into monastic history by Milton McC. Gatch, 'OE literature and the liturgy: problems and potential' (*ASE*),who points out among other things that Ælfric's 'Letter to the Monks of Eynsham' is something more complex than a summary of *Regularis Concordia,* and further that even *Exodus* has never been put squarely in a liturgical context. Making the same guess as Ruth Ames in Section 6 above he suggests that the readings of Holy Week could have come 'to stand more as types of Christ in the great drama of salvation than as types of salvation by baptism'. The 'Two Saints in the OE *Martyrology'* (*NM*) studied by J. E. Cross are Eusebius of Vercelli and Justus of Beauvais; Bede's knowledge of the former is clarified, and O.E. knowledge of the latter is put forward to the same era. Largely on the same text, the same author's '*Legimus in ecclesiasticis historiis:* a Sermon for All Saints, and its Use in OE Prose' (*Traditio*) gives a full version of the Latin sermon in question from a ninth-century Munich MS, and shows that it was known to Ælfric, the Blickling homilist, the compiler of the *Martyrology.* This latter writer need not then have used Ado's martyrology and need not be dated post-850 as Miss Celia Sisam suggested (*YW* 34.53).

[26] *Die morastischen Cantica im Mittelalter* (Münchener Universitätsschriften, Texte und Untersuchungen zur Englischen Philiologie, Band 6), ed. by Michael Korhammer. 1976. München: Wilhelm Fink Verlag. pp. xxii + 402. DM.58.

On the anonymous homilists, Jane Roberts uses the Vercelli account of Guthlac to make a tentative correction to the *Vita S. Guthlaci* in 'St. Bartholomew's Day: A Puzzle Resolved?' (*MÆ*). Paul E. Szarmach, 'MS Junius 85 F.2r and Napier 49' (*ELN*), argues that the version of the ending of Napier 49 found in Junius 85 is closer to the versions of CCCC 421 and the shortened texts than to that of the Vercelli Book; but the real conclusion is that many O.E. homilies were 'wild texts' which show 'no attempt to preserve the *ipsissima verba* of the author'. Adaptability, or carelessness? D. G. Scragg's 'Napier's "Wulfstan" homily XXX; its sources, its relationship to the Vercelli Book and its style' (*ASE*), analyses the make-up of another 'scissors and paste' homily to show an author copying both from Wulfstan *and* from a codex similar to the Vercelli Book well on in the eleventh century; virtually nothing in it is original, and its style can be intense but empty. Ten other anonymous and previously unprinted homilies are presented by A. M. Luiselli Fadda[27], from MSS including Junius 85, Hatton 114, 115, 121, and the Vercelli Book. Their themes — soul and body, Doomsday, penitence, clerical morality — are unedifying, and the presentation of them contains some evident minor errors (such as 'Hatton 114' for 'Junius 85, 86' on page 2). However, as their editor says, it is important to have these things in print so that they can be put into a historic context. Delicate scholars should remember the instructive tale from Rowland L. Collins's booklet written to accompany the Pierpont Morgan/Scheide Libraries' joint exhibition of the thirteen Anglo-Saxon MSS in America[28]. The first original MSS. in O.E. to reach America, in 1912 — a leaf from a saint's life and another from a treatise on the Franks — were lost untranscribed and have never turned up. A sad fate, to be lost after a millennium's keeping and five hundred years into the age of print!

[27] *Nuove Omelie Anglosassoni della Rinascenza Benedettina* (Filologia Germanica Testi e Studi, 1). Firenze: Felice Le Monnier. 1977; pp. xxviii + 248. 7000 lire.
[28] *Anglo-Saxon Vernacular MSS in America,* by Rowland L. Collins. New York: Pierpont Morgan Library. 1976. pp. 86, 12 plates. no price.

IV

Middle English: Excluding Chaucer

T. P. DOLAN, L. E. MITCHELL and R. W. McTURK

1. General and Miscellaneous Items

Walter Ullmann's thesis, in his study of the *Medieval Foundations of Renaissance Humanism*[1], is that 'what is commonly called renaissance humanism was an epiphenomenon, a concomitant feature and integral part of the overall ecclesiological, philosophical, governmental, and political thinking that pervaded the age' — it was a rebirth, rooted in the estrangement of Church from State. Government became secularised, and thus released itself from the vertical ordering of ecclesiastical hierarchy, and the State emerged in concept 'as the collectivized citizen'. 'The concept of the citizen was the political expression of rehabilitated natural humanity', with a horizontal ordering. The philosophical model for this new secular view was found in the writings of pre-Christian political thinkers, in particular Cicero, on such matters as *lex, ius, auctoritas, civilitas, nexus, obedientia.* In this way *Roma* was *renovata*, not out of a 'romantic-sentimental' search for a golden age, but to satisfy an urgent need for a new *scientia politica.* Ullmann instances the *De potestate regia et papali* of John of Paris, whose concern is for the *rex humanus* and *res humanae.* Literature of the first half of the fourteenth century shows this same concern — to give a humanistic place to the citizen, as a tribute to the fact that he was born through the normal course of nature, in contrast with the non-humanistic place which the Church gave him by requiring baptism for membership. Citizenship is to be seen as 'the political incarnation of *humanitas'*, and a man functions in his role as a citizen, a political animal with a civic virtue relative to his milieu (geographical, social, etc.), not the monolithic virtue promulgated by the Church. This humanistic treatment of the past contrasted with the ecclesiastical view which saw history as a reflex of the biblical events describing the course of Salvation. The study of man as an individual comes to the fore (cf. the increasing interest in biographical work). There is much political writing — but not all by men: Christine de Pisan was 'one of the earliest women to have made intelligent use of Aristotle's *Politics* and *Ethics'* (see Bornstein, below). The book's main thesis incorporates many ancillary points of interest — e.g., the fascinating suggestion as to why *Res Humanae* came so late to England in contrast with the rest of Europe (because of the institution of Parliament — the forum for debate, discussion, argument — where the citizen was already involved in the machinery of the State). This fine book will prove to be essential reading for students who need to know how and why man emerged as a focal point in mediaeval English literature.

Earl Miner contributes a soundly informed Afterword on typology

---

[1] *Medieval Foundations of Renaissance Humanism,* by Walter Ullmann. Paul Elek. pp. xii + 212. £6.95.

and figuralism in the collection of essays (originally and, in some cases, too obviously, lectures) published as *Literary Uses of Typology from the Late Middle Ages to the Present*[2]. For mediaevalists the two relevant chapters are Robert Hollander on 'Typology and Secular Literature: some Medieval Problems and Examples' (Prudentius's *Psychomachia* and Dante), and Karlfried Froehlich on '"Always to Keep the Literal Sense in Holy Scripture Means to Kill One's Soul": The State of Biblical Herm- eneutics at the Beginning of the Fifteenth Century'. Hollander discusses various types of prefiguration and postfiguration, and Froehlich offers a full analysis of the implications of 2 Corinthians 3:6 ('The letter killeth, but the spirit quickeneth'), followed by a useful discussion of such herm- eneutic features as 'double literal sense': the false (grammatical) literal sense of words, and the true literal sense, 'the one the spirit intended'.

In *The Gothic Visionary Perspective*[3]. Barbara Nolan posits and examines the affinity between art, architecture, and the written word in the manifes- tations of visions of the eschaton in the later Middle Ages (c. 1150–1400). Her thesis rests on the contention that the twelfth century introduced a concept of the apocalyptic vision that was not purely symbolic, but was also spiritually real. By considering the relationship of the mind to eternity ('anagogy') and the relationship of time to eternity ('Aevum') scholars were able to turn this perfect visionary state into a comprehensive spiritual goal for man. Artists, therefore, tried to use their art, to guide and uplift the spirit to the experience on earth of the ultimate peace and joy of this heavenly haven, the New Jerusalem. Nolan presents a history of the manifestations of the apocalyptic vision up to the twelfth century in the realms of art, and then examines in detail various later works expounding the grounds for a recognition of a new (twelfth-century) approach. Among these are the sculptural programmes of the cathedrals of St Denis and of Chartres, and MS illustrations (e.g., St John's vision of the *maiestas Domini* in B.L.MS Add. 11695). She then passes on to consider literary visions in Dante's *Vita Nuova*, the M.E. *Pearl*, and, finally, *Piers Plowman* ('the last great visionary quest of the Middle Ages', in which 'his narrator is both Everyman of all ages and fourteenth-century fallen man . . . moving towards an imminent and much-needed eschaton'). This stimulating book manages to orchestrate a great deal of disparate material in its attempt to prove its main thesis.

'What was so special about a dead man's bones . . . in the Middle Ages?' asks Ronald C. Finucane in his popular, engrossing, and readable study of *Miracles and Pilgrims. Popular Beliefs in Medieval England*[4]. Part I discusses the historical background, and describes the traffic in relics which 'emitted a kind of holy radioactivity which bombarded everything in the area', the preparation of bodies, the inspection of entrails, the boiling and disembering of bodies, the presentation of false relics, the process of canonisation, the purpose of pilgrimages, holy places (e.g.,

[2] *Literary Uses of Typology from the Late Middle Ages to the Present*, ed. by Earl Miner. Princeton, N.J.: Princeton U.P. pp. xxi + 403. £18.80.

[3] *The Gothic Visionary Perspective*, by Barbara Nolan. Princeton, N.J.: Princeton U.P. pp. xviii + 268. Frontispiece and 22 illustrations. £12.40.

[4] *Miracles and Pilgrims. Popular Beliefs in Medieval England*, by Ronald C. Finucane. London, Melbourne and Toronto: J. M. Dent. pp. 248. 16 illustrations and 5 maps. £6.95.

Compostella, Westminster Cathedral [sic], 'where the remains of St Edward the Confessor still repose', etc.). Part II deals with English Shrines ('in modern terms, faith-healing centres') and Pilgrims, and indicates the thin line dividing folk-remedies and ecclesiastically approved remedies. In his brief Part III he deals with 'The End of the Middle Ages and the Reformation' in two chapters; 'Shifting Loyalties: New Shrines and Old Saints at the end of the Middle Ages'; and 'The Destruction of the Shrines (e.g., statues of the Virgin at Worcester, Coventry, Willesden, etc.). Throughout, the style is light and boisterous ('A week before the translation, . . . Cantilupe obligingly performed his first posthumous miracle'), as are the chapter headings (e.g., 'Saints, Sickness and Snobbery: Shrines and their Clientele'). Nonetheless, the main conclusions are based on a careful consideration of seven selected English cults: Becket, Frideswide, Cantilupe, Wulfstan (of Worcester), Simon de Montfort, William (of Norwich), and Godric of Finchale and (for comparison) two French — Edmund Rich and Louis of Toulouse.

Dorothee Metlitzki divides her major study of *The Matter of Araby in Medieval England*[5] into two parts. Part I, Scientific and Philosophical Learning, deals with the transmission of Arabic culture by way of the crusades through the courts of Sicily and Spain. The treatment of Arabic studies in England takes into account the work of the early translators and then the contributions of Walcher of Malvern, Petrus Alfonsi, Adelard of Bath, Robert of Ketton, Daniel of Morley, Roger of Hereford, Alfred the Englishman, Roger Bacon, and Michael Scott. There is an account of the role played by Arabic versions of Artistotle's writings in natural philosophy and science and, in particular Adelard's treatise 'Quaestiones Naturales' with its celebration of Islamic Aristotelian thought. Part I ends with a section on 'Arabum Sententiae' in Middle English Literature, which deals in some detail with 'Scientific Imagery in "The Owl and the Nightingale"' (chiefly, the debate about the validity of astrological prediction, for which Metlitzki adduces Albumassar's *Greater Introduction to Astronomy* to demonstrate that the Owl and the Arabic treatises agree on assigning omnipotence to God: 'Al hit itid þurþ Goddes wille') and 'Scientific Imagery in Chaucer' (e.g., the star catalogues outlined for Part 3 of the *Treatise on the Astrolabe*, alchemical lore in the *Canon's Yeoman's Tale*, etc.). Part II tackles 'The Literary Heritage' under four headings: 1. Arabian Source Books ('Disciplina Clericalis', The 'Secret of Secrets', 'The Dicts and Sayings of the Philosophers'); 2. History and Romance (The Marriage Theme as a Portrayal of Christian-Muslim Relations, The Treatment of the Saracens in the English Mediaeval Romances, The Converted Saracen, The Defeated Sultan, The Saracen Giant, 'Makomet and Mede': The Treatment of Islam, The Muslim Paradise as the Land of Cockayne (seen here as 'the land of the cock', which is the guardian of paradise in the most popular account of Islamic paradisial abodes in mediaeval Europe — the *Liber Scalae*)); 3. The Voyages and Travels of Sir John Mandeville; 4. The Matter of Araby and the Making of Romance. It has been necessary to itemise the chapter- and section-headings in this way because the contents of Part II of the book, which contains Metlitzki's main independent contribution to the subject, indicate, as she seems to

[5] *The Matter of Araby in Medieval England*, by Dorothee Metlitzki. New Haven, Conn. and London: Yale U.P. pp. xiii + 320. 11 illustrations and 2 maps. £10.80.

realise herself, that 'the matter of Araby' is in no sense a body of material comparable to the matters of Troy and of Britain, and all that can be done is to check for Arabic affinities (e.g., the authentic Arabic setting of *Floris and Blancheflur,* Mandeville's use of William of Tripoli in his description of Muslim manners and customs, etc.). Consulted piecemeal, the book yields many interesting points of information (especially in the section on Romances, where we find that the mediaeval Romance writer used fantasy to spread his view of Islam, a view almost invariably itself founded on fantasy, and learn how Christian audiences were manipulated to view non-Christian people with reservation — see the description of Josian in *Sir Beues of Ilamtoun*). Sometimes the author gives the impression of having too great, and too exclusive a determination to find Arabic affinities (for instance, in ignoring the Irish connection in *The Land of Cokaygne*). Nonetheless, we are much in her debt for assembling such important information.

David C. Fowler studies the influence of *The Bible in Early English Literature*[6] in six chapters: 1. The Bible in the Middle Ages (which ends with a 'review of the biblical message of the sanctuary expressed in the stained glass windows of Fairford Church'); 2. Medieval Exegesis: Gregory's *Morals on Job;* 3. Old English Translations and Paraphrases; 4. Middle English Translations: The Wyclif Bible; 5. The Metrical Bible; *Cursor Mundi;* 6. Universal History: *The Polychronicon* (which complements his earlier work on Trevisa (*YW.* 41.66; 52.103)). The book is straightforwardly written in a flowing narrative style which extends to the bibliographical essay at the end. This replaces the more usual footnotes, which would have been more helpful, and, maybe, more accurate ('R. B. Y. Mynors', 'G. N. Garmondsway', *et al.*), though less readable. Another minor deficiency is the stand which the author takes against an anonymous modern viewpoint ('the modern interpretation', 'modern inclinations', and so on) which causes him to present some sections of the text in terms of a mediaeval/modern conflict. Another quibble is the anecdotal self-indulgence ('After the war, Mr Farmer, working steadily for 2 years, replaced the glass [of Fairford Church] single-handedly'). A much more serious reservation concerns the author's curious and unwise choice of the Authorised Version, rather than the Douai version, for translations from the Vulgate. All in all, though, this is an easy-to-read vade-mecum for the type of unsympathetic college student whose observations the author takes account of in the book (see p. 66). It is full of interesting information and covers many of the problems which recur in teaching such students (e.g., the significance of 2 Cor. 3: 6 - 'for the letter killeth, but the spirit giveth life'). It will make an excellent introduction, but perhaps will not fulfil the claims of the dust-jacket blurb: 'a scholarly book which promises to become the standard work on its subject'.

At the beginning of his very fine work on *The Medieval Leper and his Northern Heirs*[7] Peter Richards uses the diaries of the Dean of Åland

[6] *The Bible in Early English Literature,* by David C. Fowler. Sheldon Press. pp. x + 263. £11.50.
[7] *The Medieval Leper and his Northern Heirs,* by Peter Richards. Cambridge, England: D. S. Brewer Ltd. and Totowa, N.J.: Rowman & Littlefield. pp. viii + 178. £6.

(islands between Sweden and Finland) to tell the story of the mid-seventeenth-century leper hospital on the island of Gloskär (dealing with accommodation, food, etc.) whose inhabitants 'in many respects . . . lived and died in the Middle Ages', and where resources were so limited that lepers were required to bring with them wood and nails for their own coffins. Elsewhere Richards describes conditions in other institutions (e.g., at St Julian's, near St Albans) and notes that in mediaeval literature leprosy was portrayed as 'punishment meted out for moral failing' (as in Henryson's Cresseid), a view based on an incorrect interpretation of the Levitical concept of impurity. He discusses the Christian attitude to leprosy, the foundation of leper hospitals, the rarity of lepers in the fifteenth century, how leprosy thrives on poor living conditions and poor diet. We learn that leprosy was not a term applied randomly to a variety of diseases — 'the medieval leper was as real as his disease'. This most fascinating book, which should be essential reading for mediaevalists, ends with seventeen relevant documents (e.g., the Office at the seclusion of a leper; the Regulations of the leper hospital of St Julian's near St Albans, founded 1146, revised by Abbot Michael in 1344; the Regulations of the leper hospital of St Mary Magdalene, Exeter, restored early in the fifteenth century, etc.).

H. R. Ellis Davidson edits *Symbols of Power*[8], a collection of papers given at the conference held jointly by the Folklore Society and the Department of Religious Studies, Lancaster University (1973), to consider 'symbols . . . of spiritual and magical power, that energy which men have felt to be derived from a source beyond the familiar world'. The volume contains F. R. Allchin on 'Religious Symbols and Indian Thought' (utilising some of Tillich's descriptions of religious symbols in an analysis of Indian thought), M. Loewe on 'The World to Come, A Two-Thousand Year Old Painting from China'; E. J. Sharpe on 'The Old English Runic Paternoster' (based on the interpretation of the first two words of the prayer given in *The Dialogue of Salomon and Saturnus,* ed. Kemble, 1848); V. Newall on 'Icons as Symbols of Power' (with an interesting account of the iconoclast controversy, and a consideration of popular icon figures, St George, Elijah, the dog-headed St Christoper, etc.); K. H. Basford on the 'Quest for the Green Man' (with reference to the keystone Green Man at Fountains Abbey, 1483); C. Hole on 'Protective Symbols in the Home' (horseshoes, salt, animal-bones, skulls under the floor, etc.); K. M. Briggs on 'Symbols in Fairy Tales' (e.g., the small spell in Jack-the-Giant-Killer's pocket). The book is to be recommended for the wealth of fringe material which it contains for understanding folkloristic writings.

Volume II of N. R. Ker's *Medieval Manuscripts in British Libraries*[9], goes from Abbotsford ('The Hay Manuscript [in Scots] s. xv. ex. Scotland') to Keele (University Library, 'Hugo de Sancto Victore, etc.' s. xiii-xiv), and contains a list of Libraries and Manuscripts, a list of Signs and Abbreviations, Manuscripts: Abbotsford-Keele, and Addenda (one entry: Brailes. Presbytery Library). The Preface amplifies and adjusts some of the points made in the Preface to Volume I, and identifies the collections, which

[8] *Symbols of Power,* ed. by H. R. Ellis Davidson. *The Folklore Society Mistletoe Series.* Cambridge, England: D. S. Brewer Ltd. and Totowa, N.J.: Rowman & Littlefield, for the Folklore Society. pp. viii + 182. 3 illustrations. £4.50.
[9] *Medieval Manuscripts in British Libraries,* by N. R. Ker, vol. II Abbotsford-Keele. Oxford, at the Clarendon Press. pp. xliii + 999. £30.

include 22 of the 'larger' collections, mentioned in the Preface to Volume I — Eton College, Cambridge University Library, the National Libraries of Scotland and Wales; the Cathedrals at Canterbury, Durham, and Hereford; the universities of Aberdeen, Durham, Edinburgh, and Glasgow; ten Cambridge Colleges; the Fitzwilliam Museum, Cambridge. The entries include 'descriptions of binding fragment found in the capitular and diocesan records of Canterbury, Chichester, Durham, Ely, Gloucester, and Hereford'. The collections are of many kinds:- some have had the same location since the Middle Ages (Canterbury Cathedral; Eton College; Exeter Cathedral); some were formed between the late sixteenth century and 1800 (e.g., Blickling Hall, Gloucester Cathedral, etc.); some (the majority) are nineteenth- and twentieth-century collections.

J. J. G. Alexander and M. T. Gibson edit *Medieval Learning and Literature. Essays Presented to Richard William Hunt*[10] (1976) under four headings: 1. Medieval Libraries, with articles by B. Bischoff ('Die Hofbibliothek unter Ludwig dem Frommen'), N. R. Ker ('The Beginnings of Salisbury Catherdral Library'), G. Pollard ('Describing Medieval Bookbindings'), R. H. Rouse and M. A. Rouse ('The *Florilegium Angelicum:* its Origin, Content, and Influence'), and M. B. Parkes ('The Influence of the Concepts of *Ordinatio* and Compilatio on the Development of the Book'); II. History of Texts, with articles by B. C. Barker-Benfield ('A Ninth-Century Manuscript from Fleury: *Cato de Senectute cum Macrobio*'), T. Silverstein ('The Graz and Zürich Apocalypse of Saint Paul: An Independent Medieval Witness to the Greek'), A. B. Scott ('Some Poems Attributed to Richard of Cluny'), A. C. de la Mare ('The Return of Petronius to Italy'), and an anonymous article on 'La Tradition Manuscrite des "Quaestiones Nicolai peripatetici"'; III. Schools and Scholarship, with articles by R. W. Southern ('Master Vacarius and the Beginning of an English Academic Tradition'), E. Rathbone ('Peter of Corbeil in an English Setting'), B. Smalley ('Oxford University Sermons 1290–1293'), R. J. Dean ('Nicholas Trevet, Historian'), A. B. Emden ('Oxford Academical Halls in the Later Middle Ages'), and L. M. Labowsky ('An Unnoticed Lettei from Bessarion to Lorenzo Valla'). Section IV, on the Laity, contains two essays: L. E. Boyle, O.P. ('E cathena et carcere: The Imprisonment of Amaury de Montford, 1276'), and the late W. A. Pantin ('Instructions for a Devout and Literate Layman'). This most illustrious and scholarly volume, which so clearly reflects Dr Hunt's own interests and distinctions, ends with S. P. Hall's Bibliography of the Published Writings of R. W. Hunt, and three Indexes, on the Manuscripts, Personal Names, and Place-Names referred to in the text.

George Rigg contributes a sound introduction to his edition of a set of five papers on *Editing Medieval Texts English, French and Latin Written in England*[11]. Malcolm Godden concisely sketches the achievements of editors of O.E. texts (Thwaites, Wheloc, Elstob, etc.) up to the

[10]*Medieval Learning and Literature. Essays Presented to Richard William Hunt,* ed. by J. J. G. Alexander and M. T. Gibson. Oxford, at the Clarendon Press, 1976. pp. xiii + 455. 28 illustrations. £18.
[11]*Editing Medieval Texts English, French, and Latin Written in England.* Papers given at the twelfth annual Conference on Editorial Problems, University of Toronto. 5–6 November 1976, ed. by A. G. Rigg. New York & London: Garland Publishing, Inc. pp. viii + 128. $12.

present time, describes his own techniques for dealing with texts surviving in more than one manuscript ('I have tried to follow a policy of *interpreting* alterations rather than *describing* them'), and discusses work on dating and placing texts, and work on sources. Anne Hudson's memorable paper on Middle English commences with the question 'What is an Edition?' and shows the diversity of answers to it (e.g., revering 'the least whim of the scribe', as with Sisam's edition of *Havelok,* or seeing 'all scribes as interfering and incompetent dunces', as with Onions's reconstruction of the original south-eastern form of the *Owl and the Nightingale*). She goes on to instance three types of edition – those which present all the evidence (e.g., Bliss's edition of *Sir Orfeo*), and those 'based on the traditional methods of stemmatic, textual criticism'. The third type is 'hardly a type, since its essence is individuality', and here she engages in a probing assessment of Kane and Donaldson's edition of the B-text of *Piers Plowman* and finds several 'disturbing elements' (for instance, that 'emendation is carried beyond that warranted by manuscript collation or the necessity of sense'). She ends with an interesting discussion of the problems involved in her own work on Lollard texts. Ian Lancashire writes on mediaeval drama and, after looking at the problems involved in the plays' textual transmission, proceeds to discuss the advantages of different types of edition. He draws particular attention to what we can learn from mediaeval dramatic records. In his chapter on Anglo-Norman, Brian Merrilees describes early editions and the contributions made by such scholars as Bédier. Two continuing, interrelated problems are 'the status that should be accorded Anglo-Norman dialect forms and structures' and 'the nature of the versification'. George Rigg writes the final chapter on mediaeval Latin, a concise, but comprehensive discussion of the very large area covered by his subject (history, philosophy, theology, etc.), and some of the problems involved in editing texts, in particular, orthography ('to classicize or not to classicize'), and the justification for the practice of the Toronto series of putting out 'scribal editions' of texts as distinct from full critical editions. Future editors will look to this set of papers for stimullation and guidance on procedure, and for much basic information.

With the increasing interest in mediaeval rhetoric, Susan Gallick's presentation of '*Artes Praedicandi*: Early Printed Editions' (*MS*) is very useful. Her study is exploratory, to see if the interest in such works can be linked to the number of publishers' commissions to print them, but at this stage the connection does not seem very strong.

By 1430, according to John H. Fisher, Chancery English had assumed its mature form and in his astute analysis of the language of the *Rotuli Parliamentorum* he considers the relationship between 'Chancery and the Emergence of Standard Written English in the Fifteenth Century' (*Speculum*). Chancery English was an 'amalgam' (in spelling, grammar, and idiom) and ceased to represent any spoken dialect.

Paul Oskar Kristeller gives salutary advice in his 'Medieval and Renaissance Studies: Reflections of a Scholar' (*Speculum*): attention should be paid to the continuity between the Renaissance humanists and mediaeval grammarians and rhetoricians. He laments the decline of educational standards at pre-university level, and urges scholars to keep to the relevant evidence, to throw away pet ideas when refuted by the evidence, to pursue accuracy and other virtues.

Patrick J. Horner, F.S.C., presents two pieces of evidence from a fifteenth-century sermon in Laud. Misc 706 to show the rate of decrease of 'The Use and Knowledge of Spoken French in Early Fifteenth-Century England' (N&Q).

Contributing an important paper on 'Natural and Rational Love in Medieval Literature' (YES), Gerald Morgan uses what Aquinas says about 'the sensitive soul' and 'the rational soul' and their relationship with the passions to demonstrate that great mediaeval poets are clear in their apprehension of moral issues. In particular, 'fin' amors 'conceals an illicit shift from the sensitive to the rational levels'.

John A. Alford writes of the close association between 'Literature and Law in Medieval England' (PMLA) which can be exemplified from a host of references in, for instance, Piers Plowman (e.g., the devils debating their rights in the Harrowing of Hell episode). Such an association can be understood only if we appreciate that divine, natural, and positive law reflect the will of God, and are basically indivisible, with the result that when this coherence was dissolved, the legal metaphor was no longer usable in so vital a way.

With due reference to the work of earlier scholars (especially Arnold Williams, YW. 41.72; 34.64), Penn R. Szittya presents a most important and comprehensive study of 'The Antifraternal Tradition in Middle English Literature' (Speculum), which comprises both a description of the tradition and a thesis — to redefine the nature of anti-fraternalism, many premises of which were lies (e.g., the increase of their numbers, their usurping the privileges of preachers, etc.) in terms of biblical exegesis. The crucial figure is William of St Amour (De periculis novissimorum temporum) who symbolically identifies, but by inference only, friars with 'the Pharisees, the pseudo apostoli of St Paul's time, and the eschatological antichristi predicted for the last days', thereby showing them to be the symbolic anti-types to the Apostles.

A whole issue of SP is devoted to Margaret Jennings's lively, readable, and scholarly account of 'Tutivullus: The Literary Career of the Recording Demon' in folklore, art, literature, and drama, tracing the assimilative development from the older tradition to the mediaeval figure who 'recorded faults by collecting them in a sack'. His major didactic role diminished, until by 1523 in England it was of only 'nominal importance'. This most informative account is rounded off with Appendixes dealing with 'Recording Demons Named and Unnamed', 'Recording Demon Principal Appearances', and finally a 'Register of Manuscripts Cited'.

The Coming of the Book[12] (1970) is a translation of L'Apparition du Livre (1958) by Lucien Febvre and Henri-Jean Martin and, after a brief but comprehensive introductory section by Marcel Thomas on manuscripts, its chapters deal respectively with 'The Introduction of Paper into Europe', 'The Technical Problems and their Solution', 'The Book: Its Visual Appearance', 'The Book as a Commodity', 'The Little World of the Book' (dealing with The Journeymen, The Masters, From the Humanist Printer to the Bookseller of the Enlightenment, Authors and their Rights),

[12] The Coming of the Book. The Impact of Printing 1450–1800 by Lucien Febvre and Henri-Jean Martin, trans. by David Gerard, ed. by Geoffrey Nowell-Smith and David Wootton. (Foundations of History Library.) London: NLB, 1976. pp. 378. £12.

'The Geography of the Book' (The Journeys of Printers, Places to Set up Business, Geography and Publishing, Printing Conquers the World – the Slav Countries, the New World, the Far East), The Book Trade, The Book as a Force for Change.

Volume II of *Martianus Capella and the Seven Liberal Arts*[13], which contains *The Marriage of Philology and Mercury*, translated by William Harris Stahl and Richard Johnson, with E. L. Burge, is a very welcome and major contribution to mediaeval studies, which have long been in need of a vernacular version of Martianus's eccentric Latin. The text is based on Dick's Teubner edition (1925), but notes Willis's new readings, which are to be incorporated in his forthcoming edition. The footnotes, though brief, both help the reader to understand what Martianus means and give useful references to sources and affinities (e.g., under Arithmetic, a note on Euclid; under Geometry, a note on Martianus's misreading Pliny on the size of Euboea; under Rhetoric, a suggestion of another way to translate the key-word *locus* in the important section on Memory, in disagreement with Frances Yates (*YW*. 47.147, 171). The nine books deal with The Betrothal, The Marriage, Grammar, Dialectic, Rhetoric, Geometry, Arithmetic, Astronomy, Harmony, followed by an Index. Martianus's influence has long been recognised, but now a much wider audience will be able to refer to what he wrote, in this most felicitous translation.

The title of Thorlac Turville-Petre's attractively presented book on *The Alliterative Revival*[14] indicates his position in the revival/survival controversy: for him it was a 'rather self-contained movement' beginning with *Wynnere and Wastoure* (1352-3), which 'in every respect . . . is a characteristic alliterative poem; it shows the verbal resources, the stylistic techniques and the preoccupations that are the hall-marks of the poems of the Alliterative Revival'. He defines the structural and thematic similarities between the works of the revival, but as there is such a great diversity between them he selects three representative poems demonstrating three basic types: *The Wars of Alexander, Purity, Pierce the Ploughman's Crede*. The first part of the book is concerned with arguing the case for revival – there is no evidence for claiming that the tradition of alliterative verse preceding *Wynnere and Wastoure* was an ancient one: 'Classical' O.E. verse died quickly after the Conquest (probably the last poem written in the traditional style is *Durham*, which was written before 1109). The revival was established in the South West Midlands in the 1340s, and by the 1350s alliterative poetry was also being composed in the more northerly parts of the West Midlands, whence it spread north and east; in England it was a spent force by the mid-fifteenth century when the flexibility which it enjoyed during its prime was finally lost, but in Scotland the alliterative line became incorporated into rhyming stanzas and it survived till well into the sixteenth century (e.g., Dunbar's *un*rhymed *Tretis of the Tua Mariit Wemen and the Wedo*). Many interesting points

---

[13] *Martianus Capella and the Seven Liberal Arts*, ed. and trans. by W. H. Stahl and R. Johnson. (Number 84 of the *Records of Civilisation: Sources and Studies*.) New York: Columbia U.P. Vol. II. pp. v + 389. $25., £18.40.

[14] *The Alliterative Revival*, by Thorlac Turville-Petre. Cambridge, England: D. S. Brewer, Ltd. and Totowa N.J.: Rowman & Littlefield. pp. viii + 152. £7.50.

are made (e.g., the difference between *Piers Plowman* and the other alliterative poems). A few unclear sections occur (e.g., the argument for revival
based on such words as those for man and warrior (*guma/gome, secg/segge*)
which could surely be used as evidence for survival as well as the reverse).
The second part of the book, by contrast with the tautly argued first part,
appears rather random and less purposeful, but indicates salient features
of the movement. The contents of the book, which will be exceptionally
handy for students, include The Origins of the Alliterative Revival, The
Revival, Metre, Poetic Diction, The Art of Narrative, and an Epilogue:
After the Revival. A rather different view of it is offered by the contributor to section 2, below.

The self-confessed purpose of Norman Blake's cautionary study of
The English Language in Medieval Literature[15] is to warn and guide
students about the dangers of making anachronistic assumptions when
working on mediaeval vernacular literature. Developing a recent article
(*YW*. 57. 62) it shows some of the adjustments that should be made in
order to read such literature with profit. Chapter 1 on 'The Literary
Background' urges, among other things, that careful attention be paid
to the widely disparate and dispersed nature of the audiences that the
authors had in mind. Chapter 2 on 'The Linguistic Background' notes and
expounds the implications of the fact that 'the most important feature
of the English language in the mediaeval period is the absence of a
universally accepted standard'. Chapter 3 presents a most interesting
discussion of 'The Editorial Process', dealing firstly with the power of an
editor to determine how a text should be interpreted (e.g., Vinaver's
printing of *Le Morte Darthur* as eight tales, or an editor's decision to use
italics in spite of their absence in manuscripts, or replacing 'þ' by the
'th' in editing Chaucer, or Kane and Donaldson's assumptions about
Langland's metre). Such decisions materially affect the way a modern
reader approaches a text. Moreover, the modern audience should accept
that 'attention to the small details of language is hardly likely to have
been a feature of medieval reading habits'. Chapter 4 concerns 'Words,
Words, Words' (native connotation, foreign connotation, hard words
and poetic words, etc.) The main theme of the book appears again in
Chapter 5 (on word-play) which ends with an attempt to categorise
different types of word-play (e.g., acrostics: Eva/Ave; jingles: Chaucer's
seke/seeke, etc.). Chapter 6 on 'Parody' is a controversial essay which
dogmatically distinguishes between burlesque (of 'general' reference) and
parody (of 'particular' reference) on a number of counts, and then applies
the definition to selected texts (*Sir Thopas* is a parody, but the *Land of
Cokaygne* is a burlesque). Chapter 7 looks at themes (e.g., *Ubi sunt,*
Amazement, Storms) and notes that the critic should evaluate how such
conventional topics are elaborated by mediaeval authors. Chapter 8
features syntax, and the effects on it of translation and copying from
foreign material. The penultimate chapter before the conclusion covers
levels of discourse – mainly the colloquial level, the language of poetry
and prose, and ornate eloquence. Blake presents his material in a bold,

[15] *The English Language in Medieval Literature,* by Norman Blake. London
Melbourne and Toronto: J. M. Dent and Totowa, N.J.: Rowman & Littlefield. pp.
190. £7.95.

assertive, and business-like way. The inevitable generalising (e.g., over-dependence on words like 'typical', 'alien', and 'mediaeval' itself) leads to some loss of focus in the book, as do the over-compressed expression and a sprinkling of misprints (e.g., on Rolle: 'His name carved a certain cachet and authority on which others wished to capitalize on' [sic]). All in all, though, the book will provide much stimulus for enlivening seminars and classes in Old and Middle English.

M&H is devoted to 'Transformation and Continuity', with Maurice Keen on 'Huizinga, Kilgour and the Decline of Chivalry' (exceptionally useful and perceptive in linking historical events with literary trends); Kurt O. Olsson on 'Rhetoric, John Gower, and the Late Medieval *Exemplum*' (interesting discussion of the different usages of the exemplum device for moral purposes; see also section 6, below); Thomas J. Jambeck on *'Everyman* and the Implications of Bernardine Humanism in the Character "Knowledge"' (a thoughtful consideration of how a penitent should act to merit salvation, see also section II, below); Jeanne S. Martin on 'History and Parody in the Towneley Cycle' (an interesting opposition drawn between Eusebius of Caesarea's 'archetypal' view of history and Augustine's 'linear' view, and applied to this Cycle; see also section II, below); Michael Curschmann on 'The Concept of the Oral Formula as an Impediment to Our Understanding of Medieval Oral Poetry' (mostly with reference to the *Nibelungenlied*); Stephen G. Nichols Jr on 'A Poetics of Historicism? Recent Trends in Medieval Literary Study' (quite incomprehensible, making one long for that 'simpler era of literary study which had not witnessed the impact of the pretension to a literary science which linguistically-based models of structuralist poets have generated', which Nichols seems to disparage); Robert Levine contributes a review-article on 'The Pearl-Child: Topos and Archetype in the Middle English *Pearl'* with particular reference to Paul Piehler's book (*YW*. 52.84), probing the psychological approach to the poem (see also section 3, below); D. W. Robertson Jr contributes a short but swingeing review-article on D. R. Howard's *The Idea of the Canterbury Tales* (*YW*. 57.89) which he considers to have 'a diffuse and often verbose argument' and several other deficiencies (e.g., the anachronistic claim that the Franklin may be seen as a country-squire); M. L. Colker lists and summarily describes 'Some Recent Works for Palaeographers' (mainly Belgian, French, Italian, and Austrian) based on the Proceedings of Colloquia on Palaeography, noting inconsistencies which give them varying usefulness.

John Burrow's excellent annotated anthology of 7500 lines of *English Verse 1300-1500*[16] commences with a useful chronological table listing significant events and an introduction in which he distinguishes and briefly describes the three different kinds of poetry which he includes in his book: the Courtly Makers (Chaucer, Gower, Lydgate), Alliterative Poets (Langland, the *Gawain*-poet, *Wynnere and Wastoure*, etc.) and Folk Poetry (the four lyrics from the early fourteenth-century Rawlinson MS, the five lyrics from the early fifteenth-century Sloane MS, the *Corpus Christi Carol*, and *The Hunting of the Cheviot*). The spelling has been 'normalized and modernized'; the punctuation is editorial; and the notes are

[16] *English Verse 1300-1500*, ed. by John Burrow. Longman Annotated Anthologies of English Verse, Volume I. London and New York: Longman. pp. xxvii + 397. £4.50.

designed to 'provide information a non-specialist reader will need, together with a necessarily limited amount of critical comment'. Each text begins with a very useful and concise head-note. For instance, he explains the structure and meaning of Dunbar's *The Tretis of the Twa Mariit Wemen and the Wedo,* and after crediting it with an 'explosively unstable mixture of outdoor romance and domestic reality', he refers to a limited number of relevant studies, before going on to give short notes on 'Metre and Style' and then 'Text'. Shorter poems are given in full, but necessarily there have to be a good few extracts. Thus *Sir Orfeo* is given in full, but *Piers Plowman* is limited to two extracts (passus 6 and 18). This anthology, which ends with a select bibliography and an index of titles and first lines, will prove to be most useful for teaching students and is to be wholeheartedly recommended.

The second (and larger) section of Derek Pearsall's *History of Old English and Middle English Poetry*[17] is chiefly concerned with poetry written before the introduction of printing into England in the 1470s, and covers Late Old English Poetry and the Transition, Poetry in the early Middle English Period, Some Fourteenth Century Books and Writers (including the *Gawain*-poems, and the *Piers Plowman* group), Alliterative Poetry, Court Poetry, and the Close of the Middle Ages (a miscellany of features, including Lydgate, religious poetry, drama, romances, and Scots poetry). The volume ends with a short conclusion, Appendix 1 (technical terms, mainly metrical), Appendix 2 (Chronological Table), Notes, and Index. Pearsall's method is traditional — chronological treatment of the poems with suitable summaries, quotation, and running commentary, with declared (and most welcome) interest in the environment — manuscripts, historical events, social developments (e.g., the spread of book ownership in the fifteenth century), linguistic relationships (mainly Latin and Anglo-Norman). The bibliographical notes (which come as far as 1974) supporting the text show the author's judicious, balanced handling of the main critical contribution to the subject (with some piquant observations, e.g., on Robertson and his followers, p. 324). In line with recent critical trends, the author presents a sensitive plea for the fifteenth century — it is not an 'abyss', but a 'trough' in the history of English literature. The background information is usually presented in a reasoned and convincing way (with the odd exception — for instance, a curiously specific biographical note on Langland ('was a cleric in minor orders, married, without benefice, who eked out a living in London as a jobbing cleric, . . .'), whereas by contrast Lydgate's life is hardly adverted to. As a history of poetry which attempts to relate history with poetry and to show continuities and discontinuities, this book will prove very handy for students (perhaps too handy — because it does so much of their work for them and is dangerously mnemonic in its phrasing).

2. Alliterative Poetry

The most valuable sections of Thorlac Turville-Petre's fairly brief study of *The Alliterative Revival*[18] are those dealing with the origins of this

---

[17] *Old English and Middle English Poetry,* by Derek Pearsall. The Routledge History of English Poetry, Volume I. Routledge & Kegan Paul. pp. xiv + 352. £8.75.
[18] See note 14, above.

poetic movement and with its metre and diction. The author emphasises the resourcefulness and inventiveness of the poets rather than their fidelity to tradition, opting firmly for the theory of 're-invention' of alliterative techniques as opposed to that of a 'revival' of techniques derived from Anglo-Saxon poetry. His discussion of the poetry from a more literary point of view is relatively disappointing: it does not attempt to cover all the poems of the Revival, concentrating on the comparatively minor *Wars of Alexander, Purity*, and *Pierce the Ploughman's Crede*, so that one is left only with a very partial view of the poetic achievement of the Revival as a whole.

Hoyt N. Duggan studies some 'Strophic Patterns in Middle English Alliterative Poetry' (*MP*), particularly the tendency of a number of poems in unrhymed alliterative verse to fall into loose and apparently functionless 'strophes' composed of quatrains or multiples thereof. He suggests that this tendency may have its origins in Old Norse traditions of unrhymed alliterative verse.

Clifford Peterson's new edition of *St Erkenwald*[19] is to be welcomed, despite some oddities. He provides a more complete critical apparatus than that offered by Ruth Morse's recent edition of the poem (see *YW* 57.64). The account of the manuscript containing *St Erkenwald* is especially full. Also full, though very speculative in parts, is the discussion of the poem's sources, in which Peterson argues that the church liturgy, especially that for Ascension Day and Pentecost, provides 'a structural, even theological, basis for much of the poem'. Peterson's dating of the text, somewhat later than is usually supposed, is heavily influenced by his determination to prove that it and the four poems of the *Pearl* manuscript were all written by John Massey of Coton. He further defends this theory, though retracting his previous 'discovery' of a 'Massey-cipher' in *St Erkenwald* (see *YW* 55.101), in a note on 'Hoccleve, the Old Hall Manuscript, Cotton Nero A.x., and the *Pearl*-poet' (*RES*), to which Edward Wilson appends some further comments on the debate on ciphers.

Thorlac Turville-Petre also discusses 'The Ages of Man in *The Parlement of the Thre Ages*' (*MÆ*). He argues that the author of this poem constantly adapts conventional patterns of description for Youth, Middle Elde, and Elde in order to create an effect of ambiguity. Nicholas Jacobs, in a note on 'The Ottoman "Porte" in Middle English' (*N&Q*), construes the use of the word in the alliterative *Morte Arthure* as signifying 'Ottoman Government'; such a usage would suggest that the poem is unlikely to have been composed before a date well into the fifteenth century.

3. The Gawain-Poet

Charles Moorman's edition of *The Works of the Gawain-Poet*[20] is a very handsome volume, garnished with all the illustrations from the original manuscript as well as an attractively printed text, made easy to read by marginal glosses on difficult words and phrases. It is unfortunate

---

[19] *St Erkenwald*, ed. by Clifford Peterson. Philadelphia, Pa.: U. of Pennsylvania P. pp. ix + 147. $22.

[20] *The Works of the Gawain-Poet*, ed. by Charles Moorman. Mississippi: U.P. of Mississippi. pp. xii + 452. 12 plates. $25.

that it has appeared not long after A. C. Cawley and J. J. Anderson's much less lavish but at least equally useful edition of the same material (see *YW* 57.64). Both seem aimed at very much the same market, the general student rather than the specialist: Moorman refers the reader back to earlier editions and studies for detailed discussions of such matters as the grammar and vocabulary of the poems. From all but the aesthetic point of view, then, the Everyman edition must still seem better value. A. Kent Hieatt points out a number of 'Symbolic and Narrative Patterns in *Pearl, Cleanness, Patience,* and *Gawain*' (*ESC*, 1976), such as the constantly recurring opposition between cleanliness and filth, especially in relation to clothing, ornaments and vessels.

Two articles investigate the structure of *GGK*. In 'Structure and Meaning in *GGK*' (*PLL*), Robert W. Margeson writes interestingly on the apparent conflict between circular and linear patterns within the poem, each representing a powerful moral attitude: the idealistic circular view of chivalric life held by Arthur's court as opposed to the idea of the necessity for accepting the relentless linear march of time with its connotations of change and imperfection. Louis Blenkner's 'Sin, Psychology and the Structure of *GGK*' (*MP*), makes a rather over-ingenious attempt to relate the physical structure of the poem (as shown by the various manuscript subdivisions) to its metaphysical structure. Thus, for example, the three days at Bertilak's castle are seen as severally figuring forth Gawain's 'triple moral and chivalric fault of fleshly *couardise,* worldly *couetyse,* and devilish *vntrawþe*'.

Peggy A. Knapp's ambitious effort at showing that 'the conflict between chivalric nationalism and penitential Christianity informs the structure of *Gawain*' ends up by overleaping itself and falling into grandiose generalisations about 'mythic modes of thought' and 'regeneration themes' in 'Gawain's quest: social conflict and symbolic mediation' (*ClioW*). In 'Sir Gawain in a Dilemma: or Keeping Faith with Marcus Tullius Cicero' (*MP*), Theodore Silverstein suggests that the qualities listed in the fifth pentad of Gawain's pentangle constitute the parts of justice as found in the ancient moral philosophers, especially Cicero's *De Officiis* and mediaeval commentaries upon it. Joseph E. Gallagher examines the relationship between '"Trawþe" and "Luf-talkying" in *GGK*' (*NM*): in a detailed analysis of the temptation scenes, he finds a clash between Gawain's courtly love-talk and the Christian values he tries to uphold. In the end 'luf-talkyng' must be rejected as inimical to 'trawþe'. In 'The word "norne" and the Temptation of Sir Gawain' (*NM*), W. A. Gallagher proposes a radically different reading of *GGK* 1760–72 from the usually accepted interpretation, one which would lay much heavier emphasis on Gawain's sexual arousal by the Lady. Sexual innuendo is again central to Albert B. Friedman and Richard H. Osberg's 'Gawain's Girdle as Traditional Symbol' (*JAF*). They survey the magical and sexual connotations of girdles in folklore, concluding that the audience of *GGK* would have recognised the Lady's girdle as a powerful sexual symbol. In 'A Note on the Age of the Green Knight' (*NM*), Eiichi Suzuki suggests that the Green Knight is an old man – 1. 1124 should be taken literally.

'How Gawain beat the Green Knight', by Norman Lavers (*PAPA*) was not seen.

Marie Borroff has produced a delightful verse translation of *Pearl*[21], faithfully reproducing the very complex stanza-form and system of concatenation of its original, and even managing to include a fair amount of alliteration into the bargain. Such an undertaking might seem a dauntingly difficult one, but Professor Borroff is probably better equipped to succeed in it than almost anyone else, and the result is remarkably faithful to the tone of the original poem. There is a fairly brief general introduction to the poem and its background, and a note on its metrical form. In 'The Pearl-child: Topos and Archetype in the Middle English *Pearl*' (*M&H*), Robert Levine counters Paul Piehler's application of psychoanalytic commonplaces to the characterisation of Pearl in his book *The Visionary Landscape* (1971: see *YW* 52.84) with the argument that the characteristics singled out by Piehler are in fact normally attributed to other female figures, especially Mary, in many texts related to the tradition in which the *Pearl*-poet was writing. Peter J. Lucas notes of 'Pearl's Free-flowing Hair' (*ELN*) that her hairstyle is appropriate for her in each of its three fourteenth-century associations: for unmarried girls, for brides, and for queens.

J. J. Anderson provides the first new scholarly edition of *Cleanness*[22] for over fifty years. He prints a conservative text of the poem with a number of new readings obtained with the help of ultra-violet photography. The glossary and notes are largely devoted to the elucidation of the difficult language of the poem; the discussion of its literary aspects in the introduction, though brief, is also interesting; and an appendix deals with the poem's versification as well as its language. Altogether an admirable edition, that nicely complements the less specialised presentation of the same poem provided by Anderson in his and Cawley's joint edition of *Pearl, Cleanness, Patience,* and *GGK* (see the beginning of this section, and *YW* 57.64). Using *Cleanness's* alternative title, Elizabeth Armstrong's note on *'Purity'* (*Expl*) develops the point that the poem directs attention to the central idea of purity by using images that are homely and close to the audience's experience: Christ himself is seen as a fastidious householder.

Gabriella del Lungo Camiciotti writes 'Sulla Struttura e sul Significato del Poemetto Medio-Inglese *Pazienza'* (*StG*, 1975). She considers that the poet's rendering of the Beatitudes may be seen as the epitome of the poem as a whole, announcing themes that run throughout the narrative and constitute the very structure of *Patience*. In a rather slight examination of 'The Role of Jonah in *Patience'* (*LangQ*), George Sanderlin stresses the importance of the personality of Jonah as opposed to that of the narrator in the overall effect of the poem. In *'Patience:* the "Munster Dor"' (*ELN*), Malcolm Andrew suggests that the image of Jonah going into the whale's belly 'as mote in at a munster dor' points to the central symbolic paradox of Jonah's turning to God from the womb of Hell.

---

[21] *'Pearl': A New Verse Translation,* by Marie Borroff. New York: W. W. Norton. pp. xxi + 40. $7.95, pb $1.95.
[22] *Cleanness,* ed. by J. J. Anderson Manchester: Manchester U.P. and New York: Barns & Noble. pp. ix + 177. £8.50.

4. Piers Plowman

With due reference to P. M. Kean's work (*YM*. 45.71; 50.94) Charlotte Clutterbuck considers 'Hope and Good Works: *Leaute* in the C-text of *Piers Plowman*' (*RES*) and uses the contexts where the words *leaute* or the adjective *leel* appear to suggest that they may be taken as denoting hope or, at least, 'the foundation of hope'. Seen in this light, *Leaute* corrects the sins of despair and presumption in the sense that it represents 'some aspect of right — it is the hope which is justified by the good works on which it is based'.

D. C. Fowler stands by his long held view (*YW*. 42.68) that there was a B-poet, as distinct from an A-poet, in his long, painstaking review-article of 'A New Edition of the B-text of *Piers Plowman*' (*YES*) where, in his view, the lines which Kane and Donaldson regard as 'metrically defective' for the most part represent simply the alliteration of the B-poet: hence, many emendations which harmonise B with A are 'unwarranted' and the editors thereby 'enshrine their point of view, against all the manuscript evidence, in a seemingly scientific edition of the poem'. That said, his review notes inconsistencies in the editors' rationale for emending in the face of MS readings (e.g., exclusion after VI 182, but why not also VI 181–2?) and decries the absence in the Introduction of a section dealing with 'The B-Reviser's A-Manuscript'.

Adding to the growing body of material demonstrating the depth of Langland's learning, Erika C. D. Lindemann provides a concise and useful account of 'Analogues for Latin Quotations in "Piers Plowman"' (*NM*) with particular reference to thirteen quotations. She goes outside the bible to find affinities (e.g., Alain de Lille's *Liber Parabolorum,* which contains *sub molli pastore lupus . . . dilaceratur eo* (v. C X 265–6).

Raymond St Jacques gives further proof of Langland's biblical learning in his consideration of 'Langland's "Spes" the Spy and the Book of Numbers' (13: 26) (*N&Q*) where the men whom God orders Moses to send to view the promised land are described as spies. Hope is like them in the sense that his search for Christ is to be seen as a 'spying' mission.

In his detailed review-article on '*Piers Plowman: The B Version*' (*MÆ*) Derek Pearsall presents a cautious appraisal of the methods described by the editors in their Introduction to what he pointedly feels 'may well be . . . known for a long time as the Kane-Donaldson B-text, rather than as the B-text of *Piers Plowman'*. Confidence in the new edition will be undermined by the editors' use of conjectural emendations on a variety of grounds, some of which (e.g., the notional standard of higher quality alliteration) are open to serious challenge, and so the legitimacy of many of their readings (e.g., B XV 445) must be queried (see Hudson, above).

John A. Alford's stimulating consideration of 'The Role of the Quotations in *Piers Plowman*' (*Speculum*) leads him to develop a picture of the poet 'eking out his poem slowly, even tediously, while poring over a variety of commentaries and preachers' aids'. By noting how, when, and where the Latin texts are used, Alford is able to show that they are the primary elements in the structure of the poem, while 'the English functions mainly as an amplification of the texts' (see, for example, Alford's careful analysis of B XIV).

Robert L. Kelly considers that 'Hugh Latimer as Piers Plowman' (*SEL*) 'is the guise in which the sermonist addresses his countrymen as the prophet of the New Jerusalem to be achieved under King Edward', particularly in the 'Sermon of the Plow', which is distinguished above all by use of arming imagery (see Luke 7: 5, and Luke 9:62) and also by alliteration and satire. Such features can be seen as redolent of *Piers Plowman*.

5. Romances

Robert W. Hanning's *The Individual in Twelfth-Century Romance*[23] does not, of course deal directly with Middle English material, but is useful in that it provides a lively study of the origins of the twelfth-century idea of the individual and its importance in courtly romance. Texts principally referred to are Abelard's *Historia Calamitatum;* the *Life of Christina of Markyate;* Chrétien de Troyes' *Erec, Yvain,* and *Lancelot; Le Bel Inconnu. Partonopeu de Blois;* and Hue de Rotelande's *Ipomedon.* In the area of background material to Arthurian romance, it may be worth noting the re-issue (1976) of Richard Barber's *The Figure of Arthur*[24], and the appearance of Avallach Hunt's unashamedly speculative 'Who or What is "The Holy Grail"?' (*AWR*), which suggests that the Grail may be no less than the body of Our Lady, buried at Glastonbury.

'Formulaic Style in the Middle English Romance' (*NM*), by Susan Wittig, sets out to 'outline ways in which formulaic study may be extended to the analysis of the style of the Middle English Romance', but does not investigate her subject thoroughly enough to arrive at any very satisfactory proofs of her conclusion that 'the style of the poems is fundamentally stereotyped'. Paul Strohm's 'The Origin and Meaning of Middle English *Romaunce*' (*Genre*) was not seen.

In 'Havelok 2933: A Problem in Medieval Literary History' (*NM*), John C. Hirsh argues that the error of the scribe of the Laud manuscript of *Havelok* in writing and then cancelling the first half of 1.2953 twenty lines before its proper place arose not because the scribe was copying from a small minstrel's manuscript, as is usually supposed, but as a result of simple eye-skip (11.2933 and 2953 are visually very similar). His 'Additional Note on MSS. Ashmole 61, Douce 228 and Lincoln's Inn 150' (*NM*) contends that there is no real evidence for the often-repeated claim that they are of minstrel provenance. George B. Jack's 'The Date of *Havelok*' (*Anglia*) is a point-by-point reply to Herlint Meyer-Lindenberg's attempt to date the romance to the years 1203–1216 (*Anglia*, 1968: see *YW* 49. 96). Jack concludes that the date of *Havelok* 'cannot be more precisely fixed than within a time between the late twelfth-century and *circa* 1272'.

Elizabeth S. Sklar investigates 'The dialect of *Arthour and Merlin*' (*ELN*), and finds that its mixture of linguistic variants suggests a Sussex rather than a London origin both for this romance and for *King Alisaunder*. The place-name changes made by the redactor of *Arthour and Merlin* also

---

[23] *The Individual in Twelfth-Century Romance,* by Robert W. Hanning. New Haven, Conn. and London: Yale U. P. pp. xi + 303. £12.60.
[24] *The Figure of Arthur,* by Richard Barber. Cambridge: D. S. Brewer (re-issue, 1976). pp. 160. £3.50.

seem to point to an origin in south-central Sussex. Earl R. Anderson feels
that Thomas Chestre should be given more credit than he usually receives
for 'The Structure of *Sir Launfal*' (*PLL*). He finds an organised symmetry
of incidents running through the narrative, combined with a systematic
exploration of ethical problems (in particular, the theme of various kinds
of falsehood and their contrast with truth, which is represented above all
by the fairy world).

6. Gower, Lydgate, Hoccleve

Kurt Olsson provides a useful guide to Gower's *Mirour de l'Omme*
with his long article on 'The cardinal virtues and the structure of John
Gower's *Speculum Meditantis*' (*JMRS*). He notes that the poem has four
sections or 'mirrors': an allegory in which good and evil struggle to win
man's Body and Soul; an attack on the contemporary conduct and interaction of the various estates; a reaffirmation of the natural, created order,
partly through personal confession by the poet; and a life of the Virgin.
He argues that each of the four cardinal virtues (prudence, justice, fortitude, and temperance) corresponds respectively to each section, emphasising that Gower's treatment of the sections reflects the view that the
virtues were 'separate, yet interdependent'. Olsson's task, as he sees it,
is 'to discover how these mediative *specula* can change and mature the
moral vision of Gower's assumed auditor'. Olsson's views are much less
clear in his 'Rhetoric, John Gower, and the Late Medieval Exemplum'
(*M&H*), and for this reason may be ill served by an attempt at summary.
He distinguishes various exemplary modes used by Gower, finding in the
first section of the *Mirour de l'Omme* a type of *exemplum* which combines
with similitude and image to constitute *homoeosis,* and which exists in
a continuum with allegory. This leads him to distinguish between 'rhetoric
of faith', where special emphasis is placed on the meaning of an *exemplum,*
and 'rhetoric of action', where it is placed on its form, and to imply that
the latter kind of rhetoric is less likely than the former to fit the continuum
between *exemplum* and allegory. He then goes on to distinguish three
other modes which he describes as 'poetically ordered to effect an immediate choice or action in the auditor', giving examples from the *Mirour* and
the *Confessio Amantis.*

James Dean discusses 'Time Past and Time Present in Chaucer's Clerk's
Tale and Gower's *Confessio Amantis*' (*ELH*), concentrating on lines 1139–
69 of the former work and on Book VIII, lines 2745–2940 of the latter to
show that Griselda in her life and virtue 'recalls the constancy, righteousness and simplicity of the former age', while Gower as Amans, old and
feeble like the senescent world, 'is himself an emblem of the division
in love that Gower decries in his Prologue'. The passages show how Gower
and other fourteenth-century writers found that a *recherche du temps
perdu* 'leads to important insights about the self'. Dean's view that no-one
before him 'has ever accused John Gower of being a comic poet' should
be seen in relation to Anthony E. Farnham's contribution of 1974 (*YW*
55. 114).

Walter S. Phelan, in 'Beyond the Concordance: Semantic and Mythic
Structures in Gower's Tale of Florent' (*Neophilologus*) is led by a word-

frequency comparison of this Tale with Chaucer's Wife of Bath's Tale to the conclusion that 'Gower knits the story together through the word *schape* and the concepts of *covenant, strengthe,* and *trowthe'*, while 'Chaucer seems to do so with the idea of *chois* and the interplay of the words *love* and *lif'*. The two stories, he finds, are 'mythically identical', differing from each other 'only on an historical or cultural level'.

A long article by Lois Ebin shows how 'Lydgate's Views on Poetry' (*AnM*) are developed in his own digressive passages on the subject. He coins new words (such as 'aureate') and develops the meanings of words used by Chaucer (such as 'enlumyn') to define the qualities of good poetry, and is especially interested in the idea of the poet as craftsman, in amplification and high style, and in the relationship between the language of poetry and the well-being of the state.

Stanley J. Kozikowski points out in 'Lydgate, Machiavelli, and More and Skelton's *Bowge of Courte*' (*AN&Q*) that the image of Fortune followed by train of personifications occurs not only in Skelton's poem but also in Lydgate's *Mumming at London*, in Machiavelli's *Capitolo di Fortuna*, and in 'Fortune', a poem attributed to More.

In a commendable interdisciplinary contribution (also noted in section 8), 'Words and music in two English songs of the mid-fifteenth century: Charles d'Orléans and John Lydgate', David Fallows (*Early Music*) first distinguishes between a 'sung' and a 'written' version of a French poem by Charles d'Orléans in its surviving manuscripts, and notes that the music of the former version was by the fifteenth-century English composer John Bedyngham. Fitting the music to an English version of the poem preserved in British Library MS Harley 682 (and beginning 'Mi verry joy . . . '), Fallows tentatively suggests that Charles composed the poem originally in English, and that Bedyngham first set it to music in that language, perhaps in consultation with Charles. Secondly, Fallows suggests that an English song in the fifteenth-century Escorial chansonnier beginning 'Princhesse af youth . . .' derives ultimately from the opening lines of the rhyme-royal section of Lydgate's *Temple of Glas* in which the Lover declares his love. In an article noted in the next section, 'Patterns in *The Kingis Quair* and the *Temple of Glas*' (*PLL*), Alice Miskimin is prompted to compare the two poems by the fact that both are structurally based on the heptad, and both are 'divergent and independent answers to Chaucerian questions'. She finds 'the differences between the two poems . . . more interesting than their parallels'.

A. S. G. Edwards, in 'The Influence of Lydgate's *Fall of Princes c.* 1440–1559: A Survey' (*MS*) shows that for most of Lydgate's readers this poem and Boccaccio's *De casibus virorum illustrium*, on which it is indirectly based, were virtually synonymous, and that Lydgate's poem won popularity mainly by its didactic, exemplary character. This aspect of it bulks large in Peter Idley's borrowings from it in his *Instructions to his Son*, while the use made of it by George Cavendish in his *Metrical Visions* and by the authors of the *Mirror for Magistrates* shows that it also provided a model of historical tragedy into which contemporary events could be fitted.

Kathryn Walls offers a negative answer to the question 'Did Lydgate Translate the "Pèlerinage de vie humaine"?' (*N&Q*), suggesting that the ascription of the English verse translation to Lydgate originated in a misunderstanding by John Stowe – reflected in British Library MS. Stowe 952 – of a remark in the 'kalundare of John Shirley' (contained in British Library MS. Add. 29729) about a prose 'pilgrymage'. The ascription – which has never been to Lydgate's advantage – was then perpetuated by Speght's 1598 edition of Chaucer.

In 'Hoccleve, the Old Hall Manuscript, Cotton Nero A.X., and the *Pearl*-Poet' (*RES*; see also under section 2 above), Clifford Peterson argues against Turville-Petre's view (*YW* 56. 87, 96) that Hoccleve's 'maister Massy could not have been a poet'.

In 'The Iconography of Chaucer in Hoccleve's *De Regimine Principum* and in the *Troilus* Frontispiece' (*ChauR*) James H. McGregor shows that the portraits of Chaucer found in two manuscripts of the former work reflect the view that 'Chaucer is the Aristotle of this work, and Chaucer is the royal counselor whose *Melibee*, as Hoccleve interprets it, advises the Prince and serves as the prototype for Hoccleve's own work'.

Diane Bornstein illustrates 'Reflections of Political Theory and Political Fact in Fifteenth-century Mirrors for the Prince'[25] with examples from Christine de Pisan's *Corps de policie,* Richard Ullerston's *De officio militari,* Hoccleve's *Regement of Princes,* James Yonge's translation of one of Hoccleve's sources for this poem, the *Secretum Secretorum,* and finally, George Ashby's *Active Policy of a Prince*.

7. Middle Scots Poetry

Study of this subject has been greatly assisted by the publication this year of a number of works not solely concerned with it. The advantages of *A Dictionary of Scottish History*[26] and of a new, revised edition of Croft Dickinson's *Scotland from the Earliest times to 1603*[27] will be obvious. Watt's *Biographical Dictionary of Scottish Graduates to A.D. 1410*[28], dealing with the graduate class in Scotland before the foundation of its first university at St Andrews in 1410-12, includes a detailed account of the career of John Barbour. A volume of essays on *Scottish Society in the Fifteenth Century*[29] contains a stimulating survey of 'The literature of fifteenth-century Scotland' by John MacQueen. He first discusses Andrew of Wyntoun, mentioning Barbour among his predecessors and Hector Boece among his followers, and then draws attention to the intricate numerological structure of the *Kingis Quair*. He goes on to discuss the royal court, the aristocracy and the burgesses as sources for literary patronage, and emphasises the importance of the new Scottish

[25] In *Medieval Studies in Honor of Lillian Herlands Hornstein*, ed. by Jess B. Bessinger Jr and Robert R. Raymo. New York: New York U. P. (1976) pp x + 225. Frontispiece; 9 figures. $18.50.

[26] *A Dictionary of Scottish History,* by Gordon Donaldson and Robert S. Morpeth. Edinburgh: John Donald Publishers. pp. 234. £6.

[27] *Scotland from the Earliest Times to 1603,* by W. Croft Dickinson. 3rd ed. rev. & ed. by Archibald A. M. Duncan. Oxford: at the Clarendon Press. pp. xii + 442. 10 genealogical tables, 3 maps. £9.75.

[28] *A Biographical Dictionary of Scottish Graduates to A.D. 1410,* by D. E. R. Watt. Oxford: Clarendon Press. pp. xliv + 607. £30.

[29] *Scottish Society in the Fifteenth Century,* ed. by Jennifer Brown. Edward Arnold. pp. xii + 273. 14 plates, 3 figures. £11.

universities for the development of literature throughout the century. He concludes with a discussion of Henryson as an example of almost every aspect of the literary tradition apart from historical narrative. By contrast, the relevant chapters (I and part of II) of Maurice Lindsay's *History of Scottish Literature*[30] are disappointing. It is understandable, perhaps, that the approach in such a work should be descriptive rather than analytical, but if the author implies, as he does in his Introduction, that the extent of specifically Celtic influence on Scottish literature has been exaggerated, he should not hint at such influence, as he does in the context of Dunbar's 'Flyting', without saying clearly what he means by it; and his unqualified assumption that Gavin Douglas wrote *King Hart* (see *YW* 40. 93 and Florence Ridley in *Speculum* 1959) suggests inadequate research. A prose translation into Scots, dating from *c.* 1540, of Boece's *Historiae Scotorum*[31] — itself a prose work though much indebted to Wyntoun's verse *Cronykil* — is now available in facsimile.

While the subject-matter of *Bards and Makars*[32] extends into the seventeenth century and includes Scottish Gaelic, the volume nevertheless contains much that is relevant here. Adam J. Aitken writes on 'How to Pronounce Older Scots' and Hans H. Meier shows that 'Scots is Not Alone' by comparing it with its Older Swiss and Middle Low German analogues. Thomas W. Craik offers in 'The Substance and Structure of *The Testament of Cresseid*: A Hypothesis' to the effect that Henryson may have viewed his poem as an 'alternative ending' to Chaucer's *Troilus*. The *Testament*, he concludes, 'is more profitably approached as a tragic poem than as a didactic one'. Matthew P. McDiarmid finds that 'Robert Henryson in His Poems' is haunted by 'the tragedy of sin, that men made in the image of God should become "beistis Irrational"'. His paper includes a spirited attack on some recent remaks of J. A. W. Bennett on the *Testament* (*YW* 55.118). John McNamara argues for 'Language as Action in Henryson's *Testament of Cresseid*', in the sense 'that we as audience are ourselves literary creations implied by the text'. In order to readjust whatever impression of Cresseid the reader may have from other works of literature, 'the *Testament* becomes a kind of metalanguage about the literary tradition even as it generates its own language about the actions of the heroine'. Carol Mills illustrates the 'Romance Convention of Robert Henryson's *Orpheus and Eurydice*' with examples of possible influence from 'courtly romance of the Chaucerian type' and from 'the romance Orfeo tradition', particularly *Sir Orfeo* itself. Wilhelm F. H. Nicolaisen shows how 'masterful' syntactic techniques help to create a lively relationship between 'Line and Sentence in Dunbar's Poetry'. Jean-Jacques Blanchot writes on 'William Dunbar and François Villon: the literary *personae*. Towards a methodology of comparison in literature'. Ian Ross attempts to share 'Dunbar's Vision of the "Four Last Things"' (death, judgement, hell and heaven) by examining paintings, engravings, and woodcuts of his

---

[30] *History of Scottish Literature*, by Maurice Lindsay. Robert Hale. pp. 496. £8.95.

[31] *Chronicle of Scotland*, by Hector Boethius. Edinburgh, (1540?). The English Experience, no. 851. Amsterdam: Theatrum Orbis Terrarum, Ltd., and Norwood, N. J.: Walter J. Johnson, Inc. 2 leaves including modern title-page + 286 folio leaves, each reproduced, recto and verso, in facsimile. $70.

[32] *Bards and Makars, Scottish Language and Literature: Medieval and Renaissance*, ed. by Adam J. Aitken, Matthew P. McDiarmid, and Derick S. Thomson. Glasgow: U. of Glasgow P. pp. viii + 250. £15.

time, particularly those of the Early Netherlandish School. Taking as her starting-point the list of writers in the Court of the Muses in Douglas's *Palice of Honour,* Priscilla Bawcutt tentatively reconstructs 'The "Library" of Gavin Douglas', emphasising his debt to Latin (rather than Greek), Italian and vernacular writers. Anna J. Mill writes on 'The Records of Scots Medieval Plays: Interpretations and Misinterpretations', finding that the latter result from terminological confusion, careless transcribing by editors, ignorance of Latin, and failure to check the contemporaneity of manuscript sources. She also criticizes the Edinburgh section of Alan Nelson's *Medieval English Stage* (*YW* 55. 142-3). Claude Graf, in 'Theatre and Politics: Lindsay's *Satyre of the Thrie Estaitis*' compares the 1540 and 1552 versions of the play, finding the earlier one 'more topical and occasional' than the later, which he finds 'broader in scope, though also geared to the situation of pre-Reformation Scotland'. In 'Manuscripts and Prints of Scots Poetry in the Sixteenth Century' Denton Fox seeks support in the Asloan and Bannatyne manuscripts for his view that sixteenth-century Scottish manuscripts may often be copied from prints, and hence all the further removed from what the poets wrote. William Ramson, finally, 'On Bannatyne's Editing', finds that the most important ordering principle in the Bannatyne manuscript is the statement about human and divine nature which its division into five parts reflects.

Defining a Latinism as 'a lexical item of Latin origin that — whether borrowed directly or through French — betrays no sign of Gallo-Roman or Old French sound changes in its base, and so can be immediately related to its Latin counterpart', Bengt Ellenberger documents systematically *The Latin Element in the Vocabulary of the Earlier Makars, Henryson and Dunbar*[33]. He lists the Latinisms under morphological and conceptual headings, the former often revealing instances of rhyme, and gives further information about each word in an Index. In a chapter on 'Frequency' he shows, among other things, that in Henryson's *Fables* the proportion of Latinisms is higher in the Prologues and Morals than in the Fables proper, and he applies a modified version of the mediaeval stylistic scale — with an 'upper' and 'lower' middle style — to Dunbar's poems, which he divides by content into seven groups. In another chapter he attempts to clarify the term 'aureation' by investigating certain types of Latinism, including polysyllables and neologisms, in the poetic vocabulary of Dunbar. His treatment of words falling alphabetically between Pa and Pavil(l)ion may now be compared with that of the same words in the *Dictionary of the Older Scottish Tongue*[34], the relevant part of which has appeared.

In 'John Barbour and Rhetorical Tradition' (*AnM*) Bernice W. Kilman examines *The Bruce* under different headings in order to show that Barbour knew such works as *ad Herennium* and Geoffrey de Vinsauf's writings and made good use of his knowledge. 'Arrangement' is shown in the way he alters historical chronology to provide a rhythm of incident

[33] *The Latin Element in the Vocabulary of the Earlier Makars Henryson and Dunbar,* by Bengt Ellenberger. Lund Studies in English, 51, ed. by Claes Schaar and Jan Svartvik. Lund: CWK Gleerup. pp. 163. Sw. Kr. 45.
[34] *A Dictionary of the Older Scottish Tongue from the Twelfth Century to the end of the Seventeenth Founded on the Collections of Sir William A. Craigie.* Part XXIX, PA – PAVIL(L)ION, ed. by A. J. Aitken, M. A., and James A. C. Stevenson, M.A., Ph.D. assisted by Francis Bamford, M.A., and Jean K. Glass, Dip. Com. Chicago and London: The U. of Chicago P. pp. 245-364. £10.90.

comparable to the upward movement of Fortune's Wheel; 'Amplification and Abbreviation' are fully illustrated in the description of James Douglas; and the 'Style' is found to be appropriate to the poem's subject – the struggle of all classes to be free – in that it combines the high, middle and low levels recommended by the rhetoricians.

Coincidentally, Alice Miskimin also discusses numerology in the *Kingis Quair*, in her article on 'Patterns in *The Kingis Quair* and *The Temple of Glas*' (*PLL*) (see section 6 above). Her comparison of James's poem with Lydgate's is one difference between her own approach and MacQueen's in the article noted above, though among elements she has in common with MacQueen are her reference to the work of Alastair Fowler, her emphasis on the 'circular shape' of the *Kingis Quair,* and the importance she attaches to James's twice nine years of imprisonment and to his age (twenty eight) at the end of that period.

Larry M. Sklute, in 'Phoebus Descending: Rhetoric and Moral Vision in Henryson's *Testament of Cresseid*' (*ELH*), sees the 'image of Phoebus descending' 'as a metaphor for the vision of life and of human action' in this poem. Noting that Henryson's differs from most versions of the Troy story in making Calchas a priest of Venus and his relationship with Cresseid sympathetic, Sklute goes on to describe the *Testament* as 'the legend of a bad woman', comparable in form to parts of Chaucer's *Legend of Good Women,* though in purpose 'far more moralistic and far more intent on blaming women'. Henryson's narrator, Sklute finds, ' is a shrewd old man who makes up in moral righteousness for what he lacks in sexual potency'.

Roderick J. Lyall, in 'Two of Dunbar's Makars: James Affleck and Sir John the Ross, (*Innes Review*, 1976) very tentatively suggests an identification of Sir John the Ross of Hawkshead with the 'Sir John the Ross' mentioned in Dunbar's 'Flyting' and 'Lament for the Makaris', and of this Sir John's son-in-law, James Auchinleck, with the 'James Affleck' of the 'Lament'. Lyall also considers the question of whether this Auchinleck was the author of the *Quare of Jealousy* and *Lancelot of the Laik.*

In 'Two Notes on Dunbar' (*FMLS*, 1976), David W. Lindsay first interprets the 'sabot' of line 502 of the 'Tua Mariit Wemen and the Wedo' as 'Sabaoth', perhaps with connotations of 'sabbath', and secondly, reads line 129 of the same poem as 'He trowis that young folk arne yeild, quhair he gane is', meaning 'he believes that young people are impotent, where he is virile'. L. P. Harvey, however, in 'An Observation on "Two Notes on Dunbar"' (*FMLS*) objects to Lindsay's 'arne yeild', substituting 'I yerne yeild', meaning 'I pay willingly'. Though he does not discuss 'gane', he presumably takes it as meaning simply 'gone'. Lindsay then replies to Harvey briefly and inconclusively.

8. Lyrics and Miscellaneous Verse

The second edition of Richard Leighton Green's *Early English Carols*[35] makes it clear that 'the basic plan of the book remains unchanged', though much has been added to the Introduction, Bibliography of Original

---

[35] *The Early English Carols,* ed. by Richard Leighton Greene. 2nd ed., rev. and enlarged. Oxford: at the Clarendon Press, pp. clxxiv + 517. Frontispiece. £25.

Sources, and Notes, while new carol-texts have been fitted into the numbering-system of the first edition. With even more confidence than in 1935, when the first edition appeared (see *YW* 16.132–3), the editor defines the carol as 'a song on any subject, composed of uniform stanzas and provided with a burden'. In the Introduction he develops, among other things, his distinction between the burden, which is external to the stanza and is characteristic of the carol, and the refrain, which is inserted between the lines of the stanza and is characterisic of the ballad, and suggests that these two types of song have their origin in different kinds of dance. The Preface implies that not quite all the new material contained in the same editor's *Selection of English Carols* (1962) has been incorporated in the new collected edition, and expresses the hope that the *Selection* 'will not be entirely overlooked' — as it has been until now, unfortunately, by *YW*.

Greene's discussion of the carol as dance-song naturally includes a mention of the story of the dancers of Colbeck as told in Robert Mannyng's *Handlyng Synne*. Angus McIntosh, in 'Some Notes on the "Dancers of Colbeck" — James Osborn: in Memoriam' (*N&Q*), calls attention to passages where the text of this story in Yale University Library MS. Osborn 5 provides information about difficult or corrupt passages in the MS. Harley 1701 and MS. Bodley 415 versions. Greene's various studies of the lyrics of the Red Book of Ossory, including his edition of 1974 (*YW* 55.120), are among those criticised by Theo Stemmler in 'The Vernacular Snatches in the *Red Book of Ossory:* a Textual Case-History' (*Anglia*) where an analysis of the editorial handling of these fragments is offered to 'demonstrate how slow and slight the progress of scholarship sometimes is'.

Douglas D. Short, in 'Aesthetics and Unpleasantness: Classical Rhetoric in the Medieval English Lyric *The Grave*' (*SN*, 1976), demonstrates that, within its overall rhetorical pattern provided by the metaphor of the grave as a house, this poem (item 3497 in Brown and Robbins' *Index*) also shows such rhetorical figures as hypozeuxis, metalepsis, and chiastic and envelope patterning, all of which contribute to its distinctiveness.

John E. Hallwas finds that the fourth line of the final stanza of 'þu sikest sore' (*Expl*), 'þe weder is went', can mean both 'the weather has changed' and the 'Lamb (or wether) has departed', and John C. Hirsh finds that, in the third and fourth lines of the quatrain 'Me þingkit' (*Expl*), 'det' means both 'death' and 'debt', and 'lete' means both 'to give up' and 'to rent' (or 'to let').

Sarah Stanbury Smith discusses '"Adam lay i-bowndyn" and the *Vinculum Amoris*' (*ELN*), the latter being 'the chain of love which binds man to his lady, or in sacred literature, to Christ'. In Smith's view the poet 'is contrasting the literal act of taking the apple, so small a thing in itself, with the fullest implications of that action in the history of Christian loving'.

Alan J. Fletcher edits 'A Death Lyric from the Summa Predicantium, MS. Oriel College 10' (*N&Q*), the opening lines of which, in the *Proprietates Mortis* tradition, have affinities with nos. 4047 and 4033 in Brown and Robbins' *Index*, while the remainder of the poem shows other common death topics such as death's poverty and the *Memorare Novissima*.

Edward Wilson describes 'A Middle English Manuscript at Coughton

Court, Warwickshire, and British Library MS. Harley 4012' (*N&Q*), showing that these contain a number of the same items, including the lyric 'Unkind Man, Take Heed of Me' (*Index* and *Supplement* 3827), variant readings of which are given from both manuscripts. Edward Wilson also edits 'An Unpublished Passion Poem in British Library MS. Harley 4012' (*N&Q*), with detailed notes and a short introduction in which Wilson compares the poem in question (*Index* 1779) with 'Wofully araide' (*Index* and *Supplement* 497) which immediately follows it in this manuscript.

Betty Hill discusses in detail 'The Twelfth-Century *Conduct of Life*, Formerly the *Poema Morale* or *A Moral Ode*' (*LeedsSE*), attaching particular importance among its seven extant copies to the one contained in Trinity College Cambridge MS. B. 14. 52, 'as the first English verse text which can be assigned, with some confidence, to the London area'. She discusses the author's use of the first person (singular and plural), his treatment of stock themes such as the Harrowing of Hell and the Last Judgement, and his references to contemporary abuses, certain of which seem to have remained 'contemporary' during the poem's textual transmission; and she studies the poem's similarities to the Anglo-Norman verse sermon attributed to Guischart de Beaulieu, while remaining unconvinced by the attribution. Finally, she argues the case for her new title for the poem.

Kurt Olsson, in 'Character and Truth in *The Owl and The Nightingale*' (*ChauR*) first establishes that by the twelfth century, *avis* can signify, tropologically, either the human mind or pride. Asking to what extent each debater in the poem betrays these meanings, Olsson concludes that 'each descends in pride from truth, truth which begins in self-knowledge'. He calls attention to the 'need for the proper engagement of the reader' in the debate itself, warning that 'if we laugh at the cleverness alone, we are reduced . . . to a *levitas* generically like that of the debaters'.

Borrowing some of his terminology from a recent essay by D. S. Brewer (in *Geoffrey Chaucer: Writers and their Background*, ed. by D. S. Brewer, 1975), David Lampe, in 'Country Matters and Courtly Eyes: Two Thirteenth Century Middle English Debate Poems'[36], treats the mixture of misogyny and Marian praise in 'The Thrush and the Nightingale' as an example of 'official culture', and contrasts that poem with the Harley Lyric pastourelle, 'De Clerico et Puella', which he sees as a product of 'courtly vernacular culture', perhaps even of a 'counter-culture', with its thirteenth-century equivalents of the Farmer's Daughter and the Travelling Salesman.

Klaus P. Jankofsky writes on 'Personalized Didacticism: The Interplay of Narrator and Subject Matter in the *South English Legendary*' (*Texas A and I University Studies*), concentrating in particular on the narrator's treatment of the martyrdoms of St George and St Margaret in order to illustrate 'the new tone and mood of compassion and emotional involvement which he creates'.

Karl Reichl edits 'Ein mittelenglisches Marienleben aus der H. S. Add. 4122 der University Library in Cambridge' (*Anglia*). This poem, somewhat

---

[36] In *The Thirteenth Century*, ed. by Kathleen Ashley, Acta, Vol. III. Binghamton, N.Y. The Center for Medieval and Early Renaissance Studies. State University of New York at Binghamton. pp. vi + 119. see pp. 79–93.

misleadingly entitled 'Tretys of Oure Ladye howe sche was wedded', and characterised by four-beat couplets with frequent formulaic repetition of rhymes and half-lines, largely corresponds in subject-matter to Lydgate's *Life of Our Lady*, with which it seems to have shared Jacobus de Voragine's *Legenda Aurea* as one of its sources. It cannot be more precisely dated than between the mid-thirteenth and mid-fifteenth century.

Charles S. Rutherford, with *'The Boke of Cupide* Reopened' (*NM*), finds that if this poem (also known as *The Cuckoo and the Nightingale*) is viewed as a partial imitation of Chaucer and as an example of the debate genre, it emerges as a light-hearted treatment of the paradoxical nature of the lover's state.

Brian S. Lee discusses 'A Poem "Clepid the Sevene Ages" '[37], contained in Cambridge University Library MS. Ff.2.38 and also (though not always completely) in seven other manuscripts. In spite of its title and apparent comparability to Jaques' speech in *As You Like it* it deals in fact with eleven ages of man. After rejecting a cautious earlier attribution of the poem to Lydgate, Lee goes on to stress its strong moral orientation, in which respect it differs from its classical analogues and from Jaques' speech, and to compare it with its derivative, the early sixteenth-century morality play *Mundus & Infans*, in order to show what the author of the latter found necessary to change in it when converting it into drama.

Klaus Bitterling edits 'An Abstract of John Mirk's "Instructions for Parish Priests"' (*N&Q*) from Trinity College Dublin MS. 211 and corresponding to lines 410–525 of the complete text (cf *YW* 55. 124–5).

Walter Sauer edits *The Metrical Life of Christ*[38] from its one manuscript, MS BM Add. 39996, with Introduction, Notes and Glossary. He finds it likely that the poem is of north-east Midland provenance, dating from the first decades of the fifteenth century, and infers from its structural linking-techniques and stylistic repetitiveness that, for all its composite subject-matter, it is the work of a single author. He suggests the *Legenda Aurea* 'or similar book of legends' as one of its sources, but in general finds that, except where its subject-matter is biblical, the text 'evades precise source analysis' because of 'the poet's marked degree of individuality'.

Cyril Lawrence Smetana, O.S.A., also produces an edition published for the first time with *The Life of S. Norbert by John Capgrave, O.E.S.A. (1393-1464)*[39]. In this case also the manuscript (MS HM 55 in the Huntington Library, San Marino, California) is unique, though unlike the MS BM Add. 39996 it is in all probability an autograph manuscript. The Introduction gives a list of Capgrave's exant works, showing, *inter alia,* that with this edition all his vernacular works have been published; and an account of Capgrave's text in relation to the A and B versions of its main source, the *Vita Sancti Norberti*, shows that he used the B version. Textual

[37] In *An English Miscellany Presented to W. S. Mackie,* ed. by Brian S. Lee, Cape Town: O.U.P. pp. 218. See pp. 72–92. £6.50.
[38] *The Metrical Life of Christ,* ed. from MS BM Add. 39996 by Walter Sauer. Middle English Texts 5, General Editor: M. Gorlach. Heidelberg: Carl Winter, Universitätsverlag. pp. 127. DM 29.
[39] *The Life of St Norbert by John Capgrave, O.E.S.A. (1393-1464),* ed. by Cyril Lawrence Smetana, O.S.A. Studies and Texts 40. Toronto: Pontifical Institute of Mediaeval Studies, Toronto, Ontario, Canada. pp. x + 179.

and explanatory notes are given at the foot of each page, and a glossary is also provided.

John Ayto finds that 'Marginalia in the Manuscript of the *Life of St Edith*' throw 'New Light on Early Printing' (*Library*), in that certain of the marginalia in the only known manuscript (B.M. Cotton MS. Faustina B iii) of the Middle English verse *Life of St Edith*, dating from *c.* 1425, suggest that the text was prepared by a compositor for the making of a printed copy.

Richard Firth Green argues the case for William de la Pole, Duke of Suffolk, who was in custody in the Tower in 1450, for 'The Authorship of the *Lament of a Prisoner against Fortune*' (*Mediævalia*, 1976; the poem is edited by E. Hammond, *Anglia*, 1909). On the possibility that a French poem by the prisoner-poet Charles d'Orléans was originally composed by him in English, see David Fallows's article, reported in Section 6, above.

Henry Hargreaves notes and edits for the first time 'De Spermate Hominis: a Middle English Poem on Human Embryology' (*Mediæval Studies*) from the National Library of Scotland, Advocates' MS. 23. 7. 11, and concludes that it 'may not be of the highest quality as poetry, but . . . offers a valid introduction to medieval embryological thought'.

Bradford Y. Fletcher describes with a stemma 'The Texual Tradition of the *Assembly of Gods*' (*PBSA*), a fifteenth-century rhyme royal allegory numbered 4005 by Brown and Robbins. His findings make it less likely than ever that the old attribution of this poem to Lydgate is correct.

E. B. Lyle collects into one volume eight *Ballad Studies* (1976)[40], one of them (by Herschel Gower) previously noted in *YW* (45. 357) and all in some form previously published apart from Alisoun Gardner-Medwin's. Holger Olof Nygard writes on the interrelations of 'Popular Ballad and Medieval Romance' (1967); E. B. Lyle mentions *Thomas of Erceldoune* and *Thomas Rymer* in discussing 'The Wee Wee Man' and *Als Y Yod on ay Mounday*' (1973); David Buchan, in 'History and Harlaw' (1968) suggests that 'The Battle of Harlaw' and other historical ballads contain more history than is often supposed; Alan Bruford traces back to a sixteenth-century Scots ballad composed in Orkney on the basis, perhaps, of a Norse tale or ballad, the various versions of 'The Grey Selkie' (1974); Hugh Shields, in 'The Grey Cock: Dawn Song or Revenant Ballad?' extends and revises an article in French from 1974 showing that the various versions of this ballad suggest that it was originally conceived as a dawn-song of the *alba* type; Alisoun Gardner-Medwin writes on 'Miss Reburn's Ballads: a Nineteenth-Century Repertoire from Ireland'; and J. M. Sinclair, in 'When is a Poem like a Sunset?' (1965) studies the progress of Keats's 'La Belle Dame Sans Merci' as learned by heart and transmitted orally by his students.

David Buchan's lecture on 'Oral Tradition and Literary Tradition: The Scottish ballads'[41] takes the corpus of ballads recorded from Anna

[40] *Ballad Studies*, ed. by E. B. Lyle. The Folklore Society Mistletoe Series. Cambridge: D. S. Brewer Ltd. and Totowa, N.J.: Rowman & Littlefield, for the Folklore Society. pp. xii + 212. £4.50.

[41] In *Oral Tradition, Literary Tradition: A Symposium. Proceedings of the First International Symposium Organized by the Centre for the Study of Vernacular Literature in the Middle Ages. Held at Odense University on 22-23 November, 1976.* Ed. by Hans Bekker-Nielsen, Peter Foote, Andreas Haarder, Hans Freda Nielsen. Odense: Odense U. P. pp. 121.

Gordon (Mrs Brown of Falkland) as the basis for an admirably lucid account of certain characteristics of 'oral tradition' – a term which Buchan analyses carefully before going on to show 'oral formulas, oral structuring, and evidence of oral re-creation' in the style and structure of these ballads.

A volume of essays republished from *Past and Present* 1958-73[42] includes five on Robin Hood, only one of which, by T. H. Aston (from 1961) is not mentioned in the Select Bibliography of Dobson and Taylor's *Rymes of Robyn Hood*, reported last year (*YW* 57.79). Mention may finally be made of two books likely to throw light on the nature of the oral tradition underlying certain types of poem treated in this section: the second volume of *Hebridean Folksongs*, edited by J. L. Campbell and Francis Collinson[43], and the second edition of Margaret Fay Shaw's *Folksongs and Folklore of South Uist*[44].

9. Malory and Caxton

In 'The Red Knight in Tennyson's "The Last Tournament" and Malory' (*N&Q*), J. M. Gray shows that Tennyson's Red Knight 'is carefully modelled on selected details in Malory', that is, in the latter's fourth and fifth Tales.

Mary Hynes-Berry, in 'Malory's Translation of Meaning: *The Tale of the Sankgreal*' (*SP*), argues that, in adapting the *Queste del Saint Graal* for his sixth Tale, Malory 'subtracted phrases and passages that elaborated the allegorical meaning and instead brought into relief the dramatic potential of the plot'. Thus the tension in Malory 'is between good and bad' – with Lancelot as 'the best of any synfull man' – 'rather than between heavenly and earthly chivalry'. Susanna Greer Fein, in 'Thomas Malory and the Pictorial Interlace of *La Queste del Saint Graal*' (*UTQ*), defines such interlace as ' a distinct maze-like image of paths within a forest' 'the wandering through life of all mankind in search of divine salvation'. She suggests that Malory, in his sixth Tale, changed this feature of his source in two ways: first he reduced its prominence 'by omitting details of the landscape and the knight's movements over it and by adding details unrelated to the symbolic design'; and second, he thereby stressed 'the value of human bonds', and 'his feeling that man's relation to his fellow man holds an equal, if separate, importance with his relation to God'.

Phillip McCaffrey, in 'The Adder at Malory's Battle of Salisbury: Sources, Symbols, and Themes' (*TSL*) draws on literary sources from Virgil to Henryson to show that the image of a snake emerging from a bush has associations of lust and treason, and compares the Salisbury adder in Tale VIII with the serpents in Arthur's dream following his incestuous procreation of Mordred in Tale I to show that Malory uses

[42] *Peasants, Knights and Heretics. Studies in Medieval English Social History*, ed. by R. H. Hilton, Cambridge, London, New York, Melbourne: C.U.P. (1976). pp. 330. £5.

[43] *Hebridean Folksongs* II. *Waulking Songs from Barra, South Uist, Eriskay and Benbecula*, ed. and trans. by. J. L. Campbell. Tunes transcribed from recordings and annotated by Francis Collinson. Oxford: at the Clarendon Press. pp. x + 367. Frontispiece; musical transcriptions pp. 255-358. £15.

[44] *Folksongs and Folklore of South Uist*, by Margaret Fay Shaw. 2nd ed. Oxford: O.U.P. pp xiv + 342. Musical transcriptions, one map, and 32 illustrations, pp. 71-342. £12.50.

'serpent emblems' to forecast the end of Arthur's kingdom at its very beginning.

N. F. Blake, in 'William Caxton' (*Lore and Language*) sees Caxton as more of a publisher than a printer, and suggests that Chaucer, in instituting a new French style in English poetry, had done for the latter what Caxton was trying to do for English prose in publishing translations of French and Burgundian material. The inclusion of a prologue in Caxton's reprint of the *Canterbury Tales* suggests to Blake that Caxton 'felt the text had to be promoted on its second appearance'. The stylistic uniformity of Caxton's prologues and epilogues should not be allowed to conceal their diversity, which reveals itself mainly in the wide range of his patrons and in the way each book is given a particular theme for its promotion.

The Catalogue[45] of a Caxton exhibition held at the British Library in 1976–77 contains a succinct account of Caxton's printing-types and describes the various exhibits within the framework of Caxton's life, career, and importance. Among them are Raoul le Fèvre's *Recuyell of the Histories of Troy*, the first book printed in English, which the catalogue dates 'towards the end of 1474 or in the first months of 1475'; Caxton's first and second editions of the *Canterbury Tales*, together with the Ellesmere and Harley (7333) manuscripts of that work; the first edition of Caxton's translation of *Reynard the Fox;* the Egerton manuscript (1991) and Caxton's edition of Gower's *Confessio Amantis;* and the Winchester and Caxton Malorys. Also shown in the same exhibition were three works which have appeared this year in facsimile: Caxton's editions of Cicero's *Old Age* and *Friendship* (in one volume, 1481)[46] and of Lull's *Book of the Order of Chivalry* (1484)[47]; and de Worde's edition (1495) of Caxton's translation of the *Vitas patrum* wrongly ascribed to St Jerome[48].

On loan to the British Library for this exhibition were the Caxton Malory and Caxton's first edition of the *Sarum Horae*, both from the Pierpont Morgan Library in New York. These are, of course, included in Frederick R. Goff's list of 'Caxtons in America', (*Gutenberg-Jahrbuch*), the total number of which, including 'duplicates' and fragments, he finds to be 226.

B. Lindström, with 'Some Remarks on Two English Translations of Jacques Legrand's *Livre de bonnes meurs'* (*ES*) discusses Caxton's trans-

---

[45] *William Caxton. An Exhibition to Commemorate the Quincentenary of the Introduction of Printing into England.* British Library Reference Division. 24 September 1977. British Museum Publications Limited for the British Library, 1976. pp. 94. 69 illustrations. £2.

[46] *Of Old Age. Of Friendship*, by Marcus Tulius (*sic*) Cicero. W. Caxton 1481. The English Experience, no. 861. Amsterdam: Theatrum Orbis Terrarum, Ltd., and Norwood, N.J.: Walter J. Johnson, Inc. 2 leaves including modern title-page + 120 folio leaves, each reproduced, recto and verso, in facsimile. $30.

[47] *The Book of the Ordre of Chyvalry or Knyghthode*, Westmynstre, William Caxton (1484). The English Experience, no. 778. Amsterdam: Theatrum Orbis Terrarum, Ltd., and Norwood, N.J.: Walter J. Johnson, Inc. 2 leaves including modern title-page + 52 quarto leaves, each reproduced, recto and verso, in facsimile. $10.

[48] *Vitas Patrum*, by Saint Jerome (*sic*). Westmynstre, de Worde, 1495. The English Experience, no. 874. Amsterdam: Theatrum Orbis Terrarum, Ltd., and Norwood, N.J.: Walter J. Johnson, Inc. 2 leaves including modern title-page + 356 folio leaves, each reproduced, recto and verso, in facsimile. $86.

lation of 1487 in relation to the anonymous one contained in B.M. MS. Harley 149, leaving aside John Shirley's translation in B.M. MS. Add. 5467. Caxton's text is on the whole better, since he seems to have had a better copy of the French text before him though sometimes the anonymous translator is himself guilty of erroneous readings. There are occasional places where he is right and Caxton wrong, however, and he shows less willingness than Caxton to retain French words and constructions in his translation.

Eric Vickers (*Library*) replies briefly to Howard M. Nixon's article on 'Caxton, his Contemporaries and Successors' (*YW* 57. 83), answering in the negative the question of 'whether Wörth, the reputed birthplace of Wynkyn de Worde, actually was in Lorraine in the fifteenth century'.

A collection of essays by A. N. L. Munby[48a] includes two on subjects related to Caxton, one of which, from the *Book Collector* of 1963, has not previously been reviewed in *YW* (the other was reviewed in *YW* 50. 31). Here Munby (together with M. Pollard) develops the question 'Did Mr Cavendish burn his Caxtons?' which in 1813 was raised in court as a result of the refusal of the London Hope Assurance Company to honour a financial claim by the Hon Frederick Cavendish on property including two Caxtons (Gower's *Confessio Amantis* and Chaucer's *Book of Fame*) lost by him as a result of a fire at his house in Clontarf near Dublin.

10 Other Prose

In providing substantial notes on 'Some Difficult Words in the *Ancrene Riwle*' (*MS* 1976) (*bihalden, cnost & dolc, woh, schrift, fleschliche sawlen, worltliche, loke cape*), Martha Baldwin makes further corrections to M. B. Salu's translation (1955). She convincingly argues that 'an understanding of the traditional ascetic, devotional and penitential literature familiar to its author can throw light on the meaning of his terminology'. With a strongly feminist slant, Bernice W. Kliman looks at the development of attitudes to 'Women in Early English Literature, "Beowulf" to the "Ancrene Wisse"' (*NMS*) and makes a clear distinction between the Anglo-Saxon women who have to function as powerless weavers of peace in a man's world in the heroic poems, and as more positive creatures in the religious-heroic poems (e.g., Judith), and the women 'of inferior intellect and dangerous sexuality' who comprise the audience of *AR*. The distinction which Kliman draws is perhaps too simplistic, and the examples chosen too disparate, but she makes a very striking case for the influence of rabbinical and Pauline ideas on the significant change of attitude to women between the O.E. and E.M.E. periods. Providing further evidence of the *Ancrene Riwle* author's independent use of his sources (here with reference to avian symbolism), James F. Maybury writes 'On the Structure and Significance of Part III of the *Ancrene Riwle*, with some Comment on Sources' (*ABR*) and shows how the author uses biblical exegesis for his comparison of the recluse to the pelican (long associated with the recluse), and the sparrow (prone to falling sickness — cf. Neckam:

[48a] *Essays and Papers: A.N.L. Munby*, ed. with an introduction by Nicolas Barker. The Scolar Press. £10.

'morbo . . . epilemptico frequenter haec avis vexatur'). George B. Jack presents a strong case for taking '"Luste" in "Ancrene Wisse"' (NM) as a present tense form of 'indeterminate' mood, rather than as a subjunctive. He plausibly suggests that the preterite 'luste' was probably reinterpreted as a present tense (cf. 'wulle' = 'desires', indicative and subjunctive). Writing 'On Claims for Syntactical Modernity in Early English Prose' (MP) with specific reference to deficiencies in an earlier study by Fred West (MP 1973), T. P. Dolan provides evidence from Ancrene Wisse and Vices and Virtues to show weaknesses in West's argument for verb-object dominance in the period 1200–1300. AW is conservative in many respects, and VV even more so, and the rate of progress towards VO dominance should be gauged by noting the currency of non-modern word-order patterns in O.E. and E.M.E.: the methodology should concentrate on clauses where we expect change. The words 'As Seint Austin Seith' not only indicate a very common source for the author's thought in Ancrene Wisse but also, according to Cecily Clarke (MÆ), may give a clue to some stylistic features. The verbal and phrasal patterning so characteristic of AW may well have its roots in the writings of the early Fathers of the Church and 'especially' Augustine.

In an interesting paper, Richard H. Osberg tries to make perhaps too close an association between 'The Alliterative Lyric and Thirteenth-Century Devotional Prose' (JEGP): 'structural alliteration in the Middle English lyric does not derive either from the decadent long line and arcane vocabulary of the alliterative revival poems or from the octosyllabic patter and hackneyed alliterative tags of minstrel verse, but evolved rather from the rhythmical alliteration of certain veins of devotional prose'. Rosemary Woolf had briefly considered such possibilities in her study of the lyric (YW 49.92–3).

In 'The Experience of God: A New Classification of Certain Late Medieval Affective Texts' (ChauR 1976), John C. Hirsh tries to make a case, in perhaps too general a way, for classifying such writings under three headings: 1. 'Texts of Encounter' (e.g., Rolle's Fire of Love); 2. 'Texts of Adoration' (e.g., the Wooing Group); 3. 'Texts of Devotion' (e.g., Anselm's Meditations, Rolle's Form of Living, etc.). The three categories appear to be unconnected.

Peggy Ann Knapp presents a jaunty study of The Style of John Wyclif's English Sermons[49] using the five groups of sermons (MS Bodley 788) edited by Thomas Arnold, set against the background of other fourteenth-century prose writings (mystics, translators, preachers). Analysis of Wyclif's biblical quotations demonstrates the differences between his version and the two 'Wycliffite' versions (e.g., his wider use of the resources of idiomatic English). The chapter on 'The Words. Diction, Allusion and Irony' commends Wyclif's lucidity, notes the absence of personal reference and the modernity of his vocabulary, and instances his use of insult as a rhetorical device (e.g., his identification of the Pope with Antichrist). In dealing with 'The Structures: The Sermon and the Sentence' Knapp corrects some of Krapp's assertions about Wyclif (e.g.,

[49] The Style of John Wyclif's English Sermons, by Peggy Ann Knapp. De Proprietatibus Litterarum Series Practica, 16. The Hague and Paris: Mouton. pp. v + 116. DM 38.

that 'the many-membered, sprawling sentence . . . is not characteristic of Wyclif') and distinguishes other features of his style (e.g., his ubiquitous use of co-ordinating conjuctions). So far, her analysis is straightforward, but then Knapp begins to use 'a technique devised by Maynard Merlyn Eyestone for describing subordinate clause "nesting" in American English'. These obfuscating, egg-shaped diagrams also appear in an Appendix, to little purpose. From her chapter on 'The Mysti [sic] Wits: Allegory and Metaphor' we learn that 'Wyclif knew and advocated in these simple English homilies Aquinas's four levels of Biblical interpretation', and that he used metaphors drawn from the wide range of his intellectual experience (e.g., optics, geometry, botany, etc.). Images taken from Scripture, which 'might contain all four kinds of spiritual truth', are necessarily less concise than Wyclif's own inventions, which are characterised by their brevity. Towards the end of the book Knapp places Wyclif in the homiletic tradition, demonstrating both those features of his thought which take him 'far toward modern Protestantism', and those which confirm him as a conservative theologian dependent on such traditional authorities as Augustine, Ambrose, and Gregory. This book will be found patchy in its usefulness, but in highlighting many of Wyclif's distinctive features it will serve to guide the growing number of students who are turning to him for the first time.

George Wood Tuma's presentation of *The Fourteenth Century English Mystics: A Comparative Analysis*[50] (Rolle, Hilton, the *Cloud* author, Julian, Kempe) requires us to accept his thesis that it is possible, indeed necessary, to develop a critical methodology 'which would permit a consistent and relatively trustworthy basis for analysing comparatively the thought of the medieval English mystics as well as for determining the extent of their indebtedness to earlier mystics'. His methodological procedure for dealing with them is based on the commonly accepted three phases of the contemplative life – Purgation, Illumination, and Mystical Union, and is developed from Trier's theoretical model (as applied by Hatzfield to Old French mystical writings (1934)). He constructs primary and secondary 'conceptual fields' for the three phases and makes quite a good job of procrusteanising his authors, but they put up strong resistance – for instance, the major part of the *Cloud* author's thought concerns the Purgative phase, with no correspondingly thorough or systematic treatment of the Illuminative or Unitive phases. Tuma admits that his analysis 'may even be reductionist in nature', and it is hard to escape the conclusion that this is precisely what it is (see, e.g. Appendix A: 'Outline of the Primary Conceptual Fields for Purgation, Illumination and Union for the English Mystics', where the speculative nature of the preliminary analysis solidifies into rigid, mathematical patterning). The exercise, though a very interesting and courageous one, proves that the mystical writers are too disparate in range to have such a methodology applied to them. Tuma says that he has undertaken the task because 'analysis of

[50] *The Fourteenth Century English Mystics: A Comparative Analysis,* by George Wood Tuma. 2 vols. Salzburg Studies in English Literature under the Direction of Professor Erwin A. Sturzl. Elizabethan and Renaissance Studies, Ed. James Hogg. Salzburg: Institut für Englische Sprache und Literatur, Universität Salzburg. pp. iv + 400.

the thought of the mystics has been left to the theologians', who presumably are not felt to have the necessary literary skills. The answer to such a problem is obviously to rely on theologians who can double as literary critics – such as Edmund College and James Walsh (see below).

Michael G. Sargent (*MÆ*) gives a full description of 'A New Manuscript of *The Chastising of God's Children* with an Ascription to Walter Hilton'. He places MS 3084 (*c.* 1450, vellum SE Midland) of the Walker-Heneage (Button) collection in the B group as established by Bazire and Colledge (*YW*. 38.86–7). Jeanne Elizabeth Krochalis publishes '*Contemplations of the Dread and Love of God:* Two Newly Identified Pennsylvania Manuscripts' (*LCP*) and attempts to explain why six of the eleven complete MSS (including the two here) are divergent in their concluding chapters. Section 1 of this stimulating article, which contributes to our knowledge of fourteenth-century prose and its audience, considers 'the text and its tradition in general'; Section 2 describes and contains an edition of the concluding part of the University of Pennsylvania MS English 8 (early fifteenth century); and Section 3 does the same for the University of Pennsylvania MS English 2 (first half of the fifteenth century). J. A. Burrow perceptively examines 'Fantasy and Language in *The Cloud of Unknowing*' (*EIC*) with particular reference to Chapter 65. Though language is a physical activity, its use for the conveyance of spiritually apprehended concepts (e.g., non-physical symbols such as 'cloud' and 'darkness') does not compromise the spirituality of those concepts, and thus the integrity of the relationship between 'spirit' and 'letter' can be demonstrated. Toshiyuki Takamiya publishes 'Walter Hilton's *Of Angel's Song* edited from the British Museum MS Additional 27592' (*SELit*), with a very informative introduction which lists the Manuscripts and Printed Editions, noting the relationship of the manuscripts to Pepwell's Edition of 1521, and supports Horstman's ascription of the text to Hilton against Madden and G. E. Hodgson (who ascribe it to Rolle). The text (195 lines) reproduces the MS without conjectural emendation, except for correcting obvious scribal errors or omissions (when readings are suggested from Lincoln Cathedral Chapter Library MS 91), with editorial punctuation, capitalisation, paragraphing, and regularised word-division, and is followed by a list of textual variants, a table indicating a number of spelling variants in the extant version of *Of Angels' Song*, some useful notes explaining problematical words (e.g., *substance,* 'essential nature, essence'), and an Appendix giving all seven extant MS readings of the introductory portion of the printed text. In a densely argued article, J. P. H. Clark considers 'The "Lightsome Darkness" – aspects of Walter Hilton's Theological Background' (*DownR*) to support P. Hodgson's view (*YW*. 25. 67–9) that the *Scale* and the *Cloud* were not by the same author. There are similarities, but close analysis of significant expressions such as 'lighty darknes' shows that their theologies are substantially 'diverse', not least because the *Cloud's* theology owes its distinctiveness to Pseudo-Dionysus: Hilton's darkness is the 'darkness of sin', whereas the *Cloud's* darkness 'impinges on us through the ontological transcendence of God, through the excess of his light'. In a decidedly tendentious paper, Wolfgang Riehle (*NM*) returns to 'The Problem of Walter Hilton's Possible Authorship of "The Cloud of Unknowing" and its Related Tracts', and takes issue with Phyllis Hodgson's point (see above) about the differences between Hilton's vocabulary and style and those of the *Cloud* author. On the contrary, he finds 'amazing' and 'astonishing' similarities between them (e.g., the use of the concept of nakedness to denote the desired state at the initial stage of contemplation, paired words, groups of words, etc.).

B. A. Windeatt lucidly discusses 'Julian of Norwich and Her Audience' (*RES*) in the light of the differences between the earlier, shorter 'A' version of her text (MS Add. 37790) and the significantly longer version in Sloane MS 2499 which recasts and universalises the original account. Julian's changes affect the material (e.g., omitting the 'A' version's specific addresses to contemplatives), style, and diction. Edmund Colledge, O.S.A., and James Walsh, S. J., publish a tantalising account of their work in 'Editing Julian of Norwich's *Revelations:* A Progress Report' (*MS* 1976), which announces that, after establishing texts of both the longer and the shorter versions, their search for possible sources for her ideas and language proved her to have a 'minute and exact knowledge of Scripture', and that study of her quotations showed that she used no known copy of the English Bible and may have known Latin and used the Vulgate. Their article is excellent in every way, on stylistic, theological, biographical, and bibliographical issues.

Diane Bornstein edits *The Middle English Translation of Christine de Pisan's Livre du Corps de Policie*[51] from MS C.U.L. Kk 1.5, with an excellent introduction which sets the *Livre* (which she dates 1404–7) in the context of courtesy books, chivalric manuals, mirrors for the prince, and treatises on the three estates. Its author was 'France's first professional woman writer', who composed it as a guide for the moral and political education of princes of the royal blood, and in particular the French Dauphin, Louis of Gouienne. The work is divided into three parts of unequal length, becoming progressively shorter: I, addressed to the prince, the head of the body; II, addressed to knights and noblemen, the arms and hands; III, addressed to 'the universal people' (clergy, students, merchants, craftsmen, and labourers), the stomach, legs, and feet. The *Livre* is an accomplished compilation from other (mainly French) sources. Its English translation survives in one paper MS, mostly agreeing with MS 294 Musée Condé, Chantilly. Bornstein's Introduction is exceptionally informative (we learn, for instance, that Bennett's statement (in *Chaucer and the Fifteenth Century)* that the edition printed by John Skot (1521) was a 'separate version' was wrong). The section dealing with 'the Style of the Translation' (to be read in conjunction with her article – see below) presents cogent external and internal evidence (stylistic and linguistic parallels) to support her claim that the translation was made by Anthony Woodville (doublets, frequent use of 'and' as headword in main clauses, etc.). The Bibliography includes Primary and Secondary Sources. Bornstein also (*MS*) makes a major contribution to prose-style studies in her consideration of 'French Influence on Fifteenth-Century English Prose as Exemplified by the Translation of Christine de Pisan's *Livre du corps*

[51] *The Middle English Translation of Christine de Pisan's Livre du Corps de Policie,* ed. from MS C.U.L. Kk. 1.5. by Diane Bornstein. Middle English Texts 7. General Ed. M. Gorlach. Heidelberg: Carl Winter. Universitätsverlag. pp. 224. DM 64.

de policie', her editing of which has enabled her to identify use of the *style clergial* in the text. Bornstein's examples show that her translator was anything but slavish in following his source, and that he borrowed syntactical and stylistic devices which were compatible with English idiom, resulting in a blend 'that was essentially new'.

Phyllis Moe edits *The ME Prose Translation of Roger d'Argenteuil's Bible en François*[52], a thirteenth-century didactic work in prose, mainly narrative based on material in the Old and New Testaments and on legendary and apocryphal tales, from Cleveland Public Library MS Wq 091.92 – C468. The MS contains three items in English (an abridged text of the *Brut;* thirty-four lines of 'Cur mundus militat', and a reasonably accurate translation of Chapters 5–23 of the *Bible* (ff. 77r–99v). The language represents the London dialect of the second half of the fifteenth century with an admixture of several Northern words which may represent the scribe's own dialect. This edition carries the translation of Chapters 5–23 of the *Bible* with judiciously chosen notes on the text indicating the fairly frequent errors of translation and misreadings (e.g., *descendroit,* rendered as 'defende hem', probably through misreading a long 's' as an 'f'), together with a Select Glossary and Select Bibliography.

With some gratuitous remarks about himself, in an otherwise very useful and informative Introduction, James Hogg's edition of *Richard of Methley: to Hew Heremyte. A Pystyl of Solytary Lyfe Nowadayes*[53] corrects the 'obvious blunders' of W. E. Campbell's 1956 transcription, describes what little is known of the Life of Methley (real name Furth, born *c.* 1451/2 died *c.* 1527/8, became Carthusian at Mount Grace), notes his Latin translation of *The Cloud of Unknowing,* and uses excerpts from his *Scola Amoris Languidi* (1484), *Dormitorium Dilecti Dilecti* (1485), which includes a remarkable vision of the crucified Christ, and the *Refectorium Salutis* (1487), to show his spiritual development and interests. The text itself has twelve short chapters and mainly concerns the answer to Hew Heremyte's question 'how shalt thou kepe wel obedyence chastyte & poverty'.

The Liber Gersumarum of Ramsey Abbey: A Calendar and Index of B. L. Harley MS 445[54], edited and translated from the Latin by Edwin Brezette DeWindt, is a welcome alternative to the critical edition of the full Latin text originally proposed by J. A. Raftis which had to be abandoned by him and which was subsequently found by DeWindt to be unnecessary in any case. The Calendar provides a unique record of the peasantry in the Ramsey estate regions from 1398 to 1458 including details of land transfer, marriage, and exodus. While not itself a Court Book, the *Liber Gersumarum* may be used in combination with surviv-

[52] *The ME Prose Translation of Roger D'Argenteuil's Bible en François,* ed. from Cleveland Public Library, MS Wq 091.92 – C468, by Phillis Moe. Middle English texts 16. General Ed. M. Görlach. Heidelberg: Carl Winter. Universitätsverlag. pp. 111. DM 32.

[53] *Richard Methley: To Hew Heremyte A Pystyl of Solytary Lyfe Nowadayes,* ed. by James Hogg, comprising pp. 91–119 of *Analecta Cartusiana* vol. 31, ed. by James Hogg. Salzburg: Institute für Englische Sprache und Literatur, Universität Salzburg.

[54] *The Liber Gersumarum of Ramsey Abbey.* A Calendar and Index of B.L. Harley MS 445, by Edwin Brezette DeWindt. Subsidia Mediaevalia 7. Toronto, Canada: Pontifical Institute of Mediæval Studies, 1976. 2 plates. pp. vi + 455. $21.

ing court rolls to form a detailed picture of the peasant world of the fifteenth-century English countryside for the social historian. The Bibliography and Index Rerum appended to the Calendar are additional proofs of the care and diligence exercised by DeWindt throughout this edition in his compilation of much valuable information regarding the peasant life of the period so far obscured from the historian. The MS is of about the same date as its contents and is written in 'at least 17 clearly distinct fifteenth-century hands'. The text is intact, except for two missing years from the rule of the first abbot mentioned, Thomas Butterwyk, and goes on to include entries for his successors John Tychemersh, John Croyland, and John Stowe. Appendix I lists the Fifteenth-Century Abbots of Ramsey, and Appendix II gives the Acreage of Customary Units of Land of Ramsey Manorial Villages. There is a Bibliography, Index Locorum, Index Personarum, and Index Rerum (e.g., Conveyances, Leases, Marriage, Migration, Tenure, etc.).

Helen Spencer, in an attractively presented article, examines the texts in B. L. MS Harley 2276 and B. L. MS Royal 18 A xvii which constitute copies of 'A Fifteenth-Century Translation of a Latin Twelfth-Century Sermon Collection' (*RES*), a cycle comprising about sixty sermons. She notes that the incipits of the series in the two vernacular MSS correspond to those of the *de Tempore Sanctorum* in the *Filius matris* collection, which are ascribed to *William de montibus*.

After their recently completed edition, Vincent DiMarco and Leslie Perelman present 'Noteworthy Lexical Evidence in the Middle English *Letter of Alexander to Aristotle'* (*Neophilologus*) to demonstrate from the readings of MS Worcester Cathedral F. 172 that it was based on a version of the Epistola represented in a recognised sub-group of three twelfth-century MSS. They cite significant readings as evidence of the translator's literalness and misunderstanding (e.g., Latin *adhortatus est*, M.E. *'adort'*, O.E.D. *'adhort'* 1539).

11. Drama

Editions and General Studies

Two more texts in the admirable series of Mediaeval Drama Facsimiles published by the University of Leeds have appeared: No. III, *The Digby Plays*, introduced by Donald C. Baker and J. L. Murphy (1976)[55], and No. IV, *The N-Town Plays*, introduced by Peter Meredith and Stanley J. Kahrl[56]. The first prints facsimiles of the plays in Bodley MSS. Digby 133 and e Museo 160; though Furnivall's theory that the two manuscripts originally belonged together is no longer tenable, the introducers of the texts felt that it was desirable to keep the two groups of plays

---

[55] *The Digby Plays: Facsimiles of the plays in Bodley MSS. Digby 133 and e Museo 160*, intr. by Donald C. Baker and J. L. Murphy. Leeds Texts and Monographs: Medieval Drama Facsimiles III. Leeds: U. of Leeds, School of English (1976). pp. xix + facsimile. By subscription.

[56] *The N-Town Plays: A Facsimile of B.L. MS. Cotton Vespasion D VIII*, intr. by Peter Meredith and Stanley J. Kahrl. Leeds Texts and Monographs: Mediaeval Drama Facsimiles IV. Leeds: U. of Leeds, School of English. pp. xxix + facsimile. By subscription.

together for bibliographical convenience. They give a fairly brief account of the contents and scribal practices of both manuscripts, emphasising the miscellaneous nature of Bodley 133, where different items seem to have come from completely different sources. Almost no continuity of hands can be found here, except that the scribe of *The Killing of the Children* was also the scribe of the *Wisdom* fragment. The second provides a very full commentary on its highly complex manuscript, B.L. MS. Cotton Vespasian D VIII. Meredith and Kahrl have concentrated on presenting the complicated evidence for the processes involved in the compilation of the manuscript as clearly as possible. The main conclusions they feel entitled to draw are: that the *Contemplacio* group (Plays 8 – 11, 13) was originally a separate Mary play; that the first Passion sequence was originally a separate manuscript; and that the work of the B-reviser was directed primarily at once again re-grouping the plays, this time clearly for theatrical production. They have re-numbered and re-titled the plays in order to correct the obscurities of numbering and of division of plays one from another in the manuscript itself.

In 'Rite et jeu dans le théâtre réligieux anglais du Moyen Age' (*RHT*), Claude Gauvin argues that mediaeval audiences understood drama solely as 'game', as a figuring-forth of their religious beliefs, rather than as any kind of substitute for religious ritual. Carolyn L. Wightman's 'The Genesis and Function of the English Mystery Plays' (*SMC*) was not seen.

Siegfried Wenzel's note on 'An Early Reference to a Corpus Christi Play' (*MP*) claims that Robert Holcot's mention of 'ludus . . . in die corporis Christi' in his *Book of Wisdom* (c. 1335) must refer to a play rather than to a procession.

York

'From "Tristitia" to "Gaudium"': Iconography and the York-Towneley *Harrowing of Hell'* (*ABR*), by Clifford Davidson, points out that the York play and its Towneley derivative use entirely traditional symbolism (for instance the imagery of light associated with Christ as Saviour) to provide a bridge between the Crucifixion and the process of redemption. Albert F. Chambers examines the relationship between 'The vicars choral of York Minster and the Tilemakers' Corpus Christi pageant' (*REEDN*). Contemporary records show that the vicars choral contributed, as major manufacturers of tiles themselves, first to the tilemakers' own pageant and later to that produced and financed by the tilemakers and their associates. Alexandra Johnston's 'The Guild of Corpus Christi and the Procession of Corpus Christi in York' (*MS*, 1976) is not directly concerned with the play of Corpus Christi (the Guild never had anything to do with the play), but gives interesting information about the part played by the Guild in the general Corpus Christi celebrations.

Towneley

In 'Language as theme in the Wakefield Plays' (*Speculum*), Martin Stevens concentrates on the work of the Wakefield Master (he assumes that this consists of all portions of the cycle written in the Wakefield Stanza). He claims that the Master makes the use and abuse of language a major theme in the cycle as a whole, showing an overriding concern with the falsity of man's word as contrasted with the Word of God. The rather obvious point of Dorrel T. Hanks Jr's chatty article on 'The *Mactacio Abel* and the Wakefield Cycle: Study in Context' (*SoQ*) is that an individual play such as the *Mactacio* must be seen in relation to the cycle as a whole. Cain's 'type', the man who rejects salvation, recurs throughout the cycle and acts as a unifying element in it. Again focusing on the *Mactacio*, but in much more ponderous tones, Bennett A. Brockman's 'Comic and Tragic Counterpoint in the Medieval Drama: the Wakefield *Mactacio Abel*' (*MS*) attempts to propose a 'formal rationale for such readings of the humorous cycle plays' as tend to show that 'the comic establishes the plays' deepest human and theological meaning'. Robert B. Bennett's study of 'Homiletic design in the Towneley *Abraham*' (*MLS*) makes the interesting point that, of all the Middle English dramatic treatments of the story, only the Wakefield playwright's version 'attempts in any intellectually rigorous way to bring God's actions comprehensively into line with the idea of a loving and just God'.

Jeanne S. Martin's 'History and Paradigm in the Towneley Cycle' (*M&H*) summons Eusebius to the support of her argument that the form and content of the cycle plays are generated by a 'fundamentally archetypal' view of Christian history, according to which all history conforms to one basic recurring pattern, that of the struggle between God and the devil.

N-Town

Peter Meredith continues his work on the N-Town manuscript with 'A Reconsideration of some Textual Problems of the N-Town Manuscript (B.L. MS. Cotton Vespasian D VIII)' (*Leeds SE*). He clarifies some textual obscurities in the plays of the *Visitation* and the *Last Supper,* and examines the evidence provided by the play of *The Assumption of the Virgin* of the extent to which the main scribe of the manuscript as a whole was involved in revising the material he copied. In 'The Composition and Development of an Eclectic Manuscript: Cotton Vespasian D VIII' (*Leeds SE*) Stephen Spector puts forward the theory that some of the different strata of this heterogeneous cycle can be sorted out according to their characteristic prosodic forms. On the assumptions that the iconography of manuscript illuminations was closely related to that of religious stage productions, Theresa Coletti argues that the illuminations from contemporary Books of Hours offer persuasive evidence for an imaginative reconstruction of 'Devotional Iconography in the N-Town Marian Plays' (*Comp D*).

Daniel P. Poteet writes on 'Condition, contrast and division in the *Ludus Coventriae* "Woman Taken in Adultery"' (*Mediævalia,* 1975), by which he means that the dramatic form of the play must be seen, not as a developmental and causal sequence, but as a static moral structure of contrasts encompassing 'both the limitation of human perspective and the expansive divine vision encasing that narrowness'.

Chester

Kevin J. Harty does his best to show that the Chester cycle is more of an effective dramatic unit than is usually admitted: 'The Unity and Structure of the Chester Mystery Cycle' (*Mediævalia,* 1976). He lays a good deal of stress on the cycle's supposed connections with Benedictine monasticism, and finds that its unity derives from a monastically-inspired concern for prophecy, Christian perfection, and the Last Things. In 'The Chester Whitsun Plays: Dating of post-Reformation performances from the Smiths' Accounts' (*Leeds SE*) John Marshall sifts the available evidence for correcting the dating of the earliest Smiths' account for the plays as it appears in Randle Holmes' seventeenth-century transcription.

Moralities and Non-Cycle Plays

Ian Lancashire surveys the information to be found in already published 'Records of drama and minstrelsy in Nottinghamshire to 1642' (*REEDN*), and lists possible manuscript sources of fresh information. Again in *REEDN*, Robert E. Finnegan lists the references to plays to be found in the local records of 'Gloucestershire and Bristol', and John Anderson and A. C. Cawley print a facsimile of Bourne's text (published in 1736) of the now lost manuscript of 'The Newcastle Play of *Noah's Ark*'.

In '*Everyman* and the Implications of Bernardine Humanism in the Character "Knowledge"' (*M&H*), Thomas J. Jambeck argues that Bernard's concept of knowledge not only serves to clarify the apparently disparate functions of Knowledge in the play, but also helps to elucidate *Everyman's* overall doctrinal significance. Finally, Thomas J. Jambeck and Reuben R. Lee's note on '"Pope Pokett" and the Date of *Mankind*' (*MS*) suggests that the allusion in *Mankind* 140–46 must be to John Poket, prior of Barnwell Abbey. As Poket died in 1464, the play is unlikely to have been written later than that year.

V

Middle English: Chaucer

JOYCE BAZIRE and DAVID MILLS

1. General

A bibliography for the current year will be found in 'Chaucer Research, 1977. Report No.38' by Thomas A. Kirby (*ChauR*).

Several features of John H. Fisher's *The Complete Poetry and Prose of Geoffrey Chaucer*[1] will recommend it to students, particularly with its pleasing and clear layout. The *Romaunt of the Rose* has been included (because of tradition and the light the work throws on Chaucer's debt) and also the *Equatorie of the Planetis*, since there is a strong suggestion of Chaucer's authorship. In addition to some reproductions of ordinary manuscript pages, there are also diagrams from the *Astrolabe* and *Equatorie*. An explanation of the method of preparing the text for this edition is given, together with an account of the manuscripts of the various works. Points of interest in regard to the selection are: the text of the *Tales* is based on the Ellesmere MS; only the F version of the Prologue to the *Legend* is printed; and *Troilus*, while presenting the G text, is based on MS Morgan 817. Where appropriate, variant readings are recorded in footnotes, which also contain notes to the text and glosses (of necessity sometimes repeated). The purpose of including a glossary also (containing mainly non-substantive words) is not immediately obvious; in both the Glossary and the footnote-glosses omissions can be found. Each of the works is preceded by a succinct critical introduction, which concludes with a short explanatory bibliography with comments. While the later classified bibliography concentrates mainly on items between 1964 and 1974, reference is also made to bibliographies covering earlier years. Useful surveys are found in 'The Place of Chaucer' (summarising past criticism) and 'Chaucer in His Time'. Most of the edition will be readily understood by the non-specialist, but parts of the language section presuppose some knowledge of language and are not always accurate.

The impression given by John Gardner's *The Poetry of Chaucer*[2] is that the book is not so much a survey of the poetry — which the title would lead one to expect — as a collection of essays which cover aspects of the individual works that seem important to Gardner, and which also raise many points challenging the reader's understanding of Chaucer. (For example, unlike most critics, Gardner believes the *House of Fame* to have been written about the time of *Troilus* rather than of the *Parlement*). Throughout the book are illustrated topics discussed in the Intro-

[1] *The Complete Poetry and Prose of Geoffrey Chaucer,* ed. by John H. Fisher. New York, London: Holt, Rinehart & Winston. pp. xii + 1040.

[2] *The Poetry of Chaucer,* by John Gardner. Carbondale, Ill: Southern Illinois U.P. pp. xxxv + 408. $15.

duction: the nominalist position (which, Gardner maintains, Chaucer made the very heart of his comedy); love (a matter of prime importance in the poetry); and neoplatonic ideas. In the companion volume, *The Life and Times of Chaucer*[3], Gardner has allowed himself considerable freedom to speculate, and to some extent this fault is found also in *The Poetry of Chaucer*. Gardner contends, for example, that the alteration to the *Tales*, connected with Fragments II – IV, was occasioned by Chaucer's observance of Richard II's tyrannical behaviour and his desire to comment, 'discreetly and indirectly (for the most part), on Richard's ideas of proper government'. The somewhat cursory treatment of the *Tales* leads to an imbalance in the book. (Reviewed by Russell A. Peck, *Criticism*, 1978, pp. 66–8; Janet M. Cowen, *RES*, 1978, pp. 471–2.)

Robert B. Burlin examines three aspects of *Chaucerian Fiction*[4] – 'Poetic', 'Philosophic', 'Psychological' – which use the tension of narrator and narrative to realise the opposition and interpenetration of 'authority' and 'experience'; in so doing, they manifest 'the binary structure of Chaucer's imagining'. 'Experience' is endorsed in the experienced dreams of book-learned narrators, where Chaucer speculates on the poet's relation to his audience and on the value of poetry. But Chaucer also tested his techniques on the fictions of others, questioning given philosophies, as in the *Parlement* or *Troilus*. In the *Tales* Chaucer uses the fictitious Narrator and pilgrims to explore the contamination resulting from the translation of 'experience' into 'authority', for which the 'Retraction' is fitting conclusion. The thesis is at times overwhelmed and obscured by individual assessments. Of these, however, one would commend the discussion of the *House of Fame* as anti-vision; the stress on Troilus's intelligence as evidenced by the degree of his understanding of Boethius; and a sensitive reading of the *Prioress's Tale,* whose artistry might indicate that Chaucer saw the Prioress as 'a potential vessel of grace'. The chapter on the *Franklin's Tale* is adapted from Burlin's 1976 article (*YW* 48.96). (Reviewed by R. T. Davies, *N&Q*, 1978, pp. 356–8; Gloria Cigman, *RES*, 1978, pp. 469–70; G. S. Ivy, *DUJ*, 1978, pp. 12–3.)

'An extensive inquiry into the many subtle changes a *meta*-humanistic perspective works upon Chaucer's literary and critical profile' is how Raymond P. Tripp Jr describes his *Beyond Canterbury*[5]. Over half the book is devoted to an examination of the fallacious assumptions and consequences of humanist criticism and literature and a corresponding attempt to define Tripp's alternative, meta-humanism, drawing examples from Chaucer – as the first English humanist poet – and his critics. The last two chapters examine two of Chaucer's works from the meta-humanistic standpoint, finding Chaucer to be un-Boethian. In the *Book of the Duchess* the Dreamer is liberated from his near-fatal doctrinaire viewpoint and the Knight from his morbidly obsessive love through a repetitive debate of increasing vehemence as each recognises the unten-

---

[3] *The Life and Times of Chaucer,* by John Gardner. New York: Alfred A. Knopf. pp. ix + 328 + x. £7.50.
[4] *Chaucerian Fiction,* by Robert Burlin. Princeton, N. J.: Princeton U.P. pp. x + 293. £10.90.
[5] *Beyond Canterbury: Chaucer, Humanism and Literature,* by Raymond P. Tripp Jr. Onny P. Ltd. pp. vii + 239.

ability of his position. The poem is marked by its insistence on the infinity of love in its own right and the corresponding finality of death; the Dreamer recognises the fact of White's death from the start, but has to be led to an understanding and acceptance of the intense emotion which it generates in the Black Knight. The result is 'the first modern dialogue with death'. A similar thematic focus is discerned in the *Knight's Tale,* where Palamon, the archaic man, manifests a love compounded of physical desire and concern with the problems of lineage and also directed towards an object that his gaze transforms into a goddess. Arcite, in contrast, is a new man, who loves Emily as physical object but universalises that love to the point at which it can be entrusted to his spirit at his death. Arcite's tragic isolation is a key to the poem, for his attitude cannot be appreciated by Palamon or Theseus — the latter a military type of fixed character who acts brutally and with disconcerting certainty. The disruptive effects of Arcite's intrusion into Theseus's archaic world are symbolised by his funeral rites; Palamon is more in harmony with the Duke. But Theseus's final speech, so far from bringing the tale to an appropriate Boethian conclusion, merely shows 'an old man trying futilely to think his way out of himself' and 'its main business is to be the instrument on as large a scale as the framework of the tale can support *of the tragedy of the humanist condition'.*

Tony Millns believes that the technique of 'Chaucer's Suspended Judgements' (*EIC*), begun in the *Parlement* and the *House of Fame,* becomes the structural principle of *Troilus.* In this last work, the voice of the Narrator, who is sympathetic towards the lovers and avoids judgements by retreating behind sources, is distinguished from the voice of the no-less fictive Author who is heard partially in the Prologue but clearly and absolutely in the Epilogue. In the *Tales* Chaucer achieves the same effect without recourse to sources, with the absolute view of the Parson at the end followed by the Author's retraction. Just as in *Troilus* the irony of Troilus's double sorrow provides a clue to the final absolute position, so in the *Tales* the existence of ideal figures among the pilgrims, against whom the rest can be judged, similarly anticipates the final evaluation. Stewart Justman finds precedents for the tension of the principles of unity and diversity which result in the 'double standards and cacophony of voices' which characterise 'Medieval Monism and Abuse of Authority in Chaucer' (*ChauR*). In 'Chaucer's Literacy', (*ChauR*), Paul Christianson sees Chaucer's concern with the often dangerously persuasive power of language as the reason for his recurring emphasis on 'the art of reading and the artifice of writing' and his consciousness of the tasks of writer and reader. In 'The Heart: Chaucer's Concretization of Emotions' (*McNeese Review,* 1974–5), Leila Gross notes how Chaucer uses the heart as the seat of emotions in a range of physical and perceptual collocations which communicate the strength of those emotions to the reader.

J. D. Burnley's discussion of 'Chaucer's *Termes'* (*YES*) explores the word's meanings and implications both in modern register and in mediaeval *proprietas,* and demonstrates the importance of *termes* by Chaucerian examples such as the theologically allusive *termes* of *Troilus.* Paul Strohm reviews 'The Origin and Meaning of Middle English *Romaunce'* (*Genre*) and argues that Chaucer's definition of *lay* in the *Franklin's Tale* springs from a wish 'to eliminate an inconsistency in his own poetic materials'. He explains away references to *romaunce* in the *Book of the Duchess* 48 and *Troilus* II.100 as allusions to French works and suggests that Chaucer comprehends under *romaunce* only 'works written in the French vernacular and . . . popular compositions in Middle English'.

In Section I of 'Chaucer's Theseus and the *Knight's Tale*' (*LeedsSE*), Walter Scheps examines the 'Theseus tradition' of the Middle Ages, and, in II, Chaucer's Theseus, as found in *Anelida*, the *House of Fame*, and the *Legend of Ariadne*. The presentation of him in the *Knight's Tale* seems to attempt a synthesis of the disparate earlier material for characterisation and bears some resemblance to Plutarch's 'morally ambivalent figure'. 'Chaucer's Temples of Venus' (*Studi Inglesi*, 1975), by Piero Boitani, examines the three descriptions – in the *House of Fame*, the *Parlement*, and the *Knight's Tale* – first placing Chaucer in the literary tradition of inconography from classical times. In the *House of Fame* the temple represents a synthesis of traditional elements, the temple of a goddess both good and evil, which is allusively connected with the rest of the vision. Direct influence from the *Teseida* is found in the temple of the *Parlement*, though Boccaccio's meaning and method are changed. In the *Knight's Tale*, which, like the *Teseida* is a romance, not a dream poem, Boccaccio's influence is seen again, and Venus is goddess and planet. Although at some point Chaucer's path of meditation on Venus intersects that of Boccaccio, none the less it diverges considerably.

W. G. East considers Chaucer's use of '"Lollius"' (*ES*) for Boccaccio to be meant as a joke. Jerome Mandel seeks the artistic appropriateness of the connotations of the use of '"Boy" as Devil in Chaucer' (*PLL*, 1975). F. P. Magoun Jr's 'Two Chaucer Items' (*NM*) examines the meaning of two phrases, one in the *Friar's Tale*, the other occurring in four places in Chaucer's work. In 'Chaucer's Worthless Butterfly' (*ELN*) Karl P. Wentersdorf explores the uses of the butterfly image. In 'Chaucer, Alice Perrers, and Cecily Chaumpaigne' (*Speculum*) Haldeen Braddy seeks to establish Cecily Chaumpaigne as Alice Perrers's stepdaughter, and to consider Cecily's relationship to Chaucer, in support of his thesis advanced in 1946 (*YW* 27.82). E. Catherine Dunn uses Chaucer's tales of St Cecilia, Griselda, and Constance as illustrations in 'The Saint's Legend as History and as Poetry: An Appeal to Chaucer' (*The American Benedictine Review*, 1976). In the course of ' "The Boke of Cupide" Reopened' (*NM*) Charles S. Rutherford notes the work's resemblances to Chaucer's work. Several 'Chaucer Allusions: Addenda to Spurgeon' (*NQ*) are noted by Jackson C. Boswell. Hilton Kelliher suggests that the miniature in 'The Historiated Initial in the Devonshire Chaucer' (*NQ*) may represent Chaucer in the condition suggested by *The Complaint of Chaucer to his Purse*. Anthony G. Petti's *English literary hands from Chaucer to Dryden*[6] provides annotated facsimiles of two possible Chaucer holographs and of a leaf from MS Ellesmere. (Reviewed by M. Görlach, *Archiv*, 1978, pp. 406–8.) Marvin Mudrick's 'The Blind Men and the Elephant' (*HudR*) is a scathing review article on the works of some recent writers on Chaucer.

Derek Pearsall provides an excellent, though necessarily brief, survey

---

[6] *English literary hands from Chaucer to Dryden*, by Anthony G. Petti. Edward Arnold. pp. ix + 133. £14.50.

of Chaucer's background and achievement (particularly in regard to his language and techniques) in the chapter on 'Courtly Poetry' in *Old English and Middle English Poetry*[7]. Robert P. Miller's large and wide-ranging anthology, *Chaucer: Sources and Background*[8], presents a collection of extracts from works known to Chaucer or used by him, or illustrating what he would have known. Each extract, in modern English translation, is placed in its own tradition by a prefatory note. The whole should prove a useful compendium for students. Gillian Evans's *Chaucer*[9] gives a sketch of Chaucer's cultural and historical background for the general reader, with some attention to the portraits of the *General Prologue*. The first British edition of Marchette Chute's *Geoffrey Chaucer of England*[10] confirms the assessment, made unseen, of its 1946 publication as 'apparently a popular account of the poet' (*YW* 27.71).

Paul Strohm finds 'Chaucer's Audience' (*Literature and History*) most prominently among the lesser gentry, with whom Chaucer ranked socially and who would be sympathetic to the balance and open-endedness of his poetry. Thomas J. Garbaty gives a disappointingly superficial account of 'Chaucer and Comedy' in *Versions of Medieval Comedy*. A version of 'Games and High Seriousness: Chaucer'[12] by Richard A. Lanham appeared in *ES* in 1967 (*YW* 48.89). *The Matter of Araby in Medieval England*[13], by Dorothee Metlitzski (parts of which have already appeared in articles), has reference to Chaucer *passim*, considering some of his ultimate sources and scientific imagery, but naturally deals particularly with the *Squire's Tale* and the *Astrolabe*. *Figures of Life and Death in Medieval English Literature*[14] by Philippa Tristram contains useful comment on Chaucer's work *passim*.

Alan T. Gaylord's 'Scanning the Prosodists: An Essay in Metacriticism' (*ChauR*) is a critical review of studies in Chaucer's prosody. It indicates the problems to which prosodic analysis should address itself and desiderata for future work in this field. In 'Chaucer's Metrical Lines: Some Internal Evidence' (*Parergon*), Dennis Biggins analyses ll.1–100 of the *General Prologue* in the Ellesmere manuscript to demonstrate statistically the pervasiveness of the iambic pentameter line.

Geoffrey Chaucer: Troilus and Criseyde and Selected Short Poems[15] is an edition in normalised spelling of *Troilus* and some lyrics, apparently

[7] *Old English and Middle English Poetry*, by Derek Pearsall. The Routledge History of English Poetry I. Routledge & Kegan Paul. pp. xiv + 352. £8.75.

[8] *Chaucer: Sources and Backgrounds*, by Robert P. Miller. New York: O.U.P. pp. xv + 507. pb £5.75.

[9] *Chaucer*, by Gillian Evans. Authors in their Age. Blackie & Son. pp. ii + 150.

[10] *Geoffrey Chaucer of England*, by Marchette Chute. A Condor Book. Souvenir P. (E.&A) Ltd. pp. 347.

[11] *Versions of Medieval Comedy*, ed. by Paul G. Ruggiers. Norman, Ok.: U. of Oklahoma P.

[12] In *The Motives of Eloquence*, by Richard A. Lanham. New Haven, Conn. and London: Yale U.P. pp. xiii + 234. 1976.

[13] *The Matter of Araby in Medieval England*, by Dorothee Metlitzski. New Haven, Conn. and London: Yale U.P. pp. xiv + 320.

[14] *Figures of Life and Death in Medieval English Literature*, by Philippa Tristram. Paul Elek (1976). pp. xiv + 245. £9.50.

[15] *Geoffrey Chaucer: Troilus and Criseyde and Selected Short Poems*, ed. by Donald R. Howard and James Dean. New York: Signet Classic. (1976). New American Library. pp. lvi + 327. $1.95.

for the student. Donald R. Howard contributes a readable and stimulating examination of *Troilus* and James Dean the notes and apparatus.

Designed as a continuation of William R. Crawford's *Bibliography of Chaucer, 1954–63* (*YW* 48.87), Lorrayne Y. Baird's *A Bibliography of Chaucer*[16], *1964–1973* follows the earlier reference work in organisation and method, apart from certain exceptions mentioned in the Introduction. A second edition has appeared of *Chaucer*[17], bringing up to date this bibliography compiled by Albert C. Baugh (*YW* 49.100). It is a selective bibliography of 3215 items (800 new) for graduate and advanced students. A guide to *Old and Middle English Poetry to 1500*[18], provided by Walter H. Beale, devotes a section to Chaucer, containing entries of selective criticism of the last twenty years as well as of reference books.

2. Canterbury Tales

Charles A. Owen Jr's closely-argued book, *Pilgrimage and Story-telling in the 'Canterbury Tales': the Dialectic of 'ernest' and 'game'*[19], has developed to some extent, as he acknowledges, from his own earlier work, as well as from that of other writers. His thesis is that, in the course of writing the *Tales*, Chaucer shifted the emphasis from the *ernest* of overt morality to the *game* of storytelling. In support of this thesis Owen stresses the importance of the tales of the Wife of Bath – her original tale (now the Shipman's), and her present one, allotted as Chaucer's interest in her grew – together with those tales linked to them (in D and B^2), and those tales influenced by her present story (C and E-F). He adduces careful supportive evidence for the development of the earlier, more moral design to the latest, which included the supper-plan and decision concerning the number of tales to be told by each pilgrim; the latest plan also allocated certain tales for telling on the homeward journey.

This thesis lies behind the rest of the book, in which Owen comments in detail on the Fragments and on most of the individual tales. He explores the varied ways in which Chaucer presents the *Prologue*-portraits, and also considers the points in time when certain of them were written, some of them being later additions. The examination of the various tales provides some interesting and enlightening interpretations of them as tales or in regard to the teller (e.g. the *Pardoner's Tale*). The Fragments are characterised in various ways, as in the case of B^2, where the stories show a great variety of genres and are self-contained to an unusual degree, or of D, the 'most thoroughly dramatic' of all the Fragments. Throughout the discussion, note is made of the part played by the Host, his developing character, and the reasons underlying his words. The book contains useful and critical

---

[16] *A Bibliography of Chaucer, 1964–1973*, by Lorrayne Y. Baird. Boston, Mass.: G. K. Hall & Co.; London: George Prior Publishers. pp. xxiv + 287. $22 and £17.50.

[17] *Chaucer*, by Albert C. Baugh. Goldentree Bibliographies in Language and Literature. Arlington Heights, Ill.: AHM Publishing Corporation. pp. xiii + 161.

[18] *Old and Middle English Poetry to 1500. A Guide to Information Sources*, by Walter H. Beale. Gale Information Guide Library. Detroit, Mich.: Gale Research Co. pp. xxiii + 454. 1976.

[19] *Pilgrimage and Story-telling in the 'Canterbury Tales': the Dialectic of 'ernest' and 'game'*, by Charles A. Owen Jr. Norman, Ok.: U. of Oklahoma P. pp. ix + 253. £10.50 and $12.95.

annotation. (Reviewed by Donald MacDonald, *Criticism*, 1978, pp. 100-1; J. H. Fisher, *Speculum*, 1978, pp. 835-6.)

The appropriateness of Chaucer's pilgrimage-frame as thematically embodying the opposition of the remembered pietistic ideal of pilgrimage and the contemporary decline from it to *curiositas* is the theme of Christian K. Zacher's chapter, 'Curiosity and the Instability of Pilgrimage: Chaucer's *Canterbury Tales*'[20]. The old ideals of order, justice, and social harmony, are expressed in the strategically-placed tales of Knight, Chaucer and Parson, and find a counterpart in the recurring images of pacts or contracts. The spiritual goal is replaced by the game-agreement to tell tales which at once unites and divides the pilgrims. The stories range over the appropriate themes of order and disorder in human relationships, and the appropriateness of story-telling, to conclude with the Parson's assertion of a spiritual goal, a reconciliation in a 'non-tale'. Thomas Pison discusses 'Liminality in *The Canterbury Tales*' (*Genre*), regarding the work as a whole as a *rite de passage*. It manifests the dissolution of social ties and the establishment of *communitas* under the Host's direction as correlative to the transition from profane to sacred; an analogous structure, in the separation, examination, and aggregation of social claims, characterises individual tales, such as that of the Franklin.

Taking as his starting-point Hubertis M. Cummings's *The Indebtedness of Chaucer's Works to the Italian Works of Boccaccio (A Review and Summary)*, which has won almost unanimous acceptance, Donald McGrady, in 'Chaucer and the *Decameron* Reconsidered' (*ChauR*), proceeds to analyse the grounds for the belief that Chaucer did not know and imitate the *Decameron*, and also brings forward decisive evidence. In the first instance he shows that Cummings did not examine available evidence sufficiently carefully. McGrady draws attention also to Willard Farnham's 'England's Discovery of the *Decameron*' and refutes arguments that Chaucer could not have known this work of Boccaccio. Finally he devotes himself to showing how, apart from perhaps two tales, the framework and stories reflect a secondary use of Boccaccio, being grafted on to models derived from other sources.

Peter Hyland counsels caution in 'Number Symbolism in *The Canterbury Tales*: Some Suggestions'[21]. He comments on Russell Peck's use of number symbolism in discussing the prologue to the *Parson's Tale* (*YW* 48.98), offers an alternative interpretation, and then considers some other instances of such symbolism in the *Tales*.

D. W. Robertson Jr considers the importance of the work of historians in establishing connotations for 'Some Disputed Chaucerian Terminology' (*Speculum*) in the *Tales*. Chaucer was not class-conscious but made his assessments on the basis of the moral qualities and effective social contributions of his characters. Most of E. Talbot Donaldson's 'Some Readings in the *Canterbury Tales*'[22] argues for *aryue* instead of *armee* (A 60);

[20] In *Curiosity and Pilgrimage: the Literature of Discovery in Fourteenth-Century England*, ed. by Christian K. Zacher. Baltimore, Md. and London: Johns Hopkins U.P. (1976) pp. x + 196.
[21] In *The Annual Reports of The Faculty of Arts and Letters Tohoku University*, xxvi. Sendai, Japan: Tohoku University, The Faculty of Arts and Letters (1976). pp. 216.
[22] In *Medieval Studies in Honor of Lillian Herlands Hornstein*, ed. by Jess B. Bessinger Jr and Robert R. Raymo. New York: New York U.P. (1976). pp. x + 225.

in addition, three probable omissions and one probable misreading are discussed. Paul G. Ruggiers's 'A Vocabulary for Chaucerian Comedy: A Preliminary Sketch'[22] concentrates upon plot and character in the *Tales* in an attempt to establish a system of analysis for Chaucerian comedy, heavily dependent upon Aristotelean definitions.

Robert W. Hanning, in 'From *Eva* to *Ave* to Eglentyne and Alisoun: Chaucer's Insight into the Roles Women Play' (*Signs*), speculates that the Prioress, as revealed in her portrait, is endeavouring to salvage 'a positive sense of self in the face of her powerlessness in a man's world', and that her resentment is exemplified in her tale; while the Wife's relationships with men are coloured by the fact that she is 'trapped between sexual and intellectual needs'.

Using the Ellesmere order of the *Tales*, David R. Pichaske and Laura Sweetland trace the development of the Host in 'Chaucer on the Medieval Monarchy: Harry Bailly in the *Canterbury Tales*' (*ChauR*). They regard the Host as the focus of a commentary on government in the *Tales*, since he is meant to be the governor on the pilgrimage; in addition to the links, several of the tales have a bearing on this concept. As the Host changes in character, finally abdicating to the Parson, so does a real sense of community develop among the pilgrims.

Chaucer's comic tales or *fabliaux* are illustrated by the typical example of the *Miller's Tale*, where 'the articulation of the insult into a fantastic story turns it into a classically comic structure'. These tales are not connected with love nor do they fit the view that in comedy the story should have a happy ending. After a consideration of such characteristics, D. S. Brewer provides a lively account of 'Structures and Character-Types of Chaucer's Popular Comic Tales[23]. In 'Chaucer's Portraits of the Pardoner and Summoner and Wyclif's Tractatus de Simonia' (*Classical Folia, 1975*), Terrence A. McVeigh notes the uses of leprosy and of sodomy as images for simony in Wyclif's treatise, and their probable influence upon Chaucer's portraits.

Gerald Morgan's 'The Universality of the Portraits in the *General Prologue* to the *Canterbury Tales*' (*ES*) arises from his criticism of Jill Mann's claim that the portraits are at once both individual and typical. Commenting on 'Chaucer's *General Prologue*, 133–136' (*Expl*, 1976), Patrick Bowles asserts that the Prioress was sharing a communal cup. The significance for a mediaeval audience of the mention of the mouse in the description of the Prioress is discussed by Stephen P. Witte in '*Muscipula Diaboli* and Chaucer's Portrait of the Prioress' (*PLL*), with particular reference to the use of a mousetrap as a theological metaphor. After a very detailed account of 'The Making of a Fourteenth Century Sergeant of the Lawe' (*RUO*, 1975), Isobel McKenna comments that Chaucer's knowledge in this connection must have been first-hand.

Regarding 'Chaucer's Knight as Don Quijoté' (*Notre Dame English Journal*, 1976), Burton Raffel concentrates on his tale 'as a poem, as a story', not, for example, as a philosophical problem, and sees in it many parodic elements, emphasised by a deliberate and substantive use of clumsy narrative technique.

[23] In *Estudios sobre los géneros literarios* I, *Acta Salamenticensia Iussu Senatus Universitatis: Filosofía y Letras* 89, ed. by Javier Coy and Javier de Hoz. U. of Salamanca (1975).

In his discussion of 'Characterization and Syntax in the *Miller's Tale*' (*JNT*, 1975), Thomas J. Jambeck points out that, while the pilgrim's *manere* characterises both him and his tale as *lewed*, there is also a 'syntactical layer of meaning', which indicates his idiosyncratic way of regarding the world. Differences from the analogues, found in the 'window-scenes', explain the relationship between 'Art and Scatology in the *Miller's Tale*' (*ChauR*), argues Peter G. Beidler. The effect is 'to take woman down from Emily's pedestal' and also to show the Miller's contempt for Absolon, every one of whose senses is offended by the actions of Alisoun and Nicholas. Here and elsewhere in the tale is underlined the inappropriateness of Absolon's behaviour, especially as a religious official. While discussing 'The Italian Sources of Gil Vicente's *Auto da Índia*' (*Romance Philology*, 1976), Donald McGrady comments on its resemblances to the *Miller's Tale*.

After exemplifying juxtaposition in visual arts, Ronald B. Herzman proceeds to comment on the two fabliaux in 'Millstones: An Approach to the *Miller's Tale* and the *Reeve's Tale*' (*The English Record*). He concludes that a study of the fabliaux suggests that Chaucer was also a great writer of a Divine Comedy. Discussing 'The Homoerotic Underside in Chaucer's *Miller's Tale* and *Reeve's Tale*' (*Michigan Academician*), Dolores Warwick Frese remarks on the substitution in the former of the anal for the oral, which leads to the climax where the homosexual suddenly replaces the heterosexual. This 'underside' is feebly answered by the Reeve in both his prologue and his tale. Roy Peter Clark queries whether or not there is 'A Possible Pun on Chaucer's Name' (*Names*) in A 3904. Posing the question, 'Another Northernism in "The Reeve's Tale"?' (*NQ*), N. F. Blake suggests that no emendation should be made to the apparently uninflected genitive *god*.

The use made of *De contemptu mundi* reveals that for the Man of Law 'wealth is equated with good fortune and poverty with bad'. Robert P. Miller re-examines Chaucer's alterations to Trivet's tale in 'Constancy Humanized: Trivet's Constance and the Man of Law's Custance' (*Costerus*, 1975), showing that the 'Lord of Fortune' in fact rewards Custance with earthly joys, indicating that 'she is good because she is rich', and also that the wicked are punished. Unlike Trivet's heroine, Chaucer's 'humanised' Custance cannot be regarded as exemplary. In this interpretation it is possible to see as obvious the links between the tale and its prologue, which previously have been considered only tenuous. Franklin B. Williams Jr prints and comments on 'Alsop's *Fair Custance*: Chaucer in Tudor Dress' (*English Literary Renaissance*, 1976), a fragment of a version of the *Man of Law's Tale*, akin to CUL MS Ii.3.26.

'"By Preeve which that is Demonstratif"' (*ChauR*) gives example of the narrative thread, based on the ideas of *experience* and *auctoritee*, that W. G. East sees running through Fragment D. Through an examination of the Wife's 'speech acts', a means of comparison is established between her, the Hag, and Prudence in *Melibee* by Ellen Schauber and Ellen Spolsky, writing on 'The Consolation of Alison: The Speech Acts of the Wife of Bath' (*Centrum*). They conclude that Prudence and the Hag personify the mediaeval ideals of prudence and philosophy, and that the Wife, despite her efforts, represents a Lady Philosophy *manquée*. Just as the Pardoner's 'constitutional malady is a relentless obsession with the imposible', so is there 'The Impossible Dream: An Underside to the Wife of Bath' (*Moderna Språk*, 1976), argues Alain Renoir. The *wo* that she found in marriage may not have been resolved in her final reconciliation with her fifth husband, and 'her notorious promiscuity should perhaps be understood as a subconscious means . . . to an end rather than as an end in itself', in view of the several statements she makes concerning procreation. The Wife of Bath serves E. Talbot Donaldson as one entertaining corrective to pietistic generalisations about the Middle Ages in 'Designing a Camel: or, Generalizing the Middle Ages' (*TSL*).

Penn R. Szittya's 'The Antifraternal Tradition in Middle English Literature' (*Speculum*) provides some background material for Chaucer's work. Discussing 'Doubting Thomas in Chaucer's *Summoner's Tale*' (*ChauR*), Roy Peter Clark examines the relevance of the parts played by the friar and the old man, Thomas, to the gospel account of the apostle as well as to the legend of St Thomas of India.

David C. Steinmetz provides a detailed explanation of the *Clerk's Tale* as an allegorical demonstration of the nominalist doctrine of justification. He concludes in 'Late Medieval Nominalism and the *Clerk's Tale*' (*ChauR*) that, although Griselda completely exemplifies this doctrine, Walter is an imperfect symbol of God. To prove 'The Psychological Basis of the *Clerk's Tale*' (*ChauR*), E. Pearlman first subjects the protagonists to orthodox Freudian scrutiny. Their relationship is then examined in the light of Chaucer's descriptive and rhetorical attitude to psychology – with reference to Griselda's comments, to the Cupid-Psyche folk tale, and to the relationship between coloniser and colonised. In 'Re-reading Allegory: The *Clerk's Tale*' (*Paunch*, 1975), Elliot Krieger considers the *Clerk's Tale* as an expression of Chaucer's conservative neoplatonism, with Griselda representing the obedience of wife to husband, subject to ruler, and human to God. The article further indicates the applicability of mediaeval allegory on a literal level, stressing that literal absurdities cannot be considered absurd when connected to the spiritual sense. James Dean concentrates on 'Time Past and Time Present in Chaucer's *Clerk's Tale* and Gower's *Confessio Amantis*' (*ELH*), particularly the conclusion of the former work and the climax of the latter, to illustrate the attitude shared by the two writers in representing what Dean describes as 'humanistic' time. The greater part of Harriett Hawkins's 'The Victim's Side: Chaucer's *Clerk's Tale* and Webster's *Duchess of Malfi*' (*Signs*, 1975) is concerned with the former work; but they present alternative means of eliciting an audience's protests against injustice. Through an examination of the tale on a literal and human level, it is shown that Chaucer had added to his sources to emphasise Walter's behaviour as 'infuriating and reprehensible' and Griselda's 'uncritical acceptance of unnecessary suffering' as 'painful and pitiable'. Chaucer also made additions which provide strong critical comment of Walter. Shirley S. Allen's 'The Griselda Tale and the Portrayal of Women in the *Decameron*' (*PQ*) has significance for the *Clerk's Tale*.

Bernard S. Levy prefaces 'Gentilesse in Chaucer's *Clerk's* and *Merchant's Tales*' (*ChauR*) with the argument that the Wife of Bath wishes to show that a man of noble birth, but lacking true *gentilesse*, must be converted to an understanding of it by a woman like herself, who posesses it even though of low birth. However, she really equates *gentilesse* with carnal desire. The *Clerk's Tale* does in fact show what the Wife thinks she is proving, while the Merchant demonstrates that neither by inherited virtue in a man of birth, nor by natural virtue in a woman of low birth can *gentilesse* be achieved. In directing attention to 'Deluding Words in the *Merchant's Tale*' (*ChauR*), Douglas A. Burger emphasises how the gap between words and reality both influences the actual structure of the tale, with its many long speeches and rhetorical set-pieces, and also adds to the irony of which the Merchant himself is aware. Douglas Wurtele's 'Marian Overtones in Chaucer's *Merchant's Tale*'[24] traces in detail the bitterness in the Merchant's evocations of the Virgin Mary in presenting January and May. After contrasting exegetical interpretations of Canticles with January's inappropriate use of it, and after noting other ironies (such as the nominal parallel of Mary-May), Wurtele finally considers the implications of this device for the portrait of the Merchant. Wolfgang E. H. Rudat comments on 'Chaucer's Merchant's Tale, E 1263, 1854, and 2360–65' (*Expl*).

Melvin Storm comments on 'The Tercelet as Tiger: Bestiary Hypocrisy in the *Squire's Tale*' (*ELH*). Writing on 'The Chivalric Tradition and the Red and White Gown of Chaucer's Squire' (*ELN*), Robert J. Fehrenbach notes the propriety of the colours for the Squire as knight-aspirant.

Writing 'A Defence of Dorigen's Complaint' (*MÆ*), Gerald Morgan approaches the subject from a moral, not psychological, point of view, in line with rhetorical tradition. He proceeds to explain in detail the significance of the exempla (the number of which was expanded in the revised version) and 'their relationship to one another in a lucidly articulated sequence', dealing with chastity, fidelity, and honour. The conclusion examines Arveragus's response to Dorigen's dilemma. In '"To Maken Illusioun": the Philosophy of Magic and the Magic of Philosophy in the *Franklin's Tale*' (*ChauR*), W. Bryant Bachman Jr analyses the tale in a study of the tension that exists between the 'idealistic posture', found in Boethius, concerning evil, and 'the equally implacable demands of the experiential world', which 'generates the ultimate philosophical statement of the tale'. The normative forces are at the end shown to be the keeping of *trouthe* and the compassion which that produces in Aurelius and the clerk. Michael Foley examines 'Irony and Plot in the Franklin's Tale' (*The English Quarterly*, 1975), tracing a rising pattern of irony in the tale to its culmination in the Franklin's unconscious revelation that he himself does not understand the concept of *gentilesse*. In 'Chaucer and the "Breton" Lay' (*ChauR*) Emily K. Yoder questions the connection of 'Breton' with Brittany.

Discussing 'Chaucer's Pardoner and Preaching' (*ELH*), Frank V. Cespedes notes that the Pardoner's violation of the accordance of word and deed contravenes both the instructions given to preachers by

---

[24] In *The Virgin Mary in Art, Thought, and Letters in the Middle Ages and the Renaissance*, Proceedings of the Third Annual Symposium of the Ottawa-Carleton Medieval-Renaissance Club, ed. by Raymond St Jacques (1976).

preaching-manuals, and also the injunctions of St Paul's Epistle to Timothy, which provides the texts for both the tale and its prologue. Significantly the Pardoner approves the Wife's inversion of the same Epistle at III.165; and, in his final offer of relics, he recalls for the pilgrims the usual intention of the preacher. He is the reverse of the Parson, a poor exemplar but a good communicator, and is one manifestation of the general concern in the *Tales* with the interaction of fable and Christian instruction. In 'Audience and Exempla in the *Pardoner's Prologue* and *Tale'* (*ChauR*), A. Luengo argues that the two audiences for the tale — *lewed peple* and pilgrims — influenced the structure. He points to the alternation of exemplum with moral tale and the corresponding changes in terms of address, style, and selection of material. Warren Ginsberg's 'Preaching and Avarice in the Pardoner's Tale' (*Mediaevalia,* 1976) stresses the Pardoner's literal use of spiritually symbolic action and detail, symptomatic of his inner state. Like the Old Man, he is a victim of avarice, but the Old Man has finally repented, whereas the Pardoner remains obdurate. Julia Dias-Ferreira recounts 'Another Portuguese Analogue of Chaucer's *Pardoner's Tale'* (*ChauR*).

In considerable detail V. J. Scattergood defends 'The Originality of the *Shipman's Tale'* (*ChauR*) against the charge that it is a typical *fabliau.* In comparison with analogues, both the mercantile setting and the character of the merchant are developed, the latter by contrasts such as his honourable behaviour against that of the monk, not only professionally, but in regard to their relationship with each other. But there is some limiting criticism of him in the presentation of his literal-mindedness, revealed in his speech, particularly in contrast with that of the wife and the monk. '*Cosyn* and *Cosynage*: Pun and Structure in the Shipman's *Tale'* (*ChauR*) by David H. Abraham shows that although the two meanings of the words are implicit throughout the tale, that of relationship is primary in the earlier part, of deception in the later, the point of reversal coming in ll.1338–43. In ' "Taillynge Ynough": the Function of Money in the *Shipman's Tale'* (*ChauR*) Paul Stephen Schneider contends that money is a force for both good and evil in the tale, which ends on a satisfactory note. A study of 'Source and Theme in the *Shipman's Tale'* (*University of Dayton Review,* 1974) leads Joseph R. Millichap to conclude that while it is impossible to show a real source, marked differences from the analogues in characterisation increase both complexity and irony in Chaucer's version.

A symbolic meaning for 'The Mysterious "Greyn" in the *Prioress's Tale'* (*ChauR*) is denied by Albert B. Friedman, who prefers to regard the *greyn* as a necessary prop, since on its removal the child stops singing and the funeral can take place. In '*Cum Grano Salis:* a Note on the *Prioress's Tale'* (*AN&Q*), Gregory K. Jember discusses the possible connotations of salt and grain raised by *greyn* in the *Prioress's Tale* 1.662.

Ruth Van Arsdale seeks to dispel the homosexual implications of 'The Chaste Sir Thopas' (*AN&Q,* 1975), detected by George Williams (*YW* 46. 87). In 'Chaucer's Prudence as the Ideal of the Virtuous Woman' (*ELWIU*), Elisabeth Lunz argues that Chaucer's *Melibee* shows the poet utilising the traditional characterization of the virtue of Prudence to serve a new purpose, that of establishing the ideal of the virtuous woman as a reference point for the marriage group in *The Canterbury Tales*'.

In considerable detail Robert A. Pratt examines 'Some Latin Sources of the Nonnes Preest on Dreams' (*Speculum*), showing to what extent and how closely Chaucer followed the commentary by Robert Holcot on the Book of Wisdom – *Super Sapientiam Salomonis* – in the discussion by Pertelote and Chauntecleer of the latter's dream. Pratt comments on the very effective use of detailed borrowing from Holcot and other Latin sources such as Albertus Magnus. The mixed style of the tale has often been noted, and Susan Gallick develops the subject further in 'Styles of Usage in the *Nun's Priest's Tale*' (*ChauR*), where she not only discusses the varying styles of characters and narrators, but also shows that shifts in style of usage can reflect the speaker's relationship with another person or group. Wayne D. McGinnis sees 'The Dramatic Fitness of the *Nun's Priest's Tale*' (*CEA*, 1975) in aspects of the tale which suggest that the Priest may have been 'having a little fun' at the expense of the Monk and Prioress. Lawrence L. Besserman's 'Chaucerian Wordplay: the Nun's Priest and his *Womman Divyne*' (*ChauR*) deals with the semantics of B 4456, detecting 'a punning swipe at the Prioress'. John Duval's '"Si coume Renart prist Chantecler le Coc" and "The Nonnes Preestes Tale"': A Comparison' (*Publications of the Arkansas Philological Association*, 1975) not only compares the two tales, but also considers how they may have been influenced by their setting among other tales.

Albert E. Hartung employs internal stylistic evidence, textual variants, and ostensible historical allusions in his consideration of '"Pars Secunda" and the Development of the *Canon's Yeoman's Tale*' (*ChauR*). He concludes that 'Pars Secunda' was originally an earlier, separate work, and considers the process involved in adapting it to its place in the *Tales*. John C. Hirsch's discussion of 'The Politics of Spirituality: the Second Nun and the Manciple' (*ChauR*) proposes an added dimension for the Nun's tale in the circumstances of the Great Schism, and for the Manciple's in the parable of the unjust steward and its glosses. Cecilia's perfection and the Manciple's self-interested prudence offer examples of success, 'each in its own way commendable' and inter-relatable. David L. Jeffrey's first concern in 'The Manciple's Tale: The Form of Conclusion' (*English Studies in Canada*, 1976) is to examine changes made by Chaucer to the story which provide a more negative reading of the wife's behaviour and develop the relationship between Phebus and the crow (whose function is also altered); such changes undermine the connection with the Manciple's concluding moralising. The introduction of a tale about 'rash anger and precipitous judgement' as the penultimate in the pilgrimage reflects a theme of the *Tales*, beginning in the Knight's and working to a resolution in the *Parson's Tale*, the latter allowing for redemptive hope. The interpretation of the Manciple as 'a witless, almost incoherent, moralizing bore' is developed in Richard M. Trask's 'The Manciple's Problem' (*SSF*). The lack of perception to be noted in his words is reflected in those of Phebus. By its position, the tale itself has relevance to the theme of the pilgrimage as a whole.

3. Troilus and Criseyde

In *O Love O Charite! Contraries Harmonized in Chaucer's 'Troilus'*[25] Donald W. Rowe argues that Pandarus's successful direction of the idealistic Troilus and the pragmatic Criseyde to a physical, spiritual, and stylistic concord in Book III attests Chaucer's use of the *concordia discors* tradition of universal order. It suggests at once the soul's descent into sin and the soul's journey to join matter; Troilus's progress suggests movement from the hell of Book I, through the purgatory of Book II to the heaven of Book III, while the Narrator moves from superiority to identification with the lovers. The echo of these patterns in Book IV suggests the renewed operation of natural justice, and by Book V Troilus-*caritas* is distinguished sharply from Criseyde-*cupiditas*, with the Narrator reverting to his initial detachment. The poem describes both comic and tragic circles, demonstrating that the world and worldly things are valuable but only partial reflections of the eternal Good, just as poetry itself is a valuable but imperfect reflection of spiritual truth. The reader's involvement in the lovers' false paradise requires recognition of its falseness to turn him to the truth. (Reviewed by Barry Windeatt, *MÆ*, 1978, pp. 156–8.)

James I. Wimsatt's 'Medieval and Modern in Chaucer's *Troilus and Criseyde'* (*PMLA*) shares some of Rowe's observations (e.g. the hell-paradise pattern, definition of what is by what a thing is not). Wimsatt finds many mediaeval elements in *Troilus* in the evocation of epic (Dante), romance (Machaut), and philosophic demonstration (Boethius), but, noting the undermining of these frames of reference by Chaucer, he stresses Chaucer's modern technique of realism, seen in his irony and in the suggestion of everyday activity and detail. Rose A. Zimbardo's view of *Troilus* in 'Creator and Created: the Generic Perspective of Chaucer's *Troilus and Criseyde'* (*ChauR*) may also be compared with Rowe's as she finds in the ambivalent poetic structure of the poem (tragedy or romance?) an expression of the artist's ambivalent position as creator and creature. She examines the successive inadequacies of the designs imposed on the action by Troilus, Pandarus, and the Narrator, each successively encompassing the other(s) until even the Narrator's poetic reality is encompassed by the eternal reality of God. The reader must experience the human dilemma before being distanced from it in order to see the harmony of God.

Applying a Brechtian formulation of aesthetic distancing, Sheila Delany examines the various 'Techniques of Alienation in *Troilus and Criseyde'*[26]. These include the critical view of the characters which is fostered; the unexpected viewpoint to which the Narrator's voice and ambiguous syntax contribute; the emphasised artificiality of genre; and the posing of direct question. Stephanie Yearwood's discussion of 'The Rhetoric of

---

[25] *O Love O Charite! Contraries Harmonized in Chaucer's 'Troilus'*, by Donald W. Rose. Carbondale and Edwardsville, Ill.: Southern Illinois U.P.; London and Amsterdam: Feffer & Simons (1976). pp. ix + 201. £12.50.

[26] In *The Uses of Criticism*, ed. by A. P. Foulkes. Literaturwissenschaftliche Texte Theorie and Kritik Bd/vol.3. Berne: Herbert Lang; Frankfurt: Peter Lang. (1976). pp. 287.

Narrative Rendering in Chaucer's *Troilus'* (*ChauR*) concentrates upon the interrelated framing devices used to present the skeletal narrative – the five-book structure, the Narrator's techniques of narrative and commentary, and the epilogue. Book and scene division, dialogue and apostrophe are among the 'Narrative Devices in Chaucer's *Troilus and Criseyde'* (*Thoth*, 1974) discussed by Michael H. Frost, but most attention is given to the identity and function of the Narrator.

In 'Zu Chaucers *Troilus and Criseyde*, Buch IV'[27], Willi Erzgräber suggests that Book IV contains five narrative segments (perhaps deriving from Boethius's structure), and that the 'parting scene' itself consists of five sections (deriving from Boccaccio); the whole constitutes a drama of inactivity [A.J.H.]. Thomas J. Garbáty finds 'Troilus V, 1786-92 and V, 1807-27; an Example of Poetic Process' (*ChauR*) because the second passage echoes Dante and led Chaucer on from his earlier concern with tragedy to Troilus's 'cosmic and spiritual laughter'.

'A Chaucerian Crux' discussed by William Frost (*YR*) is the pun on *queynte* in *Troilus* V.543. McKay Sundwall seeks the source and suggestive force of Diomede's seizure of 'Criseyde's Rein' (*ChauR*) at V.85-91 in Benoit's four climactic examples of the same motif in the *Roman de Troie*. Lawrence Eldredge discusses 'Boethian Epistemology and Chaucer's *Troilus* in the Light of Fourteenth-century Thought' (*Mediaevalia*, 1976), arguing that 'in physically rising to a point in the eighth sphere, Troilus provides us, the readers, with an analogue to Lady Philosophy's advice to strive to see with our highest faculty'. The epilogue to John Leyerle's 'The Rose-wheel Design and Dante's *Paradiso'* (*UTQ*) suggests that the complexities of rose-wheel design are found in *Troilus*, and mainly in the character of Criseyde. W. M. O'Neil's astronomical discussion of 'The Bente Moone' (*Journal of Australian Universities Language and Literature Association*, 1975) and associated data in III.624-5 suggests 12 May, 1385, as the probable day, although the details are not precisely accurate and suggest reliance on tables rather than observation. Deborah Ellis – in ' "Calle It Gentilesse": A Comparative Study of Two Medieval Go-Betweens' (*Comitatus*) – examines the characters of Celestina (in Fernando de Rojas' *Tragicomedia de Calisto y Melibea*) and Pandarus, before concentrating on 'the interplay between the go-between and the spatial imagery' of the works.

Derek Pearsall re-assesses the connection between 'The *Troilus* Frontispiece and Chaucer's Audience' (*YES*), relating the picture to the tradition of presentation pictures. Claiming that the picture does not necessarily support a connection of Chaucer with the King and the highest nobility, he urges the importance of a Chaucer 'circle' in administrative echelons more remote from the King. James H. McGregor also considers the Frontispiece in his study of 'The Iconography of Chaucer in Hoccleve's *De Regimine Principium* and in the *Troilus* Frontispiece' (*ChauR*). Placing Hoccleve's portrait of Chaucer in the context of Hoccleve's comments on Chaucer in the text, and setting the frontispiece in the twin traditions

[27] In *Philologica Romana*, ed. by M. Bambeck and H. H. Christmann. Munich: Fink (1975).

of dedicatory and of teaching miniatures and in relation to the poem, McGregor concludes that both pictures lead to the same retrospective image — of Chaucer as a national poet, an adviser of princes, whose poetry pointed the way to the creation of a peaceful realm. John H. Fisher finds probable subjects for nearly all 'The Intended Illustrations in MS Corpus Christi 61 of Chaucer's *Troylus and Criseyde'*[22].

4. Other works

In examining 'The Parliament of Fowls: The Narrator, the "Certeyn Thyng" and the "Commune Profyt"' (*Theoria*, 1975), J. A. Kearney indicates the ways in which he thinks the theme of *commune profyt* runs throughout the work, how dichotomies — both real and apparent — are finally resolved, and how the narrator pursues his search for a doctrine of love. Judith Hutchinson, in questioning *'The Parliament of Fowls: A Literary Entertainment?'* (*Neophilologus*), shows how, stage by stage, Chaucer does not fulfil the conventional expectations his audience might have, and in the end deflects the mockery from them to the narrator. None the less he says 'something of fundamental weight lightly'. As Robert M. Jordan points out, attempts to find unity in the structure of the *Parlement of Foules* have proved unsuccessful. He suggests, in a well-argued article, 'The Question of Unity and the *Parlement of Foules'* (*English Studies in Canada*), that the poem shows discontinuity and acentricity instead of tightness of structure and relevance of all parts, as well as 'variegated, encyclopedic display' rather than economy and relevance. Discussing 'The Tragic Lovers in Chaucer's *The Parliament of Fowls'* (*Publications of the Arkansas Philological Association*), Emil A. Mucchetti sees as the link between the lovers mentioned in ll.288–94 the fact that their passion led them either to abandon *commune profyt* themselves or to cause others to do so. In the preceding ll.286–7, the moral culpability has been toned down in order to emphasise it in the following list.

Although the story of Ceyx and Alcyone, set in a 'better past', proved irrelevant for the narrator, nevertheless, despite the decline in the world from the Golden Age, Blanche and her knight show themselves as modern embodiments of *trowthe* and virtue. In 'Irony and the Age of Gold in the *Book of the Duchess'* (*Speculum*), John M. Fyler argues that in their story is found a partial consolation for the sorrow of a fallen world. Ieva Kronlins's 'The Still Point: Artifice in Chaucer's *Book of the Duchess'* (*Centerpoint*, 1974) emphasises the Narrator, the artificial structure, and the self-reflexive discussion of poetics among Chaucer's devices for distancing his subject and involving the audience in the poetic process. She is then led to an interpretation involving the Jungian process of the active imagination. Marc M. Pelen in 'Machaut's Court of Love Narratives and Chaucer's *Book of the Duchess'* (*ChauR*) discusses Chaucer's poem against the background of some of Machaut's works, finding it 'both derivative and innovative in its structures, imagery, and themes'. Writing on 'Chaucer's *Book of the Duchess:* An Art to Consume Art' (*DUJ*), David R. Aers maintains that until the end the Dreamer is unaware that the lady's death is real, since he believes that the knight's is a fictive grief. Velma Bourgeois Richmond suggests a link between 'Chaucer's *The Book of the Duchess* and *Guy of Warwick*' (*PLL*, 1975) in the Dreamer's questions concerning the Knight's lost lady.

In 'Chaucer's *fyn lovynge* and the Late Medieval Sense of *fin amor*'[22], Edmund Reiss demonstrates that *fyn lovynge* in the *Legend of Good Women* F 544 applies in all other Middle English instances to legitimate married love and to Christian charity. He suggests that the ideal evoked here increases our awareness of the inadequacies of love shown in the poem. A detailed examination of 'The medieval Cleopatra: the classical and medieval tradition of Chaucer's *Legend of Cleopatra*' (*JMRS*) leads Beverly Taylor to conclude that Chaucer has produced a 'highly ironic and condemnatory portrait' which depends on the perception of the mediaeval tradition, but plays against it.

At the end of his brief survey of secular court verse in England, 'The Vintner's Son: French Wine in English Bottles'[28], Rossell Hope Robbins hypothesises that, since Chaucer's court love-poems show the influence of the fashionable French *dits amoreux*, Chaucer may have composed, and gained his earliest reputation from, poems in French rather than English. Alfred David tells 'The Truth about "Vache"' (*ChauR*) to correct David E. Lampe's partial view of the word's significance (*YW* 54.123).

In three parts Sigmund Eisner provides instructions for 'Building Chaucer's Astrolabe' (*Journal of the British Astronomical Association*, 1975 and 1976).

[28] In *Eleanor of Aquitaine*, ed. by William W. Kibler. Symposia in the Arts and the Humanities, No.3. Austin, Tex. and London: U. of Texas P. (1976). pp. xv + 183.

VI

The Earlier Sixteenth Century

R. E. PRITCHARD

Prose

Among the most valuable books to appear during the year was Volume 12 of the Yale Complete Works of St Thomas More, *A Dialogue of Comfort against Tribulation*[1]. The introductory section provides a definitive account of the text and history of the book, by Louis L. Martz, together with versions of his earlier discussions of the design of the *Dialogue,* and 'The Tower Works'. In the first essay, Martz shows how More's art, that seems informal and extemporaneous, in the end reveals a firm structure and design; in the second, Martz analyses the *Dialogue* to show the progress, from the first book's reassertion of familiar, traditional views, through the second book's more entertaining emergence from theory into engagement with the world of everyday actuality, to the third book's encounter with the problem of persecution, and emphasis on the art of meditation, moving towards the contemplation of the Passion. Then J. F. Manley provides an interesting and convincing analysis of the three books in terms of the three virtues of faith, hope and charity – the faith that enables us to see suffering as 'a caress of God', the hope that enables us to resist temptation and have hope of heaven, and the charity that is related to grace, and associated with various aspects of the Passion. He also has a valuable essay on 'The Audience'. First, he deals with the historical and symbolic significance of the Turks, for More's contemporaries; then with More's family and friends; and then with the significance of the work for More himself. His analysis of More's use of scriptural quotations and allusions offers valuable insight into More's thinking during this last period. The volume also includes a splendid commentary, with textual notes and glossary.

Essential Articles for the Study of St Thomas More[2] provides a selection of articles dating from 1892 to 1972, with some specially written for this volume; it excludes articles that have been collected elsewhere, or that appear in the Yale *Complete Works*. The articles are arranged in four sections – fifteen biographical studies, nine on *Utopia*, thirteen on other works, and ten of general views. Of particular interest and value for the literary student are, in the first section, M. A. Anderegg's and R. S. Sylvester's discussions of early More biographies. In the second section there is an excellent review article by Arthur Barker on the Yale volumes of *Utopia* and *Richard III*. P. Albert Duhamel's discussion of the medi-

---

[1] *A Dialogue of Comfort against Tribulation,* The Complete Works of St Thomas More, Vol. 12, ed. Louis L. Martz and Frank Manley. New Haven, Conn. and London: Yale U. P. (1976). pp. clxvii + 566.

[2] *Essential Articles for the Study of St Thomas More,* ed. R. S. Sylvester and G. P. Marc'hadour. Hamden.: Archon Books. (1977).

aevalism of *Utopia*, relates it to the Scholastic Method, and shows its connection with Aristotle, Plato and Aquinas's *Contra Gentiles*. Elizabeth
McCutcheon offers an analysis of Litotes in *Utopia*. In the third section,
L. F. Dean and A. N. Kincaid have useful discussions of irony and of
dramatic structure in *Richard III*. The fourth section is less useful; in it
are Chesterton's encomium, Robert Bolt's preface to *A Man for All
Seasons*, and an extraordinary piece by G. Marc'hadour that explores
the various possible puns on, and associations of, the words 'Thomas
More'. In short, not all the articles deserve to be called 'essential', but
this remains a useful volume.

In *Moreana* (Nos. 55–6), John X. Evans argues that *Utopia* is less
concerned with an ideal political state than with the kingdom of God in
'the good and genuinely Christian heart'; thus many of the practices in
Utopia are defensible, the limitations of reason without grace are apparent, and the work looks for spiritual reformation rather than for political
revolution. Lee Cullen Khanna discusses 'The Images of Women in More's
Work', emphasising the sympathetic presentation of intelligent and virtuous women, and implicit or explicit criticism of anti-feminist values
and prejudices, in the *Utopia, Richard III* and the *Dialogue of Comfort*.
More's neo-mediaeval jokes about women are not discussed.

Alvin Vos continues his discussion of Ascham's prose (*PQ* Vol. 55),
arguing that while Ascham employed many of the rhetorical figures
that Lyly was later to take to excess, his purposes and methods were
different. While Ascham is sometimes insufficiently formal, where he
is excessively stylised this is due, Vos suggests, to an incomplete mastery
of technique. In general, as Vos demonstrates, 'the extensive parallelism
. . . is handmaid to the thought': schematisation is employed for clarification of thought, to assist comparison, analysis and judgement; of course,
not all subjects lend themselves to, or benefit from, the techniques of
parallel and contrast. Anne Drury Hall, in 'Tudor Prose Style' (*English
Literary Renaissance,* Vol. 7), discusses the struggle, in early Renaissance writers' discussions of style, between, on the one hand, their desire
for a central, clear and socially-cohesive standard in style and usage and,
on the other, their sense of linguistic variety and change, and of the
need for the extension of language to provide for new concepts and
circumstances. After a full and useful outlining of the to-and-fro of the
debate in the sixteenth century, she points to Jonson in *Discoveries* as
seeming truly central, mediating between the 'rules' and the 'publicke
riot', working towards a decent, urbane and civilising style.

Poetry

In *Moreana* (No.53) Frederic B. Tromly discusses More's 'A Ruful
Lamentation', suggesting that More, by means of dramatising the speaking
voice (speaking as from the tomb) of the dead Elizabeth York, Henry
VIII's queen, extends the didactic convention of contemporary elegies,
so that the poem transforms *contemptus mundi* materials into an elegy
that combines pathos with an implicit celebration of the subject's virtue,
producing an exhortation not merely to die well, but to live well. In
No.55, Charles Clay Doyle continues discussion of the Aesopic background

of More's *Epigrams*, relating them to versions in de Vitry's *Exempla*, Gobius's *Scala Celi*, and the *Mensa Philosophica*; these Aesopic fables were, as he indicates, the common poperty of early sixteenth-century Europe.

Helen V. Baron, in *The Library* (Vol.31), has a most interesting discussion of the manuscript of Wyatt's 'What rage' (familiar from being reproduced in Muir's edition). She shows the importance of the fact, not noted by earlier editors, that the MS. shows two colours of ink, and suggests three stages in composition. Of interest for other Wyatt poems is her discussion of the lines 'In diepe wid wound the dedly stroke doth torne/to curid skarre yt neuer shall retorne'; while Nott read these lines as, 'The stroke made a wound which, though cured, leaves a scar that never can be removed', Baron argues for Wyatt inverting the word-order (as in 'Tagus fare well, ll.1–6, and 'When Dido' ll.41–5), and reads 'The deadly stroke doth turn in to a wide wound, that shall never more return in to a cured scar'. She also discusses some important reiterated words in Wyatt's poetic vocabulary, notably '(un)kind' and 'rage'. In *Studies in English Literature* (Vol. 17), L. Nathan relates the achievements of Wyatt and Surrey to the fifteenth-century courtly lyric tradition, with its conventional limitations. Wyatt, he suggests, extended these by being particular rather than general, purporting to deal with actual life and individuals; Surrey was less innovative. Nathan finds little of interest in 'The soote seson' (of which a more provocative account appears in Alastair Fowler's *Conceitful Thought,* Edinburgh, 1975), and points to the superiority of the 'Epitaph on Clere', because of its particularity, and the pathos of its 'restrained literalness'; unfortunately, he does not mention John Fuller's excellent brief account in *The Sonnet* (London, 1972).

Frederick Kiefer, in *Studies in Philology* (Vol. 74), discusses the relation between 'Fortune and Providence in the *Mirror for Magistrates'.* The ancient and mediaeval tradition of the dominance of Fortune was dissonant with modern moralists' emphasis on Providence; sometimes, as in some emblem-books, attempts were made to conflate Fortune with Nemesis, to suggest that it was an instrument of divine justice. Where the poets of the *Mirror* felt confident about the justice of God's ways, they emphatically denied the power of Chance, and restricted the role of Fortune in the narrative; conversely, where the protagonists' ends seemed unjust, then Fortune was made the presiding deity of the poem. Thus, the relation in the *Mirror* between Fortune and Providence varies according to the circumstances of the story.

VII

Shakespeare

DAVID DANIELL and ANGUS EASSON

1. Editions

Two additions to the New Penguin Shakespeare offer excellent editions of plays with problems. Emrys Jones, introducing *Antony and Cleopatra*[1], suggests it might be seen as an essentially small-theatre work and tackles the difficulty of how one grasps a work so extensive, so various, and so fluid. He finds a sceptical viewpoint established from the opening, so that, divided, we argue about Antony as his soldiers do. Like the sea, he suggests, whose presence is much felt in the play, reality is varying and the play strives to capture the moment of 'becoming' in history. Jones then examines how Shakespeare has used Plutarch, incorporating his source's ethical concern, yet also finding ways to convey the richness of anecdote, reminiscence and allusion. His consideration of the protagonists seems finely right, his moral judgements, unlike those of some critics (see individual plays, below), being suspended, as he argues the play's movement encourages us to suspend them. In textual matters, Jones is conservative. He notes fully in the commentary (IV.xii.21) Hilda Hulme's suggestions about 'spanieled me at heels' but retains F's reading, though he emends where sense clearly demands, e.g. III.xiii.77 ('Till from' for 'Tell from'), following Kenneth Muir. If *Anthony and Cleopatra's* problems are its form and the response expected from the audience, *The Two Noble Kinsmen's* are canonical and dramatic. N. W. Bawcutt's edition[2] reflects 'the increasingly firm conviction . . . that a substantial part of the play is authentically Shakespearian'. He suggests that Shakespeare and Fletcher may have planned the whole together and gives Shakespeare those parts of the play normally assigned to him. Bawcutt sees an emphasis on 'a dignified and serious treatment of admirable human beings responding to the pressures of fate and circumstance.' He stresses ritual and considers that the excellence of Act I would be recognised more if the rest of the play were by Shakespeare, since whatever gain there is in purely theatrical terms of variety and liveliness when Fletcher takes over, 'this is paid for by a loss in significance'.

The Hayden Shakespeare Series[3], published earlier in the United States, is now available here and offers for each title an Introduction, A Note on

[1] *Antony and Cleopatra*, ed. by Emrys Jones (New Penguin Shakespeare). Harmondsworth: Penguin Books. pp. 299. pb £0.75.
[2] *The Two Noble Kinsmen*, ed. by N. W. Bawcutt (New Penguin Shakespeare). Harmondsworth: Penguin Books. pp. 249. pb. £1.25.
[3] *Hamlet; Henry V; I Henry IV; Julius Caesar; Macbeth; A Midsummer Night's Dream; Othello; Romeo and Juliet*, ed. by Maynard Jack and Robert W. Boynton (Hayden Shakespeare). New York: Hayden, London: Butterworths.

the Elizabethan Theater, a Textual Note, Commentary on the text, In the Theater of the Mind (to help realise the play on stage, since the editors see few of their readers as likely to have easy access to performance), Study Questions, and Books, Records, Films related to the text. The Series is clearly designed for American high schools and there is a concern to make the plays 'relevant'. In *Julius Caesar,* for instance, it is pointed out not only that Brutus's tragedy is almost unbearable because it gives an aura of nobility to self-delusion but also that there is no better antidote against political or moral self righteousness than a thoughtful reading of the play. Texts are the earliest good ones, though some of the regularisations seem inconsistent: if Antonio becomes Antonius, why should Calphurnia be retained? The *1 Henry IV* and *Hamlet* volumes are mean and depressing to handle, meagre in comment and annotation. The short comments and extended questions at the end do nothing to open up the plays. For a similar adolescent audience, J. H. Walter's *Richard II*[4] is full, bright and attractive, with an unusual and lively brief bibliography, and no trace of the condescension which mars the Hayden. Balz Engler's edition of *Othello*[5] places a German prose translation on facing pages with the Pelican text. Introduction, notes and commentary are in German, the whole giving a very pleasing impression.

2. Textual Matters

SQ carries a memorial tribute to Charlton Hinman, the scholar who has perphaps done most to advance our knowledge of the First Folio's production: certainly the Hinman collating machine is the most important mechanical device yet brought to bibliographical analysis. Paul Ramsey answers two questions in the negative in 'Shakespeare and *Sir Thomas More* Revisited: or, A Mounty on the Trail' (*PBSA*, 1976): can we be sure beyond reasonable doubt that addition D is Shakespeare's? and should these pages be used as a literary and textual guide to Shakespeare's practice? He goes on to look at palaeographical, orthographical and literary cases in the light of his answers. Various aspects of the Quartos receive attention. Frank E. Haggard writes on 'Type-Recurrence Evidence and the Printing of *Romeo and Juliet* Q1 (1597)' (*PBSA*), while in the same journal Mary J. H. Gross looks at 'Some Puzzling Speech Prefixes in *Richard III*'. On '*Richard III* (Q1) and the Pembroke "Bad" quartos' (*ELN*), Karl P. Wentersdorf suggests, by looking at tag phrases and their clusters as evidence for a particular reporter, that the *Richard III* text came into existence at the same time as the other bad texts of 1592–94 associated with Pembroke's men. Two books not previously reviewed may usefully be mentioned here: Robert E. Burkhart's *Shakespeare's Bad Quartos* (1974, The Hague: Mouton), still not seen, and Kristian Smidt's monograph on the Quarto copy for *Richard III*[6]. Influenced by the 1965 article on 'The Text of *Richard III*' by E. A. J. Honigmann (who later developed its

---

[4] *The Tragedy of King Richard II*, ed. by J. H. Walter. Heinemann. pp. 246. £1.25.

[5] *Othello*, ed. by Balz Engler. Berne & Munich: Francke. pp. 328. 38 Sw. fr.

[6] *Memorial Transmission and Quarto Copy in Richard III: A Reassessment,* by Kristian Smidt (Norwegian Studies in English). Oslo: Oslo U.P., New York: Humanities Press (1970). pp 93.

ideas in *The Stability of Shakespeare's Text*), Smidt looks again at the question of memorial reconstruction, and although he is less unwilling than in his 1964 book to recognise such reconstruction, he still challenges the 'bad quarto' theory. He argues that the text is not straight from the theatre; that a comparison of Q with F that does not assume F the better text removes some of the stigmas of corruption; and that there are indications that Q was at least partly set from a sound manuscript. He claims common manuscript origins for Q and F, suggests that Q is closer to the play's sources in verbal points than F, and in the study's second part considers the copy for F. Jonathan H. Spinner on another 'Bad' Quarto investigates 'The Composition and Presswork of *Henry V*, Q1' (*Lib*). He identifies a single compositor, whom he takes to be the A described by G. W. Williams in his study of the *Romeo and Juliet* Good Quarto, though there are anomalies: was A changing his habits? or was he assisted by an apprentice? Spinner takes into account evidence of type shortages and the possibility that copy was brought to the printer's shop as it was being written down. In 'Punctuation and the Compositors of Shakespeare's *Sonnets*, 1609' (*Lib*, 1975), MacD. P. Jackson examines the question of what modifications the manuscript may have undergone in the printing-house–especially interesting since Eld also published the Quarto *Troilus and Cressida*. Jackson finds two compositorial patterns in the Sonnets and advances the hypothesis that the A and B who set *Troilus and Cressida* set this quarto as well.

On the First Folio, S. W. Reid looks at 'Some Spellings of Compositor B in the Shakespeare First Folio' (*SB*, 1976), since B's work on the seven plays he set in the Folio where the copy is known may help identify his share in portions of the Folio hitherto only tentatively assigned to a particular compositor, while his spellings may help identify the copy behind other Folio plays. Fifty-five words are examined and although Reid finds that some spellings hitherto considered useful to identify B's work or copy are unreliable, he does show how both assignment and copy can be clarified by this method. On two other compositors, John S. O'Connor's 'A Qualitative Analysis of Compositors C and D in the Shakespeare First Folio' (*SB*) concludes that C is the more careless of the two, although editors have tended to emend D's work more (because his errors are the more obvious when they come). O'Connor concludes that since C makes more frequent and more serious errors, future editors should examine C's pages more closely and emend more liberally. Another corrected proof page of the First Folio has been identified (*HLQ*), in the Huntington Library's 'Church' copy, *King Lear*, p. 297, by the same hand as the previously identified sheets of *Antony, Othello, Lear* and probably *Romeo*. On a later edition, James G. McManaway in 'New Discoveries in the Third Folio of Shakespeare' (*PBSA*, 1976) reports on evidence of reprinted sheets.

The nineteenth century is the concern of two other articles in *PBSA*. Peter James Ventimiglia considers 'Shakespeare's Comedies on the Nineteenth-Century New York Stage: A Promptbook Analysis'. He takes the eight most frequently produced and finds amongst other things the marked British influence on texts; cuts of classical allusion and indecorous language; stripping away of the subplot; scenes arranged according to theatrical convenience; a sense that despite all restorations some parts of Shakespeare were not possible for the stage. This is an engaging and careful piece. John W. Velz and Frances N. Teague report 'New Information about some Nineteenth-Century Shakespeare Editions from the Letters of John Crosby'. Crosby's letters, in the Folger Shakespeare Library, were reported on in *SQ* (1976) and these are now explored further.

D. J. Lake in 'The Date of the "Sir Thomas More" Additions by Dekker and Shakespeare' (*N&Q*) examines some verbal forms to suggest that the additions in both Hands D and E are later than 1600, even several years later. In a note in *SQ*, Sidney Thomas demonstrates that in *Romeo* IV. i.83, 'chapels' is a misreading not of a Shakespearean spelling, but of a spelling of the Q1 reporter or compositor.

3. Biography and Background

S. Schoenbaum's documentary life was reviewed with very proper enthusiasm two years ago (*YW* 56). Now comes *William Shakespeare: A Compact Documentary Life*[7] to answer perhaps the only complaint about the earlier work: that it was too large for handy reading. The facsimiles of the earlier version have mostly been omitted, though the text of many of them is given. Schoenbaum has also corrected errors and added new information and reconsidered evidence, so that, for example, he presents a new interpretation of the widow's portion. Documentation is now fuller. All Shakespeareans are Schoenbaum's debtors.

We are all Leslie Hotson's debtors too, but are more cautious about some of his demands upon us. *Shakespeare by Hilliard*[8] seeks to show that the miniature portrait of 'Unknown Man Clasping a Hand issuing from a Cloud', of which the Victoria and Albert museum has one version and Hotson himself now possesses the Castle Howard version, is none other than a portrait of Shakespeare pictured as Mercury clasping the hand of Apollo. To do this, Hotson proceeds in a style which is a mixture of detective-fiction teasing and dazzling quotation. The first tends to set up a resistance to what is being argued, the second to result in a sense of skimpy material being eked out. Hotson argues that we need to try to understand what the picture might mean to the Elizabethans. What we have is the device and invention of the sitter, an Impresa-portrait. The hand from the cloud is identified as divine and details of the portrait (hat, clothes) are built up to show that the sitter is figured as Mercury. Hotson then brings in the portrait of a Youth among Roses, which he has in the past identified as Mr. W. H. Not only is it Mr. W. H.'s portrait, it is Mr. W. H. as Apollo; it is Apollo's hand in the Howard miniature; the year is 1588; there is an exchange of gifts; and the Howard portrait is a picture of Shakespeare as Mercury. Certain pieces of evidence in Hotson's chain of argument are perfectly acceptable: the poet as Mercury and, from the Folio verses, the idea of Shakespeare as Mercury the poet. But, as Hotson's own wealth of citation shows, such an idea was so commonplace

---

[7] *William Shakespeare: A Compact Documentary LIfe*, by S. Schoenbaum. Oxford: Clarendon Press. pp. xix + 376. hb £6.75.

[8] *Shakespeare by Hilliard: A Portrait Deciphered*, by Leslie Hotson. Chatto & Windus. pp. 210. £6.50.

that a Mercury-link between Shakespeare and the portrait can be only of the most tenuous, while that the sitter is presented as Mercury is readily challenged — the black and white clothes of the Youth among Roses identify him (for Hotson) as Apollo, yet the same colours identify the Howard sitter as Mercury.

S. Schoenbaum writes on 'A New Vertue Shakespeare Portrait' (*SQ*), a miniature, apparently of 1734, based on the Chandos portrait and unusual in being in profile; the portrait also appears on the dustjacket of Schoenbaum's compact version of the life. G. P. V. Akrigg supplements his book, *Shakespeare and the Earl of Southampton* (1968), by 'Something More about Shakespeare's Patron' (*SQ*), the Earl's name appearing on a French agent's list of the religious affiliations of English noblemen (the agent either knew nothing about Southampton or thought him an atheist), while part of the Earl's personal correspondence amongst the Newcastle Papers is described; nothing bears directly on Shakespeare. Although the Shakespearean link is tenuous, Wallace Shugg's 'Prostitution in Shakespeare's London' (*ShakS*) is worth mentioning, both for its gathering of material (e.g. Stowe's listing of regulations which include, 'No single woman to take money to lie with any man, but shee lie with him all night till the morrow') and its scholarly approach.

John Mortimer's *Will Shakespeare: an Entertainment*[9] is the book of the six television plays on Shakespeare's Life brought to birth by Britain's ITV and US advertising backers, and thus horrendous enough, even if delivered by John Mortimer. Here are 'the stories of those plays' tricked out, complete with every Hollywood 'Elizabethan' cliché there is ('So through piled apples and between hanging sides of beef and under cartwheels the chase continued . . .'). With relief, one turns to the late Robert Speaight's *Shakespeare: The Man and his Achievement*[10] — only to run straight into the Sonnets as 'the record of a personal experience': that they were not such a record but were written within a literary convention, he says, 'no responsible commentator believes today'. (See the notes on Stephen Booth under The Sonnets, below.) Speaight's judgements are, alas, arbitrary and shallow throughout this long book. Occasional references to performances (Speaight was an actor) are illuminating: but the book has little value compared with Schoenbaum's monumental, accurate, balanced, and even more readable *Documentary Life*. It is sad to see Speaight accepting Emilia Lanier as Shakespeare's 'Dark Lady'. He has not noticed Mary Edmund's calm correction of A. L. Rowse's misreading of the Forman MS. Simon Forman did *not* say that that woman was dark, and so Rowse's whole edifice collapses. Which brings us straight to the question of the ethics of publishing. Weidenfeld and Nicolson have produced, in *Shakespeare the Elizabethan*[11] one of the most handsome books I have ever seen. The abundant illustrations are ravishingly done, many in splendid colour, and many not normally seen. The text is written

[9] *Will Shakespeare: an Entertainment,* by John Mortimer. Hodder & Stoughton. pp. 256. £4.25.

[10] *Shakespeare: The Man and his Achievement,* by Robert Speaight. J. M. Dent. pp. 384. £6.50.

[11] *Shakespeare the Elizabethan,* by A. L. Rowse. Weidenfeld & Nicolson. pp. 128. £4.95.

by a historian of high standing. Yet over one sixth of the book is simply
not the truth, not history at all, but arrogant and ignorant fiction. Did
the publishers not know this? The author is A. L. Rowse, who presents
as historical truth, entirely from his own wilful misreading of the Sonnets
and Simon Forman, a vast imaginary edifice of a homosexual relationship
between Shakespeare and Southampton, into which come Marlowe and
Emilia Lanier. Even the beautiful pictures become suspect in their captions
– 'Forman visits the Dark Lady', 'The Dark Lady consults Forman'
(two pages of Forman's MS). Worse, the pretty water-colour captioned
simply 'The Globe Theatre' and reproduced on the back of the jacket,
sitting among all those splendid facsimiles, is a modern impression only
(acknowledged at the back of the book 'after Visscher: Rainbird Publishing Group, London') – and incidentally it makes the Globe (ITV made the
same mistake) look as if it barely held thirty-five people, not the 3500
it did. Part of Hollar is (excellently) reproduced, but someone should
have pointed out that the names of the two theatres are transposed.

A distinct oddity is *Giants of Literature: Shakespeare*[12], the English-
language edition of an Italian book, written in a tuppence-coloured style,
but with good illustrations, including some of infrequently reproduced
paintings.

So on to *terra firma* with a paperback reissue of Marchette Chute's
Shakespeare of London[13], first published in 1950, when Muriel C.
Bradbrook said in these pages that it was designed for American college
students 'and has successfully achieved its aim'. Miss Chute's ten-page
Appendix on 'The Legends' is admirably judicious. The Bibliography
has not been touched, and is now so out of date as to have a grotesque
antiquarian interest.

4. General Criticism

Not previously noticed, Leo Salingar's *Shakespeare and the Traditions
of Comedy*[14] was originally to have been on Shakespeare's comedies, with
some discussion by way of preliminary on the traditions. In the event,
Salingar found he had to explore the traditions fully and so while the
book is always tied in with Shakespeare, the point to which he is eventually driving, it stands also as earnest of the study still to come. Starting
from the familiar concept of the stage, and comedy in particular, as a
mirror up to life, Salingar notes the differences here between dramatic
theory and practice, before finding in the comic celebration with its
pastime and revelry a kind of borderland between everyday life and the
stage in which 'episodes and structural motifs in Shakespeare's comedies
are situated'. Various main topics (further broken down within the
chapters) are treated: mediaeval stage romances; 'errors', deceit, and
fortune in classical comedy; Shakespeare and Italian comedy; the Elizabethan playwright. Some discussions seem more strictly relevant than

[12] *Giants of Literature: Shakespeare*. Sampson Low. pp. 135. £2.75.
[13] *Shakespeare of London*, by Marchette Chute. Souvenir Press (E&A) Ltd.
pp. xii + 397. hb £4.95, pb £3.50.
[14] *Shakespeare and the Traditions of Comedy*, by Leo Salingar. Cambridge:
C.U.P. (1974). pp. x + 356. hb £15.

others: while New Comedy clearly has roots in the Old, Shakespeare has no connection with Aristophanes. But when Salingar looks, for instance, at *The Comedy of Errors* in the mediaeval tradition of Gower and story-telling, he shifts our perception of it from a classically-based comedy to that of a romance play, deriving from Gower but also from a native tradition of romantic drama. An always useful, often exciting book, which, through the traditions, explores Shakespeare in a critically sugges-tive way that makes us eagerly await the work on Shakespeare's comedies.

Two collections of essays by noted Shakespeareans should be recorded. Kenneth Muir's volume[15] reprints fourteen pieces, spanning 1947–76, of which nine involve Shakespeare. Even those published some time ago are not always easy of access (e.g. 'Some Freudian Interpretations of Shakes-peare' from *PLPLS*, 1952), while two pieces only now come to hand: 'This Side Idolatry', a discussion of Shakespeare's faults, and 'The Singu-larity of Shakespeare', which asks, in the context of an international gathering, 'if we strip Shakespeare of his poetry, does enough remain to justify his position as the greatest of dramatists?'. Muir's prose is work-a-day and his presentation can be skimble-skamble, but there is always sense and there are some flashes of light, as on the bedtrick in *Measure for Measure* in the first of the new pieces. Harry Levin[16] offers sixteen pieces (including one on Marlowe) plus two appendages – an afterpiece written with G. Blakemore Evans, exposing the absurdity of the 'Oxford' author-ship, and a very winning 'Induction', recounting his own experience of Shakespeare from a child, through instruction by Kittredge ('Kitty' – who also figures in *Teaching Shakespeare,* reviewed below) and the more exhilarating influence of E. E. Stoll, to his own teaching. The essays date between 1946 ('Falstaff Uncolted') and 1975 ('The Underplot of *Twelfth Night')* but unlike Muir, Levin not only provides precise references to quotations (following up a Muir lecture could be a frustrating business), he also takes account of work since first publication. A useful collection by a subtle and persuasive interpreter.

An elegant, often suggestive and perceptive study, F. W. Brownlow's *Two Shakespearean Sequences*[17] may seem based on rather odd organis-ation and certainly not all the connections claimed between the early plays and the late plays make the book cohere. But the real organising principle is found in Hamlet's advice to the players: Brownlow claims that to show 'the very age and body of the time his form and pressure' moulds the plays as well as being needful to our reading of them. He explores both how Shakespeare responded to that age and body and how we can perceive the form and pressure. Brownlow's aim (much of it successful) embodies this desire to be historically exploratory and yet also critically responsive here and now. He also draws on our sense of Shakespeare himself who, however elusive, is individually present in his own work, arguing that 'a poetic dramatist is an authority showing in his

---

[15] *The Singularity of Shakespeare and Other Essays,* by Kenneth Muir. Liverpool: Liverpool U.P. pp. 235. £9.75.

[16] *Shakespeare and the Revolution of the Times: Perspectives and Commentaries,* by Harry Levin. New York: O.U.P. (1976). pp. 324.

[17] *Two Shakespearean Sequences: Henry VI to Richard II and Pericles to Timon of Athens,* by F. W. Brownlow. London and Basingstoke: Macmillan. pp. 245. £7.95.

work things perhaps not otherwise knowable' and that, like Hamlet, Shakespeare shows himself to have an empirical, experimenting mind. The first sequence deals with *Henry VI, Richard III, King John,* and *Richard II;* the second with *Pericles, Cymbeline, The Winter's Tale, The Tempest, Henry VIII, The Two Noble Kinsmen,* and *Timon of Athens,* Brownlow urging for this last that it is perhaps truly Shakespeare's final play, unfinished at his death, though his critical argument is not dependent on chronological sequence. On *Henry VI* he writes well on the problems of shaping material from Hall's chronicle and the handling of the Tudor myth, arguing that the trilogy was planned as a whole and suggesting (see Emrys Jones on *The Origins of Shakespeare*) that the original idea was probably to mount a secular, up-to-date version of the mystery cycles. Brownlow illuminates apparently isolated episodes like that of the Countess of Auvergne in *I Henry VI* when he relates it to the sequence's depiction of the baleful influence of women. Again he is excellent on *Pericles* and *Cymbeline* as tales, and while not claiming the latter as successful he directs us to our re-reading by showing the way it requires suspension of involvement or detachment in favour of sympathetic curiosity. *The Tempest,* now falling well behind as Shakespeare's 'last' play, is not a play about an artist, but a magician (a useful corrective, still needed); *Henry VIII* is infused with irony — a convincing reading of a puzzling play. Brownlow's main theme never swamps his individual readings, which are as valuable in isolation as in sequence.

Not previously noticed is Harriet C. Frazier's *A Babble of Ancestral Voices*[18], which interestingly examines the evidence for Theobald's authorship of *The Double Falsehood.* Frazier rejects, too scornfully perhaps, linguistic evidence (it is just such fingerprints that might betray Theobald or even, just possibly, reveal Shakespeare or one of his contemporaries) but is usefully original in concentrating upon the play's context. She shows first of all that Theobald had all the period knowledge necessary to the production of the play (though she exaggerates, surely, when she speaks also of Theobald's 'remarkably sound' editing of Shakespeare's text) and plays a trump when she examines Theobald's 1715 Shakespeare imitation, *The Cave of Poverty.* Interesting again is the demonstration of the eighteenth century's interest in Cervantes and of possible influences in the choice of the Cardenio episode through French playwrights and Aphra Behn. Though detail and emphasis can be disputed, Frazier does show that Theobald had sufficient knowledge of Shakespeare and his age, had sufficient poetic skill, and was sufficiently attuned to his own times' interest in Cervantes as to be almost certainly the author of *The Double Falsehood* in its entirety.

Richard Levin follows up his earlier article (*YW* 1975) in 'Refuting Shakespeare's Endings, Part II' (*MP*), being concerned now with a modern tendency not simply to see ironies at the close but to refute the plays' final judgements, a process which demands 'nothing less than a transvaluation of the "apparent" values of the play'. The arguments are based not on questions of the dramatist's failure of intention, which Levin accepts

[18] *A Babble of Ancestral Voices: Shakespeare, Cervantes and Theobald,* by Harriet C. Frazier (Studies in English Literature, LXXIII). The Hague and Paris: Mouton (1974).

as arguable, but on the claim that Shakespeare intended the opposite of what the play's ending and the audience's common understanding have always seemed. Levin considers various strategies of these 'reversing' critics: analogy by which characters are denigrated (e.g. Pistol and Henry V); thematic homogenisation; external standards applied ruthlessly; ideas of the times (see also Levin's contribution to *Mosaic*, noticed below); revelation of secret codes (the examples on *Antony and Cleopatra* at once amuse and appal). Levin's views are salutary and should be pondered by us all. Rather different in approach is Charles Frey's 'Shakespearean Interpretation: Promising Problems' (*ShakS*), which questions whether there is little new to be said about Shakespeare. Frey finds both procedural and interpretative problems promising lines of future development, and hopes that teachers will encourage readers to acquire skill in interpreting all of Shakespeare for themselves. He also stresses the importance of Shakespeare's power of making us see things, and hopes for more exploration of truly dramatic progressions within the plays, as opposed to residual, post-play concepts. One of Frey's hopes is pursued by Elliot Krieger's 'Shakespearean Crossroads: Teaching Shakespeare through Induction' (*CE*), where the need is urged for the teacher not to state (deductive method) but to point and to allow for possibilities; examples are taken from *1 Henry IV* and *Macbeth*. Another pedagogical exercise is Kenneth J. Zahorski's 'The Next Best Thing . . . Shakespeare in Stereo' (*CE*) which discusses the playing of tapes or records followed by teaching sessions (see also *King Lear*, below).

The problem of 'structure' as a critical term is the concern of Volker Schulz in 'Conflicting Ideas of "Structure" in Literary Criticism: Reflections Based on Examples Taken from Shakespeare' (*EA*), an interesting challenge to structuralism. After considering the linguisticians' 'structure' he shows the difficulty encountered by such an idea of system when describing complex 'structures' like dramatic or narrative, exemplifying this from Sourian's structuralist reading of *Othello*. In a discussion of Sonnet 129 Schulz argues that '"structuralist" practical criticism itself disproves the notion of the literary work as a "structure", in the sense of "system"', and concludes that two different concepts of 'structure' that exist in literary criticism need to be distinguished. Less interesting is Paul N. Siegel on 'Marx, Engels, and the Historical Criticism of Shakespeare' (*SJW*), who points with admiration to Marx's and Engels's anticipation of contemporary historians (Marxist historians, oddly enough) and suggests that their passing remarks on Shakespeare give insights unknown to commentators of their own times. Unfortunately Marx and Engels wrote little about Shakespeare – Marx saw Shylock as a capitalist of 'naked self-interest' and Belmont as a 'feudal, patriarchal idyllic' picture of Christian society (contrast A. L. Morton's comment, below); his most important and extended commentary is on Timon's gold, which also provides Anne Paolucci with a text in her *Mosaic* essay. To include Engels on the basis of an allusion to Falstaff seems either an obsession with completeness or a species of desperation. More fruitful is Maqbool Hasan Khan's 'Shakespeare's Self-Revelation: A Critical Theme in the Nineteenth Century' (*Aligarh Journal*), a consideration of the approach to Shakespeare through his life (as distinct from constructing his biography from the plays).

Nicholas Brooke's British Academy Shakespeare lecture on 'Shakespeare and Baroque Art' (*PBA*), looks particularly at Bernini and his St Teresa in the Cornaro Chapel: Brooke analyses the total theatrical conception of the chapel and suggests how this may relate to features of Shakespeare's own baroque art.

Papers presented at a 1976 seminar on Shakespeare and Women are printed in *SJH*; Ursula Püschel writes on the women characters in relation to aspiration and human dignity ('Lebensanspruch und Menschenwürde: Shakespeares Frauengestalten'); Arthur Leslie Morton (the only English language contribution reproduced) considers 'The Situation of Women in Shakespeare's Time', which offers no new historical information, though he suggests that feudal not bourgeois marriage is depicted and condemned in *Romeo and Juliet* and argues that Shakespeare again and again asserts the potential equality of women, even of 'the repellent Portia'; Armin-Gerd Kuckhoff on the 'evil women' ('Versuch über die "bösen Weiber" bei Shakespeare') looks at Regan and Goneril, Margaret of Anjou, Tamora, and Lady Macbeth, amongst others; while the journeying Shakespeare heroine is Ljuben Groiss's concern in 'Shakespeares Frauen Unterwegs'; Christa Gottschalk talks as an actress of roles she has played in 'Meine Erfahrungen mit Shakespeares Mädchen- und Frauengestalten'; Hans Henning looks at Heine's book of 1838, *Shakespeare's Girls and Women* in 'Heines Buch über Shakespeares Mädchen und Frauen': and Rolf Rohmer sums up the results of the conference ('Zum Ergebnis unserer Tagung').

Ina Schabert tackles the interesting topic of use of rhyme in 'Zum Reimgebrauch in Shakespeares Dramen: Reimende Personen und reimender Autor' (*SJH*) and more specialised problems of Shakespeare's language arise in Eva Walch's consideration (*SJW*) of the practice and criticism of Shakespeare translation in East Germany ('Zur Praxis und Kritik der Shakespeare – Übersetzung in der DDR'), while Jaak Rähesoo in the same journal reviews 'The First Complete Shakespeare Edition in Estonian: Background and Perspectives'. This latter is particularly interesting (the Lear in Kozintsov's film, noticed elsewhere, is Estonian): the translation was published 1959-75, Shakespeare having been first played in Estonia in 1888 (*The Merchant of Venice*). Estonian is a language that has rapidly developed in this century, so that translations of the 1920s already seem archaic; it also tends to be a trochaic rather than iambic language. The bulk of this translation is by Georg Meri, and Rähesoo, despite reservations, clearly admires his work, though is more doubtful about the edition's critical apparatus. (On other translations see *Othello*, below). While on aspects of language, it is good to welcome the paperback edition of Hilda Hulme's *Explorations in Shakespeare's Language*[19] , reviewed here enthusiastically on its first publication (*YW* 1962). It is still posssible to feel the thrill of that Stratford moment when the witness utters 'arent the wich' (p. 17). The only pity is that Hulme has not incorporated any new work into this reprinting.

Hilton Kelliher reports on 'A Shakespeare Allusion of 1605 and its Author' (*BLJ*), contained in a letter from John Poulett of 1605, interesting because it substitutes a 'b' for 'p' ('Shackesbeare') and so may have

---

[19] *Explorations in Shakespeare's Language,* by Hilda M. Hulme. Longmans pp. xii + 351. pb £3.95.

bearing on the Revels Accounts' 'Shaxberd'. There is a photograph of part of the letter. On comparative matters, David Gervais reminds us in 'James's Reading of *Madame Bovary*' (*CQ* 1976) that Flaubert was re-reading *King Lear* as he came to the end of the novel, while Manfred Pauli comments on Sean O'Casey's attitude to tradition in '"Mein Freund Billy Shakespeare"': Anmerkungen über Sean O'Caseys Verhältnis zur Tradition' (*SJW*). A special issue of *Mississippi Folk Register* (1976), edited by Philip C. Kolin, was devoted to Shakespeare and Folklore; this was not seen, but includes articles on unnatural birth; *Macbeth; Othello; The Merry Wives;* and *The Tempest.*

In '"Now Mercy Goes to Kill"': Hunting in Shakespearean Comedy' (*DUJ*), R. S. White looks usefully at the ways the terminology and visual presentation of hunting are used to illuminate or complicate the love plot in the romantic comedies. He is excellent on the tone of *Venus and Adonis,* where the relationship between the love of hunting and the love of Adonis is shown not only to be related to the comedies but also more subtly complex than usually admitted. White writes well on *Love's Labour's Lost* and *As You Like It,* while he finds *Twelfth Night* the play that comes closest of these comedies to allowing the note of cruelty and privation in love to become dominant.

In 'Exaltation at the Close: A Model for Shakespearean Tragedy' (*MLQ*), Charles J. Sugnet, unable to accept the ideas of others, finds himself admiring rather than condemning the hero's behaviour, while remaining unconvinced that there is a benign order in the world of Shakespearian tragedy. Looking principally at *King Lear, Othello, Macbeth,* and *Antony and Cleopatra,* Sugnet divides the characteristic tragic career into three parts: the hero's presentation as an 'iconic' figure dependent on external sources of value; next, destruction of the icon to reveal a confused, suffering human being; last, admirable, exalting return to the hero's original forms of behaviour. During a general discussion, 'I Love You. Who Are You? The Strategy of Drama in Reception Scenes' (*PMLA*), Helene Keyssar draws examples from *King Lear.* Not unrelated to Sugnet's responses is James Kinnaird's analysis, 'Hazlitt and the "Design" of Shakespearean Tragedy: A "Character" Critic Revisited' (*SQ*). Kinnaird argues that when discussing the four great tragedies Hazlitt 'was engaged in a critical enterprise that his later reputation has tended to obscure and distort'. Hazlitt offers a larger study of dramatic imagination than is comprehended simply in 'character' study, demonstrating an interworking of contrast, analogy, intensive passional movement and perspective. The audience is worked upon, Hazlitt suggests, our sense and desire of the opposite good being excited in proportion to the greatness of the evil.

Ralph Berry is guest editor for the 'Shakespeare Today' issue of *Mosaic;* not unexpectedly his introduction is concerned not only with Shakespeare's capacity always to escape from the category of immediate enquiry but also with an inter-relation of academic and theatrical, borne out in the collection that follows.

Jan Kott's 'The Tempest, or Repetition' (also available in French in *Tel Quel*), whatever one's reservations (e.g. whether Prospero is Shakespeare's last ruler), explores suggestively first the correspondence between the play's action and the American discoveries, finding 'the universal history' within the story's mythic perspective: second, it shows and then exploits the repetitions of the *Æneid,* though Knott finds a most bitter reading of Vergil, a repetition without purification. Alexander Leggatt on 'The Extra Dimension: Shakespeare in Performance' is concerned with what the (unstoppable) performance insists upon, effects not always noticed in the study, where we can linger over an idea; amongst others he cites Aaron's silent presence throughout the first act of *Titus Andronicus.* A much thinner piece is Michael Goldman's 'Acting Values and Shakespearean Meaning: Some Suggestions', which urges that we pay attention to Shakespeare as a writer for actors and the ways in which he uses actors to shape audience response. Daniel Seltzer launches an attack in 'Acting Shakespeare Now' upon large-scale productions, whether by the Royal Shakespeare Company or at Stratford, Ontario, which fail to elicit a range of emotional responses that the texts require. The aim of Maurice Charney is comparatively modest, but in 'The "Now Could I Drink Hot Blood" Soliloquy and the Middle of *Hamlet'* he hits the mark to reinforce Hamlet as the revenger, who is cruel, physical, forceful. An interesting and suggestive piece by Stephen Booth, 'Syntax as Rhetoric in *Richard II'* looks at Act I's involved syntax and how this produces a reaction to character which becomes dissipated later in the play. A structuralist reading is offered by Marjorie Garber in *'Cymbeline* and the Language of Myth', ingenious (perhaps excessively so at times) but persuasive and suggestive. She argues that the play's deep structure has something to do with deciphering 'seeming', and considers how we may read its riddles and dreams, beginning with boxes and chests, going on to caves, and finding underlying them the myth of Prometheus and Pandora. In 'Shakespeare Microscopic and Panoramic', Marvin Spevack considers Shakespeare's language in the light of work on his computer Concordance. Mention should be made here of Spevack's earlier work, both about the project in 'SHAD: A Shakespeare Dictionary'[20] (with H. Joachim Neuhaus, T. Finkenstaedt) and in 'A Shakespeare Dictionary (SHAD): Some Preliminaries for a Semantic Description' *(CHum,* 1975), jointly with H. Joachim Neuhaus; and the Concordance to which two new volumes have been added[21], plus its abridged version[22]. In *Mosaic,* Richard Levin amplifies one point of his objection to those who refute Shakespeare's ending (see above). In 'Shakespeare or the Ideas of his Time' he calls in question the value of studies of ideas which then proceed to apply them to the plays: he takes Lear's abdication, the ghost of old Hamlet, and Desdemona's runaway marriage, shows that the claims made on the basis of ideas of the time are factually incorrect, and suggests that Shakespeare 'is very careful to incorporate within the play itself the relevant ideas and attitudes that he wishes to govern his audience's response.'

[20] In *Computers in the Humanities,* ed. by J. L. Mitchell, Edinburgh: Edinburgh U.P. (1974).
    [21] *A Complete and Systematic Concordance to the Works of Shakespeare,* by Marvin Spevack. Hildesheim and New York: Olms. 6 vols. 1968–70. Vol 7 'Concordance to Stage Directions and Speech-Prefixes' (1975); Vol. 8 'Concordance to "Bad" Quartos and "The Taming of a Shrew" and "The Troublesome Reign of King John"' (1975).
    [22] *The Harvard Concordance to Shakespeare,* by Marvin Spevack. Cambridge, Mass.: Harvard U.P. (1973).

Anne Paolucci's title, 'Marx, Money, and Shakespeare: The Hegelian Core in Marxist Shakespeare—Criticism', may suggest she has taken on too much: the most interesting section is a discussion of Marx on Timon's gold, handled much more subtly than Siegel's discussion noted above. The collection is rounded off by Carole McKewin who suggests in 'Shakespeare Liberata: Shakespeare, the Nature of Women, and the New Feminist Criticism' that feminist criticism is now less self-conscious and more closely related to the text, which she illustrates usefully. Altogether a number well worth reading and deserving of separate issue.

It takes five editors, not one of whom contributes an essay, to assemble *Teaching Shakespeare*[23], but if the cooks seem many, the fare is excellent, including some of the most illuminating essays on single plays this year. The essays share a concern for developing students' interests and skills beyond formal analysis. Robert B. Heilman in 'Shakespeare in the Classroom: Scientific Object vs. Immediate Experience', argues that the simple playing of records is no substitute for study, and if his style can be too 'clever', nonetheless he says useful things about not betraying Shakespeare. John W. Velz's 'Shakespeare Inferred' considers ways of encouraging students to move on their own beyond what the teacher has time or talent to do; D. Allen Carroll in 'The Presentation of Shakespeare' is concerned with the teacher as much as with Shakespeare. Norman Rabkin and Winfried Schleiner contribute to the second section, 'Shakespeare and the English Curriculum', the former on 'Shakespeare and the Graduate English Curriculum' (almost the whole book is concerned with American university students and teachers) and the latter on 'Deromanticizing the Shrew: Notes on Teaching Shakespeare in a "Women in Literature" Course', arguing that Kate in *The Shrew* is not romantic. Part Three, 'The Course in Shakespeare: Genre and Canon', offers excellent discussions of *Measure for Measure*, *Macbeth*, *King Lear*, and the early comedies by, respectively, A. C. Hamilton, Albert Wertheim, Paul M. Cubeta, and David M. Bergeron, who illuminate the problems of teaching as they explore or renew the play; one would like to be taught by any or all of them. The two longest essays come in Part Four: 'Exemplary Approaches to Particular Plays', and Ray L. Heffner Jr's 'Hunting for Clues in *Much Ado about Nothing*' might with advantage go to the barber's with Polonius' beard. Although often interesting, it seems to have little connection with teaching as such. Brian Vickers writes on 'Teaching *Coriolanus*: The Importance of Perspective', a powerful argument for Coriolanus himself, rightly stressing Volumnia's appalling breaking of her son. In Part Five the most suggestive essay is Bernard Beckerman's 'Some Problems in Teaching Shakespeare's Plays as Works of Drama'. Jay L. Halio in '"This Wide and Universal Stage": Shakespeare's Plays as Plays' is right to stress performance as a way to get across the idea that there is no one fixed version, but says little about the plays, while G. Wilson Knight's 'The Teacher as Poetic Actor' is a version of a section from *Shakespeare's Dramatic Challenge*. Beckerman shows skilfully, using *Hamlet* as his example, how engagement in a theatrical performance is a necessary

[23] *Teaching Shakespeare*, ed. by Walter Edens, Christopher Durer, Walter Eggers, Duncan Harris, Keith Hull. Princeton, N.J. and Guildford, Surrey: Princeton U.P. pp. xv + 343. $13.50, £9.10.

adjunct to, but no sufficient substitute for, a critical understanding of dramaturgic behaviour. The whole is a most fruitful collection.

Anyone who is concerned for opera and its adaptation of literary works will find things of interest in Gary Schmidgall's *Literature as Opera*[24]. Its 'opening perspective' has Chabrier considering an opera on *The Tempest* (he wanted the love story expanded, 'otherwise papa Prospero would get to be a bore'), and Schmidgall uses this unrealised project to stress how when masterly literature is considered for opera 'literary values do not necessarily loom importantly in the process'. For Shakespeare, Schmidgall concentrates upon Verdi and *Macbeth,* praising Verdi's sensitive response to the original and his 'unerring sense of precisely where theatrical interest resides'. He shows what in Shakespeare fits easily with the conventions of Verdi's own time: the structure of Lady Macbeth's first appearance is not unlike that of dramatic recitative, aria and cabaletta. Verdi's challenge, as Schmidgall proceeds to argue, was not to structure the opera but to reproduce the poetic impact of this memorable entrance. Schmidgall has incidental comments on *Falstaff, Otello* (including Rossini's), the pro- jected *King Lear*, and Britten's *A Midsummer Night's Dream*, and though he sometimes writes a little obliquely and some of his Shakespearean comments might be challenged, he should be given every credit for ven- turing so successfully into the minefield between literary criticism and musicology.

Film is an increasing concern of Shakespeareans, and Jack J. Jorgens[25] has written an excellent study of sixteen productions ranging in time from Reinhardt's *A Midsummer Night's Dream* (1935) to Brook's *King Lear* (1971). There is very little detail about choice of cast, problems in shooting, finding of locations, or costume design, though comments by directors and others (e.g. script details for *Julius Caesar* which were omitted in the final version) are included. Jorgens writes as an enthusi- ast in the best sense, his aims being to 'illuminate Shakespeare's plays by looking at various visions and revisions, translations and adaptations of them, and to help us understand and properly value cinematic works'. Jorgens is intensely aware both of Shakespeare's play and what is hap- pening to it in the visual translation, being descriptive and evocative, as on Reinhardt, where he brings out the Baroque multiplicity-in-unity, yet also technically aware, as when he observes how in Peter Hall's *Dream* the cutting of shots coincides with ends of lines or with caesuras. Zeffirelli's films of *Romeo and Juliet* and *The Taming of the Shrew* are liked (not uncritically, though he says nothing of the dramatically disastrous hand- ling of the Petruchio-Katherine wooing scene) and he strongly favours Welles' 'Chimes at Midnight' and 'Othello', characterising the latter film as one 'in which the images on the screen generate enough beauty, variety, and graphic power to stand comparison with Shakespeare's poetic images'. Sometimes memory must qualify Jorgens's response: parts of Reinhardt's *Dream* are fine, but it is disastrously caught in its time and Jorgens never notes that stage productions have the *advantage* of fading where films

[24] *Literature as Opera*, by Gary Schmidgall. New York: O.U.P. pp. xi + 431. £6.95.
[25] *Shakespeare on Film*, by Jack J. Jorgens, Bloomington, Ind. & London: Indiana U.P. pp. xii + 337. £11.25.

offer a fixed and (repetitively) static performance. There is no bibliography in view of a forthcoming one on *Shakespeare on Stage and Screen*, but cast lists are given, together with summaries of scene order and content. The photographs are blown up from frames rather than publicity stills, so that Jorgens could get the illustrative material he wanted. Though not seen, mention should be made of an issue of *Literature-Film Quarterly* devoted to Shakespeare on film.

The Introductions to each play in the Folio Society editions are now published in one volume[26], with some beautiful illustrations. Though disappointing on *Hamlet* (three miserable pages by Richard Burton) it is a book full of the unexpected, to be kept by the study armchair and picked up daily at tea-time. Flora Robson on *Winter's Tale* and her theory of affinities between the people of the play and those of Queen Elizabeth's childhood; Olivier on *Antony*, Wolfit on *Lear*, Hobson on *Measure*, Peter Brook on theatre and, incidentally, *As You Like It;* Brewster Mason on Falstaff, Nevill Coghill on *Romeo*, Gielgud on *Richard II*, Clifford Williams on *Comedy of Errors* — it is all good stuff. Possibly the most valuable to keep are Manfred Wekwerth and Joachim Tenschert of the Berliner Ensemble on *Coriolanus* and Terry Hands' loving and revelatory piece on *Merry Wives*.

Also unexpectedly good is David M. Zesmer's *Guide to Shakespeare*[27], which, though not so definitive as C.U.P.'s *New Companion*, covers similar ground and does it rather well. It has the faults and the virtues of a one-man book: some plays, one feels, are inadequately appreciated (*2 Henry VI*, for example) and there are odd remarks one wants to challenge. But Zesmer is knowledgeable, warm and witty. The notes to each chapter are full and sensible, though they should have included Schoenbaum for Chapter One, and the omission of Stanley Wells' *Bibliographical Guide* from the final list is a sin more than venial. The book is obviously aimed at the U.S. college market (more pages on *Romeo* than any other play) and it will do a lot of good there.

Kenneth Muir's long-awaited second volume of his Sources book[28] has of course been overtaken by Bullough: so he has sensibly completed his work in one thoroughly-revised volume, including new pages advising great caution in source-hunting. The whole book, however, is to this reviewer a little sterile. Muir is downright conservative about the authorship of the early histories, being numbered among the disintegrators of *1 Henry VI*, and thus ducking issues of source. Longest (and good) on *Richard II*, sensible on *King John*, he is up-to-date and judicious on *Hamlet*, though calling the influence of the disintegrators on Eliot 'baleful'.

In *ShStud*, Yoshiko Kawachi confirms the great stature of Malone in a well-documented study 'Edmond Malone and His Chronology of Shakespeare's Plays'. G. Wilson Knight's Jackson Knight Memorial

---

[26] *Introductions to Shakespeare, being the Introductions to the individual plays in the Folio Society edition 1950-76* with a foreword by Charles Ede. Michael Joseph. pp. 245. £6.95.
[27] *Guide to Shakespeare*, by David M. Zesmer. New York: Barnes & Noble. pp. viii + 472. pb $4.95.
[28] *The Sources of Shakespeare's Plays*, by Kenneth Muir. Methuen. pp. 320. pb £4.90.

Lecture[29] is entitled 'Vergil and Shakespeare' and honours the classical scholarship of his brother, while comparing the two great poets. John Dean's five-page monograph 'Shakespeare's Romances and Herodotus' Histories'[30] forces the issue. A worse sin is committed by Robert F. Willson Jr in his book *Shakespeare's Opening Scenes*[31] for he writes 212 pages of pedestrian statement of the extremely obvious, mostly simply telling the stories under fancy titles, so that *Love's Labour's Lost* is 'Utopia Violated' and *Romeo* is 'The Peacemaker's Failure' and *Tempest* 'The Boatswain's Rule'. His diagrams of staging cause hilarity. A little better is Jagodish Purkayastha's *The Tragic Vision of Life in Hamlet and King Lear*[32]. We have also received *Love and Marriage in Shakespeare* by Walter Dias[33].

Sometimes one is justified in wondering how certain books ever achieve print. We are told of John Arthos' *Shakespeare's Use of Dream and Vision*[34] that 'In these studies he refers the uses of dreams and visions and some allied matters to the metaphysics that the celebration called for in *The Phoenix and the Turtle* depends upon'. A five-page preface contains a lot of knowing remarks, largely incomprehensible ('The hope of Antipholus, Berowne's appeal to a Promethean fire, Valentine's conviction of transcendent union turn to ashes for the sixth Henry and the second Richard': 'Yet while we impose restraints upon any inclination we have to discover allegories we know that in these works thought is as profoundly engaged as it would be in philosophy, and as recalcitrant to reduction' are random, fair examples) some grotesquely mis-used punctuation and one crashing and elementary mistake of vocabulary ('discrete' for 'discreet'). The enormous first chapter has colossal notes, one six pages long, and the whole book is written with that exasperating supposedly-inclusive knowingness of the inner club. The book is *not* about Shakespeare's use of dream and vision. It is clever Mr Arthos making some very esoteric and unnecessary remarks about four plays of Shakespeare and a short poem.

How refreshing to turn to Francis Fergusson's gentle book *Trope and Allegory*[35], a brief and lucid exploration of some parallels between Dante and Shakespeare, nicely poised. Out of date on the Tudor Myth, and positively wrong about almost all the comedies, (Borachio is not seen climbing into Hero's window, for example), the book is so comfortable and open that these matters receive forgiveness. R. Kirkpatrick in *MLR* writes 'On the Treatment of Tragic Themes in Dante and Shakespeare',

[29] *Vergil and Shakespeare*, by G. Wilson Knight. Exeter: The University. pp.26. £0.50.
[30] *Shakespeare's Romances and Herodotus' Histories*, by John Dean. Salzburg Studies in English Literature. pp 5.
[31] *Shakespeare's Opening Scenes*, Robert F. Willson Jr. Salzburg Studies in English Literature. pp.217.
[32] *The Tragic Vision of Life in Hamlet and King Lear*, by Jagodish Purkayastha. Salzburg Studies in English Literature. pp.207.
[33] *Love and Marriage in Shakespeare*, by Walter Dias. New Delhi: S. Chand & Co Ltd. pp. ix + 368. Rs60.
[34] *Shakespeare's Use of Dream and Vision*, by John Arthos. Bowes & Bowes. pp. 207. £5.
[35] *Trope and Allegory*, by Francis Fergusson. Athens, Ga: The U. of Georgia P. pp.164. $10.50.

qualifying what we should understand as 'a dramatic quality'. Welcome is a second edition of Clemen's seminal book on imagery[36], with a new eleven-page introduction and minor changes, and an up-dated select bibliography.

In a journal called *Cithara* David Scott Kastan writes '"More Than History Can Pattern": Notes Towards an Understanding of Shakespeare's Romances', richly charting Shakespeare's progress from tragedy to romance, somewhat nervously dating the new transformation, where loss gives way to gain, in *Antony*. 'The key to the romance vision is the perspective that refuses to see tragic action as a fully-realized whole. The field of vision is extended so that tragedy is recognised merely as a component of a more comprehensive action that moves beyond, and through, suffering and harmony.' He gives weight to 'that perfect romance, the Corpus Christi Play'. Ingeniously and persuasively he argues for *Richard III* and *Henry VIII* as romance, and uses even the 'unresisting imbecility' of *Cymbeline* to show the patterns of innocence, fall, and redemption; the essential victory of the 'comic over and *through* the tragic'. It is a pity that St Bonaventure University could not have brought more responsible skills to the printing of this fine piece.

5. Shakespeare in the Theatre

Taking over from Peter Thomson, Roger Warren reviews the RSC season ('Theory and Practice: Stratford 1976', *ShS*) bearing in mind the advantages and disadvantages of a company committed to the work of a single dramatist: a new production can develop discoveries made in an earlier one, but the constant temptation is to avoid last time's solution, however successful. Trevor Nunn spoke of his distrust of academic clichés, an attitude which Warren feels had positive results, especially in *Macbeth*, though he challenges how far some of Nunn's statements were borne out in practice: the season did not suggest a company that had developed over several years and revealed none of the command of powerful middle-range talent the company once had, while the supporting players in *Macbeth* were so inept as to imperil entire scenes (Warren here, as elsewhere, quotes from newspaper reviews to offer opinions other than his own). *Romeo and Juliet* avoided the collapse half-way through so often fatal to the play, gaining in power and culminating in a superb, even moving final scene: Juliet began to move, unnoticed by Romeo, just before he took the poison, which intensified the pathos of the lovers' death. On *Much Ado about Nothing*, Warren would wish to see an Elizabethan production some time: out of six productions he has seen, five have been nineteenth-century. Yet he found that John Barton's Imperial India sharpened the distinction between the military and civilian worlds, though the church scene was not so effective, because there was in effect no congregation. Like most (but not all) commentators he praised Judi Dench and Donald Sinden in the leading roles. The three other main-house productions prompted Warren's thoughts about the problems of restricted repertoire. In *The Winter's Tale*,

---

[36] *The Development of Shakespeare's Imagery*, by Wolfgang Clemen. 2nd Edition. Methuen. pp. xvii + 237. pb £3.75.

Nunn carried over from his 1969 production the sudden switch of lighting to emphasise the fantasies that seize Leontes' fevered brain. The bear was a primitive folk emblem, an actor in a mask, guiding Antigonus off. The sense of effort to produce points showed in Bohemia. Altogether more problematical was John Barton's *Troilus and Cressida,* where the danger of a director's close involvement over several productions showed: because he knows it so well, Barton seemed sometimes to forget that what the audience needs is to have the main points of an exceptionally difficult text made as clear as possible. Features of the 1968 production were the nakedness of the Trojans and Myrmidons, a showily effeminate Achilles and a Thersites covered with bleeding sores and a mouth-shaped codpiece. *The Comedy of Errors,* which has been a great success in the past, took place in a cluttered Turkish market. Interpolated musical numbers were based on fragments of texts or specially supplied doggerel. Like most other reviewers, Warren's main enthusiasm is for *Macbeth* (at The Other Place) the best example of the company's developing work on a single work. Played without an interval and with outstanding performances from Judi Dench and Ian McKellen, who seemed husband and wife not only in passion but also in the quiet natural handling of their conversations, the production brought out a clash between religious purity and black magic, developed from the 1974/75 production. Warren concludes by noting that if the season 'was pretentious in theory but impressive in practice, that is surely very much the right way round'.

In *SQ* a new layout is adopted for the annual review of productions, which now includes compact production records, information as available about 1977's plans, and addresses for further enquiries. A number of accounts are compiled from or supplemented by newspaper reviews. Robert Speaight contributes what proved to be his last 'Shakespeare in Britain', since he died shortly afterwards. He catches up on the end of the 1975 Stratford season, when he saw Tony Church's production of *Richard III* (The Other Place), with Queen Margaret notable as a Chorus of moral condemnation. He reports the transfer of *Hamlet,* in London, to the new National Theatre building, where it was given entire in under four hours, unadventurous and a little dull. Claudius and the Ghost were doubled. Despite the present reviewer's deep reservations, there is no doubt about Speaight's enthusiasm for the St George's Theatre (see *YW* 1976): 'From now onwards no visitor can complain of Shakespeare's absence from the London playbills'. He describes the auditorium and the productions in superlatives: 'I have never seen a better production of *Twelfth Night*'; 'Alan Badel was the best Richard I have seen since Laurence Olivier', while *Romeo and Juliet* was also liked. At Stratford, Speaight welcomed the change of staging from the square black box to something more like the De Witt drawing of the Swan. In *Romeo and Juliet* only Ian McKellen's Romeo reached the high level he expected; *Troilus and Cressida* was interesting, but too fussy; while he notes in *The Winter's Tale* that the 'bear' carried a halberd and its severed head afterwards appeared in the hands of Time. Speaight found a notable improvement in speaking in all the Stratford productions.

Stratford 1976 is rounded off by Gareth Lloyd Evans's report on 'The RSC's *King Lear* and *Macbeth'* (*SQ*). He finds that economic constraint has proved artistic gain in the form of strong acting and unambiguous meaning. *King Lear,* in the main house, he found competent rather than triumphant, but *Macbeth* in 'one of the most exciting acting arenas in the United Kingdom' gave a sense of 'almost unbearable proximity to, and identification with, the world of the play'.

The reviews of North American productions are more extensive this year (though, ironically, economic pressures were expected to prevent some festivals being mounted in 1977). Particularly popular was *Henry V,* partly because of its celebratory qualities in the American bicentenary year, partly because of RSC's successful production (*YW* 1976), which played in New York: it was also the occasion for two of the silliest production ideas – in New York Joseph Papp had a muttering 'interpreter' throughout English/French encounters while New Jersey had all the French characters speaking in French, compounding boredom with atrocious accents and rhythms (no doubt productions of *Caesar* in Latin and *Timon* in Greek will follow!) Berners A. W. Jackson at the 'Stratford Festival, Canada' showed less enthusiasm for the proscenium stage than last year, though he found it a striking comparison when plays in the different auditoriums were seen on the same or successive days and he makes interesting observations about the different effects. *Hamlet* offered two Hamlets, each with his own Gertrude, which gave the opportunity to see the way the Prince affects the impact of the tragedy. Gertrude was deeply unhappy and sought a refuge in drink, while Berners could see no point in the pole to which Ophelia was strapped in her madness nor the resultant acrobatic activities (see Ralph Berry's *On Directing Shakespeare* below for Robin Phillips's discussion of such detail). *The Tempest* was more exciting, with Ariel white and attentive, like a tall bird, the Caliban twisted yet recognisably human. In *The Merchant of Venice,* Shylock was not softened but played as an angry and beset man, driven by hatred and a desire for revenge, while *Antony and Cleopatra* began as high comedy and ended as lyric tragedy, the protagonists two invincible egotists, dazzling performers on the world's stage. Last year's *Measure for Measure* was revived and *A Midsummer Night's Dream* doubled Theseus/Oberon and Hippolyta/Titania, the latter looking like Queen Elizabeth. The addition of newspaper reviews in *SQ* accounts helps to give perspectives on some of the productions described, though as always it is difficult to know by what standards any one festival is to be judged. At Monmouth, Maine, *A Midsummer Night's Dream, Antony and Cleopatra* (superbly mounted but disappointing performances), and *I Henry IV* were performed. At Champlain the company was amateur, *The Comedy of Errors* emphasising not merely farce but wonder and mystery: Dromio of Ephesus 'stuck his male member through a hole in the wall to prove his identity to the maids within' ('wonder'? 'mystery'?). In *Richard II* the deposed king offered no resistance to his killers. At the American Shakespeare Theatre a revival of *The Winter's Tale* again doubled Hermione and Perdita, while in *As You Like It* the English Rosalind's accent clashed with a New York Celia's. Maurice Charney in New York reviews the RSC's *Henry V* as well as a *Hamlet* which presented the Prince as an enraged Maoist, a Hamlet in the spirit of Timon. In Central Park's *Measure for Measure* the opening tableau presented a God-like Duke before whom the characters emerged from a trapdoor to form a frieze of purity or lechery, the Duke stage-managing the play. Elsewhere, at New Jersey, *The Tempest* began fifteen minutes before curtain up, with couples dancing on board a liner, the opening scene being cut entirely. The Alabama Shakespeare Festival had Antigonus pursued by a cuddly polar bear and used Mozart's music in the statue scene, while Nahum Tate quietly took over in the opening of *King Lear*, when Edgar was shown standing by Cordelia, 'mute but supportive'. Included amongst other non-textual gestures ('that have become almost commonplace', says the reviewer) was Oswald and Regan making love on a bear-skin rug throughout IV.v. At the Great Lakes *The Tempest* was remarkable for a living figurehead in the first scene and a black actress as Ariel, while *Romeo and Juliet* ended with the death of Juliet. Dallas has Free Shakespeare; not in John Russell Brown's sense, but without entrance charge, while at Odessa *A Midsummer Night's Dream* was all Bottom's dream: in the first scene Theseus and Hippolyta were bathing, the pool later providing Oberon's entrance, the mechanicals doubling as fairies, a bit like hobbits in coloured fake fur (*not* cute, we are assured). Colorado offered *King John* in a clear and open reading, as well as *The Tempest* and *The Comedy of Errors*. Stephen Booth has a long and important review of activities in California and Utah. He has strictures on a North American-Indian style *As You Like It* and praise for San Diego's *Othello* with a black actor able to show first a shadow Othello in a real world and then a real Othello in a false world. Reviews of *Troilus and Cressida* lead Booth to interesting comments on the playing of Thersites, while in Hamlet with Jon Voight he notes with approval Hamlet's 'Buzz, buzz' being taken as a stage direction for continued conversation (Elizabethan rhubarb), though he found Voight's playing a study of a leading role by an able and hard-thinking actor more interested in its dynamics than those of the whole play. He also notices the Shakespeare Society of America, one man's enterprise to stage the whole canon over three years: four plays are reviewed and cast-lists of two more given. The section is completed by Alan C. Dessen at Oregon who praises *The Comedy of Errors* as inventive and zany (Booth obviously loathed it), but found *II Henry VI* in cutting and in emphasising violence lost dramatic coherence, drive and sense. He has also a long and detailed discussion of *King Lear*. This year's summary of *SQ* may seem to emphasise oddities and eccentricities, but they seemed thick on the ground, though no doubt need for compression makes reviewers comment on unusual features and these festivals offer opportunities for experiment. *SQ* included in its Annotated World Bibliography the usual details of Productions, Staging and Stage History, and Festivals, while other publications like *ETJ* and *Plays and Players* include reviews of productions.

For Germany, Christian Jauslin surveys West Germany in 1976 (*SJH*): twenty plays are listed (though the entry under *The Merry Wives* is for Verdi's and Nicolai's operas only). *Twelfth Night* has nine productions, *Hamlet* five plus *Fratricide Revenged* and two other versions. East Germany in 1975 is covered by Armin-Gerd Kuckhoff (*SJW*), with twelve productions (only *Macbeth* of the major tragedies), photographs showing *The Merchant of Venice* and *Troilus and Cressida*.

Various articles treat aspects of production. John Turvey's 'Solving a

Problem Play' (*SJH*) records *Measure for Measure* in Greek, directed by a German, at the National Theatre of Cyprus, which he finds a producer's play; the production suggested an authoritarian state, where the Duke was a genial Father Christmas with justice in his sack and Isabella coarse, rancorous, self-absorbed, comic, stupid, hypocritical 'and only ultimately cynical'. In 'Brakedrums and Fanfares: Music for a Modern *Macbeth*' (*SQ*), John Duffy describes his experience in composing for a 1967 production and how the sounds wanted were achieved. Morris Carnovsky interviewed by Peter Sanders talks about 'The Eye of the Storm: On Playing King Lear' (*SQ*), which he did in three seasons at Stratford, Connecticut. He is interesting on his preparation and his response in action: at the end Carnovsky has no belief in Cordelia being alive, and finds the key to the interpretation of the role in 'Pour on, I will endure'. Elsewhere, Emrys James is interviewed by Michael Mullin in 'On Playing Henry IV' (*ThQ*). Some incidental remarks about Shakespearean production arise in Kenneth Tynan on 'Director as Misanthropist: on the Moral Neutrality of Peter Brook' (*ThQ*), while the running of a Shakespeare Festival is Homer Swander's theme in 'Shakespeare Gold in the Oregon Hills' (*SQ*), a tribute to Angus Bowmer who founded it forty-two years ago: the main theatre has Elizabethan characteristics and all productions are played without interval. (Bowmer's autobiography appeared in 1975[37].) Swander affirms 'The standards are professional, the budget is over a million dollars . . .'. He tells very little for the historian. For example, anxious to find out about how full a text of the *Henry VI* plays they played in 1953, one learns only that *Part One* was played in rain, which downpour gets five lines. Not a word about anything else, which is characteristic of the gushing nature of the piece.

More theoretical discussion is the concern of Joachim Kaiser's 'Geist und Buchstabe beim Shakespeare-Interpretieren' (*SJH*), on the letter and the spirit in Shakespeare interpretation, and of Hans-Joachim Heyse's 'Fragen der heutigen Shakespeare-Regie' (*SJH*), on problems of Shakespeare direction today. The different merits of film and theatre are considered usefully by J. L. Styan in 'Sight and Space: The Perception of Shakespeare on Stage and Screen' (*ETJ*). He does not see one medium as necessarily better nor that Shakespeare's images get lost when translated into visual images on the screen. His main concentration for examples is on Olivier's *Hamlet*. This ties in interestingly with Jorgens's book, noticed above.

Ralph Berry has interviewed seven directors and published the result as *On Directing Shakespeare*[38]. The book might have been more carefully prepared: not only is there no bibliography, but no notes are provided on the directors' careers or dates of the productions discussed, though some of these arise incidentally in the text. Nonetheless, this is a useful and often fascinating book. Berry feels that through the unique collective response of these people he may answer the question 'What *is* Shakespeare today?' (see the issue of *Mosaic* reviewed above). He is not concerned with technical details nor even with particular productions except by way of

[37] *As I remember, Adam,* by Angus Bowmer, Ashland, Oregon: Oregon Shakespeare Festival Association (1975).
[38] *On Directing Shakespeare: Interviews of Contemporary Directors,* by Ralph Berry. London: Croom Helm; New York: Barnes & Noble. pp. 135. £5.95.

illustration: he quotes with approval and sees as a kind of touchstone Jonathan Miller's 1971 statement that Shakespeare's plays have assumed the status of myth 'and it is the honourable fate of all great myths to suffer imaginative distortions at the hands of those to whom they continue to give consolation and nourishment'. The interviews vary: Jonathan Miller describes how he often begins from the inflation of a single line (compare Chinoy's account, *YW* 1976) and how his rehearsals proceed. Konrad Swinarski (one of the directors about whom necessary background information is not given) shows particularly how directors use Shakespeare today: he sees a homosexual contest between Bertram and Lafew to possess Parolles and in *A Midsummer Night's Dream* finds Shakespeare our Marxist contemporary. Still, the sense of someone at work is there, often fascinatingly, which is not the case, for instance, with Giorgio Strehler, whose factual knowledge of Shakespeare is odd and from whom nothing much about production comes across. Other directors include Trevor Nunn, Michael Kahn, Robin Phillips (see the review of his *Hamlet* in *SQ*, noted above), and Peter Brook — this last an excellent piece, balanced and often exciting, the interview being supplemented by an account of Brook's Paris production of *Timon of Athens*. Stanley Wells's *Royal Shakespeare*[39], a study of recent RSC productions, was not available for review.

More quirky, though not without its charms, is G. Wilson Knight's *Shakespeare's Dramatic Challenge*[40]. The book has at the back of it Knight's long experience of the stage and his own lecture/recitals; the frontispiece shows him performing Timon in 1976. The first part is the predominantly lecture material — the heroes, on poetic acting, and above all *Timon of Athens*. Wilson Knight remains true to his tragic idea that when a Shakespearian hero 'appears abrased or disintegrated, look for some grand reassertion': each character is 'run-through', and assertion about the effect and function of the verse is preferred to any close analysis, which can sink to the level of 'The Speech is one of universal interest and application'. Yet every so often comes a shaft of light, particularly when Wilson Knight gives personal details of how he tackled some line or gesture. Much on *Timon of Athens* is good, though the risible begins to break in when he describes his costuming for Timon: eventually Timon/Knight is to cast away even his loin-cloth, when the sexual organ becomes a problem, 'which flaps about regardless. Better to wear a small gold covering, suggesting Timon's soul-worth taken into death; which has been my own expedient in the recital'. But laughter here should be humane, not sardonic.

On stage history, Michael Shapiro's *The Children of the Revels*[41] surveys the organisation, performances, audience, company-styles, and the plays the 'little eyases' shone in. Little of this is directly concerned with Shakespeare, but Shapiro marshals his material well; appendixes

[39] *Royal Shakespeare*, by Stanley Wells. Manchester: Manchester U.P. £1.50.
[40] *Shakespeare's Dramatic Challenge: On the Rise of Shakespeare's Tragic Heroes*, by G. Wilson Knight. London: Croom Helm; New York: Barnes & Noble. pp. 181. £5.95.
[41] *Children of the Revels: The Boy Companies of Shakespeare's Time and their Plays*, by Michael Shapiro. New York: Columbia U.P. pp. xv + 313. $18.75.

cover song and music, recorded court performances, and repertories. Although C. Walter Hodges's paper on Shakespeare's Second Globe has been previously noted (*YW* 1973), his book published that same year has not. *Shakespeare's Second Globe*[42] is brief, but concise and scholarly. 'The Missing Monument' is the playhouse Shakespeare used (all other major theatrical periods have some theatre physically still surviving). After *Shakespeare's Globe Restored*, which looked at the first Globe, burned down in 1613, Hodges considers the evidence for the construction of the second, completed and much beautified in 1614. He shows the reliability of Hollar in his Long View of London (and the preliminary drawing), suggests a sixteen-sided building, rather larger than usually estimated, but now capable of a stage of the Fortune specifications and of the three or four thousand spectators sometimes given it. He suggests the superstructure is not a house, but simply a great open timber roof, no longer supported by posts, from which the gods might descend. He offers, convincingly, other conjectures and provides his usual splendid reconstructions, though insisting, where proper, upon the fluid nature of details. An indispensable work at all levels.

Richard J. Thornberry suggests in 'A Seventeenth-Century Revival of *Mucedorus* in London before 1610' (*SQ*) that some of the problems of the play's influence on Shakespeare's romances might be solved if, as the substantively different quartos of 1598 and 1606 hint, the play had been revived before 1606. In the same periodical, G. Harold Metz surveys the 'Stage History of *Titus Andronicus*', suggesting four periods of popularity, the modern one beginning in 1923; he notes twenty-three productions between 1951 and 1974, underlining its popularity and its stature on stage in spite of so many scholarly declarations of its unattractiveness.

Shakespeare's popularity on the nineteenth-century stage was almost matched by the burlesques of him in that period. The first three of five projected volumes, reprinting the best of these, have appeared, well selected and introduced by Stanley Wells[43]. Each volume has an introduction and the texts are well produced, though no annotation is provided. Wells sees these burlesques as attacking contemporary productions as much as Shakespeare and stresses their importance as examples of the popular theatre, though perhaps he claims overmuch when he talks of their inventiveness, wit, and shrewdness of thrust, however difficult it may be to imagine them in performance.

The plays burlesqued are the most popular: in these three volumes, sixteen burlesques take in eight plays. Poole's *Hamlet Travestie*, the great initiator, includes a drunken Gertrude (compare the Canadian *Hamlet* reviewed above), while Ophelia's madness, even when she distributes vegetables, is still almost touching. Historically the series is welcome, but the genre is one that depresses the spirit. Not available for review but

[42] *Shakespeare's Second Globe: The Missing Monument*, by C. Walter Hodges. O.U.P. (1973). pp. 100. £3.
[43] *Nineteenth-Century Shakespeare Burlesques*, introduced by Stanley Wells. Diploma Press. Vol. I *John Poole and his Imitators*, pp. xxvii + 235; Vol. II *Maurice Dowling (1834) to Charles Beckington (1847)*, pp. xvii + 310; Vol III *The High Period: Francis Talfourd (1849) to Andrew Halliday (1859)*, pp. xxii + 257.

deserving mention is a bibliography of Shakespearian burlesques, parodies and travesties by Henry E. Jacob and Claudia D. Johnson[44].

J. L. Styan aims in *The Shakespeare Revolution*[45] to offer 'to trace a revolution in Shakespeare's fortunes both on the stage and in the study during this century', one which has discovered that Shakespeare knew his business as a playwright and which has broken away from the smothering picture-frame productions of the nineteenth century to 'make it new'. The book charts the situation in the Victorian period, the various responses of those concerned with Shakespeare as scholars and actors, the activities of Poel, Granville-Barker, Nigel Playfair, Barry Jackson, Guthrie and Peter Brook. The interaction between academic study and stage is considered. Styan is properly enthusiastic about many of these ventures. He quotes Guthrie's conviction that 'a play can be best presented by getting as near as possible to the manner in which the author envisaged its performance' and, commenting approvingly on the success of Guthrie's stage at Stratford, Ontario, notes that it became the pattern for new theatre-building throughout America and England. However right Guthrie was about Shakespeare, though, Styan fails to comment on the fact that this new orthodoxy is applied to all plays alike, few of which were written for Shakespeare's stage and despite Styan's approval of the National Theatre's open stage the 'new theatre-building' has produced more problems than it can solve. This is a study of Shakespeare, though, and as such is warmly welcome.

Stephen C. Schultz delivers what he promises in 'William Poel on the Speaking of Shakespearean Verse: A Reevaluation' (*SQ*). He argues that Poel's ideas, scattered through his writings, when examined critically seem seriously deficient as a guide. He shows the inadequacy of Poel's terminology and the vagueness about how the skills needed were to be acquired. Alma H. Law writes interestingly in '*Hamlet* at the Vakhtangov' (*TDR*) about what seems a very silly production; directed in 1932 by Akimov, who wished to make Hamlet 'the hero of a lusty and witty adventure story', its ghost proved a trick of Hamlet's to get people to join his conspiracy against Claudius. J. C. Trewin and Robert Speaight 'Talking about Shakespeare' (*SQ*), opens with a tribute by Trewin to Speaight and the conversation goes back in memory to 1912: but there is little specific detail, whether on why Gielgud's second Hamlet was his best or in the comparison between Poel and Guthrie. More like a strenuous hike was the show 'Shakespeare's Memory' in Berlin, described by Klaus Peter Steiger in 'Erinnerung an Shakespeare: Die Berliner Schaubühne am Halleschenufer Spielte Shakespeare's Memory' (*SJH*) and by Peter Lackner in 'Stein's Path to Shakespeare' (*TDR*), the latter including photographs of Queen Elizabeth carried to make her Golden speech, of a naked man in a sphere (very unlike Renaissance proportions), and of what seems to be a raffia-clad Womble. The event occupied two evenings and seems to have been enjoyed.

[44] *An Annotated Bibliography of Shakespearean Burlesques, Parodies, and Travesties*, by Henry E. Jacob and Claudia D. Johnson. New York: Garland (1976). pp. 202.

[45] *The Shakespeare Revolution: Criticism and Performance in the Twentieth Century*, by J. L. Styan. Cambridge: C.U.P. pp. ix + 292. £6.50.

Ann Jennalie Cook promises 'delicious' sexual gossip in ' "Bargaines of Incontinence": Bawdy Behavior in the Playhouses' (*ShakS*) but though she prints most of the passages of invective she does little with them and it proves repetitive and unspecific. While still in the theatre, mention should be made of two historical pieces by John Orrell: 'The Paved Court Theatre at Somerset House' (*BLJ*), and in *ShS* 'Inigo Jones at The Cockpit', where he suggests that two sheets of designs by Inigo Jones, published by D. F. Rowan (*ShS*, 1970), are probably for the Cockpit in Drury Lane.

6. Individual Works

All's Well That Ends Well

The problems of the play are central to two articles. Ian Donaldson's excellent *'All's Well that Ends Well: Shakespeare's Play of Endings'* (*EIC*), without ever confusing formal intention with dramatic success, explores the problem of the ending in a play which calls attention to endings, arguing that the close is more complex than most criticism concedes and that it is the culmination of a more extended treatment throughout the play of the notion of ending. Unlike most comedies, Shakespeare's play seems audaciously to heighten the element of paradox (that their endings are an end to tension or misunderstandings), so that endings and 'last things' are concentrated on. Helena's grief seems to be for her father's death, but is actually for her hopeless love for Bertram 'and what her metaphor figures is the ending of his life', while she brings the King to realise 'it is not his prerogative but God's to declare his life at an end'. One recurrent question of the play is where the 'end' is located and it speaks 'constantly of an end which is not finally realised within its dramatic framework', a puzzling feature of what ought to be a comedy. An excellently suggestive piece. For Nicholas Brooke in *ShS* the play's name alone suffices for its title, since it expresses the exploration he feels it necessary to undertake of a play that never quite takes, never quite seems to work: the problem is just what 'working' should, for this play, consist of. He analyses the play's language to show its scepticism: reticence rather than the delusory clothing of romance is characteristic of the play. What we have is folklore material, but looked at in an unfamiliar way, to illustrate which Brooke looks at Caravaggio's picture of the Magdalen (compare his British Academy lecture, reviewed above), where the naturalism imposes a calculated frustration on the responses we would like to indulge, something he sees centrally in the play, though with no mere negation of romance.

Eliot Slater, continuing his word-analyses of Shakespeare, looks at 'Word Links with "All's Well That Ends Well"' (*N&Q*) and finds that the rarer words show a statistically significant excess of links with two plays only, *Troilus* and *Measure for Measure*. Taking all words, the links with *Measure for Measure* remain and with *Othello* rather than *Troilus*. The material evidence is against the hypothesis that *All's Well* is a revised version of a play sufficiently early to be mentioned by Meres and so is not to be identified with the lost *Love's Labour's Won*.

Antony and Cleopatra

Three articles show something of the range of possible interpretations. Richard L. Nochimson in '"The End Crowns All": Shakespeare's Deflation of Tragic Possibility in *Antony and Cleopatra*' (*English*) sees the play's world as mundane, 'inhabited by very ordinary people with inflated visions of themselves, and dominated by foolishness.' He argues that the play is much closer to *Troilus and Cressida* than *Macbeth* in mood and theme, and that it has been found a tragedy because 'assumptions about the nature of the play and the nature of the historical love relationship have created that expectation' in the minds of readers and spectators. Antony lacks firmness and fails to become a tragic figure through self-awareness. Nochimson writes sensitively on Shakespeare's use of Ventidius and Enobarbus and finds Cleopatra's behaviour vile and riggish (despite the blessing of priests). After analysis of the play's ending, he concludes that Shakespeare's 'intention seems to be to deny that theory of the nature of princes, to debunk empty symbols, to deflate the possibilities for royal grandeur'. To counter this we have an equally sprightly piece, '"Again for Cydnus": The Dramaturgical Resolution of *Antony and Cleopatra*' (*SEL*), by Duncan S. Harris. Harris admits as readily as Nochimson that the play provides little basis for secure judgement (compare Emrys Jones's introduction to his edition, above), but throughout its course the play has invited judgement and although it has refused the means with which to make it, Harris argues that the guidance exists and encourages us to take the side of the lovers. The poetry of praise makes us want to believe the lovers' claims, but only when Cleopatra arrays herself for death, as she did for Cydnus, do we have the necessary visual confirmation: 'Cleopatra's death is not an isolated moment of a peculiar kind of grandeur. The scene is the delayed presentation of Enobarbus' vision of her infinite variety'. L. T. Fitz in 'Egyptian Queens and Male Reviewers: Sexist Attitudes in *Antony and Cleopatra* Criticism' (*SQ*), not only shows the range of opinions, but also the danger of being selective. While Fitz is no doubt right in assuming that many critics are hostile to Cleopatra, it is to be questioned whether all male critics are, even if some feel personally threatened, and some critics cited are well out of date. Fitz claims that far from Antony being the play's central character, (how many people claim that, despite Fitz's assertion that it is an 'almost universal assumption'?) the inner tragic struggle is to be found not in Antony but in Cleopatra.

A less contentious reading of the play is offered in 'Images et Structure dans *Antoine et Cléopâtre*' (*EA*), by Gisèle Venet, who looks at the images of fluidity and melting one thing into another and suggests a bipolarity of structure associated with these images. Stanley J. Kozikowski on V. ii. 309-11 (*Expl*) sees the asp as Cleopatra's particular symbol of victory over Octavius and links the ass (sic) to that mentioned by Plutarch as Octavius' portent of victory. Not seen was a volume of reprinted essays in the Twentieth-Century Views series edited by Mark Rose[46].

[46] *Twentieth-Century Interpretations of Antony and Cleopatra: A Collection of Critical Essays*, ed. by Mark Rose. Englewood Cliffs, N.J.: Prentice Hall. pp. 138. hb £6.55, pb £2.15.

As You Like It

In a brief note in *ELR*, 'Telling the Trees from the Wood: Some Details of *As You Like It* examined', Eamon Grennan mentions, in the light of 'the pastoral categories among which EK distributes the poems of Spenser's *Shepheardes Calendar*' some particulars of the play. Charles Whitworth Jr's *'Rosalynde*: As You Like It and As Lodge Wrote It' (*ES*) makes timely correction of errors that some recent scholars have made in re-importing Shakespearean facts into Lodge, wrongly making Gerismond and Torismond brothers, and dukes, and Rosalynde and Alinda cousins. In *SQ*, Maura Slatter Kuhn finds 'Much Virtue in *If*'. Starting from Rosalind's exit and re-entry at V. iv. 26–105 for the wedding, she points out four accompanying problems: an impossible Elizabethan costume-change, unexplained chatter from Touchstone, a textual crux, and the lack of formal recognition of Rosalind as a girl (a point stated in all parallel 'recognition' scenes). Ms Kuhn proposes that — as Fl and F2 imply — Rosalind comes back merely tidied up, still as a recognisable Ganymede. So the following 'if's' have restored value.

Ms Kuhn develops the importance of conditionals in the play, even back to the third line of the first scene, pointing out the high absolute and relative frequency of 'if's' in this play. 'If' is the basis of Touchstone's logic-games, for example: and what emerges chimes in well with all the accepted données about this unusual play. Ms Kuhn concludes 'To employ a musical metaphor, *As You Like It* is a series of inspired improvisations in the key of If'.

A major event is the arrival of the New Variorum edition[47] of this play, a monumental xxviii + 737 large pages, with a bibliography of about twelve hundred entries, articles on music, the text on stage, performances, and all the *Dunciad*-like appearance, with two lines of play at the top of the page heading acres of small-print comment, and the play itself over well before we get half-way through the book. The New Variorum series began in 1871: an *As You Like It* appeared in 1890. We should refer to this recent volume, perhaps, as the Newest Variorum: MLA, the publishers, proudly claim it is the first to appear in the whole series since 1955, and that this volume 'makes available practically everything of significance now known about the play'. Does it help? I suspect I shall always turn first to Agnes Latham's New Arden, which does so much so deceptively easily. Do we need *every* suggestion, however dotty, about 'ducdame'? (e.g. 'damn me' pronounced by a stutterer, identified, of course, as Ben Jonson). I suppose we do. 'All the world . . . ' gets a good round set of comments, crowding the play completely off the page. The fifty pages on Characters will amuse (e.g. Shaw on Rosalind's popularity 'due to three main causes. First, she only speaks blank verse for a few minutes . . . '). There is, of course, value in such museum-work, and we must salute the curators.

Coriolanus

Joyce Van Dyke has an intriguing discussion, 'Making a Scene: Language and Gesture in "Coriolanus"' (*ShS*), prompted by what she sees as

[47] *A New Variorum Edition of Shakespeare: As You Like It,* ed. by Richard Knowles with a Survey of Criticism by Evelyn Joseph Mattern, IHM. New York: The Modern Language Association of America. pp. xxviii + 737. $50.

previously inadequate descriptions of Coriolanus as a speaker. She claims that his 'peculiarity is not an insensitivity to words; rather he is uncommonly sensitive to them', and proceeds to a fine analysis. Hermann Heuer in 'Rehabilitationen: Überflüssige Texte im *Coriolan?*' (*SJH*) attempts rehabilitation by considering 'superfluous' text in the play. Two articles cast a Germanic slant on the play. Ladislaus Löb and Laurence Lerner collaborate on 'Views of Roman History: *Coriolanus* and *Coriolan*' (*CompL*), which begins and ends with a silly statement and resolutely refuses to translate any of the German quotations but usefully compares Brecht's version with Shakespeare's, arguing that where Shakespeare's is perhaps the most pessimistic of all dramatic representations of Rome by Elizabethan dramatists, Brecht treats the topic from an optimistic view-point. There is a useful bibliography. Noel Thomas moves beyond Brecht to write 'Shakespeare's *Coriolanus* and Grass's *Die Plebejer Proben den Aufstand* – A Comparison' (*New German Studies*). He looks at the Boss's likeness to Coriolanus in *The Plebians Rehearse the Uprising* and considers other Coriolanus reminiscences in Grass's work.

B. A. Brockman's introduction to his Casebook selection[48] links the play with Jacobean political and social conflict, considers its role in political and social disturbances of the seventeenth and eighteenth centuries, then discusses the movements of criticism both in terms of pieces included in the volume and those excluded. The selections are divided chronologically: 1765 to 1919 and twentieth-century (1912 to 1971); a useful feature is the extracting of sections from a long work, so that Willard Farnham is represented by seven passages from the relevant chapter in *Shakespeare's Tragic Frontier*.

Leigh Holt's book, *From Man to Dragon: A Study of Shakespeare's Coriolanus*[49] is a well-documented and interesting study, balanced and illuminating. After an excellent opening chapter examining critical views, Holt examines 'matters of public concern (Roman and English) where . . . an image of tragic vision is molded'. He finds suggested 'the necessary articles of faith: that cities of men can in some way give birth to a dragon *and* that the cities' languages can explain the dragon, humanise him, without reducing him to a cipher in normal political, familial, military, or ethical equations. These articles subscribed to, I believe we can think of him as expanding (instead of merely violating) the demands a human being can place on himself – and as taking his stand, in the end, at the heart of terrific loss.' He finds that 'renegade Coriolanus remains Shakespeare's hero – moreover a genuine tragic hero – even as the values of the City are being established'. This is a reading of great interest.

Cymbeline

Alexander Leggatt tackles the play's peculiarities in 'The Island of Miracles: An Approach to *Cymbeline*' (*ShakS*) and the problem of its outrageously idealised view of the characters, a subject that has prompted good recent criticism (see *YW* 1976) and to which Leggatt responds well.

[48] *Shakespeare: Coriolanus*, ed. by B. A. Brockman (Macmillan Casebook Series). Macmillan. pp. 236. hb £5.95, pb £2.25.
[49] *From Man to Dragon: A Study of Shakespeare's Coriolanus*, by Leigh Holt. Salzburg Studies in English Literature. pp. 241.

He sees Britain, isolated from the normal world, as a place where strange things happen: the very beginning is extraordinary and only in Italy does Posthumus begin to be questioned. Britain seems a place where imaginations are extraordinarily vivid and active, while at Imogen's lament over Cloten's body the tendencies 'of the play to generate false images and of the characters to create false images in their minds have come together'. He suggests how this qualifies our response (he is good also on Iachimo in Imogen's bedroom) and goes on to consider how this high imagination links to the resolution of the play.

Hamlet

In *ShakS* Richard Helgerson explores 'What Hamlet Remembers', producing a suggestive analysis of Hamlet's need to remember at every level, especially arising from the encounter with the Ghost, the command to seek revenge, the precepts to the prodigal son (paralleled by Polonius to Laertes) and an archaic summons of Death, concluding with the play's appeal to 'wonder'. Also in *ShakS* Arthur Noel Kincaid, in 'Hamlet's Cue for Passion in the Nunnery Scene' analyses afresh Hamlet's apparent abrupt alteration of tone at or just after the line 'Where's your father?' Kincaid rightly disposes of the two traditions, from Dover Wilson and from a clumsy stage-habit, used to make sense of the moment. Most unconventionally, Ophelia is alone: instead of saying that her father is close at hand, she tells 'a falsehood which leaves her ostensibly unchaperoned, alone at court, apparently with no other motive than to seek out her lover (for she has brought his tokens with her). However, being what she is and forced to give a false answer, her impulse is to place Polonius imaginatively away from court and in his natural setting as she knows him. Her innocence proves her disaster in this scene.' Barbara Everett prints in *ShS* '"Hamlet": A Time to Die', part of a longer study in preparation. Asking again *why* does Hamlet delay? she splendidly points out that the Ghost is a presence that fades. So 'while he thus follows the Ghost, life becomes for him "a time to die". This is the impasse or crux on which Hamlet rests, and it makes of him a figure not unlike that image of Melancholy . . ., created at a time when the mechanical clock and the sense of History were together beginning to master Europe.' Again in *ShS*, J. Philip Brockbank, under the title 'Hamlet the Bonesetter' (setting right a time out of joint, of course) is 'importunately concerned with the lines of continuity between the tragic play and its primordial spectre, the sacrificial ritual'.

The most rewarding piece on *Hamlet* for some time is Inga-Stina Ewbank's long, dense, readable ' "Hamlet" and the Power of Words' (*ShS*). Her aim is 'to explore the part which speech plays in the life of this play'. Starting from Gertrude's re-telling of the death of Polonius at the beginning of Act IV, she moves to a rich and revealing analysis of Claudius' word 'translate'; both 'to interpret' and 'to change'. Commenting both on the extraordinary freshness of the play's language and its general belief in the importance of speaking and listening (so that 'the characters are very self-conscious speakers, in a way which involves consciousness of others') she casts light into every corner of the play. The different languages, for example, spoken in a scene like I.ii 'clearly add up to a kind of moral map. That is, the adding up is clear, the map itself not necessarily so.' Hamlet listens in a more reflective way — 'listens and evaluates as Othello does not (but Hamlet surely would have done) with Iago'. Yet human sympathy, as well as positive action, can be absorbed and lost in speech. 'Polonius' method is particularly undermining in that he lets Ophelia provide the key-words which he then picks up and translates by devaluing them'. 'So we seem to be left in the end with a long row of contradictions: Hamlet's use of language is sensitive and brutal; he listens and he does not listen; his speech is built on sympathy and on total disregard of other selves; his relationship with words is his greatest strength and his greatest weakness. Only a Claudius could pretend that these are not contradictions and only he could translate them into a simple unity.' She concludes 'we are given a very wide demonstration of the power of words to express and communicate — it is, after all, words which tell Horatio and us even that "the rest is silence" — but also, and at the same time, an intimation that there is something inexpressible and incommunicable at the heart of the play'.

Charles A. Hallett, in 'Andrea, Andrugio and King Hamlet: The Ghost as spirit of Revenge' (*PQ*) discusses briefly the pathology of 'the passion of revenge' before analysing the three ghosts, somewhat unsubtly.

In a note in *SQ* Michael Shelden sketches some of the imagery of constraint. In the same place William E. Miller shows the eyas to have disagreeable qualities suggestive for Hamlet's remarks. Hellmut Salinger in *Hamlet und sein Dichter*[50] expresses forcible rejection of the incapable, irresolute Hamlet, and shows instead a Hamlet still expressing contemporary life through a poet's soul. Richard Weisberg in *MLN* sees *Hamlet* as a formative element in Mallarmé's 'Un Coup de Dés'. R. V. Holdsworth finds two convincing echoes of *Hamlet* in *The White Devil* (*N&Q*). We have also received 'The Meaning of "Hamlet": An Approach Through Language' by Visvanath Chatterjee M.A., in the *Bulletin of the Ramakrishna Mission Institute of Culture*.

For a comparative piece on *Hamlet* and *Henry IV*, see below.

Henry IV

In 'Falstaff the Centaur' (*SQ*), Douglas J. Stewart's purpose is to suggest that there is a parallel between Hal's relation with Falstaff and the Greek mythical heroes in the Centaur's cave. To make Hal such a hero, Shakespeare made his father unhistorically old and weak, and then gave Hal the three attributes for which Falstaff is the better 'father' — uncalculating behaviour, his own standards, and an understanding of lesser men. This is a wise and lively piece. There is much interest in Falstaff's rejection: Edward I. Berry, 'The Rejection Scene in *2 Henry IV*' tries for 'a total response' to it; Lawrence L. Levin in *ShakS* considers 'Hotspur, Falstaff, and the Emblem of Wrath in *1 Henry IV*' — Falstaff as emblem, Hotspur's subjugation to the same sin, 'adversaries on a collision course', 'the comic and the tragic representations'. John P. Sisk in *SQ*, 'Prince Hal and the Specialists', argues that the modern fuss about the rejection fails to

---

[50] *Hamlet und sein Dichter*, by Hellmut Salinger. Heidelberg: Lothar Stiehm Verlag. pp. 128. DM 26.

acknowledge the many-sidedness of the Renaissance ideal, and fear of specialisation, visible both in Falstaff, a specialist in appetite, and Hotspur, a specialist in honour. Norman Sanders in *ShS* works on interchange of roles in 'The True Prince and the False Thief: Prince Hal and the Shift of Identity', leading to a discussion of 'self-definition via apparent criminality' related to his father's guilt, the rebels, and a neat understanding of what 'redeeming the time' means. Also in *ShS*, J. A. B. Somerset goes through the various theories about the rejection of Falstaff, especially finding analogues in the morality plays.

G. R. Hibbard, in '"Henry IV" and "Hamlet"' (*ShS*) draws, in an elegant essay, interesting parallels between the plays in their largeness, their structure, and their central fascinating figure, '. . . the Monarch of Wit and the Prince of Paradox'. Each gives glimpses of a biography, especially the significance of his birth. Hibbard gives an excellent account of the two plays (taking both *Henry IV*'s as one) as supreme examples of growing points where Shakespeare's art makes a sudden leap forward. He demonstrates this with reference to vocabulary, and to dramatic techniques, and verse and prose, and shows Hamlet as developed out of Hotspur and Falstaff. Commenting on the lunacy of the Ghost saying to Hamlet 'Taint not thy mind', he says 'the Ghost must have taken leave of his senses; and then one realises that to take leave of one's senses, or rather to be taken leave of by them, is the necessary first step to becoming a ghost. It is precisely its abnormal ways of thinking that makes this ghost so ghostly.' *Hamlet*, he says, is rooted in reality *via* the History plays. He illustrates Shakespeare's own knowledge of the revolutionary nature of what he had done. Daniel Seltzer, also in *ShS*, ('Prince Hal and the Tragic Style') argues that 'the felt existence of an inner life from which motivation and action both spring, one causing the other, was not, I think, a component of Elizabethan dramaturgy before a certain time in the development of Shakespeare himself'. This, so necessary for the major tragedies, happened in the late nineties, during the composition of the Henry plays; in the composition of Hal, Shakespeare 'acquired the ability to make a character change internally'. By means of a discussion of Hamlet's relationship to acting styles, and acting techniques in *Richard III* and *Richard II*, he goes on to Shakespeare's discovery that 'Our own inner concentration remains where the character's has found its greatest and deepest point of self-realization'; then fully recognising that Hal is not a tragic figure — giving comment on his speeches.

Gilian West in *ES*, unhappy with the 'ostriches' of *1 Henry IV* IV.i. 97–100, in recent emendation, suggests 'All plumed like goshawks that master the wind/Revived like eagles having lately bathed'. Peter J. Gillett approaches the same lines in a note in *SQ*, finding 'the first assurance we have received in the play, from anybody but the Prince himself, that Hal is to be transformed'. T. J. King compares contemporary Stratford accounts with Falstaff's bill in *1 Henry IV* II.iv. 509–15 and finds that though Falstaff's sack was less expensive than the local average, the quantity was unusual, though not outrageously so (*N&Q*).

Gillian West, again, castigates Henry in 'Bolingbroke at Shrewsbury: The Recreant King of *1 Henry IV*' (*Neophilologus* 1976), arguing that his futile and contemptible behaviour at the battle shows him unjustified in deposing a weak anointed King. To do this she examines changes between Holinshed and Shakespeare as well as the use of Falstaff. M. A. Shaaber in 'Pistol quotes St Augustine?' (*ELN* 1976) suggests that the obscure 'obsque hoc nihil est' (*II Henry IV*, V. v. 29) ultimately derives from Augustine on the soul.

Norman Davis in an *SQ* note courteously corrects Robert F. Willson Jr (*YW* 57.133) and George Walton Williams over the 'invention' of the name 'Falstaffe' in 1598, and by means of a document in Magdalen College, Oxford casts fresh light on the problem of that name.

Henry V

Norman Rabkin explains his title 'Rabbits, Ducks and *Henry V*' (*SQ*) in relation to drawings in which you see now a rabbit, now a duck, arguing that Henry V is a work 'whose ultimate power is precisely the fact that it points in two opposite directions, virtually daring us to choose one of the two opposed interpretations it requires of us': each has been foreshadowed in a *Part* of a previous *Henry IV* play. The piece is dense, complex, over-written and too subjective, but it usefully leads into *Julius Caesar*. William Babula's 'Whatever happened to Prince Hal? An Essay on "Henry V" ' (ShS) emphasises the very great difference between the earlier Hal and this, by means of a scene-by-scene commentary of uneven value. Andrew Gurr, also in *ShS*, shows Shakespeare using an incident from Erasmus in a way which differs radically from his version, under the title '"Henry V" and the Bees' Commonwealth'. This is a fresh and in the end cynical look at the play's views on self-interest and society, useful and up-to-date; an acerbic, and hence valuable, corrective of various critical assumptions.

Henry VI

James A. Riddell in 'Talbot and the Countess of Auvergne' (*SQ*) supports Talbot's coherence of character and style, *pace* Burckhardt, especially within the classical tradition of the magnanimous man, and compared with the ambitious men of the Temple Garden scene that follows. Talbot demonstrates the necessary qualities of humility and indifference to insult. David M. Bergeron in *TSL*, 'The Play-within-the-Play in *3 Henry VI*' notes four scenes which come in this category (for which a Player-King is normally necessary, he finds): I.iv, the killing of York, involving radical alteration of source; II.iv, 'a dumb-show with words'; III.i, 'Henry's vision of Warwick and Margaret vying for the support of the French king'; and III.ii, Edward's wooing of Elizabeth while 'Richard and Clarence play audience and comic interlocutors'. Such scenes do not occur, Bergeron claims, after Richard's 'famous, revealing, and terrifying soliloquy' because Richard, centre-stage, 'becomes the highly self-conscious artist'. James T. Henke's *The Ego-King: An Archetype Approach to Elizabethan Political Thought and Shakespeare's Henry VI Plays*[51] applies 'the Jungian theory of a collective unconscious and collective arthetypes' to the plays 'to reveal the basic psychic vision' which 'informs popular attitudes toward kingship and the state prevalent in Elizabethan England' and 'is projected

---

[51] *The Ego-King: An Archetype Approach to Elizabethan Political Thought and Shakespeare's Henry VI Plays*, by James T. Henke. Salzburg Studies in English Literature. pp. 94.

as two complementary dramas — one describing political chaos, which is superimposed upon another describing, with almost clinical accuracy, a form of human insanity'. The book is more modest and suggestive than the title might indicate, and it does illuminate: 'the image of the besieged city is a superlative metaphor for the ego's attempts to stave off the chaotic forces of insanity'. David L. Frey's book *The First Tetralogy: Shakespeare's Scrutiny of the Tudor Myth*[52] is a more main-stream study, and good to have. Sub-titled 'A Dramatic Exploration of Divine Providence' the book gives good grounds for rejecting Tillyard and 'the view that Shakespeare saw God's guiding hand in the history of England, as did the Tudor historians'. Following, but disagreeing with, Wilbur Sanders' 'natural providence' as Shakespeare's answer to growing Machiavellianism, Frey concludes 'at the heart of the Tetralogy lies the question of innocent human suffering' caught between two systems, a concern seen in the imagery and more significantly, Frey shows, in the growing qualities of the King — a portrait that was the result of very specific shaping of the sources. Noting that Tillyard 'seems to believe the myth more strongly than Henry VIII', Frey demonstrates that Shakespeare 'enlarges Richard III to nullify it, and diminishes Richmond to demolish it'. This is a lucid book, in which Frey's helpful ideas are worked out in impressive detail and with commendable brevity.

Michael Manheim's 'Silence in the Henry VI Plays' (*ETJ*) looks at the dramatic effect of characters who are present but do not speak or who make the greater effect for their previous silence, the King being chief amongst them.

Henry VIII

Tom McBride offers an interesting reading to make sense of this difficult play in '*Henry VIII* as Machiavellian Romance' (*JEGP*). Instead of judging Henry by Christian standards, McBride suggests, we must see two moral standards in the play, Christian and Machiavellian, both moral yet irreconcilable. Like Buckingham and Wolsey, the other Machiavellians, Henry too lacks an understanding of Machiavelli's advice, but unlike them he learns, dismisses his bad servant and rescues Good Counsel Cranmer. McBride links this action with Machiavelli's list of four who rose by their own virtues — Theseus, Moses, Cyrus and Romulus — all Romance figures who therefore suggest the idea of Machiavellian Romance.

King Lear

John Reibetanz begins consideration of *The Lear World*[53] with his concern for Shakespeare in his context as an Elizabethan and Jacobean dramatist, suggesting that the play draws its power from the creative re-interpretation of the dramatic traditions and conventions Shakespeare knew so thoroughly, while much of what sets the play aside from the other tragedies is what it shares with Jacobean drama. Not all the discussion

[52] *The First Tetralogy: Shakespeare's Scrutiny of the Tudor Myth; a Dramatic Exploration of the Divine Providence*, by David L. Frey. The Hague: Mouton. pp. 180. Fl. 42

[53] *The Lear World: A Study of King Lear in its Dramatic Context*, by John Reibetanz. Heinemann. pp. xi + 142. £6.80.

of Jacobean drama seems fully integrated into the book's texture, but the study as a whole is well worthwhile. Reibetanz begins by considering the play's lack of the accidentals of everyday existence, which allows it to present essentials with undiminished intensity, comments interestingly on Coleridge's opinion of the opening's gross improbability, and on the figurative characterisation. Other chapters consider the play's use of great scenes (this is linked well to Jacobean emphasis on the strong individual scene), the overall structure, characterisation, and the final scene. Good on the way this scene is 'expressly designed' to shock and overwhelm us, Reibetanz is able to qualify his earlier over-emphatic stress on the play's Christian symbolism.

A valuable and deeply suggestive book by Grigori Kozintsev, *King Lear: The Space of Tragedy* [54], is not only an account of how the Russian film was made, many fascinating insights though it offers — the Lear, an Estonian, did not speak or understand Russian well (it was his eyes that gained him the part) but insisted upon learning it properly rather than being dubbed — but also the influences upon Kozintsev. Much of the book is a meditation, showing the formative mosaic of elements from Noh drama, Kurosawa, Dostoevsky, Meyerhold, Peter Brook, and even Tolstoy who, for all his condemnation of the play, seemed to Kozintsev a presence and whose medium height (short when a giant was expected) was another influence on the choice of actor for Lear. Kozintsev also reveals how he developed the film's emphasis on the folk, the image of a scarecrow in an Elizabethan engraving being one such trigger. A book of interest to Shakespearians, film enthusiasts and observers of Russia.

James P. Driscoll in 'The Vision of *King Lear*' (*ShakS*) attempts to find new perspectives on the philosophical and religious themes by exploring the archetypal stages and patterns which structure its vision and so suggests the fruitfulness of approaches to literature through Jung. He looks at man's struggle for consciousness and psychic wholeness and man's confrontation with existential truths about injustice, death, evil, and the dark side of God. He takes the faces of Godhead and links Lear to the first three, Cordelia to all four, but shows his sensitivity by insisting that if Cordelia represents the archetype of wholeness this is not to contend that she coincides with all Jung's conceptions about this archetype nor that she resembles the orthodox Christ. A reading of the play follows, which takes full account of the darkness of its end. Philip Brockbank's 'Upon Such Sacrifices' (*PBA* 1976) is a subtle if occasionally attenuated meditation upon the end of *King Lear*. He considers the significance of sacrifice, what is meant by Lear's use of the term, the way the idea might have been given new meanings in Renaissance/Reformation England, and finds that Cordelia's innocence 'and her readiness to put herself in jeopardy, are precisely what make her a fitting sacrifice'. David Ormerod seems committed, in '"The Shadow of This Tree"; Fall and Redemption in *King Lear*' (*SJH*), to a Christian redemptive reading and may indeed be overemphasising a detail, but brings out well enough the typological possibilities of the tree under which Edgar leads Gloucester to shelter (V. ii).

[54] *King Lear: The Space of Tragedy — The Diary of a Film Director*, by Grigori Kozintsev (trans. Mary Mackintosh). Heinmann. pp. xii + 260. £8.50.

Paul Delany makes Lear's party feudal and aristocratic against the bourgeois party of Goneril, Regan and Edmund in 'King Lear and the Decline of Feudalism' (PMLA), trying to link the play with the Histories and social conflicts of Shakespeare's time to clarify its moral problems. In 'Unconscious Self-Revelation by Goneril and Regan' (SJW), Jacqueline E. M. Latham suggests that the structures of the sisters' replies to Lear's demands reveal to the audience what they are intended to keep hidden. Wolfgang Weiss's 'Redeform, Rhythmus und Character: Das Beispiel König Lears' (SJH) uses the play to exemplify deployment of rhetoric, rhythm and character. Although more concerned with pedagogy than the play, Norman N. Holland gives some interesting examples of response from students in 'Transactive Teaching: Cordelia's Death' (CE).

A crop of notes offer varying value. Winifred L. Frazer suggests that 'King Lear's "Good Block"' (SQ) at IV. vi. 185 is not an image from hat-making or preaching but equivalent to 'idea' or 'scheme': she would also break the 'hat' link by having the felt for the horses a mass of wool rather than hat-making material. In the same journal Mario L. D'Avanzo suggests the reference in '"He Mildews the White Wheat": King Lear, III. iv' is not to madness in general, but specifically to ergotism, providing links between insanity, poison, and the eating of diseased and decayed matter. Dennis R. Klinck suggests a conflation of proverbs on trusting dogs' teeth and on a tamed wolf in 'Shakespeare's "Tameness of a Wolf"' (N&Q), while Jane Donawerth's 'Diogenes the Cynic and Lear's Description of Man, King Lear III. iv. 101–109' (ELN) argues that Plato's definition of man and Diogenes' jesting response lie behind Lear's words, Montaigne's reference having triggered off memories of Erasmus or Diogenes Laertius, Lear's response to Tom then being that of a Cynic philosopher. Mathilda M. Hills on 'King Lear IV. vi. 205–208' (Expl) argues for 'which twain' being both Goneril and Regan and Adam and Eve.

Peter Milward in ShStud studies '"Nature" in Hooker and King Lear' taking up recent recognition of the importance of Book 1 of Ecclesiastical Polity for the concept of Nature in the play, arguing that Shakespeare could have understood it from mediaeval morality plays. Unlike King Leir, King Lear shows 'the condition of human nature in a pre-Christian era, while at the same time admitting an undercurrent of Biblical reference,' both O.T. and N.T. 'showing even fallen nature as pregnant with divine grace – though not as yet brought to birth in the resurrection'.

Love's Labour's Lost
Continually remarkable is the uneven quality of writing about this play. This year there are three long pieces: one good, one acceptable, and one poor. R. Chris Hassel Jr writes in ShakS on 'Love Versus Charity in Love's Labour's Lost'. Referring only to work before 1965, Hassel starts in error: 'few Shakespeareans since G. Wilson Knight' he says 'have studied Christian patterns in Shakespeare's comedies', when in fact it has most recently been hard to get away from the American discovery of Christ uncomfortably lodging in the Forest of Arden (YW 54.174) in Venice (YW 54.178; 55.220; 57.138) and in Troy (YW 54.183) to take but a few examples. In bludgeoning prose Hassel develops his theory that the play 'seems to contain an unprecedented intensity of doctrinal controv-

ersy'. But scholars, even of the early comedies, know not such a 'seems': his entire case, spread over twenty-four large pages, depends on Berowne's words at IV.iii.360, about charity and love, as evidence for the play being a statement in current, and massive, theological controversy. In saying 'The Bishops' Bible is recognizable because alone among Protestant Bibles it preferred the Catholic "charitie" to the Reformers' "love" ' Hassel ignores the headnote to Romans 13, for that passage he most uses, in the Geneva Bible, from 1560 by far the most influential Protestant Bible. That reads: 'Charitie ought to measure all our doings'. Moreover, if Berowne's short remark *is* intentionally and seriously doctrinal it is surely also with reference to the Geneva margin at 1 Corinthians 13 where the commentator differentiates the faith that shows itself in love 'and therefore is separate from charitie'. So, having forced on the play a huge construction of irrelevant doctrinal discussion, based on distortion if not actual misreading, Hassel finally refers to Shakespeare's 'so profound a religious awareness'. If this were an example of a new Christian school of interpreting Shakespeare, one would be very alarmed: but of course it is not. Much more healthily, Louis Adrian Montrose offers 'a comprehensive study' of the play, 'demonstrating the coherence of . . . structural and thematic dimensions'[55]. In 195 pages with thirty pages of notes, Montrose argues that here 'Shakespeare shapes a distinction between the imaginative world created by the characters *within* the fiction and the total imaginative form which is the play', exposing 'the self-deceptions of the characters in the process of destroying their imaginative world'. The play 'is a fictive critique of the ways in which its own characters use games, rituals, myths, social institutions, and language, as media by which to construct, explore, manipulate, and protect their reality'. He concludes, 'author, actors, and audience are social players engaged in the same kinds of strategies as those of the characters'. Though in its solemnity a little close still to its origins in a doctoral dissertation, this is to be welcomed as one of the very few full-length studies of the play. Finally, in shorter compass, John Wilders in 'The Unresolved Conflicts of *Love's Labour's Lost'* (*EIC*) writes the single best piece on the play for some time. 'The construction . . . appears to consist of an elaborate system of essentially simple contrasts, between character and character, plot and sub-plot, palace and country, and these seem to embody equally simple notions such as love and learning, action and contemplation. The more one examines the play, however, the more apparent it becomes that these are not so much contrasts as unresolved and irreconcilable opposites.'

Macbeth

Time is the concern of A. A. Ansari's 'Fools of Time in *Macbeth*' (*Aligarh Journal*), which finds the protagonist caught in an unreal and illusory conglomeration of isolated and mechanically-succeeding 'nows'. E. B. Lyle disputes direct reference to James's coronation ceremonies in 'The "Twofold Balls and Treble Scepters" in *Macbeth*' (*SQ*); rather,

[55] *'Curious-Knotted Garden': The Form, Themes and Contexts of Shakespeare's Love's Labour's Lost,* by Louis Adrian Montrose. Salzburg Studies in English Literature. pp. 222.

James was double (twofold) monarch in joining England and Scotland and treble in the formula of King of Great Britain, France and Ireland. M. E. Grenander looks at what is obviously a popular disorder in 'Macbeth IV. i. 44–45 and Convulsive Ergotism' (ELN), arguing that since the symptoms of demonic possession are consistent with those of ergot poisoning, once the symptoms of ergotism were associated with witchcraft a model was produced for responses of those who believed themselves possessed or betwitched. That it is the witch who feels the characteristic tingling or pricking, rather than the possessed Macbeth, indicates that the weird sisters are as much the victims of evil as the protagonist.

Eight essays from ShS have been reprinted[56], but as six of them are from the same volume, very little effort is saved in hunting them up. The editors have added only the briefest of introductions and no supplement is offered to G. K. Hunter's 1966 survey of Macbeth this century nor any kind of bibliography or index. Not seen was a volume of reprinted essays in the Twentieth-Century Views series, edited by Terence Hawkes[57].

John Duffy in SQ ('Brakedrums and Fanfares: Music for a Modern Macbeth') writes about the ingenuity of the author, busily taking literally the sound-imagery of the play.

Measure for Measure

In 'Measure for Measure: The Play and the Themes' (PBA 1974), J. C. Maxwell challenges received opinion about the play's handling of ideas, wondering not what sort of ideas the play embodies but how much it is concerned with embodying ideas at all. He looks at the bedtrick and betrothals of Angelo and Claudio and is acute about the complications Shakespeare had set himself. Commenting that it may be 'a profound Christian truth that Mercy should supersede Justice' he insists, though, that 'it is not well illustrated by a plea that a young man should not be executed on an obsolete technicality for sleeping with his own wife'. It is provocative in the best sense. A. A. Ansari in 'Measure for Measure and the Masks of Death' (Aligarh Review) examines how, though a comedy, the play is enwrapped in the shadow of death from beginning to end. He also claims some sympathy for Mistress Overdone. Katherine Duncan-Jones suggests in 'Stoicism in Measure for Measure: A New Source' (RES) that a work published with the 1592 edition of the translation of Garnier's Antoine and omitted in 1595 may provide the basis of the Duke's speech against fear of death.

The Merchant of Venice

A useful article is Richard Horwich's 'Riddle and Dilemma in The Merchant of Venice' (SEL). 'The attraction of Belmont's riddle', he writes, 'is that, though one risks losing everything, there is a way to win everything. In Venice, by contrast, the solutions to problems may be

[56] Aspects of Macbeth: Articles Reprinted from Shakespeare Survey, ed. by Kenneth Muir and Philip Edwards. Cambridge: C.U.P. pp. ix + 86. hb £6.50, pb £2.95.
[57] Twentieth-Century Interpretations of Macbeth: A Collection of Critical Essays, ed. by Terence Hawkes. Englewood Cliffs, N.J.: Prentice Hall. pp. 138.

almost as threatening as the problems themselves'. Horwich casts valuable light on the ring episode, which for Portia 'remedies the sole defect of life in Belmont by restoring to her what from the start she complained of lacking – the power of choice . . . According to the terms to which she bound Bassanio with the ring, she may reject him if he gives it away . . . At the same time, she makes Belmont once again a place where wishes, no matter how improbable, can come true, as all problems seem literally to disappear'. Walter F. Eggers Jr in 'Love and Likeness in *The Merchant of Venice*' (*SQ*), writes in what one may call the woolly Christian tradition, appealing at its climax to Nevill Coghill's 1940's notion of the Old and New Testaments in the play, long shown to be no more than generally suggestive. Eggers is throughout unclear: 'Now as Shylock is forced to reclaim a Christian daughter as his own, his "likeness" in Jessica is figuratively transformed by Lorenzo's love'. Matters are better with Ruth M. Levitsky's 'Shylock as Unregenerate Man' (*SQ*), which follows Shylock's 'spiritual malady and starved soul' which are, one might say, at least what one feels to be his presented characteristics. She concludes 'The Jew is *not*, then, fed with the same food as the Christian, nor is he healed by the same means. He might have been so fed and healed, for the bread and balm were offered to him before they were offered to the gentiles. And he may yet be nourished by God's grace if he will accept the Christian faith. But, barring that, he is in a pitiably hungry and diseased condition'. In *PMLA*, William H. Matchett writes 'Shylock, Iago and *Sir Thomas More:* With Some Further Discussion of Shakespeare's Imagination'. 'I want' says Matchett, 'to extend the concept of image-cluster beyond the purely verbal to include stage-images', and he says it as if this were somehow a new thing to do. The *PMLA* editor describes this essay as 'controversial but productive': in fact it is neither, being both old-fashioned and also depressing in its combination of absolute self-assurance of originality and importance, and weakness of method. *Merchant* echoes in *Othello* and *More* are a commonplace. Matchett's tissue of words in the *More* fragment to make a Merchant 'cluster' simply does not work: given the context in *More*, it is their very expectedness, not their unusualness, that is their main feature, when dealing with attitudes to strangers (it is surely unnecessary to call in Hitler's 'extermination camps' when noting Dover Wilson and R. W. Chambers on the point).

The Merry Wives of Windsor

William Carroll, in '"A Received Belief": Imagination in *The Merry Wives of Windsor*' (*SP*) has a tendency to fight old battles, in that he rather condescendingly tries to restore a supposedly inferior Falstaff to full Henriad size. This he attempts by studying 'the equivocal, subversive power of imagination' especially seen through 'Ford's relation to Falstaff, verbal style, and metaphors of playacting'.

A Midsummer Night's Dream

In *SQ*, Anne Paolucci tackles "The Lost Days in *A Midsummer Night's Dream*' – 'The dramatic action ought to cover five days; actually, only three are accounted for'. By means of ingenious elaboration of a familiar contrast between timeless, and disorientating, night-experiences and the specific time-references to day, she finds the intervals of rest 'the major clue', pointing out that 'each sleep coincides with the casting of the love-spells'. She refers to no criticism more recent than 1961, and seems unaware of the work of Emrys Jones or Stephen Fender. Leah Scragg makes a good case in 'Shakespeare, Lyly and Ovid: the Influence of "Gallathea" on "A Midsummer Night's Dream"' (ShS) for Lyly's play, already accepted as a model for part of Love's Labour's Lost, as an influence here. Supported by a number of minor linguistic echoes, the parallel is mainly of metamorphosis on every level. She notes that such intervention of Lyly between Shakespeare and Ovid possibly explains the elusiveness of the nature and extent of Ovid's influence. Hans Jürg Kupper, in 'A Local Habitation and a Name' (SJH) discusses Shakespeare's artistry in contrasting technical devices — rhyme, blank verse, and prose.

Othello

Although details may be disputed, Carol Thomas Neely's 'Women and Men in Othello: "what should such a fool/Do with so good a woman?"' (ShakS) is excellent, above all in offering new ways of looking at things. Noting how there have been 'Othello' critics and 'Iago' critics, Neely observes that most damagingly, 'both groups of critics, like both Othello and Iago, badly misunderstand and misrepresent the women in the play' (compare, though, S. N. Garner on Desdemona last year). Neely aims to show that the play's central theme is love and its central conflict is between the men and the women, linking this interestingly with some of the preceding comedies. Although one may doubt whether it is only the man's view that makes Bianca a whore, Neely convincingly shows the men fierce for reputation and full of vanity where the women are free of such tarnish.

Very different but undoubtedly interesting is Anna Kay France on 'Iago and Othello in Boris Pasternak's Translation' (SQ). Pasternak impresses his creative personality upon the work. Besides linguistic factors, Pasternak's response to character produced numerous changes; he found Iago not only unsympathetic but also unpersuasive and reduced the force of Iago's presence (France refers us to an early essay by Pasternak on the play before she goes on to the treatment of Othello and Desdemona). Rodney Poisson's 'Death for Adultery: A Note on Othello, III. iii. 394–96' (SQ) argues that the lines refer to means of disposing of Desdemona and that each of the five would be means of execution for adultery familiar to Elizabethan audiences. On '"As Liberal as the North": "Othello" V. ii. 221' (N&Q), James F. Forrest suggests 'North' here may be a metonymy for 'Satan', while in the same journal J. J. M. Tobin's 'Apuleius and "Othello"' finds links of situation and words between Psyche's lamp and the bedchamber lamp. In Expl Giles Y. Gamble on III. ii. 482–86 argues for 'minx' not only as 'wanton', but also as having animal/bestial associations, while Abby Jane Dubman Hansen links the Sagittary to Centaur, with its associations of violence and sexuality. As with Macbeth, there is a reprinted selection of essays from ShS[58], again with no added

[58] Aspects of Othello: Articles Reprinted from Shakespeare Survey, ed. by Kenneth Muir and Philip Edwards. Cambridge: C.U.P. pp. x + 110. hb £6.50, pb £2.95.

commentary or bibliography, ten pieces, seven from the same volume. Plate XIII surely shows Iago and Emilia, not Othello and Desdemona?

Pericles

Nancy C. Michael argues in 'The Relationship between the 1609 Quarto of *Pericles* and Wilkins' *Painful Adventures*' (*TSE*) that they are independent of each other and both based on a play performed at the Globe. She offers new instances of recorded stage action in Wilkins and suggests that when the original play became more complex in detail, Wilkins turned to Twine for aid.

The Phoenix and the Turtle

Placing '"The Phoenix and the Turtle" in its Dramatic Context' (*ES*), H. Straumann argues that the synthesis of true and fair, lamented by the poem but no longer possible, appears as possible in plays before 1601, but in plays after this date and in the Sonnets the values may exist separately but never together, except in the Romance, where it may be possible through luck or magic. The poem, then, represents a turning point 'both in poetic expression and in the abstract of Shakespeare's existential concept of the possible union of beauty and truth'.

Richard II

Margaret Loftus Ranald in *ELR* writes well on 'The Degradation of Richard II: An Inquiry into the Ritual Backgrounds'. She gives a most useful account of the traditions of chivalric, military and ecclesiastical degradation, especially in symbolic unclothing linked with inversion of ritual and destruction of reputation. Shakespeare, using such material, invented a ritual which 'underlines both the solemnity and the pathos of the occasion' resulting in a convincing final status as 'but a knave', Bolingbroke's 'Jack o' the clock'. In *SJW* John Scott Colley, under the title 'The Economics of "Richard II"?' takes several pages of defensive journalism about Marxist criticism to get to the play and then merely propounds a few superficial observations, concluding, 'a sophisticated and thorough Marxist approach will allow us to see Shakespeare's poetry and Shakespeare's ideas from a perspective that is both "critical" and "historical"'.

Donald M. Friedman's 'John of Gaunt and the Rhetoric of Frustration' (*ELH* 1976) challenges the usual acceptance of Gaunt's England speech, where he finds a blunting of the necessary alertness to the interplay between personality and the value it expresses. He suggests well the limitations of Gaunt's views, arguing that the 'inmost core of Gaunt's outrage appears to be not the dulling of national fame, but the fact that possession of the land has passed from the hands of its traditional owners'. Faith G. Norris (*Expl* 1976) argues superfluously that the Gardeners' scene is essential structurally and dramatically.

Romeo and Juliet

Gerald Stacy, in 'Arthur Brooke and the Lost Play of *Romeo and Juliet*' (*ES*) surveys the 'evidence' for what is apparently mentioned by Brooke in his address to the reader, and convincingly concludes that he refers not to a lost play, but to a theme found in any number of Tudor interludes, that of youth.

The Sonnets

In *PMLA*, Carol Thomas Neely writes 'Detachment and Engagement in Shakespeare's Sonnets: 94, 116, and 129'. She separates these 'three powerful and pivotal sonnets' as being not about actions 'done for or to the beloved': here the beloved is absent, the poet-lover submerged; 'the poems are deliberately impersonal, general, immobile. Not actions themselves, they are about inaction'. She points out their uniqueness in English poetry, though because they have been anthologised and much discussed they are usually taken as norms by the general reader, and critics. Each of the three, she suggests, is a model proposed as the climax of a short group. Then, within each sonnet, there is the breakdown of that model. Following each are sonnets signalling great change, in particular heightened conflict. John P. Cutts exaggerates the importance of his discovery of another Henry Lawes version of Sonnet 116, needlessly seeing alterations as the result of 'something that looks suspiciously to me like moral impediments' (*ShakS*). Philip Grundlehner in *SJH* contrasts 'renditions' of the Sonnets by Stefan George in 1909 and Karl Kraus in 1932, noting too Kraus' 'venomous attack' on George. In *Expl* Robert L. Fleissner explores nautical and naughty allusions in Sonnet 137's 'the bay where all men ride' and Heather Dubrow Ousby looks at Sonnet 125, lines 13–14. Peter M. Daly in a note in *SQ* takes up and corrects an earlier suggestion about 'compass' in Sonnet 116. Peter Jones edits a 'Casebook' in the Macmillan series[59], writing a balanced introduction which says a great deal in a small space, and printing material from 1598 to 1976, even including a specially-doctored page from Rowse in which he also vociferously dissociates 'Mr W. H.' from 'the young lord to whom Shakespeare wrote the Sonnets': (see the section Biography and Background, above). My only complaint is the absence of extracts from J. W. Lever and Stephen Booth.

Stephen Booth's own massive edition of the Sonnets[60], a milestone in Sonnet studies, is to be welcomed with arms wide open — as they will need to be, since it is a very large book indeed. It is extremely readable, and a sort of up-side-down Variorum: 'I have worked six years on the commentary to this edition, and there now seem to be few living Americans who have not read, written, or corrected some of it'.

Booth pours out a torrent of well-directed ideas in a manner which grabs the attention. In a hundred-odd pages he prints Quarto, facing a conservative modernisation, and then gets straight in to Commentary, '. . . designed not only to help a twentieth-century reader to a Renaissance reader's understanding of Shakespeare's idiom but also to answer academic questions about how the sonnets work — how they achieve the clarity and simplicity most of them have from the unstable and randomly dynamic locutions they employ. A reader who wants to know

[59] *Shakespeare: The Sonnets*, by Peter Jones. (Macmillan Casebook Series). Macmillan. pp. 258. £5.95.
[60] *Shakespeare's Sonnets: Edited with analytic commentary by Stephen Booth*. New Haven, Conn. and London: Yale U.P. pp. xix + 578. £18.

what it is that makes a sonnet he values so good will not achieve perfect understanding from this edition, but the commentary should help him to move in what common sense suggests is the most profitable direction — toward awareness of the multitudinous statements, ideas, ideals, standards and references that almost every line of the 154 sonnets contain. Four times he stops for longer essays, the longest a plea for a better criticism. Always he opens doors, again and again insisting that 'many of Shakespeare's locutions must have made his readers as uneasy as they make modern readers' as he puts it in the introduction. To check Booth on a favourite sonnet is to be repeatedly surprised by joy. On Homosexuality, he writes 'William Shakespeare was almost certainly homosexual, bisexual, or heterosexual. The sonnets provide no evidence on the matter'. And on the dreaded Dark Lady: 'She, like the male friend, may be a literary creation; if Shakespeare was talking about real people and events, we have no clue whatsoever as to the Woman's identity. Speculation on her identity has ranged from wanton to ludicrous and need not be illustrated.' What happiness!

Titus Andronicus

In *Susquehanna University Studies* (1976) Clifford Davidson offers 'A Reading of Titus Andronicus', a rather rambling essay which makes a number of comments on the play without propounding any usefully unified view.

The Tempest

The most illuminating piece is Clifford Siskin's 'Freedom and Loss in "The Tempest"' (*ShS*), which argues against Northrop Frye that far from everything being subordinate to Prospero's return, what we are involved in is a family play, where Prospero's being a widower and the marriage of Miranda are key states. Siskin argues that 'political victory and renewed friendships cannot remedy the fundamental isolation of the widower, who, even as he prepares to reveal the culminating miracle of young love, exclaims: "I/Have lost my daughter"'. As a result the play's profound nature can be comprehended without resort to extravagant allegorical speculations, while, if it is viewed in terms of familial relationships, its differences from the other romances become distinct. Two articles in *ShakS* concern Prospero's magic and the nature of his power, though neither makes reference to James Smith's discussion and only one to D'Orsay Pearson's essay (both *YW* 1974). Karol Berger in 'Prospero's Art' stresses that magic is the art and that if we want to grasp its nature with any precision, it is necessary to see what it can accomplish and by what means. The mechanism of the magic is explored in terms of Renaissance theories known to Shakespeare and his audience (above all, the Florentine Platonists), and discussion follows of the relationship between magical and political power, the play being seen as establishing a clear distinction between the unreality of the imagination and the reality of the world, a reality to which Prospero seeks to return at the end. Neil H. Wright considers 'Reality and Illusion as a Philosophical Pattern in *The Tempest*', suggesting that though this pattern is often noticed it has not been deeply probed. He proposes that the world of illusion is the play's established order, not the ordinary world of experience; that Prospero, as creator and manipulator, is not so much theurgist as maker, artist, or poet; and that the play's underlying pattern is to be found in the Renaissance concept of the poet as the teacher who alone is able to convey the highest sort of truth. Prospero uses his art, but as an aid to return to a world where the illusion of art is to be rejected.

James Hoyle's *'The Tempest, the Joseph Story, and the Cannibals'* (*SQ*) finds an analogue between Prospero and Joseph in their exile and forgiveness, linking this latter idea with Montaigne's cannibals. In *'"The Tempest" (Coral in Full Fadom Five)'* (*Expl* 1976), Abbey Jane Dubman Hansen notes that in lapidary lore, coral is good against tempests and gives fortune in travel.

Clifford Davidson writes in *The Notre Dame English Journal* (1976) on 'The Masque within *The Tempest'*, finding it 'an indicator of concealed meaning' with which one 'ought to begin any close examination'. Prospero 'appears to be drawing down celestial and divine influences in the manner of a Renaissance magus'. Davidson analyses the individual significances of the goddesses, concluding, 'Prospero's vision also involves a return to ecstatic innocence, though it may be argued that the means utilised by him in the production of this show are not so clearly guiltless'.

Timon of Athens

Arguing against seeing *Timon* as tragedy, and so raising more problems of genre than are solved, William W. E. Slights suggests in *'Genera mixta and Timon of Athens'* (*SP*) that far from ignoring genre, Shakespeare has used that tool of his craft in a far more flexible way than has generally been understood. An interesting examination of the play's elements follows to suggest how it belongs to a 'mixed genre', capable of being tragic, satiric and even mordantly comic.

Twelfth Night

In a note in *SQ*, J. F. Killeen locks 'Castiliano Vulgo' at 1.iii.42 into the context of Aguecheek's entrance with a 'talk-of-the-devil' kind of remark, reflecting the proverbial Italian dislike of Spain.

Troilus and Cressida

Tinsley Helton writes well on 'Paradox and Hypothesis in *Troilus and Cressida'* (*ShakS*). In a play where principles of discrepancy and frustrated expectation are continuously and variously operative, the tone achieved is that of paradox rather than satire. He is sympathetic towards both the lovers and good on the frustrations of action, of debate, and of set speech, concluding that Troilus by the end seems to have 'turned his back upon the problematic world of being and value and is resolved to live exclusively in the untheoretical world of action'. This new resolve of Troilus is central to Robert E. Wood's *'Troilus and Cressida:* The Tragedy of a City' (*PQ*), which argues that Hector's function is to suffer the Trojan agony, not to analyse it, and that Troilus, in taking over from the dead Hector, takes over his functions and becomes Troy, while the importance of the city mutes Troilus's claims to the stature of a self-contained tragic hero. Wood is suggestive in exploration of the pattern of crime and punishment. Grant

L. Voth in 'Ulysses and "Particular Will" in Shakespeare's *Troilus and Cressida'* (*SJW*), attacks the wily Greek whom he finds perpetually involved in misdirecting and misleading his fellow soldiers, condemning Cressida out of wounded pride and carrying out some of the most despicable of all the acts of 'general will'. If Cressida is partly rescued by this attack, Carolyn Asp's 'In Defense of Cressida' (*SP*) is a full-scale attempt to show the true pathos of the situation of a 'woeful Cressida 'mongst the merry Greeks'. It can smack of special pleading, but makes useful points. In '"Lechery eats itself": Troilus and Cressida' (*ArielE*), Leo Rockas pursues the play's parallel grouping of characters, so that the historical pattern of Menelaus and Paris in contest over a mistress has its repetition in the central dramatic contest of Troilus and Diomedes over Cressida and its parodic echo in Achilles and Ajax over Patroclus. Priscilla Martin has edited the Casebook volume[61], her introduction giving a useful summary of the play's problems. She reminds us that the first known production of the play was in 1898 (at Munich), explores the meaning of Troy in Shakespeare's time, the sources and Shakespeare's sympathies, and touches on critical aspects. The extracts, arranged in two sections as usual, range from Dryden to Mark van Doren and from Una Ellis-Fermor to John Bayley.

Important is G. K. Hunter's 'Troilus and Cressida: a tragic satire' (*ShStud*). The play, he says 'is an extreme example of Shakespeare's capacity to generate tensions and contradictions out of the material he is using: . . . attitudes of courtly love and chivalry are set beside what one may loosely call "Homeric" attitudes, to secure what the play itself calls "confounding contraries"'. Setting out 'to define what Shakespeare made of the Homer that was available to him' (a 1596 reprint of Caxton, a 1598 edition of Chaucer, as well as the 1598 Chapman) he finds that what 'Homer had to offer . . . was the knowledge that there was no order there to be destroyed, that animal violence was the rule of life and not the exception. That this was the vision of the most reverend of all writers must have come to Shakespeare with none of the glow of "a peak in Darien" but as a profoundly unliberating shock. And *Troilus and Cressida* is, I take it, the record of that shock'. Hunter goes on to analyse the longest episode the two works have in common — the visit of the Greek leaders to Achilles to persuade him to rejoin the fight, finding that 'what is left of the Homeric ethic looks like violence coupled to selfishness'. 'The shocking juxtaposition of the two visions of the Trojan world must have confirmed sharply what Shakespeare had already guessed — that the poets of the middle ages soften and sweeten our intuition of man's tragic destiny.' Thus the play is 'an experiement with the high style' in which the various languages 'are seen as languages only, impressive enough, especially to those who speak them, but fatally disconnectable from the ends towards which they are aimed'. Hence 'tragic satire'.

[61] *Shakespeare: Troilus and Cressida,* ed. by Priscilla Martin (Macmillan Casebook Series). London & Basingstoke: Macmillan (1976). pp. 253. pb £2.25.

Venus and Adonis

William Keach's aim[62] is to show 'how, and to what extent, the ambivalence of Shakespeare's *Venus and Adonis* and Marlowe's *Hero and Leander* is central to other immediately contemporary Ovidian narratives'. A long and excellent chapter on Ovid and 'Ovidian' poetry explores not only Ovid's self-consciously ironic detachment from the myths being recounted, but also the darker side, an awareness of violence and terror inherent in these myths even after they have lost their original supernatural or religious significance. Keach suggests that while the Elizabethans clearly show the ironic, witty aspects of their model, it is more difficult to evaluate their comprehension of the darker aspects of Ovid's poetry. In looking at Shakespeare's poem, Keach shows that if the reluctant Adonis did not exist before (though the aggressive Venus did), Ovid yet provided models in other episodes such as that of Hippolytus, and goes on to consider how the poem's seriousness, 'its insight into the turbulence and frustration of sexual love — is inseparable from its comedy and its entertaining eroticism', finding in conclusion that a 'surprisingly powerful sense of erotic pathos' is generated. The lack of a bibliography is a pity in such a worthwhile study.

The Winter's Tale

Nicolas K. Kiessling in 'The Winter's Tale, II. iii. 103-7: An Allusion to the Hag-Incubus' (*SQ*) finds a confusion of reference: Shakespeare alludes to the incubus who gives women children or substitutes a changeling.

---

[62] *Elizabethan Erotic Narratives: Irony and Pathos in the Ovidian Poetry of Shakespeare, Marlowe, and Their Contemporaries*, by William Keach. Hassocks, Sussex: Harvester Press. pp. xviii + 277. £10.50.

VIII

English Drama 1550 – 1660: Excluding Shakespeare

BRIAN GIBBONS and BERNARD HARRIS

1. Editions

The Complete Henslowe Papers, ed. R. A. Foakes (Scolar) will doubt-less be noted elsewhere; they are essential reading for anyone studying the drama of this period, but were not available for review. Two other editions of non-dramatic texts require mention. The Malone Society has provided a Collections volume of 'The dramatic records in the Declared Accounts of The Office of Works 1560-1640'[1]. The records for 1576–1640 were collected and transcribed by F. P. Wilson: R. F. Hill has checked, corrected and supplemented that list, and has also provided the records for the crucial years from 1560. The result is valuable, extensive evidence for the nature of the revellings at Whitehall, Hampton Court, St. James's, Nonsuch, Denmark House (Somerset House), Greenwich, Richmond, Woodstock, and Newmarket. The Latin correspondence of Albercio Gentili and John Rainolds on the subject of academic drama has been published in one of the Salzburg Studies series[2]. Some of the discussion may seem remote from stage practice, but this may be a false impression; Rainolds is often invoked in seventeenth-century theatrical debate.

Three editions have emerged in established series. N. W. Bawcutt has edited Fletcher's *The Two Noble Kinsmen*[3]. His introduction is concise and useful, and particularly helpful on the morris dance and on the possible divisions of the play between Shakespeare and Fletcher. G. R. Hibbard contributes a sound edition of Jonson's *Bartholomew Fair*[4]. George R. Price has edited Middleton and Rowley's *A Fair Quarrel*[5]. The intro-duction is modest and witty. The play has now found its way into the repertory of the National Theatre.

Three substantial editions have come from two of the Salzburg Studies

---

[1] *Dramatic Records in the Declared Accounts of the Office of Works, 1560–1640* ed. R. F. Hill. (Collections Volume X). O.U.P. for The Malone Society, 1975 (1977). By subscription.

[2] *Latin Correspondence by Alberico Gentili and John Rainolds on Academic Drama*, trans. with intro. by Leon Markowicz. Salzburg: *Elizabethan and Renais-sance Studies*, ed James Hogg. Salzburg Studies in English Literature, under the direction of Erwin Stürzl.

[3] See Chapter VII.

[4] *Ben Jonson: Bartholomew Fair*, ed. by G. R. Hibbard. Benn. The New Mermaids. pp. xxxvi + 180. pb £1.95.

[5] *Thomas Middleton and William Rowley: A Fair Quarrel*, ed. by George R. Price. Arnold. Regents Renaissance Drama Series. pp. xxvi + 138. hb £8, pb £3.95.

series[6]. C. H. Stein's edition of Greene's *James IV* is scrupulously prepared and presented; although this is a critical, old-spelling edition it would have been an advantage to have included some account of J. A. Lavin's edition. Stein is undoubtedly right to draw attention to Greene's achievement in tragicomedy several years before the genre was acknowledged in England and became fashionable. Robert J. Lordi's edition of Chapman's *The Revenge of Bussy D'Ambois* is valuable both for its text — thoroughly edited and with a most useful commentary — and for its introduction, which is a major essay on the play, detailed, perceptive, and critically stimulating. Raymond C. Shady's edition of Heywood's *Love's Mistress, or The Queen's Masque* is responsive to that difficult form, and has a full introduction, appropriately illustrated, which does justice to the work's claim[6].

2. Books and articles

Paula Glatzer has made 'the first book-length treatment' of the Parnassus plays[7]. It is an enterprise well worth undertaking. As she notes, 'The Parnassus Plays tell us more about writers and their concerns than all the rest of Elizabethan drama'. The writing is not free from jargon, but the range of reference is unusually rewarding; Daniel, Nashe, Marston are properly treated as well as the whole theme of the 'Complaint of the poet'. This is an excellent study of a topic often relegated to the margin of critical consideration — that of the profession of poetry. The analysis of *The Second Return* is especially commended. There is much to be done in research in this particular period of the early Elizabethan drama. Michael Shapiro[8] has collected articles on the child-players, published in various journals in recent years and reviewed previously. The book contains chapters on the acting companies, the place and occasion of performance, the audience, the style, and certain plays. Some of the most important questions, of acting style and audience composition and taste, are discussed with a confidence that belies the scarcity and inconclusiveness of the evidence, and it cannot be claimed that much knowledge has been added in these areas by Shapiro's work, unfortunately. Given the recent disclosures of weaknesses in T. W. Baldwin's scholarship in dealing with this subject, this remains a field in which every grain of fact unearthed could be valuable. Shapiro's book might have been improved by pruning; it goes over much ground already well studied.

Alan C. Dessen's *Elizabethan Drama and the Viewer's Eye* will be noted elsewhere; although many of its pages are concerned with Shakespeare, attention is given to short episodes from a number of other dramatists. The book is primarily concerned, as its title suggests, with the theat-

---

[6] Greene in *Elizabethan and Renaissance Studies*; Chapman and Heywood in *Jacobean Drama Studies* (ed. James Hogg). Both series may be purchased from the Universität Salsburg.

[7] *The Complaint of the Poet: The Parnassus Plays; a critical study of the trilogy performed at St. John's College, Cambridge, 1598/99 – 1601/02*, by Paula Glatzer. (*Elizabethan and Renaissance Studies*.) Both series may be purchased from the Universität Salsburg.

[8] *Children of the Revels*, by Michael Shapiro. New York: Columbia U.P. pp. xv + 307.

rical dimension of plays, and is worth consulting. Patricia S. Barry's *The King in Tudor Drama* (*Elizabethan and Renaissance Studies* 58) is well documented, and the range of the topic is exceptionally controlled and demonstrated; the chapter on 'The King defined in scene' is admirably attentive to the needs and requirements of the theatre. Marie Axton's book[9] begins by examining the succession debate and the theory, notably discussed by Ernst Kantorowicz in his book *The King's Two Bodies* (Princeton 1957), that the monarch was a body politic who never died, as well as a mere mortal who did. The importance of lawyers and the Inns of Court as active in support of drama is stressed, and these political ideas are related to private and public drama, to Inns of Court revels, Entertainments, 'The Phoenix and the Turtle', and *King Lear*. The book is of specialist interest, historical in orientation, but contains much important and valuable material.

In 'Deception through words: a reading of *The Spanish Tragedy*' (*SP*) Carol McGinnis Kay deals with Kyd's 'world of unexplained whispers, false messages, suspected letters, and lunatic ravings', and indicates the 'non-ethical basis of all human relationships in *The Spanish Tragedy*'. Frank Ardolino's '"The hangman's noose and the empty box": Kyd's use of dramatic and mythological sources in *The Spanish Tragedy* (IV. iv. vii)' notes that the dramatic source for the gallows scene is primarily a famous *commedia dell'arte lazzo* ('Pulchinello, Brigand-Chief'), and discusses, in the course of the commentary, various cruces of the Pandora myth (*RenQ*). Leonard Tennenhouse writes a trenchant note on 'Balaam and Saul and the world of *II Tamburlaine* (*NM*), and A. N. Okerlund is equally severe on the uncertain state of Marlowe criticism in his magisterial survey of 'The intellectual folly of Dr Faustus' (*SP*). Among the Salzburg Studies are four short monographs (*Elizabethan and Renaissance Studies* 71), Richard Corballis on 'Some Machiavellian moments in English Renaissance drama'; James. T. Henke's 'The devil within: a Dr Faustus for the contemporary audience'; Dorothy E. Nameri's '*As You Like It/Fantasio*: a comparative study'; and James Hogg's '*The Spanish Gipsy* and Francis Manning's *All for the better, or the Infallible Cure*'.

Jonathan F. S. Post has compiled a bibliography of recent studies in criticism of Marlowe, from 1968 to 1976 (*ELR*). This is quite full and sensibly organised, but the comments on the scope and quality of a number of entries are not at all reliable, and the reader gets no clear impression of the direction or current state of criticism of Marlowe. Geoffrey D. Aggeler sketches loosely-defined elements of satire in Marlowe's plays, and suggests, in a rather laborious and predictable article (*ES*), that Marlowe be seen (as surely he usually is) as influential in the development of tragic satire. Roma Gill's 'Marlowe's Virgil: *Dido Queene of Carthage*' (*RES*) is an elegantly written and suitably provocative account of that play. She is concerned, partly, with how Marlowe 'makes drama out of epic but, playing with fire, leads tragedy into comedy'. Her prose is subtle, and can accommodate such a transition; more impressively, she remains responsive to both Virgil and Marlowe.

[9] *The Queen's Two Bodies: Drama and the Elizabethan Succession,* by Marie Axton. Royal Historical Society.

The University of Nebraska has continued its series of bibliographies in English Renaissance Drama with *The New Intellectuals*. The book was not available for review, but if it maintains the standard of its two predecessors it will be worth attention. (It deals with Jonson, Chapman, Marston, Tourneur, and a number of minor dramatists and anonymous plays).

Peter Hyland has written an interesting book on *Disguise and Role-playing in Ben Jonson's Drama* (*Jacobean Drama Studies* 69, see note 6): the introduction is wide-ranging in its references to the subject; and although *Volpone*, *Epicoene*, *The Alchemist*, *Bartholomew Fair*, and *The Devil is an Ass*, receive the main consideration, for once the late plays are not neglected. The conclusion, that 'Jonson's use of disguise elements in his plays is not merely conventional, relating only to the mechanical needs of plot' but is part of a 'consistent and unified ethical vision', is well argued and established. A. K. Nardo writes on 'The transmigration of Folly: Volpone's innocent grotesques' (*ES*). In a fairly brief space much imbecility is compressed as the argument unfolds: that Nano, Androgyno and Castrone display no vicious motives, unlike most characters in the play, whereas they have 'all the spontaneity and vivacity that Celia and Bonario lack'; their folly commends them to us, their freedom to 'go sport' is to be seen as softening the harshness of the play's ending. Not since the proposal that Sir Politic's discovery under the tortoise-shell be seen as a triumph of human dignity has so absurd a suggestion been made about *Volpone*. R. V. Holdsworth (*Lib*) defends the reading 'does' in *Epicoene* I.iv.46, despite its implications of gargantuan appetites among the diners. John Scott Colley, in '*Bartholomew Fair:* Ben Jonson's *A Midsummer Night's Dream*' (*CompD*), argues that the play 'presents a vision of comic release and comic celebration that is unique in Jonson's canon', and that 'for the first time in Jonson's comedy, the acceptance of one's folly becomes the prelude to self-knowledge and ultimate comic transcendence'. Quarlous is important to the case. George E. Rowe has written 'Prodigal sons, New Comedy, and Middleton's *Michaelmas Term*' (*ELR*), and observes that 'Roman comedy is not the only dramatic antecedent . . . the play's lengthy complication follows the pattern of prodigal son dramas; it traces a foolish young heir's fall into misery and his gradual reformation. The presence of these two structures in the comedy is extremely important, for the responses called for by New Comedy and the parable of the prodigal are incompatible . . . by juxtaposing two contradictory structures Middleton has created a play that is deliberately ambiguous'. J. L. Simmons, in 'The tongue and its office in *The Revenger's Tragedy*' (*PMLA*), observes that 'The destructive liabilities of rhetoric, although acknowledged by classical rhetoricians, are dramatically and poetically activated in *The Revenger's Tragedy* by the biblical conception of the tongue'. He finds that the play in 'deliberate contradistinction' to Marston's *Malcontent* 'insists that a man is corrupted by the questionable methods he employs, and takes on the identity of the public role he plays'. Floyd L. Goodwyn has published a useful volume on *Image Pattern and Moral Vision in John Webster* (*Jacobean Drama Studies* 71), but perhaps the more substantial study of Webster is Isabel M. Damisch's *Les Images chez John Webster* (*Jacobean Drama Studies* 66 and 67), intellectually designed, schematically arranged, but analytically satisfying. Chapter VI in Tome II, on 'Le Mal', is especially commended.

Peter F. Mullany's book on *Religion and the Artifice of Jacobean and Caroline Drama* (*Jacobean Drama Studies* 41) has a chapter on 'Revenge and Religion' and then surveys nine plays through the period from *The Maid of Honor* to *The Virgin Martyr;* the main concerns examined are 'The religious vow', 'Divine Right and revenge', and the quarrel between Christian and Pagan.

There have been several useful and detailed notes on such matters as text, sources, dating and biography, sometimes related. R. V. Holdsworth comments on '*A Chaste Maid in Cheapside* V.ii.49–50' (*N&Q*), and T. W. Craik provides 'Notes on the text of three passages in *The Changeling*' (*N&Q*). Paul Mulholland's 'Some textual notes on *The Roaring Girl*' (*Lib*) offers a detailed and technical summary of his work on the text of this play, and his article will be required reading for future editors of this text. The same critic argues in 'The date of *The Roaring Girl*' (*RES*), with convincing use of evidence, for early 1611. D. J. Lake has made two valuable contributions to knowledge and statements of principle: an enquiry into 'The canon of Robert Armin's works: some difficulties' (*N&Q*), and into 'The date of the *Sir Thomas More* additions by Dekker and Shakespeare' (*N&Q*). In both instances the tone is severe about some present day scholarly ways, and no worse for that. The second article opens up possibilities for a date later than 1600. In similar vein Michael Scott raises the question of 'Marston's early contribution to *The Insatiate Countess*' (*N&Q*), challenging the usual date of 1607–8. Michael D. Bliss, in 'Massinger's *City Madam* and the lost *City Honest Man*' (*ELR*), conjectures that since in *The City Madam* prominent stress, both positive and ironic, falls upon the phrase 'the honest man', while the entry in the Stationers' Register is one item in a long list of play titles and was not made until 1653, there is the possibility that *The City Honest Man* is an alternative title for *The City Madam*. P. J. Finkelpearl offers a characteristically scholarly article on 'The date of Beaumont and Fletcher's *The Noble Gentleman*' (*N&Q*); he concludes that we should consider the years between 1606 and 1610. Ann Lancashire (*ELN*) notes that Chapman's name has been proposed once again as a possible author of *The Second Maiden's Tragedy;* she reviews the evidence and rejects the proposal, finding Middleton or Tourneur difficult to dismiss but Chapman indefensible as a possible author. Ruby Chatterji has indicated the problem of 'Dating the Jesuit oration used by Thomas Middleton in *A Game at Chess*' (*N&Q*). O. Rauchbauer is corrective about the source of 'The "Armada scene" in Thomas Heywood's *2 If You Know Not Me You Know Nobody*' (*N&Q*). Raymond C. Shady argues that 'The putative 1610 edition of Thomas Heywood's *Love's Mistress*' (*N&Q*) is a ghost.

There are several interesting items under the general category of biography. Robert B. Bennett has explored some of the lurid background of the Jacobean court in support of the contention that Webster's dedication of the elegy on Prince Henry ('A Monumental Column') to Robert Carr, Viscount Rochester, is a bitterly ironic gesture (*ELR*). Prince Henry's restraint, seriousness and orderly way of life were at the time contrasted to Carr's prodigality and display. Carr was suspected at the time of complicity in the murder of Prince Henry, whom he hated, though there is, in fact, no evidence that Henry was murdered. Under these circumstances, Bennett notes that Webster's dedication, with its assertion that none will grieve more deeply than Carr for Henry's death, seems 'a generous compliment from a usually contentious poet to a man who three years later will be judged guilty of murdering his former private secretary, Overbury', and it is more likely to be a concealed satiric attack on Carr. Robert F. Willson, in 'Beaumont and Jonson once more' (*NM*), draws attention to Beaumont's verse 'Letter to Ben Jonson'. R. V. Holdsworth, in 'Early references to plays by Jonson, Shirley and others' (*N&Q*), uses Robert Whitehall's pamphlet for detail. Donald S. Lawless has continued his extensive reseraches into the personal relationships of Caroline playwrights, providing 'Further notes on the Cromptons and the Massingers' (*N&Q*), using the parish registers of St Mary, Stafford; and in 'A further note on Shirley's religion' (*N&Q*) suggests that a reference in Brome implies Shirley's Catholicism. Georges Bas has examined Thomas Zouch's *Life of Walton* and the alleged friendship between James Shirley and Izaac Walton (*N&Q*) and counsels scepticism about the 'evidence' so far proffered. Allan P. Green's 'Shakerley Marmion, dramatist (1603–1639): his descent from the Marmions of Adwell, Oxon' (*N&Q*) establishes that the dramatist's great-grandfather, Henry Marmion, was the brother of Anthony of Adwell and Eastington. Green follows up a note in last year's *N&Q* with 'Shakerley Marmion dramatist: declared an outlaw in 1624?' (*YB*), citing a Chancery case of 14 June 1624 which 'shows the dramatist to have been declared a rebel some three weeks before the date of his Oxford M.A.'.

Evidence for theatre structure and acting practice are always to be welcomed. David Galloway provides further consideration of 'The "Game Place" and "House" at Great Yarmouth' (*TN*). The importance of provincial records is also shown in John Marshall's 'Players of the Coopers Pageant from the Chester Plays in 1572 and 1575' (*TN*), which avoids generalisation but makes close use of the accounts. The players 'were not professionals in the usual sense of the word'. John C. Coldewey provides further notes on 'That enterprising property-player: semi-professional drama in Sixteenth-century England' (*TN*).

Finally, two comments, social and imaginative, have been made about masques. John Orrell, in 'The Agent of Savoy at *The Somerset Masque*' (*RES*), provides a note of the circumstances of Giovanni Battista Gabaleoni's attendance at Campion's piece in 1613, and translates the text of his report, all the more revealing for being the comments of an outsider, notably from either understanding or flattery of the concept or performance. A. Leigh De Neef's account of 'Structure and theme in Campion's *Lords Maske*' (*SEL*) argues that although on the literal level of its celebration of the marriage of Count Palatine and Lady Elizabeth there are confusions and some irrelevances, because Campion has not 'focused on the occasion itself', this fact shows that the poet's interest 'lies elsewhere'. On the allegorical level too little has been understood of the figure of Orpheus. Campion 'abstracts from the synecdochic figure of the Orphic poet four separate characters representing form, inspiration, ornament, and frame'. Thus the masque is not merely a wedding entertainment, but a serious statement 'on the nature of poetry'.

IX

The Later Sixteenth Century: Excluding Drama

JOHN ROE

This chapter is arranged as follows: 1. General; 2. Sidney; 3. Spenser; 4. Poetry; 5. Prose. A selective review of books may be found in *SEL*.

1. General

This category sees the arrival of three good books: one on high life, one on low life, and one — quite simply — on life. The first is Roy Strong's richly illustrated *The Cult of Elizabeth*[1], which approaches Elizabeth I much as Frances Yates did in *Astraea* (due acknowledgement of her work is made by Strong in his preface). Strong's tack is of course much more visual, and his interesting analysis of the Queen's central and unifying role depends on his interpreting a number of key portraits and pageants. In the first half of his book, where he deals with portraits, he identifies persuasively — if a little speculatively — some of the figures in the procession picture *Eliza Triumphans,* as well as skilfully re-interpreting the Queen's litter as a canopy and establishing a plausible link with the Italian Renaissance's revival of antique triumphs. In the second half of the book, he examines events such as the Accession Day tournament, relating them in close detail to the poetry written in celebration. A particularly appealing identification is that of Essex as Hilliard's *Young Man amongst Roses.* The book is a fine example of how the art historian's discovery of what is going on in a picture serves a more general interest in how Elizabeth was mythologised, and more specifically how she stood in intimate relation to some of her principal subjects.

The low-life offering is from Gāmini Salgādo: *The Elizabethan Underworld*[2]. This is a lively, entertaining book offering a picture of the London of Shakespeare's day and recounting the activities of a number of notorious rogues and cozeners (male and female alike), some of whom provided models for Jonson, Middleton, and Dekker. Among primary sources he cites the cony-catching pamphlets of Robert Greene (an interest already familiar to readers of Salgādo's edition of *Cony-Catchers and Bawdy Baskets),* and Dekker's *Lanthorn and Candlelight.* He has also relied fairly heavily on secondary sources; but it is valuable to have research on ale-houses, prostitutes, sanitation, confidence trickery (including, naturally,

---

[1] *The Cult of Elizabeth: Elizabethan Portraiture and Pageantry,* by Roy Strong. Thames & Hudson. Illustrated. pp. 228. £11.50.
[2] *The Elizabethan Underworld,* by Gāmini Salgādo. Dent. Illustrated. pp. 222. £5.50.

magic and alchemy) côllected in one readable volume. Salgādo moves with a pickpocket's nimbleness from matters of fact to anecdote, and gives his informative, gossipy account somewhat in the manner of a latter-day John Aubrey.

Or perhaps his spirit is more akin to that of the Elizabethan lawyer John Manningham, another lover of anecdotes whose diary cum common-place-book has been freshly edited (for the first time unexpurgated) by Robert Parker Sorlien[3]. The Victorian suppressions were to do with decency rather than politics, so there are no startling revelations; but the record of coarse witticisms which entertained the student Manningham at dinner (not always as brilliant as the editor claims) emphasises that casual popular idiomatic usage was an inseparable part of the language in its most creative phase. As well as jests, Manningham recorded (some-times very fully) the sermons he attended, by Andrewes, John Spenser, and John King. Sorlien makes the very good point that this diary reveals how sermon techniques sometimes associated with the innovating Donne were developed a dozen years before he began to preach. The editor has retained Manningham's spelling with slight modernisation, and his notes on the many and various personalities and events impinging on the diarist are particularly helpful. Students of theatre myth will enjoy the Shakes-peare-Burbage anecodote, while students of Shakespeare will be teased by the brief account of a performance of *Twelfth Night* in the Great Hall of the Middle Temple.

It remains only to notice two essays. Thomas P. Roche Jr discusses the sixteenth-century holdings in the Robert H. Taylor Collection at Princeton, in 'A Library for a Sixteenth-Century Gentleman' (*PULC*). And in 'Lodowyck Bryskett, Envoy from Queen Elizabeth in Flanders (1600–1603)' (*NM*), William Schrickx delves into Bryskett's diplomatic mission and subsequent imprisonment, from which he was released in exchange for the Jesuit Ferdinand Cardin. In Brussels Schrickx has found Bryskett's passport, which shows that he had his brother Michael for company while in jail in Antwerp.

2. Sidney

Work on Sidney has picked up again after last year's brief respite, there being three critical studies and an edition. Maurice Evans has edited *The Countess of Pembroke's Arcadia*[4] with students' needs and pockets in mind. This modernised text, which comes at a tense juncture in the history of Arcadia-editing, is very welcome, but it will not please everyone. Evans has chosen to give us the hybrid *Arcadia* of 1593 ('emended in the light of the 1590 revised *Arcadia* and the 1598 folio'), retaining the later bridging interpolation in the middle of Book III by Sir William Alexander. Purists may well ask why Jean Robertson's lead was not followed by the publishers and the *Old Arcadia* printed rather than this one. But the choice of Lamb's *Arcadia,* the *Arcadia* of the centuries, is defensible on various grounds, even though it perpetuates a confusion that at last promised to

[3] *The Diary of John Manningham of the Middle Temple, 1602–03*, ed. by Robert Parker Sorlien. Hanover, N.H.: U. P. of New England, 1976. pp. xiv + 468. $25.
[4] *Sir Philip Sidney: Arcadia,* ed. by Maurice Evans. Harmondsworth: Penguin. pp. 870. pb £2.

clear. One may wonder, none the less, why the editor used as copy text Ernest Baker's 1907 edition which he acknowledges to be defective in more ways than one. Evans has modernised punctuation tactfully, in large part observing the practice of the Elizabethan compositors. He has also left alone words that were archaisms in Sidney's day, while regretting the inevitable loss in words that he has felt forced to modernise (such as 'locks' for 'lookes'). He follows the 1590 printer's practice of chapter divisions, introducing his own into the later books taken from the 1593 folio. The introduction explains and defends the tricky question of Sidney's rhetoric. All in all he presents the Countess's *Arcadia* as a solemn, heroic work (a major consideration in his choice of text) and for that reason devotes his introduction in the main to its serious rather than humorous aspects.

A. C. Hamilton is not likely to be happy with Evans's use of the 1593 folio, since for him Sidney is at his greatest in the 1590 *Arcadia,* as he says in his book *Sir Philip Sidney*[5]. This is a shrewd, solid introduction to Sidney, and fulfils its aim of showing a continuity between the life and the works (though he might have disregarded the probably apocryphal story of the glass of water). While keeping his book always at the level of introduction, Hamilton brings his learning valuably to bear on his reading of the works, and writes in an engaging, sensitive way that is bound to encourage the novice to commit himself to the Sidney Order. But the more practised Sidneian will be disappointed that he was content to leave it at that, and will wish that he had spread his wings for a more original flight, of which he was surely capable.

Dorothy Connell makes such an attempt in her book, *Sir Philip Sidney: The Maker's Mind*[6], and on the whole her daring proves worth the risk. Writing principally about the *Old* and *New Arcadias,* she takes the examples of Erasmus and Castiglione to show that the Renaissance mind, to which Sidney was the principal heir, knew how to find wisdom through folly and how a man might make himself according to his Maker's intentions. This means that for Sidney, contrary to what is usually understood by his repudiation of his past behaviour, both on his death-bed and in some of his writings, a humanist confidence in things of this world remains to the end, despite the awareness of darker realities that grows in the *New Arcadia*: 'Against the darker background of the *New Arcadia* . . . human love, foolish and fragile though it is, shines more brightly'. The fool, Basilius, is alone able to make right what the wise man, Euarchus, cannot resolve, the comic ending to the trial of the princes endorsing the important paradox of making 'the too much loved earth more lovely'. Sidney's final affirmation is that human happiness can and must be sought in this world rather than the next. The logic of Connell's argument is not always impeccable, but its thrust is compelling and should stimulate new discussion as to where the emphasis lies in some of the most important moments in the *Arcadias*.

Arthur K. Amos Jr's book, *Time, Space, and Value: The Narrative*

[5] *Sir Philip Sidney: A Study of his Life and Works*, by A. C. Hamilton. Cambridge: C. U. P. pp. viii + 216. £6.50.

[6] *Sir Philip Sidney: The Maker's Mind*, by Dorothy Connell. Clarendon Press. Maps. pp. 164. £6.50.

Structure of the New Arcadia[7], challenges the view that Sidney gave up writing the *New Arcadia* because he ran out of either time or interest. His speculation, a bold one, is that it is in some ways finished ('architectonically sound'). Investigating the structure of the three books of 1590, he finds that they correspond to the time, space, and value of his title. Book I explains spatial relationships, Book II temporal ones, and already inseparable they are summed up under the consideration of values in Book III. One of the advances Amos believes Sidney to have made in the later *Arcadia* is the 'internalization' of the reader. His argument works very well, although some of the incidents with which he illustrates his temporal theme could also serve a spatial argument – though perhaps that is the point. But it is just as well for the syllogistic neatness of this scheme that Sidney, to revert to the old-fashioned view, was unable or unwilling to finish the third book and write two more.

Margaret E. Dana, in 'The Providential Plot of the *Old Arcadia*' (*SEL*) points not to Basilius but to the 'tactful' and sympathetic narrator as the one who in reality solves the dilemma that proves too much for Euarchus. Less seriously, Wendy Gibson solves a riddle posed by Nico to Pas in the *Old Arcadia*, in 'Sidney's Two Riddles' (*N&Q*).

The question of folly comes up yet again in relation to the poems in Marianne S. Regan's 'Astrophil: Full of Desire, Empty of Wit' (*ELN*). She notes the convention of the 'foolish poet' and his recourse to the 'inexpressibility' trope (citing usefully the examples of Bernart de Ventadorn, Petrarch, and Ronsard), and argues that when Astrophil abandons the successful tactic of appearing a fool he dooms himself. Distinguishing folly from wisdom in poets, E. J. Devereux, in 'A Possible Source for "Pindare's Apes" in Sonnet 3 of "Astrophil and Stella" ' (*N&Q*), considers that Sidney admires Pindar as he mocks his imitators.

In an essay on the *Defence*, Leslie D. Foster (*HUSL*) establishes the framework of the essay as logical rather than rhetorical, and insists pertinently that the power of poetry to produce a clear moral vision was more important to Sidney than questions of how poetry is made.

G. F. Waller directs attention to the ladies of the family with two editions, one of poetry by Mary Herbert and the other by Lady Mary Wroth. In editing *The Triumph of Death and Other Unpublished and Uncollected Poems*[8] by the Countess, Waller reaffirms his belief that her importance is as a poet rather than merely as the sister to a celebrated brother. He demonstrates this in relation to her translation of Petrarch's *Trionfo della Morte*, and on a more personal note even goes so far as to suggest that she saw herself and her brother somewhat in terms of Laura and Petrarch. He also publishes for the first time some of Mary Herbert's Psalms, versions which were only rough drafts or essays, on the questionable grounds that they reveal her poetic imagination in various stages of development. In an appendix he discusses in detail a new manu-

[7] *Time, Space, and Value: The Narrative Structure of the New Arcadia*, by Arthur K. Amos Jr. Lewisburg: Bucknell U. P.; London: Associated University Presses. pp. 204. $11.50.
[8] *The Triumph of Death and Other Unpublished and Uncollected Poems by Mary Sidney, Countess of Pembroke (1561-1621)*, ed. by G. F. Waller. Salzburg: Institut für Englische Sprache und Literatur. pp. v + 228.

script of the Psalms recently deposited in the Houghton Library, Harvard. Finally, his edition includes two miscellaneous uncollected poems.

Continuing his bid to establish the poetic reputation of all members of the Sidney family, Waller also publishes Lady Mary Wroth's sequence of songs and sonnets, *Pamphilia to Amphilanthus*[9] – originally appended to the *Urania*. The editor attempts to ginger up the outdated melancholy of these poems by seeing them as a dramatic reflection of her disillusioned, personally miserable circumstances in a hollow Jacobean age, which was particularly hard on widows who aspired to write love poetry (the Duchess of Malfi perhaps?) This view would get some support from Josephine A. Roberts's 'An Unpublished Literary Quarrel concerning the suppression of Mary Wroth's "Urania" 1621' (*N&Q*). She prints two slanging verse epistles exchanged by Lady Mary and Lord Denny who, as Waller remarks, advised Lady Mary to follow the example of her 'vertuous & learned Aunt' and stick to translating psalms. Waller returns to the family once more with an essay on a poem by Robert Sidney, '"My wants and your perfections": Elizabethan England's Newest Poet' (*ArielE*) – a response to the recent manuscript discovery (*YW* 56.184).

3. Spenser

Work on Spenser this year shows an interesting division: between those still intent on pushing back the frontiers of scholarship and those (sometimes established pioneers themselves) who have begun to feel that enough is enough and that a vast potential body of readers is in danger of being left behind. However, James Nohrnberg's *The Analogy of the Faerie Queene*[10] is not a work that will brook compromise. It is not easy to do justice to the imaginative and intellectual energies active in this volume. It is not that the analogies he sets out to demonstrate, those of grace, government, and love have not been treated recently and at length by others, but that his demonstration takes on a fascinating life of its own. While possessed of an enormous scholarly capacity, Nohrnberg is not afraid of his own intuitions, so that explanations of allegory that would satisfy a Renaissance mind are none the less thrown open to later kinds of investigation. The 'typification' of a pair of lovers takes in examples from all ages – for instance, *Joseph Andrews,* Wagner, Thomas Mann ('friendship romance' verging on incest). Such classifying and categorising suggest Northrop Frye, whose presence like that of Freud can be felt at many points, and who gives the book its principles of organisation. It may be said against Nohrnberg that he does not know where to stop; his argument often seems unwilling to come to rest until he has proved that everything he has read leads to or from *The Faerie Queene.* But the scope of the enterprise will win the acclaim of frontiersmen.

Another impressive work – one more obviously designed for students' needs – is A. C. Hamilton's annotated edition of *The Faerie Queene*[11].

[9] *Lady Mary Wroth: Pamphilia to Amphilanthus,* ed. by G. F. Waller. Salzburg (see footnote 8). pp. v + 118.
[10] *The Analogy of the Faerie Queene,* by James Nohrnberg. Princeton, N.J.: Princeton U.P. pp. xxii + 870. £32.20.
[11] *Edmund Spenser: The Faerie Queene,* ed. by A. C. Hamilton. Longman. pp. xiv + 754. £25.

The advantage of this edition is that its notes are on the same page as the text, almost side by side — which further helps consultation. Hamilton has amalgamated gloss and commentary, and has tried hard to serve those approaching the poem for the first time as well as those already familiar with the text. The difficult task of appealing to different levels of readership simultaneously is managed rather well. But the good points of this edition threaten to be outweighed by its disadvantages (none of them the fault of the editor). These are: its price (no student will be able to afford it); the uneven face of the text (photographed from the Oxford Standard Authors edition); and the fact that it is not the complete Spenser (Oxford will continue to be necessary).

Michael O'Connell excitingly re-defines the concept of historical allegory in his book *Mirror and Veil*[12]. Writing a prescriptive epic in the manner of Virgil (whom O'Connell perhaps sees as more pertinent than the Italian romances), Spenser none the less brings the pressure of history to bear on his prospective patroness in ethical terms. Characters who can at different times be identified with Elizabeth suggest to her choices of behaviour which have importance for the culture which she embodies. The poem's theme of personal conflict is thus broadened to macrocosmic proportions. After Book V, however — and here readers may disagree with O'Connell's understanding of Spenser's design — loss of faith leads naturally to Calidore's retirement, from which despite the poem's overt exhortation there is no real return.

Douglas Brooks-Davies's commentary on the first two books of *The Faerie Queene*[13] (chosen because they are the most read) could not be fuller. Every possible allusion is traced, and the student will be grateful that so much of his work is done for him. On the other hand, gratitude may well give way to impatience at finding so little left to do. A serious objection to this kind of aid, excellent though it is, is that it inhibits undergraduates from risking anything so naive as a fresh thought. But perhaps that is an unreal fear. The book is more likely to be used by tutors mugging up awkward points of detail of the sort that embarrassed the author into writing it in the first place.

Peter Bayley's well-arranged collection of essays on *The Faerie Queene*[14] is made up from a rather different assumption of what students require. In his introduction he complains that the 'remarkable recent extension of our knowledge about Spenser . . . has promoted a great increase in professional academic preoccupation with *The Faerie Queene* but not, alas, made it any more popular with students and the general reader'. Therefore the critics he draws upon from the later part of the twentieth century tend to be those who write with some concern for the non-expert. Allegory is dealt with by Graham Hough and Maurice Evans, while P. J. Alpers and Martha Craig are prominent in the section on rhetoric, versification, and

[12] *Mirror and Veil: The Historical Dimension of Spenser's Faerie Queene*, by Michael O'Connell. Chapel Hill, N.C.: U. of North Carolina P. Plate. pp. xiii + 220. $14.95.

[13] *Spenser's Faerie Queene: A Critical Commentary on Books I and II*, by Douglas Brooks-Davies. Manchester: Manchester U. P. Illustrated. pp. x + 198. hb £5.75, pb £1.75.

[14] *The Faerie Queene: A Casebook*, ed. by Peter Bayley. Macmillan. pp. 253. hb £4.95, pb £2.25.

language. But a specialist writing for a large audience, Rosemond Tuve, is culled at length from the pages of her *Allegorical Imagery* to settle the question of Spenser and mediaeval romance. The good sense of Hughes, Hazlitt, and Dowden seems far from antiquated in this line-up.

Cambridge University Press have issued a paperback version of C. S. Lewis's *Spenser's Images of Life*[15], carefully edited and completed by Alastair Fowler (YW 48.195). In fact a tantalising preface leaves the reader in doubt as to what parts of the book are the editor's. The notes reproduce some interesting cancelled passages (usually brief), and record disagreements author and editor had in conversation over certain points of argument. Fowler has also rewritten the British Council monograph on Spenser[16]. While incorporating recent advances in scholarship (particularly in allegory and numerology), Fowler wears his learning lightly and presents a welcoming Spenser to the newcomer. He writes encouragingly and attractively on the experience to be got from reading *The Faerie Queene*.

Spenserians have convened once more at Kalamazoo[17]. The range of topics this year covers everything from antiquity (the Golden Age via *Mother Hubberds Tale*) through the Middle Ages (Dante and Chaucer), the Elizabethan age (for example, Shakespeare's *Midsummer Night's Dream*), to the present (Virginia Woolf). As before each paper draws a prepared rejoinder, also on record, so that the conference's dialogues are at least in part preserved for the reader. Among the contributors are: Rawdon Wilson, Humphrey Tonkin, John C. Ulreich Jr, and Elizabeth Pomeroy. Commentators include Waldo F. McNeir, A. Kent Hieatt, and Walter R. Davis.

And so to the essays and articles, of which there are many. Defying commentators who think they see more than the narrator in *The Faerie Queene*, Paul Alpers emphasises the narrator's own capacity to learn as he proceeds (*ELH*). This complex, taxing account sees a waning of rhetorical power in the later books preparing for the onset of lyricism in the *canzoni*. John C. Bean (*SEL*), gives a lucid account of the poem's movement from the colder Aristotelian virtue of temperance (Guyon) to the more generous, innocently erotic vision of chastity (Britomart) – emphasising the romantic element in neoplatonism. David R. Pichaske takes this further, in '*The Faerie Queene* IV ii and iii: Spenser on the genesis of friendship' (*SEL*), by arguing that both Plato and Aristotle, while present as influences, are transcended in the sphere of action by the Christian love ethic.

Edward Kahn's promising mathematical analysis of relationships, 'Semantic Marginal Complexity: A Model for Figurative Meaning in Literature' (*Poetics*), endorses with its figurative models more usual critical analyses, and finds interestingly that as a pair Scudamour and Amoret fall outside the pattern of love interest generally established by *The Faerie Queene*.

---

[15] *Spenser's Images of Life*, by C. S. Lewis. Cambridge: C. U. P. Facsimiles. pp. x + 144. £1.95.
[16] *Edmund Spenser*, by Alastair Fowler. Longman for the British Council. pp. 57. £0.65.
[17] *Spenser: Classical, Medieval, Renaissance, and Modern*, ed. by David A. Richardson. Cleveland, Ohio: Cleveland State U. Microfiche. $2.50.

Walter R. Davis proposes an open view of Book I, in 'Arthur, Partial Exegesis, and the Reader' (*TSLL*), by showing that allegory's fourfold working brings different levels closer at moments of crisis, allowing for the co-existence of different readings. James Neil Brown's fully documented study of the poem's use of Orpheus (*SoR*) enables him to establish the unity of the first five books, and then speculate on how preoccupations with time and ageing detach Book VI from the pattern.

Calvin R. Edwards makes the timely reminder that Britomart is not beyond criticism, in 'The Narcissus Myth in Spenser's Poetry' (*SP*), an essay which draws upon traces of Ficino discerned in *Amoretti* 35. Roger Swearingen equally insists in *SP* on the frailty of heroes: he points out that the collapse of Guyon after his exit from the Cave of Mammon underlines his insufficient human strength (the classical model of virtue shown to be inadequate without Christian fortitude).

Looking to the literary tradition of the poem, two critics find connections between Spenser and Italian writers. Timothy Cook, in an absorbing piece of detective work, 'Gabriel Harvey, "Pasquil", Spenser's Lost *Dreames,* and *The Faerie Queene*' (*YES*), links Spenser to the Italian Protestant humanist Celio Secondo Curione. Matthew Tosello, in 'Spenser's Silence about Dante' (*SEL*), admirably provides the framework connecting the two poets despite the thinness of the evidence. He argues convincingly that prudence was the reason for Spenser's silence about the Italian Republican champion of Elizabethan Puritans in their opposition to episcopacy.

Contemplating intentions, Jerry Leath Mills, in 'Spenser's Letter to Raleigh and the Averroistic *Poetics*' (*ELN*), protests that the 'twelve private morall vertues, as Aristotle hath devised' are a red herring; instead he uses the word 'pourtraict' to trace inspiration to Averroes's didactic commentary. Robin Headlam Wells (*ES*) looks usefully to Cicero for an explanation of Book VI. Ciceronian courtesy was available to Spenser from Castiglione and earlier English humanists, all of whom emphasise the part it had to play in public service.

Examining *The Faerie Queene* with a view to its influence on other plots, G. W. S. Brodsky, in '"The Changeling": A Possible Narrative Source in "The Faerie Queene"' (*N&Q*), sees some of the elements in the play as deriving from Spenser's Hellenore-Paridell-Malbecco triangle. Mark L. Caldwell compares Spenser's use of allegory with that of Phineas Fletcher (*ELH*). Distinguishing exegesis from organic rhetoric he shows how the prelude to the appearance of Mammon combines these two kinds to form a dramatic third mode.

There are several contributions on the minor poems. David W. Burchmore gives a fairly humdrum demonstration of the numerological importance of the Three Graces, in 'The Image of the Centre in *Colin Clouts Come Home Again*' (*RES*). Michael F. Dixon ambitiously but quite successfully seeks to reconcile diverse critical approaches to a text, in 'Rhetorical Patterns and Methods of Advocacy in Spenser's *Shepheardes Calender*' (*ELR*). Demonstrating how the poem's rhetoric extends its simple rustic characters into bearers of erotic, political, and aesthetic significance, he also establishes for it a 'grammatical' structure, transcending the strictly rhetorical, which orders alternatives 'in an inclusive, evaluative series'. Such a structure, he concludes ably, reveals man as a focus for unity as well as a source of diversity. Waldo F. McNeir (*Anglia*) interests himself in the poem's dramatic structure, and manages to reduce the twelve months to five acts. Though his Aristotelian tragi-comic formulation appeals to the imagination, it makes the dramatic character of the poem only intermittently apparent.

Carol V. Kaske looks for 'Another Liturgical Dimension of "Amoretti" 68' (*N&Q*), and finds it in a comparison of the sonnet with the Gospel for Holy Communion on St Barnabas's Day — Spenser's wedding day. The dimension revealed is that of the deeper integration of *eros* with *agape*.

Several contributions are made on Spenser in *N&Q*. J. N. Brown modifies a previous claim of Spenser's debt to Symphorien Champier, and alerts the reader to Ficino's 'Philebus' Commentary which both writers could have seen independently. On the subject of allusion, David Bergeron notes that John King (father of Henry) censured student delight in *The Faerie Queene*, the *Arcadia*, and the *Orlando Furioso*, in a lecture he gave at York in 1594 on the Old Testament book of Jonah. He suggests that this allusion be added to William Wells's 'Spenser Allusions in the Sixteenth and Seventeenth Century' (*SP 68*). Jackson C. Boswell has similar recommendations in 'Spenser Allusions: Addenda to Wells' (also *N&Q*).

4. Poetry

William Keach's good book, *Elizabethan Erotic Narratives*[18], proceeds from the belief that the epyllion is a serious and mature narrative verse form and not merely frivolous or 'Ovidian'. Ovid, in fact, is redefined in terms that make the Roman poet more profoundly comic than his lighter verse has the reputation for being. Sensationalism is played down in favour of a much more psychologically interesting portrayal of matters such as bestiality. As well as Ovid, Keach discusses *Venus and Adonis, Hero and Leander*, and Lodge's *Glaucus and Scylla* in the first part of his book. In the second half he charts the growth in satirical character of the epyllion with chapters on Marston, Weever, and Francis Beaumont, concluding with a neatly turned argument on their blend of satire and the erotic to dramatic and divisive effect ('the turbulence and contradition in erotic experience') compared with Spenser's synthesising eroticism. A drawback to some of his argument is his unnecessarily cautious attitude to the narrator, as in *Hero and Leander*, or his scepticism about such characters as Hero in the same poem.

What Keach has brought together Geoffrey G. Hiller puts asunder, in his anthology *Poems of the Elizabethan Age*[19]. The editor modernises spelling and punctuation, with the excepion of Spenser whose deliberate archaisms have been preserved. Distinguishing and insisting on the genres of Elizabethan poetry, Hiller places satire and the epyllion (or 'Ovidian romance') in two separate categories while calling for three more: the

[18] *Elizabethan Erotic Narratives*, by William Keach. New Jersey: Rutgers U. P.; Hassocks, Sussex: Harvester Press. Illustrated. pp. xviii + 278. £10.50.

[19] *Poems of the Elizabethan Age*, ed. by Geoffrey G. Hiller. Methuen. pp. xx + 332. hb £6.50, pb £2.95.

sonnet, the pastoral, and the lyric. Oddly enough, although this attractive collection tries to avoid the confusing character of a miscellany (which the Elizabethan to whose taste he defers would not have found strange), a miscellaneous impression is none the less created by dividing an author such as Shakespeare five ways. Conversely, while the point about genre is well taken, several poems seem to fit more than one category.

Maurice Evans has a notoriously simpler task in the printing of poems of a single, indisputable genre: the sonnet[20]. How often have attempts in this kind come to grief, yet how clever and courageous of the editor to simplify his problem by the bold stroke of eliminating the multitudinous Shakespeare. 'Elizabethan' is intended literally, and so Wyatt and Surrey are also absent. Space is made not only for Sidney, Spenser, and Drayton in full, but also for the whole of Daniel and Constable, with samplings from Barnes, Giles Fletcher, Lodge, Griffin, and William Smith. Sir John Davies's 'Gulling Sonnets' are also printed. The text is in old spelling and usefully annotated, and the editor contributes a helpful introduction on the sonnet's eternal twin theme of 'fulfilment and frustration'.

Chapman continues to command interest, though not so powerfully as in previous years. M. C. Bradbrook takes on the awkward task of writing about him in brief for the British Council[21]. This she does well while seeming more at ease in the section on the tragedies than in that on the lyrical poetry. John Huntington aims at correcting D. J. Gordon's celebrated justification of the punishment of the lovers in Chapman's continuation of Marlowe (ELR). His valuable but not entirely satisfactory reading advocates 'double vision': 'The poem treats the lovers in contradictory ways. If at some points it judges them rigorously and sees them as sinners against a world of ordered and civilised pleasures as represented by the figure of Ceremony, at other points it pities them and treats them as victims of an unjust and spiteful universe'. Huntington further discusses Chapman in the company of two of his contemporaries, in 'Philosophical Seduction in Chapman, Davies, and Donne' (ELH). Taking a similar double tack in order to solve the problems posed by Ovids Banquet of Sence (to which Donne's Extasie and Davies's Orchestra are compared), he proposes an attractive Stoic-Platonic reading in preference to the more grudging Stoic one of Kermode.

M. C. Bradbrook puts in another appearance on Chapman, but this time as the butt of Ian C. Mitchell who exposes an error she made many years ago concerning the whereabouts of Hitchin, in 'Chapman, Hitchin, and the Errors of the School of Night' (N&Q). Felicity A. Hughes, in 'Cynthia's Temple "Reextruct" in Chapman's "Shadow of Night"' (N&Q), convincingly demonstrates the numerological significance of Chapman's account in the poem by reference to Conti's Mythologia, the source-book which describes the Temple of Diana at Ephesus.

Writing on general themes, Earl Miner makes a spirited defence of an arguably outmoded critical position in 'Assaying the Golden World of

[20] Elizabethan Sonnets, ed. by Maurice Evans. Dent. pp. xxii + 238. hb £5.50, pb £2.95.
[21] George Chapman, by M. C. Bradbrook. Longman for the British Council. pp. 60. £0.65.

English Renaissance Poetics' (*Centrum*). Despite the ethical and social limitations under which the theory of mimesis thrived in Elizabethan England, its value is apparent in its insistence on the human relationship formed between author and reader or audience. His argument is simple and convincing.

Another piece of clear thinking – this time on the subject of metre – comes from Sharon Schuman, in 'Sixteenth-Century English Quantitative Verse: Its Ends, Means, and Products' (*MP*). Poets such as Campion *disguised* classical quantities as natural speech, satisfying layman and hierophant alike according to the allegorical formula for those in and out of the know.

Poly-Olbion receives its due for the first time in more than a year, in Stella P. Revard's 'The Design of Nature in Drayton's *Poly-Olbion*' (*SEL*). She singles out the river as specially important, its capacity for harmonisation within the natural landscape suggesting the wish for human harmony. A. J. Peacock (*N&Q*) illuminates Drayton's Latin descent, showing how despite its Horatianism the verse epistle to Reynolds derives from Catullus.

Margaret Maurer makes good use of the *emblem* convention to demonstrate the admonitory aspect of flattery in poems for patrons, in 'Samuel Daniel's Poetical Epistles, Especially Those to Sir Thomas Egerton and Lucy, Countess of Bedford' (*SP*).

Identification again exercises the wits of Timothy Cook, in 'Who Were Barnabe Googe's Two Coridons?' (*N&Q*). The phrase 'no kynne to me' is a vital clue: it signifies a repudiation of the murderous Marian Lord Chancellor, Richard Rich, by Barnabe Rich. A. B. Taylor, in '"Shakespeare's Ovid": Golding's "Metamorphoses" and Two Minor Elizabethan Writers' (*N&Q*), illustrates how the translator intervened to supply Ovidian details in poems by Henry Petowe and H. C. (?Henry Chettle).

David A. Roberts argues the integration of lyric impulse and didactic intention in Greville's poetry, while observing that his criticism insists on their being kept separate, in 'Fulke Greville's Aesthetic Reconsidered' (*SP*).

Finally, Charles G. Shirley Jr prints the text of the poem 'To bed I goe' (from *The Wonders of the Ayre* in the Lambeth Library collection) and dates it 1578-9, in 'Thomas Churchyard's Forgotten Bed-Grave Poem' (*ELN*).

5. Prose

Undoubtedly the most impressive edition of the year is the Folger Library's expensively produced *The Works of Richard Hooker*. The first two[22] of a projected eight volumes now appear under the general editorial direction of W. Speed Hill. These comprise the *Laws* up to and including Book V. Georges Edelen has edited the first volume (*Preface* and Books I–IV) and Speed Hill the second (Book V). The editors have worked

[22] *Richard Hooker: Of the Laws of Ecclesiastical Polity. The Folger Library Edition of the Works of Richard Hooker*. Vol. I ed. by Georges Edelen; vol. II ed. by W. Speed Hill. Cambridge, Mass., and London: Harvard U.P. pp. xi + 372; lviii + 552. £45.

scrupulously from manuscripts (including those in Hooker's hand or corrected by him) and printer's copies to establish this critical old-spelling edition. Their skill in textual bibliography is graciously displayed in their introductions and commentaries as well as in the list of non-substantive variants at the back of each volume. Volume I gives an interesting account of the 1593 folio which has been used for the *Preface* and the first four books. For Book V, Speed Hill has departed from previous editorial practice in not using the 1597 folio; he has instead used the manuscript prepared by Hooker's amanuensis, Benjamin Pullen, which contains Hooker's corrections (his non-substantive corrections are also listed at the back). This was the printer's copy, as is shown by the extensive markings for the typesetter. From a printing point of view the introduction to this volume is particularly interesting, but both editors show a thorough and reassuring acquaintance with the problems of textual editing. Hooker's marginal notes have been moved discreetly to the foot of the page where they are keyed economically to the text by superscript italic letters. The appearance of the page in Bembo Monotype is beautiful.

Also on Hooker, P. G. Stanwood and Laetitia Yeandle come up with an interesting manuscript speculation, in 'Three Manuscript Sermon Fragments by Richard Hooker' (*Manuscripta*). The three incomplete sermons are mainly in the hand of the seventeenth-century Archbishop of Armagh, James Ussher, and are generally thought to be his own. But the present authors guess on stylistic and verbal grounds that they may be Hooker's, copied from autograph by Ussher. The argument is strengthened by the fact that Ussher knew Lancelot Andrewes, possessor of some of Hooker's papers.

More printing problems come the way of J. S. Dean in 'Greek to the Popular Elizabethan Printer: Some Examples from Robert Greene's Romances' (*AEB*). He defends Greene's Greek by demonstrating that its mistakes are ones normally committed by compositors.

Again on the question of who wrote what, we find David Scott investigating a curious problem in 'William Patten and the Authorship of "Robert Laneham's *Letter*" (1575)' (*ELR*). After identifying the pseudonym Laneham with Langham (a hint from M. C. Bradbrook), he proposes Patten as the real author and helps his argument by comparing facsimile specimens of his handwriting with the letter.

Two writers tackle Lyly, and two more write on Lodge. Taking a hard look at the nasty goings-on in *Euphues,* Theodore L. Steinberg (*SEL*) argues that it is an anti-courtesy book, a parody of courtesy literature with a (superficially) Machiavellian, misogynistic hero at its centre. He finds it difficult to accept Lyly as a moralist and sees him as a satirist or parodist at best. Madelon Gohlke also recognises an unpleasant situation, in 'Reading "Euphues"' (*Criticism*), and gives a psychoanalytical explanation based on structuralism to show that breakdowns in mutual confidence are reflected in the prose style ('the disjunctive rhetoric of euphuism'). Both essays succeed in their different ways.

Lodge is easier for interpreters to deal with. Both critics writing on *Rosalind* show impatience with the effect Shakespeare has had on the work – particularly Charles Whitworth Jr, who lists some of the errors in family identification that have occurred in criticism and even editions, in *'Rosalynde*: As You Like It and As Lodge Wrote It' (*ES*). Charles Larson makes the interesting observation in 'Lodge's *Rosalind*: Decorum in Arden' (*SSF*) that there is less satire in Lodge's romance than in *As You Like It*, and reflects that the differences between his Arden and Bordeaux are stylistic rather than substantial. The values found in the countryside are an extension not a repudiation of those of the court.

Mark L. Caldwell puts together a nice argument on Fulke Greville's motivation in 'Sources and Analogues of the *Life of Sidney*' (*SP*), contending that his ambition, influenced by Camden's *Annales* and contemporary intelligencers, was to write interpretative rather than chronicle history.

Finally, there are two notes on minor figures. Alan R. Young fills in details of the life of his subject to show that he was something less than his style, in 'Henry Peacham, Author of "The Garden of Eloquence" (1577): A Bibliographical Note' (*N&Q*). And in 'The Published Writings of Sir Henry Finch' (*N&Q*), W. R. Prest identifies his man as the author of various anonymous theological tracts, proving that unlike the ordinary lawyer of his time he was capable of a wide range of thought.

X

The Earlier Seventeenth Century:
Excluding Drama

BRIAN NELLIST and NICK SHRIMPTON

This chapter is arranged as follows: 1. General, by Brian Nellist; 2. Poetry, by Nick Shrimpton; 3. Prose, by Brian Nellist. A selective review of books may be found in *SEL*.

1. General

Heimo Ertl has provided in *Die Scheinheiligen Heiligen*[1] what is in effect a massive anthology of references to Puritanism in the satirical and polemical writing of the seventeenth century, though its usefulness is somewhat diminished by the absence of an index. Organised analytically, it provides clear evidence on such topics as the variable usage of the word Puritan, the attributes of the caricature figure and such specific issues as sabbatarianism and the objections to the ecclesiastical calendar. The trivialisation of the more serious language of controversy in this literature benumbs the mind, and rather more extensive reference to secondary material might have produced a more searching analysis of the state of satire in the period.

One particular Puritan gentleman has been well served by Margaret F. Stieg in *The Diary of John Harington, M.P., 1646-53*[2]. Though his friends included Prynne, Hale and Ussher, and the editor's skill has identified a large number of slighter friends and associates, Harington's diary is a dry record of parliamentary debates and domestic events. The son of the translator of Ariosto, he seems more interested in his physical well-being and the state of his feet than in the movement of his mind or feelings. His notes for charges delivered to Grand Juries, wantonly scribbled across the best manuscript version of Wyatt's poems, Egerton 2711, are in effect amateur sermons, the product of a conservative Calvinism, which usefully articulate commonplaces about the relation of divine and human justice and the social ethics of right-wing Puritanism.

A rather more adventurous member of the gentry, John Pory, has been

---

[1] *Die Scheinheiligen Heiligen. Das Bild der Puritaner im Zerrspiegel satirischer und polemischer Literatur des 17.Jahrhunderts*, by Heimo Ertl. Frankfurt: Peter Lang, Berne: Herbert Lang. Europäische Hochschulschriften 49. pp. xii + 490. pb, no price given.
[2] *The Diary of John Harington, M.P., 1646–53 with notes for his Charges*, ed. by Margaret F. Stieg. Somerset Record Society vol. 74. pp. viii + 124. No price given.

given the detailed study that his varied life deserves by William S. Powell[3].
The translator and reviser of Leo Africanus, traveller and part-time
diplomat, first Speaker in the Assembly of Virginia, and above all writer
of news-letters with increasing regularity during the reigns of James I and
Charles I, Pory touches many areas and figures of interest to the student
of literature. The news-letters, only slightly less valuable than those of
John Chamberlain, and written in a similar chirpy style, are unfortunately
published on microfiches, precariously fitted into an envelope at the back
of the volume, surely the most inconvenient form of publication ever
inflicted on the reader. A highly detailed separate index to them, which
includes subjects as well as names, compensates for some of the difficulties
involved.

2. Poetry

William B. Hunter Jr has assembled an anthology of *The English Spenserians*[4] with the particular intention of restoring the long poem to its
proper prominence. One such work by each of his five chosen authors
(Giles Fletcher, George Wither, Michael Drayton, Phineas Fletcher and
Henry More) is accordingly printed entire, from the first text in which
their work is judged to have come to maturity. Convenient access to such
poems as *The Shepheards Hunting* is welcome. But the policy means that
there is no space at all for William Browne, without whom a volume with
this title seems seriously unrepresentative.

The longest of all Drayton's poems, *Poly-Olbion*, is examined by Stella
P. Revard (*SEL*) in an article which concentrates on his use of pastoral
for the anthropomorphic presentation of topography. The landscape thus
celebrated proves also to contain moral and political significances. A. J.
Peacock (*N&Q*) points out that Drayton's epistle to Reynolds, so often
spoken of as an Horatian poem, in fact opens with an adaptation of six
lines by Catullus. Norman E. Carlson (*N&Q*) draws attention to an authorial inscription to the Attorney-General, dated 1656, in a copy of George
Wither's *Britain's Remembrancer*. This he offers as evidence against the
belief that the poet's high opinion of his own political importance was
ridiculous. Richard Brathwait, the eulogist of Wither and Browne, is
considered in his own right by Edward M. Wilson (*N&Q*). Annotations
in a copy of the 1716 edition of the pseudonymous *Barnabae itinerarium*
confirm Brathwait's authorship and suggest the continuing popularity of
the work.

Susan Burchmore (*N&Q*) brings a numismatic expertise to the dating
of Donne's 'The Canonization'. Though the 'reall' of line 7 was an English
(as well as a Spanish) coin, none was minted with a king's face on it
between 1491 and 1606. This suggests a date as late as 1608 for 'The
Canonization'. The same poem is discussed at greater length, though less
persuasively, in Marjorie D. Lewis's contribution to *New Essays on*

[3] *John Pory, 1572-1636. The Life and Letters of a Man of Many Parts. Letters
and Other Minor Writings Microfiche Supplement*, by William S. Powell. Chapel Hill,
N.C.: U. of N. Carolina P. pp. xviii + 187. 6 microfiches, pp. 351. No price given.
[4] *The English Spenserians*, ed. by William B. Hunter Jr. Salt Lake City: U. of Utah
P. pp. |xiv| + 455. $20.

Donne[5], a volume of markedly uneven quality edited by Gary A. Stringer. The speaker of 'The Canonization' is here suggested to be the *adversarius* of 'Satire 1' arguing back in a manner suggested by Juvenal's 'Satire 3'. Thomas J. Wertenbaker (*Expl*) points out that 'A Jeat Ring Sent' is addressed to a ring which has been sent *back*. Laurence Perrine (*Expl*) correctly rebukes a previous suggestion, by Judah Stampfer, that the first four stanzas of 'Love's Diet' are spoken by a woman. Patrick G. Hogan Jr's essay on 'A Valediction Forbidding Mourning' in *New Essays on Donne*[5] is an otiose attempt to find iconographic significance in the poem. Nothing is thereby added which was not already obvious.

The literary background to three of Donne's elegies is explored by Roslyn L. Donald (*ELN*). 'The Anagram', 'The Comparison' and 'Love's Progress', she suggests, derisively combine the paradoxical encomium with the blazon, or catalogue of beauties. Possible sources for 'The Comparison' receive still more minute attention from Patricia Thomson (*N&Q*). The drops of sweat, which Dr Johnson found indelicate, prove to have parallels in both Spenser and Tasso. Thomas A. Reisner (*N&Q*) explains a hitherto puzzling allusion in lines 64–65 of 'Elegy 14'. The reference is not to a misreading of Plautus, as Grierson had conjectured, but to a Greek epigram attributed to Plato by Diogenes Laertius. Reisner provides an elegant translation, by Shelley, of the epigram in question. Edgar F. Daniels (*Expl*) quarrels with a reading of lines 37–38 of 'Elegy 18' offered in a previous issue of the same journal by R. W. French. M. Thomas Hester (*N&Q*) agrees with Milgate and Grierson that Donne's 'Satyre 2' was composed in early 1594. The poem is in his opinion, however, not centrally a response to the anonymous volume of Petrarchan sonnets, *Zepheria*. Instead it records Donne's feelings about the law after the imprisonment and death of his younger brother Henry in the summer of 1593. Heather Dubrow Ousby (*N&Q*) finds yet another parallel to the Hill of Truth in 'Satire 3' in one of Seneca's letters to Lucilius. Robert J. Bauer's article in *New Essays on Donne*[5] claims that the verse letter 'To Sir Edward Herbert, at Juliers' is a cryptic statement of Donne's aesthetic ideals. Unfortunately such an argument requires a convincing preliminary demonstration that Donne is thinking of Herbert as poet rather than philosopher. This is not supplied. Leonard D. Tourney writes more convincingly about Donne's epistles in his contribution to the same volume[5]. The letters to the Countess of Bedford, he suggests, help us to understand Donne's debt to the Petrarchan tradition. Not surprisingly, it is the parallels with such Petrarchists as Serafino, rather than with Petrarch himself, which seem most striking.

Jay Parini (*FMLS*) undertakes an extended comparison between the religious verse of Donne and Gerard Manley Hopkins without in the process saying anything new about either poet. Kitty Datta (*CritQ*) finds analogies for Donne's mingling of divine and sexual love in the writings of Ambrose, Jerome and Augustine and examines *The Anniversaries* in this light. In one of the better articles in *New Essays on Donne*[5] Paul A. Parrish compares the same poems with Donne's funeral sermons. Elizabeth

[5] *New Essays on Donne*, ed. by Gary A. Stringer. *Salzburg Studies in English Literature, Elizabethan & Renaissance Studies*, 57. Salzburg: Institut für Englische Sprache und Literatur. pp. ii + 262. pb, no price given.

Drury, he suggests, is treated in the same impersonal way as King James or Lady Danvers, and in both poem and sermon Donne addresses himself to an ideal audience which needs to be reminded rather than convinced. Michael Smalling's contribution to *New Essays on Donne*[5] is a circular argument which strives to demonstrate that Donne's aesthetic is religious because it is mediaeval and mediaeval because it is religious. Stanley Archer, in the same volume[5], rounds up the journey images in Donne's religious verse but makes very little of them once he's got them into the corral. Robert R. Owens (*N&Q*) discusses the fact that the voyage in the 'Hymne to God My God, in my Sicknesse' is a western one, rather than a conventional passage to Jerusalem through the Straits of Gibraltar, and lists some early accounts of the Straits of Magellan. Finally in an article which, unlike most of the other contributions to *New Essays on Donne*[5], is both learned and genuinely illuminating A. B. Chambers analyses 'La Corona' in the context of the liturgical use of time. The events of the liturgical year have a chronological sequence but simultaneously stand outside time in eternity. Donne's poem about those events is accordingly circular. Though sequential it has no beginning and no end, reflecting that expert interest in the ecclesiastical calendar which elsewhere provoked its author to write a poem 'Upon the Annunciation and Passion falling upon one day'.

Ben Jonson's poetry has had a thin year. Kathryn Walls (*N&Q*) argues that the 'just day' in 'On My First Sonne' is an allusion to the Mosaic law stated in Deuteronomy 15.1–2. The idea of sabbatical release, initially puzzling, becomes clear once we realise that it is applied to slaves as well as debtors. George Herbert has fared only slightly better, though he is the subject of an important and closely argued article by Ilona Bell (*MLQ*) which discusses the theological significance of *The Temple*. The work does not, as Rosamund Tuve and Louis Martz have claimed, reflect Catholic devotional practices. Instead *The Temple* is Protestant meditation, exploding the established Catholic procedures glimpsed in 'The Sacrifice' in a manner akin to Donne's treatment of Petrarchan conventions. Jeanne Clayton Hunter (*Expl*) makes heavy weather of the central image of 'The Bag', ignoring its obvious function as a post-bag in favour of an allusion to Job 14.17. Elissa S. Guralnick (*Expl*) attempts to substantiate J. H. Summers's claim that in 'Church Monuments' the dissolution of the body is enacted by a dissolution of syntax. Saad El-Gabalarry (*N&Q*) draws attention to two of Herbert's minor disciples, Cardell Goodman and Ralph Knevet, and records some faint verbal echoes of Herbert in their work. In an elegant and original article Leah Sinanoglou Marcus (*ELR*) gives a masterly account of those difficult simple poems Herrick's *Noble Numbers*. The sense in which they are noble remains a mystery until we understand their covert political significance. By asserting the importance of rote rather than extemporaneous prayer, by mocking predestination, and by celebrating traditional festivals the poems out-Laud Laud as an expression of loyalty to a beleaguered church and throne. Robert W. Halli Jr (*Expl*), more modestly, shows that Herrick's epigram 'Upon Prig' depends upon the fact that the 'chev'rell' referred to was a particularly expensive form of leather.

David C. Judkins (*ELR*) provides a useful survey of work on the Cavalier Poets (here defined as Carew, Lovelace, Suckling and Waller) since 1945. He records the diminishing sense of distinction between Cavaliers, Metaphysicals and Spenserians, and identifies an edition of Waller and a biography of Carew as the most urgent needs. Frances W. Fry (*N&Q*) finds a source for the theme and imagery of Carew's 'Aske Me No More' in Lord Herbert of Cherbury's *De Veritate*. Lovelace's adaptations of Italian material are discussed by Paulina Palmer (*CL*) in an article which draws attention to the difficulties faced by English poets who wished to combine the native line of wit with the more artificial manner of the Marinisti. Thomas Clayton, in his edition of Suckling in 1971, stated that the whereabouts of the Hopkinson manuscripts (containing some poems ascribed to 'J.S.') had been unknown since 1872. Peter Beal (*N&Q*) points out that the manuscripts are in fact in the Bradford Central Library and records the variants from the 1659 text of the five Suckling poems which they contain. Allan P. Green's 'Unnoticed Fact of the Life of Sir John Suckling' (*N&Q*) had, unfortunately, been noticed. Indeed it had actually been discussed in the same journal (by Judith K. Gardiner) as recently as 1975.

Gareth Alban Davies (*ULR*) considers Fanshawe's expertise as a Hispanist, in an inaugural lecture (to a chair of Spanish) which combines an account of the poet's career as a diplomat in Spain and Portugal with a critical analysis of his translations. The controversial conclusion is that Fanshawe's greatest achievements as a poet lie in his versions of sonnets by Gongora and Mendoza. William D. McGaw (*ELN*) suggests that the game of chess in Cowley's 'Destinie' is an image of recent historical events. Dirk Erpenbeck (*N&Q*) records the presence of a manuscript of William Strode's 'On Chloris Walking' in the Ajaaloo Museum in Tallinn. This was written in a German translator's album by an English merchant in 1637, when both men were on trade missions to the Shah of Persia in Isphahan. The text has no authority, but the circumstances of its origin have a pleasing topicality.

Though the tercentenary floodgates had not yet opened the year produced a substantial body of writing on Marvell. Bruce King's *Marvell's Allegorical Poetry*[6] is an extreme example of what William Empson long ago attacked as the neo-Christian Movement in modern literary criticism. All of Marvell's lyrics, whether ostensibly religious or not, are suggested to be pious allegories. The product of a man immersed in biblical commentaries, they supposedly present a single and coherent vision of the divine scheme. 'The Unfortunate Lover' is thus unequivocally Christ, 'The Definition of Love' describes the limitations of mystical contemplation, 'Little T.C.' is Adam in Paradise, and 'The Mower against Gardens' is a parody of Digger polemics. The argument which supports these extravagant claims is decidedly thin and Professor King fails to explain why these readings would make the poems more interesting, even if they were true.

Those who hanker after such reductive certainties will have no patience for the debate on the possible meanings of 'The Definition of Love' conducted in *EIC*. E. B. Greenwood suggested that the poem concerned a lover's wish to achieve penetrability rather than mere proximity. Since

[6] *Marvell's Allegorical Poetry*, by Bruce King. New York & Cambridge: Oleander Press. pp. 208. £3.75, $8.95.

this was possible only for the three hypostases of the Trinity the (highly Metaphysical) ambition was doomed. The late F. W. Bateson (*EIC*) responded with the rude but pertinent question 'So what?'. Can a good poem, he enquired, merely be virtuosity? Must there not be a human core? To flesh out the personal feeling which he at least sensed in the poem he speculated bravely about an affair with an unobtainable Royalist girl. Harold Love (*EIC*) poured predictable scorn on what he wittily christened 'the Dark Lady of the Definition' and argued for an unspecified third reading which was neither Greenwood's philosophical wit nor Bateson's human relationship. James Turner (*EIC*) drove some factual nails into the coffin of the Royalist romance and suggested that the love was impossible because it was imaginary, a poet's fictitious conception. The destruction of a particular biographical hypothesis does not, of course, affect the central thrust of Bateson's argument. His hunger for human rather than merely mechanical significances in poetry, and his belief that literature must be enjoyed as well as elucidated, will be even more sorely missed in seventeenth-century studies than they will be elsewhere.

C. B. Hardman (*EIC*) deals firmly with the question of whether the rowers in Marvell's 'Bermudas' are making the first landfall or merely a local trip at some later stage. Insisting that it is the latter, he writes interestingly about the poem as an original treatment of the relationship between work and praise. By an expert, and equally decisive, handling of some architectural evidence James Turner (*N&Q*) demonstrates that the dome sometimes discovered in stanza 7 of 'Upon Appleton House' is an illusion. A. J. Wilson (*N&Q*) offers a numerological reading of 'Upon the Hill and Grove at Bill-Borrow', suggesting that the recurrence of the number four displays the 'four-square' quality of Fairfax. Don Parry Norford (*MLQ*) applies a geometrical version of the same technique to 'Upon Appleton House'. Both the poem and the house are suggested to be examples of the mandala, or circle within a square. A remorselessly solemn article, it redeems itself slightly by reminding us that Maria Fairfax, for whose future Marvell entertains such high-minded hopes, in fact went on to marry the notoriously dissolute Duke of Buckingham. E. F. Daniels (*Expl*) suggests that 'distance' in line 50 of 'Eyes and Tears' might mean an interval of time rather than space. David K. Cornelius (*Expl*) makes a small contribution to the dispute about the 'Horatian Ode', on the anti-Cromwell side, by discussing the 'erect' sword in the closing lines. Dean R. Baldwin (*Expl*) claims that Marvell's use of the word 'mower' is a pun. More fruitfully, Christine Rees (*N&Q*) discusses 'A Dialogue Between the Resolved Soul and Created Pleasure' in the context of seventeenth-century versions of the Judgement of Paris.

Alan Rudrum's services to readers of Vaughan are continued (*N&Q*) by some scrupulous corrigenda to his Penguin edition. Jonathan George (*Expl*) distinguishes three levels of statement in 'The Pursuite' before choosing to concentrate on a series of rather fanciful verbal ambiguities. Eluned Brown (*E&S*) writes about Vaughan as a landscape poet, arguing that he is most the Silurist in his secular verse. The religious poems offer a 'baptized Breconshire', as much Middle-Eastern as it is Welsh.

Finally a note on the influence of early seventeenth-century poetry. B. Wallingford Boothe (*N&Q*) gives Edmund Gayton, whose *Pleasant*

Notes upon Don Quixot was published in 1654, credit for an early and important contribution to the subsequently fashionable genre of classical travesty.

3. Prose

That enterprising journal *SLitI* devotes an entire issue this year to articles on seventeenth-century prose. Alvin Vos opens the volume with a sceptical critique of 'stylistics' and its claim to be a self-sufficient discipline. What its exponents allege that they discover from the study of style, he argues, is often simply a confirmation of ideas actually based on a reading of the whole text. Their hidden assumption is often an attempt to enter the writer's consciousness and Vos offers mild rebukes to Joan Webber and Stanley Fish for respectively focusing on psychic biography and the role of the reader. The writer's own preference lies with older models of rhetorical analysis and a modesty that remains conscious of the historical perimeter encircling prose of the period. Writing if not to this brief then at least in its spirit, Ted–Larry Pebworth (*SLitI*) distinguishes between the essay and other related brief prose genres by indicating the open-endedness of the essay. Taking a large step from effect to intention, he then argues for the form as a drama of thinking and a presentation of an image of the self to the reader, more convincing in the case of Cornwallis than of Bacon, possibly.

There are interesting contributions also on the minor prose of the period. Florence Sandler (*SLitI*) recognises in the close relationship between Fuller's *Pisgah Sight* and his *Church History* a defence of the Church of England against its critics on the right hand and on the left. He maintains against the Millenarians of the late 1640s an Augustinian confidence in the historic church as a final dispensation, and against Catholics and Laudians sees in the relation of the Second Temple to the First (less glorious but less corrupt) an illustration of the church's need for constant reformation. J. Max Patrick (*SLitI*) in a study of Samuel Gott's *Nova Solyma* contrasts English with Latin utopias, the former usually limiting narrative detail, the latter realising their vision through processes of imaginative elaboration. The author indicates deficiencies in the translation by W. Begley and demonstrates the range of interests and sympathies of a civilised, moderate Puritan. Frank L. Huntley (*SLitI*) attributes to Joseph Hall the foundation of a specifically English and Protestant tradition of meditation. It derives, he argues, from Thomas à Kempis rather than Mauburnus, who is favoured by Louis Martz as a source for *The Arte of Divine Meditation*, and it continues the affective and less formalised tradition of late mediaeval piety against the rigour of the Ignatian method.

Other minor writers have received attention elsewhere. Karl Josef Höltgen (*N&Q*) has forever laid the ghost of the mysterious Mrs Henry Hawkins, wife to the Jesuit emblem writer. Possible scandal is avoided by the simple and satisfying discovery of her tombstone in Fordwich parish church which establishes unimpeachable evidence for her death after only one year of marriage and five years before her husband entered the English College. Supplementary to his study of Henry Peacham *père*,

Alan Young (*N&Q*) offers new material about Henry Peacham *fils*. Two obscure periods in his biography are illuminated, the first occupied with travels and music study in Italy before he returns to teach school in Kimbolton and the second when he continued that occupation in Lincolnshire. Yet another legendary death in poverty is brought into question by further evidence. George Sandys's refusal in the *Travailes* to accept the traditional siting of Troy on the western shore of the Troad, according to Jack E. Friedman (*N&Q*), is due to his dependence on Strabo, whom he follows closely at this point. Graham Parry (*LeedsSE*) writes an attractive article in honour of John Weever's *Ancient Funerall Monuments*. The study of tombs leads Weever into what we should now call social history, which he writes from the standpoint of a conservative Laudian. He traces the decay of chivalric manners to the growth of peaceful conditions and commercial enterprise. He also proves surprisingly well informed about mediaeval literature, in the manner of Camden.

Sir Thomas Browne has been made readily available to the general reader by Professor Patrides and Penguin Books in a large selection[7] which includes *Religio Medici, Hydriotaphia, The Garden of Cyrus, A Letter to a Friend, Christian Morals* and the tractate *On Dreams* as well as just under a hundred pages from *Pseudodoxia Epidemica,* including much of Book 1, his Baconian account of the sources of delusion. The texts are edited with the skill and formidable scholarship inevitable with this editor, complete with headnotes, footnotes that interest the reader as well as assisting him, a dictionary of names, Johnson's brief biography and a fuller bibliography than appears, for example, in the *Cambridge Bibliography*. It omits, however, Stanley Fish's trenchant criticism of Browne in *Self-Consuming Artefacts* (1973). Since the major audience for the work is likely to be new readers of Browne, it is a pity, maybe, that the introduction should sacrifice explanation to erudition, however elegant. Browne emerges as a prose Marvell, playing celestial games with the paradoxes of theology and achieving, apparently, a fusion of levity and seriousness, which the critic insists upon but does not really prove. Browne's rhapsodic imagination puts critics on their mettle and two articles this season seek to pull unity out of apparent diversity. Walter R. Davis (*SLitI*) in a close reading of *Urne Buriall* which multiplies evidence beyond the requirements of the argument interprets it as a voyage of discovery, cognate with Burton and Donne's *Devotions*. The reason, he argues, is conducted to the regions of death and the work ends with its resurrection to a fideist life. L. A. Breiner (*MLQ*), following Frank Huntley's original thesis for a close relation between *Urne Buriall* and *The Garden of Cyrus*, maintains that both works assume radical metaphors to specify the grandeur and misery of the human mind. If womb, earth and darkness confine its perspectives in the first treatise, the image of the circle and its centre, the sun and the sphere in the second almost deify the intelligence. The mind like the sphere itself is bounded by darkness but finds everywhere centres for its vision of the divine.

Burton's *Anatomy* continues to elude description. David Renaker

---

[7] *Sir Thomas Browne: The Major Works,* ed. with an introduction and notes by C. A. Patrides. Harmondsworth, Middx.: Penguin. pp. 558. pb. £2.00, $3.95.

(*N&Q*) poses the more traditional problem associated with it. Fontenelle and Burton both compare the stars of the Milky Way to the twelve thousand islands of the Maldive Archipelago. What is their common source? Richard L. Nochimson (*FMLS*) asks instead in what sense the *Anatomy* continues to interest the modern reader, and floats a precarious raft of semi-fictionalisation and 'shallow-masks' upon a tidal bore which almost swamps the argument in qualifications and concessions. The most valuable section indicates the changes made in later editions which indicate an increase in personal reference and in freedom of rhetorical display. James S. Tillman (*SLitI*) frankly admits the inconsistencies and sudden changes of register in Burton and compares them with the procedures of the contemporary satirist who includes his own shrewish malcontentedness among the absurdities that he attacks.

The uneven collection of essays on Donne from Salzburg[5] includes an original argument from Robert M. Cooper on the *Devotions* of 1624. He maintains that they involve metaphorical allusions to the contemporary state of the kingdom, the Spanish marriage escapade and the increase of the Catholic presence. The allusions to erring rulers, especially to David as divine but sinning monarch, the fear of relapse after the recovery of the body, now politic as well as every other conceivable allegory, and the dedication to Prince Charles, the author argues convincingly, express Donne's own anxieties about his relation to his royal patron and his policies. The other articles on prose in this volume lack this benefit of having something new and specific to say. Michael Hall's contribution[5] on scriptural exposition in the sermons starts with the interesting point that Donne seizes on unexpected words in his chosen text to spring a rhetorical surprise on the congregation. The later argument that Donne develops an exploratory, rather than an authoritative, hermeneutic lends itself, however, to desultory research over too wide a field. Carl Senheim[5] also, maybe, adopts too large and amorphous a thesis. Donne starts his preaching career by turning his back on his earlier interests, but as his confidence in his vocation grows recognises in his insights as poet grounds for claiming special expository skills, a sensitivity to Biblical metaphor and an ability to move as well as teach his flock.

XI

Milton

C. A. PATRIDES

1. General

Two historians lead the year's work in Miltonic studies, each with a contribution best described as rather particular. Christopher Hill, our first historian, displayed his view of Milton on two previous occasions: initially in *The World Turned Upside Down*, where several 'subversive' passages were eclectically isolated from their poetic contexts (*YW* 54.250), and next in the lecture 'Milton the Radical', where the poet was sought — and was of course found — in the radical circles of Ranters, Fifth Monarchists, Muggletonians, and the rest (*YW* 55.284). But now in devoting a book to Milton — *Milton and the English Revolution*[1] — Hill is not nearly as adventurous. The poet remains, of course, 'a radical Protestant heretic' and, in line with Hill's Marxist predilections, a man definitely attracted by 'the lower-class third culture'. However, Milton's radicalism is now seen to have had its 'limits' (to quote Hill); and in any case, though the Ranters and the rest still figure prominently, they are but part of 'the intellectual milieu' which, all too necessarily, encompasses dimensions beyond Hill's interests. *Milton and the English Revolution* is consequently a largely sane effort to place Milton within the immediate political and social context of his age, even as its thesis *qua* thesis is an important corrective to the claims of literary scholars. Yet Hill's ambitious interpretation of the poems, ventured all too often with a minimum of warrant and certainly with a political commitment bordering on monomania, will doubtless be argued for many years to come. In the end, it may be that the new Milton will prove to be but 'Hill's Milton' (as Frank Kermode already claimed in a review in *The New York Times* for 5 March 1978). It is nevertheless beyond doubt that we have gained a study which, however controversial, is major by any standards. The first 'official' response must certainly have astounded Hill, for in spite of his contemptuous remark on the 'Milton industry', his book received the Milton Society's first Hanford Award for the year's most distinguished book.

A. L. Rowse, our second historian, provides in *Milton the Puritan* a most lively 'portrait of a mind'[2]. The liveliness resides in Rowse's zestful style but especially in his intentionally sensationalised views. No sooner is the book under way than Milton ('a recognisable feminine type') is opposed to Shakespeare ('the completely released, normal, masculine heterosexual'). The opposition informs all subsequent judgements, from the conviction that Milton 'identified with the Lady in *Comus*' — 'reveal-

[1] *Milton and the English Revolution*, by Christopher Hill. Faber & Faber (1977); and New York: The Viking Press (1978). pp. xviii + 541. £12.50, $20.
[2] *Milton the Puritan: Portrait of a Mind*, by A. L. Rowse. Macmillan. pp. 297. £5.95.

ing psychologically', we are told – to the telling rhetorical question, 'Was Mary Powell rather boyish?' As Rowse has no doubt that 'Milton had rather a low view of womankind', his later discussion of *Paradise Lost* and *Samson Agonistes* advances along a predictable path. Even more offensive, however, is the simplistic dichotomy of the political realities into King and Puritans – or, in Rowse's terms, on the one hand 'the martyred King', and on the other 'tragic lunacy', the 'spirit of Puritan aggression', 'a nasty spirit'. Milton 'the defender of regicide' was in his political thinking quite simply 'a fool'. Since Milton's theological commitments please Rowse even less, they are dismissed as so much 'metaphysical moonshine'. The author of *Milton the Puritan*, it is clear, detests both Milton and the Puritans in equal measure. But in detesting them, he misunderstands them; and in misunderstanding them, he reveals the portrait of a historian sadly given to gross misconceptions rather too explicitly perverse.

The contributions to Milton studies by scholars outside Britain, the Commonwealth, and the United States, are often substantial and sometimes indispensable. Their enthusiasm, moreover, is frequently of such persuasion as to affect us for the best. A case in point is a work published last year in Italian, Loretta Valtz Mannucci's *Ideali e classi nella poesia di Milton*[3], which centres itself on *Paradise Lost* in the first instance and on *Paradise Regained* in the second to study Milton's thought in relation to its intellectual and political background, largely through the pattern of 'l'educazione dell'eroe'. The argument often depends on dimensions which are derivative. But as the work consistently refuses to forego Milton's text, it persuades so far as it attends to the details; and as it treads adventurously where others tend to walk much more circumspectly, it provides the most comprehensive vision of Milton's aspirations to have emanated from Italy in a long time.

Milton has gained a volume in the popular series 'Giants of Literature'. Initially prepared in 1968 for the Milanese publishers A. Mondatori and now translated into English, the volume is the oddest contribution we have had for some time; and it is perhaps not an accident that it appears anonymously[4]. The outline of Milton's career is innocent enough, and the glance at some of the public events in the seventeenth century is alarmingly superficial. But the volume may well be only an excuse for the collection of plates framing some 1700 lines extracted from *Paradise Lost*. If so, the reproductions of several illustrations of the poem – by J. B. de Medina in 1688, R. Westall in 1794–97, Doré in 1881, *et al.* – are an unexpected dimension. The several Blake plates in colour also surprise by their excellence, as do Fuseli's rarely reproduced interpretations of Milton's reconciliation with Mary Powell and his dream of his second wife.

Visvanath Chatterjee in 'Milton: After Three Hundred Years' (*Bull. of the Ramakrishna Mission Institute of Culture*) ventures not so much an essay as a paean of praise, endearingly attesting the author's unqualified

---

[3] *Ideali e classi nella poesia di Milton: La nascita dell'eroe borghese puritano in 'Paradise Lost' ed in 'Paradise Regained'*, by Loretta Valtz Mannucci. Saggi di cultura contemporanea, 116. Milan: Edizioni di Comunità (1976). pp. 284. L.5000.

[4] *Giants of Literature: Milton*. No author given. Maidenhead, Berks.: Sampson Low. pp. 136. £2.75.

enthusiasm for Milton. Irene Samuel in 'The Development of Milton's Poetics' (*PMLA*) visits some of the poet's occasional remarks, studies them in the light of his evolving thought, and claims that three views remained constant: the poet's high office, his inspiration, and the audience's requisite fitness. In a complementary essay, the same scholar attends more particularly to 'Milton on the Province of Rhetoric' (*MiltonS*). George W. Nitchie in 'Milton and his Muses' (*ELH*) attempts ambitiously to read the poet's development along a negative path, inclusive of his greatest poem which is here seen to pre-empt the efforts he had mounted earlier. Philip J. Gallagher in 'More Theirs by Being His: Teaching Milton to Undergraduates' (*MiltonQ*) argues in favour of 'accepting at least provisionally the premises under which Milton is operating — that his poem should be read as literal cosmic history'. In a plea of a different order, Michael Wilding in 'Regaining the Radical Milton' — part of a politically committed enterprise from Australia, *The Radical Reader*[5] — regards Milton as a radical revolutionary largely by virtue of his belief in the inner light ('frightening to the old order') and his pacifism; and provides in spite of the political thesis, some perceptive remarks on the relationship between *Paradise Regained* and *Samson Agonistes* ('Samson offers death, Christ offers life, . . . abjures force and saves mankind').

Milton's influence is being studied of late with renewed vigour, witness the noteworthy efforts by Leslie Brisman in *Milton's Poetry of Choice and its Romantic Heirs* (*YW* 54.243) and Joseph A. Wittreich Jr in *Angel of Apocalypse: Blake's idea of Milton* (*YW* 56.211). The latest endeavour, Paul S. Sherwin's study of William Collins labouring under the impact of Milton[6], maintains that the Miltonic legacy was a bequest as well as a burden. A discriminating reader of poetry, Sherwin details his argument with a commendable sense of responsibility toward his two subjects; and if he acquits himself as honourably as he does, the principal contributing factor is the economy and lucidity of his style — itself a legacy worthy of emulation by the cacophonous barbarians who surround us.

Responses to Milton over the centuries have certainly been manifold, and relevant accounts are always to be welcomed. Thus Martha W. England in 'John Milton and the Performing Arts' (*BNYPL* 1976) discusses several intriguing stage adaptations of Milton's poems during the eighteenth century, while Kenneth Friedenreich (*ibid.*) remarks on the conversion by Philippe Jacques de Louthenbourg of two scenes from Book I of *Paradise Lost* for presentation through his mechanical contraption, the 'eidophusikon'. Cowper's adverse reaction to Dr Johnson's 'Life of Milton', in a copy he owned of the *Lives*, is reproduced by J. Copley (*N&Q*). But the response of Walter Savage Landor was far more enthusiastic, witness two related studies — Charles L. Proudfit's 'Landor and Milton: The Commentators' Commentator' and A. LaVonne Ruoff's 'Landor's Conception of the Great Leader' (*The Wordsworth Circle* 1976) — which respectively trace the contours of Landor's attitudes to Milton as poet and thinker. With a respectable attention to detail when attending to Milton's text,

---

[5] *The Radical Reader,* ed. by Stephen Knight and Michael Wilding. Sydney: Wild and Woolley. pp. 240. pb $5.95.
[6] *Precious Bane: Collins and the Miltonic Legacy*, by Paul S. Sherwin. Austin, Tex. and London: U. of Texas P. pp. 137. £8.20.

Landor also drew on Milton for the formulation of his own idealistic political vision.

Dan Latimer in an attractively written essay interestingly juxtaposes Milton and Rilke in order to study, through their varying responses to the elegiac mode, their diverse articulations of patterns central to the sensibility of each[7]. Lastly, now that we no longer recklessly assert T. S. Eliot's reputed opposition to Milton, Mary Christopher Pecheux compares the two poets comprehensively no less than irenically in 'Milton and Eliot: Touched by a Common Genius' (*Greyfriar*).

2. The Shorter Poems

Four studies of the shorter poems may be recorded first: Joan Ozark Holmer's 'Milton's Hobson Poems: Rhetorical Manifestations of Wit' (*MiltonQ*), which argues the poet's early 'masterful command' of poetry's rhetorical tools; Jack Goldman's essay on Milton's two versions of Psalm 114 (*PQ* 1976), which asserts that the version into English is essentially Hebraic, and the version into Greek Christological; Gordon Campbell's provision of a context for reading the widely-unread 'Vacation Exercise' as a satire on Aristotelian logic (*ELN*); and Philip J. Gallagher's 'Milton's "The Passion": Inspired Mediocrity' (*MiltonQ*), which valiantly claims that the poem is 'a finely polished, carefully wrought, and thoroughly successful artifact', if seen as 'an inspired aesthetic success about the failure to be inspired'. In a more general study, Maurice Kelley proposes that the Trinity College manuscript of Milton's poems was secured through the offices of Daniel Skinner (*N&Q*).

Lowell E. Folsom in '*L'Allegro* and *Il Penseroso*: The Poetics of Accelerando and Ritardando' (*Studies in the Humanities* [Indiana U. of Pennsylvania] 1976) discusses briefly but ably the twin lyrics' musical associations; and Kathleen M. Swaim in 'Cycle and Circle: Time and Structure in *L'Allegro* and *Il Penseroso*' (*TSLL* 1976) advances from the two poems' diurnal imagery to their structure, here said to be circular or – better still – spiral.

Hale Chatfield in 'An Additional Look at the "Meaning" of *Comus*' (*MiltonQ*) provides not so much a look as a glance. J. Marc Blanchard in 'The Tree and the Garden: Pastoral Poetics and Milton's Rhetoric of Desire' (*MLN* 1976) argues – with a maximum of Very Impressive Terminology – that *Comus* is essentially 'the performance (*mimesis*) of a confrontation between representative signified values'. Far more ably, James S. Martin in 'Transformations in Genre in Milton's *Comus*' (*Genre*) examines the tradition of the masque in order to understand Milton's adjustment of the inherited conventions to his purposes; John D. Cox in 'Poetry and History in Milton's Country Masque' (*ELH*) argues the transmutation by the poem of the historical divorce between Court and Country as 'a pastoral metaphor pressed into service by a social reality that only casually conforms to it'; and John C. Ulreich Jr, in '"A Bright Golden Flow'r": Haemony as a Symbol of Transformation' (*SEL*) attends to the plant's

---

[7] *The Elegiac Mode in Milton and Rilke: Reflections on Death,* by Dan Latimer. European University Papers; Series XVIII: Comparative Literature, Vol. 10. Frankfurt am Main: Peter Lang; Berne: Herbert Lang. pp. 56.

several meanings inclusive of its eucharistic associations, and concludes that it adumbrates 'the redemption of matter by spirit'. Cedric C. Brown in 'The Chirk Castle Entertainment of 1634' (*MiltonQ*) gives the text of, and a commentary on, an entertainment which is said to have been made for the Bridgewater family in the same year that *Comus* was also performed; while Leo Miller notes a later venture, Anne Manning's idyllic novelette *The Masque at Ludlow* (1866), which concerns the composition and performance of *Comus* in 1634 (*MiltonQ*).

The *Epitaphium Damonis,* already available in several English versions, has now been rendered most elegantly into Italian as well: the translation is by Sergio Baldi, who also provides a scholarly introduction (*L'Albero*). *Lycidas* is discussed by Ellen Zetzel Lambert within the context of the evolving tradition of the pastoral elegy[8]; and in that light the poem is discerned to unify divergent strands of the tradition as it 'celebrates life's victory over death by being more open than any previous pastoral elegy to the destructive and painful elements in life itself'. Steven J. Lautermilch in '"That Fatal and Perfidious Bark": A Key to the Double Design and Unity of Milton's *Lycidas*' (*RenQ*) argues that the centrally-located image of the ship as *ecclesia* unifies Milton's twin aims of satire and elegy. Eric Smith in *By Mourning Tongues: Studies in English Elegy* (Ipswich: Boydell Press) devotes a chapter to *Lycidas,* discussing the poem largely in terms of the pattern of time; Joanne M. Riley considers some classical antecedents for the etymology of the poem's title (*N&Q*); and William P. Shaw focuses on the 'two-handed engine' yet again (*Modern Language Studies*).

Milton's sonnets are the subject of five essays in the tenth volume of *Milton Studies*[9]: Nicholas R. Jones's 'The Education of the Faithful in Milton's Piedmontese Sonnet', which argues persuasively that the poem is concerned with 'the efficacy of faith in relation to wisdom and zeal'; Gary A. Stringer's 'Milton's "Thorn in the Flesh": Pauline Didacticism in Sonnet XIX' ['When I consider . . .'], which maintains convincingly that the narrative is 'the consciously confected image of a spiritual question moved and answered'; Stephen Wigler's 'Outrageous Noise and the Sovereign Voice: Satan, Sin, and Syntax in Sonnet XIX and Book VI of *Paradise Lost*', which proposes that the nature of the satanic personality can be defined through a juxtaposition of the sonnet's protagonist and the epic's antagonist; Kurt Heinzelman's '"Cold Consolation": The Art of Milton's Last Sonnet', which details with precision the poet's 'singular use of the simile', mainly through the conception of the Alcestis story as an analogue of Christian salvation; and John Spencer Hill's '"Alcestis from the Grave": Imagery and Structure in Sonnet XXIII', which explicates with much sophistication the sonnet's 'tripartite typological ascent from pagan myth to Christian truth'. Elsewhere, William McCarthy in 'The Continuity of Milton's Sonnets' (*PMLA*) interestingly

---

[8] *Placing Sorrow: A Study of the Pastoral Elegy Convention from Theocritus to Milton,* by Ellen Zetzel Lambert. University of North Carolina Studies in Comparative Literature, No. 60. Chapel Hill, N.C.: U. of North Carolina P., 1976. pp. xxxiv + 238. $16.

[9] *Milton Studies,* Vol. X, edited by James D. Simmonds. Pittsburgh, Pa.: U. of Pittsburgh P. pp. 215. $14.95.

discusses all the sonnets as a potential 'sequence' in terms both of their comprehensive patterns and of their persuasively cosmic imagery, while John A. Vance in 'God's Advocate and his Pupils: Milton's Sonnets to Lawrence and Skinner' (*SAB*) expounds the three sonnets' theological orientation as examples of Christian advice.

Robert Hodge, in the composite volume of *The Cambridge Milton* which includes *Samson Agonistes* as noticed below[14], edits the sonnets and a selection of the lesser poems in English, Latin and Italian. His annotation is generally responsible, his translations are energetically colloquial, and his introductory comments zestful if rather spasmodic.

3. 'Paradise Lost'

Any list of the most discriminating studies of *Paradise Lost* in our time is bound to include Arnold Stein's *Answerable Style* (1953). Now, a quarter of a century after that notable achievement, Stein has written another major study of Milton's epic, *The Art of Presence: The Poet and 'Paradise Lost'*[10]. But the mode of articulation is radically different, in measure equal to our greatly improved sophistication — itself the contribution largely of Stein's earlier work. *The Art of Presence* impresses in the first instance by its utter lucidity; yet, oddly enough, it is a lucidity that often obscures the argument it is meant to sustain. Dense in exposition and highly elliptic in articulation, *The Art of Presence* habitually challenges the reader to discern the art of Stein's own presence. Five chapters advance with studied disconnectedness toward a delineation of the poet's 'presence' in *Paradise Lost* as a poet, attending en route to the poem's 'evolving perfection' (Ch.I), 'the constant presence of trial' (Ch. II), 'the satanic background' (Ch. III), and the infinite complexities of 'the story at the center' with its 'translation of the general laws of freedom into a convenient domestic model' (Ch. IV). The common denominator throughout is an undeviating respect for Milton's 'artistic and human generosity'. As such, *The Art of Presence* is essentially an endeavour to justify the ways of Milton to his readers; and if the style deployed is often so dense as not to be consistently 'answerable', the argument persuades to the extent that Stein's evident commitment to Milton's epic propels him from the details apprehended here with a maximum of perceptiveness to an expansive awareness of the poet-prophet's 'presence' in the artistic integrity which is *Paradise Lost*.

Mili N. Clark in a singularly sophisticated essay, 'The Mechanics of Creation: Non-contradiction and Natural Necessity' (*ELR*), dwells on the poem's more vexing paradoxes by explicating its theological claims, their philosophical implications, and the imperatives in the human condition as envisaged by Milton. R. D. Bedford in 'Milton's Logic' (*EIC*) disputes the conclusions of K. W. Gransden in 'Milton, Dryden, and the Comedy of the Fall' (*EIC* 1976), and asserts that the absurdities inherent in the story were treated by Milton much more seriously than has been claimed. J. B. Savage in 'Freedom and Necessity in *Paradise Lost*' (*ELH*) philosophises on the implications of Milton's well-attested com-

---

[10] *The Art of Presence: The Poet and 'Paradise Lost'*, by Arnold Stein. Berkeley, Calif.: U. of California P. pp. 190. $12.

mitment to freedom as conditioned by its moral texture. Michael Lieb in '"Holy Place": A Reading of *Paradise Lost*' (*SEL*) draws on Biblical precedents and their accumulated tradition to define first the metaphysical contours of topographies both divine and demonic, and next the interiorised nature of the 'Paradise within' under the impact of the poem's Christocentric burden. Harold Toliver in 'Symbol-Making and the Labors of Milton's Eden' (*TSLL* 1976) focuses on the epic language in terms of its prelapsarian gracefulness and the subsequent promise of 'new genres of reformative and moral poetry'. George E. Miller in 'Dismissive Comparisons as a Descriptive Technique in *Paradise Lost*' (*NM*) briefly considers Milton's negative syntactical strategies — '*not* this, *but* this' — in terms of the human condition before and after the Fall. Dennis H. Sigmon in 'The Negatives of *Paradise Lost:* An Introduction' (*SP* 1976) argues that the poem's numerous negative constructions, largely if not exclusively dictated by the indefinable nature of God, illumine Milton's tactics in the poem as a whole.

Sergio Baldi in 'Sulla Protasi del *Paradiso Perduto*' (*Studi inglesi* 1976–77) discourses learnedly on the convention of the initial invocation in both Milton and his predecessors. James H. Sims in 'The Epic Narrator's Mortal Voice in Camoëns and Milton' (*RLC*) discusses the nature of the invocations in *Os Lusíadas* and *Paradise Lost* in terms of their respective pleas ('the mortal cries for immortal help'). E. R. Gregory in 'Three Muses and a Poet: A Perspective on Milton's Epic Thought' (*MiltonS*) examines Renaissance interpretations of Clio to conclude that Milton's espousal of Urania represents his radical opposition to earlier claims about the nature of the heroic. Michael Fixler in 'Plato's Four Furors and the Real Structure of *Paradise Lost*' (*PMLA*) moves through Platonic notions on the energising and apocalyptic power of inspiration (*furor*) to consider the poem's four invocations as revelatory of the unity Milton posits between time and eternity.

Douglas Wurtele in '"Perswasive Rhetoric": The Technique of Milton's Archetypal Sophist' (*ESC*) competently surveys the much-discussed nature of Satan's false rhetoric. Roberts W. French notes that Satan's 'sonnet' in I, 178–91, is intentionally incomplete in that the art of creation belongs solely to God (*MiltonQ*). Jason P. Rosenblatt studies the celebrated bee simile (I, 768–75) within an expansive context that includes in the background literary allusions, and in the foreground eventual relevance to other parts of the poem (*TSLL*). Edmund T. Silk relates the congress of the fallen angels in Books I–II to Claudian's council of underworld spirits in *In Rufinum* (*MiltonQ*).

William J. Rewak, S. J., in 'Book III of *Paradise Lost*: Milton's Satisfaction Theory of the Redemption' (*MiltonQ*) revisits material widely known to everyone but himself. Michael Murrin in 'The Language of Milton's Heaven' (*MP*) asserts the importance of prophetic technique — notably Ezekiel 1.4–28 — in Milton's unprecedented delineation of the celestial regions. George Yost in 'A New Look at Milton's Paradise' (*MiltonS*) surveys the traditional materials out of which Milton created his Eden. John G. Demaray in 'Love's Epic Revel in *Paradise Lost*: A Theatrical Vision of Marriage' (*MLQ*) emphasises the masque-like elements in Milton's conception of Eden so as to suggest the beauty, but also the ephemeral nature, of prelapsarian bliss. A. James Smith in 'Sense and Innocence: Two Love Episodes in Dante and Milton'[11] asserts Milton's far more decisive endorsement of the senses in *Paradise Lost*, IV, 492–511, as against the *Inferno*, V, 127–38; but the juxtaposition of other passages would, of course, have yielded very different conclusions. Jack Goldman in 'Perspectives of Raphael's Meal in *Paradise Lost*, Book V' (*MiltonQ*) connects the episode to Jewish commentaries on the visit of the three angels to Abraham (Genesis 18.8), while Linda Weinhouse also invokes the Judaic tradition in connection with the Urim and Thummim in VI, 750–62 (*ibid.*) Anne T. Barbeau in 'Satan's Envy of the Son and the Third Day of the War' (*PLL*) emphasises the Son's creative activities in advance of his martial response to the War in Heaven and annotates Satan's self-ostracism from the hierarchical oneness of the universe.

Diane McColley in 'The Voice of the Destroyer in Adam's Diatribes' (*MP*) convincingly attributes Adam's postlapsarian denunciations of Eve not to Milton's own prejudices but to demonic instigations eventually converted to a greater good. Mark C. Miller in 'Beelzebub and Adam and "the worst than can be" ' (*MiltonS*) studies Adam's final attainment of 'conspicuously unsatanic humility' through a comparison with the demonic pride that obtained earlier. Robert L. Entzminger in 'Epistemology and the Tutelary Word in *Paradise Lost*' (*ibid.*) examines the collapse after the Fall of the 'absolute signatory system', yet its qualified restoration under the impact of Grace. Briefer contributions include annotations by John E. Gorecki on II, 1011–16 (*AN&Q*); by Theodore M. Anderson on IV, 131–45, in relation to Tasso's description of Armida's mountain in *Gerusalemme liberata* (*MLN*); by C. A. Martindale on V, 350–57, and VIII, 59–63, in relation to Homer (*N&Q*); by H. J. Real on VI, 673, in relation to *The Æneid*, IX, 227 (*N&Q*); by P. J. Klemp on IX, 510–14, which is evidently an acrostic spelling SATAN (*MiltonQ*); and by J.J.M. Tobin on X, 504 ff., where the serpentine Satan is said to be related to traditional views of the heresiarch Arius (*ibid.*)

4. 'Paradise Regained' and 'Samson Agonistes'

Andrew W. Ettin in 'Milton, T. S. Eliot, and the Virgilian Vision: Some Versions of Georgic' (*Genre*) interestingly juxtaposes the *Georgics*, *Paradise Regained*, and the *Four Quartets*, and fruitfully directs attention to analogies which readers of Milton's 'brief epic' have normally disregarded. William E. McCarron places Satan's 'persuasive Rhetoric' (*Paradise Regained*, IV, 4) within the tactics evident in the poem at large (*MiltonQ* 1976). Byne Rhodes in 'Milton's Banquet in the Wilderness' (*AN&Q*) touches briefly — but with militant piety — on the poem's spiritual dimension. John B. Dillon annotates IV, 135–37 (*MiltonQ*).

Samson Agonistes has gained a sensitive reading by an Indian critic, P. Sircar[12]; and while originality should not be sought in his argument, the reading is no less comprehensive than it is responsible, and no less attract-

---

[11] In *An English Miscellany presented to W. S. Mackie*, ed. by Brian S. Lee. Cape Town: O.U.P.

[12] *Milton's Samson: Studies in Character and Construction*, by Prabirkumar Sircar. Kalyani, West Bengal: The U. of Kalyani. pp. xi + 83. Rs. 16.

ively written than it is eminently lucid. As often remarked in these pages (e.g., *YW* 55.287), we should be disconcerted that excellence in style is so often the province rather of foreign than of native speakers of English.

Of several other studies of *Samson Agonistes*, Anthony Low in 'Milton's *Samson* and the Stage, with Implications for Dating the Play' (*HLQ*) surveys the poet's evolving view toward the theatre and concludes that 'no substantial work on the play' was undertaken before 1658. Jacques Blondel in 'La tentation dans *Samson Agonistes*' (*EA*) argues the significance of patience as articulated in *Paradise Regained*: 'he who reigns within himself, and rules/Passions, Desires and Fears, is more a King' (II, 466–67). Jean-François Camé in '*Samson Agonistes* (68–109): A Summary of Essential Elements in Milton's Imaginary Universe' (*CahiersE*) mounts a wide-ranging effort to establish through a single 'nucleus' several 'obsessive themes'. C. A. Patrides in 'The Comic Dimension in Greek Tragedy and *Samson Agonistes*' (*MiltonS*) invokes Homer as well as Aeschylus, Sophocles, and Euripides, to outline their tendency to conflate the tragic and the comic – a strategy extended by Milton in the characterisation of Harapha as of Manoa and the chorus. James Dale in '*Samson Agonistes* as Pre-Christian Tragedy' (*HAR* 1976) considers the play's Old Testamental qualities – especially the impact of Psalms – in order to assert the immediacy of its tragic nature. Mary Ann Radzinowicz in 'Medicinable Tragedy: The Structure of *Samson Agonistes* and Seventeenth-Century Psychopathology'[13] emphasises the novel psychological and dramatic theories current in Milton's day.

Heather Asals in 'Rhetoric Agonistic in *Samson Agonistes*' (*MiltonQ*) discusses Manoa as representative of epideictic rhetoric, Dalila as that of deliberative, and Harapha as that of forensic. John B. Mason in 'Multiple Perspectives in *Samson Agonistes*: Critical Attitudes toward Dalila' (*MiltonS*) surveys the diversity of available responses and warns against the adoption of any narrow viewpoint at the expense of Milton's proliferating implications. Joyce Colony in 'An Argument for Milton's Dalila' (*YR*) proposes the unexceptional thesis that Dalila is 'a powerful catalyst for Samson's transition from despair to triumph'. J. J. M. Tobin seeks antecedents for the play's sea imagery in the *Æneid* (*ELN*). Stephen P. Witte dwells on the play's form in certain instances, notably the final choral speech (*Expl*).

The Cambridge Milton for Schools and Colleges, begun in 1972 under the general editorship of J. B. Broadbent (*YW* 53.243), now allots a volume[14] to *Samson Agonistes* and those shorter poems inclusive of the sonnets which did not form part of the edition earlier devoted to the odes, pastorals and masques (*YW* 56.213). In editing *Samson Agonistes*, Broadbent introduces into the text the subdivisions concocted in Aristotle's *Poetics*. But the usual enthusiasm of *The Cambridge Milton* for an appearance of zestful modernity is here mercifully kept to a minimum, save for a section sacrificed to 'anthropological analysis'.

---

[13] In *English Drama: Forms and Development*, edited by Marie Axton and Raymond Williams. Cambridge: C.U.P.

[14] *Samson Agonistes, Sonnets, &c.*, edited by John Broadbent and Robert Hodge. Cambridge: C.U.P. pp. xiv + 235. pb £2.25.

5. Prose

Joan S. Bennett in 'God, Satan, and King Charles: Milton's Royal Portraits' (*PMLA*) — recipient of the Milton Society's first Hanford Award for the year's most distinguished article — argues in detail the impact of Milton's prose on his poetry in terms of their striking parallels concerning tyranny. Peter Auksi in 'Milton's "Sanctifi'd Bitternesse": Polemical Technique in the Early Prose' (*TSLL*) studies the antiprelatical tracts in the light of the modes of controversy characteristic of Christian reformers. James Egan in 'The Satiric Wit of Milton's Prose Controversies' (*SLitI*) briefly surveys the intentions of the polemical prose as deployed by Milton and his contemporaries at large.

Claud A. Thompson in '*The Doctrine and Discipline of Divorce,* 1643–1645: A Bibliographical Study' (*TCBS*) unravels some of the textual problems attending the treatise's four editions. John M. Perlette in 'Milton, Ascham, and the Rhetoric of the Divorce Controversy' (*MiltonS*) examines Anthony Ascham's recently discovered treatise *Of Marriage* — edited, incidentally, by Perlette himself in 1973 (*YW* 54.250) — as a possible 'oblique response' to Milton's thesis. Clarence O. Johnson annotates 'gamut' in *Areopagitica* as suggestive of Milton's anti-Catholic bias (*ELN*). Mary Ann McGuire in '"A Most Just Vituperation": Milton's Christian Orator in *Pro Se Defensio*'(*SLitI*) analyses the treatise in a desperate effort to justify its unattractive demeanour — and, in spite of Milton, succeeds partially.

Karl L. Winegardner in 'No Hasty Conclusions: Milton's Ante-Nicene Pneumatology' (*MiltonQ*) surveys some patristic attitudes toward the Holy Spirit. Gordon Campbell, finally, argues that Milton's *Index Theologicus* (now lost) was in preparation for his projected attack on the mighty Bellarmine (*MiltonQ*).

XII

The Later Seventeenth Century

JAMES OGDEN

This chapter has three sections: 1. General bibliography, anthologies, literary history and criticism; 2. Dryden; 3. other poets, dramatists and prose writers. There were fewer books than usual, but more articles than ever; research is rather heavily concentrated on the drama.

1. General

The second volume of Allison and Goldsmith's title index to Wing's *Short-title Catalogue*[1], including published and unpublished additions, will help and perhaps inspire scholarly work in our period. Responsibility for the major annual bibliography of such work has passed from *PQ* to the American Society for Eighteenth-Century Studies, but their first volume, *The Eighteenth Century: A Current Bibliography*, covering 1975, is still not to hand (February 1979). *PQ* now devotes one issue a year to review-essays on the previous year's work in the period 1660–1800, and three of those in the Fall 1976 issue must be mentioned: Philip Harth's 'Studies in Restoration Literature'; Robert D. Hume's 'Studies in English Drama 1660–1800'; and Paul K. Alkon's 'Literary Criticism and Intellectual Foregrounds'. All three discuss books relevant to our period, and Harth and Hume also comment on articles. Harth is of course an authority on Dryden, and he gives a detailed critique of Empson's 'A Deist Tract by Dryden' (*YW* 56.230), but on other poets he is sketchy, and he wrongly implies that there was little important work on Restoration prose. Hume authoritatively assesses recent specialist articles, though his description of Edward Saslow's misdating of *Albion and Albanius* as 'a howler' seems unduly censorious, since worse mistakes are made every year.

A new periodical was born, *Restoration*, edited by J. M. Armistead and David M. Vieth[2]. Early issues were essentially newsletters designed to publicise work on the period. Regular features were accounts of conference papers; critical surveys of work on special topics, such as 'Restoration Libertine Court Poetry' by John H. O'Neill, and 'Restoration Prose Fiction', by Benjamin Boyce; 'Some Current Publications', comprehensive lists of books, articles and dissertations, with notes on the scope and value

---

[1] *Titles of English Books (and of Foreign Books Printed in England). An Alphabetical Finding List by Title of Books Published under the Author's Name, Pseudonym or Initials. Vol. II, 1641–1700*, by A. F. Allison and V. F. Goldsmith. Folkestone, Kent: Dawson. pp. titles + 318.

[2] *Restoration: Studies in English Literary Culture, 1660–1700*, ed. by J. M. Armistead and David M. Vieth. Knoxville, Tenn.: U. of Tennessee. Twice yearly.

of most items; and 'Projects, News, and Queries'. I might have said that this periodical promised to be exceptionally helpful to anyone wanting to get on top of research and publication, both by giving guidance up the slope and by not adding to the pile; but in the Fall of 1978 it started publishing scholarly essays as well. Other periodicals which regularly review or mention books and articles on Restoration topics are *SEL* (Summer issue), *SCN*, *The Scriblerian*, and *The Johnsonian Newsletter; Restoration* compares well with these, especially in scope and coverage of the most recent work.

The Female Spectator[3], a handsome anthology of extracts from English women writers from Dame Julian of Norwich to Anna Seward, includes some from the later seventeenth century: Bathsua Makin, Margaret Cavendish, Katherine Philips, Aphra Behn, and Delariviere Manley. The editors supply a general introduction and brief biographies and bibliographies. In choosing extracts their criteria were quality, variety, and accessibility; so there is nothing from Dorothy Osborne, whose letters were perhaps thought accessible enough, but Bathsua Makin's elegy for Lady Elizabeth Langham and Katherine Philips's 'To Rosania and Lucasia' are published for the first time, and there are extracts from Margaret Cavendish's *Nature's Pictures* and Makin's little-known *Essay to Revive the Ancient Education of Gentlewomen* (1673). These all have enough real or historical interest to need no defensive commentary, but the editors might have explained why Mrs Behn is represented only by the prose romance *The Unfortunate Bride*, surely not one of her best efforts.

Literary Uses of Typology[4], a collection of learned papers, includes Barbara Kiefer Lewalski's 'Typological Symbolism and the "Progress of the Soul" in Seventeenth-Century Literature', Steven N. Zwicker's 'Politics and Panegyric: The Figural Mode from Marvell to Pope', and Paul J. Korshin's 'The Development of Abstracted Typology in England, 1650–1820'. Lewalski briefly discusses typology in *Pilgrim's Progress*, and Zwicker gives an account of typology in Dryden's poetry. A general essay of a very different kind is David M. Vieth's 'Divided Consciousness: The Trauma and Triumph of Restoration Culture' (*TSL*). Vieth believes the years 1660 to 1676 were a time of traumatic change, when 'a theoretically holistic culture' became 'a fragmented society'. In literature the triumphant response took the shape of 'innovative structures' that have not yet had the recognition they deserve: 'works reflecting a "providential" view of events', such as Marvell's *Horatian Ode*, Dryden's *Heroique Stanzas* and *Astraea Redux;* 'works expressing a "many-sided awareness"', such as Dryden's heroic plays and Etherege's *Man of Mode;* works that "entrap" a reader between extremes with no clear middle term', such as Rochester's *Disabled Debauchee* and *Satyr against Reason and Mankind;* and 'works written "upon nothing" or with . . . a "reversible meaning"', such as Rochester's *Upon Nothing*, and *Hudibras, The Rehearsal, Mac Flecknoe,* and *A Tale of a Tub*. This paper, when read at conferences, must have provoked discussion; or maybe it just provoked.

[3] *The Female Spectator: English Women Writers before 1800*, ed. by Mary R. Mahl and Helene Koon. Old Westbury, New York: Feminist Press, and Bloomington, Ind. & London: Indiana U.P. pp. x + 310.
[4] *Literary Uses of Typology from the Late Middle Ages to the Present*, ed. by Earl Miner. Princeton U.P. pp. xxi + 403.

(a) *Poetry*

The 'Viking Portable' anthology of *Restoration and Augustan Poets*[5], edited by W. H. Auden and Norman Holmes Pearson, is now published by Penguin. Milton and the Cavaliers are represented as well as the Restoration poets, and Auden's introduction makes points that all students of this poetry should ponder. Larry Carver's 'The Restoration Poets and Their Father King' (*HLQ*) documents the widespread use of the politically loaded title *pater patria* for the King, which led to a literary war between Court and anti-Court poets. John H. O'Neill's 'An Unpublished "Imperfect Enjoyment" Poem' (*PLL*) is an anonymous song, 'Bless me you stars', here printed from a manuscript in the Victoria and Albert Museum, and compared with poems on this un-Victorian theme by Etherege, Rochester, Aphra Behn and others. It is the last and worst of the series. Christopher Ricks's 'Allusion: The Poet as Heir', is noted in section 2 (b) below.

(b) *Drama*

Whether *RECTR's* annual bibliography of work on Restoration and eighteenth-century theatre continues to appear is uncertain; 1977 issues of this periodical were not available. Frederick M. Link's *English Drama 1660–1800: A Guide to Information Sources* (1976; *YW* 57.233) is an excellent descriptive bibliography of all substantial books and articles published before early 1974. An important bibliographical essay is Judith Milhous and Robert D. Hume's 'Lost English Plays, 1660–1700' (*HLB*), which surveys information on 92 'lost' Restoration plays, 86 of which were so designated in the Harbage-Schoenbaum *Annals of English Drama* (*YW* 45.12). Nearly a third are not really 'lost' at all; four are extant, some are extant under alternative titles, and some are 'ghosts' mentioned only in eighteenth-century playlists. The rest are lost, but this essay should help research and lead to discoveries. In an addendum Milhous and Hume note Curtis A. Price's discoveries, not of plays but of previously unrecorded titles; he describes his work in 'Eight "Lost" Restoration Plays "Found" in Musical Sources' (*Music and Letters*).

A handy volume of *Restoration Tragedies*[6], edited by James Sutherland, was added to the Oxford Paperbacks. It comprises *All for Love, Lucius Junius Brutus, The Unhappy Favourite, Venice Preserved,* and *Oroonoko.* Sutherland has collated early editions and noted major textual variants; in the case of *Oroonoko,* for instance, his text and notes are in places better than those of the more ambitious 'Regents' edition (see section 3 (b) below, and the review by John Barnard, *N&Q*, 1978). He has silently corrected printers' errors, and has modernised the spelling and 'occasionally' the punctuation; the type is excellent but the plays' readability is impaired by the abbreviation of speech prefixes. The volume includes an introduction, prefatory and occasional explanatory notes, and a bibliography. The introduction stresses that these tragedies appealed especially

[5] *Poets of the English Language. Vol. III, Restoration and Augustan Poets: Milton to Goldsmith,* ed. by W. H. Auden and Norman Holmes Pearson. N.Y.: Viking Portable Library, and Harmondsworth, Middx.: Penguin Books. pp. xliv + 622. £1.95.
[6] *Restoration Tragedies,* ed. by James Sutherland. O.U.P. pp. xii + 441. pb £2.95.

to women, here treated more seriously than in contemporary comedies; relied heavily on spectacular scenery and gorgeous costumes; and dealt with agonising choices, notably those arising from what Johnson called the 'contradictory obligations' of love, though in several plays political issues are seriously raised. It is not argued that heroic plays are not tragedies, so the lack of any specimen of that species probably arises because Oxford also publish the 'World's Classics' volume of *Five Heroic Plays*. Otherwise the choice is admirable, and the volume makes a very good introduction to a body of drama which deserves study if not revival.

'Studies in Restoration and Eighteenth-Century Drama' filled the Spring issue of *SLitI*. Of four general essays, three were on the morality of Restoration comedy. Maximillian E. Novak's 'Margery Pinchwife's "London Disease": Restoration Comedy and the Libertine Offensive of the 1670's' describes comedies and prose works by libertine royalists which sought 'to praise the city and court as the center of civilisation and to see the country as stupid, barbaric and dull'. Novak glosses over the distinction, made by dramatists if not by pamphleteers, between city and court; sure enough when he comes to Wycherley's play he makes much of the country wife's conversion to London's libertinism, but nothing of the Fidgets' exhibition of its folly. The main idea of Robert D. Hume's longwinded essay on 'The Myth of the Rake in "Restoration" Comedy' is that libertinism is treated less sympathetically than critics like Novak have thought. Many of the heroes are not genuine rakes, just men who keep mistresses; genuine rakes are either villains or are not taken too seriously. *The Country Wife* and *The Man of Mode* are unusual in seeing libertinism as the way of the world, but Horner is not taken too seriously and Dorimant is finally 'tamed'. As usual, the breadth of Hume's reading is impressive, but the soundness of his judgement is debatable (see also *YW* 57.188–9). Is there 'no hint' in *The Way of the World* that Mirabell's treatment of Mrs Fainall is rather shabby? Is Lord Foppington 'an ugly menace'? In general, Hume's resolve to call a rake a rake leaves him uninhibited by mixed feelings about Restoration comic heroes. His belief that the plays' ethics must be unacceptable to Christians is challenged by Aubrey Williams's 'Of "One *Faith*": Authors and Auditors in the Restoration Theatre'. Williams holds that both authors and auditors were familiar with Christian teaching, especially on providence and redemption; so for example when Mirabell says he is sorry and Lady Wishfort promises to 'forgive all that's past', she echoes *The Book of Common Prayer* and 'the emblematically religious elements in the scene are driven home'. Williams apparently thinks catching the echo would moderate rather than increase the audience's amusement. The fourth general essay is less controversial: Eugene M. Waith's 'Aristophanes, Plautus, Terence, and the Refinement of English Comedy' argues that the critical myths about Classical comedy (that the New Comedy was more refined than the Old, and that Terence was more refined than Plautus) encouraged the unfortunate refinement of English comedy from Jonson to Steele. Essays from *SLitI* on Dryden and Wycherley are noted in sections 2 (c) and 3 (b).

The evolution of comedy through the period was traced in three essays in other journals. Shirley Strum Kenny's 'Humane Comedy' (*MP*) develops her earlier work on Congreve, Vanbrugh, Cibber, Farquhar, and Steele (*YW* 57.189–90). These dramatists created what she calls 'humane comedy' to distinguish it from both Restoration comedy of manners or humours and Augustan sentimental comedy. Their humane outlook, complex characters, realistic dialogue, and rowdy action are their chief legacy to Fielding, Goldsmith, and Sheridan. Unhappily the boundary with earlier comedy runs right through *The Way of the World,* Lady Wishfort being typical of Restoration and Millamant of 'humane' comedy. If we must have categories three are better than two, but will this new one improve appreciation of these plays? As Ms Kenny remarks, *The Beaux' Stratagem* is already more popular on the stage than either *The Man of Mode* or *The Conscious Lovers.* A further essay at differentiating Restoration from eighteenth-century comedy is Robert D. Hume's 'Marital Discord in English Comedy from Dryden to Fielding' (*MP*). Early Restoration comedy was mostly about what leads to marriage, and not fundamentally critical of the institution, though some plays, notably *Marriage à-la-Mode, The Atheist, The Wives' Excuse* and *The Provoked Wife,* did take a hard look at what happens after marriage. After 1700 plays on marital problems become more common. Cibber in *The Provoked Husband* decides wives must obey; Fielding in *The Modern Husband* asserts the possibility of reconciliation; only Farquhar in *The Beaux' Stratagem* proposes divorce. The irony of Vanbrugh and the cynicism of Otway and Southerne may seem preferable now, but for Hume the 'wishful thinking' of the later dramatists has its attractions. A somewhat different view is taken by Robert L. Root Jr in 'Aphra Behn, Arranged Marriage, and Restoration Comedy' (*Women and Literature*). He argues that Mrs Behn stated the problem of arranged marriage more clearly than any other dramatist of the time. She found its economics disgusting, sympathised with unfaithful wives, and knew that adultery could grow from sincere love and social injustice. After 1688 most dramatists tended to support conventional morality, and only in odd plays by Southerne, Crowne, Vanbrugh, Farquhar, and 'to a lesser degree' Congreve is the injustice of arranged marriage similarly emphasised.

As a learned article which is not only more informative but also better written than the average critical essay, H. Grant Sampson's 'Some Bibliographical Evidence concerning Restoration Attitudes towards Drama' (*JRUL*, 1976) is recommended. From 1660 to 1714 both new plays and reprints were almost always published in pretty bad quartos. They were priced at a shilling till about 1700, and thereafter eighteen pence; probably about a thousand copies would have to be sold for the printer to make a profit. Sampson concludes that they were seen as convenient records of theatre performances rather than as serious literary works, which were usually issued in elegant and expensive folios and octavos.

Several articles dealt with theatre history. T. J. King's 'The First Known Picture of Falstaff (1662): A Suggested Date for his Costume' (*ThRI*) concerns the frontispiece to *The Wits, or Sport upon Sport,* where Falstaff's costume resembles that of the poet Wither in an engraving of 1635. In 1662 Wither was in jail for supporting the Parliamentarians, so 'a contemporary audience would undoubtedly associate Falstaff's costume with "the old days" before the Civil War'. John Orrell's 'A New Witness of the

Restoration Stage, 1670–1680' (*ThRI*) is the second part of an article noted in *YW* 57.189 about references to the theatre in the dispatches of Giovanni Salvetti, the Florentine agent in London. A quarrel at the Theatre Royal between Rochester and Richard Newport is described more vividly than anything that happened on the stage. John R. Spring's 'Platforms and Picture Frames: A Conjectural Reconstruction of the Duke of York's Theatre, Dorset Garden, 1669–1709' (*TN*) contends that the Restoration fore-stage projected beyond the proscenium arch, but was enclosed on both sides in such a way as to bring an actor forward out of the scenery, without placing him in the midst of his audience. Spring therefore disagrees with Edward Langhans's conjectural reconstruction of Dorset Garden (*ThS*, 1972).

(c) *Prose*

Only two articles are noted this year. Roger Thomson's 'Two Early Editions of Restoration Erotica' (*Lib*) are *The School of Venus* (1680), a translation of *L'Escole des Filles*, by Millet and L'Ange, and *Tullia and Octavia* (1684), almost certainly a translation of the *Satyra Sotadica*, by Nicholas Chorier. We do not have the books themselves, but luckily their publishers were both prosecuted, and one indictment quotes passages from *The School of Venus*, exhibiting 'a vigorous and open approach to sexual matters'. Henry Knight Miller's 'Augustan Prose Fiction and the Romance Tradition'[7] sees romance not as a primitive form of the novel but 'in terms of its own assumptions and conventions'. These are described so abstractly that I lost interest.

2. Dryden

(a) *General*

Somehow three rival bibliographies have proceeded independently: Zamonski's (*YW* 56.225), Latt's (*YW* 57.190–1), and George Hammerbacher's *A Survey of Dryden Studies: 1949–1974*[8]. This latter is a description and evaluation of recent work on Dryden, with annotated lists of 148 studies omitted or inaccurately described by Zamonski and of fifty-four more which appeared in 1974. Hammerbacher duly celebrates recent achievements: the half-finished California edition, Ward's biography, Montgomery's concordance, and a pile of critical books. Some works (*Absalom and Achitophel, Mac Flecknoe, All for Love*) have been studied too much, some (*Don Sebastian, Marriage à-la-Mode, Amphitryon*, the minor poems) not enough. When the California edition is finished, a new concordance can be made; a new edition of the letters is wanted, and a thorough study of Dryden's influence. Hammerbacher's 'An Annotated Bibliography of John Dryden' (*MP*) is a review of Zamonski. According to Hammerbacher he has not missed many important studies and has

---

[7] In *Studies in the Eighteenth Century III, Papers presented at the Third David Nichol Smith Memorial Seminar, Canberra 1973*, ed. by R. F. Brissenden and J. C. Eade. Toronto and Buffalo: U. of Toronto P. (1976). pp. xi + 262; 16 illustrations.
[8] *A Survey of Dryden Studies: 1949–1974*, by George Henry Hammerbacher. PhD, Temple University. See *DAI* 37 (1977) 7762A.

perhaps saved some good things from oblivion, but his work is full of errors, his cross-referencing is inadequate, and his index so bad that it is best ignored. Hammerbacher here lists 133 of Zamonski's omissions; thirty-three were published in 1973, but my remark that 'up to 1972 Zamonski is pretty comprehensive' (*YW* 56.225) seems overgenerous. I am not altogether humbled, since of the four items I noted as being omitted by Zamonski only one is restored by Hammerbacher.

Edward L. Saslow made a further contribution to the study of Dryden's life and thought with 'Dryden's Authorship of the *Defence* of the Royal Papers' (*SEL*). He supports Charles E. Ward against Edward Malone and Earl Miner in believing that Dryden wrote the whole of *A Defence of the Papers written by the Late King of Blessed Memory, and Duchess of York* (1686). A passage in the preface to *The Hind and the Panther* is not an acknowledgement of authorship of the third part only, and stylistic differences between the parts are not so great that Dryden could not have written them all. If the *Defence* can be accepted as Dryden's it becomes a major biographical document, as it was written soon after his conversion to Rome, and is a discussion of church authority.

David Wykes's *Preface*[9] aims 'to set out such facts, reasonable guesses, informed opinions, and personal reactions' as may help a new reader to appreciate Dryden. The book has sections on Dryden's life and character, his philosophical, religious and political beliefs, his 'craftsmanship and audience' (his literary style, criticism, and attitudes to painting and music all come in here), a critical survey of representative extracts, and a reference section (including brief biographies of some of Dryden's associates and an annotated bibliography). In some ways the book is the victim of its predetermined scheme. The idea is to present Dryden to an audience which finds it hard work simply to read old poets or even new critics. So we have a series of prefaces to the preface itself, and the main text so tricked out with sections, sub-sections, sub-headings and illustrations that in its paperback form especially the book looks like a sort of reader's digest of Dryden. The arrangement encourages repetition, and we are told three times that Dryden should not be seen as Pope's predecessor before we have fairly started. But the book is better than it looks; it gives lucid summaries of what we need to know about Dryden, and introduces his work in such a way as to leave us with something to think about. The only section likely to confuse is that on metre; Wykes rightly makes use of the idea of a 'counterpoint' of stress and metre, yet feels free to talk of spondees and pyrrhic feet. The section on representative extracts could have been improved by the inclusion of the Oldham elegy and one or two passages from the plays.

In 'Dryden, Charles II, and the Interpretation of Historical Character' (*PQ*) Richard Wendorf argues that Dryden did not simply eulogise Charles, since 'characters' of him by Halifax, Mulgrave, Evelyn, Burnet and Welwood make similar claims and criticisms. In various works from *Astraea Redux* to the dedication to *King Arthur* Dryden gave 'a just portrait of a shrewd and enigmatic king'; he was not only Poet Laureate but also Historiographer Royal.

[9] *A Preface to Dryden*, by David Wykes. Preface Books. Longman. pp. xx + 236; 30 illustrations. hb £4., pb £2.25.

(b) *Poetry*

For the second successive year no books or editions came my way. Three essays were in different ways about Dryden's debt to his predecessors and may be profitably read one after another. Christopher Ricks's discourse on 'Allusion: The Poet as Heir'[7] is a perpetual fountain of critical insight. It is about the way in which Dryden and the Augustan poets acknowledged their literary inheritance by making allusions, and comments on Dryden's ideas of the paternal nature of poetic influence, of poetical 'successions', and of patronage generally. Inevitably there is a section on Dryden and Milton, emphasising that Dryden did not come into his own as a poet till after Milton's death. K. W. Gransden's 'What Kind of Poem is *Religio Laici?*' (*SEL*) maintains that the poem's form, structure, and rhetoric are based on those Latin poems, notably the third book of *De Rerum Natura,* the third satire of Persius, and the tenth satire of Juvenal, which with their prestige could support Dryden's advocacy 'of a sane and healthy approach to "the nature of things" and . . . could give to the commonplaces in which he rests a majesty and sublimity they might otherwise lack'. His reference in the preface to Horace's *Epistles* as his model is therefore misleading. Gransden's argument is well supported by quotations of parallel passages in Dryden's own translations of the Latin poems. Robert H. Bell's 'Dryden's "Aeneid" as English Augustan Epic' (*Criticism*) is a thoughtful answer to modern critics of Dryden's translation (such as Havelock, whom Bell does not mention; *YW* 55.304). Dryden and the Augustans may have seen the *Æneid* as above all a poem celebrating 'the long glories of majestic Rome', and so may have been rather insensitive to its irony; but Dryden did render its pathos. 'He shared with Virgil a sense of the burden of the past, the private cost of public achievement, and the diminished possibilities of heroic action', though he was too sceptical by temperament to take the supernatural powers seriously. If his idea of the *Æneid* was limited, so is that of modern critics; we can enhance our sense of the poem's richness by going back to him.

Two essays on *Absalom and Achitophel* contrasted in aim and effect. A. E. Dyson and Julian Lovelock's 'Beyond the Polemics: The Opening of Dryden's *Absalom and Achitophel*' reappeared in a book of essays in 'practical criticism' meant for beginners[10]. Despite this context a host of 'facts', not all reliable, is deployed before the critique of the first 84 lines begins. As practical critics the authors are sometimes wrong, for instance about the metre of lines 67-8, and always ready to amaze the unlearned with their perceptions of ironies. The most remarkable ironies strike 'a sensitive reader' in the first ten lines, where the King is 'censured' for lacking 'deep human emotion'. Although they use dialogue form the authors are basically agreed, and they have no respect for alternative readings, supposing everyone else must be wrong since the poet has 'totally annihilated unwanted meanings'; but on their own evidence some unwanted meanings have survived, so the essay develops an unintended irony of its own. This cocksure display was first staged in *The Critical Survey*

---

[10] *Masterful Images: English Poetry from Metaphysicals to Romantics,* by A. E. Dyson and Julian Lovelock. Macmillan (1976). pp. 254. pb £2.75. [Reviewed by Allan Rodway, *MLR*, 1978.]

(1971; not noted in *YW*): did *nobody* suggest revision? Much more modest and helpful is Hannah Buchan's '*Absalom and Achitophel:* A Patron's Name or a Patriot's?' (*YES*), about line 179, of which the accepted reading is 'Usurp'd a Patriott's All-attoning Name', though the first issue of the first edition reads 'Assum'd a Patron's'. Dryden with *Paradise Lost* always in mind may have been thinking of Christ as man's 'Patron or Intercessor' (Book III, 219), but in the end he chose the more straightforwardly ironic version, and included the extra lines, 180–91, to bring out what he had originally implied, that if Shaftesbury had kept faith with Charles his role would have been more like Christ's than Satan's.

The suggestion that the 'Song for St Cecilia's Day' itself runs 'through all the Compass of the Notes' was put forward by Jay Arnold Levine (*PQ* 1965; *YW* 46.219). In 'The Musical Structure of Dryden's "Song for St Cecilia's Day"' (*ECS*) Douglas Murray develops it into an argument that the poet used the theory of the modes as a foundation. Dryden moves from the tonic in the first stanza to its octave in the last, through stanzas in the Dorian, Phrygian, Lydian, Mixolydian, Aeolian and perhaps Locrian modes. He would have us realise that 'the passionate modes, at first sight out of step with the music of the great C major scale, are merely varied arrangements of those very notes which, in the "correct" order, comprise that most orderly of scales'. It may be questioned whether Dryden was really familiar with the theory of the modes, but most of the stanzas are remarkably close to the characters of the modes as described by the early musicologists Murray quotes.

Finally three notes from *NQ*. A. H. de Quehen's 'A Parenthetical Allusion in Dryden's "To Dr. Charleton"' refers to lines 29–31, and comments that Charleton considers the question of whether blood is life's fuel or the body's food in his *Natural History of Nutrition, Life, and Voluntary Motion* (1659). Tav Holmes's 'Poppies in John Dryden's "Mac Flecknoe"' proposes that lines 126–7 suggest both Shadwell's dullness and 'his relation to Christ', because the poppy has connotations of both ignorance and the Passion. D. W. Hopkins's 'Dryden's Use of Thomas Heywood's "Troia Britanica"' argues that in translating 'Helen to Paris' for *Ovid's Epistles* Dryden used the translation of the letter which forms Canto 10 of Thomas Heywood's *Troia Britanica* (1609).

(c) *Drama*

What flocks of critics hover here today,
As vultures wait on armies for their prey,
All gaping for the carcass of a play!
(Prologue to *All for Love*)

In the last five years *All for Love* has been subject to two editions, four chapters in books, and eight articles. Antony has been identified with Dryden himself, Charles II, an oak tree, and of course Christ. If a list of moderately helpful studies of the play were wanted I could compile a longish one without mentioning the three published this year. Alan S. Fisher's 'Necessity and the Winter: The Tragedy of *All for Love*' (*PQ*) notes that the prologue offers 'such rivelled fruits as winter can afford', suggests that Dryden felt compelled to renounce the luscious fruits of the heroic play, and sees a similarity between him and Antony as 'represent-atives of a human grandeur that modernity will not tolerate'. Antony and Cleopatra will not renounce their ideals and are of necessity crushed: 'their grandeur is irrelevant to the real world but also transcends it', so they are gathered into the artifice of eternity and Caesar's triumph is but a paltry thing. This essay rambles, but does prompt thought, and is the best of the three. J. E. Tierney's 'Biblical Allusion as Character Technique in Dryden's *All for Love*' (*ES*) claims that Antony's situation in Act I parallels Christ's in the Garden of Gethsemane; so for example when Antony thinks of being 'stretched at my length beneath some blasted oak', the audience would think of Christ on the cross. Rebecca Armstrong's 'The Great Chain of Being in Dryden's *All for Love*'[11] claims that 'the Great Chain of Being serves as a framework that unifies the natural imagery, structure, and thematic conclusion of the play': so when Antony thinks of the oak, the audience would think of the hierarchy of trees, and realise that 'Antony identifies himself . . . with nature, becoming the very tree itself'. Thus the carcass of *All for Love* has been saved from vultures, but is felt to need artificial preservatives and lashings of sauce.

Four articles about the heroic plays and operas have been read. Bruce King's 'Allusion to "The Conquest of Granada" in "Taxation No Tyranny"' (*N&Q*) arises when Johnson mocks American claims to independence by associating them with Almanzor's boast, 'I alone am King of Me', which King believes Johnson assumes is comical, so the allusion supports the 'ironic' reading of heroic drama. But what does he make of Johnson's comment in the *Life of Dryden*, 'the ridiculous is mingled with the astonishing', which does not seem to support an ironic reading? David W. Tarbet's 'Reason Dazzled: Perspective and Language in Dryden's *Aureng-Zebe*' (*Criticism*, 1976) seeks to show that Dryden translated Renaissance pictorial perspective into literary terms. R. D. Bedford's 'Milton's Logic' (*EIC*) comments on K. W. Gransden's 'Milton, Dryden, and the Comedy of the Fall' (*EIC*, 1976; *YW* 57.194), an essay partly about *The State of Innocence*. Michael W. Alssid's 'The Impossible Form of Art: Dryden, Purcell and *King Arthur*' (*SLitI*) reveals 'brilliant juxtapositions and tensions of opera and drama' whereby *King Arthur* 'sustains a dichotomous texture' and 'comments on its own form, yet in so unique, so self-conscious a way as to demonstrate its incapacity to make music and drama indispensable one to the other'. Their separation may show Dryden's 'realistic awareness of an eternal dichotomy which over two and a half centuries of operatic experiment since *Arthur* has [*sic*] not yet [*sic*] resolved'. Also unresolved is the question of responsibility for the stylistic weaknesses, grammatical errors and frequent misprints in this article, since an editorial footnote thanks two Professors (of English?) for preparing the late Professor Alssid's manuscript for publication.

Of more specialised interest is Colin Visser's 'John Dryden's *Amboyna* at Lincoln's Inn Fields, 1673' (*RECTR*, 1976), arguing that this play might well have been designed to exploit the settings for *The History of Sir Francis Drake* and *The Cruelty of the Spaniards in Peru*, operas by Davenant which had already been staged at Lincoln's Inn Fields. James D. Garrison's 'A Quotation from Waller in Dryden's *Love Triumphant*'

---

[11] In *A Provision of Human Nature. Essays on Fielding and Others in Honor of Miriam Austin Locke*, ed. by Donald Kay. Alabama: U. of Alabama P. pp. xi + 207.

(*ELN*) concerns the witty adaptation of a couplet from *A Panegyric to My Lord Protector.*

(d) *Prose*

Hoyt Trowbridge's *From Dryden to Jane Austen*[12] includes his good old essays on 'Dryden's *Essay on the Dramatic Poetry of the Last Age*' (*PQ*, 1943) and 'The Place of Rules in Dryden's Criticism' (*MP*, 1946; *YW* 27.179–80), and a good new one on 'Perception, Imagination, and Feeling in Dryden's Criticism'. Broadly, the essay on 'The Place of Rules' stresses Dryden's belief in rational principles, and the one on 'Perception, Imagination, and Feeling' stresses his acknowledgement of the nonrational faculties; he is seen as avoiding the extremes of dogmatism and subjectivism. Robert G. Walker notes 'A Possible Dryden Echo in Johnson's "Life of Dryden"' (*N&Q*). Edward L. Saslow's 'Dryden's Authorship of the *Defence* of the Royal Papers' is noted in section 2 (a).

3. Other Authors

(a) *Poets*

There is remarkably little to report here, even though I include Cowley and Marvell, who do not wholly belong to the period. Cowley is the subject of a bibliography by M. R. Perkin[13], which describes in full all editions, issues and variants of separately published works, and collections and selections down to Johnson's, with reproductions of title-pages in microfiche. The book is excellent in its way but is very much a bibliographers' bibliography and has only a brief note on secondary sources.

Marvell as a Restoration literary figure is the subject of three articles. A. S. G. Edwards and R. M. Schuler's 'New Texts of Marvell's Satires' (*SB*) draws attention to a Princeton manuscript which includes 'Britannia and Rawleigh', '[Further] Advice to a Painter', the first part of 'Nostradamus's Prophecy', 'Bludius et Corona', and part of 'The Loyall Scot'. This is perhaps in some ways closer to Marvell's original text than many of the other surviving manuscripts, and in the case of 'Britannia and Rawleigh' it is superior to them. Full lists of variants are given. Annabel Patterson's 'The *Second* and *Third* Advices-to-the-Painter' (*PBSA*) argues on bibliographical and literary grounds in favour of accepting these satires as Marvell's and gives a detailed chronology of relevant political and literary events. Ms Patterson promises further study of this complicated matter in a forthcoming book, *Marvell and the Civic Crown*. Her 'Naked or Otherwise: Marvell's *Account of the Growth of Popery and Arbitrary Government* (*SLitI*) treats this pamphlet as an example of a work with two levels of meaning, and asks how we can be sure we recognise in it 'a "deep structure" . . . of political sympathy and argument, when the surface structure asserts . . . documentary plainness'? The answer is that

---

[12] *From Dryden to Jane Austen: Essays on English Critics and Writers, 1660–1818,* by Hoyt Trowbridge. Albuquerque, N.M.: U. of New Mexico P. pp. 300 $15. [Reviewed by Barry Roth, *ECS*, 1978.]

[13] *Abraham Cowley. A Bibliography,* by M. R. Perkin. Pall Mall Bibliographies. Folkestone, Kent: Dawson. pp. 130; frontispiece and 93 microfiche plates. £12.50.

'we can only be sure we know what Marvell is doing by placing it in the light of what he has done before'. I would have thought that a reader who had never heard of Marvell, however much he might expect documentary plainness in an *Account,* would anticipate *some* bias in one of *Popery and Arbitrary Government.*

Butler's *Hudibras* is related to its literary context by Heimo Ertl in *Die Scheinheiligen Heiligen*[14], a doctoral thesis on the caricature of Puritans in seventeenth-century satire and polemic. (I am indebted to Mr Stuart Low and Mr Stephen Parry for help with the translation.) *Rump* (1662), a collection of ballads written from 1639 to 1661, shows that most anti-Puritan satire was crude party propaganda; there was less demand for such stuff after the Restoration, and in transcending it Butler achieves satire of greater general availability (*'grössere Allgemeingültigkeit'*).

Rochester's ideas, according to J. W. Johnson's 'Lord Rochester and the tradition of Cyrenaic hedonism, 1670-1790'[15], evolved from hedonism through Epicureanism to Christianity, yet through the eighteenth century he was seen as the archetypal hedonist. This is a potentially fascinating legend, but Johnson is bent on deducing Rochester's ideas from conjectures about his life and dubious interpretations of his works. He believes Rochester 'conducted the secret experiments of the English public school'; perfected his knowledge of hedonism in theory and practice while on the Grand Tour; at the same time became temporarily a Roman Catholic 'to escape the Protestant emphasis on damnation'; and eventually wrote *Sodom* as an indictment of hedonism. Commenting on Johnson's paper in 'Some Current Publications' (*Restoration*) D. M. Vieth challenges him 'to produce documentation of his wild, implausible claims'. In 'The Authorship of *Sodom'* (*PBSA*) A. S. G. Edwards concludes that there is not enough evidence to identify Rochester or anyone else as the play's author. Its structure is 'inorganic', and a careful study of manuscripts suggests three authors worked on it independently.

Items of more specialised interest included B. Wallingford Boothe's 'Edmund Gayton and English Travesty' (*N&Q*): Gayton's travesties of Classical poets in *Pleasant Notes upon Don Quixot* (1654) are the most important English forerunners of Charles Cotton's *Scarronides.* Catherine Cole Mambretti's '"Fugitive Papers": A New Orinda Poem and Problems in her Canon' (*PBSA*) attributes 'To . . . Lady Boteler', preserved in a National Library of Wales manuscript, to Katherine Philips, and discusses the attribution of three poems to her by Margaret Crum in the *First-line Index of English Poetry, 1500-1800, in Manuscripts of the Bodleian Library.* Of these Catherine Cole Mambretti accepts only one, 'On the Coronation', as Orinda's. Wilson F. Engel III's 'John Oldham and the Threat of Building Paul's: A Note' (*N&Q*) quotes a letter to Oldham which mentions the deaths of three men 'by ye fall of ye ruins of Pauls'. Oldham

---

[14] *Die Scheinheiligen Heiligen. Das Bild der Puritaner im Zerrspiegel satirischer und polemischer Literatur des 17. Jahrhunderts,* by Heimo Ertl. European University Papers, series 14, vol. 49. Frankfurt am Main: Peter Lang; Bern: Herbert Lang. pp. [x] + 490.

[15] In *Studies on Voltaire and the Eighteenth Century. Vol. CLIII, Transactions of the Fourth International Congress on the Enlightenment, III,* ed. by Theodore Besterman. Oxford: The Voltaire Foundation at the Taylor Institution (1976).

probably recalled this in some lines in his imitation of Juvenal's third satire.

(b) *Dramatists*

James Howard's *The English Mounsieur* is a play of some historical importance. It was performed by 1663, and gives the earliest examples of satire on a frenchified fop and of the courtship of a 'gay couple' (unhappy term). There are also good scenes contrasting *précieuse* and rustic modes of courtship. The text has been reproduced in facsimile[16], with an introduction by Robert D. Hume. Unfortunately the 1674 quarto, badly printed in the extreme, has to be used; some reference books mention a 1679 edition, but are confusing the play with an unrelated novel of the same title.

In 'Two Plays by Elizabeth Polwhele: *The Faithfull Virgins* and *The Frolicks*' (*PBSA*) and an edition of *The Frolicks*[17], Judith Milhous and Robert D. Hume describe the work of one of the first women dramatists. The authoress remains obscure – it is not even certain that her Christian name was Elizabeth – but a signed manuscript of *The Frolicks* has turned up in Cornell University Library, and it helps to identify an unsigned one of *The Faithfull Virgins* in the Bodleian. The latter, a mediocre melodrama, was probably performed in 1669 or 1670. The former, a lively sex comedy, was written in 1671 and was the first comedy by a woman for the professional stage, but it is not known if it was performed. Milhous and Hume's excellent edition gives a conservatively modernised text and a full account of the manuscript's peculiarities, with its readings in all cases of substantive emendation. Only one needful emendation seems to have been missed: at IV 191 and 328, for '*Exit ambo*' read '*Exeunt ambo*'. There are helpful explanatory footnotes and an appendix on contemporary marriage law. A long but mostly interesting introduction covers the theatrical background, the character of the play and its stage possibilities, the origin of the manuscript, *The Faithfull Virgins*, and what is known or conjectured about Miss Polwhele.

A comparatively famous woman dramatist, Aphra Behn, was the subject of a biography by Maureen Duffy[18]. Despite enthusiastic research Ms Duffy contributes more to speculation than to knowledge. Aphra was most likely born at Harbledown in 1640, daughter of Bartholomew and Elizabeth Johnson. The family was almost certainly in Surinam in 1663 to 1664. On returning to England Aphra presumably married Mr Behn: 'it seems certain . . . that he was dead by August 1666', but it cannot be proved that he was ever alive. In 1666 she was employed by the crown as a spy in Holland. She got into debt, determined to become a professional writer, and had at least fourteen plays performed by 1682. She was

[16] *The English Mounsieur,* by James Howard, 1674, with intro. by Robert D. Hume. A.R.S., 182–3. Los Angeles, Calif.: Clark Memorial Library. pp. [xvi] + [iv] + [68].

[17] *The Frolicks, or The Lawyer Cheated,* by Elizabeth Polwhele, ed. by Judith Milhouse and Robert D. Hume. Ithaca, N.Y. and London: Cornell U.P. pp. 154; 3 illustrations. £6.50.

[18] *The Passionate Shepherdess: Aphra Behn 1640–89,* by Maureen Duffy. Jonathan Cape. pp. 324; 15 photographic illustrations, 6 text figures, endpapers. £7.50. [Reviewed by Pat Rogers, *RES*, 1978.]

admired for her wit and beauty, but was sneered at for being a writer, and defended herself vigorously. Many of the plays were more or less obvious Stuart propaganda, but in 1682 she offended Charles II by criticising Monmouth, and for a time quitted the stage to concentrate on poetry, romances, and translations. She was again short of money, and near the end of her life seriously ill, but shortly before her death she refused to support the succession of William and Mary. This book gives the fullest account of Aphra Behn so far, and the most exasperating. Ms Duffy is at her best in the more strictly biographical chapters, such as the one about Mrs Behn's love for the atheistic homosexual John Hoyle, and she does illuminate Mrs Behn's milieu and possible personal and political references in her works. But if we are to believe these works are as good as she says, more good passages should be quoted, and some idea of how they compare with the best of her contemporaries should be given. Typically, she argues that Rochester is behind Willmore in *The Rover*, but makes no comparison with Dorimant in *The Man of Mode*. And it is hard to accept *Oroonoko* as 'a masterpiece' when its title is always wrongly spelt. There is no attempt at a general assessment of Mrs Behn's work, which seems as varied as Dryden's but much inferior. In her impassioned defence of Mrs Behn against male chauvinism Ms Duffy slights earlier work, failing to mention available editions, Link's book (*YW* 49.230), and several sympathetic critical studies. Worst of all, Ms Duffy is bent on being readable, but often gets bogged down in detail, and tries to save herself with a style which is aggressively informal to the point of vulgarity. Meanwhile, in the learned journals, Robert L. Root Jr considers 'Aphra Behn, Arranged Marriage, and Restoration Comedy' (see section 1 (b) above), and Martine Watson Brownley 'The Narrator in *Oroonoko*' (*ELWIU*). For Ms Brownley 'Behn carefully develops a distinctive voice for her narrative *persona*', who unifies the story, gives it some realism, and 'offers a viable standard of judgment'.

Of this year's essays on Etherege and Wycherley, the best was Brian Corman's 'Interpreting and Misinterpreting *The Man of Mode*' (*PLL*). Corman sees the well known exchange between Steele and Dennis about this play as posing most of the questions critics have continued to discuss. He contends that Dorimant is not a heartless libertine but 'a dramatic version of a Restoration gentleman', whose relationship with Harriet moves 'almost irreversibly toward the marriage one expects at the end of a comedy'. Joseph Candido's 'Theatricality and Satire in *The Country Wife*' (*ELWIU*) notes allusions to acting and the theatre, and discusses theatrical episodes in which Sparkish, Sir Jasper Fidget and Pinchwife are held up to ridicule by other characters. Candido wrongly assumes that the theatricality must improve the satire; a fool does not necessarily look more foolish if another character remarks on his folly. Alan Roper's 'Sir Harbottle Grimstone and *The Country Wife*' (*SLitI*) sees a parliamentary debate on the Popish Plot and Wycherley's play in relation to a general idea about how words mediate between 'events' and 'issues', or facts and interpretations. Roper confesses 'I am not describing features which have escaped the attention of others', but supposes his terminology makes these features clearer. Arthur Friedman's 'Two Notes on William Wycherley' (*MP*) show that in *The Plain-Dealer* and *The Country Wife* some incidents may have been borrowed from a French source, and that in *Love in a Wood* III.ii a good guess can be made at what Ranger says in a speech omitted from the printed text.

Two farcical comedies by Thomas D'Urfey, *Madam Fickle* and *A Fond Husband*, were edited with introductions and notes by Jack L. Vaughn[19]. Professor Vaughn believes that since D'Urfey was well known and respected in his day he is unfortunate in being 'all but unknown to modern readers'; that he has been 'ignored by modern scholars'; and that 'not one of his dramatic works has appeared in print with editorial treatment since the eighteenth century'. Of these claims, the first may be allowable; the second is not really, since Vaugn's own bibliography, though incomplete, lists several modern studies; and the third is not at all, since *Madam Fickle* appears in Jeffares's *Restoration Comedy* (*YW* 55.298). Vaughn's texts are based on the first quartos, with some modification of accidentals 'in the interest of readability', and full lists of textual variants. There are detailed bibliographical descriptions of early editions. Modern readers will want more persuasive introductions and less conservative texts, and even scholars may see something farcical in such sophisticated editorial treatment of farces. The explanatory notes are helpful, and the information about D'Urfey's life and work is accurate as far as I know, but the idea of Alexander Pope writing a letter to Oliver Cromwell (p. 15) must be condemned as an improbable fiction.

A new study of Nathaniel Lee is promised by J. M. Armistead, who contributed 'Nathaniel Lee and Family: The Will of Richard Lee, D. D.' to *N&Q* and 'Lee, Renaissance Conventions, and The Psychology of Providence: The Design of *Caesar Borgia*' to *ELWIU*. The terms of his father's will suggest that Lee's madness did not estrange him from his family. *Caesar Borgia* is related to Renaissance ideas about Machiavelli, Fortune, and the New World, and Armistead argues that Lee comments on Restoration politics not through historical parallels as in *The Massacre of Paris*, but in a 'symbolic paradigm showing how Providence unfolds implications inherent in minds and hearts which flourish in all eras of intense political intrigue'. In 'Nero and the Politics of Nathaniel Lee' (*PLL*) David Scott Kastan claims this play implies parallels between the despotism of Nero and the rule of Charles II; the character Britannicus is dragged in as an embodiment of suffering Britain. Since Nero's death is not followed by the restoration of order, Lee's view of British politics must have been pessimistic.

Otway's *The Orphan* was edited for the 'Regents' series by the late Aline Mackenzie Taylor[20]. A brief introduction covers the provenance of the text and the theatrical history, sources, and interpretation of the play. Much is taken from Mrs Taylor's *Next to Shakespeare* (1950) and little is said of recent criticism. This is a pity since Marshall (*YW* 50.253) and others have answered criticisms of the characters' motivation better than Mrs Taylor does. In the text there are apparent misprints at I.54, III.310

---

[19] *Two Comedies by Thomas D'Urfey*, ed. by Jack A. Vaughn. Rutherford, Madison and Teaneck: Fairleigh Dickinson University Press, and London: Associated University Presses (1976). pp. 301+frontispiece. £7.

[20] *The Orphan*, by Thomas Otway, ed. by Aline Mackenzie Taylor. RRestDS. Arnold. pp. xxx + 118. hb £8, pb £3.95.

and IV.153, and doubtful readings at IV.152 and V.61. Annotation is adequate, and there are interesting appendixes on Otway's personal problems and the original staging. This is the only edition of its kind, but it would not be difficult for a rival series to improve on it. In 'Swift's Dismal and Otway's Antonio' (*N&Q*) A. J. Varney suggests that the literary model for Swift's portrait of the Earl of Nottingham as Dismal in *An Excellent New Song* (1711) was Otway's portrait of Shaftesbury as Antonio in *Venice Preserved*.

Another addition to the 'Regents' series was Southerne's *Oroonoko*, edited by Maximillian E. Novak and David Stuart Rodes[21]. Their text is good but not beyond criticism. Only one line seems to need emending, V.v.290, where 'let not' (Q2, 3, *Works*) improves both metre and sense, but in places heavier punctuation is desirable and at V.iii.27 it is necessary. Annotation is inconsistent: in the prologue we are told that 'mend' means improve, but not that 'strained' means bridled; in IV.i we are told that 'rotten' means unsound, but not that 'recruited' means replenished; in V.iv we are told how Parham House got its name, but a difficult stage-direction (49) is not explained. Sutherland (see section 1 (b) above) deals more satisfactorily with all these points, but Novak and Rodes's editing is better in some ways and their introduction is good. They discuss the source of the text, the theatrical history and interpretation of the play, and its relation to Aphra Behn's novella. They argue persuasively that while the tragic plot about slavery deriving from her and the comic one about marriage added by Southerne do not directly impinge on each other, 'it is the strongly worked cross-cutting and juxtaposition of the two which give Southerne's play its scope and dramatic impact', helping us to see Oroonoko as a noble idealist whose tragedy is precisely that he lives in a world of his own.

Essays on Congreve were variable in character and quality. Maximillian Novak's 'Congreve as the Eighteenth Century's Archetypal Libertine' (*RECTR*, 1976) shows that what Suckling was for the early Restoration and Rochester soon after, the archetypal libertine, Congreve was for much of the next century. The idea may be based on a misreading of his plays, but modern critics who read them as sentimental (Zimbardo), exemplary (Schneider), or providential (Williams), go too far the other way. This essay is short, sharp, and salutory. John King McComb's 'Congreve's *The Old Bachelor: A Satiric Anatomy*' (*SEL*) contends that here Congreve presents the stock characters of Restoration comedy, rake, fop, railer, and cuckold, 'as stages in a single life's progress'. Bellmour, Vainlove, Heartwell, Fondlewife and Spintext are successive metamorphoses of the libertine, and analogies between lust and other evils enlarge the satire's scope. McComb is worth reading but takes the play too seriously and puts his case too emphatically. His remark that 'the characters compose a satiric version of Jacques' famous speech on the ages of man' should have been blue-pencilled: is that speech not satiric? Sue L. Kimball's 'Games People Play in Congreve's *The Way of the World*'[11] sees the idea of life as a game in the play's structure, theme, and language, and makes interesting if debatable comments on particular phrases and general questions. Her

[21] *Oroonoko*, by Thomas Southerne, ed. by Maximillian E. Novak and David Stuart Rodes. RRestDS. Arnold. pp. xlii + 143. hb £8, pb £3.95.

readings of phrases involving the words 'deal', 'hand', and 'pass' seem at times strained, and while it may be true that Mirabell holds back his ace, the deed of gift, partly because he enjoys toying with Fainall, it is at least equally true that he must wait till the other aces have been played. Charles H. Hinnant's 'Wit, Propriety, and Style in *The Way of the World*' (*SEL*) argues that knowing Dryden's definition of wit as 'a propriety of thoughts and words' would enable a fit audience to distinguish between the play's true and false wits. Close analysis of the major figures' characteristic styles makes this essay fascinating to read but difficult to summarise. An important point is that Mirabell's gravity and Millamant's vivacity are antithetical modes of wit, which can be harmonised and must be distinguished from the corresponding modes of false wit, pedantic formalism and genteel artificiality. Hinnant rightly concludes that one reason why *The Way of the World* is a brilliant comedy is that Congreve does not separate language from serious social and moral concerns. But its language is pretty well separated from them in Carey McIntosh's 'A Matter of Style: Stative and Dynamic Predicates' (*PMLA*), which shows that predicates became more stative and less dynamic in the eighteenth century than they had been in the seventeenth. J. M. Treadwell's 'Congreve Bereaved' (*AN &Q*, 1975) shows that Congreve's father died in 1708, and his mother in 1715.

Kerry Downes's *Vanbrugh*[22] supersedes all attempts at describing Vanbrugh's buildings. It redefines the collaborative achievement of Vanbrugh and Hawksmoor at Castle Howard and Blenheim, and re-establishes Vanbrugh's personal contribution to English baroque in other houses. It also gives a mass of new information on Vanbrugh's family and domestic circumstances, but it is not a full biography and it is not concerned with the plays. More biographical information is given in Maynard Mack's '"They have actually turned me out": Vanbrugh to Marlborough' (*Scriblerian*), which includes a facsimile and transcript of a newly found letter about Vanbrugh's dismissal from the Comptrollership of the Works. Colin Duckworth's 'The Fortunes of Voltaire's Foppington'[7] is a lively account of the theatre history and dramatic quality of Voltaire's *Le Comte de Boursoufle*, a free adaptation of *The Relapse*. English critics accused Voltaire of plagiarism, ignoring both Vanbrugh's indirect debt to Molière and the whole complicated history of the cross-channel fop trade. Frank M. Patterson's 'Sir John Vanbrugh as Translator: *The Confederacy*' (*REC TR*, 1976) shows Vanbrugh not so much as a translator as a skillful adapter and improver of Dancourt's *Les Bourgeoises à la Mode*. Bertil Johansson's *The Adapter Adapted*[23] is a study of Vanbrugh's *The Mistake* and other versions of Molière's *Le Dépit Amoureux*.

Farquhar's *The Recruiting Officer* was edited for the 'New Mermaids' by John Ross[24]. An editor of this play must pick and choose between

[22] *Vanbrugh*, by Kerry Downes. A. Zwemmer Ltd. pp. xiv + 291; frontispiece, 160 plates, 20 text figures. £28.

[23] *The Adapter Adapted: A Study of Sir John Vanbrugh's Comedy "The Mistake", its Predecessors and Successors*, by Bertil Johansson. Stockholm Studies in English, vol. 41. Stockholm: Almqvist & Wiksell. pp. 76. Kr. 37.25.

[24] *The Recruiting Officer*, by George Farquhar, ed. by John Ross. The New Mermaids. Benn. pp. xlii + 141. pb £1.95.

first and second quartos; Ross's account of his problems, spread over a long introductory note and an appendix, could be clearer. The text is based on Q1, but incorporates presumably authorial revisions from Q2; some passages whose omission Farquhar may have approved are retained, and some are relegated to the appendix. Nearly all the main revisions are to do with theatrical effectiveness rather than propriety; here Ross would disagree with the 'Regents' editor (*YW* 47.219-20). Spelling has been modernised, but the rhetorical pointing of Q1 has usually been kept. In the introduction, the biographical section could have been improved by reference to a recent article by R. J. Jordan (*YW* 55.314-5). The section on the play discusses the origins of the characters in real life or theatrical types, and argues that 'the effect of each satiric attack upon the army world is modified ironically by its immediate context, and by the pervading atmosphere of good humour'. Ross sees the play as 'a masterpiece of theatre', and sketches its stage history, with useful appendixes on early staging and music for the songs. There are also a note on further reading, a map of Shrewsbury, selections from the Articles of War, and full explanatory notes; for the student, this is the obvious edition. Four minor criticisms: on p. xxxvii, for 'formerly' read 'formally'; at II.ii. 46 a note that 'a pad' is a horse, not a bedsitter, is wanted; at IV.ii.236 it might be noted that 'the carpet' is a tablecloth; and at IV.ii.286 the stage-direction 'Knocking hard' should be 'Knocking heard'. With *The Beaux' Stratagem*, *The Recruiting Officer* was found suitable for 'Casebook' treatment[25]. Richard A. Anselment examines their case-histories in his introduction, and groups diagnoses under three headings: 'Critical Comments, 1706 to 1924' (47 pages); 'Modern Studies' (1963-73, 114 pages); 'Comment on Production' (in theory, and by William Gaskill, 27 pages). Pope found Farquhar suffering from 'pert low Dialogue', but Bonamy Dobrée went to him for 'a torrent of semi-nonsensical amusement'. After the general practitioners had had their say the patient was left alone for forty years and got much better; specialists were called in, and though Professor Berman fears Farquhar is only replacing 'one world-view founded on a relativity . . . by another', Professor Rothstein assures us he is able to perform 'the adjustment of moral values . . . on a firm and flexible base'.

The scope of research on Restoration drama is shown by the number of articles on matters of limited interest. J. P. Vander Motten's 'The Earl of Dorset and William Killigrew' (*N&Q*) doubts whether the Earl was a patron of Killigrew. Patrick Thomas's 'Sir Thomas Clarges's Translation of Corneille's "Héraclius"' (*N&Q*) quotes from a National Library of Wales manuscript an anonymous 'Epilogue upon Sr. Tho: Clargis Heraclious', and suggests that it was Clarges's version, now lost, that Pepys saw staged. Robert D. Hume discusses 'Manuscript Casts for Revivals of Shadwell's *The Libertine* and *Epsom Wells*' (*TN*). Robert A. Tibbetts explains 'Queer Foliation in *The London Cuckolds*' (*PBSA*): that is, in the 1682 quarto, not in Ravenscroft's play itself. Michael de L. Landon comments on identifications with living people of characters in Crowne's *City Politiques* (*TN*). B. J. McMullin prints 'The Songs from John Crowne's *Justice Buisy, or The Gentleman-Quack*' (*RES*), seven of which were

[25] *Farquhar: The Recruiting Officer and The Beaux' Stratagem: A Casebook*, ed. by Richard A. Anselment. Macmillan. pp. 230. hb £5.95, pb £2.50.

published separately; their discovery leads to the conjecture, unusually speculative for *RES*, that Crowne may be the author of the anonymous *Feign'd Friendship*.

(c) *Prose writers*

Two biographers, Wood and Walton, were subjects of scholarly studies. Allan Pritchard's 'According to Wood: Sources of Anthony Wood's Lives of Poets and Dramatists' (*RES*; in two parts, pp. 268ff and 407ff) illustrates the range of Wood's papers in the Bodleian, shows how Wood compiled the *Athenae Oxonienses*, explains how he found out what books his authors had written, and prints some sources for the first time. The evidence of these somewhat neglected papers, Pritchard suggests, should increase respect for Wood as a genuine scholar; they are also valuable primary sources, since Wood did not use all their information. The selections deal especially with Lovelace, Shirley, Sir John Davies, Randolph, Wither, the Killigrew family, and Shakerly Marmion. Walton was a rather less scholarly biographer; Clayton D. Lein's 'Art and Structure in Walton's *Life of Mr. George Herbert*' (*UTQ*) argues that in its final version this *Life* has more art and subtlety than any of Walton's earlier works, and that its special quality comes from 'the deft interweaving of the life pattern of George Herbert with the personal vision of Izaak Walton on the nature of holy living'. The argument is persuasive except when Lein says 'we are barraged with the rhetoric of sanctity' and apparently does not mean the verb to imply criticism. Jonquil Bevan's 'Izaak Walton and his Publisher' (*Lib*) shows Walton taking a lively interest in the business of Richard Marriott, advising on what to publish, doing editorial work, and writing commendatory verses for various books. In Marriott can be seen a steady hardening of the High Church and Royalist convictions he shared with Walton. Georges Bas's 'Thomas Zouch's Life of Walton and the Alleged Friendship between James Shirley and Izaak Walton' (*N&Q*) concludes that whether Shirley and Walton were friends remains an open question.

John Bunyan: A Study in Narrative Technique[26], by Charles W. Baird, is the first book on Bunyan's literary artistry. It argues that in his five major works Bunyan gradually reduced the conflict between his didactic aims and 'the basic illusion necessary to effective narrative art'. He found less intrusive ways of pointing out the significance of his narratives, as we see in *The Holy War*, the most precise of his accounts of religious experience; and more effective means of sustaining the illusion, as we see in *The Second Part of Pilgrim's Progress*, the most fully dramatic product of his genius. The book seems to be an unrevised doctoral thesis completed around 1968, judging by its unattractive style and the lack of reference to work on Bunyan since then, and as is the way with supporters of theses Baird protests too much for his general argument to be wholly persuasive; but in close critical analyses of various passages he does help us to appreciate that Bunyan did not want art.

Students of Bunyan should not miss Robert Bell's 'Metamorphoses of Spiritual Autobiography' (*ELH*), where *Grace Abounding* is seen as a new

[26] *John Bunyan: A Study in Narrative Technique*, by Charles W. Baird. Port Washington and London: Kennikat Press. pp. |viii| + 160. $9.95.

development within its tradition. Bunyan would have liked to have been as sure as St Augustine of the distinction between himself as narrator, abounding in grace, and as subject of narration, chief of sinners. But lacking that confidence he anticipated secular autobiographies such as Franklin's and Rousseau's, and even fictional autobiographies, where in the absence of anything like religious conversion other ways of shaping experience were explored. Sheila Jackson's 'Sources for the "Wide Field Full of Dark Mountains" in Bunyan's "Pilgrim's Progress"' (N&Q) pursues the argument (YW 55.317) against Clifford Johnson and others who make molehills of the mountains. Bunyan 'used the terms *mountain* and *hill* interchangeably', and the backslider who would avoid the Hill Difficulty perishes, ironically, among 'an entire *field* of mountains, and not only that, but a *wide* field *full* of *dark* mountains'. The wording was suggested by several biblical passages. Albert B. Cook III's 'John Bunyan and John Dunton: A Case of Plagiarism' (PBSA) considers what Bunyan meant when in the verse preface to the second part of *Pilgrim's Progress* he complained of attempts 'to Counterfeit/My Pilgrim'. He is most likely to have been thinking of books by Benjamin Keach and John Dunton, especially Dunton's *Pilgrim's Guide* (1684), which contains 'out-and-out plagiarism' of both parts of *Pilgrim's Progress*.

The completion last year of the Latham-Matthews text of Pepys's *Diary* was the occasion for a lively review-article by Marvin Mudrick, 'Su Cosa Mi Cosa; or, Busy, Busy, Busy' (HudR). Neither sharing Matthews's enthusiasm for the character exposed in the diary nor accepting his comparison of Pepys with Chaucer, Mudrick would compare him with some of Chaucer's vigorous but horrifying creations, such as the Pardoner or the Wife of Bath.

Students of this period who incline to dispense with the history of ideas should at least read Donald Greene's 'Latitudinarianism and Sensibility: The Genealogy of the "Man of Feeling" Reconsidered' (MP), a devastating critique of the late R. S. Crane's influential 'Suggestions toward a Genealogy of the "Man of Feeling"' (ELH, 1934, reprinted in his *The Idea of the Humanities,* 1967; YW 48.231). Crane argued that eighteenth-century men of feeling identified virtue with good works and benevolence, preferred sensibility to stoicism, assumed such attitudes were inherent in human nature, and stressed what was called the 'self-approving joy' that comes with them; and that the source of this outlook was the Latitudinarian tradition. Greene replies that most of these ideas were part of the Christian tradition long before the days of Latitudinarianism, and that Latitudinarians certainly did not teach that the reward of virtue was self-approbation. He appeals to ecclesiastical history and common sense, pointing out that even if Latitudinarians had preached doctrines patently at variance with *The Book of Common Prayer* they would not have made much headway; 'the most influential philosophers of "innate benevolence", Shaftesbury and Hutcheson, did not get their inspiration from attending an Anglican parish church each Sunday and taking notes of the sermons'. The Latitudinarians should be thought of as Anglican divines who sought to mediate between Puritans and High Churchmen; that is, to maintain a central and truly Anglican point of view. Yet Greene does not have the last word on this subject; G. S. Rousseau's 'Nerves, Spirits, and

Fibres: Towards Defining the Origins of Sensibility'[7] takes 'sensibility' as 'a term to connote self-consciousness and self-awareness', and argues that in this sense, narrower than Crane's, it did derive from our period, from Thomas Willis's *Pathologiae Cerebri* (1667) and *Cerebri Anatome* (1664), through their influence on research on the nervous system and on Willis's pupil Locke. Willis was the first to argue convincingly that the soul is located in the brain; as the brain was understood to work through the nerves, his theory led to the ideas that man's nature is essentially nervous, and that sensibility and imagination depend on nervous delicacy.

The Locke Newsletter[27] includes a list of recent publications, articles by Eric Matthews, J. Douglas Rabb, Paul Helm, R. W. K. Hinton, and Patrick Kelly ('Locke and Filmer'), and book reviews, including a detailed one by R. S. Woolhouse on Mackie's *Problems from Locke*[28]. The efforts of Locke's friend Collins to accommodate religion and reason are the subject of an agreeably lucid essay, 'The Problematical Compromise: The Early Deism of Anthony Collins', by Robert B. Luehrs[29]. It was Collins who said of Samuel Clarke's rationalistic theology that nobody doubted the existence of God until Dr Clarke undertook to prove it.

[27] *The Locke Newsletter*, No.8, ed. by Roland Hall. York: Philosophy Department, York University. pp. 136. Free to Locke scholars.
[28] *Problems from Locke*, by J. L. Mackie. Oxford: Clarendon Press, 1976. pp. ix + 237. pb £2.50.
[29] In *Studies in Eighteenth-Century Culture VI*, ed. by Ronald C. Rosbottom. Madison, Wisc.: U. of Wisconsin P. pp. xvii + 485.

XIII

The Eighteenth Century

K. E. ROBINSON

1. General

The period continues to be indebted to the annual bibliography in *PQ*, the selective notices and reviews in *The Scriblerian* and the notices of books and articles in the *Johnsonian News Letter*. In addition there are general review essays by Patricia Carr Brückmann (*UTQ*), William Kupersmith (*PQ*) and Carey McIntosh (*PQ*), and this year's review essay in *SEL* is by Leo Braudy. 1976 saw a marked slowing down in the rate of publication on the period: the trend continues this year without the compensaion enjoyed last year in the form of the massive proceedings of the Fourth International Congress on the Enlightenment.

The most important book to be reviewed in this section is W. B. Carnochan's *Confinement and Flight: An Essay in English Literature of the Eighteenth Century*[1]. It would be no surprise to find a study of images of confinement and flight in Romantic or post-Romantic literature: W. B. Carnochan's modest book studies the handling of the images by eighteenth-century writers. He is concerned more with metaphysical than epistemological prisons, 'more, that is, [with] the state of being that generates an epistemological crisis than [with] the crisis itself', a state of being which has its genesis in 'the demolition of the closed world and its replacement by the infinite universe'. The paradoxical desire to soar and be confined is an expression of Man's reaction to the new infinitude in general and in particular 'the age . . . of perilous balances' which was the eighteenth century. Crusoe, Gulliver and Uncle Toby supply Carnochan with three 'islanders' who both do and do not want to be rescued from their isolation. *Moll Flanders* and *Tom Jones* image 'happy prisons . . . [which] lead to release and a kind of resurrection'; whilst Pope's Eloisa inhabits an unhappy prison from which death offers the only avenue of escape. *A Tale of a Tub* and *The Beggar's Opera* pull together these poles. Just as Milton's Satan could not escape his internal Hell, so the eighteenth-century quester or soarer is always brought back to the confinement of 'an unaltered self'. Caleb Williams, Tristram and Caliph Vathek all represent for Carnochan men whose flights double back upon them. In heroic opposition to these tendencies of the modern mind Carnochan sets Samuel Johnson. Yet they were tendencies characteristic of Johnson's own mind,

---

[1] *Confinement and Flight: Essay on English Literature of the Eighteenth Century*, by W. B. Carnochan. Berkeley and Los Angeles, Calif.: U. of California P. pp. xii + 201.

and Carnochan gives a sensitive account of the psychodrama played out in Johnson's life and works.

Anyone wishing to pursue the image of confinement would do well to take account of Foucault's *Surveiller et punir: naissance de la prison* which is likely, now that it is available in translation[2], to be as influential for the study of literature as Foucault's earlier study of madness. In the same vein Max Byrd (*PR*) writes of the madhouse, the whorehouse and the convent in the works of Defoe, Richardson, Hogarth, Fielding, Swift and the Gothic novelists. For Byrd these institutions are 'symbolic prisons where irrational energy was locked away from normal society'. It is a shame that this stimulating supplement to Byrd's *Visits to Bedlam* should be so short that essential distinctions cannot be developed adequately. From whorehouses we may enter the world of eighteenth-century London's homosexuals with Randolph Trumbach (*Journal of Social History*) who offers much interesting information about the role of the Societies for the Reformation of Manners in the pursuit of homosexuals as well as a geography of the homosexual sub-culture in the capital. Donald Greene (*MP*) is concerned with a more respectable man of feeling. In characteristically disputatious style Greene reassesses R. S. Crane's genealogy of the man of feeling. The outcome is more negative than positive: Greene can seem to be more interested in ridiculing his opponents than in getting at the truth. Hoyt Trowbridge's collection of old and new essays. *From Dryden to Jane Austen: Essays on English Critics and Writers, 1660-1818*[3], has not been made available for review.

Amongst a large historical literature are several items which might be found useful by those whose interests are primarily in English studies. Joseph M. Levine's study of the Dr Woodward of the *Memoirs of Martin Scriblerus, Dr Woodward's Shield: History, Science, and Satire in Augustan England*[4], provides useful background material about the relationship between antiquarian studies and science. Levine uses Woodward's *sorties* into palaeontology and natural history to show that in some hands at least antiquarian studies possessed 'a method that could be used to accumulate reliable information and to distinguish between truth and falsehood'. Woodward's own theories did not, however, escape the justified scorn of his contemporaries. H. T. Dickinson's *Liberty and Property: Political Ideology in Eighteenth-Century Britain*[5] delineates a clear picture of ideology within the period 1660-1800 (divided into smaller periods: 1660-1714, characterised as Tory and Whig, 1715-1760, Court and Country, and 1761-1800, Radical and Conservative. Historians will want to argue about the boundaries within and between Dickinson's three political eras, but the working distinctions that he offers will prove invaluable for the literary scholar. Closely related is John Brewer's *Party*

[2] *Discipline and Punish: The Birth of the Prison,* by Michel Foucault. New York: Pantheon. pp. 333.

[3] *From Dryden to Jane Austen: Essays on English Critics and Writers, 1660-1818,* by Hoyt Trowbridge. Albuquerque, N.M.: U. of New Mexico P. pp. 300.

[4] *Dr. Woodward's Shield: History, Science, and Satire in Augustan England,* by Joseph M. Levine. Berkeley and Los Angeles, Calif.: U. of California P. pp. 362.

[5] *Liberty and Property: Political Ideology in Eighteenth-Century Britain,* by H. T. Dickinson. New York: Holmes & Meier. pp. 369.

Ideology and Popular Politics at the Accession of George III[6] which will be especially welcome for the attention it pays to Burke's contribution to the concept of 'party' in pamphlets such as the *Short Account of a Late Administration* (1766) or *Thoughts on the Cause of the Present Discontent* (1770). Finally amongst the historians Paul S. Fritz's *The English Ministers and Jacobitism between the Rebellions of 1715 and 1745*[7] is worth consulting for its account of Walpole's obsession with Jacobitism and the detail it offers on his ministerial intelligence system. Fritz's work is altogether more reliable and stimulating than Betty Kemp's *Sir Robert Walpole* in the British Prime Ministers series[8]. Insufficiently evidenced, full of horrendous errors, and often unclear, Miss Kemp's study underlines the value of H. T. Dickinson's *Walpole and the Whig Supremacy*.

A *Bibliography of George Berkeley* by Geoffrey Keynes[9] supplies a full bibliographical description of all works, including translations, published in Berkeley's lifetime, and of contemporary works for and against Berkeley. There are facsimiles of the title pages of all the editions, a chronology, an index of printers and publishers and a general index. In a smaller way David Berman (*Hermathena*) also contributes to our knowledge of Berkeley with an account of Mrs Berkeley's annotations in her interleaved copy of *An Account of the Life of George Berkeley* (1776). Out of the many articles published on Hume in 1977 several are attractive for the literary scholar. Victor G. Wexler (*ECLife*) discusses eighteenth-century Scotland as seen by Hume; John R. Boatright (*RIPh*) examines Hume's account of moral sentiment, and S. A. Grave (*RIPh*) analyses Hume's criticism of the argument from design. T. E. Jessop (*RIPh*) offers a useful discussion of Hume's limited scepticism, and J. C. Hilson and John Vladimir Price (*YES*) print and comment upon two new Hume letters, to his friends Sir Harry Erskine of Alva and John 'Fish' Crauford of Auchenaimes. Best known as the irritant that caused Burke to write his *Reflections on the Revolution in France*, Richard Price is the subject of a study by D. O. Thomas, *The Honest Mind: The Thought and Work of Richard Price*[10]. Thomas illuminates the antagonism between Price and Burke, suggesting that it is unlikely that it was based simply on ideological differences; and he is interesting, too, on Burke's distortion of his adversary's case.

To Levine's study of science and history may be added Margaret C. Jacob's (*ECS*) reassessment of the role played by Newtonianism in the origins of the Enlightenment. It is especially challenging for its suggestion that the Newtonian legacy on which Enlightenment figures built 'may not have nurtured, and indeed may even have been intended to inhibit, the libertine and materialist modes of the Enlightenment'. Miss Jacob's paper is a worthy supplement to her *The Newtonians and the English Revolution*

[6] *Party Ideology and Popular Politics at the Accession of George III*, by John Brewer. C. U. P. pp. 382.

[7] *The English Ministers and Jacobitism between the Rebellions of 1715 and 1745*, by Paul S. Fritz. Toronto: U. of Toronto P. pp. viii + 180.

[8] *Sir Robert Walpole*, by Betty Kemp. Weidenfeld & Nicolson. pp. x + 147.

[9] *A Bibliography of George Berkeley*, by Geoffrey Keynes. Oxford: Clarendon. pp. 234.

[10] *The Honest Mind: The Thought and Work of Richard Price*, by D. O. Thomas. Oxford: Clarendon. pp. 366.

1689-1720. There is a related study in Bernard Fabian's *excursus* on Newton and the poet in the eighteenth century (*Medizin historisches Journal*).

Two articles are of interest on the arts of the period. Judith Colton (*ECS*) discourses on garden art as political propaganda, and Ronald Paulson (*ECS*) is responsible for a review essay with some stimulating thoughts on landscape theory.

2. Poetry

There are no anthologies to report and there is little by way of general study of the period's poetry. The most ambitious undertaking is Percy G. Adams' *Graces of Harmony: Alliteration, Assonance, and Consonance in Eighteenth-Century British Poetry*[11], which, despite its title, covers the period 1660–1800 and includes a long chapter on Dryden. Adams' opening chapter supplies the necessary definitions and a survey of the traditions of sound patterning; and, together with the chapter on Dryden, it provides a background for studies of Pope, Thomson and a bevy of later eighteenth-century poets including Young, Blair, Dyer and Johnson. Adams' painstaking analyses are always lucid and add to our knowledge of the craftsmanship of the poets concerned, but though he is consistently at pains to show that sound and sense should not be divorced, their linking in this study is disappointing. In three smaller studies Jeffrey Plank (*SBHT*) discusses John Aikin on science and poetry, and Peter Hughes (*NLH*) ties himself in knots trying to restructure the literary history of the eighteenth century. James Wooley reviews recent studies in *MP*.

There was nothing of note on Gay this year, but Garth benefits from Daniel L. McCue Jr's general account (*Bulletin of the New York Academy of Medicine*) of the man and his work as both physician and man of letters. Swift fares better with two books devoted to the poetry, though both leave a lot to be desired. Despite the increased attention to Swift's poetry in recent years, selected editions have been slow to appear. Anyone teaching Swift must have had high hopes of C. H. Sisson's selection for Carcanet[12]. These hopes are far from fulfilled. Sisson's text is unreliable and the general presentation of the poetry is unhelpful, especially for the new reader at whom the selection seems to be aimed. Inconsistent modernisation, omitted lines and stanzas, and the introduction of new variants add up to a text to which few will send their students, particularly when so little editorial help is given. There is no dating (though, with one or two exceptions the pieces are arranged chronologically), and there is no annotation. The second book is a critical study, *The Poet Swift* by Nora Crow Jaffe[13], also aimed at the beginner. If it is useful at all it will be for its account of Swift's ideas on poetry and his relation to antecedents in Donne, Butler and Rochester. Miss Jaffe emphasises Swift's

---

[11] *Graces of Harmony: Alliteration, Assonance, and Consonance in Eighteenth-Century British Poetry*, by Percy G. Adams. Athens, Ga.: U. of Georgia P. pp. xii + 253.

[12] *Jonathan Swift: Selected Poems*, ed. by C. H. Sisson. Carcanet. pp. 91.

[13] *The Poet Swift*, by Nora Crow Jaffe. Hanover, N.H.: U. of New England P. pp. x + 190.

rhetorical strategies, amongst them his presentation of a personality. Many will, however, find Miss Jaffe's rhetorical analysis unilluminating and her own critical strategy of paraphrase with occasional commentary a poor example for the student. She is, too, sadly ill-versed in recent studies of the poetry. But all is not black. Claude Rawson's Clark Library paper printed in *English Literature in the Age of Disguise*, edited by Maximillian E. Novak[14] is a much more challenging piece analysing and contrasting the nymphs of the city in the poems of Swift, Baudelaire and Eliot. Clive Probyn's (*DUJ*) essay on Augustan conversation and the poetry of Swift also sets a much better example. Probyn works from the premise that Swift's poetry 'adheres to spoken rhythms and idioms for its effect' to build up a view of the poetry as concerned with the decay of conversation. Looked at in this way 'The Progress of Love' and 'The Progress of Marriage', for example, become poems 'about human relationships which lack conversation, producing incompatibility of mind and temper'. Sidney L. Gulick (*PBSA*) challenges in a different way: he counters the argument advanced by Leland D. Peterson that Chesterfield revised Swift's 'Day of Judgment', making Swift himself the reviser.

Two new books appeared on Pope in 1977 to shed light on the man and his ideas. James Anderson Winn's *A Window in the Bosom*[15] offers itself as a general introduction to Pope's letters, though in fact it might be more properly regarded as an introduction to Pope through his letters. The maxim that a man most reveals himself in his letters in less easily applied to Pope than to most writers, given Dilke's findings in the last century. Pope's editing of his own letters and, in some cases at least, his eye for eventual publication, introduce elements of self-dramatisation unlikely in the ordinary letter. These difficulties do not shake Winn's belief that Pope valued his letters (and recalled and edited them) because they provided him with material for self-examination (though Winn is interested not just in what Pope chooses to reveal about himself but in what the letters betray about Pope's psychology). He places the letters in a tradition of public letter writing and illuminates the different sides of himself Pope presented to his different correspondents. Winn's lucid common sense makes this a book of considerable merit for the general reader (not least because of its generous quotation), but the initiated might wish that he had dealt more rigorously with the peculiar problems Pope raises. More time and thought might have been given, for example, to the differences between letters for which Pope sought public readership and those which remained unpublished in his lifetime; and he might have been altogether more alert to fact in his treatment of the Pope-Swift correspondence. Like the task facing Winn, that which the late Miriam Leranbaum set herself in *Alexander Pope's 'Opus Magnum' 1729–1744*[16] calls for considerable tact. Miss Leranbaum describes and analyses 'the evidence bearing upon the nature and scope of the ethic system that

[14] *English Literature in the Age of Disguise*, ed. by Maximillian E. Novak. Berkeley and Los Angeles, Calif.: U. of California P. pp. 316.

[15] *A Window in the Bosom: The Letters of Alexander Pope*, by James Anderson Winn. Hamden, Conn.: Archon. pp. 247.

[16] *Alexander Pope's 'Opus Magnum' 1729–1744*, by Miriam Leranbaum. Oxford: Clarendon. pp. xxii + 187.

Pope planned to erect upon the foundation of the *Essay of Man'* referred to in a letter to Swift in 1734 as 'my *Opus Magnum'*. On the basis of the considerable, though fragmentary, evidence of the ethic scheme's existence and importance for Pope from 1729 onwards, she argues that the *Essay on Man* and *Moral Essays* were conceived of as part of an interrelated whole so that each epistle was 'significantly affected by Pope's efforts to see it in relation to the larger *opus magnum* scheme'. The nature of the evidence available to Miss Leranbaum is such that a good deal of speculative interpretation is required to shape it into a coherent picture. Any picture she might have offered was bound to provoke dissent, but she works with a proper sense of the limitations of her material. Her elegantly lucid and imaginative reconstruction should stimulate intelligent discussion well beyond the limits of the book's immediate subject.

Amongst the periodical publications are several on the life and text of Pope. Alfred W. Hesse (*N&Q*) cites manuscript evidence to show Pope's role in Rowe's defection from Tonson to Lintot, whilst Richard Elias (*N&Q*) defends Pope against Dennis's charge that he had written a 'panegyrick upon himself' and passed it off as Wycherley's. He finds that though Wycherley was responsible for the piece in question ('To My Friend Mr. Pope on his Pastorals'), he unwittingly implicated Pope by his heavy reliance on Pope's *Discourse on Pastoral Poetry*. David Nokes (*N&Q*) on the other hand records an 'Ex Libris Alexandri Pope' copy of *A New Collection of Poems relating to State Affairs* (1705) in which Pope appears to have claimed a poem as his own, 'On the Death of the Queen and Marshall Luxemburgh'. This was probably Pope's first appearance in print. It is of incidental interest that whereas the volume claims to print its contents from 'their respective Originals, without Castration' Pope felt it necessary in his own copy to castrate the text of Rochester's 'On King Charles . . . for which he was banish'd the Court . . .'. Peter F. Martin (*N&Q*) sheds light on the discrepancy between Pope's reference to a quincunx in his Twickenham garden in 1733 and the absence of a quincunx in Searle's *A Plan of Mr. Pope's Garden* (1745). The difficulty disappears when it is known that 'quincunx' was fashionably applied in Pope's period to describe precisely those groves made up of rows of evenly spaced trees which are found in Searle's plan. Irving N. Rothman's *PQ* essay (*YW* 57) should now be read in the light of Martin's findings. When Dodsley published Searle's plan in 1745 he included with it the collection of verses on Pope's garden and grotto first published in 1743. Of the six pieces involved four are anonymous, but Morris R. Brownell (*N&Q*) not only suggests Walter Harte as the W.H. responsible for the Greek translation of Pope's own opening piece but supplies firm evidence to prove Nicholas Hardinge the author of both one of the two Latin translations and 'Horti Popiani: Oda Sapphica'. Still on Twickenham, Brownell (*N&Q*) reminds us of William Bowles's note to line 21 of Pope's imitation of Horace, Ode IV, i in *Works* (1806): 'His House, &c.: This alludes to Mr. Murray's intention at one time of taking the lease of Pope's house and grounds at Twickenham, before he became so distinguished'. Two letters from the distinguished Pope are brought to light by D. H. Weinglass (*N&Q*) and T. C. Duncan Eaves and Ben D. Kimpel (*N&Q*). Weinglass prints a text of a letter from Pope to Dr William Oliver (15 November, 1743) taken from a transcription made by William Roscoe; and Eaves and Kimpel give a text for a letter to John Brinsden (1741) reproduced in facsimile in *Isographie des hommes célèbres ou collection de facsimile de lettres autographes et de signatures* (Paris, 1828–30). Finally in this section on life and canon, Bertrand A. Goldgar (*MP*) provides an account of Pope and the *Grub-Street Journal* and in a magisterial Clark Library paper Maynard Mack has drawn up a finding list of Pope's library[14].

As if to bear out James Reeve's fears about Pope criticism (*YW* 57) *N&Q* allows plenty of room this year for allusion spotters, echo hunters and inveterate annotators. Oliver W. Ferguson (*N&Q*) annotates Pope's quotation from 'The Celebrated Beauties' in his 'Epistle to Augustus' (line 413), whilst Gary A. Boire (*N&Q*) notes an echo of Spenser's 'November' (lines 188–89) in Pope's 'Winter' (lines 71–2). In a second note Boire (*N&Q*) finds an allusion to *Annus Mirabilis* (lines 893–96) in Pope's portrait of Ariel confounded by the 'Earthly Lover lurking at [Belinda's] Heart'. If Boire labours the allusion's significance, at least an allusion seems possible: David M. Vieth's (*N&Q*) suggestion of an allusion to *Paradise Lost* (II, 477) in Pope's description of Belinda at her dressing table (I, 126) is very unlikely. A second contribution by the same writer (*N&Q*) is more helpful. Charles Gildon used the phrase 'Nature Methodiz'd' when discussing Shakespeare, Nature and the Rules in the preface to his *The Patriot, or the Italian Conspiracy*. Tillotson found a source for the first two lines of *Eloisa to Abelard* in lines by William Broome: A. L. Greason Jr (*N&Q*) offers a source for the fourth line in Francis Fane and Horace, in 'To the late Earl of Rochester, upon the report of his Sickness in Town . . .' and Book IV, ode i. Greason (*N&Q*) also notes a tenuous connection between lines from Sir Carr Scroope's epigram on Rochester and lines 319–20 from the *Epistle to Arbuthnot*; and F. T. Griffiths (*N&Q*) plays with bilingual and trilingual puns in the same poem. Three notes by Felicity Rosslyn (*N&Q*) are more substantial. In the first she juxtaposes passages from Cowley's *Davideis*, Book I and *Dunciad*, I, 53–66 to show how the earlier poet's 'vision of the genesis of music became Pope's nightmare of the poetry created by the Dullness'. In the other two she is concerned with Pope's *Homer*, locating the origin for Pope's *Iliad*, XXI, 412–15 in Addison's translation of *Metamorphoses*, Book III and recording several occasions on which Pope found a couplet from Tickell's *Iliad*, Book I suggestive in his own *Iliad*. On a more general note on Pope's *Homer*, H. A. Mason (*N&Q*) comments on the help Pope derived from Rapin and Boileau when 'formulating the problem of translating Homer into English'.

1977 produced fewer longer studies of Pope in the periodicals. There were two useful review articles on recent studies, by G. Douglas Atkins (*CEA*) and W. Hutchings (*CritQ*), and two articles of general interest. Ralph Cohen's Clark Library paper[14] challenges the drift of recent criticism still conditioned by what he sees as an essentially Coleridgean interest in organic imaginative unity in favour of a more mechanical view of Pope's art, closer to the earlier eighteenth-century poet's own view. In the second paper John A. Jones (*CentR*) explores the sister arts of music and poetry, concentrating on an analogy between Bach and Pope. A literary relationship, that between Donne and Pope, is investigated by Aubrey Williams in his contribution to *A Provision of Human Nature,* a festschrift for Miriam Austin Locke[17]. Williams argues that the received critical emphasis on differences of style between Donne and Pope's versifications has obscured 'the ways in which Pope's modifications involve changes in the actual subject matter of Donne's poems', particularly in the recasting of *Satyre II.* Patricia Carr Brückmann (*ESC*) is also intent on redressing a balance, urging that the importance of the ending of *Eloisa to Abelard* is underestimated. It is not surprising that Dr Johnson used the poem in his private meditations because, on Miss Brückmann's reading, it reconciles earthly and divine love, banishing 'Black Melancholy'. Friendship rather than love is central to Lawrence Lee Davidow's article on the verse epistles (*HLQ*). Concentrating on the *Epistle to Arbuthnot* Davidow pursues the theme of virtue and friendship against a background of a 'fecund epistolary tradition'. Like Cicero, Pope links the 'abuse of friendship with political corruption'; private life becomes 'the locus of real virtue' and supplies Pope with a moral norm. On the same tack Faith Gildenhuys (*ESC*) provides a companion piece for Probyn's essay on Swift's poetry, discussing the conversational style in the *Epistle to Arbuthnot.* John E. Sitter's (*SEL*) approach to the *Epistle to Cobham* is very different. He advances the view that Pope's intention is to replace the 'pseudo-scepticism of the overtly confident "you"' of the opening (Cobham in particular and the reader in general) with 'real and vigorous humility'. This humility is forced upon the reader by making him recognise that he is not free from that 'inconsistency and self-delusion [which is] mirrored in the fickleness and folly of those portrayed'. Finally on Pope, Anne T. Barbeau (*TSL*) draws attention to what she terms a 'double focus on reality' imaged in the wild and in the garden in the *Essay on Man,* and Vincent Newey (*EIC*) defends Raymond Williams's historical approach by way of a Williams-inspired account of the Man of Ross as a 'man of "small Estate"' in whom the traditional qualities of transcendent benevolence and priestly function are preserved in combination with the more practical virtues of prudence, private initiative [and] technological resourcefulness'.

It is doubtful whether there can have been a better year for Lady Mary Wortley Montagu's poetry. There could be no better editors for the essays and poetry than Robert Halsband and Isobel Grundy. Halsband's contribution to *Lady Mary Wortley Montagu: Essays and Poems and Simplicity A Comedy*[18] includes all nine of Lady Mary's essays for her periodical *The Nonsense of Common-Sense* and Miss Grundy supplies a complete collection of the poetry apart from juvenile work and fragments and passages available in Halsband's *Complete Letters*. In addition the volume contains both Lady Louisa Stuart's *Biographical Anecdotes* (and the Supplement to the *Anecdotes* written in response to their reception but suppressed before publication) and *Simplicity*. Both parts of this finely produced edition are model pieces of work. Miss Grundy's task was the more difficult in several ways, not least because of questions of

[17] *A Provision of Human Nature. Essays on Fielding and Others in Honour of Miriam Austin Locke,* ed. by Donald Kay. Alabama: U. of Alabama P. pp. xi + 207.
[18] *Lady Mary Wortley Montagu: Essays and Poems and Simplicity, A Comedy,* ed. by Robert Halsband and Isobel Grundy. Oxford: Clarendon. pp. 400.

attribution; but her account of, and solution to, the problems which faced her are lucid and tactful. The juvenile poetry composed between the ages of twelve and sixteen in the period 1701–05 is described by Miss Grundy in *YES*. She reveals that Lady Mary could describe herself with some justice as 'a Virgin muse untaught by rules of art', despite her background amongst the Wits. Despite flashes of personal experience the poems are essentially literary for Lady Mary was not without literary models (Ovid, Moschus and Halifax all inspired her). Halsband alone is responsible for *Court Eclogs Written in the Year 1716: Alexander Pope's autograph manuscript of poems by Lady Mary Wortley Montagu*[19], a very fine facsimile in a limited edition of a 1716 manuscript copy of the eclogues in Pope's 'fairest hand', with transcriptions on facing pages. Whether it was Gay or Swift who first adapted Virgil's pastorals to fashionable city life in the town eclogue, Lady Mary was quick to see the possibilites of the form. It is a shame that on this occasion Halsband was not as quick to consult with Miss Grundy about their respective notes for the poems: they are at odds on more than one occasion.

There is little to report on Johnson's poetry this year. John E. Sitter (*SP*) is interested in the explanations that have been advanced for the change in tone between *London* and *The Vanity of Human Wishes*. They fall into two broad categories: there are those which are based on a difference in the Juvenalian models and others which argue from the biography. Sitter proposes a third explanation: the difference reflects a decided shift in English poetry of the 1740s. Sitter would need to write a book to argue his thesis adequately. On a much more modest scale Carol Becker (*N&Q*) notes that lines 285–90 of *The Vanity of Human Wishes*, on avarice, have no source in Juvenal. Miss Becker posits a possible influence from *Volpone*. If Johnson attracted less attention than is normal, Churchill gets more, in the form of a general study by Raymond J. Smith in TEAS[20]. Though there is a sound text, a biography and no absence of postgraduate interest in Churchill (in America, at least), he remains a neglected author. Smith's introduction is, therefore, most welcome: it gives a sensible account of the development of Churchill's work, carefully keyed to the biography and the social and artistic background, charting his relationship to the Augustan satirists whilst insisting on his proto-Romantic antipathy to their concern for order. It would be a shame if Smith's study were overlooked because it appears in a series which has often produced less useful books.

All the studies of Gray's poetry deal with aspects of the *Elegy*. George T. Wright (*MP*) examines its argument whilst John M. Aden (*SR*) argues that it should be regarded as classical. Aden objects to the stock view of the *Elegy* as proto-Romantic. It is, he admits, a poem full of sentiment but it is sentiment that is 'eminently classical' (hence Johnson's praise and Wordsworth's unhappiness with it). This classicism is manifest in both the matter and the manner of the poem. Though Aden's sharp little piece might act as a useful corrective to those who insist on Gray's

---

[19] *Court Eclogs Written in the Year 1716: Alexander Pope's autograph manuscript, of poems by Lady Mary Wortley Montagu*, ed. by Robert Halsband. New York: New York Public Library & Readex Books. pp. x + 69.
[20] *Charles Churchill*, by Raymond J. Smith. TEAS. N.Y.: Twayne. pp. 156.

sensibility at the expense of cutting him adrift from the poetry of the earlier century, it needs to be read as a polemic which supplants one half-truth with another. The two versions of the *Elegy* (the Eton MS version and the published version) are often distinguished as the personal and the impersonal respectively. Thomas R. Carper (*SEL*), approaching the *Elegy* via the early poems, finds both versions 'intensely personal'. For Carper 'Gray's concern with parental relationships and with his position among the great and lowly in the world' which had begun to emerge in the early Eton poetry survived in strength into the *Elegy* to find in that poem its 'most affecting expression'. Last but no means least on Gray comes Roger Lonsdale's Oxford Standard Authors edition of Gray and Collins[21]. The text has been reset, there is a new critical introduction and headnotes to the poems, and both poets are given a chronological table.

Collins is also the subject of a book by Paul S. Sherwin, *Precious Bane: Collins and the Miltonic Legacy*[22]. Hazlitt once remarked that despite his 'patchwork' Collins 'has not been able to hide the solid sterling ore of his genius'. Paul S. Sherwin, who is equally convinced of Collins' genius, finds a patchwork quality in the tendency of 'poems and groups of poems [to] cultivate divergent and often contrary experiences ... single poems to be divided against themselves, pitting mood against mood, vision against vision'. A major cause of this tendency lies in the relationship between Collins' individual genius and the genius of the literary past, at its most forceful for Collins in Milton. This relationship is the focus of Sherwin's book. He distinguishes well between Collins' imitations and assimilations of Milton, with some particularly acute perceptions on the mythopoeic in the work of the two poets; but there are drawbacks. The major influence behind Sherwin's own work is Harold Bloom, the anxiety of whose influence is felt on every page of *Precious Bane*. Like Bloom, Sherwin can often lapse into jargon and portentous generalities, as, for example, in his description of 'the enlightened writer' as afflicted with a 'massive depletion anxiety'. If Richard Wendorf's little note (*N&Q*) on Collins attempts less, it is at least unpretentious. Wendorf sorts out an instance of confusion between William Collins and John Collins, the actor and songster. Two poems attributed to William in the Osborne Collection at Yale are both by John. 'The Mulberry Tree' and 'The Despondent Negro' are printed in John's *Scripscrapologia* (1804).

John Ginger begins his *The Notable Man: The Life and Times of Oliver Goldsmith*[23] in Reynold's studio on an August afternoon in 1766. That he does so shows his novelist's eye, for he immediately gives a rich picture of Goldsmith within his London context and allows himself room for some preliminary remarks about Goldsmith's puzzling character by way of a reading of the portrait. Beneath the sombre, dark aspect is 'the possibility of an explosion of laughter which will take the dim-witted

[21] *Gray and Collins. Poetical Works,* ed. by Roger Lonsdale. Oxford Standard Authors. Oxford: Clarendon. pp. 200.

[22] *Precious Bane: Collins and the Miltonic Legacy,* by Paul S. Sherwin. Austin, Tex. and London: U. of Texas P. pp. 137.

[23] *The Notable Man: The Life and Times of Oliver Goldsmith,* by John Ginger. Hamish Hamilton. pp. xv + 408.

by surprise and be quite beyond the comprehension of more stolid by-standers, who will congratulate themselves on discovering that the famous poet is a fool'. In Ginger's portrait dignity co-exists with a strain of almost child-like simplicity. The remainder of the biography traces and interprets Goldsmith's life from County Roscommon to London and fame. Ginger is always keenly aware of those aspects of Goldsmith's character which made him an outsider even when he was 'expending energy in maintaining a public image'. It is insight of this sort which makes Ginger's biography compare favourably with the recent biography by A. Lytton Sells. It compares even more favourably with Richard Ashe King's *Oliver Goldsmith*, first published in 1910 and now reprinted[24]. On a smaller scale Richard J. Dircks (*MP*) deals with the dating and genesis of Goldsmith's *Retaliation*, and Leo Storm (*SEL*) argues that the concentration on affective qualities in *The Traveller* has led to insufficient regard being paid to Goldsmith's ideas. Given Goldsmith's poverty of mind, the ideas are, as one might expect, conventional, though his articulation of them is fresh. Storm analyses the way Goldsmith incorporated the archaic political theory associated with Denham's *Cooper's Hill* and the related philosophy of the Great Chain of Being into his description of foreign cultures and the theme of liberty.

The remaining poets can be disposed of quickly. Joseph F. Musser (*Style*) finds evidence in Cowper's syntax of his relation to the Augustans, and J. Copley (*N&Q*) prints Cowper's marginal notes on Johnson's *Life of Milton*. Copley sums up the notes as in the main 'angry outbursts . . . at what [Cowper] feels to be the bias of Johnson against his hero'. C. P. Macgregor (*HLB*) reconsiders the dating of fragments B1 and B2 of Smart's *Jubilate Agno* and Marcus Walsh (*N&Q*) discusses a unique edition of Smart's *Proposals for Printing . . . a New Translation of the Psalms of David* which includes texts of Smart's versions of Psalms 45 and 148 and, uniquely, his hymn for the New Year, the opening hymn of *Hymns and Spiritual Songs*. Finally, Larry L. Stewart (*ELN*) discusses Macpherson and Burke.

3. Prose

The periodicals have attracted two books this year, *A Guide to Prose Fiction in the Tatler and Spectator* by James E. Evans and John N. Wall Jr[25] and *The Female Spectator*, edited by Mary R. Mahl and Helene Koon[26]. The *Guide* offers an introductory discussion of fictive techniques and themes, issue-by-issue summaries, an index and a checklist of recent studies. Though the summaries are reliable, there is always a worry with an enterprise of this sort that they will supplant the periodicals themselves. *The Female Spectator* provides samples of the work of twenty female writers from the fourteenth to the eighteenth centuries, including work by

[24] *Oliver Goldsmith*, by Richard Ashe King. Folcroft, Pa: Folcroft Library Editions. pp. 295.
[25] *A Guide to Prose Fiction in the Tatler and Spectator*, by James E. Evans and John N. Wall Jr. New York and London: Garland. pp. 396.
[26] *The Female Spectator*, ed. by Mary R. Mahl & Helene Koon. Bloomington, Ind.: Feminist Press. pp. 310.

Susanna Centlivre, Mrs Manley, Elizabeth Robinson Montagu and Anna Seward. What is lacking in critical introduction is compensated for with useful biographical notices. Mark Evan Johnston's paper in *Essays in Arts and Sciences* is a contribution to the study of periodical literature which also ranges outside the period: Johnston examines the influence of the *Spectator* and the *Rambler* on the handling of the narrator in the short stories of Nathaniel Hawthorne. *Newsletters to Newspapers: Eighteenth-Century Journalism*, edited by Donovan H. Bond and W. Reynolds McLeod[27] has not been received for review.

Blanchard's edition of Steele's correspondence contains eleven letters to Ambrose Philips: now they are twelve. Robert Halsband (*Scriblerian*) provides a photograph and a transcription of the twelfth letter. Brief as it is this new letter 'offers tantalizing proof' that Philips penned an anonymous pamphlet in the Bangorian controversy, *A Letter to Dr. Andrew Snape* (1717). When Steel paid a surprise visit to Stephen Clay only to find him fraught by 'the Agonies of death', he was deeply impressed by human transience. James H. Averill (*RES*) examines the impact of this experience on the *Spectator* papers of August 1711, finding them marked by a 'recurrent solemnity and consciousness of death'. Albert Furtwangler (*MLQ*) is less concerned with the man and more with the mask in his account of the genesis of Mr Spectator. Furtwangler lists the many advantages and uses of the *eidolon* of Mr Spectator and explores their development from Swift's first projection of Isaac Bickerstaff in 1708. In a second paper Furtwangler (*Wascana Review*) describes Addison's revision and editing of his thoughts on Imagination for inclusion in the *Spectator*. John C. Stephens (*N&Q*) notes that in *Guardian* No 99 (4 July, 1713) Addison defends the Whig Lord Chief Justice, Sir Thomas Parker, against attack from the *Examiner*.

Defoe's prose was no less attractive than last year. *The Master Mercury* (1704) is reproduced for the Augustan Reprint Society with an introduction by Frank H. Ellis and Henry L. Snyder[28]. This is a welcome text of a rare periodical even though numbers 3 and 6–10 are missing. Still more welcome is *The World of Defoe* by Peter Earle[29]. *The World of Defoe* is arranged into four parts. In the first, biographical, section Earle works with exemplary caution, without retreating from the task he sets himself; but in the second he is on firmer ground, charting Defoe's religious, moral and philosophical view of his world, his ideas on geography, exploration and the natures and outlooks of non-European societies. The third part is devoted to an account of the economic and social structure of Defoe's England, and the final part to the making of the individual. Though anyone looking for fresh interpretation of individual works will be disappointed, it is extremely useful to have such a coherent overall view. And in one respect at least the book is challenging, for Earle argues that though weak on fact and chronology Defoe is 'surprisingly

[27] *Newsletters to Newspapers: Eighteenth-Century Journalism*, ed. by Donovan H. Bond and W. Reynolds McLeod. Morgantown, Va.: U. of West Virginia P. pp. x + 318.
[28] *The Master Mercury*, by Daniel Defoe, intro. by Frank H. Ellis and Henry L. Snyder. A.R.S. No. 184. Los Angeles, Calif.: U. of California P.
[29] *The World of Defoe*, by Peter Earle. Weidenfeld & Nicolson. pp. xii + 353.

consistent [in ideas] for a man who wrote so much'. Where there is a clash between his ideas in one field and those in another (as in his ideas on the moral and the economic) Earle urges that the inconsistency is consistent. The opposed views of the critics inspire Geoffrey M. Sill (*ECS*). Sill finds two opposed views of Defoe's *Tour* in the approaches of its two editors, G. D. H. Cole and Pat Rogers. Whereas Cole emphasised the value of the *Tour* for students of social and economic history as 'a celebration of pre-industrial England'. Rogers stresses its literary qualities, used 'to convey a sense of England in simultaneous states of growth and decay — that is, in *process'*. In Sill's synthesis the literary art is not forgotten, but the association of growth with towns of thriving industry and decay with towns lacking such economic vitality seems to indicate 'a moral imperative pointing the way toward England's industrialisation'. Defoe's view of eighteenth-century Scotland is examined by J. A. Downie (*ECLife*); and in a further paper Downie (*PBSA*) reviews the attribution of *The Advantages of Scotland by an Incorporate Union with England*.

Amongst sundry items concerned with more minor writers, Margaret C. Katanka (*N&Q*) prints passages from the preface to Captain Alexander Smith's *The School of Venus, or Cupid Restor'd to Sight . . .* (1716) together with passages from Sir John Overbury's characters of 'A Whore' and 'A Very Whore' to convict Smith of plagiarism. Mary Klinger introduces related items for the Augustan Reprint Society: Theophilus Cibber's *Harlot's Progress* (1733) and the anonymous *Rake's Progress* (c. 1778–80)[30]. In the same series George Clarke introduces George Buchanan's *The Beauties of Stow* (1750)[31]. David Fairer (*SB*) continues his study of the Wartons with an account of the writing and printing of Joseph Warton's *Essay on Pope*.

The flood of studies of Mandeville was stemmed in 1977. M. M. Goldsmith (*JBS*) and Malcolm Jack (*N&Q*) are the only takers. Goldsmith defines and gives a historical context for Mandeville's spirit of capitalism, whilst Jack draws attention to Hutcheson's misascription of two passages to Mandeville to comment on the unrestrained dislike which Hutcheson felt for Mandeville.

The only editions of Swift and Swiftiana to appear come in the *Irish Writings from the Age of Swift* series. Volume V provides a text of Molyneux's *Case of Ireland Stated* (1698) with an introduction by J. G. Simms and an afterword by Denis Donoghue[32], and Volume VI supplies a text for Swift's own *Dialogue in Hybernian Stile Between A&B* and *Irish Eloquence*[33]. The editor, Alan Bliss, has solved the editorial problems these texts pose by printing in parallel on facing pages and printing, too, an edited text which attempts to represent Swift's final intentions. In the

---

[30] *The Harlot's Progress*, by Theophilus Cibber and *The Rake's Progress*, intro. by Mary F. Klinger. A. R. S. No. 181. Los Angeles, Calif.: U. of California P.

[31] *The Beauties of Stow*, by George Buchanan, intro. by George Clarke. A.R.S. Nos. 185–86. Los Angeles, Calif.: U. of California P.

[32] *Irish Writings from the Age of Swift: Volume V: Molyneux' Case of Ireland Stated*, intro. by J. G. Simms, with an afterword by Denis Donoghue. Dublin: Cadenus. pp. 148.

[33] *Irish Writings from the Age of Swift: Volume VI: Swift's Dialogue in Hybernian Stile Between A & B and Irish Eloquence*, ed. by Alan Bliss. Dublin: Cadenus. pp. 102.

brief notes, Elizabeth Duthie (*N&Q*) gives a source in the *Gentleman's Magazine* (1743) for the notion, picked up by Johnson, that Swift was exhibited as a humorous spectacle in his later years. Paul Sawyer (*N&Q*) deals with an actual public appearance by Swift, presenting evidence to show that the Tory journalist Nathaniel Mist was allowed a benefit at Rich's Lincoln's Inn Fields theatre (25 May 1727) which Swift attended 'as a generous gesture to Mist'. A. T. Varney (*N&Q*) suggests that Swift's representation of 'Orator *dismal* of *Nottinghamshire*' might have been influenced by Otway's portrait of a similarly foolish and corrupt orator, Antonio in *Venice Preserv'd;* and in a longer piece A. C. Elias Jr (*HLB*) reconstructs the early printing history of Orrery's portrait of Swift, which shows Orrery to have been most exercised by 'the figure he cuts as a critic of ancient history and literature'. In a second article, more directly concerned with Swift, Elias (*Scriblerian*) advances evidence to prove that Swift was Stella's writing master in the house of Sir William Temple in the late 1690s.

In the papers concerned with Swift's prose work Clayton D. Lein (*SEL*) casts the commentator of *Examiner* No 14 as a Christian humanist alarmed by the political battlefield he describes, whilst Lance Bertelsen (*PLL*) illumines Swift's careful casting of himself as Drapier. Bertelsen argues that Swift was claiming the role of satirical defender of Ireland whose cloth industry had suffered at English hands. Not only had Swift's *Proposal for the Universal Use of Irish Manufacture* concerned itself with textile manufacture but the French spelling of drapier (that is, drapier rather than draper) might suggest a pun on the French 'drapper' which Temple anglicised in his memoirs to mean 'to jeer or to satirize'. The remaining essays are concerned with *Gulliver's Travels*. The most significant is J. A. Downie's account of political characterisation (*YES*). Downie puts Case's explanation of political allusions under the microscope to distinguish between a general concern with political issues and a more specific concern with particular men. He does not deny that specific people are often involved (Oxford and Bolingbroke in the *Voyage to Lilliput,* for example), but he does question Case's claim that references of this sort are sufficiently consistent to form an allegory. In Downie's view Bolgolam, Reldressal, Munodi, and even Flimnap 'become types, symbols, not actual personalities'. By comparison James E. Gill's contribution to the literature on the *Travels* (*TSL*), concerned with 'the theme of alienation and its relationship to the norms of nature and reason', suffers from a simplifying neatness. Jenny Mezciems' essay (*MLR*) which focuses on Part III is altogether more complex — indeed it is difficult to abstract with any justice. Suffice it to say that Miss Mezciems is concerned to demonstrate the unity of the *Voyage to Laputa* by reference to the utopian tradition and that her handling of difficult material commands respect. Raymond Trousson covers related ground in his contribution to *Essays on the Age of Enlightenment in Honour of Ira Wade*[34]. He scrutinises the eighteenth-century attitude to the utopian ideal through an examinations of works by Mandeville, Prevost, Swift, and Tiphaigne

---

[34] *Essays on the Age of Enlightenment in Honour of Ira Wade,* ed. by Jean Macary. Geneva: Droz. pp. 385.

de La Roche to conclude that the age was temperamentally out of sympathy with the ideal. John B. Radner (*SEL*) is less interested in literary traditions and more in Gulliver's psychology. Radner argues that in the light of the Struldbrugg episode Gulliver's commitment to the Houyhnhnms stems not from a perception of their virtues but from a need for 'security, superiority and emotional detachment'. Sawrey Gilpin's interpretation of Gulliver is the subject of a brief article by Elizabeth Duthie (*Scriblerian*). Finally, in the only discussion of the *Tale*, Werner von Koppenfels (*DVLG*) works hard to show that the *Tale* is given unity by its imagery of aeolism and sartorism.

The only critic to approach Fielding's prose outside the novel is George H. Wolfe in his contribution to *A Provision of Human Nature*. Wolfe offers a very useful survey of Fielding's ethics in the *Champion* essays[17], finding there the first 'extended and thoughtful formulations of criteria for right behaviour'.

Boswell attracts rather more attention. *Boswell: Laird of Auchinleck, 1778-1782* edited by Joseph W. Reed and Frederick A. Pottle[35] is not yet to hand, but it is to be expected that it will maintain the high standard of presentation and editing enjoyed by previous volumes. It is supported by several articles in the periodicals. Robert H. Bell (*MLQ*) asks about the degree of artistic control in the *London Journal* and especially about what Bronson has termed Boswell's 'double consciousness' or, as Bell puts it, 'a simultaneous awareness of himself as both participant and observer'. He finds that the boundary between participant and observer 'fluctuates and becomes blurred' for Boswell is trying to create a self he does not yet know. The case is different for the *Life*. Whereas Boswell had earlier been overwhelmed by the confusing flux of experience, he transforms it in the *Life* into 'a symbolic vision . . . [of] the fragmented, fallen world in which Johnson suffered, endured, and inspired lesser mortals such as Boswell and his readers'. In a related vein William R. Siebenschuh (*MP*) enters the arena of Boswell's reliability in the *Life*, investigating the relationship between factual accuracy and literary art, and Irma S. Lustig (*PBSA*) remarks on the compiler of *Dr. Johnson's Table Talk*, 1785.

Boswell's *Journal of a Tour to the Hebrides* and Johnson's *Journey to the Western Islands* are contrasted by George H. Savage (*SEL*). He presents the latter as concerned with places visited at particular times, the former as concerned with 'the careful . . . construction of the sense of misty distance and indeterminate time'. This contrast, reflected in the form and titles of the two works, brings out the odyssey-like quality of Johnson's account of his journey. Scotland becomes for Johnson 'an island, isolated . . . static and uncultivated'. But it is also 'a sea of nearly unrelieved emptiness within which, without continual effort of the will, man will disappear'.

The latest in a distinguished line of successors to Boswell is Walter Jackson Bate in his *Samuel Johnson*[36]. Equal to his task, Bate offers a fundamentally psychological study of Johnson. He is at his best on the

---

[35] *Boswell: Laird of Auchinleck, 1778-1782*, ed. by Joseph W. Reed and Frederick A. Pottle. New York: McGraw-Hill. pp. 382.

[36] *Samuel Johnson*, by Walter Jackson Bate. New York: Harcourt Brace Jovanovich. pp. 646.

inner tensions and anxieties lurking beneath the public face. There is an especially rich analysis of Johnson's mental fatigue in the 1760s with a penetrating account of the important role played by the Thrales in his gradual rehabilitation. It is valuable to have such a psychological insight combined with Bate's known critical acumen, though John Wain's study remains for me the more impressive response to the whole man. No one has done more than Donald J. Greene to further our understanding of Johnson's politics: his efforts have their consummation in his edition of the *Political Writings* as Volume X of the Yale edition[37]. Aimed at showing that Johnson 'was as political as any dedicated moral writer can and should be', this collection of Johnson is splendidly edited and annotated and includes a very helpful chronological table placing Johnson's life and writings in the context of contemporary events. Similarly helpful is W. K. Wimsatt's introduction to *Samuel Johnson. Selected Poetry and Prose* by Wimsatt and Frank Brady[38], arranged chronologically around key events in the life. Brady's selected text provides a cross-section of the letters, poetry, Lives and *Rambler* and *Idler* papers as well as the Prefaces to the *Dictionary* and *Shakespeare* and *Rasselas*. Those teaching Johnson will find this a very welcome addition.

Two reprints of Johnson material are less suitable for the undergraduate and more for those concerned with the history of Johnson scholarship. James Macaulay's *Doctor Johnson: His Life, Works, & Table Talk*[39] and William Henry Craig's *Doctor Johnson and the Fair Sex: A study of Contrasts*[40] are both reissued in Folcroft Library editions. William Edinger's *Samuel Johnson and Poetic Style*[41] has not been available for review.

In the category of matters arising from last year's work are an important review article by Bruce King (*SR*) and an equally important review by J. D. Fleeman (*AEB*) of Helen Louise McGuffie's *Samuel Johnson in the British Press, 1749-1784: A Chronological Checklist* in which Fleeman supplies addenda. B. L. Reid (*SR*) is concerned with Johnson the man, offering a panegyric on his courage in its many forms: his pugnacity in the face of insult or attack, resoluteness before persons in high place, endurance in marriage, fortitude in poverty and sturdy spirit in illness and melancholy. Reid concentrates on the last months of Johnson's life. Charmaine Wellington (*NRam*) is exercised by a different aspect of the man, his attitude towards women's education; and Robert G. Walker (*N&Q*) quotes chapter and verse from Tillotson's *The Rule of Faith* (1666) as a possible source for Johnson's defence of Christian evidence by way of the argument that man commonly accepts as true things which are less than certain. Amongst the articles addressed to particular works, Bruce King (*N&Q*) notes an ironic allusion to Dryden's

---

[37] *Political Writings. The Yale Edition of the Works of Samuel Johnson Volume X*, ed. by Donald Greene. New Haven, Conn. and London: Yale U. P. pp. 482.

[38] *Samuel Johnson. Selected Poetry and Prose*, ed. by W. K. Wimsatt and Frank Brady. Berkeley and Los Angeles, Calif.: U. of California P. pp. 654.

[39] *Doctor Johnson: His Life, Works, and Table Talk*, by James Macaulay. Folcroft, Pa.: Folcroft Library Editions. pp. 257.

[40] *Doctor Johnson and the Fair Sex: A Study of Contrasts*, by William Henry Craig. Folcroft, Pa.: Folcroft Library Editions. pp. 283.

[41] *Samuel Johnson and Poetic Style*, by William Edinger. Chicago, Ill.: U. of Chicago P. pp. 288.

The Conquest of Granada Part I in *Taxation No Tyranny*, whilst Clarence Tracy (*N&Q*), dissatisfied with existing footnotes on Johnson's reference to 'the Pythagorean scale of numbers' in the Preface to his edition of Shakespeare, supplies an account of Pythagorean musical theory which Johnson could have known of through either Thomas Stanley's *History of Philosophy* (1665) or his association with Hawkins and Burney. Charles A. Knight (*PLL*) examines the presentation of the writer as hero in the periodical essays, and in a related piece William McCarthy (*SEL*) attends to Johnson's portrayals of poets' careers, portrayals he approached with a moral purpose. After a survey of the genre of the brief life, McCarthy demonstrates Johnson's ability to create lives which were at once particular and emblematic. Gay, for example, becomes 'the comic victim of fortune and of hope', and the *Life of Shenstone* is 'an ironic essay on the vanity of aesthetic escapism'. Michael M. Cohen (*NRam*) is more interested in the biographer than his portraits, finding him 'puzzled' in the *Life of Savage.* Though Locke's account of time would not impress the modern reader as central to Locke's contribution to thinking about poetics, Phyllis Galba (*ECS*) believes that it had a marked impact on eighteenth-century writers. Miss Galba instances Addison, Kames, Garrick and Sterne and proposes to add Johnson, especially the Johnson of *Rasselas.* Johnson, she argues, imports moral significance to the Lockean basis of succession and duration.

The basis of Mary Hyde's *The Thrales of Streatham Park*[42] is a hitherto unpublished journal, Mrs Thrale's 'Children's Book', covering the period from September 1766 to December 1778. Mrs Hyde carefully identifies every detail of Mrs Thrale's maternal effusions on her children, and every detail of the account of her mother's death and the episodes involving Dr Johnson. When Mrs Thrale's own narrative stops, Mrs Hyde takes over, to continue the family history to 1892 and the death of Augusta, the last of the Thrales. Annotation on a much smaller scale is the province of Robert M. Ryley (*N&Q*) who corrects an error in Osborn's edition of Spence's *Anecdotes.* Anecdote 951 ('He's an absolute fo–ol! I saw it the first time I was in his company, in the horrid massiveness of his look, and that impenetrable taciturnity') is taken by Osborn to refer to Warburton, but Ryley shows that Spence is quoting Warburton on Dr James Lesley, a prebendary of Durham. On the huge scale again, the Yale edition of *The Percy Letters* takes another step forward with Cleanth Brooks's edition of the seventh volume[43], covering the correspondence of Percy and Shenstone between 1757 and 1763. The clearly presented text is a symbol of the edition's quality: it has a fine introduction (which deals especially well with the question of an earlier correspondence between Percy and Shenstone), it is comprehensively annotated and it has rich supportive appendixes. The only fault that I can find is that it lacks a list of contents.

Finally on the prose, there are three items on Gibbon. *Edward Gibbon*

[42] *The Thrales of Streatham Park,* by Mary Hyde. Cambridge, Mass.: Harvard U. P. pp. 296.
[43] *The Percy Letters: Volume VII: The Correspondence of Thomas Percy and William Shenstone,* ed. by Cleanth Brooks. New Haven, Conn. and London: Yale U. P. pp. xxxiv + 324.

and The Decline and Fall of the Roman Empire edited by G. W. Bower-sock, John Clive and Stephen Graubard[44] consists of essays previously published in *Daedalus*, whilst J. G. A. Pocock (*ECS*) and James D. Garrison (*ECS*) contribute fresh studies. Pocock examines *The Decline and Fall* as in the spirit of the last years of the Enlightenment, 'the uneasy years' between the American and French revolutions. The size of the task he sets himself is not suited to a short essay and he too often drifts into generalities, but there are some illuminating paragraphs on Gibbon's systematic rejection of 'the myth of Gothic agrarian virtue' and antipathy to the thesis that commercial society is a regression from a happy agricultural society. Gibbon worked in an age of 'historical Pyrrhonism' (J. H. Brumfitt) in which historians were sceptical about the evidence of both traditional narrative accounts (especially Livy) and supplementary evidence such as medals. Garrison looks at Gibbon in this context, urging that 'Gibbon turns Enlightenment scepticism into an instrument for distilling solid evidence from such discredited materials as the panegyrics addressed to the later Roman emperors'.

4. Novel

Like 1976 this was another comparatively lean year for the eighteenth-century novel. Madelaine Blondel's two volume *Images de la femme dans le roman anglais de 1740-1771*[45] attempts to establish whether Pamela, Clarissa and Amelia are typical of the characterisation of women in the novel of the period. Her method of enquiry takes the form of a comparative analysis of a myriad of novels. Though her findings might be useful to some (to the social historian, for example), they are unlikely to satisfy the critic. If Mlle Blondel's cataloguing is inimical to the nuances of fictional creation, so is the summarising of Clifford R. Johnson's *Plots and Characters in the Fiction of Eighteenth-Century English Authors*[46]. This summary of Swift, Defoe and Richardson is a worrying enterprise. It gives no indication of how its plot summaries are to be used; but there is inevitably the danger that they will be misused as a short-cut to knowledge of the novels and narratives concerned. Though Johnson issues a caveat that there is a lot more to the works than plot, there is no attempt to indicate precisely what it is that is missed in each summary. The threat inherent in such an undertaking is far from offset by the alphabetical index of characters. In the periodicals Samuel F. Pickering Jr (*JNT*) discourses on the evolution of the genre of fictional biographies for children in the eighteenth century, and Edward W. Pitcher (*Library*) gives addenda to Robert Mayo's *The English Novel in the Magazines, 1740-1815*. By far the best general study of the novel in the period is Terence Wright's study of the emergence of a 'significant form' for the empirical relationship between man

[44] *Edward Gibbon and the Decline and Fall of the Roman Empire*, ed. by G. W. Bowersock, John Clive and Stephen R. Graubard. Cambridge, Mass.: Harvard U. P. pp. 257.

[45] *Images de la femme dans le roman anglais de 1740-1771*, by Madelaine Blondel. Lille: U. de Lille. pp. 672.

[46] *Plots and Characters in the Fiction of Eighteenth-Century English Authors: Volume I: Jonathan Swift, Daniel Defoe and Samuel Richardson*, by Clifford R. Johnson. Archon and Wm. Dawson & Sons. pp. xx + 270.

and his world in the early novel, especially in Defoe, Richardson and Sterne (*DUJ*).

There is little to report on Defoe this year. Frederick R. Karl's review article (*SNNTS*) is a reminder of richer times. Malinda Snow (*JNT*) has some fresh thoughts on the origins of Defoe's first-person narrative technique, and Manuel Schonhorn[14] looks anew at the politics of Defoe's fiction and finds a novelist suspicious of Parliamentary power and Whiggish interests. Maximillian E. Novak (*PMLA*) presents the most stimulating argument. Novak compares the general English reaction to the plague about Marseilles in 1721 with Defoe's account of the plague of 1665 in his *Journal of the Plague Year* (1722). Whereas the English concern in 1721 centred upon the problems of civil order, especially amongst the poor of London, Defoe is compassionate towards the less fortunate to the extent of being sympathetic to their spirit of rebellion. The bursting of the South Sea Bubble also informs Defoe's novel, the 'mental despair' that it generated being reflected in the *Journal*. Novak holds that on the basis of past experience Defoe prophesies that London will triumph over its adversities 'through the compassion of its citizens'.

Though Richardson enjoyed a lot of attention from thesis writers this year (no fewer than seven theses are listed in the *MHRA* bibliography), there can scarcely have been a thinner year for books and periodical essays. Rachel Mayer Brownstein (*YR*) discusses Clarissa as an exemplar to her sex, whilst Lawrence W. Lynch (*CLS*) investigates Richardson's influence on the concept of the novel in eighteenth-century France. John Traugott's Clark Library paper[14] puts Richardson in firm control of Lovelace and his reader, and Robert M. Schmitz (*PMLA*) and Judith Wilt (*PMLA*) are in contention about Lovelace's ability to control himself. Miss Wilt's modest proposal that Lovelace 'could go no further' because of impotence is not to Schmitz's liking. Though David K. Jeffrey[17] has only half an eye on Richardson, he produces the most stimulating discussion. Jeffrey works from the notion that the epistolary form involves letter writers who are both isolated and unreliable, isolated because they are separated from the present in the act of recording the past and unreliable because the past that they recount is so close to them temporally and emotionally that they cannot be completely accurate. In the light of this theory Pamela, and one of her many daughters Lydia Melford, seem to Jeffrey isolated from reality by the epistolary form which 'enables them to construct their own portraits of themselves'. Pamela and Lydia 'are aware of the artistry such portraiture involves, and they use their art to structure not only their characters but also the plots of their lives'. If Jeffrey's basic premise is difficult to accept as it stands, the perceptions that it leads him to are challenging.

Fielding is the subject of half the contributions to *A Provision of Human Nature*[17], though, these essays aside, he, too, receives less attention than has been normal. Richardson and Fielding are linked in T. C. Duncan Eaves' enquiry into the reasons behind Fielding's decision to be more consciously serious and less facetious in *Amelia* than in his earlier novels. The answer lies not in Fielding's illness, depression or gloom but in his great admiration for *Clarissa*. Eaves' great enthusiasm for his discovery betrays a curious ignorance of Fielding scholarship.

The capacity for generous critical praise which Fielding shows in his reviews of Richardson was often sadly lacking in the critical reception accorded his own works. Eugene Williamson explores this reception as a preliminary to discussing the guiding principles behind Fielding's criticism of the critics. Fielding's attacks on critical malpractice focus around three points: 'the offending critics are (1) ignorant or otherwise unqualified for their work, (2) pedantic and mechanical in their approach to literary texts, and (3) unjust in their dealings with authors'. His positives are the opposite side of these negative coins.

Whereas Williamson gives dense (but not pedantic) textual support to his account, John J. Burke Jr's discussion of Fielding's views on historiography and the extent to which they influenced his theory of fiction often cries out for evidence and for definition. The remaining two essays on Fielding the novelist in *A Provision of Human Nature* are both concerned with *Tom Jones*. Eleanor N. Hutchens addresses herself to the novel's geometry, finding that despite its formal symmetry, 'the geometry of *Tom Jones* . . . is a geometry of wrong', the geometry of the systematising Square's name, his pairing with Thwackum, and his huddled shape in the angle of Molly Seagrim's triangular attic. Natural goodness is expressed through asymmetry, as in Allworthy's Gothic house and garden. Though, ironically, Miss Hutchens can at times systematise, forcing a strict separation between the good and the bad, the symmetrical and the asymmetrical, this is an entertaining and searching paper with an eye for the telling detail.

There is less room for enthusiasm for Susan Miller's dogged account of the nature and importance of recreation in the eighteenth century and the number of ways in which *Tom Jones* might be said to involve play. In the periodicals, A. J. Hassall (*N&Q*) notes that in Fielding's description of the visit made by Tom, Partridge and Mrs Miller to a performance of *Hamlet*, which allows Fielding to compliment Garrick, the order of two major scenes in Act III is reversed, the closet scene coming before instead of after the play-within-the-play. Also writing in *N&Q*, Linda Davis Kyle presents a selective bibliography of editions and critical studies of *Amelia*. Finally, on Fielding, Hugh Amory (*HLB*) discusses the text of *Tom Jones*.

James E. Swearingen's *Reflexivity in Tristram Shandy: An Essay in Phenomenological Criticism*[47] is a difficult book, both because its method brings with it all the terminological problems of phenomenology and hermeneutics and because its single-minded pursuit of a thesis breeds a mixture of the ingenious and the freshly perceived and understood. Swearingen finds in *Tristram Shandy* a major, if unsystematic, philosophical advance. He holds that Sterne, working on the foundations of Lock's empirical study of the mind, recognises (unlike Locke) 'the richly complex processes of consciousness available to a reflective method . . . In writing his autobiography Tristram engages in a reflective explication of his own consciousness as rooted in a particular time and place'. Though blighted by obscure language borrowed from notoriously obscure thinkers, Swearingen's book deserves to be taken on its very considerable merits.

[47] *Reflexivity in Tristram Shandy: An Essay in Phenomenological Criticism*, by James E. Swearingen. New Haven, Conn. and London: Yale U. P. pp. xiii + 271.

If accepted, his phenomenological reading nullifies the opposition of philosophy to comedy.

Jeffrey R. Smitten's paper on spatial form in *Tristram Shandy* (*ArielE*) is concerned with the reflexive in a different sense. Smitten too imports a complicated terminology, defining spatial form in terms of 'reflexive reference among disconnected word groups' but his essay is simply about the role of themes and motifs in linking together apparently discontinuous material. Michael Rosenblum (*Novel*) uses *Tristram Shandy* as a focus for a general exploration of the logic of events in a narrative. Whereas mid-century writers toyed with the theme of order under threat, Sterne analysed the ways that men make their orders. 'The world as it is in *Tristram Shandy* is the representation of contingency, the operations of chance which are independent of human desire. Liberty for Sterne is our freedom and inventiveness in reading meanings into the world.' Still on *Tristram Shandy*, Richard A. Davis (*N&Q*) records unnoticed borrowings from Joseph Hall and James MacKenzie; and last but not least W. G. Day (*Library*) discusses Sterne's books.

John Ginger's biography of Goldsmith (which challenges Friedman's dating of *The Vicar of Wakefield*) is supported by three studies of *The Vicar*. Robert A. Bataille (*ECLife*) flirts with the opposition of town and country in *The Vicar*, whilst Robert H. Hopkins (*SP*) looks into Goldsmith's opposition to the Marriage Act of 1735 as it finds its way into the novel. The Act was designed to prevent clandestine marriages but it incurred an opposition which included Goldsmith who attacked the Act in both *The Citizen of the World* and his *History of England* because he felt that it drew 'an impassable line between the rich and the poor'. Hopkins gives the background to the opposition thesis that the Act was framed to stop marriage between the aristocracy and the lower classes, a thesis which gives an ironic twist to the marriage of Squire Thornhill.

On quite a different tack David Durant (*SEL*) comments on the relationship between the sentimental novel and *The Vicar*. Although the narrative style of Goldsmith's novel is that of the sentimental novel, shaping the story according to the belief that principle infuses all experience, the reader is not required to share the Vicar's experiences but to stand aside in judgement of him. Primrose is the sentimental novelist, not Goldsmith. The Vicar's failures are matched by the failure of didactic fiction within his novel. Durant sees *The Vicar* as leaving unresolved those tensions which are generated by Goldsmith's worldly irony at the expense of the sentimental, tensions such as that between principle and experience or goodness and happiness.

I have not yet seen a copy of the *British Studies Monitor* and George Rousseau's apparently provocative essay on Smollett criticism, but the *Johnsonian News Letter* suggests that it is destined to instigate a controversy about the proper approach to Smollett. Damian Grant's *Tobias Smollett: A Study in Style*[48] is based on an argument that we have not yet found a proper critical perspective for Smollett. The first part of his own attempt to erect such a perspective examines the criteria by which

---

[48] *Tobias Smollett: A Study in Style*, by Damian Grant. Manchester: Manchester U. P. pp. xii + 232.

Smollett's work has been judged, offering discussions of the implications of questions about Smollett's fidelity to fact, his moral purpose and his formal and more general artistic awareness. In the second part Grant reveals his own view built on the conviction that Smollett writes 'in a different linguistic tradition from that of his fellow novelists, especially Fielding; and exercises within this tradition a far greater degree of stylistic virtuosity'. The main exponent of the tradition before Smollett is Rabelais and since Smollett, Joyce: it is marked, according to Grant, by a delight in 'the *excess* of language, that bears witness to the vitality as well as the vagrancy of the human imagination'. It is easy to see how this tradition contrasts with the proper language of British empiricism: perhaps too easy. The most useful aspect of the third and final part of the book lies in Grant's demonstration of Smollett's register of styles suited to the subject before him, ranging from the compassionately moral to the effervescently decorative. The drawback of Grant's approach as here practised is that it is very much a matter of passages with insufficient sense of how it is that they cohere.

In three shorter studies Roseann Runte (*FR*) compares *Gil Blas* and *Roderick Random,* whilst John Sekora (*N&Q*) examines political figures in *Humphry Clinker* in the light of Smollett's work on behalf of the Bute administration in 1762–63, and Peter Miles (*N&Q*) illustrates the use made of Smollett by the radical reformers of the nineteenth century. Miles' study underlines the inadequacy of looking upon Smollett as 'Tory historian'.

Volumes V and VI of the *Journals and Letters of Fanny Burney* are the subject of a review essay by Peter Glassman (*HudR*), and the received notion that *Evelina* was inspired by Eliza Haywood's *The History of Miss Betsy Thoughtless* (1751) is reviewed by Sharon B. Footerman (*N&Q*). Miss Footerman suggests new sources in Madame Ricononi's *The History of Miss Jenny Salisbury* (1770) and Marivaux's *Vie de Marianne*. In the case of Madame Ricononi's novel the influence is 'so direct as to amount to little short of plagiarism'. Finally on Burney, Gerard A. Barker (*PLL*) compares the two Mrs Selwyns. in *Evelina* and *The Man of the World*, whilst Rose Marie Cutting (SEL) urges that Burney's preoccupation with propriety was balanced by a growing rebellion against restrictions imposed upon women, and Emily H. Patterson (*NRam*) analyses the themes of family and pilgrimage in *Evelina*.

Family is important, too, for Robert J. Gemmett in his TEAS volume on *William Beckford*[49]. In this nicely thorough study Gemmett is at his best when analysing the relationship between the repressive atmosphere of Beckford's upbringing and the oriental fantasies of his maturity. In an introductory chapter he sketches in a background of growing interest in the oriental fiction in both France and England against which he evaluates Beckford's role in 'heralding the more authentic orientalism' of later poets and scholars. Gemmett believes that Beckford's oriental fiction helped along the 'democratisation of letters in England' as well as playing a part in establishing the view that 'specific facts and unusual experiences had a dominant role to play in art'. Gemmett's study is supported by Kenneth

---

[49] *William Beckford*, by Robert J. Gemmett. TEAS. N.Y.: Twayne. pp. 158.

W. Graham's (*PBSA*) history of Beckford's design for *The Episodes of Vathek* and Theodore Besterman's transcription of Beckford's notes on a life of Voltaire[50].

Ann Radcliffe and Maria Edgeworth are represented by Malcolm Ware and Gerry H. Brookes (*SEL*) respectively. Ware takes his reader on a gentle ramble through the picturesque natural scenery of Mrs Radcliffe's novels. The scenery is used, he believes, 'to maintain a necessary distance between character and scenery' so that we enter in the novels not 'a Gothic world of tasteless horror and violence, but . . . [Mrs Radcliffe's] own distinctive world of enchantment, of mild terror, and of, certainly, romance'. On Edgeworth, Brookes contests Marilyn Butler's view that Castle Rackrent 'evolved from a fairly elaborate verbal imitation of a real man' so that the novel in contrast to Edgeworth's usual practice centres around 'the character sketch of Thady rather than a didactic theme'. Brookes prefers to see it as a moral fable designed to demonstrate by means of fictional examples that through 'quickness, simplicity, cunning, carelessness, dissipation, disinterestedness, shrewdness and blunder' the Rackrent family had destroyed itself and threatened the social order.

5. Drama

RECTR is still very late in appearing: the 1976 volume is now complete, but nothing has yet been seen for 1977. The annual bibliography by Muriel Sanderow Friedman included in the second part of the 1976 volume is, however, as useful as ever. Last year's deceleration in the rate of publication on the drama continued this year, but there are some significant items to report. The first is Volume V of *The Revels History of Drama in English* by John Loftis, Richard Southern, Marion Jones and A. H. Scouten[51], which deals with the years 1660–1750. Like Volume VI it includes a good chronological table and a selected bibliography as well as considerable illustration. The volume as a whole offers a survey of the social and literary context of the drama, a description of the playhouses and their stages, and an account of the fortunes of the major writers and actors. The parts of the volume which concern the present chapter are clear and scholarly in their presentation of wide-ranging material, but tighter editing might have reconciled contradictions between the individual contributions and weeded out repetition. Turning from the general survey to particular studies, Vincent Liesenfeld (*TN*) examines the case for the existence of legislation in 1733 aimed at regulating the stage and finds that it rests solely on a modern misdating. Calhoun Winton (*SLI*) surveys eighteenth-century dramatic use of the theme of Roman virtue, especially the theme of self-sacrifice. Also classically inclined, Anthony J. Podlecki (*RECTR*) describes and analyses Samuel Madden's portrait of Themistocles in his *Themistocles, the Lover of his Country* (1729). Portraits of Congreve in the period's drama occupy the attention of Maximillian E. Novak (*RECTR*). Novak shows that 'what Suckling was

[50] *Studies on Voltaire and the Eighteenth Century, volume CLXIII*, ed. by Theodore Besterman. Oxford: The Voltaire Foundation at the Taylor Institution.
[51] *The Revels History of Drama in English, Volume V, 1660–1750*, by John Loftis, Richard Southern, Marion Jones and A. H. Scouten. Methuen. pp. xxxi + 331.

for the very start of the Restoration and Rochester for most of the period, Congreve became for the eighteenth century, particularly the period after his death in 1729'. Sallie Minter Strange (*RECTR*) and Arnold Hare (*TN*) add to our knowledge of the performers. Miss Strange evaluates the evidence that might suggest that Colley Cibber's daughter, Charlotte Charke, was a transvestite. It seems probable that her liking for 'breeches parts' was as much, if not more, an expression of her natural flair for showmanship as it was a symptom of emotional instability. Arnold Hare gives a carefully documented account of the early career of George Frederick Cooke to complement his earlier essay on Cooke in *The Eighteenth-Century English Stage.*

Amongst the dramatists, Addison and Steele are without commentators this year and Gay fares little better with only J. T. Klein's (*MichA*) exposition of the satiric and dramatic function of the lyrics in *The Beggar's Opera.* Cibber's only taker is John W. Bruton (*SB*) who is concerned with the text of *The Double Gallant: or, The Sick Lady's Curse;* but Rowe enjoys more than his normal share of attention. James L. Harner (*Library*) discusses stop-press corrections in the first edition of *The Tragedy of Jane Shore,* and there are two books. Annibel Jenkins' *Nicholas Rowe*[52] in TEAS is most unexceptional, concentrating on the plays but failing to breathe life into them; but J. Douglas Canfield's *Nicholas Rowe and Christian Tragedy*[53] gives the tragedies a fresh edge by relating them to European theories of tragedy generally and the Christian sense of Providence in particular. Rowe's heroes are studied as champions, Saints, and reluctant and resigned penitents. If Canfield sometimes claims too much for Rowe, most of the time he shows sure judgement. There are two useful appendixes: a text of *A Catalogue of the Library of Nicholas Rowe, Esq.* (1719) and a bibliography of twentieth-century work on Rowe.

Starting from remarks on the 'Art of thriving' in *An Essay on the Knowledge of the Characters of Men* Jack D. Durant[17] comments on Fielding's portrayals of the obsessively self-interested in his drama, especially those, like Sir Avarice Pedant, who by their self-interest 'abuse and bemean others and bring all human relationships into the marketplace'. Like Satan's hypocrisy, the stratagems of the thrivers are more than a match for the trusting benevolence of the good, except in *The Fathers* in which Fielding's 'affirmative moral statement fully balances his negativeness'. Durant's demonstration that the thrivers generally have sway in the comedies sounds a timely warning to Providentialist critics. Durant himself notes that 'happy resolutions though attributed to Providence and virtue . . . seem arbitrary and wildly fortuitous'. In a minor key Graeme J. Roberts (*ES*) surveys political satire in Young's *The Brothers,* whilst Samuel J. Rogal (*BSUF*) explores anti-Methodist sentiment in Samuel Foote's *The Minor.* Robert W. Halli Jr[17] spins out an essay on mercantilism, sentiment and morality in Lillo's *The London Merchant;* and on Goldsmith Susan Hamlyn (*N&Q*) suggests a source for *She Stoops to Conquer* in an anecdote from John Quick's *Quick's Whim.* Quick, a comedian in

[52] *Nicholas Rowe,* by Annibel Jenkins. TEAS. N.Y.: Twayne. pp. 167.
[53] *Nicholas Rowe and Christian Tragedy,* by J. Douglas Canfield. Gainesville, Fla.: U. of Florida P. pp. x + 212.

the Covent Garden company and a friend of Goldsmith, played the Post-boy in *The Good-Natur'd Man*, and Tony Lumpkin.

John Loftis's study of Sheridan, *Sheridan and the Drama of Georgian England*[54] is one of the best books to appear on the eighteenth century this year. It should be useful to beginner and advanced student alike. Always in detailed control of his material, whether it be the plays or the context in and traditions against which Sheridan was writing, Loftis finds the key to a proper evaluation of Sheridan in his art of burlesque and satire, especially the former. His account of the background to this burlesque in Sheridan's Georgian predecessors strikes a fine balance between emphasising the heterogeneity of their works and abstracting some general tendencies. Against this background he devotes individual chapters to Sheridan's burlesque in *The Rivals* and *The Duenna* of dramatic formulae which had survived from the Restoration into the Georgian period, the survival of neoclassical dramatic principles in *A Trip to Scarborough* and *The School for Scandal*, his role as a theatre manager and ironical statement of his dramatic ideals in the burlesque *The Critic*, and, last of all, the change of direction in *Pizarro* in the context of Sheridan's Whig politics. Throughout these chapters Loftis is not afraid to note the weaknesses as well as the strengths: the result is a deeper understanding than any special pleading could have given.

[54] *Sheridan and the Drama of Georgian England*, by John Loftis. Basil Blackwell. pp. xii + 174.

XIV

The Nineteenth Century:
Romantic Period

PHILIP DODD, ANDREW LINCOLN, and J. R. WATSON

The chapter has three sections: 1. Verse and Drama, by J. R. Watson; 2. Prose Fiction, by Andrew Lincoln; 3. Prose, by Philip Dodd.

1. Verse and Drama

The most useful bibliographical aids to the study of the romantic period are the *MLA* bibliography and the annotated 'Selective and Critical Bibliography' in *ELN*. The summer number of *TWC* reviews books on the first-generation romantics, and provides useful 'Annual Registers' of Wordsworth and Coleridge scholarship by Eric R. Birdsall and Jane Matsinger respectively. L. W. Conolly and J. P. Wearing provide a bibliography of drama studies in *NCTR*. John O. Hayden's *Romantic Bards and British Reviewers*[1], first published in Britain in 1971 (see *YW* 52.297) has been reprinted in a new 'Landmark Edition'; it is a generous selection of reviews, if not exactly a literary landmark, and its re-appearance is welcome (even though it now costs three times as much as in 1971).

A collection of essays edited by George Bornstein, entitled *Romantic and Modern*[2], is concerned with the importance of Romanticism to Modernism. Its general thesis — that Modernism should not need to be anti-Romantic — seems a little dated; but there are some important essays by individual critics. In 'Towards a Definition of Romantic Irony', Stuart M. Sperry discusses the development of irony as a mood, or an indeterminacy, especially in Keats and Shelley. Walter H. Evert writes on 'Co-adjutors of Oppression: A Romantic and Modern Theory of Evil', which is that of the inevitable corruption of good into evil, seen both in romantic poems (such as 'Christabel' and *The Cenci*) and modern ones. Two other general essays in the volume deal with the relationship of romantic idea to form. Michael Goldman's 'The Ghost of Joy: Reflections on Romanticism and the Forms of Modern Drama' is concerned with the dramatic representation of a feeling of being cut off from the joy of life, which Goldman sees as the unfulfilled side of the romantic project of self-fulfilment. Richard Haven's 'Some Perspectives in Three Poems by Gray, Wordsworth, and Duncan' concerns the poet's relationship to the world, his language, and his audience. George Bornstein's own contribution to

---

[1] *Romantic Bards and British Reviewers*, ed. by John O. Hayden. Lincoln, Neb and London: U. of Nebraska P. pp. xx + 433. £18.

[2] *Romantic and Modern: Revaluations of Literary Tradition*, ed. by George Bornstein. Pittsburgh, Pa.: U. of Pittsburgh P. pp. xiv + 248. $12.95.

this volume is on 'Yeats and the Greater Romantic Lyric', which suggests a pattern of internal-external expression that follows the shape of imaginative experience. Other essays which refer back in some detail to the romantic poets are Herbert N. Schneidau's 'Pound and Wordsworth on Poetry and Prose', relating their ideas to the linguistic theory of Roman Jakobson. Hugo Witemeyer examines the influence of Landor's shorter poems on Pound in 'Walter Savage Landor and Ezra Pound', and Glenn O'Malley, in 'Dante, Shelley, and T. S. Eliot', relates 'The Triumph of Life' to Eliot's Dantesque passage in *Little Gidding*. James A. W. Heffernan discusses the literary reactions to both modern and late eighteenth-century politics in 'Politics and Freedom: Refractions of Blake in Joyce Cary and Allen Ginsberg': in Heffernan's summary, 'In *The Fall of America* as in the very last words of Gulley Jimson, the voice of the ancient bard continues to resonate'.

John Spencer Hill's casebook *The Romantic Imagination*[3] is a useful collection of writings by the romantics themselves (excluding Blake but being generous with Coleridge) and by twentieth-century critics. It concentrates on discussions of the romantic imagination quite narrowly, refusing to be drawn into wider considerations of romanticism and its relation to the imagination: this is in part a strength of the book, but also a limitation. It has no Victorian criticism, perhaps justifiably, but it is also rather thin on recent American criticism. It will be useful to students looking for specific references to romantic poets and the imagination. Carl Woodring's 'Nature and Art in the Nineteenth Century' (*PMLA*) also deals with the individual and his relation to the external world, concluding that both the doctrine of nature and that of art for art's sake 'are half alive'. In 'Marxism, Romanticism, and the Case of Georg Lukács: Notes on some Recent Sources and Situations' (*SIR*), Paul Breines tackles the complex relationship between Marxism and a romantic revolt against modern capitalist civilisation, using Lukács as a central figure in the equation.

Jason Y. Hall describes 'Gall's Phrenology: A Romantic Psychology' (*SIR*), outlining the theories of Franz Joseph Gall and discussing their appeal for later Romantic writers. Aaron Sheon discusses 'Multistable Perception in Romantic Caricatures' (*SIR*), relating an early nineteenth-century interest in multistable forms to an interest in the complex functioning of the eye. Introducing a special number of *TWC* on 'The Occult and Romanticism', Anya Taylor provides a useful summary of the main themes and of recent literature on the subject.

Donald A. Low's *That Sunny Dome*[4] is a fresh and agreeable book, a portrait of Regency Britain. Low is very good on his particular kind of brisk survey: he paints a Frith-like canvas, taking in the Prince Regent and his associates, the frame-breakers, the prize-fighters, the travellers and the architects. The sections on poetry and the novel are part of the genre portrait, and are no more than thumbnail sketches: but they are part of a brisk and useful introduction to the period.

It is not easy to write about G. E. Bentley Jr's monumental *Blake*

[3] *The Romantic Imagination*, ed. by John Spencer Hill. Macmillan. pp. 241. £5.95.
[4] *That Sunny Dome*, by Donald A. Low. Dent. pp. xvi + 208. £5.95.

Books[5]. Like the title, the description is unpretentious: 'Designs, engravings, Books he Owned, and Scholarly and Critical Works about Him'. The whole is a successor to the 1964 *Blake Bibliography*, and is nearly three times its size: its fascinating detail and coverage of minute particulars in the bibliographical history of the various copies suggest a life-time of meticulous scholarship. The summary of Blake criticism, up to 1973, is also astonishing in its thoroughness, reaching as it does to articles in the *Los Angeles Times, Jimbum Kenkyu*, and *Wen-hsueh Chou-K'an*. 'A Supplement to Blake Books' is provided by Bentley in *BNL*, and a long supplementary review of the work is provided in *BNL* by Robert N. Essick. Bentley also publishes a checklist of works in the Saltykov-Suchedrin Library in Leningrad, compiled by Russian writers, in *BNL*, and discusses a plagiarised article of 1834 in 'The Vicissitudes of Vision: the first account of William Blake in Russian' (*BNL*).

David Bindman's well-produced and finely illustrated *Blake as an Artist*[6] is an unusual and valuable book, which sees Blake's work through the eyes of an art historian. Bindman does not neglect the central meanings of Blake's symbols, nor his debts to Boehme and Swedenborg, but he concentrates on placing the visual art in its historical context. He is particularly good on the relation between *Songs of Innocence* and eighteenth-century book illustration, and on Blake's illustrations in relation to the art of his time, together with his influence on others. J. R. Harvey also writes on 'Blake's Art' (*CQ*), concerning himself primarily with Blake's skill in engraving and water-colours; and James Jefferys, one of the minor artists whose work lies behind Blake's 'proto-Romantic Neo-Classicism' is discussed by Martin Butlin in *BNL*. In 'Blake and the Artistic Machine: An essay in Decorum and Technology' (*PMLA*), Morris Eaves cleverly relates Blake's practice in art to his ideas about machines and their effect on man. Michael Davis has written a concise general biography in *William Blake, A new kind of man*[7]. It is a short book, and not intended for the Blake specialist: even the student who has read *Songs of Innocence and of Experience* will feel the brevity of the critical account. But as a biography, it is well done. It is well written, packed with information, sympathetic and humane, with well-chosen illustrations.

In 'Style and Epistemology: Blake and the Movement toward Abstraction in Romantic Art' (*SIR*), W. J. T. Mitchell analyses Blake's forms as abstract only in reacting against the tyranny of the eye, the single vision of materialism. In the process Mitchell uses structuralist terms to make some far-reaching observations on romantic art's combination of idealism and sensory qualities. This is one of several notable articles in a special Blake number of *SIR*; Morton D. Paley reconstructs a crucial point in Blake's development in 'The Truchsessian Galley Revisited'; David V. Erdman discusses 'The Symmetries of *The Song of Los'*, noting the connections between the two parts; and David Worrall's 'Blake's *Jerusalem* and the Visionary History of Britain' is a lucid account of Blake's use of British history and antiquities. Raymond H. Deck Jr sheds 'New Light on C. A. Tulk, Blake's Nineteenth-Century Patron', a Swedenborgian who

[5] *Blake Books*, by G. E. Bentley Jr. Oxford: Clarendon P. pp. xii + 1079. £40.
[6] *Blake as an artist*, by David Bindman. Oxford: Phaidon. pp. 256. £9.95.
[7] *William Blake, A new kind of man*, by Michael Davis. Paul Elek. pp. 181. £6.75.

was a crucial figure in the early development of Blake's reputation; and Philip J. Gallagher writes of anger made incarnate as a physical object in 'The Word Made Flesh: Blake's "A Poison Tree" and the Book of Genesis', an ingenious and convincing reading of the poem as an alternative to the priestly myth of the Fall.

Robert F. Gleckner's 'Blake, Gray, and the Illustrations' (*Criticism*), is an important study which links Blake's 'The Fly' with Gray's 'Ode to Spring' through Blake's illustrations, both the plate of 'The Fly' and the water-colour designs for Gray's poems: Gleckner suggests a redemptive force in the illustrations, and a typical reshaping of the imagery which Blake found in Gray, whose figure of Mischance is rejected by Blake. Gleckner also writes on Blake and the eighteenth century in 'Blake and Satire' (*TWC*), which points out that there has been no full-length study of Blake as a satirist, and addresses itself to his models, notably Henry Carey and Sterne; another Gleckner article, 'Blake's Miltonizing of Chatterton' (*BNL*), suggests that Blake's borrowings are less from Chatterton than from Spenser and Milton, transformed by Blake's individual usage.

Three articles on Blake appear in the 'occult' number of *TWC*. Howard O. Brogan's 'Blake and the Occult: "The Real Man the Imagination which Liveth for Ever"' makes the strong claim that all of Blake's characteristic work is occult, with a progression from Hermetic and Kabbalistic ideas towards a Christianised Gnosticism. Leonard Trawick, on the other hand, argues in 'Blake's Empirical Occult' that while Blake has many affinities with occult traditions, 'his own view of reality is ultimately inimical to them'. Jane McClellan and George Mills Harper, in 'Blake's Demonic Triad', point out that he uses the number three in unholy opposition to the divine four. At the opposite extreme from these concerns, David Punter has an illuminating discussion in Marxist terms of some passages from the prophetic books; in 'Blake: Creative and Uncreative Labour' (*SIR*), he discusses three studies of Blake which deal with his relations to the social and economic circumstances of his time, and supplies his own interpretation of Los and Urizen's work in terms of labour and product.

In 'Engineered Innocence: Blake's "The Little Black Boy" and "The Fly"' (*EIC*), C. N. Manlove proposes an ironic reading of the poems in which innocence is retained by ignoring or annihilating pain, so that it becomes self-deluding. Vivian Mercier notes two imitations of Blake, and a translation into Latin of 'The Fly', in 'Blake Echoes in Victorian Dublin' (*BNL*). In 'The Last Stanza of Blake's London' (*BNL*), Grant C. Roti and Donald L. Kent suggest an exact medical condition for 'Blasts the new-born Infant's tear'; and Mary Lynn Johnson-Grant writes of the problems of cartography and space in 'Mapping Blake's London' (*BNL*). In 'Blake's Babe in the Woods' (*BNL*), Thomas R. Dilworth notes similarities between Blake's lyrics 'The Little Girl Lost' and 'The Little Girl Found' and the old ballad. *BNL* prints a remarkable contemporary account of the Holy Thursday service from the *Monthly Magazine*.

In 'Another look at the Structure of *The Marriage of Heaven and Hell*' (*BNL*), Edward Terry Jones suggests that selected episodes of Biblical history (rather than children's primers) provide the basic structure for the poem.

Two articles on *The Four Zoas* appear side by side in *PQ*. In 'Urizen and the Comedy of Automatism in Blake's *The Four Zoas*', Martin Bidney stresses the poem's ironic comedy, and Blake's use of the comedy of situation; in 'The Dialogues as Interpretive Focus in Blake's *The Four Zoas*', Victoria Myers stresses the similarity of imagery among the Zoas (reflecting their original undivided state), but the differences in their narrations. Donald Ault's 'Incommensurability and Interconnection in Blake's Anti-Newtonian Text' (*SIR*) is a complex demonstration of Blake's interconnections between characters and events in *The Four Zoas,* and the difference between this and Newton's methods of interconnection, which involve the suppression of alternatives. Myra Glazer Schotz writes briefly 'On the Frontispiece of *The Four Zoas'* in *BNL*.

Harry White's 'Blake and the Mills of Induction' (*BNL*) argues that Blake understood that imaginative perception was the foundation of scientific progress, and that without it the movement was circular, as in Blake's image of the mill. In 'Blake's Mixed Media: a Mixed Blessing' (*E&S*), G. Ingli James discusses the practical consequences of Blake's technique, in particular the problems of inaccessibility and comparison.

Among the 'minute particulars' of *BNL* are Raymond H. Deck Jr's 'Unnoticed Printings of Blake's Poems, 1825–1851', and George Goyder's 'An Unpublished Poem about Blake by William Bell Scott'. Also in *BNL*, David Worrall notes an imaginative use in *Jerusalem* of three levels of Derbyshire, and in 'A Tentative Note on the Economics of The Canterbury Pilgrims' Ruthven Todd discusses the cost of doing an engraving. David W. Lindsay's *'The Song of Los:* on Interpretation of the Text' (*Forum*) is a close-packed brief summary of the themes of freedom and oppression, of the Fall and the Exodus. Rochelle C. Gross and C. M. Henning published a list of 'Dissertations on Blake: 1963–1975' in *BNL*. Also in *BNL*, David V. Erdman discusses additions and alterations proposed by Blake scholars in 'Preface to the Revised Edition of Blake's Notebook' and Richard J. Schroyer prefers 1788 to Erdman's 1789 in 'The 1788 Publication Date of Lavater's Aphorisms on Man'; other *BNL* articles include Raymond H. Deck Jr's 'An American Original: Mrs Colman's Illustrated Printings of Blake's Poems;. 1843–44' and Christopher Heppner's account of the Blake collection at McGill. A Liverpool subscriber to Blake's illustrations for *The Grave* is described by Dennis Read, also in *BNL*.

The Cornell Wordsworth continues with two important volumes. Beth Darlington has edited *Home at Grasmere*[8] from complex manuscript sources, printing both MS *B* and MS *D* as reading texts. Her introduction deals with the vexed question of the poem's date, and with later revisions; this edition, like the others in the series, prints photographic reproductions and transcriptions of all the early manuscripts. Stephen Parrish has edited *The Prelude, 1798–99*[9], the poem in two parts of which Parrish writes that at the end of them 'Wordsworth had reached a significant stopping place'. The chief MSS are *JJ* and *RV*, together with others

[8] *Home at Grasmere*, ed. by Beth Darlington. The Cornell Wordsworth. Ithaca, N.Y.: Cornell U.P.; Hassocks, Sussex: Harvester P. pp. xiv + 464. £16.50.

[9] *The Prelude, 1798–1799*, ed. by Stephen Parrish. The Cornell Wordsworth. Ithaca, N.Y.: Cornell U.P.; Hassocks, Sussex: Harvester P. pp. xii + 313. £12.50.

whose contents and places in the jig-saw are indicated by diagrams and a clear introduction. Jonathan Wordsworth, who introduced the two-part *Prelude* some years ago (see *YW* 54.311), now writes on 'The Five-Book *Prelude* of Early Spring 1804' (*JEGP*). He argues that it was in many ways the most impressive of the many versions: details of the MSS are followed by reconstructions of the composition, and a hypothesis about the poem's expansion which relates to the unfinished *Recluse*. The 'Penguin English Poets' edition of Wordsworth[10], edited by John O. Hayden, makes a pair of bulky volumes which, in equipment and apparatus, fit between the old Oxford double-column Wordsworth and the new Cornell edition. The text, unusually for these days but in accordance with Wordsworth's wishes. is that of the final copy printed during his lifetime (*The Prelude* remains separate in the Maxwell two-text edition, which makes the whole *oeuvre* quite an expensive three-volume operation); but, sensibly, the editor has preferred an arrangement in order of composition to Wordsworth's own ordering which has stood for so long. Although the blurb claims that only by reading the whole of Wordsworth's collected poems can the reader perceive how all-of-a-piece the work is, it is likely that the first volume (carrying everything written before the publication of *The Excursion*) will be much more thumbed, and perhaps more bought, than the second. The first volume also contains the Preface to *Lyrical Ballads* and the 1793 text of *Descriptive Sketches* (though not that of *An Evening Walk*). The second contains the Preface of 1815, and the Essay Supplementary to the Preface. Both volumes have unobtrusive and helpful notes. Frances Ferguson's *Wordsworth: Language as Counter-Spirit*[11] is a challenging and difficult book, which examines Wordsworth's use of language from a premise taken from a section of the third 'Essay on Epitaphs'. Ms Ferguson's insights are many, and the reader finds himself continually pushed into agreement and disagreement: she illuminates a number of unusual matters, such as Wordsworth's own classification of his poems, and the role of language and reading in *The Excursion*, together with more obvious examples of the epitaphic mode, such as 'We are Seven', the 'Immortality Ode', and the Lucy poems. The chapter on the Lucy poems illustrates finely the skill of Ms Ferguson's perceptions, but it also seems to be over-emphatic in its argument, as in the reading of 'Three years she grew in sun and shower', where Nature is seen as cruel.

There are two articles on Wordsworth in a special 'Language' number of *SIR*. In 'The Perfect of Experience', Julian Boyd and Zelda Boyd point out that the present perfect (such as 'And I have felt') allows a sense of continuity, and a persistence of results. James Holt McGavran Jr, in 'The "*Creative* Soul" of *The Prelude* and the "Sad Incompetence of Human Speech"', discusses Wordsworth's use of language as expressing his sense of loss and gain, sublimity and failure. The section on Newton from Book III of *The Prelude* is the subject of Michael Black's 'On Reading: Some Lines of Wordsworth' (*CR*), which relates these lines to other passages by Wordsworth in a demonstration of the 'irreducibility' of

[10] *William Wordsworth, The Poems*, ed. by John O. Hayden. Harmondsworth, Middx.: Penguin. Vol I, pp. 1066; Vol II, pp. 1104. £3.75 each.
[11] *Wordsworth: Language as Counter-Spirit*, by Frances Ferguson. New Haven, Conn. and London: Yale U.P. pp. xviii + 263. £10.80.

the text. George Watson's account of the revolutionary youth of Wordsworth and Coleridge (see *YW* 57.242) is questioned by John Beer in *CritQ*: Beer concludes that both were honourably against violence. Watson replies briefly in the same number. His article is the starting point for another study in *CritQ* by David Ellis, 'Wordsworth's revolutionary youth: how we read *The Prelude*'. Ellis not only questions some of Watson's deductions, but argues for *The Prelude* as essentially 'literary' rather than 'factual'. Barbara Gates, on the other hand, in '*The Prelude* and the Development of Wordsworth's Historical Imagination' (*EA*), argues that the poem shows a consistent historical awareness, which for the poet illuminates both place and time.

In 'Coleridge, the Wordsworths, and the State of Trance' (*TWC*), John Beer carefully surveys the interest of the two poets and Dorothy in trance-states, including Wordsworth's gradual movement towards an orthodox religious language in his descriptions of such states. Beer notes Wordsworth's unsureness about *Peter Bell* in this respect, but Charles I. Patterson Jr, in the same 'occult' number of *TWC*, writes on 'The Daemonic in *Peter Bell*', suggesting that the spirits in the poem are non-malicious: he connects them with pre-Christian spirits, and the Greek daemons found in Thomas Taylor's translations of Plato, concluding that the story of Peter's spiritual rebirth is psychologically sound.

In ' "The Thorn" and the Poet's Intention' (*TWC*), W. J. B. Owen rehearses earlier arguments about the relative importance of the story and the narrator in the poem, and expands them to conclude that the centre of the poem is the process of the mind working on the thorn to create a profound sense of tragedy. Another article by Owen, 'A Shock of Mild Surprise' (*TWC*), provides a term, 'counter-expectation', to describe the shock which assists the external world in its impact on the observer. The external world also features in a delightful short article by the late Jane Worthington Smyser, '"An eye to perceive and a heart to rejoice"' (*TWC*), which describes Wordsworth's love of the Lake District.

Andrew L. Griffin's 'Worthsworth and the Problem of Imaginative Story: The Case of "Simon Lee"' (*PMLA*) approaches the poem through the reader, who is called by Griffin 'the harried reader'; then through the narrator, who is seen to be wrestling with his difficulties; and then through Wordsworth, who is seen as being in progress towards a state of 'silent thought'. This is interesting, mainly becasue it leads Griffin to a comparison of 'Simon Lee' with 'Tintern Abbey', which is seen as having the same mixture of affirmation and uncertainty. In '"Michael", Luke and Wordsworth' (*Criticism*), Peter J. Manning presents a bleak but effective view of the poem as concerned with the insufficiency of nature and the betrayal of one generation by another, so that the poem becomes 'an elegy for the securities we all no longer know'. A more benevolent view is taken by Fred V. Randel in 'Wordsworth's Homecoming' (*SEL*), which considers the poems of journeying and return, and emphasises the importance of the arrival in Grasmere in 1799. The local landscape is also the subject of Geoffrey Little's '"Tintern Abbey" and Llyswen Farm' (*TWC*), which suggests a possible location for the poem.

In 'The Lucy Poems and Wordsworth's Dream Vision' (*ArielE*), James W. Pipkin relates the poems to the romantic theme of dream and awakening in the manner of Keats. J. R. Watson's 'Lucy and the Earth Mother' (*EIC*) suggests that the poems reflect man's nostalgia for the lost paradise and the myth of the *terra genetrix*.

Arnold B. Fox and Martin Kallich write on a Wordsworth sonnet in 'Wordsworth's Sentimental Naturalism: Theme and Image in "The World Is Too Much With Us"' (*TWC*). In 'The Two Contrasts of Wordsworth's "Westminster Bridge" Sonnet' (*TWC*), Patrick Holland points to the contrast between city and country, but also, more importantly, to the contrast between the city early in the morning and later, in its normal ugly state.

An interesting essay on Wordsworth's Scottish poems is Jeffrey C. Robinson's 'The Structure of Wordsworth's *Memorials of a Tour in Scotland, 1803*' (*PLL*), which suggests that the walking tour becomes a part of a journey towards self-discovery and imaginative confidence; while in 'Wordsworth's Yarrow and the Poetics of Repetition' (*MLQ*), Ronald Schliefer writes of beginnings and endings in Wordsworth, of his use of echoing structures, and of the need to reconfirm the self, which is found in the Yarrow poems.

Two articles deal with criticism of Wordsworth. In 'The Unmerited Contempt of Reviewers: Wordsworth's Response to Contemporary Reviews of *Descriptive Sketches*' (*TWC*), Steven E. Sharp examines Wordsworth's sensitivity to hostile notices in the *Critical Review* and the *Monthly Review*. In 'Friendly Persuasion: Lamb as Critic of Wordsworth' (*TWC*), John I. Ades notes that Lamb has recently been underestimated as a critic of Wordsworth because of his sense of fun, and points to some distinguished examples of his work.

Ronald Tetreault prints a new letter of 1824 from Wordsworth to Thomas Clarkson in *MP*: this suggests that Wordsworth was cautious before the enthusiasm of the anti-slavery movement. In 'Tragedy and Wordsworth's Sublime' (*TWC*), W. P. Albrecht analyses Wordsworth's essay 'The Sublime and the Beautiful', and places it in the eighteenth-century and romantic traditions. Jack Benoit Gohn points to Lockhart as the author of a Wordsworth parody in 'Who Wrote *Benjamin the Waggoner?* An Inquiry' (*TWC*).

Coleridge's Poetic Intelligence[12] is a very exact title for John Beer's new study, which deals with the complex formulation of ideas within the poems. Beer's literary detective work is intricate and impressive: it leads him into romance, science, mesmerism, theories of the effect of heat and cold upon the intellect, and into an account of the development of Coleridge's mind and spirits up to 1805. Beer establishes his thesis firmly at many points, and shows that Coleridge's thought is closer to his poetry than might have been supposed; but perhaps the chief excitement of the book is in its teasing out of references to the mysterious workings of the human mind, and the connections of these to 'Kubla Khan', 'Christabel', and 'The Ancient Mariner'.

J. Robert Barth's *The Symbolic Imagination*[13] is subtitled 'Coleridge

[12] *Coleridge's Poetic Intelligence*, by John Beer. Macmillan. pp. xviii + 318. £8.95.

[13] *The Symbolic Imagination*, by J. Robert Barth, S.J. Princeton, N.J.: Princeton U.P. pp. xii + 155. £7.80.

and the Romantic Tradition'. The tradition to which Barth is referring is that of romantic literature as religious and mysterious: in this context symbol becomes vital, as it is through symbol that man encounters the mysterious and transcendent. The symbol, in Barth's reading, is thus sacramental. This theory allows him to provide some illuminating readings of Wordsworth, though only of one kind of Wordsworth, the poet of 'Tintern Abbey' and some parts of *The Prelude*. Both here, and in the interpretations of Coleridge, Barth emphasises the relationship between the imagination and the mysterious, in a way which has clear theological parallels: 'symbol reveals the deepest mysteries of human life, but respects their ultimate resistance to revelation'. The consequences of this argument are far-reaching, and lead to a particular kind of understanding of 'The Ancient Mariner' and 'Kubla Khan'; while throughout the book, Barth's tendency to emphasise the transcendent is accompanied by a very down-to-earth sense of the progression of poetic language, from eighteenth-century figures to romantic metaphor. In the process, he has some useful insights into Coleridge's antipathy to allegory, which is also the subject of John Gatta Jr's 'Coleridge and Allegory' (*MLQ*). Gatta argues that Coleridge was by no means so simply hostile to allegory as the well-known passage from *The Statesman's Manual* suggests.

Morality is implied in so many of Coleridge's writings, that a book entitled *Coleridge the Moralist*[14] comes as something of a surpise. Yet Laurence S. Lockridge has succeeded in producing a most enlightening study, in which Coleridge appears more than a little Blakean, a figure who believed that prudence and duty were obstacles to a true and creative morality. It is good to see Empson's theory about 'The Ancient Mariner' taken seriously in this context, though Lockridge's reading of Geraldine in 'Christabel' seems to me too simple. Throughout, Lockridge relates Coleridge's thinking to the German tradition and to the British, showing how he developed his own emphasis on joy, freedom, and the community.

There are no rivals to Kathleen Coburn's *In Pursuit of Coleridge*[15] as the most delightful book of the year in this period. It is splendid reading for an academic evening off, a celebration that is at once joyful and modest. It could so easily have become a chronicle of triumph, but it turns out to be quite different, a record of happy accidents, unexpected friendships, understated hard work, and a particular kind of life-style in which the hectic life of a travelling scholar is refreshed by periods of tranquillity on a lake island. It is a record of determination and kindness, and finally a brief celebration of Coleridge himself.

Several articles deal with the relationship of Coleridge to other figures. In 'Coleridge, Chemistry, and the Philosophy of Nature' (*SIR*), Trevor H. Levere considers Coleridge's preference for the science of Davy over that of Dalton, and outlines Coleridge's impressive attempts to find a unity in different sciences. One of the authors whom he read, Lorenz Oken, is discussed by Pierce C. Mullen in 'The Romantic as Scientist:

[14] *Coleridge the Moralist*, by Laurence S. Lockridge. Ithaca, N.Y. and London: Cornell U.P. pp. 294. £9.25.
[15] *In Pursuit of Coleridge*, by Kathleen Coburn. The Bodley Head. pp. 202. £4.50.

Lorenz Oken' (*SIR*). In 'Coleridge, Joseph Gerrald, and the Slave Trade' (*TWC*), Peter Mann describes Coleridge's disillusion with Gerrald (whom he had praised in a 1795 lecture) because of his curious involvement with slave trade interests. John Beer's 'Coleridge, the Wordsworths, and the State of Trance' (*TWC*), mentioned above, notes the early influence on Coleridge of Thomas Beddoes. The jokey title of P. M. Zall's latest offering in his series 'The Cool World of Samuel Taylor Coleridge' (*TWC*) is 'Do Ye Ken Tom Poole?' It is, as usual, full of zest and enjoyment in its account of 'the town radical in residence'. Another in the series is concerned with the *Anti-Jacobin* and George Canning. Rosemary D. Ashton's 'Coleridge and *Faust*' (*RES*) is an account of Coleridge's ambivalent attitude to Goethe's drama, which suggests that his failure to come out in its favour was due to his sensitivity 'to the confused attitudes prevailing in England towards *Faust* and German literature as a whole, and to his nervous desire for financial success, celebrity, and excellence'.

In 'Words and "Languageless" Meanings: Limits of Expression in *The Rime of the Ancient Mariner*' (*MLQ*), Raimonda Modiano investigates the conflict between what happens to the mariner and his account of it: the account has to give the original experience a coherence and meaning which it did not originally possess. Among other things, Modiano notices an interesting change in the language used by the mariner after the intervention of the wedding guest in Part IV. Elizabeth Chadwick's 'Coleridge's Headlong Horsemen: Insinuating the Supernatural' (*TWC*) deals with the influence on Christabel of Bürger's '*Lenore*' and '*Der wilde Jäger*'. John L. Mahoney's '"The Reptile's Lot": Theme and Image in Coleridge's Later Poetry' (*TWC*) deals with the unhappiness of Coleridge's later years and the poetic expression of despair, hope, and resignation.

Anthony John Harding describes 'Coleridge's College Declamation, 1792' (*TWC*), an undergraduate exercise in Latin, and prints the text. In 'Coleridge on the King's Evil' (*SIR*), H. J. Jackson discusses the fragmentary 'Essay on Scrofula' and relates it to the *Theory of Life*, published posthumously in 1848.

Volume 7 of Leslie Marchand's new edition of *Byron's Letters and Journals* is called *Between Two Worlds*[16]. It deals with the year 1820. The two worlds are those of England and Italy, the England of Murray and the Italy of Teresa Guiccioli. The letters to England are full of buoyant energy, containing much information about the composition of *Don Juan* and about Byron's life at Cambridge. The Italian letters are accompanied by a translation, and the edition also has brief biographical sketches of Count Gamba (Teresa's father) and Count Pietro Gamba Ghiselli (her brother). Marchand's editing is, as usual, unobtrusive and accurate, though I suspect that the painter of the frontispiece is mis-named. Doris Langley Moore's study of Byron's legitimate daughter, *Ada, Countess of Lovelace*[17], is a detailed account of an extraordinary life, which began with the over-protectiveness of Lady Byron and ended in a secret passion for gambling on the horses. It is an interesting story in its own right, and has

[16] *Between Two Worlds: Byron's Letters and Journals,* Vol. 7, ed. by Leslie A. Marchand. John Murray. pp. iv + 282. £6.50.
[17] *Ada, Countess of Lovelace,* by Doris Langley Moore. John Murray. pp. 397. £9.50.

some retrospective significance in regard to the character of Byron, since it demonstrates with great clarity Lady Byron's relentless manipulation. If the narrative seems occasionally to be clogged with detail, this was probably inescapable.

The word 'indispensable' is used in the preface of Oscar José Santucho's *George Gordon, Lord Byron: a comprehensive bibliography of secondary materials in English, 1807-1974*[18], and for once it is fully justified. The immense volume of criticism on Byron is daunting, even to read through as a list of titles: its paths are neatly charted in an essay by Clement Tyson Goode Jr. This traces various stages in the historical process of receiving Byron: from lifetime and aftermath, through decline and revival of interest, to modern critical beginnings and, *enfin*, to what Goode sees as the golden age of Byron scholarship and criticism, from 1957 to 1972. The essay is of great usefulness and interest, not only as a guide to the material which follows, but also as permitting an understanding of attitudes to Byron at different times; the book thus becomes a bibliography which is also a true survey of a critical heritage.

'The Literary Find of the Century' is Elma Dangerfield's grand title for her brief description in *The Byron Journal* of the newly-discovered Byron letters to Scrope Davies and Charles Matthews, together with the lost MS of Canto III of *Childe Harold's Pilgrimage*. Another piece of textual work in *The Byron Journal* is Jerome J. McGann's 'The Murray Proofs of "Don Juan" I–II'. This journal also contains a number of articles describing the effect on different countries of Europe of Byron's death. Douglas Dakin gives a disappointing summary of 'The Political Influence of Byron's Death on Britain', concluding that his writings continued to be a source of inspiration, and that Byron was an internationalist. More informative than this is Charles E. Robinson's corresponding essay on America, which demonstrates interesting links between Byron, Daniel Webster, and Edward Everett, the American philhellene. Giorgio Melchiori traces the influence of Byron's death on Italy, especially on the *Risorgimento* and Cavour, and Ernest Giddey does the same for French-speaking Switzerland. These contributions were given at a seminar at Missolonghi, described in this number of *The Byron Journal* by M. Byron Raizis.

J. Michael Robertson, in 'Aristocratic Individualism in Byron's *Don Juan*' (*SEL*), explores Byron's deliberately cultivated uniqueness, in which he can use both his knowledge of the aristocratic world and his sense of apartness from it. Two plays about Venice are discussed by the late John Jump in 'A Comparison of "Marino Faliero" with Otway's "Venice Preserved"' (*The Byron Journal*), who concludes that it is the vigour and eloquence of the speeches which distinguish Byron's play. In 'Byron on Joanna Southcott and Undeserved Salvation' (*KSJ*), Frederick L. Beaty notes Byron's consistent attacks on the selling of 'passports to heaven', and relates this to Byron's other views on eternal life.

Minor Byron matters include Guy Evans's description of two of Byron's

[18] *George Gordon, Lord Byron: A comprehensive bibliography of secondary materials in English, 1807-1974*, by Oscar José Santucho, with a Critical Review of Research, by Clement Tyson Goode Jr. Metuchen, N.J.: Scarecrow P. pp. xiv + 641. $22.50.

servants, Vasili and Dervish Tahir, in 'Byron's Albanians' (*The Byron Journal*); and Charles W. Smith's 'Seventeen Guns for the Baron: A New Description of Lord Byron's Visit to the *Constitution'* (*KSMB*). The latter notes Byron's high reputation in America, and provides some intricate details of naval etiquette to demonstrate Byron's reception on board two American warships. A kind of review-forum is held in *SIR*, with brief essays by George M. Ridenour, Jerome J. McGann and Donald H. Reiman, occasioned by the publication of McGann's *Don Juan in Context* (see *YW* 57.245f.) Ridenour and McGann differ in their interpretation of Byron's place in the romantic movement; Reiman stresses the importance of epic in any assessment of *Don Juan*, and notes the poem's epic inclusiveness.

Like Frances Ferguson's book on Wordsworth, mentioned above, Stuart A. Ende's *Keats and the Sublime*[19] is a product of the Yale school of romantic criticism: not surprisingly, perhaps, it identifies a highly sophisticated problem and discusses it in complex terms. The poet's conflicting needs, according to Ende, are 'to be sublimed in the ecstasy that is poetic fire, and to retain one's sentient being'. It begins with a difficult chapter on the self and the external world, using Freudian terminology to suggest the conflicting and changing relationship between the two. The examination of Keats's poetry which follows stresses the problem of love, a submission to the sublime and an awareness of what is involved in this: he is particularly good on *Hyperion* and on the 'Ode to Psyche', though the reading of the 'Ode to a Nightingale' seems to this reader to be over ingenious. However, the book ends with a coda on Yeats, in which the approach seems fully justified: it would be perverse to say that Ende is better on Yeats than on Keats, but there is a sense in which Yeats is more suited to his particular method. Helmut Viebrock has written a selective account of Keats scholarship from its beginnings to the present, covering the most important critical and methodological approaches to his work[20]. The greater part of Professor Viebrock's book deals with the critical discussion concerning Keats' major poetical works and his letters. There are three separate essays on the key concept of Beauty and Truth, on Keats in interdisciplinary research, and on Keats and Romanticism. [H.C.C.]

John Kinnaird's 'Hazlitt, Keats, and the Poetics of Intersubjectivity' (*Criticism*) questions the idea that Hazlitt was one of the fathers of the doctrine of 'pure poetry', and emphasises Hazlitt's recognition of the movement of poetry towards 'intersubjective humanity'; Kinnaird argues for this as an influence on Keats's *Odes*. In 'The Performing Narrator in Keats's Poetry' (*KSJ*), William C. Stephenson argues that Keats uses the narrator to undercut his myths in 'The Eve of St Agnes', 'Lamia', 'Hyperion', and 'The Fall of Hyperion'.

Gail McMurray Gibson's 'Ave Madeline: Ironic Annunciation in Keats's "The Eve of St Agnes"' (*KSJ*) argues that the poem echoes ironically the Annunciation by Gabriel to the Virgin Mary. This points up the essentially

[19] *Keats and the Sublime*, by Stuart A. Ende. New Haven, Conn. and London: Yale U.P. pp. xviii + 201. £9.
[20] *John Keats*, by Helmut Viebrock. Darmstadt: Wissenschaftliche Buchgesellschaft (Erträge der Forschung 67). pp. 135.

temporary human love of the poem. Leon Waldoff mounts a strong defence of Porphyro in 'Porphyro's Imagination and Keats's Romanticism' (*JEGP*), suggesting that he embodies Keats's concept of the seizing, active imagination.

Eugene Green and Rosemary M. Green write on 'Keats's Use of Names in *Endymion* and in the Odes' (*SIR*), showing the progression of Keats's art from a rhetorical use of names to a more significant employment of them. In 'Strategies of Time in Keats's Narratives' (*SEL*), Jacqueline Zeff concentrates on *Endymion* and *Lamia* and suggests that Keats's narrative technique is undervalued, since critics have preferred to concentrate on details of imagery and on decorative effects. In 'Keats's "Hymn to Pan": A Debt to Shaftesbury?' (*KSJ*), Robert M. Ryan suggests a source in 'The Moralists', a philosophical dialogue in Shaftesbury's *Characteristics*. Judith Driscoll suggests that both Lamia and Apollonius are right in their respective spheres in 'Form and Fancy in Keats's *Lamia* (*SoRA*). Her point is that Lamia belongs in a pastoral world of beauty, but that there is a finer visionary state which comprehends the agonies of human strife. In 'The Refining of Lamia' (*TWC*) Coleman O. Parsons deals with a large corpus of serpent literature, and Keats's individual use of the tradition.

Leon Waldoff adds the 'Ode to Psyche' to the usual ode-sequence by emphasising the conception of Psyche as a dying immortal in 'The Theme of Mutability in the "Ode to Psyche"' (*PMLA*). There are two notes on the connection between Keats and Coleridge: Donald Lange prints a new letter of 1848 from John Hamilton Reynolds to Richard Monckton Milnes, which suggests that there were two meetings between Keats and Coleridge (*MLR*). In 'An Echo of Keats in "The Eolian Harp" ' (*RES*), John Barnard argues that Coleridge is echoing 'Sleep and Poetry', rather than the other way round.

A poet who was powerfully influenced by Keats is described by Priscilla Johnston in 'Charles Jeremiah Wells: An Early Keatsian Poet' (*KSJ*), which argues for some recognition of Wells as a poet. Stanley Jones prints a snippet from the *Courier* as 'A Glimpse of George Keats in Philadelphia' (*KSMB*).

In the field of Shelley studies, this is clearly Timothy Webb year: he has published two major books on the poet, together with a selection of the verse. The more specialised book, *The Violet in the Crucible*[21], is a study of Shelley and translation; there is meticulous attention to detail and a graceful account of the place of translation in Shelley's work. Webb discusses translations from Greek, German, Spanish, and Italian: particularly interesting are the sections on *Faust* and its parallels with *Adonais*, and on Dante and his influence on *Epipsychidion*. It would have been very easy to make this highly technical work dull and pedantic; Webb has succeeded in presenting Shelley as translator with grace and enthusiasm. In his other book, which is a more general study entitled *Shelley: A Voice Not Understood*[22], Webb is anxious to remove the myths which have accumulated around the poet. He clears the ground by disposing of the

[21] *The Violet in the Crucible*, by Timothy Webb. Oxford: Clarendon P. pp. xiv + 364. £12.
[22] *Shelley: A Voice not Understood*, by Timothy Webb. Manchester: Manchester U.P. pp. viii + 269. £11.95.

assumptions that Shelley was somehow ethereal, and that his poetry was a projection of his own ego. He then turns to politics and religion, demonstrating Shelley's own Christian mythology of Christ as revolutionary, and his attachment to the Greek example of what man ideally might become. Finally he shows Shelley's attachment to the idea of an active and animate nature, and the relation of this to the rest of his thought. Webb writes clearly and briskly: this is a book which is a splendid corrective to sloppy thinking about Shelley, or to a too-easy acceptance of received ideas about him. The sections on religion, in particular, seem to me to illuminate Shelley's deep and serious, almost Blakean, interest in Christianity.

Webb's *Shelley, Selected Poems*[23] is a useful and representative selection, which is more balanced than the Penguin one because it contains some of the political poetry. It also includes *Julian and Maddalo,* and part of *Prometheus Unbound.* The introduction is a highly compressed version of *A Voice Not Understood,* and none the worse for that: it discriminates nicely between the true and the false Shelley, the Shelley of myth. It also contains a very useful and substantial bibliography.

Ingrid R. Kritzberger's *"A Thousand Images of Loveliness" in Percy Bysshe Shelley's Love Poetry*[24] concentrates on *Epipsychidion* and *The Revolt of Islam,* but also takes in some of the shorter poems. It deals briskly with images for the beloved, musical images, and synaesthetic effects.

Martha Banta provides an ingenious comparison between poetry and paintings in 'Adonais and the Angel: Light, Color, and the Occult Sublime' (*TWC*), in which the 'angel' is Turner's 'The Angel Standing in the Sun': by using Blake's 'Glad Day' as a third reference point, Banta contrasts Shelley's sense of incompleteness and rebellion with Turner's vision of what she calls 'the occult sublime'. Norman Thurston's 'Shelley and the Duty of Hope' (*KSJ*) underlines the excitement of choice and hope which is found in Shelley's poetry. Harry White's account, 'Shelley's Defence of Science' (*SIR*) emphasises the importance for Shelley of an imaginative science, which transcended any limiting idea of material progress.

Two articles deal with Shelley's poetic language. Susan Hawk Brisman's '"Unsaying His High Language": The Problem of Voice in *Prometheus Unbound*' (*SIR*) is a densely-packed argument which suggests that Prometheus moves from a defiant and denunciating mode to a poetic and compassionate one, in stages which are carefully plotted. Richard Cronin's 'Shelley's Language of Dissent' (*EIC*) discusses the question of the radical poet's need to use conservative language, placing it within the context of the romantic poet's love-hate relationship with language.

In 'Poetry as Subversion: The Unbinding of Shelley's Prometheus' (*Anglia*), Leonard N. Neufeldt suggests that *Prometheus Unbound* is an attack upon mental order, doctrine and ideology, setting up against Jupiter images of change, growth and movement; this is reflected in the freedom and virtuosity of the language of Act IV. Frederic S. Colwell argues for the dismissal of an attractive idea in 'Shelley's Asia and Botticelli's Venus: an Infectious Shelley Myth' (*KSMB*). Richard Cronin,

[23] *Shelley, Selected Poems,* ed. by Timothy Webb. Dent. pp. xl + 232. £1.75.
[24] *"A Thousand Images of Loveliness" in Percy Bysshe Shelley's Love Poetry,* by Ingrid R. Kritzberger. Salzburg: Romantic Reassessment, 69. pp. vi + 96. £4.60.

in 'Shelley's Witch of Atlas' (*KSJ*), re-examines the comic technique of the poem, seeing it as 'a skeptical myth designed to explore the function of poetry'.

Claude Brew offers an amalgamation of two essays (following F. L. Jones — *SP* 1948) and a revised text as 'A New Shelley Text: Essay on Miracles and Christian Doctrine' (*KSMB*). E. B. Murray provides 'Annotated Manuscript Corrections of Shelley's Prose Essays' in *KSJ*. Neville Rogers describes the four poems (two previously unknown) in 'The Scrope Davies "Shelley Find"' (*KSMB*); a sonnet by Shelley's friend, Horace Smith, on 'Ozymandias' is printed in *KSJ* by M. K. Bequette. R. Stanley Dicks prints a poem which may be an elegy on Shelley by Mary in *KSMB*. Gabriel Gersh contributes a review article on Richard Holmes's *Shelley: The Pursuit* in *ArielE*.

William St Clair's *Trelawny, The Incurable Romancer*[25] is an entertaining and informative book which seeks to disentangle the reality from Trelawny's own legend. Trelawny was such a deceiver and self-deceiver, playing the part of a corsair with such abandon and fantasy, that his biography almost exists in two simultaneous accounts — his own, and the correct one. St Clair has done his work well, and by using a good deal of unpublished material he has presented an account which is useful, scholarly and yet unpedantic.

Terence Bareham's *George Crabbe*[26] approaches the poet, fruitfully, through the background of his age and ideas. Bareham is very good at the foundations of moral and spiritual belief which lie beneath Crabbe's poems: as he says, 'the poet and the parson are one'. To this end he examines not only Crabbe's life, but the pattern of clerical lives around him, and the result is a genuine understanding of the major values of the poetry. Bareham even does his best with less promising material when he considers Crabbe on politics and madness, ending with a mature consideration of Crabbe's art. There are occasional misprints, and dashes into modish colloquialism, but this is a book which has a spirit of generous appreciation and helpful scholarship.

Kenneth Curry's *Robert Southey: A Reference Guide*[27] will from now on be the obvious first step for any student doing research on Southey. It contains a list of writings by Southey, an annotated list of writings about Southey from 1796 to 1975, a list of doctoral dissertations, and an author-subject index.

Two books on Scottish poets deserve a mention here. Douglas Gifford's *James Hogg*[28] contains a lucid chapter on Hogg's poetry and drama, in which Gifford emphasises the narrative element in Hogg's work: he sees Hogg as moving from poetry to fiction, where his greatest achievement lies. Catarina Ericson-Roos's *The Songs of Robert Burns*[29] is subtitled 'A Study of the Unity of Poetry and Music'. It fulfils this purpose

---

[25] *Trelawny, The Incurable Romancer*, by William St Clair. John Murray. pp. xii + 235. £7.50.

[26] *George Crabbe*, by Terence Bareham. Vision P. pp. 245. £5.95.

[27] *Robert Southey: A Reference Guide*, by Kenneth Curry. Boston, Mass.: G. K. Hall. pp. xx + 95. $12.

[28] *James Hogg*, by Douglas Gifford. Edinburgh: Ramsay Head P. 1976. pp. 240. £4.95.

[29] *The Songs of Robert Burns*, by Catarina Ericson-Roos. Uppsala: Studia Anglistica Upsaliensia, 30. pp. x + 144. Price not stated.

well, showing how the music assists the words and how the words suit the music. There have been literary studies of the songs before, and musical studies of the music: this book combines the two, and provides some genuinely illuminating commentary. Also in Scotland, Joseph Kestner's 'Linguistic Transmission in Scott: *Waverley*, *Old Mortality*, *Rob Roy*, and *Redgauntlet*' (*TWC*) begins with the oral transmission of Scott's poetry, although its main subject is Scott's fiction.

Christine Brinkmann's book on English Romantic drama[30] concentrates on works intended to be read rather than performed. The striking preference by Romantic writers for this type of 'play' is explained with reference to a divergence of the authors' aims and the expectations of the theatre-going public. Particular attention is paid to Lamb, Coleridge, and Byron, whose *Manfred* and *Marino Faliero* are discussed in detail. An inventory of dramas between 1784 and 1828 is appended.[H.C.C.]

Patrick O'Neill provides 'A Note on Bains' Calendar of Theatrical Performances in Toronto, 1809–1828' (*NCTR*), adding some further information (see *YW* 56.294). Charles H. Shattuck gives a fascinating, sad, and sometimes hilarious account of 'The Romantic Acting of Junius Brutus Booth' (*NCTR*), describing an English actor in America who was usually eccentric and occasionally quite mad.

2. Prose Fiction

If Scott is still neglected by modern readers, at least he is not being neglected by scholars. This year he has been well served by two works of devoted scholarship, both of which explore virtually unmapped territory. In *'The Siege of Malta' Rediscovered*[31] Donald E. Sultana makes a painstaking study of Scott's last and unpublished novel. The first part of his book gives a moving account of Scott's last journey around Europe, during which the novel was conceived and completed. In the second part Sultana describes the manuscript and gives a detailed précis of the novel, with extensive quotations. Passages which call for no editing are transcribed *literatim*. The précis, Sultana ruefully admits, is 'the only practicable and readable version in which it can come to light'. By examining the biographical context of the novel he is able to illuminate several different aspects of the work: he refutes Lockhart's assertion that it was written 'in spite of all remonstrances' (Scott's publisher had offered £2000 for the manuscript); he explores the relationship between one of its central themes ('changed manners') and Scott's interest in the Reform Bill; he traces the process by which the work degenerated from novel to chronicle, as Scott – perhaps under pressure to meet the publisher's deadline, and desperate to get home again – focused increasingly on the drama and heroism of the siege at the expense of his original characters. A fine balance between sympathy and cool critical sense helps to make Sultana's study a particularly engaging work. He makes no elaborate claims for the novel, but insists that it is by no means a work of shame.

[30] *Drama und Öffentlichkeit in der englischen Romantik,* by Christine Brinkmann. Frankfurt am Main: Peter Lang (Anglo-American Forum 7). pp. 248. Sfr. 50.
[31] *'The Siege of Malta' Rediscovered,* by Donald E. Sultana. Edinburgh: Scottish Academic P. pp. xii + 215. £7.50.

The Walter Scott Opera[32] by Jerome Mitchell is an erudite study of the fifty or so operas that have been based on works by Scott. Mitchell attempts to show in some detail the way in which a novel, poem, or historical work has been interpreted and adapted for the operatic stage, and also to define those qualities in Scott's works which made them suitable for opera. He emphasises the importance of the pictorial qualities of the novels, Scott's fondness for 'theatrical' set pieces like Rebecca's trial scene, the boldly drawn characters whose soliloquies sometimes possess 'a structure quite similar to that of the conventional recitative, cavatina or cabaletta', and the central importance of 'opposing fanaticisms' in Scott's fiction. The breadth of Mitchell's knowledge is impressive, and so is his attention to detail. The scope of the study is wide, and as a result this is a book of greater literary interest than its title might suggest.

George W. Boswell sets out to abstract Scott's 'personal beliefs' from the novels, and duly marshals quotations to illustrate Scott's views on such things as gambling, pastoral scenery and religious fanaticism (*SCB*). Unfortunately Boswell's attempt is rather too slight to shed much new light on either the novelist or the novels. *The Supernatural Short Stories of Sir Walter Scott*[33], edited by Michael Hayes, contains five stories, including 'Wandering Willie's Tale'. The edition has no notes, and the briefest of introductions, but it does have a useful glossary.

Two more biographical studies of Jane Austen have appeared this year. *A Little Bit of Ivory*[34], by Elfrida Vipont, is an attempt to give the sense of what life in the Austen household would have been like. This is not a scholarly work (some members of the Austen family hover just this side of caricature in the book), but it does offer a very lively introduction to the subject. *Jane Austen*[35], by Margaret Llewelyn, is a rather more substantial work. Llewelyn is ostensibly concerned with the personality of the novelist, but it would be more accurate to say that Jane Austen's opinions are its primary subject. Some readers may find Llewelyn's method of arranging snippets from the letters and novels under such headings as 'Immorality', and 'The Poor', rather disconcerting, but this does help to bring into focus Austen's views on subjects ranging from current affairs to children's games. In each case the quotations are allowed to speak for themselves as much as possible, and may be identified readily through the source notes. There are brief notes on other members of the Austen family, a genealogical table, and even a chart setting out the available evidence about the novelist's mysterious love affair. The book may prove to be a useful reference work for students.

Marian E. Fowler makes an illuminating study of 'The Feminist Bias of *Pride and Prejudice*' (*DR*). She suggests that certain terms such as 'elegant female' and 'rational creature' would have carried special connotations for Austen's first readers, because they were key phrases in a contemporary debate about the role and education of women. Having

---

[32] *The Walter Scott Operas*, by Jerome Mitchell. Alabama: U. of Alabama P. pp. xiii + 402. $17.50.

[33] *The Supernatural Short Stories of Sir Walter Scott*, ed. by Michael Hayes. Calder. pp. 217. £5.25.

[34] *A Little Bit of Ivory*, by Elfrida Vipont. Hamish Hamilton. pp. 148. £3.25.

[35] *Jane Austen*, by Margaret Llewelyn. Kimber. pp. 189. £3.95.

examined the models of female conduct offered in courtesy books, and the arguments made against the superficialty of female education by such feminists as Mary Wollstonecraft and Priscilla Wakefield (whose battle cry was 'woman as rational creature'), Fowler goes on to suggest that *Pride and Prejudice* shows the liberation of Elizabeth Bennet from the female stereotype of her society. Elizabeth develops from an 'elegant female' (a role assumed for Wickham's sake) to a 'rational creature' (in her revised assessment of Darcy), and thus is able to become fully herself. In an article entitled 'Moral Geography in Jane Austen' (*UTQ*) David Jackel suggests that there is no clear precedent for Jane Austen's use of particular locations to focus the central issues of her novels. He examines in some detail the structural function of Pemberley in *Pride and Prejudice*, and comments briefly on the use of locations in the other novels.

In *Jane Austen's 'Emma'*[36], Douglas Jefferson considers the significance of a single work in the development of English fiction. On the one hand he draws attention to the continuities between Austen's fiction and that of her major predecessors in the eighteenth century (in particular, the continuities of style). On the other hand he attempts to define her originality. In her novels the reader has the sense of 'stretches of time belonging to the characters ("their day") in which their role . . . is primarily that of being themselves'. They are clearly conceived in relation to a community, which means that even the minor characters transcend fixed literary categories (Mr Elton, for example, is not simply a comic character, as it is his job to officiate at Emma's wedding). Jefferson is particularly good at showing the relationship between convention and originality. He makes a detailed analysis of the plot of *Emma* in order to show that, while it remains 'very near to the logic of ordinary life', it depends quite heavily on a device taken over from artificial fiction – multiple misunderstanding. He sees Emma as the first in the long line of faulty heroines in English fiction. The study is concise and lucid, and makes a welcome contribution to the subject.

Bruce Stovel (*DR*) attempts to trace the 'real plot' of *Emma*, which he finds beneath the complicated surface events. He argues that many of the events in the novel are really caused by Emma's unacknowledged response to Knightley. This concealed relationship is carefully counter-pointed by the secret engagement of Frank Churchill and Jane Fairfax. Stovel also suggests that some characters are used to embody aspects of Emma herself: Mrs Elton, for example, is Emma's 'vain spirit'.

Stein Haugom Olsen, in his article 'Do you like Emma Woodhouse?' (*CQ*), challenges the critical assumption that sympathetic characters are the exponents of acceptable moral standards, while unsympathetic characters embody negative values. He suggests that to judge Emma the reader has to relate her to the scheme of values that has been established in the novel, but that he does not have to share this scheme himself; and he argues that the reader's personal attitude to Emma has no role to play in his evaluation of her (although sympathy or antipathy may interfere with the proper evaluative process). The issues raised in his discussion seem too large for the limited space Olsen has at his disposal in the article, but

[36] *Jane Austen's 'Emma': A Landmark in English Fiction,* by Douglas Jefferson. Chatto & Windus, for Sussex U.P. pp. 89. hb £3.00, pb £1.50.

he gives an effective account of the way in which Austen's 'evaluative machinery' is built up in the novel. Helen Dry considers the relationship between syntax and point of view in *Emma* (*SIR*). In a detailed, orderly and perceptive analysis, she identifies the rhetorical devices used in the novel to express two main points of view (Emma's and the narrator's), and she examines the way in which Emma apparently usurps the narrator's role as the novel progresses.

Elizabeth Jenkins makes a genial survey of Austen's novels in order to demonstrate that 'the whole human condition' is mapped out in them (*EDH*). Examining the familiar charge that Austen's world is without pain or passion, she draws attention to the sufferings of female characters such as Marianne, Fanny, and Jane Fairfax, and also to the novelist's ability to evoke through dialogue and gesture the sexual excitement of her characters. D. G. Kendall suggests that the term 'Co-' used by Lady Denham in *Sanditon* is short for 'Co-heiress' (*N&Q*), while Elaine Noel-Bentley notes a third reference to *Sir Charles Grandison* in Austen's letters, to be added to the two noted by R. W. Chapman (*N&Q*).

A completed version of *The Watsons*[37], by 'Jane Austen and Another', has a postcript which discusses the relationship between the unfinished narrative and the circumstances of its composition, and points out that this is the second continuation of the novel to be based on Catherine Austen's novel *The Younger Sister*.

Nicholas A. Joukovsky has edited an unpublished manuscript of Thomas Love Peacock, under the title 'A Dialogue of Idealities' (*YES*). This is a revised and expanded version of the untitled work published as 'A Dialogue on Friendship after Marriage'. Joukovsky describes the manuscript, dates it 1859–62, and provides textual notes. Norma Leigh Rudinsky suggests that Asterias in *Nightmare Abbey* is a caricature of the Scottish baronet Sir John Sinclair (*N&Q*).

Mary Shelley continues to receive generous attention. Safaa El-Shater's study of the novels[38] begins with a rather disarming admission: 'I have given a summary of each of them considering that all, with the exception of *Frankenstein*, are now mere bibliophile's items'. The study cannot really be described as an attempt to resurrect the novels. El-Shater continually acknowledges their faults: the loose construction, excessive use of coincidence, padding, and the 'increasing conventionality' of the later works. Even in the discussion of *Frankenstein* she argues that the use of the epistolary technique is pointless, that the author's social views are inadequately related to the central theme, and that the novelist has failed to exploit the potential for direct conflict between the two antagonists. But the study does justice to the historical interest of the novels. El-Shater explores their relationship with the works of the great Romantics, their biographical content, the apparent recurrence of Shelley and Byron in different disguises (she detects the hand of Shelley himself in *Valpurga*). It is a study which gives the novels a dusting, but which leaves them, critically speaking, more or less where they were.

Charles Schug considers the way in which each of the three narrators

---

[37] *The Watsons*, by Jane Austen and Another. Peter Davies. pp. 235. £3.90.
[38] *The Novels of Mary Shelley*, by Safaa El-Shater. Salzburg: Romantic Reassessment. pp. 172.

in *Frankenstein* uses his narrative to establish a sense of order and logic in his own experience (*SEL*). According to Schug, the reader's experience of conflicting points of view in the novel makes preconceived standards of judgement seem inappropriate. The form is thus well suited to the theme, as the novel argues for 'sympathy' and for the 'suspension of moral judgement'. Leslie Tannenbaum argues that Mary Shelley is engaged in a continual dialogue with Milton in *Frankenstein* (*KSJ*). In his interpretation, based on an examination of the verbal echoes of, and allusions to, *Paradise Lost,* the novel shows that man is completely responsible for his fallen condition, and is doomed to remain fallen as long as he attempts to build a morality on empirical grounds.

Alethea Hayter's edition of Maturin's *Melmoth the Wanderer*[39] has an admirably lively introduction, in which Hayter surveys Maturin's life, assesses the strength and weaknesses of his novel and discusses its influence. She draws attention to the contrast between the author's 'daylight tastes' (the pleasures of wit and good company), and the 'night side of his personality' (of which he was frightened, and which found expression in his romances). In Hayter's view, the strengths of the novel arise from Maturin's interest in the tyrant-victim relationship, and in the psychology of prisoners. She condemns the 'Chinese-box perversity' of the narrative method, the limp ending, and Maturin's failure to emphasise the potentially climactic moments of choice in the novel. As a sustained design the novel fails, but its personification of an element in the human subconscious is an enduring imaginative achievement. In contrast, Jack Null seeks to defend the design of the novel, by clarifying the relationship between its form and theme (*PLL*). Taking 'The Wanderer's Dream' as his starting point, he attempts to reconstruct Melmoth's life history, and finds a 'definite and consistent' chronology which suggests careful planning. Null discusses the way in which Maturin uses conventional motifs of the gothic novel to make a profound statement about the role of human suffering in salvation, and shows how this theme is developed in the diverse parts of the narrative. His case for the thematic unity of the novel is quite effective, but a fuller treatment of the subject would have been welcome.

3. Prose

Mary Wollstonecraft is the obvious example of a writer whose status has been radically revised in the light of current social and political concerns. She now enjoys a reputation which not only sanctions the publication of her fiction and most important non-fiction (see *YW*, 1975 and 1976) but also makes feasible *A Wollstonecraft Anthology*[40] and *Mary Wollstonecraft: An Annotated Bibliography*[41]. The anthology, which has been designed 'to suggest Wollstonecraft's literary powers, her use of a wide range of styles, and her philosophical progress, especially in her

[39] *Melmoth the Wanderer: A Tale,* by Charles Maturin, ed. by Alethea Hayter. Harmondsworth, Middx.: Penguin. pp. 720. pb £1.95.

[40] *A Wollstonecraft Anthology,* ed. by Janet M. Todd. Bloomington, Ind. and London: Indiana U.P. pp. x + 269. £11.55.

[41] *Mary Wollstonecraft: An Annotated Bibliography,* by Janet M. Todd. N.Y. and London: Garland, 1976. pp. xxxi + 124. £12.

understanding of women and of emotion', includes pieces from such writings as *Thoughts on the Education of Daughters* as well as from more famous works. A chiefly biographical introduction, and a bibliography, frame the extracts, which are grouped under five headings. It is a pity none of the important works is given entire. Janet M. Todd, who edits the anthology, is also responsible for *Mary Wollstonecraft: An Annotated Bibliography*. She includes works by Wollstonecraft and 'most of the critical and biographical comment written on her in English between 1788 and 1975'. The introduction, which surveys the literature contained in the bibliography, devotes twice as many pages to 'Biographies' as to 'Historical and Critical Studies', an index of the kind of attention Wollstonecraft has so far received. Todd's introduction to the bibliography is reprinted in *BSM*, with a short list of post-1975 studies.

Two interesting articles offer further clarification of the composition of Cobbett's radicalism, and renew the reader's understanding of the interpenetration of religious and political beliefs in the period. In 'A Re-examination of William Cobbett's Opinions of Thomas Paine' (*JRUL*), Claribel Young attempts, with fine narrative skill, to refute the received belief that, after early hostility to Paine, Cobbett became his 'sincere admirer'; and in 'William Cobbett, George Houston and Freethought' (*N&Q*), J. R. Dinwiddy sheds light on Cobbett's views on religion, which 'have been something of a mystery'. Some letters of Cobbett, which offer information on various topics, including his health in later life, are briefly discussed by John W. Osborne in 'Some New Cobbettiana' (*JRUL*).

The major contribution to Hazlitt scholarship this year – and for several years – is James A. Houck's *William Hazlitt: A Reference Guide*[42], a chronological survey of writings about Hazlitt which appeared between 1805 and 1973. Offering 'descriptive rather than evaluative' annotation, especially generous in the case of books and articles which centre on Hazlitt's ideas, it seems impressively complete, includes a complex index which facilitates cross-reference, and contains a thoughtful introduction, which provides an explanation of the contents of the guide, and some notes on the history and possible directions of Hazlitt scholarship. Not only may it be referred to for material on its subject, but also may be *read* as a work which charts Hazlitt's changing reputation over one hundred and fifty years. Terry Eagleton's stimulating 'William Hazlitt: An Empiricist Radical' (*Blackfriars*, 1973), which Houck records, and which seems to have escaped all the annual bibliographies, is certainly worth notice in *YW*. Hazlitt is committed to the preservation of 'the imagination as a political force', and demonstrates 'a quite remarkable intuitive grasp of the internal relations of literary style, theories of knowledge, ideological consciousness and political practice', according to Eagleton, who argues his case with cogency and spirit despite the lack of space to substantiate all his claims. In a speculative and interesting piece, 'The Discovery of the Future and Indeterminacy in William Hazlitt' (*TWC*), which supports part of Eagleton's thesis, Donald M. Hassler argues that *An Essay on the Principles of Human Action*, with its hypothesis that the imagination

[42] *William Hazlitt: A Reference Guide*, by James A. Houck. Boston, Mass.: G. K. Hall & Co., and London: George Prior. pp. xx + 268. £14.95.

works 'independently of selfish behavioral "causes" to produce products that had not existed previously', marks a break with the generally deterministic preconceptions and beliefs of eighteenth-century theorists.

Hazlitt's relationship with Wordsworth, his influence on Keats ('Ode to a Nightingale' is 'an almost perfect illustration of Hazlitt's idea of a poem'), and romantic and modern notions of poetry, are among the issues discussed in 'Hazlitt, Keats, and the Poetics of Intersubjectivity' (*Criticism*) by John Kinnaird, whose central concern is Hazlitt's conception of the imagination. In another long, well-documented article, 'Hazlitt and the "Design" of Shakespearian Tragedy' (*SQ*), John Kinnaird argues that *Characters of Shakespear's Plays,* and other writings, suggest Hazlitt is interested in the function of character within the design of the plays, and not merely, as often has been supposed, with the psychology of individual figures. Stanley Jones continues his regular contribution to Hazlitt studies with two articles: 'Some New Hazlitt Letters' (*N&Q*), in which he prints a number of unpublished letters, the most interesting of which shows Hazlitt at a crucial moment in the '*Liber Amoris* affair, and gives an almost unique glimpse of him as a father'; and 'Hazlitt's Missing Essay "On Individuality"' (*RES*), in which he challenges the received belief that the essay was never written, persuasively arguing, from external and internal evidence, that the essay is none other than 'On Reason and Imagination', the subject of which was admirably suited to Hazlitt's distressed state of mind. In *Hazlitt*[43], a pamphlet which replaces that of J. B. Priestley in the same series, R. L. Brett sets Hazlitt's writings in a biographical context, but adds nothing to our knowledge of Hazlitt, and fails to substantiate with argument his conviction that Hazlitt's achievement lies 'in his essays and his literary criticism'. Brett, a reliable critic, seems defeated by the constraints of the series to which he contributes. In 'Shelley, Hazlitt and Keats', a section of Patrick Parrinder's *Authors and Authority: A Study of English Literary Criticism and Its Relation to Culture 1750-1900*[44], Hazlitt is praised as an intelligent and incisive polemicist, and as a fine literary critic of 'realistic fiction and the meditative or musical lyric'.

Hazlitt's reliance on Holcroft's *fictional* writings in his compilation of the later parts of Holcroft's *Memoirs* is the subject of John Thieme's 'Hazlitt's Biographical Method in "Holcroft's Memoirs"' (*N&Q*); the importance to Hazlitt of Joseph Fawcett, his 'first real preceptor in literary taste' is discussed in Edmund G. Miller's 'Hazlitt and Fawcett' (*TWC*); and Hazlitt's art criticism is briefly mentioned in Helene Roberts's '"Trains of Fascinating and of Endless Imagery": Associationist Art Criticism before 1850' (*VPN*).

Articles by Winifred F. Courtney and Peter A. Brier challenge in important ways the received critical view on Lamb. Recording the recent discovery of some copies of the Bath newspaper, *The Albion,* which date from the time of Lamb's contribution to it, Winifred Courtney, in the

---

[43] *Hazlitt,* by R. L. Brett. Writers and their Work 256. Harlow, Essex: Longman, for the British Council. pp. 40. £0.60.

[44] *Authors and Authority: A Study of English Literary Criticism and Its Relation to Culture 1750-1900,* by Patrick Parrinder. Routledge & Kegan Paul. pp. viii + 199. £3.75.

first, and most substantial, of her three essays in *ChLB*, offers a complete list of the articles in *The Albion*, which she believes may be attributed to Lamb, and reprints the most important of them, 'What is Jacobinism?' The piece, which shows Lamb 'for the first time writing a serious essay entirely on a political subject', could hardly have been written by the Charles Lamb of Hazlitt's imagination, who 'prefers bye-ways to highways'. In the next two articles Courtney reprints other pieces by Lamb from *The Albion*, and, in the light of other scholars' comments, revises some of her initial assumptions. If her articles implicitly suggest Lamb's kinship with the radical writers of his own age, Peter Brier's 'The Ambulant Mode: Pantomime and Meaning in the Prose of Charles Lamb' (*HLQ*) sees a close similarity between the literary effects of Lamb's familiar essays and the dramatic effects which a modern radical author, Artaud, championed in 'The Theatre of Cruelty'. Brier offers a dense and illuminating argument, the strength of which resides not so much in its comparisons of Lamb and Artaud, but in its careful establishment of the 'pointed theatricality' of Lamb's essays.

Wayne McKenna contributes two pieces to *ChLB*: 'Charles Lamb on Acting and Artificial Comedy', in which he discusses the influence of the theories of acting in 'Stage Illusions' on 'On the Artificial Comedy of the Last Century'; and 'Charles Lamb on Bensley', in which he focuses on 'On Some of the Old Actors'. The subject of John I. Ades's 'Friendly Persuasion: Lamb as Critic of Wordsworth' (*TWC*) is exactly what its title would lead one to expect (see above, p. 263).

When so little modern criticism of Leigh Hunt is easily available, James R. Thompson's *Leigh Hunt*[45] is welcome, even if the conventions of the Twayne series ensure that Hunt's least and most considerable works are given almost equal space. Although Thompson rehearses Hunt's involvement with Shelley and Keats, he does not allow primacy to the biographical context, and concentrates on Hunt's contribution to the literature of his age, claiming that he 'was one of the masters of nineteenth-century nonfictional prose, especially in the familiar essay'. Thompson offers a more substantial account of Hunt's fine autobiography than is to be found elsewhere, but even here, with a book which he claims is one of the best nineteenth-century autobiographies, the lack of space means he is not able to give the work the attention it deserves. 'Leigh Hunt', an essay by R. H. Horne, Hunt's immediate predecessor as editor of the *Monthly Repository,* was published last year (*BI*, 1976). David R. Cheney's 'Leigh Hunt — Sued for Debt By a Friend' (*BI*) has not been available for review.

William Ruddick has intelligently and with care compressed *Peter's Letters To His Kinsfolk*[46], 'into a selection equal in length to one of its original three volumes'. The annotated selection, which is based on the second edition, tries to preserve 'as much of the documentary material as seemed likely to be of immediate interest to the modern reader'. Lockhart's work, first published in 1819, is well worth attention: it may be understood, as Ruddick suggests in his able introduction, as the culmi-

[45] *Leigh Hunt,* by James R. Thompson. Boston, Mass.: Twayne. pp. 176. £5.50.
[46] *Peter's Letters To His Kinsfolk,* by John Gibson Lockhart, ed. William Ruddick. Edinburgh: Scottish Academic P. pp. xxiii + 204. £3.95.

nation of a period of Lockhart's self-examination and as a work of cultural criticism. Indeed its ability to fuse cultural criticism and self-exploration is its real achievement.

Without regard 'to chronology or the particularity of texts', V. A. DeLuca, in 'Motifs of Convergence in De Quincey's Imaginative Prose' (*ESC*), tries to identify one of the persistent patterns of De Quincey's literary imagination: the pattern of convergence, which represents 'the very pattern of the mind's operation in its most heightened moments'. In 'On the Incompleteness of the *Confessions of an English Opium-Eater*' (*TWC*), David F. Clarke argues that, in the 1856 edition of his works, De Quincey placed at the close of the *Confessions* 'The Daughter of Lebanon', with its unambiguous Christian optimism, 'so that the world of more or less unalleviated suffering' represented in the *Confessions* 'would not remain as his final statement about the nature of existence'.

XV

The Nineteenth Century: Victorian Period

LAUREL BRAKE and OWEN KNOWLES

This chapter is arranged as follows: 1. Verse, by Laurel Brake; 2. The Novel, by Owen Knowles; 3. Prose, by Laurel Brake; 4. Drama, by Owen Knowles. A comprehensive bibliography appears in *VS*, annotated guides in *VP* and *SEL*, and specialist lists in *VPN, BIS,* and *NCTR*.

1. Verse

Barbara Hardy has collected nine previously published articles on feeling in poetry[1] including two on Clough and Hopkins and an inspired introduction on the advantage of lyric as a genre. Of its kind this book is outstanding for the genuinely common concern of its subjects which range from Donne's work to Plath's, and for the sustained quality of the essays which stem prodigiously from insightful practical criticism and unfailingly mirror the complex experience of the text and genre. For the author the strength of Clough's poetry lies not in its intellect but in its combination of lyric with argument, narrative with lyric, and irony with passion, and in Hopkins, memorably, 'passion judges and analyses passion'.

John Holloway discusses Tennyson, Arnold, Clough, Browning, and Hardy in *The Proud Knowledge*[2]. Each chapter deals with a new way of constructing a poem which appeared in English verse between 1620 and 1920; all reflect the pursuit of the self and an individual notion of truth or the theme of the soaring mind, and the theme proves to have characteristic imagery. In 'Paracelsus' and 'Dipsychus' disintegration of the quest myth is evident: 'Paracelsus', in its reduction of the quest to an evolutionary drive common to all, transforms Romantic myth into a Victorian one, and in 'Dipsychus' the higher self is identified with ordinariness and the spirit with cynical self-indulgence. Tennyson's 'The Holy Grail' is dual in character; on one level it repudiates the idea of the quest but it can also be read as a quest poem. Description of another kind of poem, concerning the failed self and the re-enactment of its regeneration, involves discussion of 'To Marguerite—Continued', 'Thyrsis', and *Maud* on which Holloway is particularly sustained and good. 'St Simeon Stylites', 'Andrea del Sarto', 'The Bishop Orders His Tomb', 'Dis Aliter Visum', 'Childe Roland', and 'How It Strikes a Contemporary' figure in a chapter on the

---

[1] *The Advantage of Lyric: Essays on Feeling in Poetry*, by Barbara Hardy. Athlone. pp. 142. £5.50.
[2] *The Proud Knowledge*, by John Holloway. Routledge. pp. 264. £6.75.

poem of the featureless or 'zero' life; in a last suggestive chapter Holloway reads Hardy's verse — 'the application in literature of the democratic idea' — in terms of its break with the tradition of 'the proud knowledge' which implies an outstanding subject and author: in Hardy both are commonplace, the poet a nobody. This is a good generic study, and the author's command in detail of the whole range of English poetry gives rise to fresh categories and telling connections.

Eric Smith publishes a series of studies of 'Lycidas', Gray's 'Elegy', 'Adonais', 'The Scholar-Gipsy', 'Thyrsis', and *In Memoriam*[3]. In an introduction called 'The Context' he muses on the nature of elegy, relating it to pastoral and noting particularly its dual role as memorial and self-expression, and this in itself is very useful for students of the genre. The following essays on Arnold and Tennyson relate specific poems to the tradition by way of their continuities, digressions, and developments. In connection with the conclusion of 'The Scholar-Gipsy', he notes a new defensive post-romantic aspect of pastoral in the Tyrian trader's purposeful rather than escapist flight and *In Memoriam* occasions interesting deliberation on the changing relation of the poet and speaker in the poem, the growth away from the purely expressive view of poetry with which the speaker begins. This interesting book is marred by a total disregard of lineation in quotations and by frequent errors.

The Victorians' feelings about feelings in poetry — the predisposition toward emotion and the distrust of it as reflected in Victorian literary criticism — are Isobel Armstrong's subject in *VPN*. Noting a common association by critics between feeling correctly and seeing the external world accurately, she examines their idea of imagery and the theory of symbol latent in it. Mill, Carlyle, G. H. Lewes, Keble, Dobell, A. Hallam, Ruskin, and certain critics of emotion in the spasmodics and *In Memoriam*, serve to illustrate the distinctions, rather than the continuity, between nineteenth- and twentieth-century understanding of symbol and aesthetics. The author's reticence to throw Victorian literature on the bandwagon of modernism is rare and welcome, and only one of the many pleasures of this piece. In an article paired in *VPN* with Professor Armstrong's, Maurianne Adams contests the notion of a single dominant set of assumptions in Victorian criticism of poetry, and debates the alternatives of a plenitude of traditions or a minority tradition. Her illustrations come from pre-Victorian and Victorian criticism of Coleridge by David Masson, John Wilson, Lockhart, Symons, Swinburne, Mill, W. J. Fox, and others; she discovers a diverse defence of a view of poetry among critics which, in its welcome of the highest poetry as an allegory of the state of one's mind, is antithetical to Arnold's call for objective poetry, and to Wordsworth's insistence on truth to nature. Describing in the same periodical the declining status of the poet in the Utilitarian climate of the early nineteenth century, H. B. de Groot touches on the influence of W. J. Fox on J. S. Mill and R. Browning.

The relation between painting and poetry is studied by Kenneth R. Ireland who discusses the wider implications of *Sight and Song* (1892), a volume of poems by Katharine Bradley and Edith Cooper, two authors

[3] *By Mourning Tongues. Studies in English Elegy*, by Eric Smith. pp. 149. Ipswich: Boydell P., and Totowa, N.J.: Rowan & Littlefield. £5.

writing under the single pseudonym Michael Field. All of the titles of the poems allude to works of art, largely of the Italian Renaissance; Ireland searches for a coherent structure among them, assesses their degree of objectivity, the differences between the media, and the qualities of the genre of picture-poems, and the advantages of their collection into a narrative-descriptive cycle (*VP*). To readers of the same periodical David R. Ewbank offers a series of parodies of the major Victorian poets (including M. Goose) which he dubs, in a Coleridgean preface, fragments of a new Lamb cycle to which 'discovery' he invites other scholars to contribute.

By comparing 'Balder Dead' with an eighteenth-century Arthurian poem by Richard Hole which, in Percy's Mallet, has a common source, Paul Dean reveals Arnold's achievement in avoiding antiquarian or academic poetry (*N&Q*). Alice N. Stitelman examines lyrical process in 'The Buried Life', 'Dover Beach', and 'Palladium', and reveals an intimate personal inquiry, thought in process, in a poet usually viewed as a philosophical lyricist with final schematised conclusions (*VP*). In *ELH* David Trotter plumbs Arnold's 1849–53 elegiac and lyrical poems for their hidden 'sense of person'. Arnold's preference for separating energy from judgement and thus resolving anxiety is analogous to the Victorian notion of home as a blank place, of praise and peace. Sources of Arnold's thought are located in Rousseau and Borrow, and Arnold's wanderers and gypsy are contrasted with Wordsworth's to the extent that Trotter moots 'two divergent lyric traditions', one emphasising imaginative effort or recognition, the other internal wandering and the pathos of infrequent possession. To conclude Trotter notes Arnold's echoes of Shelley in 'Stanzas from the Grande Chartreuse' and Shelley's continued exposure to risk through effort in his poems, a posture Arnold rejects. Of interest are Trotter's speculations on the implication of simile for Arnold in connection with that poem. Keble's lectures on poetry (1831–41) – which Trotter regards as representative of the culture of the day – reveal a similar search for a unifying identity behind the diversity, and Trotter explores Arnold's belief that language distorts rather than reveals this self in 'The Buried Life'. This is a meandering, if rich article. Anthony Kearney traces the reason for an adverse opinion of Arnold of a former devotee: John Churton Collins, Professor of English and self-appointed watchdog of all matters concerned with its study, remembered Arnold's rejection of his request for support of the establishment of a new School of English at Oxford in 1886 (*N&Q*). Roger P. Wallins shows briefly that lines 1–10 of 'Dover Beach' serve to modify the appearance of calmness by using the same meter for the reality of 'the grating roar of pebbles' as for the initial description of peace (*The Arnoldian*).

In *ELN* Christopher Clausen reprints from *Buddhism,* September 1903, 'The Golden Temple', the last poem of Sir Edwin Arnold who was editor of the *Daily Telegraph* and author of *The Light of Asia* (1879), a popular and influential life of the Buddha in blank verse.

Elizabeth Barrett Browning's political poem *Casa Guidi Windows* has been edited by Julia Markus for the Browning Institute[4]. Marcus reprints the 1856 version which appeared in the fourth edition of *Poems*

---

[4] *Casa Guidi Windows,* by Elizabeth Barrett Browning, ed. by Julia Markus. N.Y.: The Browning Institute. pp. xliii + 130. $10.

and provides a list of some variant readings from the 1851 edition and manuscripts. Markus also publishes for the first time Robert Browning's copy of Field Talfourd's portrait of E.B.B. (which is described by William Peterson in an article cited below), and, in an appendix, a transcription from and a photograph of an 1847 holograph letter of E.B.B.'s on which she has sketched the view of the Risorgimento crowds from her window. The poem is so heavily annotated that the decision to put the notes at the back rather than on the page seems justified. These annotations and the detailed textual notes reflect the editor's determination expressed in the introductory re-evaluation of the poem that E.B.B. and this poem be accorded serious scholarly attention and respect. Markus's case — the intelligence and liberality of E.B.B.'s view of the Risorgimento compared with that of her contemporaries, the empirical basis of the poem, and the poet's notion of the centrality of the poet/artist — succeeds in making the poem more accessible but not better in quality. The editor's implication that E.B.B.'s 'daring subjectivity' or 'confidence' or 'political engagement' in itself makes this poem atypical in its period and therefore good is unacceptable, and typifies the tendency of the editor to make too great a claim for her subject. But the edition is exemplary and handsome, and the poem interesting.

Sven Backman assesses Elizabeth Barrett Browning's considerable influence on Wilfred Owen, not noted elsewhere, and stresses the significance of her experiments in rhyming technique for Owen in 1917 (*SN*). A version of the familiar portrait of E.B.B. by Field Talfourd, Robert Browning's copy, is described, reproduced, and traced from its inception to its recent appearance by William S. Peterson in *BIS*.

BSNotes is lively, and keeping up with the formidable standard seen in previous volumes; it publishes trenchant reviews occasionally and wry editor's notes regularly. The December number, the last under Arthur Kincaid's direction, contains an index to Volumes 1-7. In *BSNotes* Elizabeth Berridge makes an effort to reinstate 'Aurora Leigh' in the histories of English poetry and in the syllabus, and C. Casten explores the unconventional posture of the speaker in her autobiographical narration; she notes the structural problems of a poem in which the author sacrifices realism at several points in order to delay the appearance of the final Aurora, mature in her knowledge and judgement, until the last. Moreover, much of the strength of the poem derives from our almost uninterrupted experience of the impassioned voice of Aurora and her disturbed consciousness, and the absence of any narrative plateaux. As an alternative to the recurring figure of the powerless female in the 1838 and 1844 volumes, Sandra M. Donaldson draws attention to E.B.B.'s two sonnets to George Sand, 'A Desire' and 'A Recognition', which present strong and capable, though feminine women, and presage *Aurora Leigh* (*SBC*). Increased attention to E.B.B.'s poetry is attributable in part to the rise of Women's Studies and feminist presses, and it is to this phenomenon that we owe the sketch of the life and work of Constance Naden (1858-1889), the feminist poet and philosopher, by Philip E. Smith and Susan Harris Smith in *VP*.

John Maynard's *Browning's Youth*[5] expands on the poet's largely

[5] *Browning's Youth*, by John Maynard. Cambridge, Mass.: Harvard U.P. pp. xix + 490. $20.

undocumented life up to the age of 22, or the mid 1830s, and the work benefits from the roomy sense that pressing facts and abrupt opinions are not competing for the author's and reader's attention. Its leisurely yet concrete speculation, its interest in re-evaluation of received traditions (such as the linking of specific works with certain biographical figures, for example), its space for areas of evident significance (such as the nature of Browning's experience of Shelley or of the sciences or history), make it an adjunct to Irvine and Honan's recent biography. Divided into three parts, 'Early Environment', 'The Development of a Poetic Nature', and 'Education', it treats place and family; the influence of the Flower sisters and Shelley, and 'Pauline'; and Browning's private, institutional, and self-education. It is fully annotated, generously illustrated, and well written; while some 350 pages long, it is worth reading for its portrait of early nineteenth-century life as well as for its adumbration of the background of Browning's later work and the emergence of his creative interests. Contemporary and post-war literary criticism of *The Ring and the Book* are methodically contrasted by Ezzat A. Kattab[6].

Bernard R. Jerman provides a detailed account of Browning's last autumn in Venice, his death in December, the funeral, and the public tributes (*AN*). Two of three items in *BIS*, 1976, are based on Browning's correspondence. T. J. Collins, assisted by W. J. Pickering, introduces and edits the extant fraction of the poet's lively letters (1874–89) to the Rev. J. D. Williams, a classical scholar who read Browning's work admiringly but critically. Of the thirty-eight letters, thirty-three are published for the first time. The other correspondence, between the Brownings and Mrs Kinney, an American, poet, essayist, and journalist, serves as a record of their friendship in an informative piece by Ronald A. Bosco, which includes nine uncollected complete letters (1853–1871) and six undated fragments. Bruce S. Busby reprints an undated letter in the Huntington collection from John Forster to William Harrison Ainsworth acknowledging the poet's contribution to the prose life of Strafford, and dates it 10 June 1836 (*SBC*).

The cartoon of Browning which appeared in *Vanity Fair* in November 1875 by 'Ape' or Carlo Pellegrini is discussed by Jerold J. Savory, who also reproduces the verbal satiric portrait originally accompanying it, in *SBC*. Philip Kelley introduces a reprint of Sotheby's catalogue for the sale in 1937 of the papers of Lt-Col Harry Peyton Moulton-Barrett, the nucleus of which is manuscripts and letters left in London by E.B.B. when she left with Robert in 1846. Kelley indicates the present location of the lots where known (*BIS*). In *SBC* Jack Herring reports on the progress of the Ohio/Baylor edition of Browning; Morse Peckham, who has withdrawn his *Men and Women* volumes from the edition and resigned from the project, reiterates his discovery of the gross inaccuracy of Volumes 1 and 2 which remained unnoticed by eminent reviewers. He suggests despairingly a proper editorial procedure for that edition and outlines plans for a better one – involving emending a copy of the copy-text marginally – which, having tried for a new edition of *Sordello*, he discusses.

⁶ *The Critical Reception of Browning's 'The Ring and the Book': 1868–1889 and 1951–1968*, by Ezzat A. Kattab. Salzburg: Institut für Englische Sprache und Literatur, Universität Salzburg. Romantic Reassessment 66. pp. iv + 214.

That the double frame of 'My Last Duchess' points to its meaning is Joshua Adler's view in *VP*, where he goes on to reveal links between this pattern of self-enclosure and the preoccupation of Victorian literature with culture and ethics, and with the valuation of spontaneity over a static, self-imprisoned mode of life. S. H. Aiken shows how character and meaning in 'Childe Roland' derive from the structural development of the imagery which both reveals Roland's inner transformation and expresses and explains his changed vision of the world (*BIS*). How *King Lear* and Shelley's 'The Triumph of Life' contribute to the craft and meaning of the same poem is Mario D'Avanzo's subject in *SEL*. While Shelley's poem provided Browning with 'an august high philosophical seriousness' and an ultimate antitype to Roland in Shelley's Rousseau, *King Lear* provides a more positive model for Roland in Edgar, his fortitude, pride, isolation, and the comfort of fellowship. Judith Weissman reveals a relation of interest between the self-created hells of 'Childe Roland' and 'The Statue and the Bust' in *Concerning Poetry*: 'the true cause of the experience of damnation in both poems is the participation of the character(s) in a corrupt political order', and these political meanings reveal an ethical side to Browning's Christianity.

The alienated poet of Books I and XII of *The Ring and the Book* is interpreted as a response to reviews of Browning's work and to the Roman public viewed in relation to the British, in a useful piece by Kay Austen in *SBC*. Margaret Doane enters the debate 'Is Guido Saved?' in *SBC* with an affirmative, resulting from her identification of interior and exterior monologues signalled by double spacing in Book XI, whereby Browning moves Guido to self-knowledge and eternal salvation. Richard D. McGhee draws on recent adaptation of Yeats's theory of masks for discussion of Browning's poetry to comment on the same question, in connection with the paradoxical movements of Guido's second monologue as described by Langbaum (*YW* 53.324f.) McGhee uses a Kierkegaardian analysis of Guido's double masks − of truth and aesthete − to show that Langbaum's affirmation of Guido's salvation is correct (*BIS*). In Guido's two monologues Joseph A. Dupras detects a characteristic use and abuse of 'old saws' about spiritual renewal and the hereafter which obliquely disclose his spiritual bankruptcy (*Renascence*). John Woolford takes a close and vigorous look at Browning's philosophy of extremity as reflected in the poet's pronounced interest in death-bed utterances in *The Ring and the Book, Ivan Ivanovitch,* and other poems (*BSNotes*).

Stephen C. Brennan sees Andrea del Sarto's monologue as a complex rationalisation of an intolerable situation, and denies Andrea any tragic suffering by preferring literal to ironic readings where supportive evidence is available (*SBC*). Andrea's allusion to the New Jerusalem before he sends his wife out to meet 'the cousin' is noted by George V. Griffith in *VP*; the hope is squelched because the allusion is the culmination of a series of references in the poem to walls, which symbolise Andrea's weaknesses. A similar technique is employed by Michael Bright who suggests, also in *VP*, that the frequent references to John the Baptist in 'Fra Lippo Lippi' call attention to important similarities between John and Lippo. The allusions not only contrast the asceticism of the saint with the worldliness of the friar but emphasise Lippo's prophetic roles as messenger of light and herald of flesh and spirit reconciled. In two notes in *SBC* Allan C. Dooley identifies another detail from Vasari in 'Fra Lippo Lippi' in the reference to Judas, and responds to William S. Peterson's work on the proofs of *Men and Women* (*YW* 56.311). The same author claims that the 1885 edition of the *Poetical Works* is a new edition, not a second printing of the collected edition of 1863 as it has been regarded (*PBSA*). The revisions are not drastic, but many punctuation changes make the characters more coherent.

Ashby B. Crowder takes issue with David Eggenschwiler's suggestion (*YW* 51.312) that the thinker himself has fabricated the excuses he attributes to Porphyria in lines 21–30 (*SCB*). Instead he argues that Porphyria's lover may be consciously mocking in these lines, and is not insane but outraged and frustrated. In *BIS* Crowder reconsiders painstakingly the entire process of revision of *The Inn Album* from the manuscript through the Revised Edition of 1888/9, and corrects J. M. Hitner's description in *Browning's Analysis of a Murder* (1969). 'Swine's snout' in 'Soliloquy of the Spanish Cloister' is identified as an allusion to Proverbs 11.22 by Mario D'Avanzo in *SBC*. D. W. Griffith's 1909 film *Pippa Passes*, described shot by shot and placed in a generic context, by Edward Guiliano and Richard C. Keenan, also occasions an interesting discussion of Browning as a cinematic poet in 'Fra Lippo Lippi' as well as in *Pippa Passes* (*BIS*, 1976).

The implications of an allusion to *Don Quixote* (i.11) in the opening of *Sordello* (lines 2–9) are spelled out in *MLN* by Mark Hawthorne: the two heroes and two creative acts are thus compared, and the relation between the narrator and the audience is mooted. In *VP* Leo Hetzler re-examines Browning's attitude towards Napoleon III as indicated by his and E.B.B.'s letters, to understand better 'Prince Hohenstiel-Schwangau' (1891). He concludes that the poem was Browning's attempt to present a tragic story of achievements and failures. Joseph Korg, in *VP*, also stresses Browning's art. Drawing a clear line between factual and fictional material in 'By the Fireside', Korg observes how Browning shapes authentic emotions derived from personal experience into poems of independent status and general significance. 'Pauline', 'Sordello', *The Ring and the Book,* and 'One Word more' also figure in a more general discussion of impersonal and subjective in Browning, with reference to Nietzsche's notion of the impersonal lyric.

Browning's reworking of the source of 'Beatrice Signorini' in *Asolando* is assessed by B. A. Melchiori, particularly with relation to the topical question of the nude in art – a theme mooted earlier in 'Fra Lippo Lippi' and *Parleyings* which is subsumed in this poem by a dominant attention to the theme of rival (male and female) artists such as Browning and E.B.B. (*BSNotes*). A second reading of this poem in *BSNotes*, by John G. Rudy, proceeds through a comparison of Francesco Romanelli and Stephen Dedalus to identify a theory of art in the poem which endows all the *Asolando* poems with an enhanced moral and philosophical range addressed to the aestheticism of the day and anticipating the thought of early twentieth-century artists. In the same journal C. Casten traces the interwoven fancies and facts promised in the sub-title of *Asolando* as two different kinds of perception in 'Flute-Music, with an Accompaniement' and the 'Prologue', and in a study of 'Inapprehensiveness' Malcolm Hicks finds ironic possibilities which jeopardise the adequacy of a strictly biographical interpretation.

It is Bruce Morton's suggestion in *N&Q* that the reference to 'the Bridgewater Book' in 'Mr Sludge, The Medium' is to *Comus* and *its* Earl of Bridgewater, rather than to books resulting from the later Earl of Bridgewater's legacy to the Royal Society in 1829. Details of Miltonic allusions in 'Bishop Blougram's Apology' are shown by Michael J. O'Neal to support the view of the poem elucidated by Arnold Shapiro (*YW* 53.325), who argued that Browning continually undermined the bishop's rhetoric by frequent references within it to the Gospel of St John. O'Neal subsumes Blougram's references to sheep into a pastoral theme derived from St John by way of 'Lycidas'; parallels with 'Paradise Regained' suggest an association of Blougram with Satan (*VP*). Charles F. Thomas identifies St. George's Cathedral, Southwark, as the setting for the poem (*SBC*), although it has already been mooted by Robert G. Laird (*YW* 57. 268).

In a somewhat rambling if probing article on *Fifine,* Lee Passarella draws attention to the poet's criticism of the imaginative life (*SBC*). William Whitla particularises the context of Browning's treatment of Don Juan in an informative piece on the same poem which recounts the Byron scandal and castigates his defenders such as Alfred Austin (*BSN*). Mark Siegchrist considers thematic coherence in the *Dramatic Idyls,* 1879, and the second series in 1880, and traces in 'Pan and Luna', the last Idyl, its links to the work as a whole (*VP*). Yao Shen contends that the eagle feather in the fourth stanza of 'Memorabilia' alludes to Keats, not Shelley, and that the poem is a tribute to both poets (*SBC*). Treating the motif of lofty diction in 'The Glove', David Sonstroem argues in *VP* that the buffoonery of style derives from tension between tone and rhythm, and even reflects ironically on Ronsard, the jocular narrator of the poem, as well as on his objects within the poem. The mystical elements of *Saul* are highlighted in D. Douglas Waters's attempt in *BIS* to clarify the theology and establish the unity of the poem. Waters's examples of Christian mysticism should be compared with the analysis of neoplatonic hermetic elements in the poem by C. Dahl and J. L. Brewer (*YW* 56.309).

Three critics examine Browning's influence on twentieth-century authors; Stephen Brown notes similarities between 'A Toccata of Galuppi's' and 'The Love Song of J. Alfred Prufrock' in *BSNotes*, while William T. Going comments on the 'many facets' of Gabriel Conroy's allusions to Browning in Joyce's 'The Dead' (*PLL*). Unacknowledged echoes of Browning in Frank Tuohy's biography of Yeats are catalogued by James McNally to show the extent to which Yeats and Pound unconsciously absorbed Browning (*SBC*).

Robert H. Tener publishes a new letter (3 February 1849) from Clough to Walter Bagehot, which shows Clough, conscience-stricken, offering to give Bible-readings to the pupils at University Hall, after refusing to lead them in prayer (*N&Q*). In the same journal Christopher Murray regards the pun on Philip Hewson's name, son of Hew, as a direct hint of the autobiographical nature of that character in the *Bothie*, and argues that a similar pun on the heroine's surname, Mackaye = son of Aoidh (or Hugh), shows their essential equality and unity. Clough's repeated use of the Eden myth and the related story of Jacob, Rachel, and Leah, in *The Bothie* and 'Adam and Eve', is traced by Paul Dean and Jacqueline Johnson in *DUJ*.

The third number of *ELT* comprises Mary O Connor's heavily annotated bibliography of writings about John Davidson (errata appear in No 4); in her introduction the author reviews Davidson's reputation, and considers his influence on modern writers and influences upon him, particularly Nietzsche. The annotations for each entry include full summaries of arguments and a brief evaluation. While O'Connor's bibliography is otherwise informative, it seems anomalous to refer to the 1940 *CBEL* instead of *NCBEL* (1969) in a list including works up to 1974. Meandering towards detailed comments on art and nature in John Gray's *Silverpoints*, Linda C. Dowling in *VP* notes disapprovingly that critics, largely ignoring the poems, have focused on the appearance of the volume and the life of its author, aspects on which she too lingers. But she ultimately describes qualities of the poems which reveal Gray's scepticisim about the power or point of art.

In the Preface to *Thomas Hardy*[7] Norman Page justifies his book's existence by claiming to treat Hardy's total *oeuvre*, unlike many writings on Hardy, and to use as yet unpublished material. Far from being empty formalities these factors pervasively inform the nature of what follows; and Page's view of individual works and genres is, among other things, comparative, moving outward to questions of narrative strategies in other of the novels or poems. The book contains chapters on Hardy's life and career, major novels, minor novels, short stories, non-fictional prose, and verse, but Page unfailingly overcomes the format of a critical primer and even the limitations of space: his prose is good and brisk, and he writes intelligently and provocatively. He is notably aware of previous and present-day work on Hardy which he manages to indicate and address himself to without pedantry, and the bibliographical notes are alive with judgements and suggestions of work yet to be done. The last chapter considers various problems raised by the verse — its defiance of contemporary orthodoxy, its biographical and fictive elements, the difficulties of its chronology, its relation to the fiction, and its narrowness of range. Page's *Thomas Hardy* is an uncommonly good and lively introduction to its subject.

Susan Dean attempts to provide a perspective which renders *The Dynasts*[8], Hardy's project of nearly forty years, accessible and defensible. While acknowledging its spiritual (though godless), historical, and biographical elements, she subsumes them to the notion of the poem as vision in action, and interprets its shaping as visual, an ordering in the feeling present of distanced impressions or flat paintings. The poem represents not merely the action of the war with Napoleon but the watching of that action, which Hardy's epic machinery effects. The poem is analogous to a narrative experience in a diorama, in which apparently solid views fade into one another and reappear, so that perspectives

[7] *Thomas Hardy*, by Norman Page. Routledge. pp. xiii + 195. £5.50.
[8] *Hardy's Poetic Vision in 'The Dynasts': The Diorama of a Dream*, by Susan Dean. Princeton U.P. pp. x + 319. £12.40.

easily and frequently change and play off one another. Chapters on various perspectives of the poem, that of the brain-image and the spirits, the characters' notion of free will, the non-human lives (e.g. horses in battle), and, on the periphery, wild nature noticed by the poet but not yoked to his meaning, comprise a book which does meet successfully many of the problems that *The Dynasts* presents. The poetry is studied from Hardy's own standpoint by Birjadish Prasad[9] to see if Hardy's professions are borne out in his practice. As in other Salzburg Studies, this work originates in a thesis which has not been updated, the most recent reference in the bibliography being a work of 1955, but it does, atypically, have an index.

James Richardson[10] explores the dualism in Hardy's verse; the intransigence of the inevitability of the self and the possibilities which take shape only against the limits of that stubborn necessity give rise to Hardy's 'constant and passionate concern' with what might have been. Hardy's self-division is compared with Browning's and a kinship in their styles is shown to reflect their similarity: 'possibilities preserve the sentence of monolithic Hardy, and necessity anchors the protean Browning'. A chapter on 'Style and Self-Division' precedes one on 'Hardy's World', in which Richardson examines the poet's 'religion of nostalgia' and use of 'the communal role of memory'. *The Poetry of Necessity* is the work of an especially young critic who is very conscious of other critics of Hardy and who stays strictly within his brief, but within these limits the exegesis is sensitive and of interest.

R. A. Burns provides a very basic reading of the imagery of 'The Darkling Thrush' in *Concerning Poetry*. Hardy as a balladist is the focus of Maire A. Quinn's brief estimate of 'The Sacrilege' in *THY* (1976). Lloyd Siemens looks interestingly if briefly at the diverse ancestry and descendants of 'the President of the Immortals' in Hardy's poetry and discovers the trope of the anthropomorphic God in more than twenty-five poems (*Four Decades*). In the same journal (1976) Siemens explores the extent to which the harshness and metrical asymmetry of Hardy's verse should be taken as a conscious reaction against the music of Victorian poetry of affirmation. Noting Hardy's proclivity to experiment with poetic form and diction, Siemens specifies carefully the influence of William Barnes, the older Dorset poet whose poems Hardy reviewed, edited, and read to London audiences. In *VP* W. J. Keith provides a fascinating comprehensive history of Hardy's 1908 edition of William Barnes's poems, and an assessment of the critical implications of Hardy's audacious and far-reaching omissions and alterations.

K. G. Wilson muses on Hardy's relationship with a contemporary, the novelist Mrs Henniker, noting particularly her literary debts to Hardy as well as their similar 'emotional imaginativeness'. But Wilson also finds a probable source of Hardy's 'Had you wept' (1914) in one of Mrs Henniker's translations in 1893, from the Spanish of G. Becquer (*THY*). Brief reviews by G. Stevens Cox of Hardy in the auction rooms and book-

[9] *The Poetry of Thomas Hardy*, by Biriadish Prasad. Salzburg: Institut für Englische Sprache und Literatur. Universität Salzburg. Romantic Reassessment 57. pp. iv + 412.
[10] *Thomas Hardy: The Poetry of Necessity*, by James Richardson. Chicago and London: U. of Chicago P. pp. 143. £8.20.

shops, and of books, appear in *THY* along with queries stemming from work in progress. The history of the formation of the Thomas Hardy Society Ltd in 1967 is recorded in *Four Decades*, 1976, by T. R. Wightman.

Bernard Bergonzi produces a workmanlike and reliable critical biography of Hopkins[11], the first for many years; it incorporates information from the more recent editions of Hopkins's letters and journals, together with his sermons and devotional writings within the confines of the Masters of World Literature Series which consists of lightly annotated somewhat brisk biographies by reputable scholars directed largely to sixth-formers, university students, and the general reader rather than to other scholars. Professor Bergonzi's Life is lucid, direct, discerning, and disinterested, qualities particularly welcome in studies of Hopkins.

Hopkins's opinion, in a letter to Bridges, that 'the poetical language of an age should be the current language heightened' provides the basis for James Milroy's study[12]. In the first part Milroy examines Hopkins's notion of 'current language' (i.e. speech) in connection with his linguistic interest and the linguistics of his time, for it is in these — culled from the poet's early diaries and letters — rather than in his links with literary tradition that Milroy believes the springs of his poetic language lie: in the second part the author charts the methods used by Hopkins to heighten current language, and in an appendix he comments at length on words used in the poetry in rare, special, or non-standard senses. Milroy's current field is the empirical study of language variation, and he has much to say of general interest about Victorian literary conventions of language and Victorian speech and dialect. Moreover, Milroy writes clear critical rather than linguistic technical prose, and his discussion of Hopkins is fluent, informed, and unfailingly lively. My principal cavil is the lack of an index.

Stephan Walliser devotes an entire book-length study[13] to 'That Nature is a Heraclitean Fire', offering chapters on the circumstances of its composition, a line-by-line interpretation, the development of Hopkins's sonnet form, rhythm and other structural parts of rhetoric, imagery, Heraclitian philosophy, Christian concepts, the sonnet in relation to Hopkins's diaries and the earlier poetry, and a final reading. This work is so overly methodical that the prose has a staccato quality.

In an ambitious and weighty article Jerome Bump finds a precise nineteenth-century context for Hopkins's imagery in Tractarian mediaevalism (Pusey's and Keble's) rather than in Ruskin's Protestant version of Gothic (*VP*). From this tradition comes the faith in the typical and the typological representation modes of mediaeval art in Hopkins's poetry, as well as from Hopkins's readings of Herbert and the metaphysical poets. 'Rosa Mystica', a poem of the early 1870s, illustrates how Hopkins acquired a mediaeval capacity to use language to transcend the world with the aid of Tract 89, and in reaction against Swinburne's pagan mediaevalism. Hopkins's technique of multiple denotations and their unification, charac-

[11] *Gerard Manley Hopkins*, by Bernard Bergonzi. Macmillan. Masters of World Literature Series. pp. xviii + 202. £7.95.
[12] *The Language of Gerard Manley Hopkins*, by James Milroy. André Deutsch. The Language Library. pp. xiv + 264. £7.95.
[13] *'That Nature is a Heraclitean Fire and of the Comfort of the Resurrection': A Case-Study in G. M. Hopkins' Poetry*, by Stephan Walliser. Berne: Franke Verlag. The Cooper Monographs, 26. pp. 197. Sfr. 28.

teristic of mediaeval typology, is facilitated by highly structured phonic repetitions. In the third and final part of this article, Bump argues that Hopkins's sacramental poems of nature, such as 'The Starlight Night' and 'Hurrahing in Harvest', have Victorian mediaevalist origins.

Robert C. Wilson undertakes a study of comparable elements in Hopkins's poetry and the art of painting, and suggests a method for analysis of the poetry's 'literary pictorialism' in *Thought* (1976). Biographical information and descriptive passages from the letters and journals reveal Hopkins's early and strong critical interest in visual art; Wilson also notes the general influence of the aesthetics of Walter Pater and John Ruskin, and the more far-reaching imprint of the Pre-Raphaelites whose 'mechanical and stylized' symbolism Hopkins's sacramentalism transcends. Invoking the ideas of recent theoreticians of comparative literature (such as G. Giovanni, R. Wellek, and John Bender), Wilson detects an affinity between Hopkins's poetry and painting which is deeper than any one-to-one correspondence: he imitates the world through visual imagery that imitates visual perception, and seems like a picture as well as conveying some essential meaning. This Wilson demonstrates with reference to specific poems including 'That Nature is a Heraclitean Fire', 'Inversnaid', and 'Epithalamion'.

In *VN* Thomas A. Zaniello approaches inscape and instress afresh through epistemology at Oxford as reflected in Hopkins's published and unpublished *Oxford Essays* (1864-8). Sources of inscape are detected in Hopkins's undergraduate probings into Cyrenaic hedonism, Eastern philosophy, associationism, and Greek philosophy more generally. The future poet's response to contemporary works of Max Müller, John Grote, and Ruskin, the coinciding of his essay on Cyrenaicism and Pater's 'Conclusion' (1868), and his thinking on Hobbes and Parmenides, plainly show the evolution of his vocabulary from his reworking of the English empiricist tradition as seen in contemporary Oxford intellectual life.

Margaret C. Patterson focuses on the achievement of the young Hopkins in one of the early poems, 'I am like a slip of comet' (1864), in *HQ*, and Patricia L. Skarda examines three pieces of juvenilia – two stories and a playbill – of the Hopkins family, from the Collection of the Humanities Research Centre at Austin, Texas, also in *HQ*. In a short note in *Concerning Poetry* Edward Proffitt tries to resolve conflicting traditions of interpretation of 'the ooze of oil/Crushed' from 'God's Grandeur' by offering a third alternative – 'a drop of either oil tar or sea oil' 'crushed' by a finger. The same author interprets the 'dead letters' of the terrible sonnets biographically, claiming that read like this, the metaphor brings the octave to the proper pitch of grief rather than to anti-climax (*HQ*).

In a closely argued essay in *HQ* Michael R. Baker meditates on the Logos in *The Wreck*, and to the same periodical David Anthony Downes contributes a centenary estimation of grace and beauty in *The Wreck*. The piece would serve as a good introduction for new readers of the poem. In *EA* R. Gallet examines the link between 'La Construction de "The Wreck of the Deutschland" et la Notion de "Correspondence"'. In a reading of stanzas 25-28 of the poem Edward Proffitt delineates the debate concerning the sanctity of the tall nun, whom Hopkins finally venerates and deals with as a saint though with perhaps deliberate obscurity, as in Catholic doctrine private moral certainty suffices for private, though not for public, veneration (*ELN*). A French root for 'unchancelling' in Stanza 21 of *The Wreck* is suggested by Margaret M. Smith in *N&Q*. 'Carrion Comfort' is placed by Alan M. Rose in *VP* within the meditative tradition as described by Martz, but he regards it as subjected by Hopkins to 'artful disordering'; Jay Parini brings to the familiar stress on Hopkins and the meditative tradition a comparison between Donne's Holy and Hopkin's 'terrible' sonnets and a distinction of these poems from confessional poetry (*FMLS*).

A specific debt of Hopkins in 'Spring and Fall' to the earliest extant 'lullai' carol is noted by C. Anthony Giffard in *VP*. In 'Hopkins' Linguistic Deviations' Joseph Korg (*PMLA*) finds that the poet's principal mode in the mature poems is not mimetic but linguistic, and that language is used to reshape reality according to linguistic principles. In this clear and erudite piece, Korg links Hopkins's speculations about art in prose before his conversion to the developing conception of language as an autonomous organic structure of the period. In *Renascence* a relation between Hopkins's interest in alchemy and his theology of art is described by James Leggio who looks closely at the conclusion of 'That Nature is a Heraclitean Fire' for illustration. Hopkins's efforts to connect the eucharist with the sciences are also explored by Leggio who examines Hopkins's dealings with physics and biology, and the consequence in his poetic diction (*HQ*). In 'The Burden of Theological Metaphor in Hopkins', in the same journal, Paul L. Mariani probes a deeper kind of dynamic metaphor in connection with th last two sonnets, 'The Shepherd's Brow' and 'To R. B.', which are linked by the complex metaphor of the human breath and encode a psychological and religious resolution.

Hopkins's latest return to a portrayal of humanity in 1887 is shown by William B. Thesing to raise dark and disturbing questions (*VP*). Thesing tellingly supplements Bell G. Chevigny's outline (*YW* 46.276) of the phases of the inscapes of humanity with the poet's own categories from a letter of 1879; he proposes a fourth additional one for 'Tom's Garland upon the Unemployed' in which the structure of feeling concerning Victorian social problems explodes into chaotic syntax. 'Henry Purcell', 'Felix Randal', and 'Harry Ploughman' are also treated in detail. In an erudite and convincing article Norman White describes 'Epithalamion' as an exception to the close correspondence of the 1884–89 poems with the physical circumstances in which they were written, and stresses its biographical rather than poetical importance (*HQ*). By examining the tradition of the epithalamium in Theocritus and Catullus, with its pagan and sexual associations, White shows why such a subject resulted in a poem uncompleted by Hopkins whom the subject eluded.

Four articles on the biography of Hopkins appear in *HQ*. The first, on biographic materials, priorities, and techniques, by Alison G. Sulloway, examines sixteen existing works for successful methods. Richard F. Giles reports on progress toward the 'definitive' biography, two of which are under way, and notes wryly the existence of Jesuit and non-Jesuit critical camps. R. K. R. Thornton links the theme of estrangement in the poems with the sense of estrangement from his secular family felt by Hopkins after his conversion. The poet's day-to-day life as an Oxford under-graduate (1863–67) in connection with his formal studies is sketched by Rev Michael Allsopp. *HQ* also includes a chronological bibliography of criticism about Hopkins between 1967 and 1974 by Susan I. Schultz; in *VP* John Thiesmeyer carefully reviews Tom Dunne's *Gerard Manley Hopkins: A Comprehensive Bibliography* (1976), and Philip Dacey offers 'The Peaches', a poem dramatising the relations of Bridges with Hopkins.

Ellen Friedman ponders the recurring dual perspective in Housman's poetry and, with the aid of R. D. Laing's definition of 'schizoid', examines not only the movement from life to loss, but the hidden celebrations of loss by the survivor speaker (*ELT*). A personal account of the formation of the Housman Society and its activities by J. M. C. Pugh appears in *Four Decades*, 1976. The *Housman Society Journal* contains a useful review of studies of Housman since 1973 in which B. F. Fisher IV reiterates his objections concerning the selectivity of Maas's edition of the *Letters*, and publishes a new letter (1935) about musical settings for the poems. W. Keats Sparrow offers a brief analysis of Housman's last lecture, 'The Name and Nature of Poetry', finding it more comprehensive than its 'bipartite title' suggests by revealing a third section. Two articles on *A Shropshire Lad*, 35 and 51, by John H. Gottcent and Frank R. Giordano Jr explore Housman's skill with sound, and with art and imagination respectively. In *Four Decades* Gottcent looks mainly at Housman's complex use of wrenched allusion, when the poet twists his sources for ironic effect. Back in *HQ* K. L. Mix considers the provenance of Laurence Housman's *An Englishwoman's Love Letters* and Richard P. Graves publishes poems by Housman's grandfather and a letter from Housman's brother, Herbert. Anne Born examines *The Were Wolf* (1890), the first book (for children) by Clemence Housman, author, suffragist, housekeeper for Laurence, and his literary collaborator.

Angus Wilson's biography of Kipling[14] is a great pleasure to read; its elements are thoroughly integrated: facts of the life and Wilson's careful familiarity with Kipling's work, his profound knowledge of nineteenth-century literature and history, and his experience as a novelist which enables him to dramatise and place episodes quietly and fittingly, and to create a tone which accommodates alike his personal judgement and his continual turning to the work, of which there is much satisfying interpretation. The format is critical not scholarly, in that the notes are relatively few and undetailed, but there is a very full index and use of unpublished sources.

Kipling as the poet and prophet of transport technology emerges from Christopher Harvie's interesting study in *VS*. He considers 'The Sons of Martha' together with poems and stories which manifest Kipling's commit-ment not to romanticism and anarchy but to an alternative interpretation of society and its control by the selection and management of technology. This article is lucid and wide-ranging, specific and contextual, a model of its kind. An episode in Indian history — an account of the conduct of native 'followers' of European regiments during the Indian Mutiny of 1857 — is identified by Mukhtar Ali Isani as the origin of 'Gunga Din' in

[14] *The Strange Ride of Rudyard Kipling. His Life and Works*, by Angus Wilson. Secker & Warburg. pp. xiv + 370. £6.90.

VP; perhaps communicated orally to Kipling by Lord Roberts, accounts of the event appeared in published form only after 1890. In a revealing piece on day and night in Kipling's stories and poems (*EIC*), Janet Montefiore regards the division of life into the worlds of action and dream, day and night, white and black, as his way of partially transcending the limitations of the imperialist middle classes from which he spoke. She examines the incidence of these worlds and their languages. In the *Kipling Journal* Joseph R. Dunlap compares Kipling's love of rural Sussex with Morris's similar feeling for Kelmscott in Oxfordshire, while Hayden Ward examines Kipling's critical response, 'The Last of the Light Brigade' (1891), to Tennyson's poem; Dorothy Adelson writes on Kipling's sister 'Trix', author of two novels, *A Pinchbeck Goddess* (1897), and an earlier pseudonymous one, *The Heart of a Maid* (1890), which is revelatory about the course of her unhappy life, beset by chronic breakdown; Ace G. Pilkington seeks for didactic elements beyond the practical advice on the surface of *Stalky & Co* as a clue to its basic structure, while Sir Cyril Pickard compares his experience of the Great Road with Kipling's descriptions of it.

Delbert R. Gardner's book[15] acknowledges its thesis origin in the Preface, but nowhere does it say that the thesis was written in 1963 or that it has not been updated. In the intervening eleven years two biographies, two relevant theses, some articles, the Critical Heritage volume on Morris, and *Victorian Scrutinies* have appeared, and the publication of the *Wellesley Index* and *VPN* has meant that studies of Victorian literary fame which involve the periodicals can never again be as straightforward as they could in 1963. The author's statistical analysis of a wide range of periodicals, while not his only method, tends to lump critics and periodicals together, with not enough allowance for the weight or complexity of ideas each review reflects. His sandwiching of a description of the critical reception of Morris's work between a brief introductory survey of Victorian poetry and criticism and a final summary of Morris and the reviewers makes the limitations of the horizontal chronicle both evident and inevitable. Thus Gardner says little of moment about the periodicals or individual critics (and then largely in passing), or even about Morris, relying mainly and heavily as he does on previous criticism. What the book does offer is a collation of certain materials which reflects, in ways yet to be interpreted adequately and fully, Victorian ideas about the nature of poetry.

It is a pleasure to record the publication and current availability of a revised edition[16] of E. P. Thompson's view of William Morris's life and work, first published in 1955. For this revision Thompson has cut out two appendixes and what he regards as moral and political 'intrusions', and added a lengthy postscript in which he considers recent Morris studies — notably those of Stanley Pierson, Paul Meier, Miguel Abensour, and John Goode — and the implications of the reception and use of the first edition by successive critics. Thompson concludes that 'We have to make

[15] *An 'Idle Singer' and his Audience. A Study of William Morris' Poetic Reputation in England, 1858–1900*, by Delbert Gardner. The Hague and Paris: Mouton (1975). Studies in English Literature 92. pp. 135. DM36.

[16] *William Morris: Romantic to Revolutionary*, by E. P. Thompson. Merlin P. pp. xiv + 825. hb £10, pb £3.90.

up our minds about William Morris. Either he was an eccentric, isolated figure, personally admirable, but whose major thought was wrong or irrelevant and long left behind by events . . . On the other hand, it may be that Morris was a major intellectual figure.'

A telling parallel between 'Rapunzel' and Joan of Arc is detected by Ramona Denton in Morris's reference to Rouen in his poem of the fairy-tale, in which he transforms the secular legend into a tale of Christian martyrdom and deliverance (N&Q). Frederick Kirchhoff takes issue with the commonly-held view that Morris's art led him to socialism and contends that they were alternative solutions to the problem of the gap between the actual world and visionary happiness. Viewing Morris's literary development as a process of experiment and self-correction, Kirchhoff considers Love is Enough, the most clearly transitional of the earlier poems, as an illumination of a crisis, and not as E. P. Thompson believes a regression, in Morris's development as a socialist. Because the poem makes explicit and therefore untenable the death wish of the earlier poetry, it makes possible the profounder later writings (VP). Following Pater's lead, Margaret A. Lourie applies a post-Freudian understanding of dreams to 'The Blue Closet' and to six other pre-rational poems from The Defence of Guenevere which resemble it in their displacement of thought by visual certitude (VP). The life-denying element of Morris's inwardness, which contrasts with Arnold's association of poetry with life, culminates in Yeats's early work on which Lourie comments. The Journal of the William Morris Society contains three items of scholarly interest: Ruskin's Lectures on Architecture and Painting (1854) are seen as a possible source of Morris's and Webb's plans for the Red House by Jacques Migeon; J. R. Ebbatson finds an important source of Morris's interest in the romance form, in News from Nowhere and the short epic romances, in Richard Jefferies's After London, or Wild England, which Morris read in 1885; a manuscript by Morris from the British Library is published in the Journal by J. M. Baissus; it describes a boating expedition 'with critical notes'. George P. Landow presents a newly discovered letter of 1882 from Morris to Swinburne about Malory in reply to a query for a commissioned life of Mary Queen of Scots in the Encyclopedia Britannica (N&Q). The sources of tension — mainly financial — between Morris and Burne-Jones in the late 1860s and early 1870s in connection with the Firm, are once again recorded by John Le Bourgeois (N&Q). In DUJ E. P. Thompson wittily and indignantly defends his Appendix to William Morris, Romantic to Revolutionary against the charge of Le Bourgeois (YW 57.301) that he has wrongly discredited John Bruce Glasier's biography, William Morris and the Early Days of the Socialist Movement (1921), and that he 'chose to overlook' other pertinent material. Thompson regards Bourgeois's criticism as 'unjustified, inaccurate and ill-informed'.

In his study of Christina Rossetti[17] Ralph Bellas concentrates on the poetry and to a lesser extent the prose, rather than the life, but the endeavour is dogged by over-inclusiveness and lists appear frequently. Presumably this book is directed at undergraduate readers who are thought to require a brief overview, an annotated bibliography, and a chronology,

---

[17] Christina Rossetti, by Ralph A. Bellas. Boston: Twayne. TEAS 201. pp. 139. $7.50.

all of which it provides. Bellas is methodical and clear, but contents himself largely with indicating broad themes and types. Because the book doesn't presume familiarity with Rossetti's work, plots, arguments, and subjects are summarised.

In *ELN* D. M. R. Bentley reveals D. G. Rossetti's debt to the Aldine edition (1499) of Colonna's *Hypnerotomachia Poliphili*, in particular to its wood-cut of the tomb of Adonis, for 'Arthur's Tomb' (1854-5), Rossetti's first painting of an Arthurian subject, 'Jenny', and *The House of Life*. The same author in *N&Q* shows classical themes and images hitherto unnoted in Rossetti's 'The Song-Throe' (1880), later sonnet LXI in *The House of Life;* in *VP* he probes 'Ave', Rossetti's Marian poem, and several related pictures (reproduced in *VP*) for insights into the poet's handling of religious themes in that poem, which was written as a prologue for a series of designs, and in poetry and painting. If we acknowledge Rossetti's involvement with Anglo-Catholicism from 1843, 'Ave' can be seen as a sincere orthodox hymn to the Blessed Virgin.

John Adlard writes a short illustrated monograph[18] on Owen Seaman (1861-1936), the author, who launched his career as a parodist in the 1890s on the occasion of the race for the Laureateship after Tennyson's death, and who in 1906 later became editor of *Punch,* having been on its staff since 1897. The amount of material, which in Chapter Two and elsewhere dissolves into near notes, overwhelms the reader — and Adlard, who is also at times precious and coy. But the material itself is of considerable interest to students of literature and of the periodicals, and Adlard implies through quotation of an unpublished letter of Pearl Craigie's (the nineties novelist known as John Oliver Hobbes), that Seaman was James's model for Densher in *The Wings of the Dove.* Conspicuously absent in this otherwise handsome volume, and from a series on neglected writers is a bibliography.

Leslie Brisman makes use of T. S. Eliot's diagnosis of Swinburne's characteristic preoccupation with the abstract sense of words to transcend his judgement (*GR*). She takes Eliot's quarrel with Swinburne as his quarrel with the whole of the Romantic tradition, and examines in *Atalanta in Calydon* Swinburne's treatment of the issues Eliot makes explicit. Announcing in *N&Q* the acquisition of his 101st copy of the first edition of *Atalanta in Calydon*, John S. Mayfield observes that the accepted figure of one hundred for the original printing is mistaken. Taking as given that the diffuse effect of Swinburne's verse is deliberate, a result of its subject-matter and craftsmanship, Antony H. Harrison looks closely at the poet's view of language as reflecting the evanescence of man's self-expression. With illustrations from *Poems and Ballads*, Harrison details Swinburne's techniques of suspending or dissolving precise meaning in his poems while magnifying their expressive force (*VN*). R. Keith Miller offers a short piece on Swinburne's religious thought which is primarily manifest in his mythic vision of nature in the poems (*ArielE*), though also in his notions of morality, love, death, and time. In *1837-1901* Jill Forbes, writing sensibly on 'Why did Swinburne write Flagellation Poems?', reviews and rejects the main attitudes of previous criticism toward these works,

---

[18]*Owen Seaman: His Life and Work,* by John Adlard. The Eighteen Nineties Society. Makers of the Nineties. pp. viii + 139. pb £4.65.

and suggests fairly persuasively that the primary determinant of these pieces is literary.

In *The Poetry of Tennyson*[19] A. Dwight Culler takes a well-paced and perceptive look at Tennyson from the poet's earliest fascination with the magical power of language to traffic between the worlds of the seen and unseen to his disillusion with language and the imagination in the *Idylls*. In singling out less well-known works for the purposes of his argument, Culler usefully calls the reader's close attention to overlooked poems. Chapters on the apocalyptic, pastoral, and socio-political elements of the poetry, precede a description of certain poems after 1833 as Alexandrian, short, highly wrought poems or long composite works. The remainder of the volume is given over to essays on single poems or groups – the English Idyls, *The Princess, In Memoriam, Maud,* and *Idylls of the King*; in these chapters Professor Culler is, among other things, interested in Tennyson's framing of poems, and his gradualist and catastrophic assumptions, and he succeeds fully in engaging the reader in his wide-ranging and seasoned readings. He is particularly good on connections between poems, continuities, and genre.

Artem Lozynsky and John R. Reed edit a contemporary account by Horace Traubel of a Whitman disciple's visit to Tennyson in August 1891[20]. Richard Maurice Bucke's and Tennyson's common interest in spiritualism and evolution is evident in their conversation, which touched on immortality and thought-transference, and American pirating of poetry. Traubel's interview with Bucke provides a vivid portrait of the aged Laureate. Details of Tennyson's use of the church bells motif in his early and late poetry are related to its appearance in the concluding epithalamium of *In Memoriam* by Elizabeth Waterston in *DR*.

In a short, provocative note in *VP*, P. D. Edwards tests his contention that Tennyson was accorded a freedom of reference to the physical aspects of sex denied to most Victorian authors (novelists in particular) by contrasting poems of the Laureate's alluded to in the novel *Not Wisely but Too Well* with the limitations of this successful novel about 'fast' heroines. That Tennyson's creation was largely preconscious is Peter J. Gillett's conclusion in *VP*, after having interestingly pieced together evidence about his creative methods and experiences. Patrick Scott uses Mrs Clough's record of the family's visit to Freshwater in the spring of 1861, previously inaccessible, to portray relations between the two poets, and to reveal Tennyson's comments on *Essays and Reviews,* and Clough's reaction to a reading of *Maud (TRB)*. He also speculates that Clough's experiments with classical metres in English, largely unpublished, may have contributed to Tennyson's subsequent interest in translation of Greek metres into English poetry. In the same periodical William B. Thesing identifies four stages in Tennyson's attitude to the city which reflect contemporary historical situations, with 'Timbuctoo', *Maud,* the *Idylls,* and some late poems figuring significantly in the argument.

'*In Memoriam* as a whole is clearly not a pastoral elegy' proclaims Ian

[19] *The Poetry of Tennyson,* by A. Dwight Culler. New Haven, Conn. and London: Yale U.P. pp. x + 276. £10.80.
[20] *A Whitman Disciple Visits Tennyson,* ed. by Artem Lozynsky and John R. Reed. Lincoln, Lincs.: Tennyson Society. Tennyson Soc. Monographs No. 8. pp. 44.

H. C. Kennedy at the beginning of his piece on that poem and that tradition in *VP*. Tennyson intensifies the personal grief by demonstrating the inadequacy of the formal conventions of pastoral to express it and simultaneously the use of the conventions establishes a *public* context for the grief. While considering very much the same practitioners of the genre as Eric Smith does, he examines in detail the presence of 'Adonais' in the last third of *In Memoriam*. In a persuasive effort to avoid the schism between system and conviction posited by most critics of *In Memoriam*, H. Kozicki (*SEL*) examines the kind of meaning elicited from the past by the persona of the poem. He moves into happiness, not through recognition of design or supernaturalism, but through 'his willed construction of "meaning" in the disastrous past, and his faith in a God that is totally unknown except through . . . his consciousness and this past'. For Kozicki *In Memoriam* is the 'Way of the Historian' who sees as an artist. In a close reading of *In Memoriam* xv, Raymond G. Malbone views it as straightforwardly descriptive (*Expl*). Noting Tennyson's rejection of an ornate style for the expression of grief in *In Memoriam*, Marion Shaw suggests that he turned instead to popular hymns as models of form, imagery, and declarations of faith and doubt (*VP*).

Replying to Jonathan Wordsworth's recent essay on 'Maud' (*YW* 55.412), Frank R. Giordano suggests that the answer to the confused hero's question 'Was it he lay there with a fading eye' (II, 1.29) when he looks down at Maud's wounded brother, may be Maud as Wordsworth suggests, but also may be his father or himself. Giordano defends Part III of the poem from Wordsworth's indictment, as the fulfilment of the speaker's suicide mission (*N&Q*). A colourful unpublished letter from Benjamin Jowett to Tennyson praising 'Maud' and damning the critics is presented and commented on by James O. Hoge Jr in *N&Q*.

J. M. Gray shows that Tennyson's use of Malory as a source of the Red Knight in *The Last Tournament* is not confined to Malory's Tristram, but also extends to Malory's tale of Beaumains or Gareth (*N&Q*), and the same author writes on Tennyson's use of 'vicious quitch', the garden weed, in *Geraint and Enid* (*TRB*). In *VS* Henry Kozicki attempts to supply a systematic historical explanation for the *Idylls* by tracing Tennyson's preparatory reading of history and theology — notably Hegel, Lecky, and Giordano Bruno — in the 1850s. His account of the fall of Camelot through the conflict between individual freedom and historical necessity, helps substantiate recent criticism which tends to view Camelot as an archetypal civilisation, not merely a correlative of private spiritual conflict. Viewed in isolation from the other *Idylls*, poems of the Tristram group — 'Balin and Balan', 'Pelleas and Ettare', and 'The Last Tournament' — have predominantely psychological concerns; for Kerry McSweeney in *VP* they reveal Tennyson's simultaneous attraction to and repulsion from a naturalistic acceptance of life.

TRB contains sections on research in progress and recent publications, as well as notes by G. Edward Byron on the recorders of the poet's dialect poems, and on the preparation of a forthcoming second edition of J. Carter's and G. Pollard's *An Enquiry into the Nature of Certain Nineteenth Century Pamphlets* (1934), which will incorporate the results of four working papers (1967–70), two dealing with Tennyson. Catherine B.

Stevenson briefly examines Hallam Tennyson's schoolboy notebook (1866–72) for glimpses of his father's opinions after *The Princess* on the extension of women's rights, with which Tennyson is shown to sympathise (*TRB*). The provenance of a letter of 1874 from Tennyson to an unnamed person, published by Hallam in *A Memoir*, is revealed by David Staines in *N&Q* to be the first draft of a letter to Benjamin Paul Blood (1832–1919), an American philosopher and 'pluralistic mystic'. The sonnets of Charles Tennyson Turner, Tennysons's brother, published between 1830 and 1880, are J. R. Ebbatson's subject in *VP*. In a compelling biographical article on Arthur Hallam and Emily Tennyson in *RES* Jack Kolb offers an alternative to the *Memoir,* and concentrates on the chronology and complexion of their relationship; in rejecting December 1829 as the date of their first meeting, and favouring April 1830, he establishes Fanny Kemble as the object of Hallam's sonnet of December 1829, 'How is't for every glance of thine', on which the earlier date is based. In his exploration of the implications of the new date, Kolb argues that the families of the two lovers had grounds for objecting to the precipitous engagement, and notes that tensions in the relationship do not inspire confidence in its future had Hallam lived. Kolb also identifies an anonymous sonnet in *Fraser's* (February, 1833), 'On an old German Picture of the Three Kings of Cologne', as Hallam's, with the aid of an unpublished letter in the Wellesley College Library (*VP*). This confirms doubts recently cast on Hallam's 'renunciation' of poetry in 1831. The death of Sir Charles Tennyson this year is reflected in the contents of *TRB*, which includes the text of an Address written by the Poet Laureate and Hallam Tennyson, delivered at Somersby Church, and a supplement to the existing bibliography of Sir Charles (Tennyson Society Monographs, No.6, 1973) by Lionel Madden, its author.

In *N&Q* William Lutz publishes two pieces on the death of James Thomson; he locates the gravestone in Highgate Cemetary, correcting Imogene Walker's account in her biography, and documents physiologically the last weeks of Thomson's life, concluding that Thomson died of cancer rather than of alcoholism or pessimism.

At last a book of quality on Oscar Wilde's *oeuvre* has appeared. Rodney Shewan's *Oscar Wilde, Art and Egotism*[21] is adept, full, and informed. He largely rejects the well-tried psycho-sexual approach and focuses on the works, which he regards as Wilde's expressive medium for self-investigation. Stressing Wilde's classicist/humanist education of the 70s, Shewan depicts him as 'continually veering between life and art, passionate commitment and dispassionate contemplation, the ecstasy of Romantic moments and the timeless spectating of the all-knowing critic', tensions reflected in his love of paradox. He begins with a discussion of the early poems, criticism, and fiction under the heading 'Art and Pastoral', and moves to two chapters on 'Crime and Egotism' in which the nineties criticism, *The Picture of Dorian Gray,* and the woman hero in the dramas *Vera, The Duchess of Padua,* and *Salome,* figure. He concludes with two chapters on the comedy of manners which he suggests confirms Wilde's 'gradual change from Romantic posturing in verse and tragedy to social sparring

[21] *Oscar Wilde. Art and Egotism,* by Rodney Shewan. Macmillan. pp. xx + 239. £8.95.

in prose, eventually in stage comedy dominated by the dandy', and a final essay on *De Profundis* and *Ballad of Reading Gaol*, works in which Wilde is shown to revert to an introspective Romantic posture. Shewan draws on unpublished material and uses the early poems, lectures, and book reviews, and lesser-known works carefully and fruitfully. The illustrations are relevant and not well-known; all in all the book is the best we have.

2. The Novel

Three main trends are discernible in this year's published work. There are several good contextual studies of single authors or groups of authors, in some cases the contexts being very wide indeed — the Victorian publishing trade, foreign authors and literatures, nineteenth-century social and religious movements. It has also been a good year for bibliographies of criticism on the major novelists — Thackeray, Dickens, George Eliot, and Mrs Gaskell. Finally, and more predictably, there is no waning in the amount of Dickens criticism being published, an increasing proportion of it seemingly committed to refining upon the refinements of earlier critics: this year there are thirteen volumes for review and the usual large number of articles.

(a) General

In a long and closely detailed study[22], Patricia Thomson traces the impact and influence of George Sand in Victorian England, with the valuable intention of reminding us how powerful a phenomenon George Sand was and how numerous the English Sandists. Dr Thomson's opening chapters show Sand's prominence in reviews and effect upon literary and radical circles: from letters, memoirs, and journals, Thomson shows the more sensational sides of the Frenchwoman's impact, an impact deriving variously from the addictive effect of her poetic style, her appeal as a writer of 'naughty books', the blazing reputation of the woman, and the earnest feminism and socialism which attracted a youthful avant-garde. Later chapters convincingly show the depth and extent of Sand's influence upon a number of more or less devoted proselytes — Elizabeth Barrett, the Brontës, Arnold, Clough, George Eliot, Hardy, and Henry James. Combining historical and comparative methods, Thomson argues for new continuities underlying Victorian literature which link it, through Sand, to European Romantic traditions: in doing so, she forcefully challenges the common view of the Victorian writer as 'insular' and 'provincial'.

J. A. Sutherland's *Victorian Novelists and Publishers*[23] is an original and engrossing study of the interactions between art and trade from 1830 to 1870. The first part of the book surveys the organisation and development of publishing and distribution during this period. Important circumstantial factors are measured to show their power in shaping the single novel and the literary career — such factors as the power of contract, the forms in which fiction was printed, the influence of Mudie's

[22] *George Sand and the Victorians: Her Influence and Reputation in Nineteenth-century England,* by Patricia Thomson. Macmillan. pp. ix + 283. £6.95.
[23] *Victorian Novelists and Publishers,* by J. A. Sutherland. Athlone, 1976. pp. 251. £7.

Circulating Library, author-publisher relations, and 'railway reading'. By concentrating on selected houses — Bentley, Macmillan, Blackwood, Smith Elder, Chapman and Hall — Sutherland is able to distinguish between their commercial policies and explore the extent to which the publisher was artistic patron as well as commodity merchandiser. In the second half of his study, Sutherland focuses upon particular novelists, novels and careers in relation to prevailing conditions in the book trade. He considers Thackeray's *Henry Esmond,* Kingsley's *Westward Ho!* as a planned best-seller, the publishing careers of major and minor writers (Trollope, Lever and Ainsworth), Dickens as a publisher, the process of marketing *Middlemarch,* and Hardy's efforts to break into print. Sutherland's general approach to the economics of the Victorian book trade owes something to (and complements) earlier studies by Kathleen Tillotson and R. D. Altick. His original contribution is to have made such telling use of publishers' records to support ambitious literary conclusions. A further bonus is Sutherland's crisp prose and his eye for the amusing literary anecdote.

Accommodating eighteen essays by American critics, *The Worlds of Victorian Fiction*[24] will be of interest to specialists and advanced students. Dissimilar in range and approach, these essays are designed to relate to the idea of a fictional 'world' (as reflected in a genre or motif throughout the period, in a single author, or single work) and grouped by the editor, Jerome H. Buckley, to throw light on the plurality of Victorian worlds. The collection opens with three views of the Dickens world by Melvyn Haberman, Barbara Charlesworth Gelpi, and Harry Levin (who detects a myth embracing 'The Uncles of Dickens'). Then follow three rewarding essays on George Eliot. Henry Auster writes on 'George Eliot and the Modern Temper' as revealed in her preoccupation with creative imagination and unity of being in the later novels. Robert Kiely examines 'The Limits of Dialogue in *Middlemarch*', stressing the frequency of breakdown in dialogue which points to a 'darkening Victorian vision of reality'. J. Hillis Miller concludes this section with 'Optic and Semiotic in *Middlemarch*'. A third section collects single essays on other Victorian novelists — Thackeray, Charlotte Yonge, Trollope, Meredith, and Gissing. Notable among these is Donald D. Stone's 'Trollope, Byron, and the Conventionalities', in which an unusual pairing yields unexpectedly rich rewards. Finally, there are a number of essays which range synoptically over such areas as Arthurian fiction, urban literature, and science fiction. Three of these in particular combine useful survey with fresh insight. John Maynard helpfully isolates problems connected with the historical novel, ranging through Scott, Bulwer-Lytton, Dickens, George Eliot, and Conrad. U. C. Knoepflmacher considers 'The Counterworld of Victorian Fiction and *The Woman in White*', examining some of the ways in which Victorian novelists 'repudiate yet indulge rebellious attitudes at odds with the dictates of accepted behaviour'. Ellen Moers is both amusing and informative in her survey of 'Performing Heroism: The Myth of Corinne', in which she shows that for literary women Mme de Staël's Corinne exerted the fascination of a 'female Childe Harold'.

[24] *The Worlds of Victorian Fiction,* ed. by Jerome H. Buckley. Harvard English Studies 6. Cambridge, Mass.: Harvard U.P. (1975). pp. x + 416. hb £12.30, pb £3.40.

Robert Lee Wolff has not been able to make use of Valentine Cunningham's work on Victorian dissent[25], but his encyclopaedic study of novels of faith and doubt[26] is a valuable companion to the former and possibly of greater value to the student as an introductory guide. Including discussion of over a hundred major and minor novels, Wolff provides a very clear delineation of the various phases of religious debate during the period, of underlying doctrinal and liturgical issues, and varieties of belief and unbelief. He also shows the ideas of more important figures (Newman, F. D. Maurice, Disraeli, Froude, W. H. Mallock, Mrs Ward) being espoused or attacked by a host of lesser writers. Each of his chapters treats its selection of novels chronologically, and novels are grouped in terms of Catholic and Anti-Catholic, Low, Broad and High Church, the Fiction of Dissent, and Varieties of Doubt. A historian by training, Wolff succeeds admirably in subordinating individuals and individual novels to his historical overview: in particular, he identifies a gradual movement among believers and unbelievers alike towards philanthropy and social action in the later part of the century. In dealing with minor figures, Wolff performs some valuable rescue-work and also writes wittily on the 'popular pathology' in religious novels he cannot rescue.

Gains and losses of a different kind are John Lucas's concern in *The Literature of Change: Studies in the Nineteenth-Century Provincial Novel*[27]. He claims that the Victorian provincial novel is uniquely well placed to record the nature of social change and to register its impact upon individuals and patterns of living. In particular, he focuses upon the relationship between social change and the individual experience of alienation and loss of selfhood, an experience he links with the dilemmas of women in these novels. Excluding the example, though not the influence, of George Eliot, Lucas chooses to emphasise the achievements of Mrs Gaskell, William Hale White and Hardy. His reading of the first two novelists is appreciative, vigorous and cogent. Lucas stresses the 'anarchic tendencies' in both writers which lead them to question awkwardly their own liberal pieties, and their sensitivity to the meaning of social change in individual and historical terms. In Mrs Gaskell's case, prominence is given to the subtlety of social and historical imagination revealed in her later works (*A Dark Night's Work, Sylvia's Lovers* and *Cousin Phillis*), though there is also a chapter comparing her attitudes to working-class life in *Mary Barton* with those of Engels. Lucas's later chapter on Hardy is narrower in focus: a tendency to judge Hardy's novels by the effectiveness of their heroines turns out to be severely limiting, as is most evident in his account of *Jude*. It means, unfortunately, that Hardy's importance in the tradition so vigorously described by Lucas is only obliquely and intermittently realised.

T. B. Tomlinson's general study gives the impression of being a potpourri of essays gathered under the umbrella-title, *The English Middle-*

[25] *Everywhere Spoken Against: Dissent in the Victorian Novel,* by Valentine Cunningham. Oxford: The Clarendon Press, 1975. pp. xv + 311. £7.50.

[26] *Gains and Losses: Novels of Faith and Doubt in Victorian England,* by Robert Lee Wolff. New York and London: Garland. pp. xiv + 537. £10.50.

[27] *The Literature of Change: Studies in the Nineteenth-Century Provincial Novel,* by John Lucas. Hassocks: Harvester P.; New York: Barnes & Noble. pp. xii + 217. £8.50.

Class Novel[28]. Among other things, Tomlinson's failure to define clearly what he means by this kind of novel and the attitudes it reflects leaves his overall intentions irritatingly vague. An equally basic objection is that Tomlinson, in generally following the tracks of the Leavises through Jane Austen, Dickens, George Eliot, Conrad and James, feels no obligation to argue for his own 'tradition' and to define the terms appropriate to it. In the absence of any clear guidance (especially on matters of social history), the reader finds himself with much of the hard work to do. Tomlinson offers only limited aid — some incidental subtleties, some incidental banalities ('What Jane Austen added to literature, on the other hand, was not what the Elizabethan dramatists had added'), and a good deal of unsifted and directionless generalisation.

In his preface to *'New Women' in the Late Victorian Novel*[29], Lloyd Fernando makes the large claim that he wishes to refute a 'common fallacy' that the major novelists of this period were only marginally interested in the woman question. After the enormous amount of feminist criticism since the late sixties, does any such fallacy still exist? Much of this criticism goes unnoted by Fernando. He refers to a publication of 1962 as a 'recent essay', and seems to have missed such a central item as A. R. Cunningham's 'The "New Woman Fiction" of the 1890's' (*VS*, 1973). Elegantly written though it is, Fernando's study proves to be disappointingly generalised where others have already been thorough and precise: it is perhaps only in his chapter on George Eliot and her concept of 'emotional intellect' that he achieves an extended and integrated argument. The works of the other writers are sampled in a more conventional survey which is disappointingly removed from the surrounding context of debate.

Two wide-ranging works include substantial sections on Victorian novelists. A. O. J. Cockshut's *Man and Woman: A Study of Love and the Novel, 1740-1940*[30] contains some odd groupings, which often seem more convenient to the writer in ordering his material than they are illuminating for the reader. There are chapters on 'The Realists' (Thackeray and Mrs Gaskell), 'The Pessimists' (J. A. Froude, Emily Brontë, Swinburne and Hardy), and 'The Optimists' (Kingsley, Grant Allen and Havelock Ellis). David Skilton's *The English Novel: Defoe to the Victorians*[31] incorporates chapters on Dickens and the literature of London, the condition-of-England novel, Victorian views of the individual, and a selection of late Victorian writers.

There are a number of general articles this year. In 'Balzac and British Realism: Mid-Victorian Theories of the Novel' (*VS*, 1976), Walter M. Kendrick writes on ambivalent mid-century responses to a writer whose art compelled admiration, but whose 'disreputable' realism conflicted with prevailing views of the moral function of fiction. Changes of sensibility

[28] *The English Middle-Class Novel*, by T. B. Tomlinson. Macmillan, 1976. pp. 207. £7.95.

[29] *'New Women' in the Late Victorian Novel*, by Lloyd Fernando. Pennsylvania State U.P. pp. xiv + 168. £10.30.

[30] *Man and Woman: A Study of Love and the Novel, 1740-1940*, by A. O. J. Cockshut. Collins. pp. 221. £4.50.

[31] *The English Novel: Defoe to the Victorians*, by David Skilton. Comparative Literature Series. Newton Abbot, Devon: David & Charles. pp. 200. £6.50.

are examined which account for Balzac's later 'emergence' at the expense of George Eliot and Trollope. Harold Orel offers a compressed survey of 'The Victorian View of Russian Literature' (*VN*), though he covers ground explored more fully in Gilbert Phelps's *The Russian Novel in English Fiction* (1956).

Konrad Gross has edited a collection of essays in German and English on the Victorian social novel[32]. The first three essays are on 'Exoticism and Social Literature at the Beginning of the Victorian Age' (J. -P. Hulin), 'Truth and Propaganda in the Victorian Social Problem Novel' (S. M. Smith), and on 'The Representation of the World of Work in the Victorian Social Novel' (K. Gross). There are fourteen essays on specific works of fiction by Dickens, the Brontës, Elizabeth Gaskell, George Eliot, and others. The book concludes with a discussion of more general topics such as 'The Presentation of the East End in Fiction Between 1880 and 1914' (E. Domville) and 'Henry James as a Social Critic' (C. Oliver). There is a select bibliography compiled by the editor. [H.C.C.]

Frau Noll-Wiemann's book on nineteenth-century fiction[33] looks at the Victorian concept of the artist in eighteen representative works of fiction. Among the novelists discussed in detail are Disraeli, Thackeray, Dickens, George Eliot, Shaw, Hardy and Gissing. The author arrives at a classification of types of artists in fiction. There is a separate chapter on the impact of Goethe's *Wilhelm Meister* on the English literary scene. [H.C.C.]

John Killham examines 'The Idea of Community in the English Novel' (*NCF*). He applies Ferdinand Tönnie's distinction between *Gemeinschaft* and *Gesellschaft* to a number of nineteenth-century novels, including *Adam Bede* and *The Mill on the Floss*, in the course of challenging Raymond Williams's use of community as 'a value term defined in particular relation to the working class'. In *NCF* Peter K. Garrett conducts an enquiry into the effect of certain types of multiple plot. He identifies in some novels a 'dialogical' form which is characterised by a double logic or a dialogue of structural perspectives. Their form 'is neither single nor multiple focus but incorporates both', and it is 'the inter-action and tension between these structural principles' which prevent such novels from resolving into any single, stable pattern or meaning. In 'Heart of Stone: An Emblem for Conversion' (*VN*), C. S. Vogel considers variations of hard- and tender-heartedness in relation to the process and emblems of conversion. *Adam Bede* and *Jane Eyre* (and *Maud*) figure as characteristic examples of the transformation of the undeveloped heart. In *PQ*, James D. Merriman surveys 'The Other Arthurians in Victorian England'.

(b) *Individual novelists*

Many of the qualities John Carey most admires in Thackeray — wit, trenchancy, prodigality, raciness — are also present in his splendid study, *Thackeray: Prodigal Genius*[34]. Carey's important work grows out of his

---

[32] *Der englische soziale Roman im neunzehnten Jahrhundert,* ed. by Konrad Gross. Darmstadt: Wissenschaftliche Buchgemeinschaft (Wege der Forschung 466). pp. 472.

[33] *Der Künstler im englischen Roman des neunzehnten Jahrhunderts,* by Renate Noll-Wiemann. Heidelberg: Carl Winter Verlag (Anglistische Forschungen 117). pp. 226.

[34] *Thackeray: Prodigal Genius,* by John Carey. Faber & Faber. pp. 208. £6.95.

admiration for the 'joyfully proliferating imagination' found in Thackeray's work before 1848, after which there is, in his opinion, a marked decline and sad capitulation. Carey emphasises the high-spirited radical verve and quick, reflexive style in Thackeray's early sketches, essays and burlesques, writings which appear to constitute a breeding-ground for *Vanity Fair*. Chapters on light and colour, food and drink, commodities, theatre, and time, indicate the stress he wishes to place on the fullness and prodigality of Thackeray's response to tactile things. There are some brilliant insights into Thackeray as 'the novelist of commodities, and of people appre-hended through them', into the 'backstage region' of his imagination aroused by the theatre, and the 'epicurean imaginings' associated with his view of food. The Thackerayan style admired by Carey combines imagistic vividness, flashlight impression and impromptu metaphor: these features, he suggests, embody a response to the unruly 'friskiness' of life. In two final chapters, Carey extends the larger implications of his thesis in a consideration of *Vanity Fair* and Thackeray's later decline. This study should gain new readers for Thackeray by its buoyant enthusiasm as much as its shrewd insight. Specialists will also find themselves returning to his works with freshened appreciation of the man who 'laughed, and ate, and drank, and threw his pearls about with miraculous profusion'.

A further volume to record this year is John Charles Olmsted's anno-tated bibliography of twentieth-century criticism on Thackeray[35], which lists over a thousand items — books, articles, reviews and biographies.

In 'The Uses of Memento Mori in *Vanity Fair*' (*SEL*), Bruce Redwine writes perceptively on the strategies used by Thackeray to shock and unsettle the reader into a new awareness of mortality. He traces the disquieting effect of *memento mori* in deathbed scenes, emblems and imagery, and Thackeray's subversion of the traditional happy ending. Winslow Rodgers reviews the kinship between 'Thackeray and Fielding's *Amelia*' (*Criticism*), arguing that *Vanity Fair* was 'a successful creative response' to Fielding's novel. In particular, its example prompted Thackeray to expand 'the implications of the mixed narrative mode into a thorough-going narrative self-consciousness that questioned all of the resources of the novelist and made every point of view a possible moral vantage point'. In 'Thackeray's Mirror' (*TSL*), Jerry W. Williamson's immediate subject — the relation between text and illustrations in *Vanity Fair* — is interestingly linked with the technique of ironic mirroring in the novel as a whole. The mirror, an emblem common to text and drawings, has the dual function of showing truth or flattering the self-delusion of the characters. Mirrors held up to the reader are more impudently puzzling and provoca-tive. Distorted by irony, they work through undermining and reversal of expectations, making 'participation in folly easy while gently condemning our willingness to participate'. Williamson concludes that the novel gives us 'a mirror in the Holbein and Erasmian tradition, for Thackeray constantly sticks out his tongue at us'.

In 'Clio's Heroes and Thackeray's Heroes: *Henry Esmond* and *The Virginians*' (*English*), Andrew Sanders claims for Thackeray a serious and informed view of history, though it is a sceptical view yielding no

[35] *Thackeray and His Twentieth-Century Critics: An Annotated Bibliography, 1900-1975*, by John Charles Olmsted. Garland Reference Library of the Humani-ties 62. New York and London: Garland. pp. xxvi + 249. $27.

neat conclusion other than that 'unheroic mankind is constant only in its shortcomings'. In his analysis of the features which make *Henry Esmond* a superior historical novel to *The Virginians*, Sanders stresses the consistency of Thackeray's attempt to secure familiar rather than heroic history: he argues that 'our judgement of Thackeray's fiction, and especially of his historical fiction, must be relative to his belief in human equality and human imperfection'. In *EA*, Michael C. Kotzin shows one of the ways in which Thackeray served as 'the Master's master' in '*The American* and *The Newcomes*', while Pierre Nordon offers 'Regards sur *Barry Lyndon*' in the light of Kubrick's film adaptation.

Ina Ferris (*NCF*) identifies signs of technical breakdown and failure of narrative control in *Lovel the Widower,* which, she believes, reflect Thackeray's own increasing weariness and scepticism. She concludes that 'Thackeray's scepticism pushes him into narrative experiment, but the same scepticism ensures that these experiments will be conducted in a vacuum'. *N&Q* includesl three items of Thackerayana: David A. Roos publishes the contents of 'A New Speech by Thackeray', delivered at the Royal Academy of Arts in 1863; Mark A. Weinstein offers 'A Thackeray Letter Dated and his Verses Explained', while Edgar F. Harden writes on 'Thackeray's *Rebecca and Rowena*: A Further Document'.

In 'Two Against Rome: A Family Contribution to Victorian Anti-Catholic Fiction' (*DUJ*), Shirley Foster writes interestingly on William Sewell and his sister, Elizabeth, as an example of 'family writing'. She shows how their respective novels, *Hawkstone* (1845) and *Margaret Percival* (1847), contribute to the body of Victorian anti-Catholic propaganda novels and also illustrate the workings of a close literary relationship.

A notable event in Dickens scholarship has been the publication of a fourth volume in the monumental Pilgrim Edition of his letters[36]. Containing over a thousand letters, over 250 published for the first time, this volume covers the years 1844–46. A large part of this period coincides with an unprecedented pause in Dickens's creative life, between the end of *Chuzzlewit* and the beginning of *Dombey*, when he took up residence in Italy. Hence, there are a large number of travel letters, extracted from Forster's *Life,* which were to be the basis of *Pictures from Italy*. In her helpful introduction, Kathleen Tillotson points to other projects and interests broached in the letters of this period – Dickens's plan to establish a periodical under his own control, his design to set up an 'Asylum' for reclaiming prostitutes, his interest in the condition-of-England question, and experiences as an amateur mesmerist. Editorial standards and presentation are excellent, though unfortunate misprints have crept in – for example, an appendix listing the contents of Devonshire Terrace before the house was let prior to Dickens's departure for Italy in 1844 is headed '1854'.

Many users of R. C. Churchill's *A Bibliography of Dickensian Criticism, 1836–1975*[37] may agree with Philip Collins in finding it 'a useful, unusual, engaging, sometimes amusing, sometimes irritating book' (*The Dickensian,*

[36] *The Letters of Charles Dickens, Volume 4 (1844–1846),* ed. by Kathleen Tillotson. Oxford: The Clarendon Press. pp. xxiv + 771. £20.
[37] *A Bibliography of Dickensian Criticism: 1836–1975,* by R. C. Churchill. New York and London: Garland, 1975. pp. xiv + 314. $34.

1976). Given Churchill's desire to assert the importance of early twentieth-century criticism — from Chesterton to the mid-thirties — he might have been expected to defend that view and set out clearly the principles upon which his selection of items depends. In the absence of any such guide, the reader must detect Churchill's biases for himself — one of them being a rather cool regard for American scholarship. In other ways, there is an attempt to reflect the full variety of Dickensian criticism. An opening section lists bibliographies, journals, letters etc. The body of the work is then divided into general criticism, criticism of particular works, and criticism organised around fifty important aspects of Dickens. Then follows a section listing critical comparisons of Dickens with other writers.

Fred Kaplan makes an original and engaging contribution to Dickens studies with his *Dickens and Mesmerism: The Hidden Springs of Fiction*[38]. He begins with an outline of mid-century 'mesmeric mania' and then shows how closely Dickens was in touch with it — through his friendship with John Elliotson, his reading, attendances at public demonstrations, and his own sessions as an operator with Madame de la Rue. Kaplan's early chapters are valuable both as a general survey of the popular scientific culture of the time and as a context appropriate to Dickens's works. The later chapters, in which Kaplan attempts to press home his thesis that mesmerism provided Dickens with 'a language and an imagery that could be dramatically utilized in fictional creations', are stimulating but tendentious; the reservations made in the final chapter should figure more prominently in the main body of his study; if they are admitted, what becomes of the claim that mesmerism represents *the* hidden springs of Dickensian fiction? However, Kaplan leaves one in little doubt that it is a powerful and important tributary.

Literary confession, as defined by Barry Westburg in *The Confessional Fictions of Charles Dickens*[39], shows time as growth, and growth as structure, this continuum being most in evidence in the self-conscious developmental narrative, which shows 'the truth of a whole life' from childhood to maturity, and in which time, growth, and identity are mutually implicated. These assumptions lead Westburg to claim that *Oliver Twist, David Copperfield* and *Great Expectations* form an integrated 'confessional series': each of them he sees as preying upon and deconstructing its predecessor and marking a crisis in the process of growth as depicted by Dickens. Westburg's heavy structuralist apparatus does not disguise the fact, however, that he arrives at an uneasy conflation of characteristics associated with the first-person narrative, elements in the novel of 'growing up', and problems of time and identity common to *all* of Dickens's fiction. Nor does there seem to be much justification for over-systematising the connections between three novels. Westburg is most leaden when invoking such allies as Rank, Lacan, Merleau-Ponty, and Lévi-Strauss to clarify such matters as the 'subjectivity/objectivity split' in *David Copperfield*; and most rewarding when engaged in direct critical analysis.

[38] *Dickens and Mesmerism: The Hidden Springs of Fiction*, by Fred Kaplan. Princeton U.P., 1975. pp. xv + 250. £5.95.
[39] *The Confessional Fictions of Charles Dickens*, by Barry Westburg. N. Illinois U.P. pp. xxiii + 223. £7.

In *The Dickens Myth: Its Genesis and Structure*[40], Geoffrey Thurley attempts to show the power throughout the Dickens *oeuvre* of the rags-to-riches myth lived out by most of the central characters. As seen by Thurley, this myth also embodies the most basic desires, fears and wishes felt by Dickens and his age. Freudian and Marxist terminology allows him to define its twin aspects: it is both a 'primal fantasy' which 'fulfills a deep-seated need in Dickens ... to re-enact, and thereby reaffirm, his emergence from the abyss of penury and degradation' and also expresses the universal fears and desires of Victorian capitalist society. Hence, Dickens is presented as the kind of artist who, in sharing the nightmares of his age, is 'the leading point of society's coming-to-consciousness of itself', Dickens's greatness being 'vitally connected with his own participation in the dynamic growth of Victorian capitalism'. Combining the traditional insights of Chesterton with elements of a structuralist approach, Thurley provides a fresh and vigorous reading.

The same can hardly be said of Jane Vogel's *Allegory in Dickens*[41], an ill-balanced, inordinately long and diffuse book, two thirds of which is a character-by-character analysis of *David Copperfield*. Her pursuit of Dickens the Christian allegorist often reads like a spoof-version of the frenetic critic in action: '"J" of J. Steerforth, we suggested, has multiple religious meanings, Jove-Jehovah and possibly ironic *J*esus ones, *J* symbolizing the many ways man's soul Steers Forth from Greek, Roman, and Hebrew times on . . . Sinister, blighting "J" characters fill the novel, AND NO OTHER KIND!' Elsewhere she falls into near-Jabberwocky: 'Poor Pip, poor mankind, in B.C.s ancient and extant so endlessly punished from above, and, in penetential [*sic*] performance, endlessly self-punishing.' Readers who join Vogel in what she calls her 'maiden-voyaging book' should be warned of the stormy waters ahead.

Harald William Fawkner's thesis as announced in his eye-catching title, *Animation and Reification in Dickens's Vision of the Life-Denying Society*[42], owes a good deal to J. Hillis Miller's study. Fawkner's method of juxtaposing examples from widely different novels, however, throws interesting light on the relationship between Dickens's expressionistic devices and his social indictment. Helpful, too, is the clear and systematic consideration he gives to varieties of animism, dehumanisation, and transformations involving both. He avoids being narrowly trapped by his thesis, and writes well on Dickens's city, his fragmented characters, stylistic ingenuities, and love of Gothic asymmetry. Dickens's imaginative universe in final form is found to be 'a world of meaningful, not destructive, transformation: one of coherence and of harmony between the organic and the inorganic'. In a short monograph, Gordon Spence gives a straight-forward expository account of Dickens as a familiar essayist[43]. An open-

[40] *The Dickens Myth: Its Genesis and Structure*, by Geoffrey Thurley. Routledge & Kegan Paul, 1976. pp. xi + 379. £9.75.

[41] *Allegory in Dickens*, by Jane Vogel. Alabama: U. of Alabama P. pp. xvi + 347. £8.75.

[42] *Animation and Reification in Dickens's Vision of the Life-Denying Society*, by Harald William Fawkner. Uppsala. Acta Universitatis Upsaliensis: Studia Anglistica Upsaliensia 31. Stockholm: Almquist & Wiksell. pp. 164. pb £6.85.

[43] *Charles Dickens as a Familiar Essayist*, by Gordon Spence. Salzburg Studies in English Literature: Romantic Reassessment 71. U. Salzburg. pp. vi + 159. pb.

ing chapter offers definitions and a survey of immediate predecessors (Lamb, Leigh Hunt, and Washington Irving). Spence then works chronologically through *Sketches by Boz, Household Words* and *The Uncommercial Traveller*. The newly revised and abridged edition of Edgar Johnson's *Charles Dickens: His Tragedy and Triumph* (Allen Lane) has not been available for review.

Dickens Studies Annual, Volume 5[44] and *Volume 6*[45] have a somewhat predictable format − in each, a psychoanalytic approach to Dickens, an essay on wise fools and clowns, the woman question, Gothic in the later novels, and a general gravitation towards myth, symbolism, and character-doubling. The first volume includes 'The Intelligibility of Madness in *Our Mutual Friend* and *The Mystery of Edwin Drood*', in which Lawrence Frank offers a long and rewarding analysis of Dickens's handling of Gothic motifs. Christopher Mulvey considers '*David Copperfield*: The Folk-Story Structure', claiming that Dickens anticipates Joyce in the elaboration of a mythic narrative. Other interesting essays are Stanley Tick's 'Toward Jaggers', and Nina Auerbach's 'Dickens and Dombey: A Daughter After All', in which she discerns a dialectic based on the conflict of male and female principles. In *Volume 6*, William M. Burgan offers a scholarly and cogent study, 'The Refinement of Contrast: Manuscript Revision in *Edwin Drood*'. William J. Palmer's claim in 'Dickens and the Eighteenth Century' that Dickens's vision, even in his later novels, is of a consistently optimistic, eighteenth-century cast is not really persuasive, but he writes well on the nature of benevolence in the early novels. Frank Edmund Smith gives a clear formal reading in 'Perverted Balance: Expressive Form in *Hard Times*'.

The Dickensian contains a number of valuable articles: on Dickens's uncollected speeches in separate contributions by Philip Collins and David A. Roos; Carlyle's influence on the early Dickens by F. S. Schwarzbach; the significance of 'chair-bound' characters by M. J. Lesser; Gothic conventions in *Little Dorrit* by David Jarrett; difficulties of reading and writing among Dickens's characters by K. H. Strange; and on time and the city in *The Chimes* by Alexander Welsh.

General articles on Dickens are scarce this year. Most important of these is N. N. Feltes's clear and stimulating account of Dickens's response to social and historical process. In 'To Saunter, To Hurry: Dickens, Time, and Industrial Capitalism' (*VS*), he discusses the meaning of 'commodity-time' as determined by the Victorian labour-market and the Ten Hours Movement, and its relation to private time 'owned' by the worker. The consequent historical shift in the perception of time is evident, Feltes claims, in *The Old Curiosity Shop* and *Dombey and Son*, whose temporal forms enact 'the very forms of the struggle to seize or place the new commodity-time in relation to the time rhythms of normal human life'. The appeal of *Robinson Crusoe* for Dickens is G. W. Kennedy's subject in 'The Uses of Solitude: Dickens and *Robinson Crusoe*' (*VN*). Though not one of Dickens's favourite books, *Robinson Crusoe* fascinated him as

[44] *Dickens Studies Annual, Volume 5*, ed. by Robert B. Partlow Jr. S. Illinois U.P., 1976. pp. xviii + 215. $15.
[45] *Dickens Studies Annual, Volume 6*, ed. by Robert B. Partlow Jr. S. Illinois U.P. pp. xix + 210. $15.

a work associated with the innocent childhood magic of fairy tale. Its more far-reaching influence was as 'the essential, almost mythic, image of the self in isolation' to which Dickens constantly turns in exploring the blessings and dangers of solitude. Philip Collins offers 'Some Unpublished Comic Duologues of Dickens' (*NCF*). These duologues evidently belong to the last decade of Dickens's life and were written, Collins surmises, for private performance at some house party.

How was it possible for an obscure young newspaper-reporter to write, in his early twenties, such a brilliant and popular work as *Pickwick Papers?* In engaging with this question, Duane DeVries offers the fullest and most systematic study of Dickens's apprentice years yet written[46]. After an opening survey of the stages in Dickens's creative and professional development up to 1833, DeVries gives detailed study to sketches and tales written between 1833 and 1836. These he treats as early exercises in the craft of fiction which foreshadow the techniques, styles, and tones of voice of the later novelist. Sketches are studied in the order of their publication, in relation to traditions available to Dickens, and in the light of revisions he undertook when preparing them for inclusion in *Sketches by Boz*. A disappointing feature of the book is the limited range of DeVries's commentary, which draws too repetitiously upon the language of the school-report — Dickens makes 'significant improvement', shows 'undoubted promise', or is found 'needing to do more'. However, in giving such systematic consideration to all of the available evidence, he undoubtedly adds to our knowledge of the emergent novelist.

Julian W. Breslow considers the function of 'The Narrator in *Sketches by Boz'* (*ELH*), arguing that he emerges as a consistent and reliable character who 'provides the reader with an authoritative perspective from which to view and judge the world of the *Sketches'*. He is also 'a model for all the characters who wish to flee their dull routines'. James A. Davies writes on 'Negative Similarity: the Fat Boy in *The Pickwick Papers'* (*DUJ*). In 'A New Theatrical Source for Dickens's *A Tale of Two Cities'* (*N&Q*), Fredric S. Schwarzbach suggests that 'Monk' Lewis's Gothic melodrama, *The Castle Spectre* (1797), should be added to already established sources. In *N&Q*, Robert W. Duncan speculates upon the source for Madame Defarge's knitting methods in the same novel. Cinematic adaptations of Dickens's novels figure centrally in two articles in *HSL*, David Paroissien's *'The Life and Adventures of Nicholas Nickleby*: Alberto Cavalcanti Interprets Dickens', and Ana Laura Zambrano's *'David Copperfield*: Novel and Film', in which she compares David Selznick's 1935 production with Delbert Mann's of 1970.

In his short study of *David Copperfield*[47], Philip Collins clearly and helpfully isolates the novel's leading qualities. His first chapter directs attention to Dickens's handling of memory, the relationship between novelist and hero, and the effect of serialisation upon a novel whose structure combines elements of the *Bildungsroman* and social chronicle. The later chapters — which move from the treatment of childhood

---

[46] *Dickens's Apprentice Years: The Making of a Novelist,* by Duane DeVries. Hassocks: Harvester P.; New York: Barnes & Noble, 1976. pp. ii (unnumbered) + 195. £6.95.

[47] *Charles Dickens: 'David Copperfield',* by Philip Collins. Studies in English Literature 67. Edward Arnold. pp. 64. hb £3.30, pb £1.70.

experience to the adult David, and then to the world in which he observes and participates — incorporate a number of apt comparisons with other contemporary novels. This study provides both stimulus and responsible guidance for the student.

Bleak House is undoubtedly a favourite novel with Dickens scholars this year. There is much of the relaxed critical exercise about Robert Newsom's attractive, but inconclusive study of *Bleak House* and its tradition[48]. His intention is to provide an extended gloss on the phrase, 'the romantic side of familiar things', which he sees as a central imaginative principle in all of Dickens's works. An interesting analysis of the first chapters of the novel shows how Dickens 'imposes upon the reader a kind of unsettled and unsettling double perspective which requires us to see things as *at once* "romantic" and "familiar"'. There follow penetrating insights into how structure enforces effects of circular mirroring, spatial relatedness, suspended animation, and the feeling of *déjà vu*. Unfortunately, Newsom too speedily sets his leading idea in a larger context where it is allowed to randomly accrete more nebulous meanings. However, despite its loose ends, Newsom's study is a suggestive and well-written speculative essay: its basic perspectives are intelligently conceived and fruitfully applied to the novel.

Articles on this same novel include 'G. M. Reynolds, Dickens, and the Mysteries of London' (*NCF*), in which Richard C. Maxwell Jr discusses Dickens's adaptation in *Bleak House* of the conventions of urban Gothic, a form popularly associated in the 1840s with the tales of G. M. Reynolds. Dickens's use of the conventions (manipulation of legal secrets, bureaucratic mystery, faceless professionals and their 'paperwork') to confront deformations of private and public life in a mass urban society is shown to anticipate the findings of the modern sociologist. *NCF* also includes 'Narrative Form and Social Sense in *Bleak House* and *The French Revolution*', in which Jonathan Arac juxtaposes two works to show the presence of Carlylism in a major Dickens novel and to define a common ground which history and the novel share in Victorian writing. Like N. N. Feltes above, Devra Braun Rosenberg (*VN*) is concerned with Dickens's 'experience of historical tension and transition' between two conceptions of time. She proposes that Esther's story is made up of 'synthetic picture-moments', which depict time as linear progression and resemble the moments of kinetic summary in Victorian narrative painting. For the third-person narrator, on the other hand, time exists as 'a growing present that continuously changes shape with the accretion of new visual fragments'. This apprehension of time as 'uneven, incremental growth' is closer, Rosenberg feels, to that of the Impressionists. Judith Wilt writes on 'Confusion and Consciousness in Dickens's Esther' (*NCF*). Treating *Bleak House* as a fictional autobiography in which Dickens projects himself into a female and adopts a 'sister' voice, she explores Esther's confusion as a positive strategy for living in a chaotic world, a confusion 'deployed to allow her to keep active, to "do some good", and to win and give love'. She further suggests that, through Esther's doubt and confusion,

---

[48] *Dickens on the Romantic Side of Familiar Things: 'Bleak House' and the Novel Tradition*, by Robert Newsom. New York and London: Columbia U.P. pp. xiv + 173. $15.

Dickens was 'truest to his autobiographical voice in *Bleak House*, which is narrated from a position of restlessness and broken off when rest threatens'. Finally, Albert D. Hutter offers 'The High Tower of His Mind: Psychoanalysis and the Reader of *Bleak House*' (*Criticism*), in which he links the process of reading with the process of Bucket's detection, and both with the process of growth from infant to adult understanding.

In '*Hard Times*: The News and the Novel' (*NCF*), Joseph Butwin analyses the several ways in which original readers of the novel were encouraged to see it as a form of journalism to be read continuously with *Household Words*, in which it first appeared. Each instalment has both the status of a leading article and the special identity of a signed novel. Dickens exploits his journalistic context to suggest a continuity with other articles in *Household Words* and to tease the reader with 'fictions that retain the latent authority of fact'. Thomas M. Linehan discusses the relationship between 'Rhetorical Technique and Moral Purpose in Dickens's *Hard Times*' (*UTQ*), stressing the 'illustrative and didactic unity' which results from Dickens's single-minded aim of tracing all the ruinous features of society to a single cause, the pursuit of Fact. In '"Divorce and Matrimonial Causes": An Aspect of *Hard Times*' (*VS*), John D. Baird shows how closely Dickens's concern with marriage and divorce law in the novel relates to attempted legislative reform during the 1850s.

Ira Bruce Nadel (*Criticism*) discusses the place of art and the artist in the society and commercial world of *Little Dorrit*. Art-objects, she claims, generally function 'as symbols of the role of the artist and the state of the imagination in a world morally infected with the fever of speculation and the disease of hypocrisy'. In 'Pip the obscure: *Great Expectations* and Hardy's *Jude*' (*CQ*), Philip Collins fruitfully compares attitudes and themes in two novels concerned with young men, both orphans and of working-class origin, whose growing up involves leaving the country for the town in order to realise social ambitions. Hardy's description of *Jude* as 'a tragedy of unfulfilled aims' can also be compared, he feels, with the ironic view of 'great expectations' in Dickens's novel. Ian Ousby examines contrasts and juxtapositions of 'Language and Gesture in *Great Expectations*' (*MLR*). He shows how spoken language, invariably associated with bullying or interrogation, is inferior to gesture as a medium for communicating true feeling. Peter Lewis surveys 'The Waste Land of *Our Mutual Friend*' (*DUJ*), using T. S. Eliot's poem to illuminate both Dickens's concern with spiritual sterility in the 'unreal city' and his mythopoeic methods. In 'Marriage in the Symbolic Framework of *The Mystery of Edwin Drood*' (*SNNTS*), Ina Rae Hark claims that the question of Rosa Bud's marriage is inextricably bound up with the deeper meaning of the novel. She examines likely pairings through an analysis of the novel's themes and its relation to preceding Dickens works.

Wilkie Collins figures in two interesting articles this year. J. A. Sutherland draws upon manuscript evidence in examining 'Two Emergencies in the Writing of *The Woman in White*' (*YES*) and their consequences for the novel as a whole. The first emergency shows Collins improvising brilliantly, the second explains the plot-muddle he produced in working towards the dénouement. Walter M. Kendrick writes perceptively on 'The Sensationalism of *The Woman in White*' (*NCF*), showing how it satisfies mid-

Victorian criteria for the 'novel of incident' *and* the 'novel of character'. Yet he feels that it does so in contradictory and ambivalent ways, being 'founded in the realistic faith which it violates', and deriving its sensations 'from tricks with its own nature as a text'. A reprint of the 1887 edition of Collins's *Little Novels* is now available in paperback[49].

Donald Sultana's study of Disraeli's journey to the East (1830–2), previously noted in *YW* 56.330, is now published in a new and revised edition, with a chapter added on Disraeli in Albania[50]. In ' "From his own Observation": Sources of Working Class Passages in Disraeli's *Sybil*' (*MLR*), Martin Fido questions the importance of the novel's established sources. He points to a Blue Book of 1843, *The First Report from the Midland Mining Commissioners, South Staffs*, as Disraeli's essential source, and to William Dodd's *The Factory System Illustrated in a Series of Letters to Lord Ashley* (1842) as an important subsidiary source.

Tom Winnifrith's running quarrel with Brontë biographers and the Brontë cult leads him in the opening chapters of *The Brontës*[51] to adopt a rather negative approach and a magisterial tone. Biography is introduced to show its limitations as a critical aid, the juvenilia are severely downgraded ('fustian novelettes'), and the poetry cursorily surveyed. In his subsequent analysis of the novels, on the other hand, Winnifrith does not argue at all clearly for his view, that some Brontë novels lie outside the nineteenth-century realistic tradition and are nearer to 'cosmic allegory' or 'romance'. At one point he is content to refer to 'cosmic gropings', at another he leaves us with the conclusion that 'any attempt to give a total picture of *Wuthering Heights* is bound to be incoherent, because in the last resort *Wuthering Heights* is incoherent'. Even more confusingly, Winnifrith can be found to criticise major Brontë novels for forsaking the canons of realism. This study will certainly curb the wayward excesses of the beginning student, but offers little in the way of positive and varied stimulus.

Psychological, feminist and biographical interests are effectively combined in Margaret Blom's introduction to Charlotte Brontë's life and work[52]. Agreeing with the many critics who see Charlotte's overt and poetic treatment of sexual passion as her original contribution to the novel, she stresses the psycho-sexual perplexity and conflict arising from the heroine's quest for a soul-mate. Emphasis also falls on the degree to which the self-divided heroines — they desire 'both to be supremely independent and to be merged, twinned, with another' — reflect Charlotte's own exacerbated conscience. In her analysis of the juvenilia and novels, Blom writes well on underlying sexual ambiguities and myths, 'finely differentiated degrees of emotional pain', and on Charlotte's interest in the woman question.

One of Enid L. Duthie's leading claims in *The Foreign Vision of*

[49] *Little Novels*, by Wilkie Collins. New York: Dover Publications. pp. 244. pb £2.

[50] *Benjamin Disraeli in Spain, Malta and Albania, 1830–32: A Monograph*, by Donald Sultana. Tamesis Books, 1976. pp. ix + 78. £6.

[51] *The Brontës*, by Tom Winnifrith. Masters of World Literature Series, general ed. Louis Kronenberger. Macmillan. pp. viii + 181. £5.95.

[52] *Charlotte Brontë*, by Margaret Blom. New York: Twayne (TEAS). pp. iv (unnumbered) + 176. £4.95.

Charlotte Brontë[53] is that Charlotte's Brussels period 'was as important for her intellectual and artistic maturation as for her emotional development' and had an important fertilising effect upon her art. The main stress of her first three chapters falls on Charlotte's encounter with elements of European culture, the Napoleonic legend and French Romanticism, bringing to light the numerous ways in which M. Heger 'helped to form an author'. Duthie then goes on to show the influence and effect of the Brussels experience on Charlotte's art – on setting, culture, and characters. A final chapter measures the influence of the French language and its importance in encouraging 'a more exacting appreciation of the "mot juste"'. Operating within modest limits, Duthie's is a clear and reliable assessment of influences which result in the 'fusion of European overtones with the art of an English novelist'.

In 'Resistance, Rebellion, and Marriage: The Economics of *Jane Eyre*' (*NCF*), Nancy Pell argues that Charlotte's romantic individualism is controlled and structured by 'an underlying social and economic critique of bourgeois patriarchal authority'. Elements of this critique are traced in Jane's resistance to male pressures, in allusions to actual historical events involving regicide and rebellion, and in the dynamics of Rochester's two marriages. Examining the economic basis of Jane's 'strategies for life', Pell finds a rubric for the whole novel in the heroine's determination to 'keep in good health, and not die'. In *Novel*, Peter Grudin writes on *Jane Eyre* as 'a didactic novel which subordinates the values of passion to those of restraint', maintaining that the ethical principles flatly asserted by Jane when she leaves Rochester are figuratively affirmed through the depiction of the mad Bertha. He concludes that by 'illustrating through Bertha the consequences of unrestrained passion, and by linking Bertha to Jane, this novel substantiates, by illustration, the premise upon which its didacticism is built'. In '*Jane Eyre* and the World of Faery' (*Mosaic*), Robert K. Martin offers an ingenious reading of fairy-tale motifs and their significance in the novel, invoking the stories of Cinderella, Bluebeard, Briar Rose *et al.* Norman Vance offers a brief note on 'Charlotte Brontë's Mr. Brocklehurst' in *N&Q*.

Using evidence derived from Charlotte Brontë's discarded manuscript fragments, Jean Frantz Blackall (*JEGP*) makes the intriguing suggestion that Dickens's *Bleak House* may have exerted a seminal influence upon *Villette* at a time when Charlotte Brontë was struggling to begin the novel. Her dissatisfaction with Esther, Blackall further claims, may have prompted her to fashion a contrasting alternative in Lucy Snowe.

Anne Smith introduces a volume devoted to *The Art of Emily Brontë*[54], which includes three essays on the poetry (by Robin Grove, Rosalind Miles and Barbara Hardy) and five essays on *Wuthering Heights*. Keith Sagar writes at length, but inconclusively, on 'The Originality of *Wuthering Heights*', with frequent references to D. H. Lawrence. An interest in Emily's Romantic inheritance is common to J. F. Goodridge's 'A New Heaven and a New Earth' and T. E. Apter's 'Romanticism and

[53] *The Foreign Vision of Charlotte Brontë*, by Enid L. Duthie. Macmillan, 1975. pp. xiii + 237. £7.50.
[54] *The Art of Emily Brontë*, ed. by Anne Smith. Vision Critical Studies Series, general ed. Anne Smith. Vision, 1976. pp. 246. £5.25.

Romantic Love in *Wuthering Heights'*, the latter showing how the novel contains a vision of both the potency and destructiveness of romantic passion. In 'Divided Sources', Philippa Tristram draws upon Blake's poems in her analysis of Emily's fidelity to a form of childhood experience which is 'fiercely sustained in despite of time and change'. Finally, Colin Wilson offers 'A Personal Response to *Wuthering Heights'*, which he sees as 'a piece of brilliant juvenilia' rather than a great novel.

BST contains a number of interesting articles, including Ruth Hook's address on 'The Father of the Family', previously unpublished letters by Charlotte, an account of the relationship between Charlotte and George Smith, and a note on similarities between *Jane Eyre* and *Aurora Leigh*. There are two other short notes of some significance. In 'Some Sources of *Wuthering Heights'* (*N&Q*), Patrick Diskin established important parallels with a number of tales and a novel published in the *Dublin University Magazine* between 1835 and 1840. In *TLS* (25 March), Alan Shelston publishes 'A Letter from Charlotte Brontë' (dated 28 May 1853), which offers a sidelight on her attitude to the role of the novelist.

Students of Elizabeth Gaskell have the double fortune of two excellent bibliographic guides to secondary criticism, Robert L. Selig's *Elizabeth Gaskell: A Reference Guide*[55], which covers the period from 1848 to 1974, and Jeffrey Welch's *Elizabeth Gaskell: An Annotated Bibliography, 1929-1975*[56], which begins where Northup's 1929 bibliography ends. Over their chosen areas, both volumes offer a comprehensive listing of books, articles and dissertations arranged according to their year of publication. Selig's compilation in particular, with more than three times as many items as any previous Gaskell bibliography, is an invaluable reference work.

Unfortunately, there is little to recommend in K. C. Shrivastava's full-length study of Mrs Gaskell's novels[57], a study with most of the characteristics of a poor graduate thesis: it is badly outdated, full of rhapsodic prose, repetitious, and naive in its underlying assumptions. Articles include Michael D. Wheeler's valuable descriptive analysis of 'Mrs Gaskell's Reading, and the Gaskell Sale Catalogue in Manchester Central Library' (*N&Q*). In *BST*, Enid L. Duthie draws attention to similarities between 'Henry James's *The Turn of the Screw* and Mrs Gaskell's *The Old Nurse's Story'*.

Charles Lee Lewes, the son of G. H. Lewes, donated over two thousand volumes owned by his father and George Eliot to the Dr Williams's Library, London. These are now definitively catalogued and annotated by William Baker[58], who also introduces and classifies the volumes. In

[55] *Elizabeth Gaskell: A Reference Guide*, by Robert L. Selig. Reference Guides in Literature Series. Boston, Mass.: G. K. Hall. pp. xviii + 431. $30.

[56] *Elizabeth Gaskell: An Annotated Bibliography, 1929-1975*, by Jeffrey Welch. Garland Reference Library of the Humanities 50. N.Y. and London: Garland. pp. xii + 139. $18.

[57] *Mrs Gaskell as a Novelist*, by K. C. Shrivastava. Salzburg Studies in English Literature: Romantic Reassessment 70. U. Salzburg. pp. xi + 245. pb.

[58] *The George Eliot-George Henry Lewes Library: An Annotated Catalogue of Their Books at Dr. Williams's Library, London* by William Baker. Garland Reference Library of the Humanities 67. N.Y. and London: Garland. pp. lxix + 11 plates + 300. $35.

addition to illustrating the range of their reading, Baker's catalogue records marginal comments, inscriptions and markings by both writers which, in some cases, suggest possible debts and sources. Certain chances seem to have been missed in Constance Marie Fulmer's *George Eliot: A Reference Guide*[59], an annotated bibliography covering the period from 1858 to 1971. Though Fulmer's listing of primary items is comprehensive, she seems to have missed many general studies in which George Eliot figures importantly, and her annotations for full-length studies of George Eliot are invariably brief and scrappy.

Robert Liddell's *The Novels of George Eliot*[60] has many of the virtues of an introductory author-guide — including long plot-synopses and exposition of background facts — but with the significant difference that it is also 'a protective and partial depreciation — a jettisoning of false and exaggerated claims, and an admission of weaknesses'. No doubt the introductory reader will be challenged by a study which is based upon a strong antipathy to George Eliot's puritanism, didacticism, and 'dullness'. Nor will Liddell have any truck with modish approaches: he returns to plot-character analysis, adopts a Jamesian 'aesthetic' standpoint, and discovers a neglected aspect of George Eliot's ethical thought in her interest in casuistry. Unfortunately, Liddell's preference for the gentleman-critic's leisurely and cultivated insight at the expense of anything approaching rigour tends to limit the value of his guidance: what he describes as his 'old-fashioned approach' turns out to be an odd combination of close story-telling, provocative half-truth, dismissive aside, and puckish devil's advocacy. His study will (by deliberate design?) irritate many more readers than it persuades.

Though Laura Comer Emery has not been able to consult Ruby V. Redinger's reconstruction of George Eliot's emergent psychic history (see *YW* 57.285), her psychoanalytic study, *George Eliot's Creative Conflict: The Other Side of Silence*[61], forms an interesting companion-piece. Emery focuses on the persistent latent needs, fantasies, and regressions which lie beneath the 'manifest' level of George Eliot's novels; she also wishes to examine the relationship between such latencies and the defensive and expressive mechanisms at work in the fiction. Her larger thesis is that George Eliot, in giving release to her unconscious needs through fiction, undergoes a painful process of self-confrontation, psychic readjustment and growth (beginning with inadequately controlled fantasy in *The Mill on the Floss* and culminating in the 'inner equilibrium' achieved in *Middlemarch*). Emery is most illuminating when she escapes the reductive tendencies inherent in her neo-Freudian approach and gives full consideration to the relationship between latent and manifest levels in the fiction. At such points, she has an interesting perspective to apply to long-standing problems — the ending of *The Mill on the Floss*, problems of over-idealisation, and examples of defensive moralisation.

General articles include Bonnie S. Zimmerman's '"Radiant as a Dia-

[59] *George Eliot: A Reference Guide*, by Constance Marie Fulmer. Reference Guides in Literature Series. Boston, Mass.: G. K. Hall. pp. xvi + 247. $20.

[60] *The Novels of George Eliot*, by Robert Liddell. Duckworth. pp. 193. £7.95.

[61] *George Eliot's Creative Conflict: The Other Side of Silence*, by Laura Comer Emery. U. of California P. pp. 235. £10.

mond": George Eliot, Jewelry and the Female Role' (*Criticism*), in which she discusses the thematic and symbolic significance of jewellery in relation to the multifaceted roles of George Eliot's useful and ornamental women. In *VN*, Charles Burkhart discusses 'George Eliot's Debt to *Villette*', noting points of likeness between Dr John and Lydgate. John R. DeBruyn offers 'George Eliot and Alice Helps: Two Unpublished Letters' (*N&Q*).

Joseph Wiesenfarth presents an edited and annotated version of 'George Eliot's Notes for *Adam Bede*' (*NCF*). These notes, he points out, show how extensive research supplemented personal experience in the creation of characters and incidents. His commentary identifies the sources of George Eliot's reading and the use she makes of it in the novel. In *ELN*, David Moldstad writes briefly on echoes connecting 'George Eliot's *Adam Bede* and Smiles's *Life of George Stephenson*'.

R. P. Draper has compiled a useful and well-balanced casebook on *The Mill on the Floss* and *Silas Marner*[62] (though F. R. Leavis, who is a connecting link between many of the modern essays, is not included). Reviews, opinions and criticism are arranged chronologically, with an afterword by the editor. Modern judgements are represented by Joan Bennett, Jerome Thale, R. H. Lee, Laurence Lerner, Barbara Hardy, David Carroll, and Henry Auster. In 'Authority in *The Mill on the Floss*' (*PQ*) Janet H. Freeman considers the narrator and her intense experience of retelling the story to be central to the meaning of the novel and its problematic ending.

In 'George Eliot's Florentine Museum' (*PLL*) Ann Ronald follows George Eliot's laboured research into Florentine history and examines her over-liberal use of paintings and sculpture to communicate period flavour in *Romola*. The result is 'a novel structured like an art museum', in which George Eliot seems 'so busy designing characters who pose for portraits . . . that she forgets to create lifelike people'. Jane S. Smith writes lucidly on 'The Reader as Part of the Fiction: *Middlemarch*' (*TSLL*), showing how the creation of an ambiguously defined audience is intrinsic to its meaning and technique. She identifies the dialogue between narrator and reader as a 'discursive' plot, and proceeds to analyse its effects in making the fictive reader George Eliot wants. Some of these discursive elements are also considered by Eve Marie Stwertka in 'The Web of Utterance: *Middlemarch*' (*TSLL*), though she is more concerned with how the narrator 'authenticates the word'. In her view, the spoken word is central to the novel's purpose of affirming reality, and making and mending relationships. Dialogue not only weaves connections, but also 'constitutes the dialectic which precedes synthesis and makes for progression'. In 'A Probable Source for Dorothea and Casaubon: Hester and Chillingworth' (*ES*), R. K. Wallace speculates upon the possible influence of Hawthorne's *The Scarlet Letter*. David R. Mesher throws further light on George Eliot's knowledge of Jews and Judaism in an analysis of 'Rabbinical References in *Daniel Deronda*' (*N&Q*).

In 'Charles Kingsley's Fallen Athlete' (*VS*), Henry R. Harrington writes perceptively on Kingsley's use of sport, soldier-athletes, and the sporting attitude appropriate in war as a way of focusing the moral and social

---

[62] *George Eliot: 'The Mill on the Floss' and 'Silas Marner', A Casebook*, ed. by R. P. Draper. Casebook Series. Macmillan pp. 260. hb £5.95, pb £2.50.

awareness of his characters. The exalted sporting moment allows the manly Christian to transcend the frustrations of everyday life, though in returning to those frustrations he also undergoes a 'saving fall': 'Within Kingsley's private theodicy, the fallen athlete and the manly Christian are one in a fictional world redeemed by his faith in "feminine virtue"'. Popular mid-century reading is surveyed by Sally Mitchell in 'Sentiment and Suffering: Women's Recreational Reading in the 1860s' (*VS*).

Trollope's star continues to rise. This year sees the appearance of three full-length studies, each of which makes arduous but rewarding reading. A full response to Trollope, it appears, demands a discursive chronicle form of criticism, with a leading thesis but many parallel subplots. The most synoptic of these, R. C. Terry's *Anthony Trollope: The Artist in Hiding*[63], is a work of devoted consolidation, correction and re-emphasis. Beginning with two chapters on the man and his literary reputation, Terry then attempts to show the 'inner world' of the novels by reference to a scheme of thematic concerns — love, marriage, the home life, unmarried people, and the life of the gentleman. These all receive subtle and extended treatment, Terry's emphasis falling on Trollope's 'hidden' imaginative range and understanding. Social interests are not ignored. There is a valuable chapter on Trollope and Ireland, and Terry later considers Trollope's enquiry into what should constitute the good life in a just and equitable society. Terry's detailed and appreciative study has a twofold value: it convincingly analyses the reality-in-depth which Trollope achieves at his best and, by focusing upon Trollope's handling of personal and domestic life, emphasises his grasp of the underlying and unchanging elements of human behaviour.

In his rewarding study of Trollope's formal rhetoric, *The Novels of Anthony Trollope*[64], James R. Kincaid concurs with Terry in finding a commitment to fixed, traditional values (Kincaid stresses the omnipresence of pastoral and gentlemanly ideals). In other respects, Kincaid updates Trollope's achievement and subjects his work to a searching formal analysis. Assessing the sophisticated use Trollope makes of the 'mixed' chronicle form, Kincaid sees him as 'both the most conventional and most modern of writers', because 'his formal patterns both adhere to conventions . . . and at the same time force convention to abandon all its old reliances'. In both confirming *and* radically modifying or disrupting the conventions of pastoral and romantic comedy, Trollope's novels are seen to have a mediate position between the closed forms of his predecessors and the open narrative forms of a later time. Kincaid suggests that such modifications are brought about in three ways: by the transformation of beginnings and endings, the interposition of a narrator who sets up a counter-pattern to conventional comedy, and by the use of subplots which stand in satiric or parodic relationship to the more conventional main plot. In the end, he argues, 'we are engaged in reading a Trollope novel not in the simple and final subversion of the main action but in the richer and more demanding *process* whereby the conflict between

[63] *Anthony Trollope: The Artist in Hiding*, by R. C. Terry. Macmillan. pp. xi + 286. £8.95.
[64] *The Novels of Anthony Trollope*, by James R. Kincaid. Oxford: The Clarendon Press. pp. xiii + 302. £9.75.

art and life is carried out'. Kincaid then focuses on Trollope's manipulation of comic patterns and expectations, stressing the movement in his fiction from romantic comedy to the highly ironic comedy of accommodation, and discovering that the most important variation occurs when the parodying of comic myths leads to more 'open' forms.

John Halperin's *Trollope and Politics: A Study of the Pallisers and Others*[65] is a massively detailed survey which presents the added difficulty of eye-strainingly small print. Trollope's interests would have been better served, one feels, by a shorter and shapelier volume. It is true that Halperin has a wide brief. He is concerned with what the Palliser novels tell us about 'the politics of the time, the role of individuals in politics and of politics in the lives of individuals, and the way in which politics and social systems interact and inter-depend'. Combined with this, there is an account of Trollope's activities as a Liberal candidate in Beverley and his use of that experience in *Ralph the Heir*. Halperin also identifies conclusively the politicians and parliamentary issues of the time which Trollope used in his novels. Yet the view underlying this medley of interests is basically a simple one: 'Trollope was by no means the Victorian Barry Goldwater; in terms of what most Victorians thought, his own thinking was less reactionary than simply normal.' Too much of what follows is a massive extension of this proposition, and inevitable *longueurs* arise because Halperin dwells too repetitiously on Trollope's view of the political rough-and-tumble, partisan politics, parliamentary in-fighting, political rhetoric and expediency. The extraordinary industry which has gone into the making of this study is impressive, but it has also resulted in a good deal of inert detail and, in turn, a cumulative dullness.

'Trollope and Romanticism' (*VN*) is a theme taken up by David R. Eastwood, his main emphasis falling on Trollope's detached or playfully ironic undercutting of romantic conventions. In 'Trollope, James, and the International Theme' (*YES*) John Halperin surveys their common interest and possible 'dialogue' in international subjects, and suggests that in *The Portrait of a Lady* James may in part be responding to *The Duke's Children*, concluding that 'James took from Trollope as much or more than Trollope took from him'. In *SEL*, George Butte writes on 'Ambivalence and Affirmation in *The Duke's Children*'. *N&Q* offers two short notes: John Halperin writes on 'The Composition of Trollope's *Lord Palmerston*', while P. D. Edwards draws attention to 'Some Misdated Trollope Letters'. In *VPN*, Edwards also contributes 'Trollope's Working Papers as Evidence of His Contributions to *Saint Pauls*'.

There is not a great deal to record on Meredith this year. David Williams's *George Meredith: His Life and Lost Love*[66] is a readable, briskly narrated biography centred upon Meredith's two marriages. While Williams has little new information to offer, he writes shrewdly on the progress and after-effects of Meredith's first marriage. He also offers a succinct account of Meredithian literary effects, particularly of the preciosity and 'strut' of his style. Students of Meredith now have *A Dictionary*

[65] *Trollope and Politics: A Study of the Pallisers and Others*, by John Halperin. Macmillan. pp. x + 318. £8.95.

[66] *George Meredith: His Life and Lost Love*, by David Williams. Hamish Hamilton. pp. xii + 227. £7.95.

of the Characters in George Meredith's Fiction[67], which covers all his fiction, short stories, and incomplete sketches. Each character is identified by the work(s) in which he or she appears, and then related to the plot and other characters. In *N&Q*, M. Y. Shaheen publishes 'A Meredith Letter to Leslie Stephen'.

Rita Gnutzmann writes on narrative technique in George Meredith[68] arguing that his work contributed significantly to changes in the development of the novel as a literary genre. Meredith's use of a form of 'stream of consciousness', his rejection of plot, and his use of mythology place him at the very point where Victorian fiction is superseded by the modern novel. [H.C.C.]

Hardy is the subject of two collections of essays this year. *Thomas Hardy After Fifty Years*[69], edited by Lance St John Butler, includes a variety of essays by contributors who attempt to measure Hardy's significance fifty years after his death. Contributors include F. B. Pinion, R. M. Rehder, Robert Gittings, David Lodge, Lance St John Butler, F. E. Halliday, R. C. Schweik and John Fowles (who writes on *The Well Beloved* in terms of 'the psychosis of the writing experience'). The main strength of the volume lies in its middle section. Here, Michael Alexander writes forcefully on modern and traditional aspects of Hardy's poetry in 'Hardy Among the Poets'. In 'Some Thoughts on Hardy and Religion', T. R. M. Creighton examines Hardy's religious dilemma, pointing to an unresolved conflict in his fiction between 'pre-lapsarian intuition and a conscious mind committed to frustrating it'. Michael Irwin and Ian Gregor concentrate on the beginning and end of Hardy's career (*Desperate Remedies* and *The Well Beloved*), showing the difficulties which complicated his search for a fictional method, why his method should have led him to the idea of Wessex, and why that idea was abandoned in favour of an apparently new development. Mark Kinkead-Weekes gives detailed attention to D. H. Lawrence's *Study of Thomas Hardy*, showing how Lawrence's sustained dialogue with Hardy led to revolutionary changes in his own fiction. He agrees with Ian Gregor's view that 'Where *Jude* ends, *The Rainbow* begins'.

F. B. Pinion's *Thomas Hardy: Art and Thought*[70] is a loose miscellany of long essays and short explanatory notes on topics as wide as Hardy's humour, pictorial art, and use of myth, and as narrowly focused as Hardy's bird imagery, and the influence of *Clarissa* upon *Tess*. In the absence of any overall view of the relationship between Hardy's art and thought, the volume falls rather uneasily between introductory survey and specialist reference companion. Yet Pinion throws up a number of fresh possibilities and provides a rich sampling of illustrative detail. There is an underlying

[67] *A Dictionary of the Characters in George Meredith's Fiction*, by Maurice McCullen and Lewis Sawin. Garland Reference Library of the Humanities 48. New York and London: Garland. pp. xii + 194. $21.

[68] *Der Wandel der Erzählkonventionen vom Viktorianismus zur Moderne. Untersuchungen zum Prosawerk George Merediths*, by Rita Gnutzmann. Frankfurt am M.: Peter Lang (Angelsächsische Sprache und Literatur 53). pp. 170. Sfr. 38.

[69] *Thomas Hardy After Fifty Years*, ed. by Lance St John Butler. Macmillan. pp. xiv + 153. £7.95.

[70] *Thomas Hardy: Art and Thought*, by F. B. Pinion. Macmillan. pp. x + 214. £7.95.

interest in the wide range of influences upon Hardy – including Shake-speare, Richardson, Goethe, Hugo, Shelley, Swinburne and Wilkie Collins. Interrelations of imagery and idea also receive extended treatment, and Pinion writes particularly well on Hardy's early fiction. For Norman Page's *Thomas Hardy*, see Section 1 above.

Articles of a more general nature include Devra Braun Rosenberg's 'The Shifting Balance of Community, History, and Nature in Thomas Hardy's Wessex Novels (1874–1896)' (*DUJ*), in which she shows how growing dissonance between nature and culture in the large community is mirrored in the increasingly problematic careers of Hardy's main individuals. In 'Hardy's Wordsworth: A Record and a Commentary' (*ELT*), Peter J. Casagrande provides useful evidence of Wordsworth's omnipresence – as a point of reference and departure – in Hardy's own process of self-definition as a writer. Hardy's problems as a serial writer in conforming to the demands of conventional moral opinion are considered in Robert A. Draffen's 'An Aspect of Hardy's Fiction' (*THY*, 1976). M. D. Wilkie publishes and examines 'Thomas Hardy's Correspondence with Sir George Douglas (*VN*), which extends from 1888 to 1924 and offers glimpses of Hardy's literary tastes and standards. The association between Hardy and Israel Zangwill is the subject of Bernard Winehouse's 'Thomas Hardy: Some Unpublished Material' (*N&Q*). In 'Thomas Hardy's Financial Exigencies' (*VN*), William J. Hyde discusses Hardy's parsimony in the light of his early experience of poverty and later belief in charity and altruism. He concludes that Hardy's concern for acquiring money is consistent with that of his characters for whom money is 'a socially compulsory means to an end', and provides 'a measure of fulfilled resolve'. Robert C. Schweik takes aim at critics who take their fictions too seriously (*ELT*).

In *THY*, 1976, Lawrence Jones considers the influence of the *Spectator*'s reviewers upon Hardy's fiction from 1870 to 1875. This same critic discusses parallels between 'The Music Scenes in *The Poor Man and the Lady*, *Desperate Remedies* and *An Indiscretion in the Life of an Heiress*' (*N&Q*). George Wing offers 'A Romantic "Sort of Warehouse"' (*THY*, 1976), in which he writes perceptively on the uneasy combination of romantic and visionary modes with a society fable in *A Pair of Blue Eyes*. He has an excellent analysis of Henry Knight as 'a man so morally blinkered that his design for purity ends in moral atrophy'. In 'Thomas Hardy's "Mellstock" and the Registrar General's Stinsford' (*L&H*), Jeanne Howard dutifully compares the social structure of Hardy's fictional village in *Under the Greenwood Tree* with that of Stinsford, the model for his novel. Census schedules over a period of thirty years are used to show Hardy's methods as a social historian. In the end, however, 'Accurate "history" strains against a wistful "pastoral"'.

In *N&Q* there are two articles on classical influence in Hardy's later novels. Jeremy V. Steele shows how Hardy incorporates echoes from Ovid's *Fasti* in *Tess*, while L. M. Findlay discusses Hardy's familiarity with Horace and his use of the *Carmen Saeculare* in *Jude*. Richard Hannaford offers 'Ragnarok in Little Hintock: Norse Allusions in *The Woodlanders*' (*THY*, 1976). Jane Millgate writes on 'Two Versions of Regional Romance: Scott's *The Bride of Lammermoor* and Hardy's *Tess of the d'Urbervilles*' (*SEL*), the former a work known and admired by Hardy. Affinities between the two, both direct and ironic, lead her to conclude that in *Tess* 'the example of Scott fused with the locally-derived idea of the decline of the d'Urbervilles to provide the necessary bridge to a literary mode of greater antiquity, elevation, and resonance'.

Mrs Humphrey Ward is very fortunate in having William S. Peterson as an interpreter of her aims and achievement. His meticulously researched study, *Victorian Heretic: Mrs Humphry Ward's 'Robert Elsmere'*[71], is more comprehensive than its title suggests. The first part of the book explores the successive stages of her intellectual and spiritual history which have a direct bearing upon *Robert Elsmere*. There are chapters on her childhood and Arnoldian heritage, her juvenilia and early interest in 'the psychology of unbelief', her formative period in Oxford and early writings as an essayist. Then follow chapters on the novel itself — analyses of its germination and development during revision, its dialectic, reception, and sequels. Appendixes reproduce details of the *Robert Elsmere* notebook and provide a comprehensive bibliography. Peterson teases out the many-faceted significance of the novel for its age and writes shrewdly on Mrs Ward as displaying 'the conservative moral sensibility of a Charlotte Mary Yonge overlaid with the incisive, uncompromising influence of a Mark Pattison'. The success of *Robert Elsmere* led to the commissioning of an analogous novel in a Jewish setting, the result being Israel Zangwill's *Children of the Ghetto* (1892). This novel is now newly reprinted[72], with a helpful introduction by V. D. Lipman who explains why the Jewish situation in England around 1890 called for a novel of this sort and why Zangwill was the man to write it.

A fair amount of journal-space is devoted to other minor writers of the later decades. Bram Stoker makes an appearance in two articles this year. Joseph S. Bierman considers 'The Genesis and Dating of *Dracula* from Bram Stoker's Working Notes' (*N&Q*). Stoker's concern with the *fin de siècle* wasteland, Jekyll and Hyde repression, and the quest for redemptive knowledge is the subject of '*Dracula:* The Gnostic Quest and Victorian Wasteland' (*ELT*) by Mark M. Hennelly Jr. In 'Blackmore's Letters to Blackwood: The Record of a Novelist's Indecision' (*ELT*), Max Keith Sutton shows how Blackmore's failure to repeat the success of *Lorna Doone* largely stems from his difficulties in meeting the demands of serial publication which were 'unsuited to his health, his working habits, and his weak artistic conscience'. In *N&Q*, R. A. Copland offers 'A Side Light on the Butler-Darwin Quarrel'.

The current state of George Moore studies is reviewed in 'George Moore and His Critics' (*ELT*) by Charles Burkhart, who also points to areas of future research. An important collection of Moore's letters is published and edited by J. G. Riewald in 'From Naturalism to Lyrical Realism: Fourteen Unpublished Letters from George Moore to Frans Netscher' (*ES*). Written between 1885 and 1891, they form a substantial addition to the relatively scarce letters from the first phase of Moore's literary career. In corresponding with Netscher, a Dutch supporter of Zola, Moore

[71] *Victorian Heretic: Mrs Humphry Ward's 'Robert Elsmere'*, by William S. Peterson. Leicester U.P., 1976. pp. x + 259. £3.50.

[72] *Children of the Ghetto*, by Israel Zangwill, ed. with intro. by V. D. Lipman. The Victorian Library Series. Leicester U.P. pp. 410. £6.

expresses his position in the controversy about naturalism, reveals a growing disillusion with Zola, and expresses his own impulse towards lyrical realism. In *PLL*, W. Eugene Davis offers '"The Celebrated Case of Esther Waters": Unpublished Letters of George Moore to Barrett H. Clark', letters concerned with a possible adaptation of Moore's novel which the two men planned for the American stage. This correspondence of 1922 shows 'an early amiable collaboration, subsequently strained and ultimately dissolved'. Richard Cave gives new details about 'George Moore's "Stella"' (*RES*), the pseudonym of Clara Louise Christian. A talented painter, she accompanied Moore to Ireland in 1901, and helped him, Cave suggests, to a recovery of self-confidence and 'to find a new subject and a new simple, lyrical style with which to express it'.

'Gissing's work offers an unrivalled challenge to biographical criticism to show what it can do,' writes John Halperin in 'How to Read Gissing' (*ELT*). In his view, the idea of 'the novelist as biographer' reaches its apotheosis in the works of Gissing who not only uses fiction as a release for obsessions with class, sex, money and exogamy, but also re-enacts in his own life inventions from his fiction. The latest critic to take up the biographical challenge is Michael Collie in *George Gissing: A Biography*[73], though, unlike Halperin, he is sceptical about using Gissing's fiction as direct autobiographical evidence. Collie's opening chapter sets down the assumptions underlying his view of Gissing: 'His bohemian nature did not express itself in frivolity, iconoclastic behaviour, non-conformity, but in detachment from society that was concealed beneath an apparent conformity, in a loneliness which left him free to write, and in sets of nihilistic rejections which he never reconciled with his unwillingly acknowledged needs and desires.' Such a view determines the developing pattern which Collie is able to discern in Gissing's troubled and hectic life: in one direction, it leads him to acknowledge the tenacity with which Gissing pursued his independence as a man of letters; in another, to stress the 'horrifying discrepancies between his public and his private life'. The evidence is ably assembled, and the discussion ranges through Gissing's attitudes to women, sex, marriage, class, and money.

The Harvester Press continues to reprint Gissing's novels in handsome modern editions. This year's titles include *The Whirlpool*, edited by Patrick Parrinder[74], and *The Emancipated*, edited by Pierre Coustillas[75]. Each volume contains an introduction, notes, and bibliography. Among many articles in *The Gissing Newsletter*, the most notable are Bernard Winehouse's 'George Gissing and Israel Zangwill: Some Unpublished Letters Describing their Acquaintanceship', and Francis Noel Lees's 'A George Gissing Centenary'.

'Kipling on technology is not Kipling at his best,' writes Christopher Harvie in '"The Sons of Martha": Technology, Transport, and Rudyard Kipling' (*VS*). Yet the obsession with technology in Kipling is central, Harvie claims, to his alternative view of society based on new work-

[73] *George Gissing: A Biography*, by Michael Collie. Dawson. pp. 189. £7.
[74] *The Whirlpool*, by George Gissing, ed. with intro. by Patrick Parrinder. Hassocks, Sussex: Harvester P. pp.: xii + 467. £6.95.
[75] *The Emancipated*, by George Gissing, ed. with intro. by Pierre Coustillas. Hassocks, Sussex: Harvester P. pp. xxiv + viii + 469. £6.95.

disciplines, integration of specialised skills, and organised technocratic community. In dramatising the relations between new technology and political power, Kipling also stresses 'the importance of pre-technical values and relationships in holding industrial society together'. Janet Montefiore considers 'Day and Night in Kipling' (*EIC*) in relation to other divisions which make up his 'two worlds' — action and dream, white men and native Indians, and men and women. In particular, she is concerned with the strengths and limits of 'daytime language' (arising from the world of work and effective organisation) and the meaning of the Indian's 'night-time language': 'If the "daytime" language gestures towards the unsaid, the "night-time" language points to the unsayable: what is genuinely inexpressible because outside normal consciousness.'

3. Prose

This section has five categories: a) Bibliography and general works; b) Individual authors; c) Periodicals and history of publishing; d) Visual art; e) Social History.

(a) *Bibliography and general works*

R. B. Freeman's annotated bibliographical handlist, *The Works of Charles Darwin* (1965)[76], appears in a second revised and enlarged edition. It contains all the British and foreign books, pamphlets, and circulars by Darwin seen by the author, or seen reliably recorded, from 1835 to 1975, as well as a list of papers, notes, and letters which originally appeared in serials. Frederick J. Bethke's *Three Victorian Travel Writers*[77] is an annotated bibliography of criticism on the travel writings of Mrs Trollope, Samuel Butler, and Robert Louis Stevenson. Next to the novel, travel writing was the most popular genre of the period, and the critical responses recorded here indicate the range of expectation and interest it aroused in its adherents and denigrators.

Jerome McGann contributes a crusty annual review article to the nineteenth-century number of *SEL* in which he suggests that a Marxist reading is required to make some better sense out of the ambiguity of Tennyson's endings. In *Libri* W. Boyd Rayward reports on nineteenth-century developments in bibliography in Britain, in particular *The Bibliotheca Britannica* by Robert Watt, William Thomas Lowndes's *The Bibliographer's Manual of English Literature,* the British Museum catalogue and the Royal Society *Catalogue of Scientific Papers,* though in spite of these achievements no national system of bibliography emerged. The first numbers of the *Victorian Studies Bulletin* (edited by Lynne Sacher, 820 West End Avenue, New York, New York 10025) appeared this year: they provide a diverse listing of events and publications in the field; *VSB* welcomes news and contributions. The September number of *VPN* is dedicated to Esther and Walter Houghton, creators and editors of the *Wellesley Index,* and Scott Bennett provides a checklist of their respective

[76] *The Works of Charles Darwin,* by R. B. Freeman. Folkestone, Kent: Dawson; and Hamden, Conn.: Archon. pp. 235. £10.

[77] *Three Victorian Travel Writers: An Annotated Bibliography of Criticism on Mrs. Frances Milton Trollope, Samuel Butler, and Robert Louis Stevenson,* by Frederick Bethke. Boston, Mass.: G. K. Hall. pp. xviii + 203. $20.

writings. A fifth number of *VS* called a 'Supplement' contains brief descriptions of the contents of each article appearing in its pages between 1957 and 1977, as well as a cumulative index, lists of staff, and two retrospectives on the history of the periodical by Michael Wolff, a founder, and Martha Vicinus, the current editor.

In the same periodical Linda C. Dowling argues that the Aesthetes' version of the eighteenth century served their quarrel with the contemporary stress on inward experience and notions of seriousness and substance in art. The eclectic Queen Anne style of buildings of Norman Shaw, objects of the Century Guild, and Beardsley's drawings, reflect their view of the previous century as one of social forms and elegant surfaces, avoidance of appeal to human verities, and impersonality. The article suffers badly from the failure to define 'Aesthetes', and careless use of its related forms, so that Pater, Beardsley, and Wilde are, but Morris, Rossetti, and Burne Jones are not, and 'Aesthetes' eventually emerges, in the first part, as meaning for the author's purposes anti-Gothic and pre-Raphaelite. A similar imprecision characterises the second section. Eventually Dowling (wisely) abandons 'Aesthetes' altogether, and collapses to 'the revivalists turned to the eighteenth century for relief from an aesthetic culture'. The interdisciplinary nature of this article — its constant alternations between visual art and literature, and its resulting *mélange* of chronologies and terminology — is a primary cause of the confusion that plagues it. As eclectic as, but less harmonious than, the Queen Anne style, the piece goes on to include Austin Dobson (an 'English Parnassian'), Ernest Dowson (a 'Decadent'), Wilde, and Yeats. Humphrey House commented that the *Germ* resembled a 'Puseyite parish magazine' and in *DR* D. M. R. Bentley considers the evidence for the alleged common inclination of the PRB toward Puseyism and the Oxford Movement; the author finds the lives and works of D. G. Rossetti, Millais, H. Hunt, and James Collinson all implicated.

In Anne Rouxeville's dutiful catalogue of the reception of Flaubert in Victorian periodicals in *CLS*, George Saintsbury, writing in the *Fortnightly* and the *Academy* in 1878, emerges as the author's prime sustained and serious British defender during his lifetime. The curve of the reaction, from repulsion to somewhat grudging praise, reflects the response to realism in fiction between 1857 and 1900. Noting the triumph of Nature which began the nineteenth century and the triumph of art at its conclusion, Carl Woodring, in *PMLA*, ponders the meaning of nature for the Romantics and the spur to positivist faith in objective reality afforded by the discovery of photography between 1837 and the 1850s. But Darwin's view of the rule of nature as one of chance set nature back, and left a great opening for art which the primitive craftsmanship of the preRaphaelites, and the critical stress on the interrelatedness of various forms of art reflect, until in Wilde art is seen to be completely divorced from nature. Woodring finally notes wryly that we have inherited simultaneously both the environmental and the aesthetic traditions without choosing between or reconciling them.

Lawrence J. Starzyk[78] examines the dialectical process, particularly

[78] *The Imprisoned Splendour: A Study of Victorian Critical Theory*, by Lawrence J. Starzyk. Port Washington, N.Y. and London: Kennikat P. pp. xii + 200. £8.90.

its philosophical and psychological underpinnings, on which early Victorian critical theory rests, and thereby chronicles what he treats as the Victorian response to and modification of romanticism. The first three chapters deal with the critical disarray in the early part of the period and the nature of the 'unpoetic' modernity, and the last three with the critics' vision of how art is to survive these strictures, by means of imaginative reason and regarding positively the notions of the poet as outcast, and poetry as a spiritual cult. Arnold, Mill, Carlyle, Ruskin, and Macaulay figure principally in this study, Dallas, Newman, Keble, Lewes, and Browning less — which concludes that the supremacy of a dual self is the controlling principle of early Victorian theory. This book is verbose, and the prose laborious and clichéd, but for the energetic and patient, Starzyk's exegesis has moments of interest.

(b) *Individual authors*

The last volume of R. H. Super's splendid edition of *The Complete Prose Works* of Arnold[79] gathers in one volume late essays on education, politics, and literature that have appeared recently in diverse sources; two pieces are reprinted for the first time (including an informative survey of Victorian elementary and secondary education), and reports on public lectures and brief notes by Arnold for the press also appear. It contains too the customary apparatus of last volumes — Additions and Corrections and an Index — but also a useful checklist of manuscripts of Arnold's prose works and a title index which includes all the titles by which a work was known in Arnold's lifetime. In the Introduction Super defends his choice of the New York Edition (Edinburgh, 1883–4) and denies allegations of a recent reviewer (*N&Q*, 1972) concerning the number of substantive variants and accidental anomalies of that edition. Super's volumes with their full critical and explanatory notes have been invaluable to students and scholars, and it is to be hoped that the work of other Victorian writers of non-fictional prose whose writings are even more inaccessible than Arnold's were before this edition, will eventually be rediscovered and accessible through such an edition. Both publisher and editor merit commendation for this ambitious project.

Victor N. Boutellier's study of Arnold's criticism[80] does not originate in a thesis; it *is* one which was completed before 1974 and which therefore the author tells us in a note in the bibliography 'could not' take two significant books into account. Boutellier's attempt to disclose the 'hidden dualism of "imaginative reason"' which unifies the apparently diverse criticism remains well within the confines of the familiar and occasionally stumbles even there. Between the introduction and conclusion are laboured chapters on 'Criticism of Life', 'Imaginative Reason' as the method of a new critical theory, 'Disinterestedness', and 'Urbanity'. In as far as Boutellier considers the criticism as a whole, his work reflects the current revival of interest in Victorian prose criticism as a significant genre.

[79] *The Last Word*, Vol. XI of *The Complete Prose Works of Matthew Arnold*, ed. by R. H. Super. Ann Arbor, Mich.: U. of Michigan P. pp. xii + 698. $18.50.
[80] *Imaginative Reason: The Continuity of Matthew Arnold's Critical Effort*, by Victor N. Boutellier. Swiss Studies in English 94. Bern: Francke Verlag. pp. viii + 236. SFr. 28.

The Fall number of *The Arnoldian* celebrates the completion of R. H. Super's edition of Arnold's prose. Jerold Savory writes an appreciation of Volume XI, *The Last Word,* and in a useful evaluation of the complete edition John P. Farrell stresses the scope, thoroughness, and reliability of the annotations. In the same number Douglas Bush surveys Arnold's various preoccupations in the prose as parts of a larger theme, the humanisation of man in society, which Arnold is shown to regard as manna for the faithful and defence against the Philistines. James McNally reports on a letter of December 1867 from Arnold to George Lillie Craik, an employee at Macmillan's concerning an advertisement for *Schools and Universities on the Continent* which Arnold thought, with horror, ascribed a novel (!) to him (*The Arnoldian*).

In the first number of *Prose Studies. 1800–1900* (Department of English, The University of Leicester) David J. DeLaura identifies sources not in Super for Arnold's term 'imaginative reason' and considers the tradition of which it is a part. In concluding his account of the tradition of the imaginative reason and its cognates, with its use in De Quincey, Newman, Henry Taylor (1849), Ruskin (1856), Pater (1867), and John Morley (1870), DeLaura views it as the focus of the most serious thinking on the nature of the role of poetry and of the mind in the nineteenth century. Another aspect of the relation between Newman's and Arnold's thought is treated by DeLaura in *The Arnoldian* where he interprets a great shift in modern culture, Newman's nightmare vision of a future wholly irreligious and God-denying, as a response to the arguments of *Literature and Dogma* (1873), a response echoed by T. S. Eliot, of whose extensive reading of Victorian prose-writers DeLaura reminds us.

Writing on Arnold and the Irish question in the same periodical, Thomas S. Snyder outlines Arnold's pronouncements on Celtic literature, land tenure, religion, a Catholic university, and Home Rule which Arnold opposed with notions of local provincial government; there too, the object of Arnold's allusion at the beginning of 'On Translating Homer' to rejoinders to his high esteem for criticism is identified for the first time by Robert H. Tener as an article in the *Spectator* (29 June 1861), probably by R. H. Hutton, and Dennis Chaldecott provides an extended abstract of his research on Arnold, civilisation, and the United States.

In *CLAJ* the resemblances of thought and action in the lives of Edmund Burke and Walter Bagehot are elementarily paralleled by Francis L. Davis.

I Too Am Here, a selection of Jane Carlyle's vibrant letters[81], is organised topically and chronologically, from her courtship through her marriage to her final breakdown and short-lived recovery. It is a handsome volume, with the letters based on manuscript sources rather than on Froude's edition, a lively biographical introduction, headnotes for sections, illustrations and suggestions for further reading, but no footnotes or other scholarly apparatus, all of which the editors leave to the emerging Duke-Edinburgh edition.

Charles R. Sanders has collected and revised eleven of his published essays[82]; seven treat Carlyle and his friends who include Coleridge, Leigh

[81] *I Too Am Here. Selections from the Letters of Jane Welsh Carlyle,* intro. and notes by Alan and Mary McQueen Simpson. Cambridge: C.U.P. pp. xx + 307. £6.50.
[82] *Carlyle's Friendships and Other Studies,* by Charles R. Sanders. Durham, N.C.: Duke U.P. pp. x + 342. $14.75.

Hunt, Byron, Tennyson, and Thackeray, and the remaining four Mill's *Letters*, Tennyson, The Ancient Mariner and Coleridge's theory of poetic art, and 'Two Kinds of Poetry'. The essays concerning Carlyle touch closely on matters of biography, and also on Carlyle's own portraits of his contemporaries. *Carlyle and His Contemporaries*[83] has been compiled by John Clubbe in honour of Sanders, and it includes a biographical essay about him, and a list of his publications. Clubbe has set out to create 'a genuine reevaluation of Carlyle's position within nineteenth-century English culture'; half of the sixteen essays focus on Carlyle and the other half on his impact on his contemporaries. Ian Campbell writes on Carlyle's religion, and four essays on Carlyle and contemporary attitudes treat his traffic with Goethe as Scientist (Carlisle Moore), the Saint-Simonians (K. J. Fielding), the Logic-Choppers Mill and Diderot (Edward Spivey), and Godefroy Cavaignac, Carlyle's French republican acquaintance, whom Frederick W. Hilles suggests exemplified for Carlyle the hero as revolutionary. Janet Ray Edwards writes on Carlyle's use of fictional devices between 1830 and 1843 for his literature of belief; where she regards fiction as his dominant mode Richard Altick assesses the topicality of *Past and Present* as a technique. The contemporary critical reception of *Latter-Day Pamphlets* (1850) is shown by Michael Goldberg to illustrate the changing response to Carlyle, and David J. DeLaura concentrates on the anti-poetic climate at the beginning of Carlyle's career in the 1820s and 30s as background to Carlyle's attempt to eke out a role for the future of poetry; his inability to accept Goethe's aesthetics is part of the period's inadequacy in the face of the notions of culture and aestheticism. DeLaura's piece is an outstanding contribution to this volume. Carlyle's relationships with various figures are described by Gordon S. Haight (the Leweses), Ruth apRoberts (Trollope), George A. Cate (Ruskin), Lionel Stevenson (Meredith) and Clyde de L. Ryals (Browning in 'Aristophanes' Apology'). Parodies of Carlyle are examined as commentaries on Carlyle's style by G. B. Tennyson, and the editor of the volume shows what the literary artistry of Froude's biography of Carlyle reveals about Froude's biographical techniques. This collection contains essays of considerable interest and merit, and it is indexed, which is welcome.

In 'The Editor as Reconstructor' (*BSUF*), Stephen L. Franklin considers the implications for artistic expression of Carlyle's historical notion of time in *Sartor Resartus:* 'The Editor is the outward vesture or clothing of the professor. The Editor's reconstruction of Teufelsdrockh reveals him to be the outward vesture and Carlyle's creative solution to the historical dilemma of the age.' In *DQR* Winnifred Janssen offers an elementary reading of *Sartor* which might prove useful to new students of Carlyle, and in a review article in *UTQ* Brian John reconsiders Carlyle in the light of *Carlyle and His Contemporaries*.

By examining the history of science, economics, and politics of the period, Michael S. Helfand shows that the common understanding of T. H. Huxley's lecture of 1893, 'Evolution and Ethics', is mistaken. Rather than neutral to any specific political position, humanist, and anti-science, the lecture is a culmination of a series of essays in which Huxley

[83] *Carlyle and His Contemporaries*, ed. by John Clubbe. Durham, N.C.: Duke U.P. 1976. pp. xxiv + 371. $15.75.

used the policy of natural selection to justify a Liberal imperialist policy (*VS*). In *EA* William Baker publishes and annotates seven letters from G. H. Lewes to George Crabbe – son and biographer of the poet – which reveal the 'intellectual ethos of the late 1840s'.

Volume Four of Macaulay's *Letters*[84] begins with the author's move to the Albany in September 1841, and coincides with his period in Parliament as M.P. for Edinburgh (until 1848), his steady contributions to the *Edinburgh Review* (until 1844), and the writing and publication of the first and second volumes of the *History of England* in 1848. The letters, some published in part or whole before in diverse places, and others never yet in print, are distinguished in style and informative, particularly about the workings of the *Edinburgh Review* and Whig politics; Macaulay emerges as compassionate, generous, and frank. Pinney's annotations are unfailingly tactful and full, and the volume is pre-eminently enjoyable. Kenneth Young's essay on Macaulay[85] replaces G. R. Potter's in the WTW series. A snappy biography precedes sections on Macaulay's politics, *ER* essays, and poems, and two evocative ones on the *History of England* and its reception. Young is especially alive to Macaulay's language and narrative methods.

In *Travels into the Poor Man's Country*[86] Anne Humpherys pieces together in the first chapter the little that is known about the life of Henry Mayhew who, like Coleridge, lived a life of unfinished projects which, however fragmentary and otherwise flawed, have commanded respect and admiration. The bulk of this attractive book is given over to an assessment of Mayhew's three greatest projects – his letters to the *Morning Chronicle* (1849–50), *London Labour and the London Poor*, and his survey of London prisons – and essays on his style and art, on his influence on Kingsley, and on the parallels of his work with Dickens's. Humpherys argues that Mayhew's combination of empathy (at times amounting to identification) with and distance from his abject subjects in the social surveys, novels, and educational books, reflects his ambivalence towards his own class, particularly his father. Besides providing the most sustained modern published account of Mayhew, this book looks closely at details of Victorian publishing and journalism. The contemporary illustrations, notes, bibliography, and index are commendable.

James McDonnell undertakes close textual criticism of Chapter Five of Mill's *Autobiography* in order to reveal Mill's crisis as a serious quasi-religious and vocational trauma. Linking it with a common pattern of spiritual development, he shows that one or more preliminary conversions preceded the definitive change (*MLR*). In *VPN* John M. Robson attempts to describe the significant factors in nineteenth-century periodical contributions by a single author, here J. S. Mill. This basic information is known to anyone who has already worked with material from the periodicals, but the piece is a good introduction for those new to the subject.

In 'Newman and the Victorian Cult of Style' (*VN*) David J. DeLaura

[84] *The Letters of Thomas Babington Macaulay,* Vol. IV, ed by Thomas Pinney. Cambridge U.P. pp. xii + 407. £19.50.
[85] *Macaulay,* by Kenneth Young. Longman for the British Council. WTW 255. pp. 59. £0.60.
[86] *Travels into the Poor Man's Country, The Work of Henry Mayhew,* by Anne Humpherys. Athens, Ga: U. of Georgia P. pp. xiv + 240. $12.50.

persuasively argues that an influential view of Newman's style as the new mode developed in the 1860s, and that the ethos of Pater's stylism of the eighties and nineties represents a narrowing and refining of Newman's ideas. He highlights Arnold's, John Campbell Shairp's, and R. C. Church's roles in investing Newman's style with specific meaning and authority. General as well as specific conclusions, concerning the nature of auto-biography as well as the *Apologia*, emerge from Michael Ryan's resonant discussion of the identity of good and bad writing – God's voice and man's passions – in that work (*GR*). The passage in Chapter V describing the implications of the empty mirror reflects the *apocarteretic* pattern of abandoning hope in one direction in order to turn to another for help.

L. M. Findlay, in *VSAN* (1976), records and discusses F. T. Palgrave's scant marginalia of 1851 in J. J. Winckelmann's *The History of Ancient Art Among the Greeks*. Palgrave's first essay on art criticism in 1855 adopts a different approach from Winckelmann's, being 'densely factual' rather than 'mannered impressionism'. In *VN* John O. Waller also repro-duces and briefly discusses Palgrave's marginal notes on *In Memoriam*, found in a first edition in the Tennyson Research Centre. Addressed to Tennyson himself, the notes may have influenced some of the poet's revisions in 1855 for the sixth edition.

Gerald Monsman has published the first substantial critical biography in English of Walter Pater for over seventy years[87]. It focuses equally on Pater's fiction and the theme of the Aesthetic hero, common to both the life and the art. Lumping together Pater's 'reviews, lectures, critical appreciations, unfinished fiction, and other fragments', Monsman con-siders the artist at the expense of the critic, and makes a distinction which seems particularly inappropriate to Pater's work, however much limited space required a principle of selection. By page 70 we have reached *Marius* and the Aesthetic hero, but in addition to the expected chapters on the hero in *Marius* and the short portraits, and the obligatory 'Pater and the Modern Temper', Monsman gives us an essay on *Plato and Platonism* which affords an example of a non-fictional Aesthetic hero, and occasion to discuss certain aspects of Pater's style. Although Monsman's book is scholarly, contains new information, and unfamiliar sources, it is only intermittently addressed to scholars; its abbreviated bibliography, com-pressions, and nods to the basic events in the period make clear its intended audience is also, and perhaps primarily, undergraduates. In short, the work is uneven because its audience is so wide, but it is also tantalising in some of its judgements, queries, and allusions, and gives scholars much to contemplate. And in the absence of abundant biographi-cal information Monsman has stoutly and wisely resisted depending on the fiction for an account of Pater's inner life.

After surveying the diverse and long-lived influence of Walter Pater's 'Conclusion' to *Studies in the History of the Renaissance,* Alan W. Bellringer traces Pater's successive emendations of it between 1868, when it appeared in a review of the poetry of William Morris, and 1893, in its final form in the fourth edition of *The Renaissance*. Bellringer considers the by now well-documented changes after the first edition in 1873, but also

[87] *Walter Pater,* by Gerald Monsman. Boston, Mass.: Twayne. TEAS 207. pp. 213. $7.95.

notes the existence of a deeply-felt paragraph in the review version omitted in 1873 which leaves the first edition 'Conclusion' without the evidence of Pater's own emotional commitment to his argument (*PS*). Richard Della- mora (*UTQ*) shows Pater's essay on Leonardo (1869) to be modernist, to afford guidance to contemporary artists. Although Pater accepts classical forms of beauty, he views the truths they communicate as immoral. Pater's classicism in comparison with Ruskin's is decadent. He is, however, dissatisfied with art that is only profane, and he combines elements of culture to create something like a sacred image. Christopher Ricks's 'Pater, Arnold and Misquotation' (*TLS*, 25 November) is a sus- tained and vehement attack on Pater, as a critic whose notion of criticism encroaches on the artist's territory of creation, and whose practice, for Ricks, is uncomfortably close to a parasitical dependence on works of art through what Ricks deems 'misquotation'. Ricks's strident tone is perhaps better understood when we realise that behind Pater for Ricks lies the criticism of Harold Bloom and his school.

Affirming the typicality of Impressionism in Pater's thought against Wellek's denial, and the positive value of it against the disapproval of T. S. Eliot, and Wellek and Warren, Paul Zietlow demonstrates how Pater's impressionism inevitably emerges from his notions of historical process and belief in the vitality of intellectual and imaginative effort (*ELH*). In his historical relativism, Pater challenges Arnold's fixed, pre- conceived notions of criteria for culture, and the vitality principle coin- cides with Hopkins's notion of structures charged with energy. Because of the transience of moments of culture, culture survives only to the extent that it is recreated as an impression. This is a significant and complex re- consideration of Pater's impressionism. In a piece on Arthur Machen's nine- ties novel *Hill of Dreams* (published 1907), John Batchlor briefly notes Machen's debts to *Marius* and *Studies in the History of the Renaissance (Journal of the Eighteen-Nineties Society)*. *News of Pater Scholarship* (Department of English, UCW, Aberystwyth, and Department of English, University of Arizona, Tucson) published its first number this year.

The diary of William Michael Rossetti[88], art and literary critic, editor, and brother of Christina and Dante Gabriel, appears for the first time, briefly introduced, edited, and fully annotated by Odette Bornand. For the most part the diary entries refer to people and events, many of them illustrious, and to articles and literary projects, and only secondarily to works of art and literature in any detail. But the diary contains numerous facts of interest to students of mid-Victorian figures who, beside Rossetti and his family, include Swinburne, W. G. Scott, E. J. Trelawny, James Thomson, Millais, Morris, and Whitman. Details of illnesses, visiting, move- ments, publishing projects and arrangements (including WMR's persistent work on Shelley), and various doings of servants, give a good indication of day-to-day, middle-class literary life in the period.

Positing Wordsworth and Dante as two poles of Ruskin's thought concerning Nature, Martin Bidney examines Dante's role in Ruskin's imaginative development regarding Nature. He detects Dante's influence in its three discernable stages, as seen in *Modern Painters, Deucalion*

[88] *The Diary of W. M. Rossetti. 1870-1873*, ed. by Odette Bornand, O.U.P. pp. xxiv + 302. £12.50.

(1875–83), and 'The Storm-Cloud of the Nineteenth Century' (1884), and stresses the duality of Dante's concept of nature, the Hellish as well as the Edenic (*TSLL*). John Hayman emphasises Ruskin's concern with the structural rather than the ornamental aspects of architecture in *The Stones of Venice*, Vol. I, in which Ruskin tried to settle his basic ideas about architecture, and in the three unpublished notebooks in which he prepared for it. Although in his later work Ruskin gives precedence to delight from decoration over that derived from usefulness or structure, such a dichotomy characterises much of his work on architecture and reflects the larger conflict of his life between economics and aesthetics (*BNYPL*). In *ELN* Hayman refines our responses to Ruskin's article 'The Three Colours of Pre-Raphaelitism' (1878), published in the *Nineteenth Century*, by showing it in its periodical context as a reply to W. H. Mallock's satiric piece, 'A Familiar Colloquy', in the August number of that periodical.

Billie Andrew Inman illustrates the primacy of reason rather than personal preference in Ruskin's art criticism by examining the premeditated reversal in 1871 of his previously favourable judgement of the paintings of Michelangelo, from the development of his condemnation of the Renaissance in 1849 to the gradual extension of it from architecture to painting, and from Raphael to Tintoretto and Michelangelo (*PLL*). David Sonstroem (*VS*) attempts to reinstate 'Of Queens' Gardens' by refuting Kate Millett's influential attack on it in *Sexual Politics*: Millett's misreading originates in her naive inability to find social compassion outside equalitarianism, in alliance with a hierarchic social philosophy, and Ruskin reshapes and revivifies sexual stereotypes in order to advance his social principles by enlisting his audience of women. With women ruling and rigorously educated according to Ruskin's blueprint, they are to rescue humanity as a whole, a high function which discredits Millett's charge of insincerity against Ruskin. In *PS* Donald Wesling uses the descriptive prose of an American, John Muir (1838–1914), which he compares with that of Ruskin, as the focus of a discussion on the method of such prose, and the reason for its rise and decline within Muir's life-time. John Hayman (*EA*) publishes and comments on Ruskin's letters to Rev Walter Brown, his tutor at Oxford (1841–1852?), which treat of theology; and in *N&Q* Margaret Berg clarifies an obscure reference to Ruskin in a letter (December 1859) from Rossetti to William Allingham, concerning the absence of poems by Rossetti in *Nightingale Valley* (a selection of poetry edited by Allingham), for which Ruskin had criticised the volume.

The passage of Henry Salt (1851–1919), until 33 a master at Eton, to the pursuit of socialist and pacifist ideas as a reformer and the founding of the Humanitarian society in 1891 is traced by George Hendrick in a modest critical biography[89]. Author of books on Shelley, Tennyson, R. Jefferies, and James Thomson among others, Salt was personally intimate with Shaw and Edward Carpenter, while he knew Morris, Swinburne, and Meredith; considerable space is devoted to the relationship of Kate Salt, Henry's wife, with Edward Carpenter and with Shaw, who possibly wrote *You Never Can Tell* on a theme which she suggested.

[89] *Henry Salt: Humanitarian Reformer and Man of Letters*, by George Hendrick. Urbana, Chicago, Ill. and London: U. of Illnois P. pp. 228. £7.

Hendrick draws on Salt's periodical articles in radical publications of the 1880s and 1890s as well as from Salt's own *Humanity* and *The Humane Review,* and appends two of Salt's one-act propaganda plays, 'A Lover of Animals' and 'The Home Secretary's Holiday'. There is no bibliography.

Richard Simpson as Critic[90] is a good collection of periodical articles — otherwise scattered and inaccessible — by a Victorian scholar-critic (1820–76), for which preservation and publication the Routledge Critic Series should be praised. David Carroll's selection includes reviews, history of ideas articles, studies of single authors, and four essays from *Chronicle* (1867–8), two on genre, signed 'Scholasticus'. Simpson, a Tractarian who became a Liberal Catholic, is best known as a critic of Shakespeare and the biographer of Edmund Campion, but it is clear from this volume that his critical essays are among the most rigorous and philosophic of the Victorian literary criticism still buried in the periodicals. Moreover, he is one of the few Victorian critics to write at length on Jane Austen, George Eliot, Thackeray, Newman, Browning and Tennyson, the nineteenth-century novelists and the genre, as well as on poetry. The editor's intro-duction is particularly concerned with the Liberal Catholic periodicals background, and his headnotes and annotations for the essays (which are complete) are properly informative. Given the inaccessibility of these essays and their high quality, this volume will be prized by students of the period.

The interests of Leslie Stephen's *Mausoleum Book* (1895)[91] are many, and Alan Bell in his shrewd introduction adumbrates them; they include insight into Leslie Stephen's psyche, marriages, and professional roles as journalist, critic, and editor; and into the past family life as he saw and presented it to his family in this book after the death of Julia Duckworth Stephen in 1895, forty years before Virginia Stephen Woolf wrote *To the Lighthouse,* her version of the Stephen family. Bell has opted for a read-able rather than a scholarly edition, in that he has omitted 'the distracting cross-references to the volume of Extracts', which is an extant 'Calendar of Correspondence' prepared by Stephen; though both the cross-references and the calendar would have been welcome additions to this volume.

In *TLS* (16 Dec.) Alan Bell writes informatively, using unpublished writings, on Leslie Stephen and the *D.N.B.*, the inception of the *Dictionary* and Stephen's gruelling and eventually debilitating stint as editor, during which, his biographer tells us, 'He never complained; he swore'. A subtle reference to Plautus's *Aulularia* by Swinburne in *Under the Microscope* is identified in *VP* by Clyde K. Hyder who suggests that it illustrates the poet's intimate knowledge of the classics.

Diverse writings by Arthur Symons[92], largely on his contemporaries, have been painstakingly and usefully collected from recondite sources, about half unpublished; as a result we have between hard covers new material from Symonds on André Gide, Edmund Gosse, Toulouse-Lautrec, Herbert Horne, Oscar Wilde and Lillie Langtry, Jarry, Charles Condor the

[90] *Richard Simpson as Critic,* ed. by David Carroll. Routledge & Kegan Paul. The Routledge Critic Series. pp. x + 355. £9.50.
[91] *Sir Leslie Stephen's Mausoleum Book,* intro. by Alan Bell. Oxford: Clarendon P. pp. xxxi + 118. £4.25.
[92] *Memoirs of Arthur Symons. Life and Art in the 1890s,* ed. by Karl Beckson. University Park, Pa. and London: Pennsylvania State U.P. pp. x + 284. £10.15.

painter, and various music-hall and ballet girls, and more familiar material on Pater, Swinburne, Whistler, Beardsley, and Bernhardt. Beckson's introduction explains the complicated provenance of these *Memoirs,* some of which originated in a volume Symons prepared in the 1920s and 1930s but never published, and the full annotations include details of sources and allusions. Symons's reminiscences are always evocative and affectionate, without blunting their critical edge by nostalgia. This collection provides a detailed portrait of the artistic life at the turn of the century, and should become, like Holbrook Jackson's *The Eighteen Nineties,* a standard work for the study of the period.

Symons's seventeen music-hall poems written between 1891 and 1894 are somewhat dutifully described in the context of the nineties and Symons's position as music-hall critic by Earl F. Bargainnier in *Four Decades.* Kerry Powell understands Symons, in *The Symbolist Movement in Literature* (1899), the poems, and other essays, to use symbols to create illusion merely as escape, rather than to glimpse as Coleridge did, a transcendental order. That this is typical of the Decadents, Powell argues by brief allusions to Wilde, Huysmans, Dowson, and Johnson (*Renascence*).

(c) *Periodicals and history of publishing*

Sarah Freeman's biography of Isabella ('Mrs Beeton') and Sam Beeton[93] treats the childhood and upbringing of both figures, their life together as wife and husband and fellow publishers and journalists, and Sam's life after her death at twenty-eight. Sam Beeton founded and published the *English Woman's Domestic Magazine, The Queen,* and *Boy's Own Magazine,* and Isabella contributed a great deal to the first two; out of the first stemmed *Household Management,* which appeared in part issue and was compiled for the middle-class woman. The author examines Isabella's sources and methods, and observes the interesting and anomalous relation between family and professional roles in Mrs Beeton's life; she emerges as a working mother and as an equal partner in the family business. The considerable interest of this well written and researched volume lies equally in its account of the history of publishing and in the personality and situation of Isabella Beeton as a Victorian woman.

Associationist art criticism before 1850 is Helene Roberts's subject in *VPN*; she describes the ideas of Archibald Alison, its principal exponent in the field of fine arts; periodical articles of the period (including reviews of Alison), which served to define and disseminate it: and notions of associationist critics such as Francis Jeffrey, John Landseer on Turner, William Hazlitt, and Mrs Jameson, and of its opponents such as Thackeray, Ruskin, and George Stewart Mackenzie.

Noting that *Essays and Reviews* was conceived initially as a periodical, or one of a series of volumes, Josef L. Althoz suggests that consideration of it as a periodical illuminates aspects of its character and the reaction it provoked (*VPN*). Although the essays were signed, unlike many periodical articles of the day, the authors were held collectively responsible for the volume by the critics as though it had the monolithic character of a periodical without signature. Altholz goes on to examine the provenance

---

[93] *Isabella and Sam. The Story of Mrs Beeton,* by Sarah Freeman. Gollancz. pp. 336. £6.95

of this new kind of book in connection with the *Oxford and Cambridge Essays* and the *Westminster Review*, its reception, and the eventual liberation of the English essay from its long imprisonment by the periodical. This is a well-written, informative, subtle, and fascinating piece. In *N&Q* David R. Cheney corrects a misattribution of a poem 'Moonrise', in *Household Words*, thought by Anne Lohrli to be by Adelaide Anne Proctor but in fact by Edmund Ollier. The correspondence involved illustrates some of the contemporary problems of anonymity in the periodicals. The influence of the *Spectator*'s reviews on the early novels of Hardy is assessed carefully by Lawrence Jones. The comparison of the young author with George Eliot, which ranged from presumed debts to identification of the anonymous author of *Far From the Madding Crowd* as George Eliot, resulted in Hardy's renunciation of sheep and shepherds in *The Hand of Ethelberta* (*THY*, 1976). Joanne Shattock (*VPN*) investigates the making of editorial policy in the quarterlies in the 1840s and 50s through examination of practice in the *North British Review* under Alexander Fraser, editor from 1850, who throughout his editorship remained largely at the mercy of his various contributors. Expediency not policy ruled the day, and rather than 'tight little ships' the quarterlies should be regarded as collections of 'essays by divers hands', a significant conclusion that sits uneasily beside the assumptions of Altholz's piece. Were periodicals viewed as monolithic by mid-century readers?

Eloise M. Behnken briefly surveys the attitudes towards education of women in *The English Woman's Journal* (1858–63) in *BSUF*, while in an informative piece in *DSN* Dorothy Deering reveals how Dickens regularly used *Household Words* and *All the Year Round* as editor to shape attitudes towards the English language and to equip his middle-class readers linguistically for success. John Bush Jones surveys nineteenth-century printers' manuals in order to explore the extent to which printers used authors' indifference or expectation as a justification for assuming responsibility for accidentals rather than following the copy (*PBSA*). Jones's findings, that from 1808 arbitrary correction was resisted, contrast with those of John Thorpe in *Principles of Textual Criticism* (1972), and show at least that no satisfactory generalisations can be made on this matter. The publishing fortunes of the Mitchell family of Newcastle-upon-Tyne who created a weekly newspaper, the *Tyne Mercury* (1802–46), and a literary monthly, the *Newcastle Magazine* (from 1821), are described and assessed by Maurice Milne in *VPN*, and in the same journal David Roberts examines the social conscience of the *Quarterly*, *Blackwood's*, *Fraser's*, the *English Review*, *Oxford and Cambridge Review*, the *British Critic*, the *Christian Remembrancer*, and the *Dublin Magazine*, that is, the Tory periodicals of the 1840s. He argues that a group of sixty-nine named reviewers among those on which the periodicals drew for their articles commonly reflected the 'intellectual outlook and social ideas' of Burke, Scott, Coleridge, Wordsworth, and Southey. These ideas included approval of capital punishment, inequality, a feudal organic society, and eventually voluntarism; they viewed the Anglican Church as the agent of social change and education. But the '"true conservative principle" was "a *vis inertiae*"'. Roberts looks briefly at the class and occupation of the reviewers, who are from the upper classes and rurally educated, and attributes the appalling inadequacy of the Tory social conscience of the 1840s to the paternalist assumptions and borrowed rhetoric. This is a long and compressed article, uneven and inadequate in its treatment of a huge subject, but important nevertheless; it creates, in its cumulative catalogue of policies, a poignant background for the restraint of Dickens and Elizabeth Gaskell, and optimism of Disraeli in the forties and fifties. The fifth section of an article on press prosecution in the eighteenth and nineteenth centuries by Donald Thomas (*Lib*) includes instances involving Disraeli and Newman, both of whom were charged with criminal libel, and in *1837–1901* Ian Keil describes the brief life (October–December, 1876) of *Loughborough Home News and District Intelligencer,* a weekly intended for the newly literate, working-class reader, with its enclosed weekly magazine from London, *Hand and Heart,* which catered particularly for his family.

(d) *Visual art*

Vern G. Swanson's thorough and well-written study of Alma-Tadema and his work[94] is generously illustrated with black and white photographs on every page, and thirty-two large colour plates, so that the book serves as a valuable visual reference work as well as the most detailed monograph to date. Beside offering a full biography, Swanson writes on 'The Aesthetic Basis' of the work and on its 'Content and Style', and concludes with a brief estimate of the changing reputation of the painter between 1870 and 1977. This volume also includes a catalogue of Alma-Tadema's numbered works with location when known, and a full bibliography for further study.

Margaret Jones Bolsterli[95] suggests that the vision of community of the early inhabitants of Bedford Park and of Jonathan Carr, its builder, is part of the nineteenth-century genesis of the present-day notion of the suburban community. For this study of the history of culture, the author draws on the 'house' monthly, *The Bedford Park Gazette* (1883-4), the local press, various memoirs, and Moncure Conway's autobiography and pieces in *Harper's Magazine.* She considers the foundation and architecture, the shaping forces of community (a club, the church, the Chiswick School of Art, the artist residents), and its pursuit of 'corporate happiness'. The debate over women's rights in the community between 1882-4, the activities of the Calumet, a male conversation club, and the Dramatic Club to which W. B. Yeats and John Todhunter belonged provide real insight into this utopia of the middle class.

Mark Girouard's rich study of the 'Queen Anne' movement[96] has diverse interests: it is broad yet largely unsuperficial when it comes to architecture, though the first chapter giving the literary background to 'sweetness and light' is breezy to the point of inaccuracy in quotation and conception. The throwaway tone of too much of the prose throughout is offensive as is this description of Whistler's new independence of Rossetti who, 'busy doping himself to death with chloral at Kelmscott or Cheyne Row, was a spent force'. But the book is imaginatively and very generously illustrated, and the author's combination of learning, visual taste, and

[94]*Sir Lawrence Alma-Tadema,* by Vern G. Swanson. Ash & Grant. pp. 144. £3.95.

[95]*The Early Community at Bedford Park,* by Margaret Jones Bolsterli. Routledge. £7.50.

[96]*Sweetness and Light. The 'Queen Anne' Movement. 1860–1900,* by Mark Girouard. Oxford: Clarendon P. pp. xviii + 250. £15.

enthusiasm is evident in the organisation of the volume. He treats origins, the first buildings of the style in the sixties and early seventies, and some theories behind them; these, which stress stylistic continuity rather than divorce, the vernacular, and the notion of architects and house-buyer as artists, compare interestingly with some of the literature of the period. But the bulk of the work treats public buildings; domestic architecture by Shaw, Stevens and others and the interiors; Bedford Park and Tite Street, two Queen Anne communities; the style's shops, pubs, and seasides; and its form in America. This work thoroughly acquaints the reader with the eclectic language of the late nineteenth-century style.

(e) *Social history*

Dolf Sternberger's book[97], written in 1938, appears in English for the first time, with the subtitle 'How 19th Century Man Saw Himself and His World and How He Experienced History'. Sternberger, a political scientist, newspaper publisher, and a member of the German Academy, has written a series of historical essays which draw on European history, literature, and art. They are learned, leisurely, digressive, and the combination of such a method with relatively unfamiliar material results in a book whose perspectives are both strange and familiar — Sternberger's categories roughly coinciding with those of British and American literary and social histories but the manifestations of the categories being new. His 'aspects' include 'natural/artificial', trains and steamers, 'Genre', Evolution, 'The Higher', 'Inside the Home', and 'At Night'.

Portrait of An Age[98] appears in a new edition introduced and annotated by George Kitson Clark, with a biographical memoir by Sir George Clark. Young's work is particularly suitable for such an edition, as its many quotations and allusions were without references, and made *Portrait of an Age* inappropriate for students unacquainted with the period. The editor's notes occupy half the volume and provide background and full quotation where the text warrants it; they enhance the work through their corrections and framework, and increase its accessibility and value.

Oliver MacDonagh's well-written and well-conceived book is intended for undergraduates[99]. It is arranged topically, with chapters on factory legislation, coal mining, Poor Law, public health, Ireland, the Civil Service, and local government. This is useful for the student who goes to such a volume as background to a particular aspect of literature. Unlike a general history of the period, which offers a paragraph or even a few sentences on such topics, *Early Victorian Government* is comparatively full, with indication in notes and bibliography of where to pursue subjects further.

R. J. Morris uses the first cholera epidemic in Britain in 1832 as an historian's means of testing aspects of the working and quality of British society — its technology and resources, its administrative skills, its values and cohesion in the face of crisis and disaster[100]. His chapters on the approach and outbreak of the disease; the failure of containment; the

[97] *Panorama of the Nineteenth Century*, by Dolf Sternberger and transl. by Joachim Neugroschel. Oxford: Blackwell. Mole Editions. pp. 214. £10.

[98] *Portrait of an Age. Victorian England, by G. M. Young*, intro. and annotated by George Kitson Clark. O.U.P. pp. 423. £16.50.

[99] *Early Victorian Government. 1830–1870*, by Oliver Mac Donagh. Weidenfeld & Nicolson. pp. xii + 242. £6.95 and £3.75.

[100] *Cholera, 1832*, by R. J. Morris. Croom Helm. 1976. pp. 235. £7.50.

victims; class, power, and cholera; religion and morals; medicine and science; and the later epidemics, reflect this framework and provide an illuminating view of the society depicted in the works of Dickens and others.

David Philips probes the question of the relation between increasing industrialisation and increasing crime in a book on crime and authority in the Black Country[101]. He asks what sort of offences were increasing, how effective were the police, who were the offenders and their victims, and what were the motives of the offenders. He concludes that property offences rather than crime in general increased, but notes that what was criminal was what the authorities defined as criminal, and that the criminal Justice Act of 1855 made prosecution easier. Still very few violent crimes came to court, and public disorder, taken as a whole, never posed a serious threat to social order. This study is a statistical one, and for that reason it distances and minimises the experience of industrial unrest (which gave rise to, and perhaps grew out of fears of the middle classes), and perhaps usefully shows its comparative infrequency.

The Army in Victorian Society[102] is an intelligent social history which stresses the links between the character of the military establishment and its parent society, so that the reader, beside learning a great deal about army matters such as officer recruitment and the purchase system, also deepens her knowledge of more general aspects of Victorian society such as professional education, the search for professionalism, the notion of honour, and the impact of the defeat of the Army in South Africa. This book provides much pertinent information for readers of Henry Esmond, The Newcomes, and Maud, in as far as its sociological orientation touches on matters which concern Victorian authors as well as soldiers, and still engage their critics.

G. I. T. Machin's Politics and the Churches in Great Britain[103] is a scholarly work of substance in which the aspects of the Anglican clergy considered by Peter Hammond and Brenda Collom (below) appear in a wider context of church, state, and politics. The various ecclesiastical reforms and reactions to them, involving Irish Church Reform, Dissent, the Oxford Movement, the Church of Scotland, the Unitarians, Catholics, and Jews are treated chronologically, in conjunction with parliamentary disputes, pressure groups, and the attitudes of politicians and clerical spokesmen. The author makes use of manuscript material and contemporary sources, and the bibliography is full and useful.

Peter C. Hammond, himself a vicar, seems to conceive of his book on The Parson and the Victorian Parish[104] as an explanation of a system and a world for neophytes; beginning with the appointments of parsons through patronage, he goes on to describe Income, The Parsonage, The Church, The Sermon, The Dead, Visiting, Schools, The Wider Church,

---

[101] Crime and Authority in Victorian England. The Black Country. 1835-1860, by David Philips. London: Croom Helm, and Totowa, N.J.: Rowman & Littlefield. pp. 321. £8.50.
[102] The Army in Victorian Society, by Gwyn Harries-Jenkins. London: Routledge, and Toronto and Buffalo: U. of Toronto P. Studies in Social History. pp. xii + 320. £5.50.
[103] Politics and the Churches in Great Britain. 1832-1868. by G. I. T. Machin. Oxford: Clarendon P. pp. xii + 438. £15.
[104] The Parson and the Victorian Parish, by Peter C. Hammond. Hodder & Stoughton. pp. viii + 224. pb £3.50.

and the Secular World. This study, while straightforward, is not without colour and a certain stoical, wry pleasure in the human record. Brenda Colloms[105] portrays the Victorian country parson by accretion, through a series of descriptions of specific if representative Anglican parsons, including Patrick Bronte; John Mitford, a man of letters; William Barnes; Charles Tennyson Turner; Francis Kilvert; R. W. Dixon; and Baring-Gould, writer of 'Onward Christian Soldiers', and author. Two introductory chapters, containing the history of the status of parsons since Chaucer and shorter sketches of a mixed bag of clerics, provide a loose context for the biographies which follow.

For his monograph on Bentham's political thought[106] James Steintrager uses manuscript material as well as published works. He regards himself as a revisionist and defends the complexity and irreducible nature of Bentham's political thought by determining Bentham's understanding of events which shaped his thought and his manner of presentation. Steintrager begins with Bentham's concern with 'The Metaphysics of Jurisprudence', and chapters follow on the extent of his understanding of the obstacles to reform; polity and economy; the forces making Bentham a Democrat; and his eventual advocacy of radical, pure representative democracy. Steintrager is alive to the inadequacies of Bentham's position but sees too its strengths, and he is questioning and provocative.

J. B. Schneewind presents an historical study of Henry Sidgwick's *Methods of Ethics* (1874)[107], which was the first systematic attempt to answer important objections to utilitarianism. In the course of this careful and scholarly study, the author traces Sidgwick's intellectual development, and that of British ethics from Reid and Bentham to the writing of the *Methods;* Coleridge, Whewell, Grote, Godwin, and Mill figure in this first part as well as Reid and Bentham. A detailed interpretation of the *Methods* occupies the substantial second part of the volume; a third shorter part examines the influence of the *Methods* and its relation to Evolutionism and the Idealism of F. H. Bradley and T. H. Green, and takes a brief look as well at Sidgwick's later *Outline for the History of Ethics* (1878, 1886).

Popular Education and Socialization in the Nineteenth Century[108] is a collection of essays which explore how various types of elementary education prepared working-class children for life and labour in industrial capitalist society. Education is a prevalent theme in Victorian novels and part of the more general consciousness of the condition of England. Some of these articles reveal not surprisingly the political content of popular education and make pertinent background to the work of Henry Mayhew, Carlyle, Arnold, Newman, and Mill. The editor writes on 'Popular education, socialization and social control: Spitalfields 1812-1824' and J. M. Goldstrom on 'The content of education and the socialization of the working-class child 1830-1860'. Two other pieces on similar subjects are 'Ideology and the factory child: attitudes to half-time education' by

[105] *Victorian Country Parsons,* by Brenda Colloms. Constable. pp. 288. £6.50.
[106] *Bentham,* by James Steintrager. Allen & Unwin. Political Thinkers. pp. 133. £7.50.
[107] *Sidgwick's Ethics and Victorian Moral Philosophy,* by J. B. Schneewind. Oxford: Clarendon P. pp. xvi + 465. £17.50.
[108] *Popular Education and Socialization in the Nineteenth Century,* ed. by Phillip McCann. Methuen. pp. xii + 276. £6.90.

Harold Silver, and 'Socialization and the London School Board 1870–1904' by David Rubenstein. Attendance figures are studied by Beryl Madoc-Jones (in Mitcham 1830–39) and W. E. Marsden (Merseyside 1870–1900), and Simon Frith, J. S. Hurt, and Ronald K. Jones examine aspects of utilitarian notions of education in their respective 'Socialization and rational schooling . . . Leeds before 1870', 'Drill, discipline and the elementary school ethos', and 'Socialization and social science: Manchester Model Secular School 1854–1861'.

In *The Collier's Rant*[109] Robert Colls aims at a blend of labour and social history of the Newcastle colliery community which is exploratory and provocative rather than highly finished. Rejecting the methodology of the empiricist historian who tends to atomise society and treat its aspects in isolation and the Marxist who imposes his own class-consciousness on history and selects material accordingly, Colls uses popular songs and verse to get at a wider truth about miners' lives than either of the above methods allows. His readings, which rely heavily on assessments of myth, image, and reality in the texts, examine contemporary collections of songs and are of considerable interest to readers of any popular literature. It is of particular pertinence to the study of 'dialect' characterisation in novels and verse, and of the use of such popular songs by Elizabeth Gaskell, for example, in *Mary Barton*. This labour and social history is also a history and criticism of literature.

Four essays on nineteenth-century miners, quarrymen, and saltworkers[110] comprise the most recent volume in the History Workshop Series. Raphael Samuel writes on 'Mineral Workers' in general, Merfyn Jones on the slate quarrymen of North Wales, Brian Didsbury on the Cheshire saltworkers, and Dave Douglas on 'The Durham pitman' and on 'Pit talk in county Durham'; the method here is empiricist with emphasis for the most part on the workplace — trade unionism, job control, social relations at work, in the family, and in the community. This book provides details of the work process and conditions which constitute part of the 'condition of England' from the workers' perspective.

Frank E. Huggett's *Life Below Stairs*[111] is a serious and scholarly illustrated work on the neglected subject of domestic servants in Victorian and Edwardian Britain. It makes explicit and more general connections between factors which in the context of a novel often appear specific to character and plot. Thus the endangered morality of Jane Eyre after leaving Rochester emerges as not only specific to her character development and the novel's narrative, but as part of a common social phenomenon in which dismissed servants often experienced great hardship which sometimes ended in the brothel or the workhouse. Huggett does not himself discuss servants in literature, but this resourceful book offers the reader some knowledge with which to judge the kinds of truth represented by Dickens, Thackeray, and George Eliot, for example, in their portrayal

---

[109] *The Collier's Rant. Song and Culture in the Industrial Village*, by Robert Colls. London: Croom Helm, and Totowa, N.J.: Rowman & Littlefield. pp. 216. £6.50.

[110] *Miners, Quarrymen and Saltworkers*, ed. by Raphael Samuel. London and Boston: Routledge. History Workshop Series. pp. xvi + 363. £6.50.

[111] *Life Below Stairs. Domestic Servants in England from Victorian Times*, by Frank E. Huggett. John Murray. pp. 186. £4.95.

of servants. As Huggett contends 'The history of domestic service . . . must be concerned with masters and retainers as well as mistresses and maids and at a deeper level probes into the fundamental role of women in society'.

More than a third of *Biography of a Victorian Village*[112] is occupied by a generous introductory essay on the Victorian village, the Agrarian and industrial revolutions, and the life of the Rev Richard Cobbold whose verbal and visual account in 1860 of the houses, trades, neighbourhoods, and parishoners of Wortham, Suffolk follows in print for the first time. Both parts of this volume are valuable and concrete contributions to our understanding of rural life in mid-century.

G. E. Mingay surveys the developments of life in rural Victorian England through examining in a general way the various social groups of countrymen — landowners, farmers, labourers, industrial workers, professional people, tradesmen, and craftsmen[113]. Not for the specialist, *Rural Life in Victorian England* offers a readable general description of its subject based on standard sources for the most part. The final chapter, 'The End of the Old Order', makes a companion to Hardy's views of the significance of change, as does Geoffrey Robinson's book: *Hedingham Harvest*[114] is a personalised account of late Victorian rural life in northern Lincolnshire distilled from material related to the author by numerous relatives.

The Victorian Lady[115] is an attractively designed book with interesting plates and a slipcase; its text is informed without being scholarly or thorough, either in its use of material or in its choice of sources. It does not confine itself to High Society; the middle-class lady and working-class woman are much in evidence, if not the focus. The range of chapters — on education; getting married; marriage; childbearing and abortion; motherhood; the household; good works; the invalid; legal and economic status; work; piety; amusement; the lady traveller; costume; make-up, and hygiene — indicates the scope of this work, and, given its length, its limitations. It presents a readable overview of Victorian middle- and upper-class ladies, and one emerges with an outline of the subject but insufficient details of the sources of some of the most informative material. This volume has the air of a gift book for late twentieth-century ladies who prefer untaxing but not unintelligent reading.

Annual outings of one days's duration are Alan Delgado's brief[116], and railway and steamer excursions, the questions of the desecration of the Sabbath and of safety, the outing of the firm, and the children, the Sunday School trip, and the visit to an exhibition, the employer's house, the tattoo, or a picnic, are the nineteenth-century diversions considered.

[112] *The Biography of a Victorian Village,* by *Richard Cobbold,* ed. by Ronald Fletcher. Batsford. pp. 168. £5.50.

[113] *Rural Life in Victorian England,* by G. E. Mingay. Heinemann. pp. 212. £5.95.

[114] *Hedingham Harvest. Victorian Family Life in Rural England,* by Geoffrey Robinson. Constable. pp. 208. £5.50.

[115] *The Victorian Lady. Victorian High Society,* by Barbara Rees. London and N.Y.: Gordon and Cremonesi. pp. 164. £12.50.

[116] *The Annual Outing and Other Excursions,* by Alan Delgado. Allen & Unwin. pp. 173. £4.95.

A list of sources is supplied, although there are no notes to this text, which is clearly intended for the casual reader.

Time to Spare in Victorian England[117] is designed as an introduction to the leisure-revolution for general readers. The authors, who concentrate on developments in Sussex, note two important Victorian achievements – the acceptance of a clear cut distinction between work and leisure which is different from the exertion-repose concept before, and the development of a regular annual timetable of holidays and time off work. Chapters on the development of time to spare; seaside holidays, domestic entertainment in the older 'public' tradition of the country house and in the new notion of the privacy of the family; the pub; theatrical entertainments; music; elevating institutions; and physical recreation are supplemented by contemporary photographs of leisure activity in Sussex.

The unpleasantness of travel by railway before 1870 when even first-class carriages lacked sleeping and dining-cars, lavatories, corridors, and adequate light and heating, emerges vividly from Jeoffrey Spence's short introduction to 144 annotated photographs of Victorian and Edwardian trains, trainmen, stations, and passengers[118].

In 'Victoriana' (*CQ*), a review article, Laurence Lerner tries to determine the relation of literature to social history, and his remarks on critical method are of considerable moment as well as his judgements of the books under review. Dennis Smith provides a structural analysis of Francis Adams's *History of the Elementary School Contest in England* (1882), a work representative of the provincial Dissenters' advocacy of mass education for the working and middle classes against which Arnold directed bitter attacks. Taking issue with Terry Eagleton's notion of the resort of nineteenth-century bourgeois ideology to Romantic humanism typified in Arnold, Smith stresses the importance of religious modes of thinking, a latent structure of Adams's book which, as a whole, is also deeply anti-aristocratic and confident in the people, unlike Arnold (*PS*).

In *N&Q* David Rubenstein catalogues the activities of S. S. Buckman (1860–1929), the geologist, and Lady Harberton, in connection with the movement for rational dress in the 1890s, and discloses the contents of the S. S. Buckman papers, which include the complete run of the *Rational Dress Gazette* (1898–1900) and many accounts of cycling accidents. The Autumn number of *VS* is devoted to Victorian leisure. It includes articles on the problem of leisure for the middle class (Peter Bailey), women's recreational reading in the 1860s (Sally Mitchell), cycling in the same decade (David Rubenstein), mesmeric performers (Terry M. Parssinen), and Kingsley's fictional vision of the manly Christian as the fallen rather than successful, 'muscular' athlete. Peter Bailey's interesting introductory piece contends that while finding leisure irresistible the Victorian middle class regarded it as a 'dangerous frontier zone which outran the writ of established law and order'. Increased contact between classes in leisure pursuits gave rise to the repugnance of the middle class towards the pleasures of the populace, and it is in this context

---

[117] *Time to Spare in Victorian England*, by John Lowerson and John Myerscough. Hassocks, Sussex: Harvester. pp. viii + 151. £4.95.

[118] *Victorian and Edwardian Railway Travel*, intro. and compiled by Jeoffrey Spence. Batsford. 144 plates. £4.25.

that Bailey places Arnold's notion of that class. Recent writing on Victorian women is the subject of an informative and very wide-ranging review article in *VS* by Jill Roe who assesses the present state of methodology, topics, and interpretation in the field.

4. Drama

Some of this year's most valuable articles are of interest to students of the period generally as well as to drama-specialists. Two essays of this kind are included in *English Drama, Forms and Development: Essays in Honour of Muriel Clara Bradbrook*[119]. Gillian Beer considers 'Coming Wonders: uses of theatre in the Victorian novel', showing how some of the best novelists (James, Thackeray, Dickens and Charlotte Brontë) draw upon 'the ideal of performance to give them access to areas of human needs and behaviour which will not yield themselves to the more meditative processes of narration'. Beer writes clearly and sensitively on the way in which the novelists' treatment of the individual, the notion of 'life as a play', and role-playing is linked to manifestations of theatre.

In 'Social environment and theatrical environment: the case of English naturalism', Raymond Williams's stimulating and open-ended enquiry into why serious naturalism appeared so late and in such limited forms in England leads him to survey changing relations between society and drama in the nineteenth century. After defining one kind of naturalism as a form demonstrating 'the *production* of character or action by a powerful natural or social environment' and presenting 'a specific physical environment as symptomatic or causal', he moves on to the interaction of dramatic form, theatres, and audiences in the century as a whole. His enquiry leads him through the purely technical effects of naturalism in spectacular and 'lifelike' productions, types of mid-century radical melodrama, domestic naturalism (and its limited form in T. W. Robertson), and the later problem play where naturalism is muted and overlaid by the preoccupation with polite society. He concludes with an assessment of Shavian drama: 'It is unquestionably the most effective body of drama of the period, but it never attempted, in any sustained way, the specifically naturalist conjunction of philosophy and form, and it was supported in this by the reaction against naturalism which was already evident in the avant-garde theatre elsewhere.'

Kurt Tetzeli V. Rosador throws welcome light on 'Victorian Theories of Melodrama' (*Anglia*), theories which he finds to be 'descriptive, not normative; derived from theatrical practice, not from general principles'. However, a variety of obscure sources yield surprising consistency, and his survey covers the most important theoretical concerns — the hybridism of melodrama, its domestic and episodic 'situations', theatricality, reliance upon stereotypes, dream-character, and its amusement and escapist functions. Rosador's is a clear and helpful introduction which should be useful to all students of the period.

'The Victorian audience, like the world of Disraeli's novel, was also two nations, and it is now time that we accorded the second nation its

[119] *English Drama, Forms and Development: Essays in Honour of Muriel Clara Bradbrook*, ed. by Marie Axton and Raymond Williams. C.U.P. pp. x + 263. £7.50.

rightful place in theatre history', argues Michael R. Booth (*ThRl*). Pointing to the sheer bulk of East End theatrical entertainment in the mid-century, Booth discusses the composition and tastes of working-class audiences.

In 'Trouble Up at t'Mill: The Rise and Decline of the Factory Play in the 1830s and 1840s' (*VS*), Sally Vernon surveys the evolution of a small but significant body of plays which adapt the devices of domestic melodrama to deal popularly with factory conditions, industrial strife, the condition of the labouring poor, and the relationship between protest and crime. In some of these plays, and despite managerial caution and official censorship, there is a 'stark realism that compares well with and complements the rather different approach of the industrial novelists of the 1840s'. Two review-articles include a wider review of the period's drama and of the current state of research. In 'A Great Reckoning in a Little Room: *English Plays of the Nineteenth Century*' (*NCTR*), James Ellis discusses some general features of Victorian drama, including its pervasive domesticity, punning and word-play, the development of scenic and psychological realism. David Mayer points to areas of future research in 'Some Recent Writings on Victorian Theatre' (*VS*).

Victorian actors, actresses and acting-styles continue to be popular subjects, with a welcome emphasis in this year's articles on lesser known performers. Joanna Richardson's *Sarah Bernhardt and Her World*[120] recreates the legend of 'the queen of actresses' through a collection of photographs, posters and programmes. Her text extends the period atmosphere by being constructed around numerous eye-witness accounts and extracts from Bernhardt's memoirs. Yet it is difficult to respond freshly to memorabilia already over exposed, and Richardson's book differs very little from William Emboden's earlier pictorial album[121]. In *Fanny Kemble*[122], Dorothy Marshall follows Mrs Kemble's career as an actress, authoress and abolitionist against the background of nineteenth-century England and America. Though this study adds little to the factual knowledge of her life, it has the new interpretative emphasis given by the biographer's English perspective and her stress upon Fanny's English background. Detailed and well written, Marshall's work is a useful complement to Fanny Kemble Wister's *Fanny: the American Kemble* (1972).

Harold J. Nichols (*NCTR*) considers 'The Acting of Thomas Potter Cooke', one of the most popular melodramatic performers between 1820 and 1850. Nichols examines his melodramatic acting, the nautical roles which gained him the nickname of 'Sailor' Cooke, and the contemporary trends he represents — glorification of the British navy and the influence of a romantic aesthetic. An interesting article by David L. Rinear, 'From the Artificial towards the Real: The Acting of William Farren' (*TN*), sees Farren, the early Victorian comic performer, as a transitional figure in the movement from eighteenth-century artificial conventions towards more realistic styles of acting. In 'Helen Taylor's

[120] *Sarah Bernhardt and Her World,* by Joanna Richardson. Weidenfeld & Nicolson. pp. 232. £6.
[121] *Sarah Bernhardt,* by William Emboden, with an intro. by Sir John Gielgud. Studio Vista, 1974. pp. 176. £4.95.
[122] *Fanny Kemble,* by Dorothy Marshall. Weidenfeld & Nicolson, pp. vii + 280. £6.50.

"Experimental Life" on the Stage: 1856–58' (*NCTR*) Christopher Kent follows the career of John Stuart Mill's step-daughter, who was drawn to the stage as a way of satisfying her need for personal independence. Her letters reveal glimpses of the provincial theatre world of the 1850s and show the strained relationship between Helen and her mother, two of the century's most prominent feminists. Richard Foulkes writes on 'Helen Faucit and Ellen Terry as Portia' (*TN*), examining their contrasting performances and written views of the interpretative possibilities embodied in Portia.

Roy Busby's *British Music Hall: An Illustrated Who's Who from 1850 to the Present Day*[123] is a handsomely produced and illustrated guide to music hall performers, which is also more comprehensive and systematic than any of its predecessors. An introductory chapter sketches the evolution of music hall and the growth of London halls. Entries are clear, detailed and informative, much material having been culled from Victorian newspapers and journals. Graphics, chiefly in the form of signed photographs, give a pleasant period-flavour and offer an amusing visual reminder of long-forgotten speciality acts. The whole volume combines elegant memorial with substantial information.

In '"Disillusioned Bards and Despised Bohemians": Michael Field's *A Question of Memory* at the Independent Theatre Society' (*TN*), Jan McDonald examines letters and documents relating to a production of 1893. These documents reveal a good deal about the Society's practical problems at all levels and its day-to-day operations. Russell Jackson surveys in detail 'The Shakespearean Productions of Lewis Wingfield, 1883–90' (*TN*), examining Wingfield's work as an archaeological 'advisor'. In 'An American Actress at Balmoral' (*ThRI*), Michael Jamieson recreates a command performance before Queen Victoria at Balmoral in 1893, an occasion felt to be 'a significant step in the fashionable London actors' campaign for respectability and official recognition'. The play performed was *Diplomacy*, an adaptation of Sardou's *Dora*, and the cast contained some of the most skilled players of the day, including the American actress, Elizabeth Robins. In *NCTR* Richard Foulkes writes on connections between 'Samuel Phelps's *Pericles* and Layard's Discoveries at Nineveh'.

Dickens's interest in popular entertainments is reflected in two articles this year. In 'Charles Dickens and Shakespeare; or, The Irish Moor of Venice, *O'Thello*, with Music' (*The Dickensian*), Charles Haywood examines the surviving manuscript portion of Dickens's early Shakespearian burlesque, a portion which appears to constitute the whole of John Dickens's part as 'The Great Unpaid' (the Duke of Venice). The entire facsimile text in Dickens's numbered sequence is presented, then transcribed and re-arranged in acting sequence, with music and lyrics added. In *Dickens Studies Annual, Volume 5*, Joseph Butwin relates the world of Sleary's Horse-Riding in *Hard Times* to Dickens's ambivalent portrayal of clowns from the *Sketches by Boz* onward, noting Dickens's association of 'death and comic folly' and his fascination with the contrast between clownish mask and reality.

[123] *British Music Hall: An Illustrated Who's Who from 1850 to the Present Day*, by Roy Busby. Paul Elek, 1976. pp. 191. £12.50.

In his clear and balanced assessment of Wilde's plays[124], Alan Bird shifts attention away from the Wilde legend to emphasise his versatility and development as dramatist and serious man of the theatre. Bird considers Wilde's entire dramatic output, allowing a chapter to each play (its sources, performance, reception, and subsequent history), and concludes with a review of projects unfinished at Wilde's death. This is carried out with an admirable balance between text and theatrical context. There is a thorough analysis of the early plays in relation to Wilde's ambition to succeed in the 'literary' theatre of his day, and interesting claims are made for the artistic originality of *Salome*. Additionally, Bird's consideration of Wilde in relation to 1890s commercial theatre — its actors, staging, theatres, and audiences — leads to a careful description of the Wilde comedy in performance as a social and theatrical 'occasion'. Though claiming that Wilde's plots are 'less sentimental and more socially critical than is generally admitted', Bird emphasises 'the movement beyond plot as a restraint' towards an exclusively verbal drama which anticipates later developments.

Oscar Wilde: Two Approaches[125] brings together two papers read at a Clark Library seminar in 1976. In 'A Late Victorian Love Affair', Richard Ellmann traces the destructive course of Wilde's relationship with Lord Alfred Douglas, and explores the literary manifestations of the homosexual theme in the works of Wilde and others. John Espey outlines 'Resources for Wilde Studies at the Clark Library', with detailed consideration of textual problems associated with *The Picture of Dorian Gray*.

Christopher S. Nassaar writes on Wilde's influence in 'Vision of Evil: The Influence of Wilde's *Salome* on *Heart of Darkness* and *A Full Moon in March*' (*VN*), finding in Conrad's story 'largely a thematic repetition and partly a criticism of *Salome*', and in Yeats's play that *Salome* functions as the writer's 'antithetical Mask'. *ELT* contains two articles on Wilde's literary criticism: in 'Oscar Wilde, His Criticism and His Critics', Bruce Bashford considers the problems posed by Wilde's elaboration of 'a subjectivist perspective into a theory of criticism'; while George Stavros considers 'Oscar Wilde on the Romantics'.

---

[124] *The Plays of Oscar Wilde*, by Alan Bird. Vision Critical Studies Series, general ed. Anne Smith. Vision. pp. 220. £5.40.

[125] *Oscar Wilde: Two Approaches; Papers read at a Clark Library Seminar, April 17, 1976*, by Richard Ellmann and John Espey. William Andrews Clark Memorial Library, U. of California. pp. vii + 56. pb.

XVI

The Twentieth Century

MAUREEN MORAN, SUSAN PAINTER and
JAMES REDMOND

This chapter has the following sections: 1. The Novel, by Maureen Moran;
2. Verse, by Susan Painter; 3. Prose Drama, by James Redmond. The footnotes in section 3 deviate from normal *Year's Work* practice, and the
Editor will welcome readers' comments.

1. The Novel

This has been an excellent year for students of Joyce and Woolf, and in
addition there is some illuminating general work. Neglected figures, such
as Dorothy Richardson, are beginning to attract attention.

(a) General Studies

David Lodge's *The Modes of Modern Writing*[1] is an absorbing attempt
to discover 'a comprehensive typology of literary discourse . . . one capable of describing and discriminating between all types of text without
prejudging them'. To this end, Lodge opens his book with an examination
of the nature of literature and, more particularly, the nature of fiction.
A study of a variety of texts by George Orwell, Michael Lake, Oscar Wilde,
Arnold Bennett, and William Burroughs reveals that it is often difficult
to classify a modern literary work which is neither a wholly realistic
imitation of life nor a solely autonomous structuralist unit. What Lodge
desires is a synthesis of the realist and formalist approaches '– one which
is based on linguistic form but which is applicable both to literature
approached through its content and to literature considered in terms of
its form. The solution is revealed in the second part of this study when
Lodge discusses Roman Jakobson's distinction between metaphor (a
selection and substitution based on similarity) and metonymy ('a relationship of contiguity'). These terms may be applied to a study of literature
in general, for 'literature itself is metaphoric' (because interpreted) and
nonliterature is metonymic. Similarly, realistic fiction can be seen initially
as metonymic, although ultimately interpretation converts this illusory
'part of real history' into metaphor. The final part of this book is devoted
to an application of these distinctions to modern fiction and it is here that
Lodge is most persuasive in encouraging us to see the value of his typology.
The work of Joyce, for example, is shown to have a secure metonymic
basis, but the stylistic discriminations which Joyce makes between the
consciousness of, say, Stephen and that of Bloom may be more readily
understood when one perceives that Joyce is 'varying the proximity of

---

[1] *The Modes of Modern Writing: Metaphor, Metonymy, and the Typology of
Modern Literature*, by David Lodge. Edward Arnold. pp. xvi + 279. £9.50.

the discourse to the metaphoric and metonymic poles'. An extended analysis of 'England, My England' illustrates Lawrence's direction of an ostensibly metonymic text towards prophetic metaphor. Virginia Woolf's development towards a symbolic presentation of experience is also clearly related to the modernist tendency to move from the metonymic mode to the metaphoric. The works of Greene, Orwell, Isherwood, Waugh, and Larkin are treated in a similar way. This new typology begins to break down, however, when it is applied to the postmodernist fiction of writers like Beckett, Barth, Fowles, Pynchon, Robbe-Grillet, Nabokov, and Vonnegut. Such novelists use metaphoric and metonymic modes in radical ways, refusing 'to choose between these two principles of connecting one topic with another'. Yet Lodge provides a salutory warning for those who would extend the iconoclastic postmodernist experiment indefinitely. The metaphoric and metonymic forms are the central devices for imposing order on a text. Once fiction expels these, 'it would truly abolish itself, by destroying the norms against which we perceive its deviations'.

Keith M. May discovers similarities between fiction and psychology in the twentieth century[2]. Beginning with Hardy's examination of 'the burden of consciousness', the lack of freedom which man suffers because his finer conscious perceptions 'are disconnected from . . . the laws of Nature', May notes a growing interest among novelists and psychologists in the unconscious self and its influence on behaviour. In the early part of the twentieth century, Freud's conclusions about repressed instinctual drives and the 'non-rational' basis of our impulses and aspirations are reflected in the work of novelists such as Conrad, Kafka, Mann, and Joyce. But some novelists could not accept Freud's schema. Lawrence, for example, saw the unconscious as 'the "spontaneous life-motive"' which *defied* analysis and which should be allowed to assert itself. Indeed, Lawrence is much closer to Jung in his notion of the 'Self' 'as a mid-way point between consciousness and the unconsciousness'. True individuation is possible only if man is aware of 'his own "dark" aspects of Shadow and Anima' as well as his more accessible ego. This preoccupation with the unconscious gradually gives way to 'problems of personal identity' and perception as recorded in the work of Proust, Woolf, and neo-Freudians such as W. R. D. Fairbairn. Images are given to 'the core of selfhood' in an effort to stabilise a fluid consciousness in a shifting environment. Eventually, existentialists such as Sartre replace the unconscious by defining man 'in terms of what he wills for the future'. Hemingway's stoic hero is a direct expression of such an approach. May concludes with a succinct overview of current psychological notions of the self 'as whole, purposeful, and self-determining within the limits of natural law'. Some contemporary novelists respond to this new awareness by creating fantasy or by limiting themselves to a realistic treatment of 'the phenomenal world'. But the most truthful presentation of man in literature is that which is mid-way between these approaches. Iris Murdoch, Angus Wilson, and Bernard Malamud thus provide for May the most fruitful treatment of the modern theme of selfhood for they show man's relationship to nature through 'responsible self-choice and disinterested

[2] *Out of the Maelstrom: Psychology and the Novel in the Twentieth Century,* by Keith M. May. Paul Elek. pp. xvi + 135. £5.50.

personal perception'. By portraying 'the freedom of necessity', they most clearly capture the current response to the nature of man and his quest for self-liberation. May's book provides a useful and comprehensive analysis of modern psychological theories and their appearance in fiction. It is also worth noting that difficulties arising from attributions of direct influence are avoided, since May quite rightly feels that similar conclusions are often reached independently by novelists and psychologists in response to a changing environment. A valuable bibliography is included in this volume.

In *Linguistics and the Novel*[3] Roger Fowler argues convincingly that the linguistic techniques so important to modern novels can in fact be useful starting-places for interpretation and criticism. He detects a basic relationship between the structure of a sentence and the structure of a text. Since 'the elements of novels are structurally analogous to the components of sentences', it is possible to assert that 'the compositional structure of a novel is realized in, and can be studied in, the actual sentences of its linguistic surface'. In addition to outlining key linguistic structures and relationships, Fowler offers some practical criticism in terms of linguistic analysis by examining passages by a variety of writers including David Storey, D. H. Lawrence, George Eliot, Hemingway, Fielding, Dickens, Henry James, Joyce, Thackeray, Amis, Golding, and Christine Brooke-Rose. Novel criticism becomes a matter of decoding structural patterns; even creativity itself can be explained in terms of coding: 'The novelist needs to draw simultaneously on a vast battery of codes as s/he constructs the sentences which give shape to his or her ideas.' Such emphasis on coding and decoding does somewhat detract from the complexity of the imaginative process, but it is useful to be reminded that literary communication is indissolubly bound to 'the principles of structural organization which exist in the writer, the reader and the community'. There are good suggestions for further reading at the end of Fowler's volume.

Scott Sanders in *TCL* draws attention to a 'left-handed' trend in modern literature. This is a movement against the rational and towards the mythic, the religious, the occult, and the instinctive. Such a tendency is clearly 'a reaction against the social and cultural forms of a rationalized world'. In *GaR* Herbert N. Schneidau looks at the concern with style in modern writing and finds Joyce's case instructive. For Joyce a fact or detail or object may be expanded through an exploitation of 'stylistic potentialities' so that it takes on universal significance. Joyce is a 'preeminent' modernist for he uses style to transform daily reality into sacramental nourishment.

Some interesting thematic studies have emerged this year. In his examination of love in the novel from 1740 to 1940[4], A. O. J. Cockshut detects a new consciousness of sexual passion in twentieth-century literature. With the disappearance of Victorian conventions and complacencies, novelists applied the new desire for freedom to sexual morality. Writers like Olive Schreiner, Edith Ellis, and Havelock Ellis proclaimed new sexual

---

[3] *Linguistics and the Novel*, by Roger Fowler. New Accents Series. Methuen. pp. xiv + 145. hb £4.25, pb £2.
[4] *Man and Woman: A Study of Love and the Novel 1740-1940*, by A. O. J. Cockshut. Collins. pp. 221. £4.50.

doctrines, but it was Lawrence who truly developed 'the positive spiritual possibilities of the relations between the sexes'. Total sexual abandonment and licence were not the solution, but an intense relationship held the key to fulfilment. Cockshut also includes chapters on the homosexual and the lesbian in fiction. There is some attempt by Rolfe, Forster, and Hall to give homosexuality and lesbianism 'a spiritual dimension and religious sanctity'. Jeffrey Meyers also examines the portrayal of homosexuality in literature[5]. He touches on a number of modern novelists including Conrad, Forster, T. E. Lawrence, and D. H. Lawrence, and generally demonstrates a preference for the imaginative and ambiguous depiction of homosexual love over grosser, more explicit portrayals. In most cases the homosexual relationship is seen as unsatisfactory. In Conrad's *Victory*, for example, the homosexual character is isolated from life in an emotionally sterile existence. In Forster's novels, where homosexuality is, according to Meyers, a persistent theme, sterility and degradation are also inherent in the lives of homosexuals. For example, Rev. Beebe, a somewhat ambiguous character for Meyers, is ultimately seen as 'anti-vital'. Moreover, *Maurice*, Forster's justification of homosexual love, is judged a banal and artistically weak book. Meyers examines T. E. Lawrence's 'sexual pathology' in *Seven Pillars of Wisdom*, and finally moves on to the ambiguous treatment of homosexuality in the novels of D. H. Lawrence. Homosexual love in Lawrence is seen to grow out of frustrated heterosexual relationships, and Meyers claims that it is only when the male character achieves a sexual power that 'can dominate the woman at will that he loses his fear of woman and with it his need for homosexual love'. Meyer's approach is not really one of rigorous textual analysis; he has demonstrated an important theme for modern literature but more work must certainly be done, with particular reference to an author's portrayal of homosexuality.

Lars Hartveit[6] has chosen six novels to demonstrate the art of persuasion in fiction: *Pamela, Silas Marner, The Mayor of Casterbridge, A Passage to India, Brighton Rock,* and *A Clockwork Orange.* He suggests that all artists have strategies which shape and control the reader's response to the work. Forster, for example, maintains a complex and elusive design in *A Passage to India*. Negative and affirmative forces are juxtaposed in 'a dialectic pattern' which is revealed when language of reason and prophetic language exist together. The duality and ambiguity thus created reflect Forster's 'deeply disturbing, yet humane view of the human predicament'. The section on *Brighton Rock* is more unusual. Here Hartveit centres on the visual, documentary approach to narration which really depends on subtle, selective patterning by Greene. Metaphor, rather than direct, authorial comment, serves to guide the reader. *A Clockwork Orange* at first sight seems to lack effective controls on reader response to its nightmare vision. But Hartveit argues that careful narrative structuring enables us to see the human element in Alex. Indeed, an aesthetic value scale related to 'the aesthetics of form' replaces the ethical

    [5] *Homosexuality and Literature 1890–1930*, by Jeffrey Meyers. Athlone P. pp. vi + 183. £6.95.
    [6] *The Art of Persuasion: A Study of Six Novels*, by Lars Hartveit. Oslo: Universitets Forlaget. pp. 152. pb £6.

value system associated with real life. While Hartveit adds little that is radically new to our understanding of these novels, he modestly draws attention to the importance of form and language as 'persuasive elements' in fiction.

More stimulating is Robert Langbaum's *The Mysteries of Identity*[7]. Langbaum locates the modern element in literature in individual identity as it is treated by Wordsworth, Arnold, Eliot, Beckett, Yeats, and Lawrence. As confidence in society and in man's relationship with nature waned, there was a corresponding 'loss of confidence in the individual and individual effort'. Yeats and Lawrence tried to reconstruct the self; the former by reference to 'the religion of art', the latter by reference to 'the religion of love'. Langbaum's consideration of Lawrence is thoughtful and well-presented. Lawrence sought to recover the self by obliterating self-consciousness, the product of the divided self. Sexual relationships are a means of moving back to our real unconscious connection with the animate and inanimate worlds of being, but only if domination and exploitation are expunged. Indeed, it is a recognition of man's connection with the natural animal world which first aids in the movement to unconsciousness, as Lawrence's poetry suggests. Once such a state is realised, Lawrence moves imagistically from animals to gods, indicating the new 'human individuality' which awaits his characters. Langbaum thus identifies a basic pattern of rebirth 'through connection with a more primitive mode of existence' to an 'impersonal phase of identity' where a personal relationship can be 'sealed'. For Lawrence, identity is not a question of consciousness or unconsciousness, but of 'a reciprocal flow' between these two states, 'a sexuality that heightens consciousness all over the body'. The chapters on *The Rainbow* and *Women in Love* are particularly useful. Ultimately, Langbaum argues, love for Lawrence is a 'self-creating' activity, and the realisation of identity is a continuing 'transformation of unconsciousness into consciousness involv[ing] a return to the matrix from which our individuality emerges so that we remake our individuality'.

John Alcorn and Glen Cavaliero both consider aspects of the natural world in modern fiction. In *The Nature Novel from Hardy to Lawrence*[8] John Alcorn defines a theme and technique – the 'naturist' tradition – which developed from Hardy and culminated in Lawrence. Instinct, 'sexual liberation', and 'a world of physical organism' were set up in opposition to 'Christian dogma', 'abstractions', and the ethics of commercial society. Technically, these new preoccupations were reflected in 'a loose plot structure, built around an elaborately described landscape'. Hardy initiated the trend by his presentation of a new relationship between character and landscape. In this world 'subconscious forces' took the lead, and erotic and sensual metaphors suggested man's oneness with the lower orders of the natural world. The concrete, natural, and spontaneous became superior to the conventional and abstract. In addition a concern with place symbolised 'the hope of building a society more responsive to human nature'. Alcorn shows how a new generation of writers developed from Hardy's

[7] *The Mysteries of Identity: A Theme in Modern Literature*, by Robert Langbaum. O.U.P. pp. xii + 383. £8.50.
[8] *The Nature Novel from Hardy to Lawrence*, by John Alcorn. New York: Columbia U.P., and London: Macmillan. pp. x + 139. £7.95.

position. These naturist authors wished to depict that neglected aspect of man which connects him to the physical world. To accomplish this end, they utilised a language which identified 'human emotions and attitudes' with elements in the natural world. Such interest in the natural world related to man and the accompanying sense of a 'spirit of place' led to a number of travel books which used place and nature as 'a literary means of probing into non-conceptual and instinctive areas of human experience'. Travel writers like Norman Douglas, W. H. Hudson, and H. M. Tomlinson eschewed a mechanical cause and effect narration for a 'sub-rational narrative sequence'. This tradition influenced Lawrence who also fought against destructive causality and scientific determinism; he wanted instead to forge a new link between landscape and eros which would show human communication to be rooted 'not in conscious spiritual "meanings", but in unconscious physical organism'. New Criticism which valued art more than life, and existentialism which saw absurdity everywhere, put an effective end to this naturist tradition, but Alcorn in his business-like way, calls for its return if the vitality of English fiction is to be renewed. This study is an intelligent and illuminating work.

Glen Cavaliero[9] argues for the intrinsic merit of novels about country life in the early decades of the twentieth century. Rural fiction from 1900 to 1939 showed a distinct development from romanticised nostalgia, rural fantasies, and the cult of the primitive peasant to the awareness of specific regions, the battle against industrialism, and the realistic and practical treatment of country life. The relationship between man and nature became increasingly important so that the solitary rural experience was eventually viewed as a means to heightened spiritual awareness. Despite Cavaliero's painstaking thoroughness in dealing with this rural tradition, he fails to convince that there is much literary merit inherent in its products. With the possible exceptions of Constance Holme and T. F. Powys, few rural writers considered here rise above the narrowly provincial and some seem very simplistic indeed. These writers may bear consideration for historical reasons since to some extent they reveal social and artistic tastes and trends; but they have no profound vision to offer the contemporary reader on the matter of social change and man's true relationship to the natural world.

Social and political concerns in the novel are also subjects for several general studies this year. John Atkins[10] provides an analysis of Elizabeth Bowen, L. P. Hartley, Rosamond Lehmann, Christopher Isherwood, Nancy Mitford, and C. P. Snow with special reference to the 'social milieu' which interests each writer and to the criticism which each offers concerning English society. This is a disappointing study, however. Little new insight into the work of these writers is tendered, and at times the book develops into a non-literary compendium of class attitudes or − as is the case with Isherwood − a consideration of a novelist's own psychological and social development. Atkins concludes that these essentially middle-

[9] *The Rural Tradition in the English Novel 1900–1939*, by Glen Cavaliero. Macmillan. pp. xiv + 240. £8.95.

[10] *Six Novelists Look at Society: An Enquiry into the Social Views of Elizabeth Bowen, L. P. Hartley, Rosamond Lehmann, Christopher Isherwood, Nancy Mitford, C. P. Snow*, by John Atkins. John Calder. pp. 284. £6.95.

class novelists have been conditioned by their background to ignore the working classes. Nevertheless, all see that something is wrong with the basic inegalitarian nature of English society.

J. A. Morris, on the other hand, provides a much more coherent and entertaining assessment of the effect of political commitment (or lack of it) on literature in the twentieth century[11]. Morris detects a three-stage movement from 1880 to 1950. The social malaise of the late nineteenth century led to an increasing *'stylistic* awareness of social and political realities'. There was a marked trend toward realism (as in the work of Bennett, Galsworthy, and Orwell) which paralleled a heightened social awareness. Such realism could even prevent sentimentality; Morris points to Robert Tressell's *The Ragged Trousered Philanthropists* as a case in point. Political commitment and idealism began to replace religious fervour and writers of the Left and of the Right began to emerge. Moreover, style and ideology were firmly linked. Literary and political innovation can be detected for example in the Auden - Spender — Day Lewis group. But after 1939, a gradual dissociation of politics and literature accompanied a general air of disillusionment. Inner debate rather than 'direct participation' became the norm, and more abstruse literary modes such as allegory, anti-utopias, and fable were popularised by Huxley, Orwell, and Golding among others. Modern society seemed to promise a total absorption by the totalitarian state: 'the flight from commitment left an inspirational vacuum which has been filled by uncertain views of the kind of society which comforts and titillates but does not civilize, and which menaces by its size and its systematization of mankind.'

Two studies of the colonial experience have appeared. D. C. R. A. Goonetilleke's *Developing Countries in British Fiction*[12] establishes that much English fiction set in developing countries has universal implications as well as 'local' significance. Conrad, for example, uses these far-away countries as testing grounds for his characters and their moral values. While his work is marred at times by conventional prejudice, he is sympathetic to races exploited by imperialism. Nevertheless, his work transcends the political to encompass the personal and the universal dilemmas of experience. Kipling is viewed predictably as an imperialist in his attitude to India. Forster is portrayed more sympathetically for in *A Passage to India* he saw the need for change in that country, but in Goonetilleke's opinion his depiction of Indian social complexities is sadly oversimplified. Lawrence's attitude to emerging countries is related to his cultural primitivism which sought vitality unmarred by the destructive forces of civilisation. Joyce Cary is praised for his 'lucid, concrete and assured' presentation of African realities but must ultimately be censured for his paternalism. In his over-all approach Goonetilleke admittedly seeks out social attitudes by examining literary qualities but his conclusion reveals that his major concern is with the authenticity of portrayal: 'whether or not a writer, in presenting the country in his work, develops the perspectives proved (or being proved) right by history,

[11] *Writers and Politics in Modern Britain (1880-1950)*, by J. A. Morris. Hodder & Stoughton. pp. vii + 109. pb £1.75.
[12] *Developing Countries in British Fiction*, by D. C. R. A. Goonetilleke. Macmillan. pp. x + 282. £8.95.

is usually a sign of the degree of success or of failure of his art'. M. M. Mahood has a twofold purpose in *The Colonial Encounter*[13]. She wishes to compare novels from different cultures to show that 'we do not need to change our criteria in approaching Third World novels' and she also hopes to contrast treatments of 'the experience of colonial rule and its aftermath'. Six novels are examined in a lively way with emphasis on form: *Heart of Darkness, Arrow of God, A Passage to India, The Man-Eater of Malgudi, The Comedians,* and *The Mimic Men.* The ambiguities of Conrad's novel are well presented as are the mythic and satiric elements in Narayan's work. Naipaul's skilful rendering of a narrator in the process of creation is discussed in an illuminating way, but the analyses of *A Passage to India* and *The Comedians* are rather ordinary and the consideration of Achebe's novel is somewhat scientific and anthropological in its approach. Mahood concludes that all six novelists — be they expatriate or indigenous — 'see the colonial encounter as a painful disruption', and she provides a timely reminder that these novelists have the political courage to sympathise with the exploited. Colonialism is not simply used as a metaphoric vehicle for self-exploration.

Mosaic issued a special number entitled 'Faerie, Fantasy and Pseudo-mediaevalia in Twentieth-Century Literature', and it contains a number of essays pertinent to modern fiction. Frank Bergmann notes the influence of George MacDonald and the German romantics — Friedrich de la Motte Fouqué, E. T. A. Hoffmann, and Novalis — on Tolkien's essay 'On Fairy-Stories'. While all insist on the 'transcendental' element in fairy-tales, Tolkien goes further by seeing the myth-maker as an active 'sub-creator'. Anthony Ugolnik develops this notion of the myth-making artist, and relates Tolkien's Secondary World to his linguistic aesthetic which is 'based upon the song and reflects a medieval consciousness of language'. John K. Crane closely examines T. H. White's *Mistress Masham's Repose, The Godstone and the Blackymor,* and *The Elephant and the Kangaroo.* He finds that White writes fantasies of the here and now so that his vision may be more readily applied to reality. The ways in which White used the Arthurian legend and made it his own are considered by François Gallix, and Colin N. Manlove writes on key themes in *The Once and Future King.* Tensions between realism and idealism in White's own vision are revealed in the conflict between straight narration and moral-ising; also the movement towards life is counteracted by an apparent fascination with death. The importance of 'personality' and 'apex-thought' to Powys's *The Complex Vision* is revealed by G. Wilson Knight, elements of wit and ingenuity in the unsophisticated fantasy of E. Nesbit are discussed by Colin N. Manlove, and Ursula Le Guin's iconoclastic and gloomy *Earthsea* trilogy is viewed by T. A. Shippey as 'a parable for our times'.

A number of memoirs and period studies have provided some fascin-ating insights into twentieth-century literature. Wendy Baron has produced a most interesting biography of Ethel Sands, the expatriate American painter[14]. This book, based on Ethel Sands's largely unpublished letters,

[13] *The Colonial Encounter: A Reading of Six Novels,* by M. M. Mahood. Rex Collings, pp. viii + 211. £4.75.
[14] *Miss Ethel Sands and Her Circle,* by Wendy Baron. Peter Owen, pp. xx + 300. £8.50.

reveals her as a 'hostess of genius' with important links in Chelsea and Bloomsbury. An energetic woman with a great zest for life, Ethel Sands played a significant role in the cultural life of London early in this century. She knew James, Fry, Yeats, Moore, Strachey, Stein, Bennett, Virginia Woolf, and Vanessa Bell among many others and was often instrumental in introoducing these figures to each other. Although the biography does become a jumble of comings and goings towards the end, it is a particularly detailed and astute assessment of the London artistic and cultural world in the early twentieth century.

Martin Green's lengthy study of post-1918 decadence[15] promises much. It is to be, he suggests, an analysis of a particular 'imaginative temperament' which arose in reaction to the pre-World War One life of action in which men were required to be 'fathers – husbands – masters'. Disillusionment with such ideals and with the value system which had tolerated, even encouraged, the War, gave way to a decadent fascination with idleness, fashion, gossip – to 'a preliminary period of genial anarchy'. Green identifies three major manifestations of this cultural movement – 'the dandy', 'the rogue', and 'the naif'. However, once this identification has been made, the book becomes little more than a parade of names, with brief biographical snippets and some superficial glances at the literary productions of these decadents. Green's major concern is with behaviour, sexual and otherwise, but even a partial list of the figures he discusses – Buchan, Moore, Douglas, Firbank, Huxley, Greene, Waugh, and Isherwood – suggests the rich field for literary consideration which awaits the rigorous and dedicated critic. The study ends with the rise of 'an anti-dandy centre' in English imaginative life and the increasing influence of Orwell, Leavis, Amis, and Wain. Even so, Green admits that in these later years distinctions are more difficult to draw for the anti-dandy of one moment becomes the dandy of the next.

William H. Pritchard intends his survey of English writing between the wars[16] as an introduction to a number of works with no particular 'over-arching idea'. Yeats, Joyce, and Pound are excluded from this survey on the grounds that they dwelt not in England but in 'the realm of myth and heroic literature'. Instead, Pritchard looks at the writing of Lawrence, Lewis, Bennett, Huxley, Waugh, Orwell, Powell, and Greene among others with the hope that he can recapture the experience of reading these works. The specific commentaries on novelists are neither detailed nor profound. Pritchard does draw attention to works which he feels are unjustly neglected, such as Huxley's early novels and Lewis's *Tarr*, but he is inclined to single out great moments in the fiction or make rather general comments about the relative merit of the novel in question. The book is helpful in reminding one of the great variety of fictional modes operating in this period – fantasy, satire, moralism – but as an introduction to the main themes and techniques of a number of novelists it is rather weak and unspecific. Some assessment of the quality of a novelist's informing idea is attempted, but too often the flippant comment suffices for specific analysis tied to the text. Pritchard criticises Lawrence, for instance,

[15] *Children of the Sun: A narrative of 'decadence' in England after 1918*, by Martin Green. Constable. pp. 552. £7.50.
[16] *Seeing Through Everything: English Writers 1918-1940*, by William H. Pritchard. Faber & Faber. pp. 234. £5.95.

noting that 'his fervent self-righteousness in the great cause makes us want to pick holes in his vision'.

The National Book League has produced a catalogue[17] to accompany its 1976 exhibit on the Bloomsbury Group. Quentin Bell supplies a concise introduction noting the main interests of the exhibition: the relationship of the Bloomsbury movement to Post Impressionism and the portrayal of 'the point at which the visual aesthetic of the group meets that literary form through which it is most commonly approached'. Each section of the Catalogue is prefaced by a brief and helpful note; some literary texts, paintings, sketches, and photographs are reproduced; and notes of a biographical nature are appended to catalogue entries where appropriate. The exhibition devoted sections to a number of artists and writers, including Duncan Grant and Vanessa Bell, Lytton Strachey, and Leonard and Virginia Woolf (and the Hogarth Press).

Derek Stanford's memoirs[18] of literary life from 1937 to 1957 in England form not only an attractive personal history but the story of the rise and fall of a literary generation and a literary tradition, for this volume is primarily a survey of the 'neo-romantic period'. In addition to recalling his own encounters with figures like Christopher Fry, Muriel Spark, Herbert Read, Dylan Thomas, John Heath-Stubbs, and Roy Campbell, Stanford also charts the rise of small artistic groups which combined 'revolution and aestheticism' as a reaction against philistinism, Marxist aesthetics, and social realism. With the publication of *The New Apocalypse* an alternative to the Auden-Spender-Day Lewis group became a possibility. Emphasis was placed on a 'sense of the organic world' and the neo-romantics soon formed a recognisable literary group. The influence of little magazines and anthologies on the literary directions of the time is also suggested by interesting portraits of Tambimuttu and Charles Wrey Gardiner. Although much of Stanford's interest lies with poetry, this is a useful book for anyone wishing an account of literary impulses during and after the Second World War.

In *Under Siege*[19] Robert Hewison investigates the effect of the Second World War on cultural life in Great Britain. The physical difficulties involved in artistic activities such as book production are well detailed. More importantly, Hewison gives a thorough account of the emotional response to the war and how the alternating moods of depression and exhilaration affected writers and readers alike. He touches briefly on Blitz fiction by novelists giving vent to intense feelings (William Sansom, James Hanley, Robert Greenwood, Elizabeth Bowen) and then examines the problems encountered by writers in the Services, considering poetry from the Forces in some detail. Hewison detects a general shift in prose writing from documentary realism to inner reflection and nostalgia. Evelyn Waugh is a good example. A similar movement can be seen in poetry where 'a return to the spiritual and cultural values that had been crushed by the

[17] *The Word and The Image VII: The Bloomsbury Group*. The National Book League in association with The Hogarth Press. pp. 38 + 16 plates. 1976. pb £2.
[18] *Inside the Forties: Literary Memoirs 1937-1957*, by Derek Stanford. Sidgwick & Jackson. pp. viii + 242. £6.95.
[19] *Under Siege: Literary Life in London 1939-1945*, by Robert Hewison. Weidenfeld & Nicolson. pp. x + 219. £6.

mass-mobilization of society' is advocated by the neo-romantics and an imagistic portrayal of personal feeling is urged by the apocalyptics. Short sections on art, painting, music, and the theatre round out the survey. A very clumsy and imprecise system of notes which leaves some quotations unidentified mars this otherwise revealing work.

Robert Martin Adams[20] writes briskly on new trends in fiction in the post-Joycean age. He feels that many novelists after Joyce either react against his work or demonstrate his influence. Adams begins his study by making a number of generalisations about Joycean fiction with its disregard for plot and new concern with process and 'psychological inwardness'. He traces the reception of Joyce's work and the growing awareness that Joyce was a novelist who had true depth, true awareness of 'the visionary substructure of human life'. Adams suggests that various patterns and structures used by Joyce to achieve this depth are employed by many of his successors. Eliot, Updike, Robbe-Grillet, Murdoch, and Nabokov freely use myth and paradigmatic devices. Equivocation, encyclopaedic details, and minimalist fiction as employed by Beckett and Borges all have roots in Joyce's novels. But it is in the realm of language that Joyce's greatest influence can be felt. Virginia Woolf's use of the inner monologue to suggest the texture of experience makes *Between the Acts* the 'most essentially Joycean' of her books. Nabokov, Faulkner, Gadda, Broch, and Döblin also reveal verbal similarities to Joyce. Beckett is investigated as another experimenter with language, but whereas Joyce aimed for the comprehension of infinity, Beckett strives to deprive language of its resources in order to reach 'the absolute zero of non-experience'. 'Fringe-Joyceans' like Burgess, Durrell, Pynchon, Barth, and O'Brien are also cited as bearing Joyce's stamp in various ways. Although this is a book of discussion and suggestion rather than analysis and commentary, Adams's conclusion is convincing. Joyce is viewed as a renewer of language, and *Ulysses* is seen as a twentieth-century landmark because it 'constantly invited the reader to look under or behind the surface'.

Married to Genius[21] is a biographical assessment of 'the relation between emotional and artistic commitment in the marriage of nine modern writers: Tolstoy, Shaw, Conrad, Joyce, Virginia Woolf, Katherine Mansfield, D. H. Lawrence, Hemingway, and Fitzgerald'. Despite this claim by Jeffrey Meyers, his book adds little to our appreciation of the fiction or to our understanding of the creative impulse behind it. His main theory is that an artist creates from life; the novelists considered 'used their personal experience in marriage for the themes and characters of their fiction'. Each chapter of this work thus becomes a biography of a marriage with reference to the literature to corroborate attitudes and observations. Meyers questionably assumes the autobiographical nature of works like *Ulysses* and *The Secret Agent* and uses the novels to reveal his subject's opinions on marriage, love, and personal relationships. Banal literary and psychological observations are the result. Interesting use is made of letters and diaries in order to produce readable biography, but

[20] *Afterjoyce: Studies in Fiction After Ulysses*, by Robert Martin Adams. New York: O.U.P. pp. xiv + 201. $10.
[21] *Married to Genius*, by Jeffrey Meyers. London Magazine Editions. pp. 214. £5.75.

there is little regard for the imaginative process which transmutes life into art.

Fiction written in English but produced outside Britain continues to be of interest. Shatto Arthur Gakwandi[22] attempts to assess 'the major concerns of African fiction' as well as the African response to the West. He provides succinct literary analyses of major African novels by Ferdinand Oyono, Alex La Guma, Chinua Achebe, Mongo Beti, Peter Abrahams, T. M. Aluko, Wole Soyinka, Ayi Kwei Armah, Cameron Duodu, Ngugi, and Sembene Ousmane. While these novelists all deal with different situations in different ways, there is an overriding concern with the colonial experience and the problems of contemporary society once colonialism has been abolished. The main mode adopted — that of 'social realism' — demonstrates the influence of European fiction on African writing. Gakwandi concludes that the novel form satisfies a need in African writers to 'search for the basis of a sense of community'. Only the novel 'can evoke the whole way of life of a people at a given time'. Dennis Duerden[23] explores the roots and relationship of pre-industrial African art and modern African literature. Myth and ritual and the conflicts inherent in power distribution (priest, king, and elders) form central concerns for writers like Achebe and Elechi Amadi. The essential dualism in African society — the tension between the desire of the individual for self-expression and the need to conform to the community — is captured in African fiction, drama, and poetry. Old forms and techniques from oral literature are adapted by sophisticated writers like Khadambi Asalache as a means of defining self and the relationship to the group. In fact both literary works and visual art tend to the making of 'oneself visible'.

Jane Lagoudis Pinchin's *Alexandria Still*[24] is a densely-written examination of the influence of Alexandria and Cavafy on Forster and Durrell. Pinchin begins with a sensitive introductory chapter on the city itself and attempts to capture something of that mysterious essence of place which appealed to the three writers under discussion. The section on Cavafy's relationship to Alexandria centres on his historical and love poems which stir a sense of 'our communal past' as well as on Cavafy's links with the Hellenistic tradition. In Forster's *Alexandria* Pinchin sees 'religion, love, and the relationship between East and West'. Homosexual, Hellenistic, and sensual elements link Forster to Cavafy together with 'a delicate irony' which makes 'larger historical and social pulls seem truly subordinate to the personal'. Indeed, Forster's changing attitude to history and Hellenism stems largely from his contact with Cavafy and Alexandria. Similar creative techniques in the treatment of 'history and fiction' with emphasis on character also show the sensibility shared by Forster and Cavafy. Durrell's Alexandria is an altogether shabbier and harsher place. Like Cavafy, Durrell uses historical figures to give credibility to imaginary

[22] *The Novel and Contemporary Experience in Africa*, by Shatto Arthur Gakwandi. Heinemann. pp. iv + 136. pb £1.90.

[23] *African Art & Literature: The Invisible Present*, by Dennis Duerden. Heinemann. pp. xiv + 169. £4.95.

[24] *Alexandria Still: Forster, Durrell, and Cavafy*, by Jane Lagoudis Pinchin. Princeton Essays in Literature Series. Princeton, N.J.: Princeton U.P. pp. xiv + 245. £10.20.

characters, but there is a basic difference in his conception of the hero. For Cavafy the hero is a man like all others; for Durrell, the artist is a hero whose struggles with life have an epic proportion. Consequently, Durrell sees the artist as a promising figure of affirmation and healing. There is a good account of echoes of Cavafian poems in *The Alexandria Quartet* and a thoughtful indication of the subtle influence of Cavafy's 'sense of loss' on Durrell's writing. While this is not really a thorough comparative study, the work on Durrell and Cavafy is illuminating. Two appendixes deal with the history of the translation of Cavafy's poems and the chronology of *A Passage to India*. There is an extensive selected bibliography.

In *Meanjin Quarterly* Michael Cotter looks at the response to Aboriginal life in Thomas Keneally's *The Chant of Jimmie Blacksmith*, Randolph Stow's *To the Islands*, and Patrick White's *Riders in the Chariot*. All are attracted by the 'organic' nature of Aboriginal cosmogony. *ArielE* has produced a Caribbean Literature number. Frank Birbalsingh demonstrates that Samuel Selvon's *A Brighter Sun* virtually created a new West Indian literary renaissance despite the repetititve themes and treatment in later Selvon novels. Edward Baugh argues that the preparation of the cuckoo meal in *In the Castle of My Skin* is a symbol 'of the deep and secret moral and spiritual strength of the people' because it embodies the main values of the island — 'tradition, community, self-respect, creativity and work'. Mythological elements in the drama of Derek Walcott are examined by Robert D. Hamner, and Wilson Harris's latest fiction is analysed by Hena Maes-Jelinek: Harris uses painting as a metaphor for vision both of 'man's fall and fear of extinction' and also of 'resurrection and survival'. John Thieme investigates the 'psychic division' of characters in Garth St Omer's fiction. 'Inner awareness' yields only 'anguished emancipation'. Jean Rhys is the subject of two concise essays. Michael Thorpe shows that Rhys uses and transcends elements of *Jane Eyre* in *Wide Sargasso Sea* to present 'a many-sided and complete study of tragic incompatibilities'. In some ways Rhys's novel serves as a subtle commentary 'on the short-comings of *Jane Eyre*'. Louis James considers Rhys's output as a writer about the Caribbean. In her work there is a deepening response to the West Indian dilemma. Finally, Anthony Boxill considers some of the European sources for V. S. Naipaul's work and concludes that Naipaul is not really a part of either the European or the Indian literary tradition. His is a West Indian tradition all its own, although his portrayal of West Indian problems has a universal appeal and application.

Ann Boutelle in *DR* notes the many conscious and unconscious allusions to Dorian Gray in Canadian fiction, although she can offer no satisfying reason for this occurrence. Also in *DR* Nancy W. Fraser examines the development of realism in Canadian literature of the 1920s. Realism was useful in defining the Canadian consciousness and in recording man's response to his environment. Gradually, a sense of belonging emerges. Patrick Monk offers some lively observations in *ArielE* on the use of Africa in the fiction of Dave Godfrey, Audrey Thomas, and Margaret Laurence. Africa serves as a Jungian 'Shadow' of Canada, giving Canadians an ancestry with humankind and delineating aspects of fertility and sexuality repressed in Canadian experience.

Andrew Carpenter[25] has collected some illuminating papers from the 1976 conference of the International Association for the Study of Anglo-Irish Literature. A. Norman Jeffares offers some suggestions on the ways in which Anglo-Irish writers (Swift, Goldsmith, Maturin, Yeats, Cary, and Moore for example) have responded to 'the physical entity of Ireland'. Often Ireland is used romantically; sometimes it provides a symbolic escape to a timeless, visionary realm. It may be employed as a contrast to human behaviour or as a reminder of an earlier heroic age. Robert O'Driscoll looks at some of the key ideals of the Celtic Literary Revival, and F. S. Lyons argues that the myth of Parnell often serves a complex function in works by Yeats, Joyce, Moore, O'Faoláin, O'Connor, and O'Casey. The legendary Parnell serves as a 'Messianic symbol', a 'touch-stone for various kinds of disenchantment', or an image of betrayal. Ann Saddlemyer believes that Synge's heightened sensuous response to Ireland is linked to his awareness of the infinite in man and nature. Richard Wall draws attention to Joyce's use of Anglo-Irish dialect to avoid limitations in the English language, to add an 'Irish ethos' to his work, to 'multiply the meaning of the text', and to convey 'comic tone'. Brian Coffey considers Denis Devlin as a poet of distance, and Michael R. Booth writes on 'Irish landscape in the Victorian theatre'. A double perspective in the work of Seamus Heaney, Tom Kinsella, and John Montague is identified by Andrew Carpenter. Such writers are both within and outside the landscape; this stance enables them to perceive their dualistic and uncertain Irish society. In *IUR* Patrick Rafroidi detects 'the dual forces of provincialism and feminism' in writers like Joyce, Edna O'Brien, and Brian Moore. In the same journal Terence de Vere White provides some short anecdotes on the real Richard Irvine Best who appears as a character in *Ulysses* and *Hail and Farewell,* and who was an acquaintance of many figures involved in the Irish literary renaissance.

Essays by Norman Wilson, Douglas Gifford, Iain Crichton Smith, Albert D. Mackie, Frank Thompson, Allen Wright, and Stephen Mulrine have been collected[26] to serve as an assessment of Scottish writing from the end of the Second World War to the present day. Of greatest interest is Douglas Gifford's survey of modern Scottish fiction. He notes two traditions: one involves satire on Scottish mores, and the other presents a vision of an earlier and simpler Scottish Golden Age. In such a short space, Gifford can do little more than touch on a number of writers and works, hinting at trends and pointing out excellence. There are valuable lists of Scottish publishers, literary journals, newspapers, pseudonyms, and a 'Who's Who' of living Scottish writers at the end of this book.

Considerations of minor and 'popular' fictional genres round out the general studies for this year. Julia Briggs provides an entertaining and detailed account of the English ghost story in *Night Visitors*[27]. In her introduction she offers some perceptive comments on the main reasons for the popularity of this genre, especially from 1850 to 1930. The ghost

[25] *Place, Personality and the Irish Writer,* ed. by Andrew Carpenter. Gerrards Cross, Bucks.: Colin Smythe. pp. 199. £7.50.
[26] *Scottish Writing and Writers,* ed. by Norman Wilson. Edinburgh: The Ramsay Head Press. pp. 127. £3.95.
[27] *Night Visitors: The Rise and Fall of the English Ghost Story,* by Julia Briggs. Faber. pp. 238. £6.95.

story was not only a source of spine-tingling entertainment but an expression of man's alienation from an environment seen increasingly as bestial and hostile. Even serious writers could use supernatural tales to probe themes of death and evil. But with the advent of Freud's scientific investigations into inner life, the appeal of the ghost story began to fade. The book traces this 'rise and fall' beginning with the ghost story as presented by Lucian, Apuleius, Dickens, Walpole, Emily Brontë, Lamb, and Scott. The growing obsession with psychic phenomena, the revival of religious mysticism, and the increasing importance of science all influenced the treatment of ghostly elements in nineteenth-century fiction. In addition Briggs convincingly demonstrates that *fin-de-siècle* decadence gave rise to a demonic aspect in supernatural stories. She expands this argument through a lengthy analysis of Wilde's *The Picture of Dorian Gray* with its emphasis on the inner conflict in man between the base and higher instincts. Briggs also notes that exotic settings were an important means of heightening mystery in the stories of W. W. Jacobs and Kipling. Chapters are devoted to various specialists in the genre (including Henry James, Vernon Lee, M. R. James, and Kingley Amis) and to the psychological ghost story and its concern with madness and obsession. After the First World War, ghost stories became a macabre mix of comedy and terror and the genre went into decline. This book shows that ghost stories, while often dismissed as slight, can be legitimately used to probe serious themes; to this end Briggs makes a strong case for the excellence of de la Mare's stories with their profound investigation of 'loneliness, silence and death'. The epilogue provides a helpful evaluation of the use of ghost story devices by poets such as Hardy, Yeats, and Eliot.

Paul A. Carter examines magazine science fiction over the past fifty years[28]. Main themes of such fiction are outlined: space travel, time travel, anti-fascism, the evolution of man, feminine liberation, 'artificial humans', and the collapse of civilisation. By dealing with the work of such accomplished writers as C. S. Lewis, Asimov, E. E. Smith, Heinlein, and Ursula Le Guin, Carter is able to show that science fiction reflects themes of interest in real life — in scientific, political, and social spheres. He also provides some tantalising observations on the way in which the stylistic changes in science fiction stories parallel developments in other fictional forms. Even the 'New Wave' of science fiction writers utilises 'avantgarde "mainstream" literary techniques' to break down the distinction between science fiction and fantasy. Robert Scholes and Eric S. Rabkin provide a useful starting-place for the study of this genre in their examination of science fiction with literary merit[29]. The book touches very briefly on a great many authors including C. S. Lewis, Poe, Huxley, Asimov, Clarke, Brunner, Vonnegut, and Le Guin. The book is divided into three sections. The first is an account of science fiction as 'the history of humanity's changing attitudes toward space and time'. Main preoccupations, techniques, and approaches are summarised, and although there is little that is new, it is helpful to have science fiction set against

[28] *The Creation of Tomorrow: Fifty Years of Magazine Science Fiction*, by Paul A. Carter. New York: Columbia U.P. pp. xi + 318. $16.20.
[29] *Science Fiction: History, Science, Fiction*, by Robert Scholes and Eric S. Rabkin. O.U.P. pp. x + 258. hb £8.50, pb £1.50.

a general literary and social background. Section II is an exploration and simplification of scientific advances and theories which have proved significant for science fiction. In the final part important themes and techniques used in science fiction are investigated. There is a largely descriptive account of ten representative science fiction novels to illustrate the problems and main concerns of this genre. The bibliographies are extensive.

Bruce Merry studies twentieth-century 'espionage narratives' in order to define the basic elements of the spy thriller[30]. Certain ingredients seem necessary — an exotic setting, suspense, violence, a cultivated hero, and a simplistic conflict between Virtue and Evil. Complex structures to provide a series of uniform plot permutations are also noticeable in this escapist and essentially unrealistic genre. Merry ranges over a number of themes and authors (Le Carré, Fleming, Buchan, Greene, Chandler, and Conrad for example) in an effort to show the ways in which spy fiction feeds the fantasies of the reader. Donald McCormick's *Who's Who in Spy Fiction*[31] opens with a brief account of the development of the genre. The list of contributors draws on all nationalities; each entry includes biographical detail, light-hearted plot summaries and brief commentary. There is an appendix listing 'abbreviations, titles and jargon' current in the factual and fictional worlds of espionage.

The following books were not made available for review: M. Berger's *Real and Imagined Worlds: The Novel and Social Science* (Harvard U.P.); M. Bradbury's *The Novel Today* (Manchester U.P.); T. D. Clareson's *Many Futures, Many Worlds* (Kent State U.P.); Rupert Croft-Cooke's *The Green, Green Grass* (W. H. Allen); A. Diamond and L. R. Edwards's *The Authority of Experience: Essays in Feminist Criticism* (U. of Massachusetts P.); D. L. Higdon's *Time and English Fiction* (Macmillan); Ellen Moers's *Literary Women* (W. H. Allen); J. E. Caerwyn Williams's *Literature in Celtic Countries* (U. of Wales P.).

(b) *Authors*

Kate Turkington has provided a sensible introduction to Chinua Achebe's first novel, *Things Fall Apart*[32]. The book is divided into sections on structure, theme, characterisation, language, and style. Turkington argues convincingly that the novel is important not only because it gives 'an authentic picture of the traditional Igbo life' and presents the universal problem of the individual in conflict with society, but also because it is a stunning artistic achievement. Detachment, realism, expert characterisation, deft control of images, and the use of 'rhythmic cadences' are important elements in Achebe's originality and artistry. Ponnuthurai Sarvan provides a brief note in *SSF* on Achebe's 'Girls at War'. The story is not about war, but rather concerns Nwankwo and society in general.

Lucky Jim is the subject of Richard Fallis's article in *SNNTS*. Fallis suggests that the novel is popular because it is 'a version of heroic fantasy

---

[30] *Anatomy of the Spy Thriller*, by Bruce Merry. Dublin: Gill & Macmillan. pp. vi + 253. £6.95.
[31] *Who's Who in Spy Fiction*, by Donald McCormick. Elm Tree Books, Hamish Hamilton. pp. iv + 216. £4.95.
[32] *Chinua Achebe: Things Fall Apart*, by Kate Turkington. Studies in English Literature Series, No. 66. Edward Arnold. pp. 64. hb £3.50, pb £1.95.

cast into superficially realistic situations' which simply provide material for Jim's 'fantasy life'. In *CritQ* W. Hutchings surveys Kingsley Amis's comic talent. Amis uses farce and satire to proclaim 'common-sense values, an insistence on life, and a hatred of death'.

Laura Barge has a sharp essay in *PMLA* on thematic unity in Beckett's later fiction. Beckett's heroes constantly search for 'metaphysical reality'. Hoping to find it in human consciousness, they retreat inwards only to be ironically crucified on 'the nothingness at the core of the self'. This journey into the inner self is reflected in images such as those of nature and light and in the increasingly chaotic and confused narrative voice. These questing heroes are also the subject of another essay by Laura Barge in *SAQ*. Four Beckett stories – 'The Expelled', 'The Calmative', 'The End', and 'First Love' – mark a distinctive transition point, for with these stories Beckett's undecided heroes give way to those who actively seek 'metaphysical reality'. The stories are also transitional in their obsession with mortality, with the fact of physical death as a symbol for the impossibility of being and of selfhood. There seems no end to exile and alienation. In a complex article in *FMLS* Leslie Hill presents Beckett's novel trilogy as 'a spiralling sequence of fictions' which can be read on two levels. The novels may be seen as 'arbitrary linguistic fictions' or as 'anagogic retracings of their own enigmatic point of origin in the life of the self'. Elliot Krieger (*MLN*) studies the relationship between reader and text in *Texts for Nothing*. The reader is aware of other readers forming a community based on the same confrontation with the same text. Once read, 'the *Texts* make us acutely aware of having read, of having created a process where only stasis existed objectively'.

J. G. Riewald has selected, introduced and annotated a collection of Beerbohm's literary caricatures[33]. His use of Beerbohm's own words in the commentaries on the drawings underlines the relationship between Beerbohm the writer and Beerbohm the caricaturist. The drawings themselves are wonderful examples of technical mastery and complexity, and also serve as brilliant and perceptive comments on the writers Beerbohm portrays. Chesterton, Wilde, Arnold, Henry James, Conrad, H. G. Wells, Arnold Bennett, and Aldous Huxley are among those treated in this humorous and mocking way. Unfortunately, the caricatures are reproduced in black and white only.

An exchange of letters between Israel Zangwill and Arnold Bennett is the subject of Bernard Winehouse's commentary in *N&Q*. Zangwill draws attention to an error in Bennett's presentation of an orthodox Jew in *Elsie and the Child*, and Winehouse supplies a brief account of the relationship between Zangwill and Bennett.

Stephen Gray (*ESA*) provides the topical background necessary for an appreciation of Herman Bosman's stories in the Johannesburg weekly, *The Forum*.

Victoria Glendinning's biography of Elizabeth Bowen[34] is a sound portrayal of a writer of great 'perception and sensibility' who provides

[33] *Beerbohm's Literary Caricatures: From Homer to Huxley*, selected, introduced and annotated by J. G. Riewald. Allen Lane, pp. 295. £7.50.
[34] *Elizabeth Bowen: Portrait of a Writer*, by Victoria Glendinning. Weidenfeld & Nicolson. pp. x + 261. £6.50.

the link between Virginia Woolf and novelists like Iris Murdoch and Muriel Spark. Glendinning presents Bowen as a formidable if somewhat reticent woman — a skilful artist who put writing before her own emotional gratification, a sympathetic, witty, and tactful hostess, and a figure who embodied many of the important perceptions and approaches of the Anglo-Irish literary tradition. There are brief but useful comments on the novels and stories, and good account is given of the ways in which Bowen made imaginative use of material from her life. Bowen's many friends and acquaintances also make appearances. The Oxford circle of Maurice Bowra and the London literary world peopled by such writers as Virginia Woolf, Rosamond Lehmann, and T. S. Eliot emerge clearly from this biography and serve as backdrops against which this neglected novelist is set to act out her life-long struggle between living and creating.

In *DR* D. J. Dooley and Laurence Ricou have both commented on Ernest Buckler's *The Mountain and the Valley*. Dooley finds the obtrusive style centrally related to David Canaan and his capacity for perception and communication. Similarly, Ricou analyses key passages to show that the style reflects David's consciousness. Style also reveals that David remains a child in many ways, even in adulthood.

Richard J. Buhr has provided a brief introduction to Gilbert Cannan and an annotated bibliography of writings about him in *ELT*.

Ingvar Söderskog analyses Joyce Cary's 'To Be a Pilgrim'[35] in an effort to show Cary as a technical craftsman by paying close attention to his narrative technique. The background to Cary's own philosophies of freedom and art, his use of symbolic form, and his concept of allegory are usefully set out before Söderskog embarks on a discussion of the novel itself. There is a pedestrian plot summary followed by an extended analysis of the relationship of author and speaker which reveals much about technique and theme. Söderskog discovers that Cary's use of ironies and paradoxes in the novel elicits a complex response from the reader, demonstrating how difficult it is to make an 'unequivocal judgment' about Wilcher. The narrator and the narrative line are both ambiguous so that duality and divided vision characterise the novel. Indeed such technical duality echoes the thematic conflicts between 'spirit and sentiment', 'detachment and attachment', faith and faithlessness, and the claims of society and the needs of the creative individual. Söderskog also sees another purpose served by the novel's ambiguity. Since the novel renders inflexible judgement impossible, it is 'an object lesson in the toleration that makes the basis of Cary's ideal of freedom'. In the course of a review essay in *LMag*, John Mellors provides an overview of Cary's work and his 'nonconformist' spirit. D. J. Conlon's *G. K. Chesterton: The Critical Judgments 1900-1937* (Antwerp Studies in English Literature) was not available for review.

Charles Burkhart has provided a 'discursive' account of Herman Schrijver, Nancy Cunard, and Ivy Compton-Burnett[36] — an energetic

---

[35] *Joyce Cary's 'Hard Conceptual Labour': A Structural Analysis of To Be A Pilgrim*, by Ingvar Söderskog. Gothenburg Studies in English 36. Göteborg, Sweden: Gothenburg University. pp. iv + 176. pb Sw. Cr. 60.

[36] *Herman and Nancy and Ivy: Three Lives in Art*, by Charles Burkhart. Victor Gollancz. pp. 126. £5.25.

and convivial, if somewhat idiosyncratic, trio. Burkhart reminisces about his three friends and reprints Schrijver's essay on Nancy and memoir of Ivy together with excerpts from correspondence. Ivy emerges at best as a rather lovable monster, characterised by an unsentimental negativeness on the one hand and by a provincial banality on the other. Yet she could be witty and dynamic as well. Burkhart was clearly not at ease with such a disconcerting figure, but he does convey a sense of her vocation as a novelist: 'The shape of her life was the shape of her novels.'

Nigel Stewart's collection of four Conrad tales[37] — 'An Outpost of Progress', 'Karain: A Memory', 'The Secret Sharer', and 'The Planter of Malata' — is a good selection for the general reader or young student beginning work on Conrad. Stewart's introduction to the text is primarily biographical but he does outline the major themes raised in the stories with emphasis on 'human solidarity' and 'fidelity to a code of conduct'. Each tale is followed by a very simple commentary which stresses such technical matters as characterisation and point of view. There are also a few suggestions for further reading. The book is most useful, however, for its hints about the ways in which the individual tales prefigure more important works by Conrad.

The Conrad volume in the Writers and Their Work series has appeared[38]. C. B. Cox approaches Conrad as a writer of great imagination, but as a man troubled by doubts, confusions, and tensions concerning his own identity. There is much biographical information and a tendency to discover autobiographical elements in the fiction. Cox provides separate examinations of *Heart of Darkness, Lord Jim, Nostromo, The Secret Agent,* and *Under Western Eyes* since these works mark Conrad's major achievement as a novelist. Emphasis is placed primarily on character and the search for a stable psychological identity, but Cox also gives some indication of the plurality of interpretations possible for Conrad's work. Ironic conflicts and impressionistic techniques are also noted. Cox usefully concludes by suggesting some of the ways in which Conrad comes to terms technically with the meaninglessness of the universe around him, and also asserts that the novels are compelling because of their blend of human dignity and nihilism. This brief monograph is a helpful starting-place for the student or non-specialist, provided one takes account of the insistence on a biographical and psychological approach.

H. M. Daleski's *Joseph Conrad: The Way of Dispossession*[39] is an illuminating study of a pervasive theme in Conrad's art. In *A Personal Record* Conrad himself averred he had 'a positive horror of losing even for one moving moment that full possession of myself which is the first condition of good service'. Daleski argues that this notion of 'self-possession' was crucial for Conrad's life and fiction and serves indeed as the foundation of his ideals of civilisation, 'fidelity, solidarity, duty, discipline, courage, endurance'. Daleski diligently traces the development of the theme of self-possession from *The Nigger of the 'Narcissus'* to *Under*

[37] *Selected Tales from Conrad,* ed. and with an introduction and commentary by Nigel Stewart. Faber & Faber. pp. 224. pb £2.25.
[38] *Conrad,* by C. B. Cox. Writers & Their Works Series. Harlow, Essex: Longman. pp. 43.
[39] *Joseph Conrad: The Way of Dispossession,* by H. M. Daleski. Faber & Faber. pp. 234. £5.95.

Western Eyes. Ironically, Conrad most frequently deals with his theme in a negative way, showing the loss of self through 'passion', 'panic', 'spiritual distintegration', and 'suicide'. Moreover loss of self-possession often leads to disastrous 'counter-possession' and the physical and spiritual annihilation of the self. Daleski's argument is not quite so convincing when he begins to consider the way in which a man can regain self once 'possessed' by destructive forces. The solution, he asserts, is to be found only in Razumov, though it is prefigured in Dr. Monygham. Abandonment is paradoxically the way back to self-possession. A character must release himself from what possesses him; he must renounce his 'preoccupation with self-preservation' and embrace self-effacement. Yet the benefits of self-possession seem bleak indeed. The redeemed character attains a self-knowledge which makes his miserable life bearable, and which is 'the only sort of triumph to be wrested ashore from an engulfing darkness of the spirit'. This is a well-written and sensitive account of Conrad's major novels and represents the best work on Conrad done this year.

A number of perceptive articles have appeared in *Conradiana.* In the first issue Emily K. Dalgarno examines various Conradian manuscripts and letters to show Conrad's concern for 'a rational ordering of manuscript, typescript, serial and various book versions' although subject to pressures of time and money. The same author also examines the involvement of Conrad's agent, James Pinker, in the writing of *The Secret Agent.* Commercial pressures meant that the book did not accurately reflect Conrad's intentions. Neill R. Joy argues persuasively that the 'Preface' to *The Nigger of the 'Narcissus'* is an important expression of Conrad's aesthetic. The 'Preface' clarifies the way in which life is transmuted by the artistic process so that it becomes 'an integrating symbol' significant of a higher truth. A good account of the textual history of the 'Preface' is given, and Joy demonstrates that Conrad emended it to bring it closer to his novel in terms of imagery and theme. Donald W. Rude, Kenneth W. Davis, and Marlene Salome have discovered a missing link in the textual evolution of *The Nigger of the 'Narcissus'.* A little known American serial version shows the novel 'in an early, intermediate form'. *Under Western Eyes* is evaluated by Roderick Davis in an effort to show that Conrad's modifications of that novel are in line with his changing conceptions. A history of the variants in the collected edition text of *Almayer's Folly* is provided by David Leon Higdon and Floyd Eugene Eddleman who seek to determine the extent of authorial revision.

The second number of *Conradiana* opens with a reprint of Conrad's first known interview. E. A. Bojarski suggests that Conrad seemed hesitant to discuss his Polish background for fear it would have an adverse effect on his popularity. Juliet McLauchlan skilfully argues that *Heart of Darkness* is really very coherent in form, content, and symbolic pattern. She feels that Kurtz's 'real deficiency is of humanity, of soundness of heart'. Only Marlow can attempt to rescue Kurtz for only Marlow, 'the fully human', can detect the human potential in Kurtz. Pedro Calderon de la Barca's play, *La Vida es Sueno,* had an influence on the 'psychological realism' and 'existential philosophy' of the 'destructive element' passage in *Lord Jim,* according to Gloria L. Young. Cedric Watts offers some 'absurdist descriptive techniques' such as 'empirical hyperbole' and 'reductive reification' which he feels are useful for analysing Conrad's style. Robert Chianese applies Sartrian existential philosophy to *Arrow of Gold* in an effort to establish the importance of that novel. He detects a basic conflict between existence and essence. Characters seek to avoid consciousness by becoming objects. Ultimately, the novel demonstrates 'the recognition of the freedom to exist as humanity's only unalienable right'. The rendering of the voyage in *The Nigger of the 'Narcissus'* reveals a tension between the judgements of the narrator and his sentimental feeling according to Michael P. Jones. This work, the last in which Conrad would treat an idealised and heroic community of the sea, sees the sacrifice of judgement to sentiment. Wilson F. Engel III supplies a brief note on *Heart of Darkness*. Marlow's reference to Falernian wine suggests affinities with Horace. Lewis E. Birdseye feels that the unpopular tale 'The Return' reveals one of Conrad's central concerns: 'the curse of facts and the blessing of illusions'. Santord Pinsker's admirable commentary on 'Amy Foster' centres on Conrad's uniquely modern awareness of the fragility of words. The story is a concrete embodiment of Conrad's 'distrust in the efficacy of language itself'. Peter J. Lowens shows through an unpublished letter that *The Rescue* was completed while Conrad was in pain from gout. J. C. Hilson and David Timms confirm in a note that Conrad did follow sources for the person of Gobila but changed them for artistic purposes in 'An Outpost of Progress'. The proper person of Gobila appears in *The Secret Agent*. The usual reviews follow.

In the third issue, Thomas R. Dilworth looks at the narrator and image patterns in 'The Secret Sharer'. The narrator achieves an 'understanding of humanity' through his compassion for Leggatt. *Under Western Eyes* is the subject of several interesting studies. Harriet Gilliam emphasises the importance of Faustian references and diabolic imagery in this novel which concerns the tragedy of man's confrontation with the daemonic. Ronald Schleifer, on the other hand, believes that the novel deals with 'the problematical nature of fictional narrative' which should be simultaneously public (giving 'outward voice to experience') and private (professing that 'inwardness of suffering that experience occasions'). The ultimate vision of the world which Conrad offers is one 'both public and private'. Jeffrey Berman and Donna Van Wagenen suggest Dostoevsky as a probable source for Peter Ivanovitch in *Under Western Eyes*. In a difficult but rewarding article Eric K. Hatch treats Jim and Marlow as archetypes for artists. Marlow is an artist in as far as he searches for truth 'flickering in illusion'. Jim's idealism 'exposes reality only by denying it' — 'a deliberate and artistic act'. The perception of character is an important issue in *Victory*. Henry J. Laskowsky analyses the portrayal of Axel Heyst in that novel and concludes that *Victory* may be read as 'a dramatic realization of George Berkeley's belief that "to be is to be perceived"'. Donald W. Rude and David Leon Higdon produce the 1976 Conrad bibliographical checklist. Useful reviews are also to be found in this number.

The quality of articles on Conrad which appeared elsewhere was uniformly high. In *CompL* Frederick R. Karl notes the importance of the Conrad-Gide relationship which he charts through their correspondence. Gide was perceptive in his appreciation of the anarchy and involuntary actions to be found in Conrad's fiction. Roger Little (*MLR*) provides some notes on Alexis Leger (Saint-John Perse) and his impressions of Conrad. Little also prints an uncollected letter from Leger to Jean-Aubry about Leger's encounter with Conrad in England. In *YES* Cedric Watts prints two unpublished letters exchanged by Conrad and R. B. Cunninghame Graham. Both men gained something from their friendship; Cunninghame Graham piqued Conrad's interest in the 'aristocratic subversive' and provided life-patterns and historical background for *Nostromo;* Conrad encouraged Cunninghame's idealism. William A. Covino writing in *MFS* finds dark humour and 'comic indirection' important devices by which Conrad comes to terms with the malevolent universe and the purposelessness of existence. The element of courageous mockery in the face of chaos is often disregarded in Conrad's fiction, and this lively article deserves to be noted. Chinua Achebe (*MR*) reads *Heart of Darkness* as expressive of the West's view of Africa as 'a place of negations', and Ian Watt (*SoR*) examines the blend of impressionism and symbolism in the novella. The use of both features emphasises the lack of communication and solipsism present in the work.

An illuminating essay by Wallace Watson in *JNT* details the influence of Maupassant and Flaubert on Conrad's early attempts to find a narrative voice. Oblique techniques for achieving detached aesthetic distance in the handling of point of view were clearly derived by Conrad from French novels. Daniel R. Schwarz supplies two articles. In *ArielE* he writes on the weary, doubting and ineffectual protagonists of *Almayer's Folly* and *An Outcast of the Islands*. By means of the narrator, Conrad detaches himself from these protagonists in such a way that the novels become 'acts of initiation for the artistic self Conrad was trying to create'. In *Renascence* Schwarz analyses *The Shadow-Line* as typifying a more positive and objective belief in the value of moral abstrations like 'courage, duty, and responsibility' for the development of character. Cedric Watts (*CritQ*) notices some static mirror-patterns of likeness and contrast in 'The Secret Sharer'. Such structuring devices generate tension and counterpoint in the tale between optimism and pessimism. Harriet Gilliam in *NCF* examines Razumov's attitude to and experience of time in *Under Western Eyes.* Flux is everywhere and Razumov can cope with the fact of change only by submitting to it entirely. But 'when rid of all illusion and nakedly confronting temporal existence itself, [he] knows only how to die, not how to live'. Clarence B. Lindsay detects a moral point in 'Youth' (*CR*). However, the tale does not treat a single moral lesson which Marlow learns while maturing; 'rather the significance lies in the older Marlow's moral discernment as he remembers his youth and confronts its loss'. Conrad is presenting 'an accomplished moral harmony rather than dramatizing a moral struggle'.

In *N&Q* S. T. Fisher shows that in a letter Norman Douglas claimed that *South Wind* was drastically cut.

Nicholas Utechin's quaint pamphlet, *Sherlock Holmes at Oxford*[40], attempts to establish Holmes's university during the 1870s by an elaborate game of clue-spotting in the Sherlock Holmes canon. Demolishing rival

[40] *Sherlock Holmes at Oxford*, by Nicholas Utechin. Wolfson College, Oxford: Robert Dugdale, pp. 26. pb £0.75.

claims en route Utechin triumphantly concludes that the detective's fine intellect was 'moulded in part by the religious foundation that was St John's College, Oxford'. There are some contemporary photographs and an interesting digression on Oxford in the 1870s. Ronald Pearsall's *Conan Doyle: A Biographical Solution* (Weidenfeld and Nicolson) was not seen.

Patrick O'Flaherty examines three novels by the neglected Margaret Duley in *DR*. He finds her the only novelist to perceive the Newfoundland identity with accuracy.

Mervyn Horder's collected *Memoirs and Critiques* of Ronald Firbank[41] is an essential volume for the much-needed critical reassessment of that elusive and mysterious figure. There is much in the way of anecdote and reminiscence in this book. Horder reprints the inaccessible Ifan Kyrle Fletcher *Memoir* which also includes observations by Vyvyan Holland, Augustus John, Osbert Sitwell, and Lord Berners. Other valuable reminiscences are provided by contemporaries including Grant Richards, Nancy Cunard, Siegfried Sassoon, Wyndham Lewis, Harold Acton, and Harold Nicolson. There are critical assessments too, representing the spread of opinion from 1924 to 1967 on Firbank's artistic achievements. Here again Horder selects what is not readily available today, and one welcomes the perceptions of Evelyn Waugh, E. M. Forster, Edmund Wilson, Ellis Waterhouse, and the like. Narcissistic, vague, and unconventional as Firbank was, one can agree with Edmund Wilson that 'it is a good thing to have Firbank revived'.

Igor Webb's 'Marriage and Sex in the Novels of Ford Madox Ford' (*MFS*) investigates the influence of 'troubadour romance' on Ford's fiction. The same pattern of 'constructive' love in illicit relations and 'destructive' love in marriage seems to exist in both the romances and Ford's novels, but Ford's heroes do come to learn that even a mistress demands a destructive 'personal commitment'. Valentine Wannop is a symbol for liberation in the *Parade's End* tetralogy, according to Marianne De Koven in *ELT*. Tietjens's love for her helps him to become 'an active participant in the determination of his own fate'. The Penguin edition of Ford's *Memories and Impressions* was not available for detailed review.

Two more volumes in Oliver Stallybrass's admirable Abinger edition of Forster[42] have appeared. The cost of each volume is high, but the superb standards of editing and production go a long way to justifying the price. *The Lucy Novels* show Forster at work in the early stages of composition leading to *A Room with a View*. The 'Old Lucy' version is the fuller, although it is further from the finished novel. 'New Lucy' is very melodramatic indeed with its depiction of George crushed by a tree after an unsuccessful elopement. In both cases, however, it is valuable for the scholar to have access to Forster's working sketches and notes on plot, character, and reactions. There is a lucid introduction from the editor who draws attention to such felicitous images as that of Miss Alan gather-

41 *Memoirs and Critiques*, ed. with intro. by Mervyn Horder. Duckworth. pp. xii + 227. £5.95.

42 *The Lucy Novels: Early Sketches for A Room with a View*, by E. M. Forster, ed. by Oliver Stallybrass. Edward Arnold, pp. xii + 132. £12.50. *A Room with a View*, by E. M. Forster, ed. by Oliver Stallybrass. Edward Arnold. pp. xx + 237. £7.95.

ing up her 'shawl of disapproval'. The same sound scholarship is much in evidence in the Abinger *A Room with a View*. Once again a sensitive introduction precedes the text. Stallybrass traces the novel's pre-history and tactfully suggests Forster's own concern with its thinness, despite his satisfaction with the characters. Indeed, in a 1958 assessment by Forster of his novel (printed as an appendix in this volume) Forster damns his work with faint and ironical praise, calling it his 'nicest' novel. Stallybrass draws attention to the superb characterisation and to the complex structuring and intricate symbolic patterning of the novel. The textual notes are full and pertinent, and interesting general notes are supplied on real-life personages, places, and works of art which appear under one guise or another in the novel. Frederick P. W. McDowell aims for 'completeness' in his annotated bibliography of writings about Forster[43]. It is a pleasant task to report that he appears to succeed. Forster entries from every conceivable source are noted, including reviews, 'letters to the editors of major newspapers and journals', encyclopedias, anthologies, and foreign language works. The abstractions and critical comments are precise and helpful, the chronological arrangement is sensible and the cross-referencing reflects a unity of critical judgement. The indexes are also thorough. A quiet introduction systematically outlines Forster's literary career and the three-phased critical reception of his work. McDowell concludes that Forster's reputation is being re-established 'on a firmer, less arbitrarily defined basis'.

The first volume of P. N. Furbank's biography of Forster[44] is a remarkable achievement. It is a justly tempered and well-written examination of the man, not just of the novelist. Close attention is paid to Forster's writings, letters, and diaries but there is no attempt to read the novels as autobiographical treatises. This volume deals with Forster's life from birth to the age of thirty-five. As a child, surrounded by women, he was considered 'delicate' and cossetted. His unpopularity at school, his close relationship with his mother, and a curious sexual encounter with an unknown man are tactfully presented, as is the general 'problem' of Forster's homosexuality. Due consideration is given to the influence of Cambridge on Forster and to his imaginative awakening in Italy and Greece. Forster's developing attitude to his role as a novelist will interest scholars and critics. *The Longest Journey* was produced by a novelist convinced he was offering 'hope and salvation to humanity'. But Forster gradually grew discontent with his work. With the publication of *Howards End* he was troubled by the effects of popularity, depressed by fears of creative sterility, and frustrated by a teasing love affair and his mother's morbidity. With his new novel 'Arctic Summer' it became apparent that Forster was increasingly concerned with issues of 'human conduct', and with the tension between the 'socially useful man' and 'the chivalrous man'. Erotic short stories served as a literary and emotional therapeutic exercise for a time, but Forster needed fresh impressions and new imaginative stimulation. These he found in India, but when he returned his old

[43] *E. M. Forster: An Annotated Bibliography of Writings About Him*, ed. by Frederick P. W. McDowell. De Kalb, Ill.: Northern Illinois U.P. pp. x + 924. 1976. $30.
[44] *E. M. Forster: A Life*. Volume One: *The Growth of the Novelist (1879–1914)*, by P. N. Furbank. Secker & Warburg. pp. xvi + 272. £6.50.

doubts assailed him. Edward Carpenter encouraged Forster to write *Maurice* and Forster seized the opportunity as a chance to transform his creative talents. Unhappily, no imaginative release occurred and with the coming war, Forster abandoned writing for a job. Furbank, invited by Forster to write the biography, is clearly knowledgeable of and sympathetic towards his subject — but he never allows an adulatory or personal tone to obtrude. This is indeed a masterly work and one awaits the next volume with impatience.

G. K. Das[45] investigates Forster's interest in India which was filtered into many of his writings, including his letters and diaries. Certain common themes in Forster's writings on India form the central strand of Das's book. While Forster took an interest in the political problems of India he also was concerned with more permanent elements in Indian society, including history, religion, and cultural achievements. Forster's actual experience of British India also helped to strengthen his own dislike of imperialism and to define his notions of democracy and liberal individualism. Forster is portrayed as a sensitive recorder of the Indian scene — not just of Princely India or British India — but of the whole country. Nowhere is this more evident than in *A Passage to India* which, for Das, 'stands out as the most distinguished achievement among contemporary literature about India'. Moreover, Forster looked to the future of India, again a unique departure from the contemporary approach. Das also provides an appreciation of Forster's creative relaying of the truth about Indian religions and prints (as appendixes) Forster's tribute to Mahatma Gandhi, and an account of Das's 1968 interviews with Forster. While this study does not provide any original approaches to Forster's work, it does perform a valuable function in reminding readers of Forster's continuing interest in India and of the similar concerns to be found in the Indian and non-Indian writing.

Peter Widdowson provides a brisk and readable account of *Howards End*[46] as a novel about 'the pressures of social and cultural change'. But this short study is not limited to a sociological approach. Widdowson neatly relates the liberal-humanist crisis in the twentieth century to the 'crisis of the place of realism in fiction'. He argues that Forster has to remake reality into fantasy in the novel so as not to expose 'the inefficacy of liberal-humanist values'. In this way the failure of liberalism coincides with 'the inadequacy of empirical realism'. Widdowson substantiates his case by depicting the social and cultural milieu in England at the beginning of this century. There are chapters on Forster's liberal-humanist values and on his attitude to fiction and realism. The better part of the book is devoted to an analysis of Forster's handling of material to reveal a vision of society in *Howards End*. Tension is at the heart of the novel. At a conscious level Forster urges a connection between Helen's idealism and Leonard's 'unquenchable individual life', but there is also unconscious significance. By omitting whole sections of society 'Forster tacitly admits that his vision could not accommodate them'. This explains the curious

[45] *E. M. Forster's India*, by G. K. Das, with a foreword by John Beer. Macmillan. pp. xx + 170. £7.95.
[46] *E. M. Forster's Howards End: Fiction as History*, by Peter Widdowson. Text and Context Series. Chatto & Windus and Brighton: Sussex U.P. pp. 124. hb £3.50; pb £1.75.

blend of realism and fable in the novel: 'only by an idealisation of reality can the "inner life" assimilate the "outer"'.

A double issue of *CERVE* is devoted to Forster. Some brief observations by Charles Mauron on various elements in Forster's personality and writing are printed posthumously. Emphasis is placed on the psychoanalytic perspective. Alina Szala writes on Forster's view of civilisation as beneficial in *Where Angels Fear to Tread*. The healthy Italian civilisation which is tolerant and natural is contrasted to the narrow, destructive English civilisation. Forster's relationship to the Bloomsbury Group is once more treated, this time by Elizabeth Heine who finds Forster used Bloomsbury aesthetic and moral values 'for his own purposes'. The influence of Meredith on Forster with special reference to *Howards End* is the subject of John H. Stape's thoughtful article. Themes, values and techniques are held in common by the two writers. Henri Quéré takes a structuralist approach to *Howards End,* emphasising the importance of a dialectic pattern in the novel. Dennis Altman assesses Forster's own notion of homosexuality in the course of insisting that all of Forster's works should be interpreted in terms of his homosexuality. The novelist was forced to be false to himself by portraying heterosexual relationships. Moreover, 'Forster's inability to transcend the limits of British liberalism . . . also explains his failure to deal with homosexuality except obliquely or in escapist fiction'. Evelyne Hanquart discusses the correspondence between Forster and J. R. Ackerley, and Philippe Daumas supplies a note on Forster's 'Recommendations on the Government of Egypt' which demonstrates the same 'anti-imperialist' stance found in *A Passage to India* although Forster did not fully 'grasp the gravity of the colonial situation'. Joseph Dobrinsky argues that Forster's treatment of love and friendship in *A Passage to India* culminates in his handling of the Hindu theme. G. K. Das investigates Forster's attitudes to a variety of gods throughout his life. The synthesis between reality and idealism in *A Passage to India* is discussed by Vasant A. Shahane who sees the pattern of synthesis and anti-synthesis repeated in ever widening circles in the structure of the novel. Finally, Sujit Mukherjee develops an interesting notion by examining the influence of *A Passage to India* on later Anglo-Indian fiction. Forster's treatment of themes ranging from the imperial to the universal can be seen to have started distinct trends in thematic treatment and characterisation.

Robert K. Martin adopts a familiar stance when he claims in *KanQ* that Forster's writing is everywhere 'permeated with a strong homosexual sensibility'. Such an awareness prompts Martin to examine Forster's attitude to and use of Greece in his fiction. Greece becomes a place of harmony and freedom where homosexual relationships are accepted. Martin also studies the homosexual element in 'Ansell' which is read as 'a diary of the soul'. A rather weak article by Visvanath Chatterjee in *Parnassus* calls unconvincingly for a re-appraisal of *A Passage to India* on the grounds that Forster has gone 'astray' in an attempt to write a new kind of serio-comic novel where the story and philosophy are not well integrated and where the real India is oversimplified. G. K. Das suggests some actual sources for Professor Godbole in *RES*, and James S. Malek provides a Jungian interpretation of 'The Other Boat' in *SSF*. Cocoa represents Lionel's 'Shadow'; Lionel's 'strangulation of Cocoa is a form of self-murder'. Also in *SSF*, John H. Stape finds neglected merit in 'The Other Side of the Hedge'. Forster's handling of symbols, allusion, and a mythological framework points to his concerns and techniques in the main novels. Francis King's *E. M. Forster* (Thames & Hudson) was not made available.

Students of John Fowles will want to examine the revised version of *The Magus*[47], published this year with a foreword by Fowles explaining his changes and discussing his current feelings about the book. Many of the revisions are of a stylistic nature and eradicate awkwardness, but Fowles has also introduced a more realistic 'erotic element'. The ending has been rewritten to suggest more clearly that we have witnessed illusion. Nevertheless, the essential elusiveness of the work remains and Fowles preserves his main interest in the concepts of God and free will. True freedom 'can never be absolute freedom'. For this reason Fowles cautions his readers to recall the rejected title of the novel — 'The Godgame'. In the foreword he acknowledges both conscious and unconscious influences, such as Alain-Fournier's *Le Grand Meaulnes*, Richard Jefferies's *Bevis*, and *Great Expectations*, and he asserts that Nicholas Urfe should be seen as a 'partial Everyman of my own class and background'. Also of considerable interest to Fowles scholars is a collection of French essays on *The French Lieutenant's Woman*[48]. Lucien Le Bouille notes Fowles's continuing interest in the masque, in mystery, and in the continuity beneath changing appearances. Dominique Catherine and Ginette Emprin decide that the narrative technique of the novel brings the narrator, the characters, and the reader into a special relationship in which they reach similar conclusions with regard to the true meaning of freedom. Contrasting pairs of characters and the key relationship of Charles and Sarah are the concerns of Jean-Claude Castangt and René Gallet. Sarah is clearly the pivotal figure. The same authors examine mysterious symbols of place, of land, and sea in another essay. Elisabeth Hellegouarc'h and Sylviane Troadec study the novel as an accurate historical portrait of the Victorian period and find it inadequate. Most interesting of all contributions, perhaps, is John Fowles's response to these critical essays which also suggests his own vision of himself as a writer, as a 'socialist realist' 'helping the reader teach himself'. This is why he finds mystery such fertile ground. He discusses avantgarde fiction briefly and concludes: 'I do not think the middle-class novel . . . is exhausted as a means of communication'.

Brian Friel's treatment of disillusionment and the gulf between wives and husbands in 'Among the Ruins' and 'Foundry House' is the subject of an article by Edmund J. Miner in *KanQ*. In *Studies* (Dublin) J. B. Lyons surveys Oliver St John Gogarty's literary output from 1918 to the 1930s. His fame rests on his autobiography, *Tumbling in the Hay*, which is disguised as an impressionistic novel.

[47] *The Magus: A Revised Version*, by John Fowles with a foreword by the author. Jonathan Cape. pp. 656. £4.95.

[48] *Etudes sur The French Lieutenant's Woman de John Fowles*, compiled by Jean-Louis Chevalier and Le Centre d'Etudes et de Recherches Anglaises et Nord-Américaines de l'Université de Caen. Caen: CRDP. pp. 67.

Mall Mölder Stålhammar makes a good effort at deciphering the complexities of Golding's *The Spire* in her analysis of the imagery and metaphorical language of the novel[49]. The study is fairly pedestrian in its
summation of scholarly approaches to imagistic criticism, in its chapter
on 'critical appraisals of *The Spire*', and in its survey of the narrative contents of the work. However, once the analysis of the central images commences the argument becomes more interesting. Image clusters from
nature, animation, and artefacts are used to represent the mind and feelings of characters, to reveal interrelations between characters, and to
support the central vision of the complexity of life with its dualism of
spiritual and physical needs. Jocelin is shown to accept this complexity
by the end of the novel in his awareness of the appletree. Self-develop-
ment and the artistic theme are also shown to be similar. Jocelin's work,
mind, and will 'are represented as gaining independent life' while the
created artefact becomes 'independent of its creator'. Finally, Jocelin
humbly comes to accept life and responsibility.

In *Theoria* Kolawole Ogungbesan analyses Nadine Gordimer's *The
Lying Days* and finds that Helen's quest for identity has implications
for South African society as a whole. Disillusionment and exile promise
'the beginning of a new life'.

Laura Krugman Ray examines Kenneth Grahame's *The Golden Age*
in *ELT*. While there are clear references to Wordsworthian themes and
Dickens's attitudes to childhood, Grahame's work lacks the 'depth and
range of his models'.

Henry Green's first novel, *Blindness,* has finally been reissued[50].
This is an important occasion, for Green's sensitive treatment of an artistic
youth accidentally blinded has been unavailable for some years. Also reprinted is a miscellaneous collection of essays by Graham Greene[51].
The volume includes a personal reminiscence, 'The Lost Childhood',
which includes an account of Greene's early inspiration to write on reading
Marjorie Bowen's *The Viper of Milan*. The second section of the book
is comprised of short essays and book reviews on varied literary figures
such as Chesterton, Ford Madox Ford, Rolfe, Maugham, and De La Mare.
As we might expect, these assessments are acute and succinct. Section
Three is devoted to varied perceptions of disparate figures from Titus
Oates to Norman Douglas and Fidel Castro. There is a personal postscript on a return to Sierra Leone.

Antonie Weber writes on Greene's 'Catholic' novels, *Brighton Rock*
and *The End of the Affair*[52], with the aim of elucidating 'the interrelationship between [his] concept of reality and his narrative technique'.
Greene extensively uses traditional fictional patterns to express his beliefs.
All his novels have more or less the same underlying structure and express
an unchanging outlook. [H.C.C.]

[49] *Imagery in Golding's The Spire,* by Mall Mölder Stålhammer. Gothenburg
Studies in English 37. Göteborg, Sweden: Gothenburg University. pp. 140.
[50] *Blindness,* by Henry Green. Hogarth P. pp. 254. £3.95.
[51] *Collected Essays,* by Graham Greene. Harmondsworth, Middx.: Penguin.
pp. 345. pb £0.95.
[52] *Die Erzählstruktur von Graham Greenes katholischen Romanen,* by Antonie
Weber. Bern: Francke Verlag (Schweizer Anglistische Arbeiten 95). pp. 173. SFr.
28.

Sr Teresita Fay and Michael G. Yetman usefully remind us in *Renascence* that Scobie should not be judged solely on his view of himself in *The Heart of the Matter*. Pity is an important value in the novel. When pity and love are applied to an assessment of Scobie, it may be argued that 'Greene might possibly imply that Scobie's sort of corruption is humanly praiseworthy'. Even Scobie's death may be seen as heroic since it is selfless, not escapist. At any rate Scobie's intentions need to be examined more fully. David Leon Higdon takes a different view when he examines Greene's 1971 revisions of *The Heart of the Matter* for the Heinemann-Bodley Head Collected edition (*SB*). Most of the corrections sharpen style and focus. Some changes help to clarify Greene's misunderstood intentions regarding Scobie. He is stripped of some of his earlier 'religious perceptiveness' and is made 'less attractive because less comprehending and less anguished'.

John Payne has compiled a usefully thorough bibliography of all important writings by W. H. Hudson[53], including his contributions to periodicals and translations of his books. The entries are extremely detailed and the annotations give a good idea of Hudson's concern with the publishing of his work, especially with respect to illustrations. There is also a valuable list of books about Hudson. Alfred Knopf's short foreword provides information on both the American publishing history of *Green Mansions* and John Galsworthy's own deep appreciation of Hudson's achievement.

In a paperback re-issue of *The Doors of Perception* and *Heaven and Hell*[54] Huxley gives an account of his mescalin experience and the significant change it made in his perception of 'the realm of objective fact'. The man spurred to drug-induced vision will be 'better equipped to understand the relationship of words to things, of systematic reasoning to the unfathomable Mystery which it tries, forever vainly, to comprehend'. *Heaven and Hell* serves as a sequel to the very personal recollections of *The Doors of Perception* and treats the new understanding of inner self and the vision of others which mescalin provides. Huxley analyses various 'vision-inducing' objects, substances, and actions, discusses the difference between visionary heaven and hell, and attempts to define visionary as distinct from mystical experience.

Bharathi Krishnan[55] wishes to claim that in Huxley's novels the hero's quest for 'the modes and principles of right conduct and harmonious living' parallels the author's formal experimentation and quest for a satisfactory structure and technique. However, this relationship is not clearly developed at all times. Instead, the novels are grouped and rather simplistically discussed according to structuring devices and techniques such as the use of literary allusions, recurrent character types, and animal imagery. Krishnan identifies 'house-party novels', those with a 'multiplicity of situations', conversion novels, and utopian novels. The study

[53] *W. H. Hudson: A Bibliography*, by John R. Payne, with a foreword by Alfred A. Knopf. Folkestone, Kent: William Dawson, and Hamden, Conn.: Archon Books. pp. xvi + 248. £10.
[54] *'The Doors of Perception' and 'Heaven and Hell'*, by Aldous Huxley. Frogmore, St. Albans, Herts.: Triad/Panther. pp. 143. pb £0.60.
[55] *Aspects of Structure, Technique and Quest in Aldous Huxley's Major Novels*, by Bharathi Krishnan. Stockholm: Uppsala. pp. 181.

is really an examination of the seeker in Huxley's novels and the extent to which the quester reveals Huxley's own personal solutions to the problems of modern life. *Eyeless in Gaza* is viewed as the 'exemplary' novel of questing for it provides a positive triumph 'in Anthony's private and public worlds'. By reference to an incident involving Sir George Sitwell, Jerome Meckier (*MFS*) is able to demonstrate Huxley's 'satiric imagination at work' in *Crome Yellow*. Sources are developed and transmuted so that Sir George becomes a model for Henry Wimbush.

Christopher and His Kind[56] is a fascinating but curious autobiography by Christopher Isherwood. Isherwood eschews first person narration but looks back with wry, mature amusement at a younger, harrassed self objectified dispasssionately as 'Christopher'. Despite this distancing effect which seems to enhance the discrepancy between the public Isherwood of the fiction and the private Christopher, Isherwood insists that the book is 'as frank and factual as I can make it'. However, fact and fiction merge in the people he encounters and the characters who come to people his novels of this period. The book begins with Isherwood's departure to Berlin for the first time and ends with his emigration to America. In the course of the autobiography Isherwood reveals his key concerns of this period in his life – his preoccupation with the rights of the individual, his hatred of fascism, his homosexuality, his growing commitment to pacifism. More unusual are his explorations – from a detached viewpoint – of his early use of the 'camera' narrator and of his utilisation of the bizarre as a source for fiction. In addition the somewhat impressionistic accounts of Germany *in extremis*, of wartime China, of literary giants like Auden, Forster, and Spender help in the delineation of a period and a man. While Isherwood's autobiography charts well-trodden ground it does so with originality, insight, and humour. Unfortunately, Jonathan Fryer's biography of Isherwood[57] travels over familiar territory in an all too predictable way. Fryer insists in his introduction that he wishes to show that there is more to Isherwood than the Berlin stories or the pacifism or the homosexuality. Instead Fryer hopes to persuade the reader that Isherwood has made a distinctive contribution to twentieth-century life. Yet the biography covers Isherwood's life in a most ordinary way, noting his growing distaste for the middle-class Establishment, his early literary attempts, his frustration in London, and his move to Berlin. Isherwood's homosexuality receives much attention. There is no analytical account offered of the fiction or drama, and hence no challenging assessment of Isherwood as a contributor to the modern literary tradition. While Fryer admits that Isherwood is his favourite novelist, he does not succeed in producing a biography that captures anything new about the identity of either man or writer. Journalistic clichés abound and, although interviews, letters, and manuscripts provide source material, Isherwood's own published accounts of events are used frequently and rather uncritically. The Penguin issue of Isherwood's *Lions and Shadows* was not seen.

[56] *Christopher and His Kind: 1929-1939*, by Christopher Isherwood. Eyre Methuen. pp. 252. £4.95.
[57] *Isherwood: A Biography of Christopher Isherwood*, by Jonathan Fryer. New English Library. pp. 300. £7.50.

In a thoughtful essay in *CritQ* Patrick Parrinder assesses B. S. Johnson as an experimental novelist. This is a good account both of Johnson's 'conscious aesthetic' and his Puritan imagination. Another overview is to be found in *Crit* where Robert S. Ryf views the fragmented technique as a means of exploring the chaos of experience. Johnson's solipsism conflicts 'with his insistence on telling the truth'.

Some of the best work on James Joyce in recent years has appeared this year. An excellent consideration of Joycean fiction is provided by C. H. Peake's dual study of Joyce as 'citizen' and 'artist'[58]. Peake insists that his book, based on a series of lectures first delivered at Birkbeck College in 1963 and since extensively revised, is aimed at 'interested readers rather than specialists' but all will be rewarded by his unobtrusive yet sound critical approach. The book is essentially a close reading of the narrative fiction in chronological order with emphasis on Joyce's methods and vision, though Joyce's own schemes, letters, and other writings are used to support his general thesis. Peake believes that much of the complexity of technique and structure in the stories and novels stems from Joyce's complex vision of the polarity between man as artist and man as a member of society. Beginning with *Dubliners* there is a sharp differentiation drawn between Joyce's 'vision of the nature of the artist and his vision of the nature of the city'. Of real interest is Joyce's detached artistic eye of judgement which presents the disease of urban life. (Here Peake's detailed analysis of 'The Dead' must be singled out for its sensitivity.) *A Portrait of the Artist as a Young Man* is dedicated to the study of 'an artist's nature' which must avoid those nets which might entrap his soul. Stephen's artistic detachment is, however, only a stage in the artist's movement to maturity. Joyce must himself learn that the opposite natures of 'citizen' and 'artist' should interact for true success. This indeed is the vision in *Ulysses*. Peake reserves his most extensive and intensive analysis for this novel, showing how the central action, structure, style, and content are all related to moral vision. The kinship between citizen and artist is seen in 'the spiritual father-son relationship' of Bloom and Stephen. The 'social animal', confused but 'capable of concern for others', must complement the isolated, 'self-contemplative' individual. Yet 'opposition' becomes the 'healthy state'. The strivings of citizen and artist are in different directions. Domination of one nature by another is a guarantee only of paralysis. Peake also provides a refreshing interpretation of Molly's final soliloquy. She demonstrates simply that 'the moral and spiritual purposes which trouble and motivate Stephen and Bloom are comparatively inactive'. Molly becomes just another element — 'instinctive and amoral' — in Joyce's world. The final chapter suggests the ways in which Joyce expands his dual theme in *Finnegans Wake* to present a broader view of 'a fundamental opposition within our nature'. Peake's analyses are thorough, his arguments convincing, his book well-written. Readers of Joyce in any capacity will be grateful for this volume.

Bernard Benstock's *James Joyce: The Undiscover'd Country*[59] is a lively examination of the theme of self-exile in Joyce's works. Like Peake

[58] *James Joyce: The Citizen and the Artist*, by C. H. Peake. Edward Arnold. pp. x + 369. £9.95.
[59] *James Joyce: The Undiscover'd Country*, by Bernard Benstock. Dublin: Gill & Macmillan; New York: Barnes & Noble. pp. xx + 201. £8.50.

Benstock sees a tension in Joyce's works based on a fundamental duality — the isolated, alienated artist allied to a wide literary tradition is at odds with the writer aware of his national ties and of 'the history of his people residual in himself'. The characterisation of Stephen and Bloom reveals, for Benstock, Joyce's own ambivalence towards his roots. In his portraits of the developing artist Joyce is aware of the value of isolation and defiance which spur on 'egoistical growth' but, even so, by *Ulysses* he realises that 'a consciousness of others becomes essential to the functioning artist'. Shem the Penman is Joyce's final sardonic portrait of the successful artist both separated from the world and linked to all humanity. In many ways, Benstock's approach is quite similar to that of Peake, but Benstock's volume lacks the thoroughness and, to some extent, the delicacy of perception which so distinguishes Peake's work. There is much good commentary on the interaction of characters but surprisingly little on complex patterning and language; ultimately one's understanding of Joyce is not considerably enhanced.

Dolf Sorensen has produced an interesting book on Joyce's aesthetic theory[60]. The first section is devoted to the development of Joyce's ideas based on 'essays, notebooks, letters, *Stephen Hero, Exiles*'. Sorensen traces the influence of such disparate figures as Aquinas, Vico, and Ibsen on Joyce's notions of beauty and art. Detachment, truth and humanity, classical and romantic tempers, 'the concepts of stasis and kinesis': all contribute to Joyce's overriding concern in fiction — 'the portrayal of a truthful, realistic picture of human beings in their attempts to come to terms with life'. The second part of the study is an examination of this theory as Joyce applied it in *Dubliners, A Portrait, Ulysses,* and *Finnegans Wake*. The author himself acknowledges the superficiality of this section. It is only necessary to say that Sorensen reads the novels as statements of Joyce's aesthetic (finding in *Ulysses* and *Finnegans Wake* theory and practice perfectly fused in content and structure) but little original insight into the fiction is provided. Still, this short book — really an extended essay — is a sign of a fruitful area for further research.

Richard Ellmann and Michael Groden both offer some thoughtful work on *Ulysses*. Ellmann[61] traces Joyce's response to his sources and 'how he made his book express his aesthetics and his politics as well as his epic theme'. Such a study, it is hoped, will define Joyce's consciousness or 'movement of the mind'. What is particularly novel is that Ellmann draws on Joyce's book collection formed between 1900 and 1920 and still virtually intact. He is able to show Joyce's use of Homeric commentators and post-Homeric accounts of Ulysses's final voyage in his great novel. To the linear or horizontal dimension of Homer's work Joyce added a subjective, vertical movement by introducing allusions to *Hamlet*. At this point Ellmann draws again on the library to discuss the many writers who used or commented on *Hamlet* and who subsequently influenced Joyce. Joyce's collection of books on politics demonstrates a lively political awareness, and this Ellmann also feels is borne out in *Ulysses*. Admit-

---

[60] *James Joyce's Aesthetic Theory: Its Development and Application*, by Dolf Sorensen. Amsterdam: Rodopi. pp. 96. pb Hfl. 20.

[61] *The Consciousness of Joyce*, by Richard Ellmann. Faber & Faber. pp. x + 150. £5.50.

tedly this study is limited in scope. The significance of Joyce's remodelling of his sources is never really probed, though Ellmann does see *Ulysses* as both a self-expressive, original experiment and also an age-old monument impregnated by memories from the vast worlds of life and literature. However, the real value lies in Ellmann's indication of Joyce's sources for *Ulysses*, and scholars will be particularly pleased with his listing of almost 600 items in Joyce's library left in Trieste in 1920. Michael Groden[62] amasses some convincing evidence to support his contention that Joyce's interests and intentions altered during the composition of *Ulysses*. Concern with story and character marked the first stage (up to 'Scylla and Charybdis') but gradually Joyce became more and more obsessed with style and structure so as to reflect a new encyclopaedic vision: 'individual and even national history gave way to a larger view in which any specific individual or situation recreates archetypal patterns from the past'. This is not the whole story. Joyce revised earlier stages to suit his later concerns. However, Groden cleary demonstrates that the different stages of composition and revision are clearly discernible, as with the 'Aeolus' episode which is a microcosm of the whole process of composition. In a straightforward and workmanlike way, Groden examines Joyce's method of constructing an episode, including his use of source material. Different drafts and worksheets are scanned to chart Joyce's attempt 'to create a new style for *Ulysses*'. The book reveals much about Joyce's surprisingly cautious process of composition, and also aids in interpreting that complex novel since Joyce's 'refusal to confine the contents of *Ulysses* to a closed fictional world forces us to look beyond the book for its meaning'. An ambiguous interpretation would seem to be supported by reference to Joyce's methods of composition. There is an excellent appendix on 'the early texts of *Ulysses*' as well as a valuable bibliography.

Therese Fischer-Seidel[63] collects eleven previously unpublished or recently revised essays on *Ulysses*, reflecting recent trends in West German Joyce criticism. Fritz Senn points to thematic links between *Ulysses*, *Dubliners*, *Portrait*, and *Finnegans Wake;* Hans Walter Gabler discusses criteria for an authentic version of *Ulysses;* Philip F. Herring reconstructs the book's genesis; Rosemarie Franke gives an account of the novel's reception in German-speaking countries; Eberhard Kreutzer writes on puns and the problems they pose for the translator; Ulrich Schneider looks at allusions to the Old Testament; Arno Esch evaluates the importance of Homer for the work; Viktor Link analyses the Circe-chapter; Franz K. Stanzel contributes two essays on Joyce's narrative technique; and the editor concludes the volume with a study on the function of 'stream of consciousness' in the novel. [H.C.C.]

Some interesting essays appear this year in *JJQ*, in addition to the usual helpful reviews. In the Fall number Daniel L. Moore reports on the 1976 James Joyce Colloquium at Buffalo. Albert Wachtel examines the importance of Simon Dedalus's resolution 'never to peach on a fellow'

---

[62] *'Ulysses' in Progress*, by Michael Groden. Princeton, N. J.: Princeton U.P. pp. xiv + 235. £10.90.
[63] *James Joyces 'Ulysses'. Neuere deutsche Aufsätze*, ed. by Therese Fischer-Seidel. Frankfurt am Main: Suhrkamp. pp. 377. DM12.

in *A Portrait of the Artist as a Young Man*. Stephen's adherence or non-adherence to this maxim (as it is explored in the first chapter) clearly shows his development and rebellion against his father. The 'Eumaeus' episode of *Ulysses* is the subject of Brook Thomas's illuminating piece. At the same time as it 'masquerades as a Bloomesque narrative', the episode serves as Joyce's comment 'on the linguistic technique he uses to create his character'. Margaret Honton disagrees with Hugh Kenner's contention about Molly's role-playing. Honton does not see Molly in the posture of a conquered woman. She either fantasises as 'the *prima donna*' or is in reality the active partner in sexual relations. Bernard Benstock does well to remind us to concentrate on what Stephen's villan-elle expresses about its creator. Effort is wasted in abstractly trying to evaluate its merit. Joseph C. Voelker suggests with some originality that Molly Bloom is closely related to Giordano Bruno's concept of divinity in Nature. Alan M. Cohn provides a supplemental checklist for Joyce scholar-ship for 1974 and William M. Schutte continues his index of recurrent elements in *Ulysses* with an examination of the 'Calypso' episode. There are also some brief notes of merit. David Weir relates 'A Little Cloud' to St Ignatius's structure of meditation in an effort to reveal the story's irony. R. Bruce Kibodeaux analyses the neglected 'Counterparts', Harold I. Shapiro cites *Fors Clavigera* as a possible source for 'Stephen's theory of literary kinds' in *A Portrait*, and Ruth Bauerle offers a source for Simon Dedalus's song in the same novel. Yet another reason for the choice of 16 June as Bloomsday is suggested by William P. Keen. This time the Wars of the Roses are involved. Richard M. Kain finds music hall allusions in *Ulysses*. Victory Pomeranz offers two notes on *Ulysses*: one on a possible source for John Alexander Dowie, the other a clarification of 'Stephen's use of turf terminology'.

The Winter number is a 'Reminiscences Issue'. Willard Potts and the editors explain the connection of Alessandro Francini Bruni with Joyce and thus prepare the way both for a translation of Bruni's eccentric caricature of Joyce at the Berlitz School in Pola and for Bruni's more straightforward recollections of Joyce and his good-natured, 'almost childlike' enthusiasms. Willard C. Potts also introduces the reminiscences of Ole Vinding, a Danish journalist who spent time with Joyce in Copen-hagen. Vinding reveals Joyce as a perpetually youthful and curious figure, obsessed with his work on *Finnegans Wake*. Arnold Goldman offers a brief checklist of Ole Vinding's writings about Joyce. M. S. Byram con-siders Tom Kristensen's critical review of Joyce and *Ulysses* and finds it sensitive and perceptive. With this number Alan M. Cohn's Joyce check-list commences quarterly publication so that it can be kept up to date. William M. Schutte's index of recurrent elements in *Ulysses* is concerned with the 'Lotus Eaters' episode.

A *Finnegans Wake* issue appeared as the third number. Bernard Ben-stock provides a concise survey of *Wake* scholarship since the 1960s, noting new trends and approaches. Morris Beja applies the notion of 'multiple personality' to the *Wake*, and J. L. Baird and Coilin Owens look to mediaeval sources for a detailed eucharistic image in *Finnegans Wake*. Marion W. Cumpiano offers a highly entertaining and original article on Joyce's hidden and oblique references to salmon in the *Wake*.

The salmon allusions are used to objectify Irish history and the cosmic cycle of birth, death, and rebirth. Barbara DiBernard writes an illuminating article on the many allusions to alchemy in the *Wake*. Alchemy becomes a metaphor for the transmutation involved in 'the artistic process' and for the 'artist as forger' touching his own unconscious. There is also an appendix of major alchemists to whom allusion is made in *Finnegans Wake*. Blake makes an important appearance in the *Wake* in terms of his heretical concept of God and his 'scatological interest in bodily functions', according to James D. Wallace. Franklin Walton investigates Wilde's presence in the *Wake* as 'the dark, fallen side of HCE'. Lorraine Weir believes that the philologist Marcel Jousse and his theory of the relationship between gesture and language influenced the structure and linguistic evolution of the *Wake*. Alan M. Cohn provides the current Joyce checklist, William M. Schutte reports on the 'Hades' episode in his series on the recurrent elements in *Ulysses,* and Ruth von Phul adds a note on Bloom's encipherment of Martha Clifford's name in the 'Ithaca' episode.

In the Summer number Hugh Kenner argues perceptively that what characters do not say in *Ulysses* is significant, especially where Bloom is concerned. John Henry Raleigh takes exception to Carl Niemeyer's 'A *Ulysses* Calendar' in *JJQ* (Winter 1976) and suggests his own chronological arrangement of the Blooms' memories of their pasts. Florence L. Walzl examines the complex 'life chronology' in the arrangement of the 1906 *Dubliners*. This chronology matches the dominant theme of psychological and moral paralysis for generations. There are three articles to supplement the 1976 *JJQ* 'Joyce and Modern Psychology' issue. Mark Shechner introduces the essays by Jeanne McKnight and Jane Ford, calling attention to their general place in psychoanalytic criticism of Joyce. Jeanne McKnight explores the gradual understanding which emerges concerning Stephen's identity. Stephen's relationship with his mother is the basis for his psychological struggle and 'oral-narcissistic dilemma'. Release comes through writing. Jane Ford quietly suggests that 'sin, guilt, and incest' lie at the heart of *Ulysses*. In addition to Alan M. Cohn's 'Current JJ Checklist' and William M. Schutte's study of recurrent elements in the 'Aeolus' episode, there are some brief notes. Frederick V. Wellington follows Hugh Kenner's lead and explores the significance in the narrative gap between Chapters Four and Five in *Ulysses*. Joseph C. Voelker examines the case of Florence Elizabeth Maybrick, a convicted murderess, mentioned by Molly Bloom. Heather Dubrow Ousby and Ian Ousby supply a 'Note on *Ulysses* and *Arden of Feversham*', and Myron Schwartzman discusses Shaw's attitude to *Ulysses* and an unpublished letter to John Quinn from Joyce. Joyce's portrayal of Shaw in *Ulysses* ironically supports Shaw's own reaction to the novel.

Of the general articles on Joycean matters printed elsewhere the most challenging is Stephen Tapscott's study of Joyce's liberating influence on William Carlos Williams's *Paterson*. Thematic and linguistic similarities are suggested in this article in *ArQ*. J. J. M. Tobin notes in *AN&Q* that Joyce had a special familiarity with Palestrina. In *SSF* Richard D. Beards argues that supposing Tierney a Jew in *Dubliners* reinforces main themes of 'betrayal, and usurpation by foreigners' in that work. *Dubliners* is also the subject of an agreeable essay by Richard Douglas Jordan in *DUJ*.

Jordan suggests that critical confusion about the tales stems from a 'conflict between the realistic and symbolic aspects of Joyce's technique'. He analyses 'The Dead' to demonstrate the ambiguity which arises. Linda Bennett compares *A Portrait* to *Confessions of a Young Man* in *Studies* (Dublin). Rather surprisingly, Moore's influence appears to be primarily stylistic, as in the use of the interior monologue. Joyce is a stronger and more disciplined artist but without Moore, Joyce's work could not have been so rich. J. Delbaere-Garant has a difficult essay on *A Portrait* in *RLV*. Delbaere-Garant argues that the work has a spiral structure winding into *Ulysses*, but it is also self-contained. Stephen, a Christ figure is locked within Christian tradition and needs the Jewish Bloom and Homeric epic to broaden his perspective. Eric Gould (*ES*) uses Lévi-Strauss's anthropological view of myth to probe the girl in the strand epiphany in *A Portrait*. He concludes that the novel is less an example of the usage of archetypes of myth than a recreation of 'the *form* of mythic thought' through repetitive elements. Victory Pomeranz (*MFS*) offers some suggestions about the ways in which Bloom 'modified' the truth about the pornographic book, *Sweets of Sin*. In *BNYPL* Myron Schwartzman examines notebooks, early manuscripts, and the published version of the 'Nausikaa' episode to reveal Joyce's intentions and methods. From revisions it is clear that Joyce had 'the whole section of text in mind' as he worked. John Tessitore (*ELN*) clarifies a communion reference concerning Stephen's mother in *Ulysses*. In the course of an assessment of Eugene Jolas and *transition* in *TriQ*, Michael Finney looks at the relationship between Jolas's nihilistic attitude to language and Joyce's intentions in *Finnegans Wake*. Finney warns readers not to confuse or equate the two as early critics did. Nathan Halper (*PR*) writes about some obscure references to Pound in *Finnegans Wake*. In *TriQ* David Hayman traces the influence of Joyce's *Wake* on twentieth-century writers. Beckett, Burgess, and Christine Brooke-Rose are among novelists he examines briefly. Hayman concludes 'the potential of the *Wake* has yet to be fully realized' but it has been significant in linguistic areas, in a renewed concern for universals, and in the sublimation of 'structure, harmony, and radiance in order to avoid the appearance, if not the fact, of aesthetic control'. In the same issue Philippe Sollers records his own observations on Joyce's intentions and accomplishments in the *Wake*, with particular reference to language. Also in *TriQ* Haroldo de Campos surveys Brazilian writers who seem to be influenced by the *Wake*. The following books on Joyce were reported but not seen: Michael Henry Begnal's *Narrator and Character in 'Finnegans Wake'* (Associated University Presses), Adaline Glasheen's *A Third Census of 'Finnegans Wake': An Index of the Characters and Their Roles* (U. of California P.), Jack Lindsay's *Decay and Renewal* (Lawrence & Wishart), Margot Norris's *The Decentered Universe of 'Finnegans Wake': A Structuralist Analysis* (Johns Hopkins U.P.), and Thomas F. Staley and Bernard Benstock's *Approaches to Joyce's 'Portrait': ten essays* (Feffer & Simons).

In *IUR* Janet Egleson Dunleavy argues for seeing depth in the work of Mary Lavin. Fleeting fragments in her fiction may be recognised as having a timeless universal truth of human nature about them. As a consequence, Lavin's work is 'elusive, tantalizing, and seductive'.

DHLR opens its first issue with a highly commendable essay by Charles

L. Ross on Lawrence's indebtedness to Greek tragedy in general and to Euripides in particular. A number of elements from classical tragedy appealed to Lawrence, such as the use of sacrifice as a means to rebirth, the notion of a communal initiation into manhood, and the employment of animals as significant of 'universal, instinctive energies'. But it is to the principles of ritualistic structure and characterisation that Lawrence is particularly attracted. He utilises such ritual elements as *'agon, pathos, dance, threnos* and *sparagmos'* for organising 'scenes and the inter-relations of characters in formal ways'. Ross writes clearly on this complex subject and succeeds in giving a vivid impression of the importance of the Greek tragic ritual to Lawrence's art. Jerome Mandel's article is also interesting. He suggests that *Lady Chatterley's Lover* is really a 'transmuted and modernized' version of the tale of Tristan and Isolt. Robert H. MacDonald's study of the imagery of 'The Man Who Died' is a rather disjointed examination of Lawrence's use of language and imagery to convey the themes of cosmic harmony and regeneration. David Ellis challenges the normal reading of *Sea and Sardinia* as 'casually written' and existing 'only at the minimum level of self-expression'. Ellis feels the book is a *tour de force* because it demonstrates Lawrence's talents as a writer. Lawrence captures the instant brilliantly and yet also uses this presentation to give us insight into the narrator. Moveover, he gives the reader more 'freedom of interpretation' than is usually found in autobiographical travel books. Jacqueline Gouirand offers a bibliography of Lawrence 'translations, criticism and scholarship published in France, 1927-1976', and Richard D. Beards provides a checklist of Lawrence scholarship for 1976. There are also good book reviews, news of research in progress, and other items of interest to students of Lawrence including the first issue of *The D. H. Lawrence Society Newsletter* which is being published under the aegis of *DHLR* for the present time. This newsletter gives details of conferences, meetings, books, films, and the like of relevance to Lawrence.

In the second issue G. B. Crump provides a lucid extended analysis of three modern American romantics — Kurt Vonnegut Jr, Ken Kesey, and Wright Morris — as a means of shedding light on Lawrence's own romanticism and its influence. Several elements emerge as defining Lawrence's romanticism. He views 'man as a living part of a living, and therefore changing, universe'. His attempt to balance the individual's desire both for separateness and also for 'unity with transpersonal forces' involves a repudiation of technology, democracy, and transcendental idealism. Instead, Lawrence is committed to 'life and experience'. Vonnegut and Kesey share Lawrence's hatred of the 'modern democractic machine civilization' and Morris opts for a 'renewed awareness of life's inherent possibilities'. The German elements in the shorter fiction intrigue James F. Scott since they reveal Lawrence's 'ethnic and racialistic assumptions' noticeable in all the fiction, particularly in his treatment of the German relationship to Europe and the difference between north and south Germany. Lawrence saw a link between culture and 'the physical bonds of race'. Such 'ethnic impulses' come to the fore in 'moments of historical crisis'. But Scott advises that Lawrence failed to understand 'the real machinery of social change' and fabricated 'pseudo-causes for events'. In a closely reasoned essay Gregory L. Ulmer tries to defend Lawrence's critical and theoretical writings from the charge of eccentricity by relating Lawrence's theories to German art criticism. Lawrence's aesthetics centre on the concept of *kunstwollen* or 'will to form' as developed by Wilhelm Worringer. Conscious and unconscious volition become 'the basis for Lawrence's theory of interpretation', and style is centred on 'the shifting relations between man and his natural environment'. Nevertheless, many modernists saw the new age as a 'geometric' one, not Lawrence's ideal 'return to the body'. Paul G. Baker sees *Aaron's Rod* as a unique blend of form and theme most clearly illustrated by the characterisation of Aaron. By studying the evolution of this character from typescript to the final version of the novel, Baker demonstrates that Lawrence's distancing techniques emphasise Aaron's misanthropic withdrawal from commitment. Sadanobu Kai, Yasuichirô Ohashi, Taiji Okada, and Tohru Okumura compile 'a checklist of D. H. Lawrence articles in Japan, 1968–1975'. The usual news, notes, and reviews follow.

The third number is devoted to 'psychoanalytic criticism of the short stories'. Murray M. Schwartz outlines Lawrence's relationship to the science of psychoanalysis and provides a helpful bibliography on psychoanalysis and literature. When looking at 'The Man Who Loved Islands' David Willbern discovers 'a disquieting image' of Lawrence in the islander. Moreover as the islander's character regresses to a blank nothingness, he becomes 'a pure white screen for our projections'. Richard P. Wheeler argues that 'phallic narcissism' is a significant neurosis in 'Tickets, Please'. By obliquely objectifying a personal experience in John Thomas, 'Lawrence is able to identify with the whole unconscious situation, with both poles of the mother/infant unity'. 'The Fox' clearly shows pre-oedipal conflicts, according to Judith G. Ruderman. The engulfing mother threat is more obvious than erotic sexual domination. Lawrence's ambivalent attitude to women as seen in the fiction is the subject of a useful article by Gordon D. Hirsch. He discovers that Lawrence's response to women entails a splitting of the male image into intellectual and vitalistic men; both masculine types are vulnerable. Lawrence criticism in Italy from 1924 to 1976 is listed by Simonetta de Filippis, while Fleda Brown Jackson provides a bibliography of dissertations and theses on Lawrence. The second issue of *The D. H. Lawrence Society Newsletter* printed with this number of *DHLR* contains some reminiscences by people who knew Lawrence.

Stephen Gill (*EIC*) provides a close reading of 'The Industrial Magnate' chapter of *Women in Love* in an effort to show that Gerald is Lawrence's despairing picture of 'modern industrial man'. Gerald is 'an exemplar of subjugated everyman'. In *ELN* Keith Cushman coherently argues that the minor 'Fly in the Ointment' has a 'psycho-sexual undercurrent' which surfaces in the major work. Contrast between attractive memories and unpleasant reality signifies Lawrence's essential conflict between 'the two halves of himself' which struggle towards 'self-integration'. The myth of Brynhild transmitted through Ibsen influenced Lawrence, according to Mitzi M. Brunsdale in *WHR*. The 'goddess' who rejected the physical desires of the unconscious was a destructive and doomed figure. Only the woman who embraces sexual love can become 'the necessary mediatrix to the creation of both art and life'. *Sons and Lovers* and the draft novel,

'The Sisters', bear striking similarities to Olive Schreiner's *The Story of an African Farm*. This possible influence is noted by Christopher Heywood in *ELN*. Susan Thornham usefully reminds us in *DUJ* of the ways in which Lawrence and Freud disagreed. Lawrence offered individual fulfilment through adherence to the life-force. Freud could only view this life-force as 'primitive and dangerous'. In *N&Q* G. Peter Winnington claims that Lawrence's definition of male and female principles, especially in *The Rainbow*, owes much to Ferdinand Tönnies' *Gemeinschaft und Gesellschaft*. In *The Journal of the D. H. Lawrence Society* J. R. Ebbatson investigates the symbolic meaning of the peacock scene in *The White Peacock*. It symbolises 'both the "dreaming woman" in her "paradise reserved" . . . and the passionate sensuality and degradation of the "terrible dukedom of desire" '. Ebbatson also locates sources for the peacock imagery in such varied writers as Tennyson, George Moore, George Eliot, and Mrs Rachel Taylor. The same author also writes on *The White Peacock* in *N&Q*. Here the influence of Watts-Dunton's *Aylwin* on Lawrence's novel is explored. Ebbatson contributes another source study on Lawrence to *ArielE*. He presents an interesting argument to the effect that Hardy's *Two on a Tower* was a possible influence on *Lady Chatterley's Lover*. Similarities between characters and the symbolic handling of landscape are noted, although Ebbatson concedes that 'the differences, centering upon Lawrence's critique of industrialization, are crucial and massive'. Suzanne Wolkenfeld (*SSF*) offers 'Sleeping Beauty' as a source for the mythic structure of 'The Fox' although she acknowledges that Lawrence darkly ruptures the myth with his 'vision of the conflict and uncertainty of real life'. Lawrence's view of Etruscan society is the subject of Billy T. Tracy's pithy article in *TCL*. Although Lawrence disliked some conclusions in George Dennis's *The Cities and Cemeteries of Etruria*, Tracy argues that *Etruscan Places* is definitely indebted to Dennis. Yet once again Lawrence's genius and vision gives his work originality; his interest was in 'the Etruscan mode of consciousness' and 'his aim was to recover the living universe of archaic man'.

The Middle Eastern scholar Desmond Stewart surveys T. E. Lawrence's life in his biography[64] but adds little that is new. The standard picture of Lawrence the vulnerable outsider is painted, and there is much on Lawrence's sado-masochistic tendencies and the way 'he metamorphosed guilt and failure into a myth of degradation and torture'. Stewart attempts to identify 'S.A.' of the dedication to *Seven Pillars of Wisdom*, although there is little use made of this information in the commentary on Lawrence's book. Indeed, Stewart appears alienated by the prose style of *Seven Pillars*, seeing in it the qualities of Georgian poetry which 'represented the anaemic old age of Victorian vigour'. While this book is written in an interesting way, it does not really provide a deep analysis of Lawrence. In *Solitary in the Ranks*[65] H. Montgomery Hyde provides an informative and sympathetic account of Lawrence's self-effacing career as an airman and private soldier following his desert exploits. Hyde bases his biography

[64] *T. E. Lawrence*, by Desmond Stewart. Hamish Hamilton. pp. xii + 352. £7.50.
[65] *Solitary in the Ranks: Lawrence of Arabia as Airman and Private Soldier*, by H. Montgomery Hyde. Constable pp. 288. £6.95.

largely on Lawrence's correspondence, and an excellent portrait emerges of a courageous, sincere, and intelligent man. Lawrence's acquaintance with such literary figures as Shaw, Yeats, and Forster is duly noted. In *AI* Thomas J. O'Donnell views *Seven Pillars of Wisdom* and *The Mint* as 'a single confessional project' with sado-masochistic overtones. The hero is a 'radical' example of 'a divided self'.

Nancy Shields Hardin writes briskly in *TCL* on the 'open-ended' Sufi teaching story and its relation to the fiction of Doris Lessing. Her novels and stories embody some Sufi concepts. They nourish the imagination and also make the reader uncomfortable as they emphasise the need to break out of programmed roles. Michael L. Magie has a long but stimulating article in *CE* on Doris Lessing and the 'self-divided' Romantics. Special treatment is accorded *The Golden Notebook, The Four-Gated City, Briefing for a Descent into Hell,* and *The Memoirs of a Survivor* in an effort to determine the nature of Lessing's quest for the self. Magie asserts that against her own desires for the illusions and 'foolish consolations of Romanticism' Lessing pits a vision of 'cultural hopelessness' in her fiction, demonstrating 'the morally obtuse and stunting consequences' of these ideas.

Walter Hooper has edited some collected stories and unfinished pieces by C. S. Lewis[66]. The fragment of an interplanetary novel, *The Dark Tower*, is published for the first time. While not perhaps on the same level as Lewis's space trilogy, it is good entertainment. Standard concerns of Lewis – the discernment of appearance and reality, the nature of myth, and the capturing of sharp image pictures – can be seen in several of the stories, together with Lewis's attempt at experimentation with the stream of consciousness technique. Portions of an unfinished novel are reprinted together with notes by Roger Lancelyn Green and Alastair Fowler on conversations they had with Lewis about the work. The sub-title of Sheldon Vanauken's account of his married life provides a perfect key to the subject[67]. This is a moving rendering of a couple's growth towards Christian commitment and their efforts to come to terms with a death which would mean the end of their worldly relationship. Of particular interest is their warm friendship with C. S. Lewis which began while the Vanaukens were in Oxford. Previously unpublished letters from Lewis dealing with the struggle for faith, the nature of Christianity, and the problems of death and grief are included.

Michael Beatty writing in *Theoria* relates Wyndham Lewis's early fiction to the first four stories of *The Wild Body*. The organisation of *The Wild Body* suggests a new discovery 'of an integrated language of satire'. As Lewis returns 'to the raw elements' of the early fiction, a movement may be detected 'from the Vorticist attack onto the more personal defensive'. *The Revenge for Love* is arguably Lewis's best novel. This is the position of George Woodcock in *QQ*. Woodcock discusses Lewis as a political critic, satirist, and Vorticist painter, and he also portrays the useful tension maintained by Lewis 'between the abstract visual images of human beings and the naturalistic plausibility of the plot. . . between

---

[66] *The Dark Tower and Other Stories*, by C. S. Lewis, ed. by Walter Hooper. Collins. pp. 158. £3.95.

[67] *A Severe Mercy: C. S. Lewis and a pagan love invaded by Christ, told by one of the lovers*, by Sheldon Vanauken. Hodder & Stoughton. pp. 238. £5.50.

the bogus values of the fashionable Bohemian world and the genuine feeling that inspires both Margot's love for Victor and Percy's remorse'. Students of Vorticism and Lewis's place in that movement will find Wylie Sypher's long review article on Vorticism and the Machine age valuable (*SR*).

In *JNT* Eric S. Rabkin considers David Lindsay's *A Voyage to Arcturus* as a work which draws on the science fiction tradition but also on 'metaphysical fantasy'. Lindsay's work is a serious myth, 'a moral odyssey' rather than a simple entertainment.

Some incisive work has been done on Malcolm Lowry. In the *Journal of Commonwealth Literature* Tony Bareham sees Lowry's 'Englishness' as of particular importance. Lowry's works have the tone of alienation which one would expect from an Englishman abroad. But they also demonstrate an awareness of Old World failings, especially 'the unthinking cruelty of stock response'. An extremely illuminating article by Jonathan Arac on *Under the Volcano* is to be found in *PMLA*. Arac suggests that the complexity of the novel can in part be explained by using Mikhail Bakhtin's definition of Menippean Satire and its mode of the carnival. This is indeed a convincing argument which helps to account for many of the confusing elements of Lowry's work, including the difficult structure which Arac likens to the Ferris wheel. In *Novel* Charles Baxter studies *Under the Volcano* and discovers that 'the metaphor for a certain kind of creative act is arson, which forces the object to burn with significance and light but which also decomposes both the sign and the thing signified'. He also suggests that the Consul has affinities with the romantic visionaries. He is 'the man who desires vision but who loses control once inside the dream-world'. The ironist element in the Consul destroys the symbolist.

In *Crit* F. C. Molloy treats John McGahern as a social novelist. In McGahern's works a variety of techniques like flashbacks, imagery, and rhythmical prose are used to convey characters at odds with their society.

C. K. Stead has provided a valuable service by editing selections from the letters and journals of Katherine Mansfield[68]. The book reveals the singular unity of Mansfield's creative vision. Suffering, loneliness, and a vivid regret for the passing of life are clearly present but offset by a satirical, wry and witty 'comic talent'. There are interesting letters to S. S. Koteliansky, Middleton Murry, Virginia Woolf, and William Gerhardie, and both letters and journals reveal literary tastes, expectations, and aspirations: 'To write something that will be worthy of that rising moon, that pale light.' There are helpful biographical notes appended to each section and C. K. Stead supplies a useful introduction which summarises Middleton Murry's sentimentalising treatment of Mansfield's unpublished material. Stead also traces the genesis of the *Journal* and *Scrapbook* published by Murry. Peter Alcock reads Mansfield's New Zealand stories biographically in the *Journal of Commonwealth Literature*. They are founded on 'the troubled childhood sources of her own adult personality' and reflect a New Zealand preoccupation with 'vanished innocence sharing the ruin of adult bewilderment'.

[68] *The Letters and Journals of Katherine Mansfield: A Selection*, ed. by C. K. Stead. Allen Lane, and Harmondsworth, Middx.: Penguin. pp. 285. hb £5.75, pb £0.95.

In *Ariel* K. S. Narayana Rao considers 'religious elements' in the novels of Kamala Markandaya, culminating with a discussion of Hindu and Christian interaction in *Two Virgins*. Markandaya's contribution lies in her admirable documenting of religious aspects of the Indian scene.

Anthony Curtis's *Somerset Maugham*[69] is a popularly written and rather standard biographical study. Noting the autobiographical nature of much of Maugham's work, Curtis sets out to demonstrate 'where the fact ends and the fiction begins'. This in effect comes to mean a study of the events in Maugham's life with a few interesting and rather elementary comments on literary influence and on Maugham's use of the novel-form as a means of charting 'his own emotional and intellectual progress'. Maugham's increasing bitterness and peevish nature assume primary importance in the later stages of the book. There are good sketches delineating Maugham's social milieu and copious photographs and illustrations, but the biography is really useful only as an introduction. It provides no new insights and its assessment of Maugham's literary achievement as a brilliant occupier of 'the middle ground' is common-place. Mollie Gillen's *The Wheel of Things: A Biography of L.M. Montgomery* (Harrap Books) was not available for review.

Robert Sullivan's interview with Brian Moore (*LMag*) covers the pessimism of the novels, Moore's handling of the 'writer-hero', and the change from 'realism' to 'fantasy' in the fiction.

Some valuable writing on George Moore can be found in the periodicals this year. Charles Burkhart in *ELT* surveys the direction and state of Moore scholarship and suggests directions which it might profitably take. In *RES* Richard Cave gives a detailed account of the life of Clara Christian who appears as 'Stella' in *Hail and Farewell*. There are some fascinating indications of her influence on Moore's artistic development. *RS* contains an illuminating article by G. A. Cevasco on the thematic, stylistic, and aesthetic influence of Huysmans on Moore, especially in *A Drama in Muslin, A Mere Accident,* and *Mike Fletcher*. Although Huysmans's influence on Moore waned through the years, even later novels like *Evelyn Innes* and *Sister Teresa* show certain religious elements that can be traced back to Huysmans. Fourteen unpublished letters from George Moore to Frans Netscher are collected and printed by J. G. Riewald in *ES*. Riewald notes that the letters provide much information on the debate between naturalism and Moore's 'lyrical realism'. I. A. Williams's *George Moore* (Bibliographies of Modern Authors, Norwood) was not seen.

In *Meanjin Quarterly* Jim Davidson records an interview with Frank Moorhouse in which Moorhouse's desire to get back to 'the essential Australian' is fully detailed.

David Monaghan argues in *SSF* that the structure of Alice Munro's *Lives of Girls and Women* embodies her belief that growing older brings confinement with the greater responsibilities and traps of death, family, 'religion, love, and sex'.

Readers and students of Iris Murdoch will be glad to know that more and more attention is being devoted to her fiction. In *ConL* Michael O. Bellamy prints an interview with Murdoch which covers such influences

[69] *Somerset Maugham*, by Anthony Curtis. Weidenfeld & Nicolson. pp. 216. £6.50.

on her novels as nineteenth-century fiction, Sartre, and Wittgenstein. Murdoch sees herself as a realist capturing some of the eccentricity of real people. This interest in psychological reality is pursued by P. A. Packer in *DUJ*. Packer investigates Murdoch's treatment of love and her depiction of emotional entanglements. Suffering and love seem to go together in Murdoch fiction. Moreover, she provides excellent portrayals of that almost incomprehensible selfless love which can promote rebirth and new perception. In *Crit* Ann Gossman draws attention to the use of 'icons and idols' in *A Severed Head*. She finds that they 'reinforce an ethical theme stated as a parable' in *The Sovereignty of Good*. Characters are attracted to the fire of the psyche; but they must learn that '"false love moves to false good. False love embraces false death."' In other words they must not worship false icons, but learn to embrace 'the light of the sun', true reality, and true goodness which depends on humility. Lorna Sage (*CritQ*) gives an overview of Murdoch's work and analyses *Henry and Cato*. Sage feels that the total complexity and 'impenetrability of life' is not really what is found in Murdoch's novel. Rather she fashions 'the illusion of a three-dimensional moral world'. Margaret Scanlan looks at Murdoch's ability to wed ideas and fiction in *Renascence*. After analysing *The Sovereignty of Good*, *An Accidental Man*, and *The Sacred and Profane Love Machine*, Scanlan sensibly concludes that Murdoch is not simply didactic; nor does she oversimplify. Instead she deals with complex aspects of the human predicament: 'that suffering must not be romanticized, that the ego must be transcended, and that serious artistic or intellectual work contributes to both of these ends'. Zohreh T. Sullivan writes twice on Murdoch's Gothic fiction. In *MFS The Flight from the Enchanter*, *The Unicorn*, and *The Time of Angels* are seen to reveal that the solipsism of certain characters develops into fantasy world distortions of life. Murdoch's Gothic techniques – such as movement to a closed structural pattern – reflect these distortions. The Gothic novel tradition is thus useful because of its portrayal of 'the dangers of fantasy, and the problem of the discovery of others'. *The Time of Angels* is also Sullivan's subject in *ArQ* and the point made is similar. Gothic techniques are used consciously to express such philosophical themes as the dangers of introspection and solipsism.

Colin Middleton Murry has published a sequel[70] to his account of his childhood. In *Shadows on the Grass*, John Middleton Murry's efforts at establishing a pacifist community farm in East Anglia and Colin's tempestuous relationship with his father comprise most of the text. Quotations from John Middleton Murry's own works and journals together with Colin's memories from a different perspective enhance our awareness of John Middleton Murry as an isolated figure, a 'high-handed' and inept judge of people, an emotional blackmailer who used psychological pressure for his own ends. John Middleton Murry's literary tastes and attitudes are also revealed. Although the work branches out to deal with Colin's life at Oxford, his marriage, and early attempts to establish himself as a writer and teacher, his real concern is his relationship with his father.

In the *Journal of Commonwealth Literature*, Bruce F. Macdonald

[70] *Shadows on the Grass*, by Colin Middleton Murry. Victor Gollancz. pp. 190. £4.95.

investigates the influence of Seepersad Naipaul's 'They Named Him Mohun' on his son's *A House for Mr. Biswas*. The differences not only illustrate V. S. Naipaul's more realistic analysis of the Trinidad community but also show his own distinctive creativity.

Two selections of Flann O'Brien's 'Cruiskeen Lawn' work have appeared[71]. In *The Best of Myles* there are some Keats and Chapman stories, some Plain People of Ireland creations as well as other miscellaneous fanciful anecdotes and ironic observations. Most of the work dates from the Second World War. O'Brien's comic genius is also brilliantly displayed in *The Hair of the Dogma*. Written between 1947 and 1957, the short discursive pieces in this collection range over such subjects as 'the Irish', 'the Dublin man', James Joyce, the 'space race', town planning in Dublin, and the Abbey Theatre.

Maurice Wohlgelernter has written the first extended critical treatment of Frank O'Connor[72]. This is a painstaking attempt to define the unique consciousness of O'Connor, but the book is well-written and quite suitable for the reader seeking a straightforward introduction. Yeats felt O'Connor did for Ireland what Chekhov did for Russia. With this in mind, Wohlgelernter sets out to determine O'Connor's place in Irish life, in the historical and intellectual events of his age. He looks at those who influenced O'Connor, and then moves briskly into a discussion of O'Connor's fictive treatement of political, religious, and family elements in Irish life. There is a valuable chapter on O'Connor's unorthodox and inconsistent criticism and also a section on O'Connor's involvement with the Irish theatre. Ultimately, this study is most valuable for what it illuminates − O'Connor the man, the interpreter and lover of his country, and the perceptive and witty recorder of Irish follies and tragedies. Yet, as Wohlgelernter points out, O'Connor's work has a universal appeal based on his solid understanding of human nature as well as on his remarkable skill as a storyteller.

Charles Scruggs (*SAQ*) suggests some surprising relationships between *A Tale of a Tub* and *Animal Farm*. Both Swift and Orwell have a common cause − 'to free man from the delusions of cant and hypocrisy', to uphold 'the common decency of the common man'. Both rejected those who diverged from 'normal patterns of human behaviour'. Cleo McNelly's article in *CE* will be of special interest to teachers of Orwell. McNelly argues that a reassessment of the teaching approach to Orwell is needed − one which acknowledges the influence of class and race 'presuppositions' on his style. Such awareness should enable the teacher to use Orwell as a starting-place for debate.

Only one issue of *The Mervyn Peake Review* (Spring) was available for detailed assessment. It is primarily a biographical number and contains reproductions of a few Peake drawings. Eric Drake offers some observations on the possible influence of Taoist texts on Peake's work. The substance of a talk given by John Watney on 'planning and writing' his

[71] *The Best of Myles: A Selection from 'Cruiskeen Lawn'*, by Flann O'Brien, ed. with a preface by Kevin O'Nolan. Picador. pp. 400. pb £1. *The Hair of the Dogma: A further selection from 'Cruiskeen Lawn'*, by Flann O'Brien, ed. with a preface by Kevin O'Nolan. Hart-Davis, and N.Y.: MacGibbon. pp. vi + 183. £5.
[72] *Frank O'Connor: An Introduction*, by Maurice Wohlgelernter. New York: Columbia U.P. pp. xxiv + 222. $12.95.

biography of Peake is printed, and the publication of this biography provides an opportunity for reviews and reminiscences by Maeve Gilmore, Gordon Smith, Peter McKenzie, Emil Karafiat, and G. Peter Winnington. Colin Greenland writes on the smashing-of-the-vase symbol in Peake's writing, and reviews of relevant books are provided by various contributors. There are some helpful notes on work in progress as well as reminders about recent and forthcoming publications.

Hilary Spurling's *Handbook to Anthony Powell's Music of Time*[73] is intended for the serious student and casual reader alike. Admirably thorough, it contains a 'Who's Who' character index of fictional and real-life people who appear in the novel series. Valuable notes are given with reference to significant events involving the character in question. There is an index of writers, magazines, articles, Biblical texts, hymns, songs, and books which appear, and also an index to works of art in the novels and their creators. Fictional and actual places are also listed. Every reader will welcome the chronological synopsis of Powell's *Dance* and there is a short informal essay on the structure and patterning of the novels. Humour and the function of characterisation in the novels are also dealt with in a compressed way. Kerry McSweeney suggests some weaknesses in *Hearing Secret Harmonies* (*SAQ*) but feels the novel demonstrates the distinction of the other works in the *Music of Time* series. Powell is rated as 'the peer of Thackeray'.

The Powys Newsletter prints Powys's own preface for the 1957 Japanese edition of selections from *The Meaning of Culture*. Ichiro Hara comments on John Cowper Powys's reputation in Japan and adds a few details on his acquaintance with the writer. Darrell Emmel contributes an article on *Morwyn* as a 'harrowing-of-hell fantasy'. Psychic transformation can help us escape our own unpleasant sadistic hells but only if the unconscious is reached. R. L. Blackmore supplies photographs of Powys's visit to Arnold Bennett. The text compares Louis Wilkinson's expurgated account of the visit with Powys's actual version. David A. Cook writes thoughtfully on Powys's 'spiritual debt' to Hardy and the sense of place in the Wessex novels. Neither novelist is simply a nature writer. They are both 'bards'. Daniel Booth contributes a lively essay entitled 'Teaching *A Glastonbury Romance* to Secondary School Students', there are notes on Powys activities in London, France, and England, and corrections are given for an earlier entry on 'The Powys Collection of E. E. Bissell'. Linden Peach accomplishes three tasks in his *AWR* essay. He examines 'In Defence of Sensuality' and 'A Philosophy of Solitude' as essays which supplement the *Autobiography*, draw together aspects of Powys's self-discovery during the writing of *Wolf Solent*, and demonstrate similarities to Lawrence in their sensibility. Peach concludes that both essays show that 'the prime objective of a person's life is the development of his own unique, individual consciousness'.

William Hunter's study of T. F. Powys[74] is little more than a descriptive essay which attempts to trace Powys's developing maturity. Hunter

[73] *Handbook to Anthony Powell's Music of Time*, by Hilary Spurling. Heinemann. pp. xx + 330. £7.50.
[74] *The Novels and Stories of T. F. Powys*, by William Hunter. Beckenham, Kent: Trigon P. pp. 34. £2.

praises Powys's sincerity and his effective prose style, and notes that
Death and Love are 'the two great realities' for the novelist. Brief space
in this very brief book is given over to a consideration of Powys's achievement in the short story genre.

J. B. Priestley's 'final chapter of autobiography'[75] is a discursive collection of random reminiscences and observations. The tone is sardonic
and at times boastful, at other moments bitter. Yet the felicitous turns
of phrase are still there, hidden gems among many platitudes. Priestley
comments on his early childhood, his feelings about death, the creative
process, his dreams. This is not a coherent autobiography. Those who are
devoted to Priestley will want to read it, and scholars will insist on mining
it, but it is not the best work from the master's pen. Kenneth Young has
written an introductory monograph on Priestley[76]. He sees this novelist
as a 'teller of tales' rather than as a visonary. Such an approach is echoed
in his rather pedestrian handling of Priestley's non-fiction, novels, and
plays in addition to his matter of fact sketch of Priestley's life and literary
career. Young writes in the popular vein, deftly summarising but attempting to do little more than that: 'We sweep swiftly through the centuries'.
Some themes are noted and Priestley's versatility as a dramatist is suggested but there is no sustained critical analysis. Yet Young's concluding
judgement on Priestley suggests there *is* much to analyse: 'He has stimulated thought, political, sociological, literary; entertained us mightily
with his Bayeux tapestry'.

B. L. Reid (*SR*) thinks that V. S. Pritchett's reminiscences reveal 'a
personality but not really a whole person'.

In *N&Q* Robert Barker suggests a source for the South American
section of Read's *The Green Child* which demonstrates that the novel
was not written as 'automatically' as Read claimed.

Brian Taylor considers landscape in the fiction of Ulster novelist
Forrest Reid in *IUR*. Reid sees 'life through an awareness of immanence'
– an awareness which is perfectly expressed in Reid's presentation of
landscape.

The neglected Dorothy Richardson is given full-length biographical
treatment by Gloria G. Fromm[77]. This is a thorough and readable book,
despite occasional misprints and a haphazard system of noting sources.
Fromm gives a detailed account of Richardson's life, travels, and marriage
to artist Alan Odle. More important, however, is her systematic tracing
of the genesis and development of *Pilgrimage,* Richardson's monumental
serial novel. Although emphasis is on the use of real-life experience in the
novel series, Fromm never reads *Pilgrimage* as 'poetic' autobiography.
One is left with a picture of a woman who dedicated her life and art to
the struggle for selfhood and the problems of the emerging woman.
Indeed such dedication interfered with Dorothy Richardson's complete
commitment to art and appears to be the most significant reason for her
failure to become a great artist. Nevertheless, a strong and persuasive

[75] *Instead of the Trees: A Final Chapter of Autobiography,* by J. B. Priestley.
Heinemann. pp. iv + 152. £3.50.
[76] *J. B. Priestley,* by Kenneth Young. Writers & Their Work Series. Harlow,
Essex: Longman. pp. 56.
[77] *Dorothy Richardson: A Biography,* by Gloria G. Fromm. Urbana and Chicago,
Ill. and London: U. of Illinois P. pp. xx + 451. £10.50.

case is made for Richardson as a pioneer figure in modern fiction.

Meticulous research has clearly gone into Miriam J. Benkovitz's biography of Baron Corvo[78]. Benkovitz has based her account of this outrageous figure on interviews, notebooks, memoirs, letters, unpublished essays, and his fiction. This is not a critical biography; rather, it is an attempt to expose the real man behind the myth. Frederick Rolfe is not more attractive than Corvo; he is more pathetic. The chequered career of the seminarian, photographer, homosexual, pederast, and writer reveals a man who failed at every endeavour and who was frequently homeless and friendless (often with good cause). However, there is a spark of creativity, of inventiveness, of resourcefulness which gives this figure an enduring fascination. Comment on the fiction is necessarily limited but thoughtful, and the many photographs are revealing.

In *IShav* Alex Seabrook investigates Saki's 'The Infernal Parliament' as an anti-Shaw story and shows other points at which Saki satirises Shaw and his beliefs. Robert B. Harmon and Margaret A. Burger have compiled *An Annotated Guide to the Works of Dorothy L. Sayers* (Garland Publishing) but this was not available for review.

Cherry Wilhelm (*ESA*) argues that Pauline Smith's linguistic structures reflect her creative use of a form of English she learned as a child in the Karoo.

Muriel Spark's *The Driver's Seat* departs from her usual omniscient point of view, while *The Abbess of Crewe* returns to this practice. Lotus Snow in *RS* attempts to account for this change by viewing the omniscient narrative as a device to create 'the context of mythology'. By creating a mythological rather than realistic framework Spark 'can apprehend a universe governed by immutable principles; she can select from the contemporary scene the topical themes that lend themselves to measurement against those principles'.

Stephen Spender's autobiography[79], first published in 1951, has been issued in paperback. While this is essentially a study of the development of a poet from 1928 to 1939, Spender's quiet observations on writers like Auden, Lawrence, Isherwood, and Virginia Woolf are important.

Virginia Woolf specialists will be interested in the publication of *Sir Leslie Stephen's Mausoleum Book*[80]. This is the 'intimate history' of Stephen's married life written for his children after the death of his second wife. Alan Bell's sensitive introduction makes an understandable plea for the recognition of Stephen's book as a work of great artistic integrity in its control of powerful passion. The major part of the work is devoted to Woolf's second marriage to Julia Duckworth. Self-recriminations on Stephen's part abound. He expresses sorrow for the emotional burdens he visited on Julia and also bemoans the low quality of his own literary talents. At the end a few diary notes for the period 1895–1901 are added, again for the sake of his children. The *Mausoleum Book* offers good insight into Virginia Woolf's family background; Alan Bell is right to

[78] *Frederick Rolfe: Baron Corvo. A Biography*, by Miriam J. Benkovitz. Hamish Hamilton. pp. xvi + 332. £6.50.

[79] *World Within World: The Autobiography of Stephen Spender*, by Stephen Spender. Faber & Faber. pp. x + 349. pb £2.95.

[80] *Sir Leslie Stephen's Mausoleum Book*, by Sir Leslie Stephen, with introd. by Alan Bell. Oxford: Clarendon P. pp. xxxiv + 118. £4.25.

call attention to the obvious influence of Stephen's recollections on *To the Lighthouse.*

Augustine Martin eschews the romantic anecdotes promulgated by James Stephens about himself in his valuable critical study of Stephens's writing[81]. Instead he concentrates on defining Stephens's creative imaginative impulse. Martin touches on the experimental prose fiction and the poetry, noting fantasy formats, journalistic techniques, distinctive elements like parody and satire, the comic idiom and possible influences on Stephens's complex 'patterns of myth, doctrine and symbology'. At the heart of some of the tales is 'a complex vision of human psychology', but Stephens is most important as a relentless experimenter 'with form, language and narrative techniques'. For this reason Martin concludes that Stephens like Joyce is an artist 'in a radical sense', whose best work lies in his prose narrative: 'Here his mythic imagination and his narrative inventiveness achieved a series of remarkably original fictions.' Martin's book is indeed an admirable critical survey, but it covers so much material that there is need for further, more detailed work.

Angela Thirkell, the grand-daughter of Sir Edward Burne-Jones, the mother of Colin McInnes, and a novelist in her own right, has been largely forgotten. Margot Strickland has attempted to remedy such neglect by a biography of this writer of 'middle-class novels for middle-brow tastes'[82]. Written in a chatty and disjointed fashion, this work details the life of an irrepressible, humorous, and rather sardonic woman who published thirty-five novels, many autobiographical to some extent. Unfortunately, or perhaps necessarily, there are numerous accounts of books published and friends met but little analysis of Thirkell's literary merit or even substantiation of her son's claim that 'hers was the tragedy of the inarticulate heart'.

In *SSF* James A. Davies argues that Dylan Thomas's 'One Warm Saturday' can best be understood when seen in relation to Tennyson's 'Maud'. The problems of 'adolescent infatuation' form the basis of both works, and the need to reject romantic relationships creeps in to both poem and story.

Tolkien's *Silmarillion*[83] has finally been published. Edited by Christopher Tolkien, this work contains Tolkien's detailed mythology which forms the background to his writings. *The Silmarillion* actually contains four additional shorter works so that the whole story is present from the myth of creation through the War of the High Elves to the end of the Third Age. Indeed, the last tale, 'Of the Rings of Power and the Third Age', puts the War of the Rings in the context of the whole history of the Elves. Tolkien conceived this work early in his career but constantly altered it in line with his other mythological stories. Christopher Tolkien has done an excellent job of editing the complex variants and providing indexes of names, genealogical tables, a note on pronunciation, and an appendix on 'Elements in Quenya and Sindarin Names' for those inter-

[81] *James Stephens: A Critical Study*, by Augustine Martin. Dublin: Gill & Macmillan. pp. xii + 177. £8.50.

[82] *Angela Thirkell: Portrait of a Lady Novelist*, by Margot Strickland. Gerald Duckworth. pp. x + 182. £5.95.

[83] *The Silmarillion*, by J. R. R. Tolkien, ed. by Christopher Tolkien. George Allen & Unwin. pp. 365 + maps. £4.95.

ested in Eldarin Languages. Although lacking the narrative energy and characterisation of the mythological novels, *The Silmarillion* reflects Tolkien's philological and scholarly interests at the same time as it demonstrates the tremendous feat of formulating a new mythology of creation. As Christopher Tolkien claims, these old legends 'became the vehicle and depository of his [Tolkien's] profoundest reflections'.

The publication of *The Silmarillion* eclipses Jim Allan's attempt[84] to speculate on the contents of Tolkien's work. Allan provides a framework for Tolkien's tales pieced together from all information available before *The Silmarillion* became public. It is of course supplanted by the greater detail and artistry of *The Silmarillion* but Allan does try to suggest relationships between elements in Tolkien's work and aspects of older myths.

A good account of Tolkien's life by Humphrey Carpenter[85] is based on letters, diaries, manuscripts, and reminiscences. Carpenter insists that a critical analysis of the fiction lies beyond the scope of this authorised biography but he does outline some of the influences on Tolkien's imagination and indicates Tolkien's own attitude to his fiction. Tolkien's relationship to his mother and his feelings of pessimism and religious fervour after her death are shown to have had an important effect on his sensibility. Early interests in nature, drawing, and philology are clearly demonstrated, and Carpenter lucidly charts the beginnings of Tolkien's mythology and its development in the fiction. Even more interesting from the point of view of biography is the picture which emerges of a self-effacing but rather stubborn procrastinator, determined to keep his personal and academic lives separate, determined also 'to express his own moral view of the universe' in his fiction as well as to find a vehicle for his created languages. This admirable biography may not totally reveal the man; such a complex figure as Tolkien will always be inscrutable to some extent. But it does provide a thorough picture of Tolkien's personal, academic, and literary life. The appendixes include a genealogical table and chronology of events in Tolkien's life as well as a list of his published writings.

The catalogue of an exhibition of Tolkien's drawings[86] held at the Ashmolean Museum and National Book League in 1976 reprints a selection of drawings and contains an introduction by Baillie Tolkien and a biographical note by Humphrey Carpenter. The drawings show Tolkien's interest in colour and detail, but also reveal an imagined world which is not wholly naturalistic. Divided according to specific works such as *The Hobbit* and *The Lord of the Rings*, Tolkien's art work is useful as it provides 'a coherent set of images and details of what [his imaginary world] looked like'. Ruth S. Noel's *The Mythology of Middle-Earth* (Thames & Hudson) was not made available for detailed examination.

Chikwenye Okonjo Ogunyemi compares Amos Tutuola's *Feather Woman of the Jungle* and Charles W. Chestnutt's *The Conjure Woman*

[84] *A Speculation on The Silmarillion*, by Jim Allan. Hayes, Middx.: Bran's Head Books/The Tolkien Society. pb £1.
[85] *J. R. R. Tolkien: A biography*, by Humphrey Carpenter. George Allen & Unwin. pp. viii + 287. £4.95.
[86] *Catalogue of an Exhibition of Drawings by J. R. R. Tolkien at the Ashmolean Museum and National Book League, 1976-7*. Ashmolean Museum, National Book League, and George Allen & Unwin. 1976.

in *ArielE*. Both writers are romantics with 'common roots steeped in realism' and a common concern 'about man in society, about man in a hostile environment, and the ways for man to survive'. The source of their fascination lies in 'their Africanness' and Ogunyemi uses Tutuola's novel as a touchstone for an assessment of Chestnutt's work.

A Little Order[87] is an enjoyable selection from Evelyn Waugh's journalistic writings, ranging from the early 'beastly little articles' written to order for monetary reasons to more idiosyncratic later works which are elaborate and clearly devoted to Waugh's particular preoccupations. The selections, edited by Donat Gallagher, are arranged in categories which are purely personal and self-revealing, or those which suggest literary, political, or religious positions. Although some of the pieces are admittedly slight, they all contain traces of the shrewd (and often sardonic) observer of the novels. Of particular interest are Waugh's comments on writers which influenced or attracted him because of careful craftsmanship as well as theme – Firbank, Greene, Wodehouse, Beerbohm, and Huxley, for example. Waugh's review of *The Heart of the Matter* (which is seen in theological as much as literary terms) will interest students of Greene as well as those of Waugh.

Christopher Sykes's biography of Waugh (1975) has been issued in paperback[88]. This is a sympathetic – at times almost deferential – study of Waugh based on thorough research into correspondence, written material, reminiscences, and Waugh's own autobiography. Sources for quotations are not provided, however, a fact which certainly detracts from any scholarly pretensions the biography might have. On the whole, this is a readable account of a many-faceted artist and his myriad poses: dilettante, squire, cynic, faithful Catholic, wit, and drunkard. Extensive details on the composition history of Waugh's work are supplied together with numerous anecdotes concerning the public and private man. Sykes also attempts to account for Waugh's grotesque self-hatred and self-caricature in real life. At times, it may seem that he has allowed friendship to negate some of Waugh's more unpleasant characteristics – 'an arrogant man . . . but he was never a conceited man' – but Waugh scholars will welcome this fruitful source of information.

In the *EWN* Spring issue, Sister Thérèse Lentfoehr describes a 1949 meeting with Waugh. He seemed charming and gracious with 'no feet of clay'. Jeffrey M. Heath supplies 'The Year's Work in Waugh Studies' and Jeanne Clayton Hunter offers a short note on Waugh's ironic use of language as '*non*-communication' in *Decline and Fall*. Such usage points up alienation rather than social interaction. In the Autumn number Donat Gallagher makes a biting attack on Sykes's biography, noting factual and interpretive errors. Harvey Sheleny compares *Brideshead Revisited* with James's *The American*, suggesting that James's book was probably a literary model for Waugh's novel. Donald Greene argues that Father Rothschild in *Vile Bodies* is probably modelled on Father Holt in *Henry Esmond*, and Jeffrey Heath compares variations between the manuscript

[87] *A Little Order: A Selection from His Journalism*, by Evelyn Waugh, edited by Donat Gallagher. Eyre Methuen. pp. xvi + 192. £5.95.
[88] *Evelyn Waugh: A Biography*, by Christopher Sykes. Harmondsworth, Middx.: Penguin. pp. 619. pb £1.75.

version of *Scoop* and the first edition. He finds the revised ending vastly superior. Other variations show the novel's affinity with *A Handful of Dust.* Charles Hutton-Brown writes in the Winter issue on 'hagiographical influence' in *Brideshead Revisted:* 'It seems that Waugh sought to embody a stylized martyrdom in each of the Flytes to illustrate that spiritual fulfilment, and the true demonstration of spiritual inheritance is only possible at the expense of temporal life.' Robert Murray Davis locates some interesting variants from the first edition of *Vile Bodies* in the incomplete typescript at the Humanities Research Center in Texas. Hans Otto Thieme supplies a supplementary checklist of Waugh criticism and Gene Phillips provides a brief note supporting Donald Greene's earlier article.

D. S. Savage surveys Waugh's fiction intelligently in *CR.* He detects an uncertainty of feeling in the novels and a disconcerting childishness in many of the characters. Even satire is used to prevent the author from confronting reality in a meaningful way. 'Perhaps this explains why the novels tend to fall into two species, those which attempt a serious representation of life and those in which a comic excision of feeling trivializes the subject and conceals the extent of the writer's involvement in it.' Yet this distinction also breaks down in its turn and 'the same disoriented and ambiguous Waugh emerges in both serious and satirical works'. The trivialisation of life and death in *The Loved One* becomes an 'objective correlative for his own increasing confusion between death and life, between the living and the unliving, the un-dead'. In *SHR* Robert Murray Davis reveals a theological dimension to *Vile Bodies* by a study of title, theme, and structure. T. D. Rogers prints a letter from Waugh in *N&Q.* This letter was contributed to a 1930 souvenir programme of the Oxford Preservation Trust matinee. Waugh suggests Oxford might be beautified by the application of dynamite to a few of the uglier parts of the city.

The neglected later fiction of H. G. Wells is analysed with care by Robert Bloom[89]. In an effort to render 'the experience of reading' these last novels, Bloom offers specific and detailed break-down of *The Bulpington of Blup, Brynhild, Apropos of Dolores, The Holy Terror, Babes in the Darkling Wood,* and *You Can't Be Too Careful.* A splendid initial chapter outlines Wells's own view of the novel 'as a heuristic and civilizing force' provided it is a 'novel of social, cultural, political, and intellectual discovery ... intensely and directly concerned with the life of its time'. Gradually in these later novels Wells came to accept the Jamesian emphasis on characterisation and personality and even considered abandoning the novel form altogether in favour of biography and autobiography. Bloom argues elegantly that these last novels show Wells's usual concern with ideas and experience but they also have a more insistent and consistent 'aesthetic direction' seen in the attempt to integrate ideas 'more intimately' with the technical elements of the novel. Bloom's work is also a thematic study, concerned with Wells's successful portrayal of 'the dimensions and consequences of egotism, the inexorable obtrusion of the self, most narrowly conceived, on life in general'. This personal theme is expanded to take on universal significance in Wells's last novels.

[89] *Anatomies of Egotism: A Reading of the Last Novels of H. G. Wells,* by Robert Bloom. Lincoln, Neb. and London: U. of Nebraska P. pp. x + 196. $10.95.

Bloom's work is also sound in its tactful acceptance of Wells's artistic decline, attributed, Bloom feels, to the failure of the novel genre to satisfy Wells's purpose. This is a workmanlike and sensible study.

Helmut Jansing's study of Wells's 'scientific romances'[90] argues that 'they are characterised by an attempt to fuse the prevalent features of the traditional Gothic Novel and of Utopian fiction'. Wells's novels combine an exciting horror story with a didactic aim, confronting the reader with issues such as vivisection, life on Mars, and the ideas expressed in T. H. Huxley's writings. Wells tries 'to relate his treatment of science and technology to the prevalent issues of his own time'. [H.C.C.]

Selections from the writings of Rebecca West have been collected in one volume[91]. This book serves as an excellent introduction to her work for all her many literary facets are represented: early fiction, biography, political and crime journalism, history and travel writing, and the later fiction. Rebecca West's powers of characterisation and description as well as her shrewd historical grasp and telling wit are clearly demonstrated. A concise critical introduction by Samuel Hynes notes West's main concerns and achievements. Hynes finds her work suffused with a 'steady moral seriousness' and detects a key antithesis 'between the will-to-die, which is male and creates poverty, war, and the ruin of civilisations, and the will-to-live, which is female, and bears and nourishes'.

Patrick White's *Riders in the Chariot* is viewed as symptomatic of a disturbing trend in modern Australian fiction which is obsessed with disintegration, decay, and the repulsive in humanity. Brian McFarlane argues in *CR* that White savours 'what is grotesque and maimed and disgusting about human life'. In *Meanjin Quarterly* Elizabeth Perkins sees 'the Great Australian Emptiness' in White's 'A Fringe of Leaves'. But also present is an attempt 'to form a recognisable and compelling pattern' of human intercourse.

The unpublished conclusion to *The Once and Future King* has appeared. T. H. White's *The Book of Merlyn*[92] was written during the Second World War and is certainly didactic anti-war propaganda. According to Sylvia Townsend Warner's admirable introduction, Merlyn becomes White's mouthpiece. He is filled with spleen and 'fury against the human race, who make war and glorify it'. In the book, Arthur, facing final defeat at Mordred's hands, journeys to the animal world to get a different perspective on man and hence find an answer to war. It is clear that White expresses ideas at the expense of art. When he does remember his duty to the narrative, he recaptures some of his old Arthurian magic.

P. G. Wodehouse's last and incomplete novel, *Sunset at Blandings*[93], has been issued with a long essay and notes by Richard Usborne. Sixteen out of a projected twenty-two chapters are here, together with familiar

[90] *Die Darstellung und Konzeption von Naturwissenschaft und Technik in H. G. Wells' 'scientific romances'*, by Helmut Jansing. Frankfurt am Main: Peter Lang (Angelsächsische Sprache und Literatur 45). pp. 233. sfr. 36.-

[91] *Rebecca West: A Celebration: Selected from her writings*, with a critical introduction by Samuel Hynes. Macmillan. pp. xx + 780. £8.50.

[92] *The Book of Merlyn: The Unpublished Conclusion to The Once and Future King*, by T. H. White, with a prologue by Sylvia Townsend Warner, illustrations by Trevor Stubley. Austin, Tex. and London: U. of Texas P. pp. xxii + 137. £5.25.

[93] *Sunset at Blandings*, by P. G. Wodehouse, with notes and appendixes by Richard Usborne, illustrations by Ionicus. Chatto & Windus. pp. 213. £3.95.

characters, situations, and themes. Usborne's descriptive essay on the novel includes a skeletal outline of the plot to come and detailed observations on the characters based on Wodehouse's own notes. There is also a useful account of Wodehouse's 'method of composition'. Wodehouse addicts will enjoy the brief appendixes on the topography of Blandings Castle and 'The Trains Between Paddington and Market Blandings' as well as the helpful (though at times inconsequential) 'notes to the text'. Unhappily the work clearly shows the need of Wodehouse's exquisite refining touch, but it is invaluable to those who desire an example of his 'Work in Progress'. Owen Dudley Edwards presents 'a critical and historical essay' on P. G. Wodehouse[94] which deals with Wodehouse both as a reporter of 'literary manners and fashions of his day' and as 'a writer of varied themes and moods'. Edwards begins with the 'Edwardian Wodehouse' who had a debt to Conan Doyle and detective fiction, moves steadily through his school stories and on to a consideration of Wodehouse's use of the mock-heroic and the comic novel form. Recurrent themes such as the fear of excess are isolated, but the main concern is with Wodehouse's treatment of social phenomena and problems. For this reason, the essay really seems to by-pass the question of Wodehouse's literary and artistic value, although there is an appendix on the textual revisions in *Leave It to Psmith* which demonstrate 'Wodehouse's perfectionism as a novel-writer'. Still, it is useful to have Wodehouse set in a social-historical context.

There has been some exciting work done by Virginia Woolf scholars this year, much of it concerned with the publication of her own writings. Mary Lyon[95] has edited a number of reviews and articles written by Virginia Woolf which have not been republished in book form. These informal essays are divided into two sections — 'literary matters' or 'writers' and portraits of individuals. The topics cover such diverse subjects as 'Impressions at Bayreuth', Coleridge as critic, and considerations of Sheridan, Thoreau, Sassoon, Melville, Jane Austen, and Theodore Roosevelt. Virginia Woolf's comments on the importance of place to writers like Thackeray, the Brontës, and Edward Thomas are also of interest. As a whole the collection displays Virginia Woolf's unique gift for presenting inner sensations and shrewdly pinpointing the essence of a work or man. As Mary Lyon comments: 'she had the imaginative capacity to place herself in a previous literary period and savour the total atmosphere of that era'. More important, Virginia Woolf achieves in her criticism what for her *defined* critical excellence: 'it is good criticism because it makes us turn to think about the book under consideration'.

The first of a proposed five volumes of Virginia Woolf's diary has been issued[96]. This is the diary which she kept almost continuously after her marriage. Quentin Bell argues in his introduction that the diary is indeed useful for biographical and historical information. Yet it is also a masterful 'literary achievement' in its own right thanks to the beautiful writing

---

[94] *P. G. Wodehouse: A Critical and Historical Essay*, by Owen Dudley Edwards. Martin Brian & O'Keeffe. pp. 232. £4.

[95] *Books and Portraits: Some further selections from the Literary and Biographical Writings of Virginia Woolf*, ed. by Mary Lyon. Hogarth P. pp. x + 221. £5.50.

[96] *The Diary of Virginia Woolf, Volume I: 1915–1919*, ed. by Anne Olivier Bell with introd. by Quentin Bell. Hogarth P. pp. xxviii + 356. £8.50.

and sense of 'immediacy' which is conveyed. The social and cultural scene is clearly set in the introduction. Victorian prohibitions and conventions still operate even in the early decades of the twentieth century and their existence makes the vitality of the diaries all the more apparent. But in addition to dynamic energy and freedom there are depression and melancholy: 'I wrote all the morning, with infinite pleasure, which is queer, because I know all the time that there is no reason to be pleased with what I write, & that in 6 weeks or even days, I shall hate it.' There are many ordinary events — a visit to the dentist, a dinner party — interspersed with acute perceptions of nature, lively literary gossip, and incisive vignettes of literary figures like T. S. Eliot and Lytton Strachey. This diary, superbly annotated by Anne Olivier Bell, gives a striking picture of an era, of a circle, of a novelist, and of a woman. It can only whet the appetite for further volumes.

The third volume of Virginia Woolf letters[97] covers the period of *Mrs. Dalloway, To the Lighthouse,* and *Orlando.* More significant, perhaps, the letters also cover the period when Virginia Woolf fell passionately in love with Vita Sackville-West. As we have come to expect, there is little actual information about her own work, but amidst the cattiness and trivia, there is warmth and thoughtfulness (as in the letters to the dying Jacques Raverat), vitality, and a confident flippancy ('I rather want novels to depress me . . . So I expect the books I write to be depressing and full of horrid monsters'). There is the same shrewd judgement operating on her literary colleagues; she sees, for example, the danger of Forster's relationship with his mother: 'his mother is slowly dispatching him, I think — He is limp and damp and milder than the breath of a cow.' Yet Virginia Woolf could be generous elsewhere about Forster's ability to lay 'hold of the thing I have done'. The vitality and confidence in her judgements could be related to the fact that during this period the Woolf establishment and Hogarth Press flourished. Virginia's personal relationships were also strong. Her devotion to Vanessa is clearly established and her deepening relationship with Vita Sackville-West is traced within these pages. Here can be found strong feeling sometimes sentimentalised in its depiction. More important is the fact that both women seemed intellectually stimulated by the mutual passion — Virginia Woolf's creative response was *Orlando.* (Vita Sackville-West's attitude to the novel is shown by her interesting letter to Virginia published in the appendix.) As usual, the editing and production of the book are of the highest standard. The letters are indeed an outstanding contribution to Woolf studies.

A paperback edition of *A Room of One's Own*[98] has been issued and will be welcomed by those wishing ready access to Virginia Woolf's plea for the liberation of women so that their true creative and intellectual potential can be realised.

George Spater and Ian Parsons have made intelligent use of the Woolf archives at the University of Sussex and of personal photographs and diaries of Leonard Woolf in order to create an intimate picture of daily

[97] *A Change of Perspective: The Letters of Virginia Woolf: Volume III: 1923–1928,* ed. by Nigel Nicolson; assistant ed. Joanne Trautmann. Hogarth P. pp. xxiv + 600. £12.50.
[98] *A Room of One's Own,* by Virginia Woolf. St. Albans, Herts: Triad/Panther. pp. 108. pb £0.60.

married life in the household of Leonard and Virginia Woolf[99]. The authors trace the early years, family background and upbringing of Leonard Woolf and Virginia Stephen, showing the importance of such groups as the Cambridge Apostles in their lives. The uncertain 'harrowing courtship' of Leonard and Virginia is sensitively handled, as are Virginia Woolf's mental depressions. Leonard Woolf clearly emerges from the homely domestic details, the accounts of friends, and the description of literary careers, as the stable regulating force in Virginia's life. There is, of course, little critical commentary on Virginia Woolf's fiction, but by setting the scene in which much of her work was written, Spater and Parsons have done an admirable service.

Hermione Lee's assessment of the novels of Virginia Woolf[100] is a stimulating introduction to the fiction. The nine novels are critically analysed with attention to the ways in which technique is used for the portrayal of vision. In her introduction Lee considers Virginia Woolf as a modernist who attempted to express 'the life of the mind through physical images' suggesting 'a secular faith in the value of the seen and felt'. This approach is developed throughout the book in which a chapter is devoted to each novel, although links between all the novels are noted. The elusiveness of the self and the difficulty of personal relationships are themes which Lee considers. But these concerns are subsumed by the larger polarity between the chaotic real world of social communication and the harmonious visionary realm of the silent inner self which can exist on a higher impersonal plane, making sympathy possible. Throughout the novels there is a constant struggle to reconcile this duality stylistically, as seen in the mingling of realistic and metaphoric modes. Ironically, the duality is resolved only by the acceptance of death in this transient real world. Such acceptance gives meaning to experience and freedom from the bondage of personality. It is indeed refreshing to find such intense but straightforward concentration on technique and method of presentation. This study certainly succeeds in its aim of 'turning attention back from the life to the fictional work'.

VWQ is appearing spasmodically. In the double issue available for review there are some useful articles, although creative arts, 'Women in Music', book reviews, and Asian poetry in translation take up a good deal of space. Michael Holzman identifies some omissions in *Virginia Woolf and Lytton Strachey, Letters* due to Leonard Woolf's editing of the correspondence. Unflattering remarks about personalities are among items expunged. Elizabeth Steele, Karen Reynders, and Judith Lange offer an annotated index to *Orlando* which follows up the entries in Virginia Woolf's own 'mock-scholarly' index and also treats all capitalised nouns in the text. John Lehmann gives a fuller account than is found in his autobiography of the resumption of his association with the Hogarth Press in 1938. Carole O. Brown writes well on *The Voyage Out* as a reflection of Roger Fry's influence on Virginia Woolf in technical as well as theoretical ways. Fry's 'An essay in Aesthetics' really outlines the

[99] *A Marriage of True Minds: An Intimate Portrait of Leonard and Virginia Woolf,* by George Spater and Ian Parsons. Jonathan Cape and Hogarth P. pp. xiv + 210. £5.95.
[100] *The Novels of Virginia Woolf,* by Hermione Lee. Methuen. pp. xiv + 237. £5.50.

stylistic devices of *The Voyage Out*. Joan Givner discovers that Katherine
Anne Porter and Virginia Woolf both produced work entitled *The Leaning
Tower*. While no direct influence is possible, both writers are concerned
about the place of the artist in time of war. The typescript will of Sir
Leslie Stephen is reproduced.

An excellent Virginia Woolf number devoted primarily to *The Years*
and *Three Guineas* appeared as the Winter issue of *BNYPL*. Louise A.
DeSalvo locates early notebook and diary entries recording Virginia
Woolf's first thoughts on *The Years*. 'Dante's effect on the mind' was
originally an important consideration. Joanna Lipking sees *The Years*
as satire of 'the rigidity of conventional roles . . . [of] the human need to
cut a figure'. The central structure is based on satiric opposition between
'institutional and spiritual' most noticeable when the characters view
monuments and religious edifices. The scorn in *The Years* and *Three
Guineas* causes Beverly Ann Schlack to argue that Virginia Woolf's stance
is not that of a delicate sensibility. Rather she has courage and integrity
'and confers intellectual honor upon those of the oppressed who find their
reality too real for evasion, or victory, or laughter'. Madeline M. Hummel
explores the epistolary form in *Three Guineas*. This format gives all the
advantages of a dialogue together with a high focusing of material which
serves as a vehicle for the narrator's anger. *Three Guineas* shows that
'intellectual liberty is best strengthened by negating those platitudes which
in the past have stood for "freedom"'. Victoria S. Middleton argues in
an original way that *The Years* is deliberately flawed. 'The novel teaches
the adverse effects of constraints upon selfhood and creativity. Paradoxically, she achieves the proof of her thesis about politics and art by means
of a superbly calculated tour de force, an anti-novel.' *The Years* was first
called *The Pargiters*. Mitchell A. Leaska explores the meaning of 'pargeter'
and relates it to the curiously elliptical novel. He concludes that the novel
is both fiction and autobiography which accounts for its emotional substructure. Present suffering became 'punishment for the Past. And what
greater torment could this woman endure than to feel purged of her
creative powers'. Sallie Sears examines the relationship between sexuality
and power in *The Years* and *Three Guineas*. Masculinity is presented as
death-dealing and cruel. Femininity is more capable of intimacy. The
womanly desire is for escape from the 'suffocating "private house"'
for which men believe women are trained. A thorough consideration of
the drastic final revisions of *The Years* is Grace Radin's valuable contribution to the issue. She reprints galley proofs of the two episodes which
are extensively altered and concludes that 'the loneliness and self-question-
ing of the unpublished episodes deepen the significance of [Eleanor's]
vision at the end of the novel'. Margaret Comstock shows that the form of
The Years complements its anti-fascist political vision. The reader must
think out and understand the pattern if the novel's truth is to be grasped.
Finally Jane Marcus discusses the connection between Greek drama,
Wagnerian opera, and *The Years*. Woman is seen as a 'vessel of life' and
a death-rebirth motif is clearly present. Operatic echoes can be found
in the form of 'a Dantean downward-moving spiral' tracing the downward
impetus 'of British life until the mid-nineteen-thirties'. This article is
continued in the next issue of *BNYPL*. Scattered but tantalising notes

and observations enable Marcus to suggest that *The Years* is 'a female epic'.

Alex Zwerdling (*Novel*) cautions sensibly against too positive a reading of *Between the Acts*. It is not so much a 'celebratory work affirming unity and continuity' as an attempt to capture 'the sense of a once vital cultural tradition that has lost its authority and connection with the present'. Fragmentation, not synthesis, is the dominant characteristic. In *MLQ* Richard S. Lyons attempts to clarify the intellectual structure of *Between the Acts* and to highlight 'its significance in the larger pattern of Woolf's works'. Woolf's main concern in her novels is with the significance of the moment. But in *Between the Acts* she explores the present related to a personal and historical past. However, history offers no answer to the meaning-of-the-moment question. Even religion and art provide only ambiguous and tentative solutions — a fact reflected in the structure. Given such inconclusiveness Lyons decides that the novel is singularly modern in its confrontation of absurdity and despair. In *ConL* Carol Ohmann sees *Jacob's Room* as a criticism of Western civilisation and culture which are all too often damaging. The novel proclaims 'a set of anti-traditional attitudes' which would be developed in the later fiction. Alex Zwerdling (*PMLA*) also looks at Virginia Woolf's criticism of society, this time in *Mrs. Dalloway* which he reads as a study of the 'governing class'. Clarissa plays a pivotal role in the movement toward a changed society which will be 'less hostile to the buried life of feeling in every human being'. Paul West's weak article in *SoR* looks at Virginia Woolf as a prophet and creator of the future in *Orlando*. In *Studies in Interpretation* (II) Judith Espinola examines the 'controlling narrative presence' in *To the Lighthouse*. Like a film camera this omniscient narrator provides a new quality of perception reflected through the eye of a character then 'refracted' through the narrative voice. In other words the narrator, 'as a controlling force and speaking guide who serves as the "semi-transparent envelope"... conditions the form of the novel'. Michael Kreyling examines the influence of Virginia Woolf on Eudora Welty in *SoR* by a comparison of *To the Lighthouse* and *The Optimist's Daughter*. Jane Lilienfeld in *TCL* argues that *To the Lighthouse* has autobiographical overtones. The relationship between Mrs Ramsay and Lily Briscoe is like that between mother and daughter. 'Laying Lily's obsession to rest about the Ramsays' marriage perhaps helped Virginia Woolf to diffuse her own obsession with her parents' marriage.' Also in *TCL* Jack F. Stewart examines the symbolic purpose of light and the lighthouse in *To the Lighthouse:* 'The voyage to the Lighthouse is any activity of consciousness that reaches out toward the Light, follows a direction, seeks integration.' A frequently neglected aspect of Virginia Woolf's writing is considered by René Wellek who examines her value as a critic. In a brisk article (*SoR*) he suggests that her main intention was to grasp an object fully. But he also discovers that she was attracted by 'the universally human' in an author. His conclusion is sound and well-supported. While Virginia Woolf offered no new theories she remains a critic useful for her characterisation and evaluation of main novelists like Austen, Meredith, Hardy, Conrad, Bennett, Wells, D. H. Lawrence, and Huxley.

2. Verse

Several interesting general studies merit review this year. Peter Levi's *The Noise Made by Poems*[101] is an articulate and fascinating inquiry into certain fundamental issues such as how music relates to poetry, how to understand poetry, how poetry expresses the world, what we can mean by poetry and what it is for. The vastness of the investigation does not lead to dullness and pretentiousness; on the contrary the book is lively and rewarding, drawing on many examples to make its undogmatic points. A sample of Levi's style will speak for itself: 'There are no languages, so far as I know, and no human societies have been discovered that I have ever heard of, without some kind of poetry. . . . If poetry is natural and universal, arising inside every language, and if there are many languages inside which we know how poetry behaves, then it ought not to be hard to say what poetry is. Roughly we recognize it by the noise it makes.'

In *Professing Poetry*[102] nine of John Wain's lectures given as Oxford Professor of Poetry are to be found, together with his 'account of what the Oxford Chair is, what it feels like to take it on, what kind of situations and what kind of people the Professor tends to find himself among'. The volume concludes with nine of Wain's recent poems. The lectures cover the subjects of W. H. Auden, Emily Dickinson, Philip Larkin, William Empson, and Edward Thomas, as well as the wider areas of 'Alternative Poetry', 'On the Breaking of Forms', 'Reflections on the First Night of Comus', and 'Poetry and Social Criticism'. The narrative is interwoven with the lectures, describing how particular subjects were chosen and tracing the circumstances leading up to the delivery of the topics. The friendliness and warmth of this approach should appeal to the general reader and the specialist alike.

The Poet in the Imaginary Museum[103] brings together hitherto uncollected pieces of literary criticism by Donald Davie. Written between 1950 and 1977, the essays have not been revised for their inclusion; postscripts have been added where Davie finds comment appropriate. The subjects range from general topics to specific commentaries: 'The Translatability of Poetry' and 'Poetry and the Other Modern Arts' are side by side with pieces on T. S. Eliot, J. M. Synge, and W. B. Yeats among others. This volume will be read to illuminate the evolution of Davie's thinking over more than a quarter of a century and will be valued for its incisive content. Bernard Bergonzi's 'Davie, Larkin, and the State of England' (*ConL*) brings into focus the contrast between the two poets: 'Larkin stays still, does not travel, rereads Hardy; and writes about what he sees. Davie moves on, reads many literatures — though returning constantly to Pound, the master voyager of modernism — and longs for the heroic and the imaginatively possible, as well as what is actually and inescapably there.'

Essays on Twentieth-Century Poets[104] contains a selection of George Fraser's essays spanning the period 1947 to 1976. Under scrutiny are

[101] *The Noise Made by Poems*, by Peter Levi. Anvil Press Poetry. pp.103. £3.25.
[102] *Professing Poetry*, by John Wain. Macmillan. pp.x + 396. £6.95.
[103] *The Poet in the Imaginary Museum: Essays of Two Decades*, by Donald Davie. Ed. by Barry Alpert. Manchester: Carcanet. pp.xxi + 322. £6.
[104] *Essays on Twentieth-Century Poets*, by George Fraser. Leicester U.P. pp.255. £3.95.

W. B. Yeats, Ezra Pound, T. S. Eliot, Robert Graves, W. H. Auden, Louis MacNeice, William Empson, Stephen Spender, Lawrence Durrell, Dylan Thomas, Norman MacCaig, Keith Douglas, Thom Gunn, and Philip Larkin. The criticism is made especially personal on account of the frequent acute observations of those poets with whom Fraser was acquainted; invariably these anecdotes capture character in miniature sketches: 'Eliot suddenly made a royal entrance. . . . He was wearing patent leather shoes and I noticed how lightly he moved on the balls of his feet, like a cat.' Both The Critical Heritage Series and The Critical Idiom series are added to. Timothy Rogers edits *Georgian Poetry 1911-1922*[105]. This valuable collection of reviews and articles refers to those forty poets whom Edward Marsh included in his anthology *Georgian Poetry*. An introduction charts the background to the Georgian literary scene, paying particular attention to contemporary literary magazines. The collection covers critical commentaries from 1912 to 1959. A useful appendix offers brief critical and biographical details of the contributors to *Georgian Poetry*. A select bibliography is included.

Peter Faulkner's subject is *Modernism*[106]. The two decades 1910–30 and the positions of T. S. Eliot, Ezra Pound, James Joyce, Virginia Woolf, and D. H. Lawrence are emphasised, while W. B. Yeats is shown to be an important precursor of English literary Modernism. A final chapter examines the post-1930 attitude towards Modernism. Arnold P. Hinchcliffe's subject is *Modern Verse Drama*[107]. The work of T. S. Eliot and Christopher Fry is examined in some detail, while many dramatists, including W. B. Yeats, W. H. Auden, and Christopher Isherwood, are briefly touched on. These dramatists are seen to have paved the way for the innovations of Beckett, Pinter, Wesker, and Arden.

The summer issue of *ConL* is concerned with the post-war lyric in Britain and America. Three papers are of interest here. Michael Wood's 'We All Hate Home: English Poetry since World War II' takes the view that banality has dominated British poetry since the death of Yeats: 'The distinctive sentiment in the work of Philip Larkin, Donald Davie, Charles Tomlinson, Thom Gunn, Ted Hughes, and Geoffrey Hill is a sense of crowding; of litter, both material and moral; of cheapness and indifference to cheapness; and, above all, of the oppressive, inescapable, thoroughly internalized presence of others.' Philip Larkin, Charles Tomlinson, Ted Hughes, and Geoffrey Hill are examined for their 'variety of English responses to the English condition'. Lawrence Kramer's 'The Wodwo Watches the Water Clock: Language in Postmodern British and American Poetry' suggests that 'postmodern American poets have by and large kept up the passionate belief in language as mediation – in the ability of language to confront, interpret, and even to re-enact experience – that marks the modernism of their precursors, Pound, Williams, Eliot, Stevens, Crane, and, adoptively, Yeats and Auden. . . . Recent British poets, on the other hand, seem deeply distrustful of the intersection

[105] *Georgian Poetry 1911-1922*, ed. by Timothy Rogers. Routledge. pp.xvi + 435. £7.50.
[106] *Modernism*, by Peter Faulkner. Methuen. The Critical Idiom series. pp.x + 86. hb £2.35, pb £1.20.
[107] *Modern Verse Drama*, by Arnold P. Hinchcliffe. Methuen. The Critical Idiom series. pp.80. hb £2.35, pb £1.20.

between language and reality, and appear to see the process of using language as a hard struggle against what seems its futility or vulnerability'. Philip Larkin, Geoffrey Hill, and Ted Hughes are scrutinised in the light of this statement. M. L. Rosenthal writes on 'Modern British and American Poetic Sequences'. The genre is defined: 'a grouping of mainly lyric poems and passages, rarely uniform in pattern, tending to interact as an organic whole'. Austin Clarke's 'Mnemosyne Lay in Dust', Basil Bunting's *Briggflatts*, David Jones's *Anathemata*, Thomas Kinsella's *Notes from the Land of the Dead*, John Montague's *The Rough Field*, and Ted Hughes's *Crow* are mentioned in comparison with American examples of the genre. Rosenthal notes that 'It is unfortunate that our criticism should have become so abstracted that a whole major genre could evolve, mature, and metamorphose without even being noticed'.

In *MBL* Michael J. Collins looks at 'The Rhetorical Double in Modern British Poetry', attempting to demonstrate, by such examples as Wilfred Owen's 'Strange Meeting' and 'The Show', Philip Larkin's 'Mr. Bleaney', Geoffrey Hill's 'September Song', and Gerard Manley Hopkins's 'Felix Randal' that 'the double is as useful and important a device for the poet as it is for the dramatist or the writer of fiction'.

Brian Gardner's *The Terrible Rain*[108] is an anthology of Second World War poetry representing 119 poets. The policy in selection is explained: 'I have tried to capture something of the flavour, as well as of the best poetry, of 1939–45. This, I hope, has excused me from a too-slavish respect for reputations, and allowed the inclusion of some lesser-known and forgotten poets; also, of some poetry of lesser quality perhaps that is valid in the context.' The poets include John Cornford, W. H. Auden, Louis MacNeice, Sidney Keyes, and Keith Douglas. The selection leads us through the history of the war, ending with two extracts from a poem attempting to respond to Hiroshima: Edith Sitwell's 'The Shadow of Cain'. This is a volume of great interest, with well-chosen poems and a sensitive introduction.

It is important to draw attention to the continuing issue of contemporary verse by Carcanet New Press. Volumes published this year include *Living Together*[109] by Edgar Bowers, *Affinities*[110] by Charles Boyle, *Paradise Stairway*[111] by Glen Cavaliero, *'In The Stopping Train' and Other Poems*[112] by Donald Davie, *Real Estate*[113] by Michael Hamburger, *Consequently I Rejoice*[114] by Elizabeth Jennings, *The Garden End*[115]

[108] *The Terrible Rain: The War Poets 1939–1945*, ed. by Brian Gardner. Magnum Books. Methuen. pp.xxv + 227. £0.85.
[109] *Living Together: New and Selected Poems*, by Edgar Bowers. Manchester: Carcanet. pp.84. £2.90.
[110] *Affinities*, by Charles Boyle. Manchester: Carcanet. pp.56. £2.
[111] *Paradise Stairway*, by Glen Cavaliero. Manchester: Carcanet. pp.54. £2.
[112] *'In The Stopping Train' and Other Poems*, by Donald Davie. Manchester: Carcanet. pp.55. £2.
[113] *Real Estate*, by Michael Hamburger. Manchester: Carcanet. pp.96. hb £2.50. pb £1.95.
[114] *Consequently I Rejoice*, by Elizabeth Jennings. Manchester: Carcanet. pp. 70. hb £3, pb £2.
[115] *The Garden End: New and Selected Poems*, by Peter Jones. Manchester: Carcanet. pp.116. £2.90.

by Peter Jones, *Fools' Paradise*[116] by Grevel Lindop, *'Pataxanadu'*[117]
by Christopher Middleton, *The New Divan*[118] by Edwin Morgan, *At
The Edge*[119] by Neil Powell, *From the Other Country*[120] by Andrew
Waterman, *Soundings*[121] by Daniel Weissbort, *The Winter's Task*[122]
by Robert Wells, and *The Dwelling-Place*[123] by Clive Wilmer. The valuable
magazine *Outposts,* edited by Howard Sergeant, continues to publish
contemporary verse. Readers of contemporary Irish verse may also be
interested in the poem *Siege!*[124] by Desmond Egan published by The
Goldsmith Press.

The *English Auden*[125] brings together a substantial selection of the
early writings: *Poems, Look Stranger!, The Orators,* and *Journey to a War*
are reprinted in their entirety. From the volume *Another Time* those
poems written before Auden's arrival in America are included. The volume
also contains extracts from *Letters From Iceland,* some uncollected and
some previously unpublished poems, excerpts from plays (including
extracts from an unpublished draft of *On the Frontier* and from the
unpublished *The Enemies of a Bishop* and *The Chase*), some essays and
reviews, journal entries, and a chapter from an unpublished book. The
published version of 'Paid on Both Sides' and the unpublished early
version are both here, aiding comparison. This is a valuable edition, admirably complementing the *Collected Poems.*

Martin E. Gingerich's *W. H. Auden: A Reference Guide*[126] is an
annotated bibliography of criticism covering the years 1931–1976.
Thoroughness rather than exhaustiveness is claimed for the guide. Clearly
set out, with an introduction that briefly charts the trends of Auden
scholarship, this book will be of use and interest.

Edward Callan's 'W. H. Auden's First Dramatization of Jung: The
Charade of the Loving and Terrible Mothers' (*CompD*) argues that 'Paid
on Both Sides' is derived from Jung's *Wandlungen und Symbole der
Libido.* The theory dramatised in Auden's play is that of the 'dual nature,
or "ambitendencies" of the libido whereby it energizes not only man's
instinctive urges but his creative consciousness also'; this notion 'was
the fundamental cause of the parting of the ways between Freud and
Jung'. Callan maintains therefore that there is 'a need for some reassessment of the common assumption among critics that Auden, at the outset,

---

[116] *Fools' Paradise,* by Grevel Lindop. Manchester: Carcanet. pp.64. £2.
[117] *'Pataxanadu' and Other Prose,* by Christopher Middleton. Manchester:
Carcanet. pp.107. £2.90.
[118] *The New Divan,* by Edwin Morgan. Manchester: Carcanet. pp.118. hb £3,
pb £2.
[119] *At the Edge,* by Neil Powell. Manchester: Carcanet. pp.61. £2.
[120] *From the Other Country,* by Andrew Waterman. Manchester: Carcanet.
pp.63. £2.
[121] *Soundings,* by Daniel Weissbort. Manchester: Carcanet. pp. 64. £2.25.
[122] *The Winter's Task,* by Robert Wells. Manchester: Carcanet. pp.63. £2.
[123] *The Dwelling-Place,* by Clive Wilmer. Manchester: Carcanet. pp.59. £2.
[124] *Siege!,* by Desmond Egan. The Curragh, Co Kildare: The Goldsmith P.
pp.34. £0.50.
[125] *The English Auden: Poems, Essays and Dramatic Writings 1927–1939,*
ed. by Edward Mendelson. Faber. pp.xxiii + 469. £8.95.
[126] *W. H. Auden: A Reference Guide,* by Martin E. Gingerich. Boston, Mass.:
G. K. Hall + Co. pp.xii + 145. $15.

was primarily indebted to Freud'. In *PMLA* Peter E. Firchow has a long paper: 'Private Faces in Public Places: Auden's *The Orators'*. The psychological teachings of Homer Lane and John Layard are investigated as influences on the shaping of *The Orators*. In *N&Q* Elizabeth Salter connects 'Henry Adams and W. H. Auden: *The Age of Anxiety'*.

Michael Hamburger examines 'The Poetry of Samuel Beckett' (*PN Review*) stressing that 'The true difficulty over Beckett's poems . . . has to do with silence, exile, reduction, and bilingualism'.

Edwin Brock's *Here. Now. Always.*[127] is a collection of prose pieces and poems encapsulating autobiographical experiences from childhood to marriage. The events are captured simply, often amusingly, sometimes poignantly, and the book will be of interest to followers of Brock's verse.

Karl Muller's 'Basil Bunting's Linguistic Poetics' (*FMLS*) argues that, under the influence of Pound, Bunting aimed, both in theory and in practice, to regenerate poetic language from the weaknesses prevalent in the nineteenth century. A development is noted: 'By shifting from images to language as a system, he had overcome imagistic weakness in structure and thematic scope. . . . Bunting has gained a voice of his own. His later long poems *The Spoils* and *Briggflatts* have a stronger coherence than Pound's *Cantos* and treat a subject matter which is free from the influence of his master.' Donald Davie's 'English and American in Briggflatts' (*PN Review*) categorises Bunting's poetry as 'Anglo-American': American in technique but profoundly English in sensibility. Bunting's position as an English poet among the otherwise all American 'objectivist' group is investigated. It is suggested that 'for the English poet the writing of poems is a public and social activity, as for his American peers it isn't'. *Briggflatts* is admired: 'It is writing of this quality . . . that English poetry needs to assimilate and build on'.

Edward Levy writes on 'The Poetry of Charles Causley' (*PNReview*). 'A Ballad for Katharine of Aragon' gives us 'a world of lovelessness, violence, indifference and disappointment' central to the poems as a whole. An analysis of some key poems leads to the conclusion that 'Causley's strength lies in the abundance and variety of his work, in the spontaneity which makes possible the changes of register which we find there, in his capacity for making poems in different registers, sometimes for adults, sometimes for adults and children'.

In 'The Religious Lyrics and Satires of Austin Clarke' (*Hermathena*) Daniel J. Murphy explores Clarke's poetic analysis 'of the impact of religion on his childhood, of the developing polarities of reason and faith, of sense and spirit, and of the problems of human suffering, hatred and pride with which each is closely associated'.

There are three books concerned with T. S. Eliot for review this year. In *T. S. Eliot's Personal Waste Land*[128] an important new interpretation of *The Waste Land* is argued. James E. Miller Jr shows that Eliot's friendship with Jean Verdenal was at the heart of the impulse to write the poem. The early 'Ode' is examined as 'an introduction to Eliot as a confessional poet'. The manuscripts of *The Waste Land* are scrutinised in

[127] *Here. Now. Always.*, by Edwin Brock. Secker & Warburg. pp. 153. £3.90.
[128] *T. S. Eliot's Personal Waste Land: Exorcism of the Demons*, by James E. Miller Jr. Pennsylvania State U.P. pp. xi + 176. £9.10.

sections of close analysis. A passage in 'Little Gidding' is suggested to be 'a kind of coda to the Eliot – Verdenal relationship'. Biographical detail is handled with admirable sensitivity; it is stressed that 'what actually happened, if anything, between Eliot and Verdenal has not been of primary concern here: rather, Eliot's imaginative transfiguration of the relationship in the shaping of his poetry has been the focus of attention'. This is a lucid study, firmly establishing the personal mood of *The Waste Land*.

Lyndall Gordon's excellent biographical study[129] works towards Eliot's conversion to Anglo-Catholicism, aiming to 'trace the continuity of Eliot's career and to see the poetry and the life as complementary parts of one design, a consuming search for salvation'. The important American experience of Eliot's childhood and student years is examined in detail. The period of 1911–14 is exposed as a time of great spiritual awakening during which Eliot already contemplated conversion. His first marriage is represented as 'the secret inferno to be traversed before he might be worthy of the genuine awakening only Christianity could supply'. Three appendixes are provided: a selected list of Eliot's reading in mysticism (1908–14), a section on 'Dating *The Waste Land* Fragments', and 'A Note on *The Waste Land* and *Ulysses*'. Biographical sources are noted.

In '*Ulysses*', '*The Waste Land*', *and Modernism*[130] Stanley Sultan demonstrates how 'certain qualities of *The Waste Land* placed in a certain light reflect a rich set of similarities between it and *Ulysses*, and that set of similarities illuminates Modernism as a whole'. An artistic practice, a thematic purpose, and a conception of art and the artist are shown to be common to both works. The Notes of *The Waste Land* are seen to function as part of the Modernist allusive method. The religious nature of *Ulysses* is exposed and compared with that of *The Waste Land*. The inconclusive ending and the manipulation of the narrative point of view are seen to be characteristics of Modernism shared by Joyce's novel and Eliot's poem.

William Arrowsmith's 'Daedal Harmonies: A Dialogue on Eliot and the Classics' (*SoR*) models itself on the 'Dialogue on Dramatic Poetry' in order to examine Eliot's poetic use of the classics; 'Dans le restaurant' is the focus of the examination. Doris L. Eder's 'The Exile of T. S. Eliot' (*UDQ*) is a biographical piece, concluding that 'Eliot came to regard England as home and put down roots there: England suited his formal, conservative, traditional, and elitist temperament. He saw England as the bridge between the Old World and the New, and he saw himself as a mediator between old and new, past and present.' Christopher Heywood's 'Francis Hodgson Burnett's *The Secret Garden:* A Possible Source for T. S. Eliot's "Rose Garden"' (*YES*) deals with 'Burnt Norton', relating the writing of the poem to the crisis in Eliot's life which followed the collapse of his first marriage. In 'The Plan of *The Waste Land*' (*MBL*) F. C. McGrath finds the structural key of the poem in Jessie Weston's *From Ritual to Romance:* 'the structural progression . . . follows the archetypal pattern of the fertility rites, with the significant alteration that in Eliot's *Waste Land* there is no resurrection'.

[129] *Eliot's Early Years*, by Lyndall Gordon. O.U.P. pp.xii + 174. £4.95.

[130] '*Ulysses*', '*The Waste Land*', *and Modernism*, by Stanley Sultan. Port Washington, N.Y.: Kennikat P., and Folkestone, Kent: Bailey Bros. & Swinfen. pp.xii + 92. £5.50.

There are five pieces on Eliot in *N&Q*. Nancy K. Gish indicates the error of the omission of the apostrophe in the line 'Hurry up please it's time' in nearly all editions of *The Waste Land* and she points out that this has led to false interpretation of the line. Robert Bluck's 'T. S. Eliot and "What the Thunder Said"' traces the source of the three Sanskrit words at the end of *The Waste Land*. Timothy Materer's 'Chantecler in *The Waste Land*' elucidates the cock's cry in section V with reference to the play *Chantecler* by Edmond Rostand. Geoffrey Carter's 'The Question of T. S. Eliot's Erudition' notes that some famous lines in *The Waste Land* are based on a mistranslation of Dante. Grace B. Briggs relates Stevenson's *The Ebb-Tide* and Eliot's *The Hollow Men*.

Michael T. Beehler writes on *'Murder in the Cathedral:* The Counter-sacramental Play of Signs' (*Genre*), while Louis Tremaine contributes to *MW* 'Witnesses to the Event in *MaQṣat al-Hallāj* and *Murder in the Cathedral*'. In *NMAL* Carol Weiner examines '"Sometimes Hesitating at the Angles of Stairs"': Becket's Treasonous Thoughts in *Murder in the Cathedral*'. Mabel C. Donnelly considers 'The Failure of Act III of Eliot's *The Cocktail Party*' (*CLAJ*). Leo Hamalian has a paper in *ColL:* 'The Figures in the Window: Design in T. S. Eliot's *The Family Reunion*'.

Stephen Brown has 'A Reader's Note on Similarities between Browning's "A Toccata of Galuppi's" and Eliot's "The Love Song of J. Alfred Prufrock"' in *BSNotes*. In *MLS* James C. Haba writes on '"Till human voices wake us and we drown": Community in "The Love Song of J. Alfred Prufrock"'. Elizabeth Oakes notes 'Prufrock and King Arthur' (*NConL*). Peter A. Martin examines '"Son of Man" in the Book of Ezekiel and T. S. Eliot's *The Waste Land*' (*ArQ*). Sanford Pinsker has 'Eliot's "Falling Towers" and the Death of Language: A Note on *The Waste Land*' in *CP*.

Jack Behar looks at 'Eliot and the Language of Gesture: The Early Poems' (*TCL*) while Zohreh Tawakuli Sullivan examines 'Memory and Meditative Structure in T. S. Eliot's Early Poetry' (*Renascence*). Arthur E. Walzer finds 'An Allusion to *Paradise Lost* in Eliot's "Gerontion"' (*NMAL*). Roger Sharrock considers '*Four Quartets* as a Post-Christian Poem' (*AJES*), and F. R. Leavis contributes to the same periodical 'Eliot's Permanent Place'. Muhammad Ismail Bhatti studies 'Matthew Arnold as T. S. Eliot's Predecessor' (*Explorations*). In *AN* Meta Grosman assesses 'T. S. Eliot on the Reader and Poetry'. In *Thought* James Torrens has a paper: 'Eliot's Poetry and the Incubus of Shakespeare'.

Mary Byrd Davis's *James Elroy Flecker*[131] argues that 'The traditional view of Flecker as a creator of superficial beauty is a distortion.' The scope of Flecker's work is emphasised: the books, contributions to period-icals, unpublished letters, and manuscripts are examined in an attempt to trace Flecker's development as a writer. It is concluded that, had he survived to make further literary achievements, 'Drama is the area in which Flecker would in all probability have made his greatest contribution to English literature'. A check list of Flecker's contributions to periodicals is provided. In *DUJ* the same critic writes on 'James Elroy Flecker's *Don Juan*' as 'a version which retains a close kinship with the traditional story but which is both modern and original'.

[131] *James Elroy Flecker: A Critical Study*, by Mary Byrd Davis. Poetic Drama and Poetic Theory Series, vol.33 Salzburg: U. of Salzburg: pp. viii + 264.

In *CSR* Stanley M. Wiersma considers 'The concept of Law in Christopher Fry's *Curtmantle*'. Anthony S. G. Edwards offers 'Further Addenda to Higginson: The Bibliography of Robert Graves' (*PBSA*).

In 'An Odd Angle: The Poetry of Geoffrey Grigson'(*Agenda*) Humphrey Clucas analyses Grigson's statement 'I think the best poems are immediacy [sic]' with special reference to 'Viper's Bugloss', 'Repetition in a Yew Tree'. 'I Love You', 'Angles and Circles', 'The Oculi', 'Encouragement, on a Leaf', and 'No Sprinkling of Bright Weeds'.

Patrick Swinden's 'Thom Gunn's Castle' (*CritQ*) details the development of the poetry to *Jack Straw's Castle*, detecting a 'narrowing concern with the self as a "pinpoint of consciousness"' and concluding that 'In his overriding preoccupation now with what lies beyond or beneath consciousness, Gunn really has reached a time when words no longer help'. Catharine R. Stimpson's 'Thom Gunn: The Redefinition of Place' (*ConL*) unravels the multiple sense of place in the poems: the body, the external physical world, and the mental landscape are the themes examined in this context.

Robert Buttel's study of Seamus Heaney[132] (1975) contributes to the Irish Writers Series edited by J. F. Carens. The volume opens with an account of Heaney's awakening to poetry, stressing the affinities felt with Robert Frost and Ted Hughes. *Death of a Naturalist, Door into the Dark,* and *Wintering Out* are examined in detail. It is concluded that 'Seamus Heaney's best poems define their landscape and human experience with such visceral clarity, immediacy, and integrity of feeling that they transcend their regional source and make a significant contribution to contemporary poetry written in English.' In *Éire* John Wilson Foster writes on 'Seamus Heaney's "A Lough Neagh Sequence": Sources and Motifs'.

In *IowaR* A. K. Weatherhead has a paper on Geoffrey Hill, while Igor Webb's 'Speaking of Holocaust: The Poetry of Geoffrey Hill' appears in *UDQ*.

Norman F. Davies assesses 'The Poetry of Ted Hughes' (*MSpr*). Claire Hahn writes on 'Crow and the Biblical creation narratives' (*CritQ*). She argues that 'the persistent and ironic parallels between the Biblical accounts of Creation, Redemption, and Apocalypse and the story of *Crow* . . . create more than unity; they are a scaffold giving structure to the volume and their narratives provide a counterpoint of comment on the history of Hughes' mythical bird'. In *CritI* Seamus Heaney's 'Now and in England' looks at Hughes, Hill, and Larkin. In 'Crow: Myth or Trickster?' (*Theoria*) Geoffrey Hughes writes on the verse and its critical reception with terseness and stringency, deciding that Ted Hughes 'has joined the very big crowd of trend-poets whose work is a loud and confused echo of a destructive reality which is created as much as it is perceived'. Brenda Megerle has a paper in *SHR:* 'Ted Hughes: His Monsters and Critics'.

René Hague's *A Commentary on 'The Anathemata' of David Jones*[133] is an extremely valuable elucidation of a potentially obscure text. We are led through the poem by a scholarly and sympathetic commentator;

[132] *Seamus Heaney*, by Robert Buttel. Associated University Presses and Lewisburg: Bucknell U.P. 1975. pp. 88. £2.
[133] *A Commentary on 'The Anathemata' of David Jones*, by René Hague. Wellingborough, Northants. Skelton's P. pp. xii + 264. £8.

comparisons with Jones's other poetry are made; unfamiliar vocabulary is carefully annotated; mythic references are located. Included are a number of comments made by David Jones who was able to approve a substantial amount of this guide. René Hague also has a long and intricate paper in *Agenda* — 'Myth and Mystery in the Poetry of David Jones' — where definitions of myth and mystery are analysed, David Jones is quoted on the subjects, and his use of myth is examined. There are two other articles on Jones in *Agenda:* Peter Orr writes a memoir and Colin Wilcockson traces Jones's affinity with William Morris. In passages of *The Anathemata* and *The Sleeping Lord* there are verbal parallels to passages of Morris concerning the dilemma to which Jones refers as 'The Break', the breaking for the artist of links with the past, 'occasioned primarily by the consequences of the industrial revolution, notably in the divorcing of the manufacture of useful artifacts from the artistic impulse to beautify what we make'. In 'David Jones's Use of a Geology Text for *The Anathemata'* (*ELN*) Thomas R. Dilworth writes on the relationship between Part 1 of the poem and William Whitehead Watt's *Geology for Beginners* (London, 1929), a work not acknowledged as an influence, yet one which contributed very importantly to the general tone as well as to the specialised vocabulary of the first Part. Roland Mathias's *David Jones: Eight Essays on His Work as Writer and Artist*[134] (1976) has not been available for review.

Julian Croft has written on *T. H. Jones*[135] for the Writers of Wales series. The poetry is divided into two sections for the purpose of critical examination. The first period, 1946–1959, 'is one of experimentation with technique and consolidation . . . influences are obvious, and the reader often has the feeling that he is reading a highly competent poet who is more interested in his craft than in making immediate his experiences'. In 1959 T. H. Jones took up a lectureship in Australia, and the second period of his poetry began, with a new style and a new emphasis on 'the element of punishment and inevitable retribution and destruction'. It is concluded that 'In his synthesis of Eden, Wales, love and exile, T. H. Jones constructed an impressive vision of the deracinated post-war man attempting to find a permenent and satisfying myth which could produce a state of peace, contentment, and love to calm the storms of war and personal despair.' A select bibliography is provided.

Darcy O'Brien's introduction to Patrick Kavanagh[136] (1975) sees the poet as 'part of a general literary reaction against mythopoeic notions of Irishness'. The book is more biographical than critical; *The Great Hunger* and *The Green Fool* are examined in some detail. Kavanagh's autobiographical novel *By Night Unstarred*[137] is now available. Peter Kavanagh has distilled two incomplete novels by his brother to arrive at this version. An introduction and epilogue fill in the details of the poet's life. John

[134] *David Jones: Eight Essays on His Work as Writer and Artist*, ed. by Roland Mathias. Llandyssul, Wales: Gomer. 1976. pp.144.

[135] *T. H. Jones*, by Julian Croft. U of Wales P. 1976. pp.123. £1.

[136] *Patrick Kavanagh*, by Darcy O'Brien. Associated University Presses and Lewisburg: Bucknell U.P. 1975. pp.72. £2.

[137] *By Night Unstarred*, by Patrick Kavanagh, ed. by Peter Kavanagh. The Curragh: The Goldsmith P. pp.199. £4.50.

Nemo edits a Patrick Kavanagh number of *JIL*.

Erwin Otto has written a monograph on Brendan Kennelly[138]. The book presents Kennelly's aesthetics, the importance of Irish history and present politics for his work, and defines his particular contribution to Anglo-Irish literature. A major section deals with Kennelly's poetry and there is an appendix printing fifty-one of his poems in the original English. [H.C.C.]

In *IowaR* Merle Brown writes on 'Larkin and His Audience'. In *SoR* John Press has a paper 'The Poetry of Philip Larkin'; Larkin has affinities with and owes debts to Tennyson, W. B. Yeats, and Thomas Hardy.

Erik Frykman's brief study of Norman MacCaig's verse[139] examines the major thematic preoccupations and the image patterns. Recurring subjects include the poet's art, love, death, space, and time. It is found that 'by far the greatest number of metaphors in MacCaig's verse are based on various forms of humanisation of animals or objects'. 'A Man in Assynt' is looked at in detail as a longer poem that embodies some of MacCaig's main characteristics.

In *JIL* Conrad A. Balliet has an interview 'Micheál MacLiammóir Recalls Maud Gonne MacBride'. In *EI* Honor O'Connor considers 'The Early Poetry of John Montague'. A. C. Hixson's *Edwin Muir: A Critical Study*[140] has not been available for review. *IUR* has a Richard Murphy special issue. Maurice Harmon introduces the poet and his background, and provides a biographical note. Seamus Heaney examines the poetry. J. G. Simms's 'The Battle of Aughrim: History and Poetry' analyses the historian's view of the battle, then turns to the view in Murphy's poem on Aughrim, concluding that 'His presentation is subjective, but the subjectivity is balanced'. Anthony Whilde's 'A Note on the Storm Petrel and Corncrake' provides background to the birds that inspired poems. Jonathan Williams writes thorough explanatory notes in 'A Glossary to *The Battle of Aughrim* and *The God Who Eats Corn*'. Mary Fitzgerald has compiled 'A Richard Murphy Bibliography'. In *WLT* Michael J. Collins writes on 'The Anglo-Welsh Poet John Ormond'.

Sven Bäckman relates 'Wilfred Owen and Elizabeth Barrett Browning' (*SN*). Owen's interest in the writings of Elizabeth Barrett Browning may have led to his experiments with pararhymes and half-rhymes. In *N&Q* Dominic Hibberd notes some crucial books that were in Wilfred Owen's possession. William Cooke relates 'Wilfred Owen's "Miners" and the Minnie Pit Disaster' (*English*). In *LHY* A. Banerjee has a paper: 'Wilfred Owen: A Reassessment'. In *EA* Bernard Winehouse discusses two unpublished early poems by Isaac Rosenberg.

Included in the interesting anthology *Myth and Reality in Irish Literature*[141] is an essay by Henry Summerfield on 'AE as a Literary Critic'.

[138] *Das lyrische Werk Brendan Kennellys*, by Erwin Otto. Frankfurt am Main: Peter Lang (Angelsächsische Sprache und Literatur 39). pp.352.

[139] *'Unemphatic Marvels': A study of Norman MacCaig's Poetry*, by Erik Frykman. Gothenburg: Acta Universitatis Gothoburgensis. Gothenburg Studies in English 35. pp.70. Sw. Cr. 50.

[140] *Edwin Muir: A Critical Study*, by A. C. Hixson. New York: Vantage. pp.247.

[141] *Myth and Reality in Irish Literature*, ed. by Joseph Ronsley. Waterloo, Ontario: Wilfrid Laurier U.P. pp.xiv + 329. hb $9.50, pb$7.

Robert Bernard Davis's *George William Russell ('AE')*[142] has not been available for review.

Merle Brown's 'Stress in Silkin's Poetry and the Healing Emptiness of America' (*ConL*) argues that 'Jon Silkin's poetry hinges on an acute stress between imaginative realization and ideological commitment. . . . His American poems . . . articulate his release from the confusions of his latest English poetry and at the same time signal a sharp and profound openness and repugnance before the new land'. The poetry written on Silkin's return to England after a year in Iowa is seen to be remarkably different from the early poems.

In *Agenda* Stephen Wade writes on 'Stevie Smith and the Untruth of Myth'. His thesis is that 'By using humour, absurdity, repetition and patternless lines ending in rhymes, Stevie Smith convinces us that myth is no more than a fascinating untruth – or perhaps half-truth.'

Augustine Martin's study of James Stephens[143] examines the entire canon. The profound early influences of Browning and Blake are traced, and the development to Stephens's late mystical poetry is documented. However it is in the prose narrative that Stephens is seen to excel, and the work in this area is discussed in detail. It is argued that 'Stephens was an artist of the utmost individuality whose life was a persistent, arduous and frequently brilliant experiment with experience and form'. In *MSpr* Birgit Bramsbäck writes on 'The "Dublinscape" of James Stephens'.

Paul Ferris's illuminating biography of Dylan Thomas[144] takes into account fresh material both American and British, including BBC archive information, unpublished manuscripts and letters, and the fruits of interviews with about two hundred people. Extensive notes indicate the sources of information. Intelligent and sensitive, the book is a welcome addition to the documentation of Dylan Thomas's life.

R. B. Kershner Jr contributes to the series The Poet and His Critics a volume on Dylan Thomas[145]. The series assesses and categorises critical viewpoints on selected modern English and American poets. Kershner's aim is twofold: 'The book should serve both as an introduction to the major areas of investigation for the reader whose interest in Thomas has no specific focus, and as a guide to more intensive studies for the reader who wishes to become acquainted with work already done upon a single aspect of the poet's writings.' An introduction surveys the major areas of critical response to Thomas's poetry and prose. Commentaries with a biographical and psycho-analytical emphasis are then explored. The view of Thomas as a religious poet is investigated and it is suggested that this is 'the most significant and controversial thematic aspect of Thomas's poetry'. An important critical approach involves placing Thomas in literary contexts: he is examined as a twentieth-century poet, as a Welsh poet, and in comparison with the romantic and metaphysical poets; two sections investigate the work of critics on this aspect. A final chapter summarises

[142] *George William Russell ('AE')*, by Robert Bernard Davis. Boston, Mass.: Twayne. pp. 163.

[143] *James Stephens: A Critical Study*, by Augustine Martin. Dublin: Gill & Macmillan. pp.xii + 177. £8.50.

[144] *Dylan Thomas*, by Paul Ferris. Hodder & Stoughton. pp.399. £7.50.

[145] *Dylan Thomas: The Poet and his Critics*, by R. B. Kershner Jr. Chicago, Ill.: American Library Association. 1976. pp.xiii + 280. $14.95.

and evalutates critical opinions of Thomas's poetics. A bibliography is provided at the end of each chapter. An appendix offers a list of 'basic sources for Thomas': a discussion of bibliographical material, together with an annotated list of Thomas's major works and some secondary sources. In addition we are given a chronology of Thomas's life, and an 'Index of Explications' which provides references to articles or books in which individual poems are fully discussed.

James A. Davies investigates the relationship between 'Dylan Thomas' "One Warm Saturday" and Tennyson's *Maud'* (*SSF*). It is proposed that 'an awareness of this relationship is basic to a full understanding of the story's meaning'. Paul J. Ferlazzo contrasts 'Dylan Thomas and Walt Whitman: Birth, Death, and Time' (*WWR*). Richard A. Davies writes on 'Dylan Thomas's Image of the "Young Dog" in the *Portrait'* (*AWR*). The irony of Thomas's 'young dog' pose is brought out: 'There is a pattern in Thomas's parade of youthful versions of himself but it is not the one that is generally emphasised. The pattern is one of a gradual loss of courage and boldness, a consequent increase in fears and terrors, until the young dog is fully metamorphosed into a "terrified prig of a love-mad young man"'. Dominick Hart explores 'The Experience of Dylan Thomas's Poetry' (*AWR*). Thomas's purpose is to make the reader feel or experience a unity in the universe. Hence if we analyse the poems on an intellectual level, we pull apart what Thomas is attempting to lock together: 'Thomas's poetry does not depend on an intellectual similarity between the forces of sex, death and God precisely because *similarity* marks the limit of intellectual comprehension. Rather Thomas's poetry depends on an emotional and visceral acknowledgement that these forces somehow exist one within the other in a way that surpasses our and even the poet's understanding.' Carroll F. Terrell writes on 'Thomas's "Over Sir John's Hill"' (*Expl*). In *AR* William F. Van Wert has a paper: 'Dylan. A Documentary'. Stan Smith writes on 'A Public House and Not a Hermitage: Nature, Property and Self in the Work of Edward Thomas' (*CritQ*).

Belinda Humfrey's 'The Gap in the Hedge: R. S. Thomas's Emblem Poetry' (*AWR*) contrasts Wordsworth's and R. S. Thomas's 'way of seeing essential man'; it is shown that Thomas has more in common with Traherne, Herbert, and Vaughan. In particular the emblematic poems dealing with a figure framed by a void are dwelt on: in 'Sea-Watching', for example, 'A passing gap, a fleeting absence of words, pictorially visible within the poem, conveys the poet's glimpse of eternity through mere supposition, through "it might have"'.

In *CritQ* Ruth Grogan writes on 'Charles Tomlinson: Poet as Painter'. Paul Mariani examines 'Tomlinson's Use of the Williams Triad' (*ConL*), arguing that the 'experimentation with the Williams triad may, in the long run, have helped him to loosen his own rhythms and to return to a blank verse mode now notable for its delicate suspension, its phrasal modification, its hesitating stresses'. *PNReview* celebrates Charles Tomlinson's fiftieth birthday. A tribute from Michael Schmidt heads the celebration: 'His independence, his tenacity, and his formal and thematic quests benefit all of us ... by providing distinctive poems, new and unexpected formal models, fresh approaches to poetry, and an example of poetic integrity within the living English tradition.' Five of Tomlinson's recent poems and an interview with him follow. A collection of tributes by fifteen writers, critics, producers, and readers (including Peter Levi, John Press, and Ronald Hayman) forms the bulk of the material, while Tomlinson's most recent graphic work is presented on adjacent pages.

Ruth Pryor's 'The Pivotal Point in Poetry: Vernon Watkins and the Taliesin Legend' (*AWR*) explores the significance of the figure of Taliesin in the poetry, taking as a starting-point Watkins's note on 'Poet and Goldsmith': 'this poem is about Taliesin looking at the created universe from the standpoint of Christian faith, which I call the pivotal point between one way of writing and another'.

The late Curtis B. Bradford's *W. B. Yeats: The Writing of 'The Player Queen'*[146] is in the series Manuscripts of W. B. Yeats, of which David R. Clark is the General Editor. This extremely valuable series is the product of painstaking scholarship. The evolution of the drafts of *The Player Queen* is especially interesting: revised again and again throughout Yeats's career and reflecting Yeats's developing ideas with regard to the 'system' with each successive draft, it was imperative to include the play in the series. Thus it is all the more distressing to discover that the publishers have failed to reproduce most of the corrections made by the General Editor in checking galley proofs of the book. After Bradford's decease it was Professor Clark's repeated effort to obtain page proofs. The effort remained in vain. In a letter Professor Clark has advised this reviewer that neither his galley proof corrections nor those corrections made by Russell K. Alspach have been preserved in their entirety. A section of Professor Clark's letter should be quoted in this regard in order to exonerate him from responsibility for errors.

'In the "Acknowledgements" I thank various persons, noting particularly that "Brig. Gen. Russell K. Alspach has very carefully checked line numberings to indicate similarity or identity of various lines . . . to those numbered in *The Variorum Edition of the Plays of W. B. Yeats.*" Alas, although the publishers printed this sentence, they failed to print most of General Alspach's corrections. I owe it to General Alspach (and to the reader) to correct the impression that the line numberings in Bradford's book have behind them the authority of the editor of the *Variorum.* I apologize to Professor Alspach (and to the reader) for the discrepancy, but the publishers left me helpless in the matter. If the publishers did not approve my emendations, they could have dropped me as General Editor; there was no contract with me. It is very strange that they have retained my designation as General Editor and then, without any communication, have ignored my corrections.'

It is extraordinary that a volume with such potential, worked on with such dedication, should have been abused in this way. The bulk of the text presents manuscripts representative of the play's development; an introductory chapter comments on Yeats's progress in writing *The Player*

[146] *W. B. Yeats: The Writing of 'The Player Queen'*, ed. by Curtis Bradford. Manuscripts of W. B. Yeats series. Dekalb, Ill: Northern Illinois U.P. pp.xxvi + 483. $30.

Queen. The elements from various drafts retained in the finished play, and those elements rejected, are tabulated, as is the information on the parts of the play covered by each manuscript. Bradford has commented at length on some of the drafts. The 1919 productions of the play are examined and the reviews of the first performances of it in London and Dublin are discussed. The additions that appear in the 1922 Macmillan texts, the development of the unicorn symbol in Yeats, and its meaning in the play, are investigated. It can only be re-iterated that this very commendable scholarship has been sadly treated by the publishers.

The two-volume edition of *Letters to W. B. Yeats*[147] contains a selection of over five hundred letters, the majority of which have never been published in full. The years 1886 to 1939 are spanned and the many correspondents include J. B. Yeats, George Russell, Maud Gonne, George Moore, and Gordon Craig. The editors' criteria in selection were 'first, to represent the range of Yeats's interests and, second, to imply through letters from artists, writers, and critics the development of Yeats's aesthetic'. Explanatory notes head each letter. The volumes are fascinating despite the enforced omission of letters from T. S. Eliot, Joyce, Synge, O'Casey, Lady Gregory, and Ezra Pound.

Richard J. Finneran edits *The Correspondence of Robert Bridges and W. B. Yeats*[148]. In this slim, illustrated volume are included twenty-seven letters from Bridges, fifteen letters from Yeats to Bridges, as well as a single letter to Mrs Robert Bridges. The editor's aim has been 'to present the letters in the form in which they were written' thus preserving idiosyncratic spelling and punctuation. An introduction traces the relationship between the two poets; a new perspective is gained when we read Bridges's comment: 'Yeats . . . is a true poet, and delightful company, but he is in great danger of fooling himself with Rosicrucianism and folk lore and erotical spiritualisms. It is just possible that he may recover'. In an appendix Yeats's 1897 article on Bridges is reproduced from *The Bookman*. Two further appendixes note the Yeats volumes in Bridges's library and the Bridges volumes in Yeats's.

E. H. Mikhail's *W. B. Yeats: Interviews and Recollections*[149] brings together a hundred biographical pieces on Yeats. The two volumes include accounts by John Masefield, Sean O'Casey, William Rothenstein, and Edmund Dulac. A. Norman Jeffares introduces the volumes, stressing that the collection 'throws light upon the authors as well as the poet himself'. The editor declares his aims: 'The present collection of interviews and recollections is a small effort to contribute to Yeats scholarship. It is hoped that it will constitute an added source of material for future biographical research.' However, in support of the argument that the collection is aimed at the school and undergraduate markets rather than the biographical scholar, see Warwick Gould's long review in *English*.

A. Norman Jeffares edits the W. B. Yeats volume in The Critical

[147] *Letters to W. B. Yeats*, ed. by Richard J. Finneran, George Mills Harper and William M. Murphy. Macmillan. 2 volumes. Vol 1: pp.xvii + 302. £10. Vol 2: pp.xi + 325. £10.

[148] *The Correspondence of Robert Bridges and W. B. Yeats*, ed. by Richard J. Finneran. Macmillan. pp.xviii + 68. £6.95.

[149] *W. B. Yeats: Interviews and Recollections*, ed. by E. H. Mikhail. Macmillan. 2 volumes. Vol 1: pp.xvi + 197. £7.95. Vol 2: pp.xi + 227. £7.95.

Heritage Series[150]. Included are 115 pieces of criticism written between 1884 and 1939, spanning Yeats's literary career. Appropriately enough, the volume commences with some words of J. B. Yeats on his teenage son's efforts at composition, noting that 'His bad metres arise very much from his composing in a loud voice manipulating of course the quantities to his taste'. W. H. Auden's poetic tribute to Yeats concludes the chronological series of critical extracts. The editor provides a useful introduction, as well as a depressing note: 'Because of the high fees asked by some authors, publishers or agents it has not been possible to include some criticism which the editor would have liked to make available in this selection.' Critics represented include Cleanth Brooks, Edith Sitwell, Lytton Strachey, I. A. Richards, and T. S. Eliot. A select bibliography is provided.

Barton R. Friedman's *Adventures in the Deeps of the Mind*[151] studies the Cuchulain plays (including *Deirdre*) as 'a paradigm of Yeats's struggle . . . to find a genuinely dramatic mode adequate to his aspirations for the stage'. A preliminary chapter sketches in the background dramatic theory, emphasising Yeats's 'ultimate conception of the stage . . . as a mirror of mind'. There follows an analysis of each of the six plays.

The second volume in the series Irish Literary Studies concerns *Yeats and Magic*[152]. Mary Catherine Flannery is careful to specify the distinction in Yeats's thinking between magic and mysticism: 'he saw a subtle but important difference between being a mystic and being a magician: the mystic passively submits to a system while the magician is a creator, a controller of systems . . . his idea of a magician is strikingly similar to his idea of a poet; all poets share some power of the magician and the greater the poet the more conscious he will be of the links between magic and poetry'. Concentrating mainly on the early prose, and using a chronological approach, the development of Yeats's interest in theosophy and cabbalism is traced. There is a section on Yeats and Blake, followed by emphasis on the evolution of Yeats's concern with Irish mythology in particular. By 1889 Yeats had begun 'to integrate his interests and goals, attempting to become one man – an Irish poet, using Irish subject matter, welding into his technique and statements the substance of magic and mythology'. When Yeats stated the three 'doctrines' of his belief in magic in the 1901 essay 'Magic' the importance lay in the public declaration of the hitherto private conviction. By the time of the first draft in 1912 of 'Ego Dominus Tuus' Yeats had achieved the integration begun in 1889.

There are several papers on Yeats in the anthology *Myth and Reality in Irish Literature*[153]. Norman H. MacKenzie links 'Hopkins, Yeats and Dublin in the Eighties'. Denis Donoghue considers 'Yeats: The Question of Symbolism'. Balachandra Rajan contributes 'The Poetry of Confron-

[150] *W. B. Yeats: The Critical Heritage*, ed. by A. Norman Jeffares. Routledge. pp.xvi + 483. £8.25.
[151] *Adventures in the Deeps of the Mind: The Cuchulain Cycle of W. B. Yeats*, by Barton R. Friedman. Princeton, N.J.: Princeton U.P. pp.xiii + 151. £7.50.
[152] *Yeats and Magic: The Earlier Works*, by Mary Catherine Flannery. Gerrards Cross, Bucks.: Colin Smythe. pp. 165. £6.50.
[153] *Myth and Reality in Irish Literature*, ed. by Joseph Ronsley. Waterloo, Ontario: Wilfred Laurier U.P. pp.xiv + 329. hb $9.50, pb $7.

tation: Yeats and the Dialogue Poem'. Joseph Ronsley looks at 'Yeats as an Autobiographical Poet'. David R. Clark discusses 'After "Silence"', The "Supreme Theme": Eight lines of Yeats'. Shotaro Oshima's 'Between' Shapes and Shadows' comments on the Noh drama of Japan with relation to Yeats. Thomas Kilroy compares 'Two Playwrights: Yeats and Beckett'.

Samuel Levenson's biography of Maud Gonne[154] is aimed at the general reader rather than the scholar. The lack of notes is frustrating in a book full of quotation, and the style is journalistic. Certain crucial areas in the relationship of Maud Gonne and Yeats do not receive sympathy, the mystical faith is dismissed as 'rigmarole', and Yeats emerges as slightly ridiculous: 'Yeats could spend hours, even days, weighing the value of one word in a poem as contrasted with another, but he could postulate, without a hint of skepticism, all-encompassing ideas about man and the universe that defy both belief and understanding.' The public Maud Gonne is more objectively documented, and it is concluded that 'Though Maud thought long and seriously about political problems, she turned out in the end to be more of a propagandist than a fresh political thinker or effective organizer'.

There are two papers on Yeats in *MBL*. Laurence Perrine considers 'Yeats's Response to the Experience of Rejected Love'. It is shown that Yeats 'believed in commitment and passionate attachment' and that the cynical view of love in 'Never Give All the Heart' is not Yeats's considered judgement. James Lovic Allen writes on 'Yeats and Modernism'. His subject is how far Yeats can be regarded as a modernist. Issues taken into account are whether modernism is essentially an extension of Romanticism, whether form or content defines a modernist work, whether the early, the middle, or the late Yeats should be considered in this regard, and whether Yeats's editing of the *Oxford Book of Modern Verse* helps us to arrive at conclusions. It is seen that Yeats is 'more nineteenth century and non-modern as a man and a poet than twentieth century and modern'. Both these critics have also contributed to *CP:* James Allen's paper is '"Horseman, Pass By!"': Metaphor and Meaning in Yeats's Epitaph' and Laurence Perrine's is 'Yeats's "Supreme Theme"'.

William C. Barnwell has written three papers on Yeats. For *SAB* he has looked at 'The Rapist in "Leda and the Swan"'. In *ELN* he examines 'The Blandness of Yeats's Rhadamanthus', arguing that, in 'The Delphic Oracle Upon Plotinus', the word 'bland' should be read more positively than our contemporary usage of the word suggests. In *SoR* Barnwell interviews 'James Dickey on Yeats'. Three areas of discussion are focused on: the importance of the System, the place of Yeats in our time, and Yeats's attitudes to sexuality, experience, and closed forms in writing.

Michael North's 'Symbolism and Obscurity in "Meditations in Time of Civil War"' separates the 'true Symbolist symbols' from the 'emblems' in that poem. In *EA* Pierre Danchin's 'A Propos de l'acceuil de W. B. Yeats par la Critique Anglaise' replies to M. F. G. Atkinson's 1976 *EA* article: '"Mighty Beautiful Stuff": Two New AE letters and Some Footnotes to the Irish Renaissance'. Danchin believes that Atkinson has misrepresented Francis Thompson's attitude to Yeats. Richard J. Finneran's 'On Editing Yeats: the Text of *A Vision* (1937)' (*TSLL*) details the

[154] *Maud Gonne*, by Samuel Levenson. Cassell. pp.xi + 436. £6.95.

discrepancies between *A Vision's* three printed editions, Yeats's own annotated and corrected copies, and the proofs printed after Yeats's death and corrected by his wife and his editor at Macmillan. The problems of editing an acceptable edition are examined, and it is pointed out that the process of revision made by Mrs Yeats and Thomas Mark 'extended to most, if not all, of the Yeats texts published from 1949 to 1962'. Finneran stresses therefore that 'we need to determine in detail the authority for the changes in these texts', and especially we need to do so with regard to the text of the poems.

Daniel Lenoski investigates 'The Symbolism of Rhythm in W. B. Yeats' (*IUR*). The prose writings are adduced to demonstrate that Yeats quested for musical and symbolic structure in his works. Noh drama was the climax of that quest. In *N&Q* David Parker writes on 'Yeats's Lapis Lazuli'. The Chinese carving given to Yeats has a precise symbolic significance: 'the lapis lazuli was designed to remind observers of a state of blessedness associated with longevity or immortality or both'. Yeats was very likely aware of the meaning of the carving and consciously exploited it in his poem.

There are two papers on Yeats in *SR*. Samuel Hynes's fascinating 'All the Wild Witches: The Women in Yeats's Poems' makes the point that 'in Yeats's mind the sexual interaction of male and female was a paradigm of the creative process'. The actual women, as distinct from the earlier poetical figures who enter the poetry by the time of *In the Seven Woods*, 'engage the imagination of the poet, and out of that engagement come the poems ... sex is a metaphor, and the sexual woman — old or young, historical or mythical, crazy or sane — is the muse of all creation'. The poems are scrutinised for their attitudes to sexual love. In the late love poems Yeats very often assumes the persona of a woman: 'in his last years Yeats's imagination had become like a marriage bed — a coupling of male and female, a solved antimony. Perhaps that is why those last poems are the greatest lyric poems of our time'.

James Olney's amusing 'W. B. Yeats's Daimonic Memory' (*SR*) suggests that 'Yeats's ability to forget things, by virtue of the strategic uses to which he put it, in the end became virtually a faculty in itself — the opposite counterpart, as it were, of the faculty of memory'. The device of employing adroit syntax 'that, by being simultaneously assertive and hesitant, contrives to say something and *at the same time* deny it' and that subsequently implies that Yeats 'never said what he said, never denied what he had said, and is even now not denying either his statement or his denial' is investigated in the prose. The strategy of forgetfulness is employed especially when anything to do with the occult is in question. The use of rhetorical questions in the poetry becomes another 'device for slipping the literalist noose'.

Steven Helmling's 'Yeats's Esoteric Comedy' (*HudR*) discusses a 'uniquely Yeatsian comedy ... of ironic self-discovery in which the play of contradiction and inconsistency come to have considerable exploratory value'. We are also made aware of a 'comedy of ambiguity, issuing from an awareness that "discovery" is never complete or final'. We are invited to acknowledge that the humour in Yeatsian accounts of the occult is conscious: 'Viewed in this way, the Gulliverian poker face ... pushes the events we are reading about gently but firmly in the direction of the ludicrous and the incredible; toward a comic response, that is, and toward fiction.' The use of the fictional characters Robartes and Aherne is in particular seen as a comic distancing technique, and Helmling goes on to say, 'If I were not reluctant to plunge into the stuff of Yeatsian esoterica proper, I might be tempted to suggest a comic reading of the whole of *A Vision*'. It is argued that Yeats intended us to see that 'Fact and fiction ... exist on a continuum, rather than in an either/or relationship ... we are invited to indulge freely both our belief and our doubt, our urge to revere and our impulse to mock'.

Hiromu Miyauchi's 'The Byzantium Poems: A Verbal Criticism' (*SELit*) contends that the conflict of Yeats's vacillation between the natural world and the aesthetic-spiritual world 'constitutes an integral part of the Byzantium poems'. Miyauchi examines Yeats's 'subtle change in attitude towards the two worlds with special reference to the language which reflects it'. There follows a very close and intricate analysis of the poems with the emphasis on 'Byzantium'.

In *Studies* there are two papers on Yeats. Mark Mortimer's 'Yeats and Synge: An Inappropriate Myth' questions whether Synge's decision to go to the Aran Islands was motivated by Yeats's famous advice. It is impressed on the reader that 'the time has come to cease the parrot repetition of what is at best highly doubtful and at worst a complete distortion of the available evidence. Synge's decision was taken in the context of a family connection, a knowledge of Irish, an interest in Brittany and a yearning to discover in his own country a primitive, unspoiled civilisation. It was taken nearly eighteen months after his meeting with Yeats ... in full independence of mind.' Hilary Pyle's '"Men of Destiny" – Jack B. and W. B. Yeats: The Background and the Symbols' shows that parallel symbols and literary motifs can be traced in the work of the two Yeats brothers. The images of the rose and the clown are seen to be important in this context. The work done in collaboration is examined in a very interesting section which takes into account Jack's backcloth design for *The King's Threshold*. It is seen that 'the closest emotional bond between the two, other than their love of Sligo, was their devotion to the idea of an Ireland free from foreign domination'.

Warren Leamon has a paper in *SWR*: 'The Tragedy of Dogmatism: Yeats's Later Plays', and, in *MD*, he writes on 'Theatre as Dream: Yeats's Stagecraft'. In *LWU* Stuart Hirschberg considers 'The Visionary Landscape of Yeats's "The Tower"'. For *C&L* David Leigh has written '"The Whirl Becomes a Sphere": Concept and Symbol in Yeats's Poetry of Beatitude'. Jon Lanham considers 'Some Further Textual Problems in Yeats: *Ideas of Good and Evil*' (*PBSA*). John Montague looks at 'Faces of Yeats' (*EI*). In *Expl* Virginia D. Pruitt comments on Yeats's *The Wind Among the Reeds*. Two articles link Yeats and T. S. Eliot: David Rogers's 'Yeats and Eliot on "Traditional Culture": A Few Long Thoughts' (*Spirit*) and Joanne Seltzer's 'The Kings of the Cats: Eliot and Yeats' (*Pre-Raphaelite Rev.*). In *CLAJ* Gary and Linda Storhoff have a paper: '"A Mind of Winter": Yeats's Early Vision of Old Age'. Eriko Takada looks at 'The Quest of William Butler Yeats for Human Integrity' (*Bull. of Seisen Coll.*, Japan). Mary Helen Thuente writes on 'W. B. Yeats and Nineteenth-

Century Folklore' (*JIL*). In *Views of the Irish Peasantry: 1800–1916*, edited by Daniel J. Casey and Robert E. Rhodes, John Unterecker writes on 'Countryman, Peasant and Servant in the Poetry of W. B. Yeats'. In *A Festschrift for Edgar Ronald Seary: Essays in English Language and Literature Presented by Colleagues and Former Students*, Robert O'Driscoll writes on ' "The Second Coming" and Yeats's Vision of History'. The periodicals *Éire*, *CJIS* and *Mosaic* should be consulted by Yeats scholars for their interesting selections of papers on Yeats.

3. Prose Drama
N.B. The footnotes in this section deviate from normal *Year's Work* practice, and the Editor will welcome readers' comments.

Modern Drama, The Journal of Beckett Studies, The Sean O'Casey Review, and *The Shaw Review* should be consulted for bibliographical lists and for specialist review articles. *Who's Who in the Theatre*[155] enters its sixteenth edition with a new, improved typeface. The biographical entries cover the theatre in the United States, Australia, and Britain; there are cast lists and production details covering five years in New York, London, Chichester, and the Stratfords of Ontario and Warwickshire; there is useful information about theatres and repertoires. *Theatre Quarterly* continues to publish *Theatrefacts*[156], with detailed information on theatres opening, re-opening, planned, threatened, saved, and demolished; on companies, festivals, exhibitions, publications, and obituaries.

European Drama Criticism: 1900–1975[157] usefully lists books, articles, sections of books and reviews on the main playwrights including Shaw, Yeats, O'Casey, Synge, Beckett, Arden, Behan, Bolt, Osborne, Pinter, Stoppard, and Wesker. In *Stage Scenery, Machinery and Lighting*[158] Richard Stoddard offers selective lists of books, articles, pamphlets, and catalogues covering a very wide range of theatrical periods and practices. In *London Theatre: from the Globe to the National*[159] James Roose Evans offers a good-natured, enthusiastic introduction to the subject, with some interesting pictures. In *Mosaic Theatre*[160] Lael J. Woodbury offers a well illustrated essay on the creative use of 'theatrical constructs', with the broad argument that new technical resources in today's theatre might liberate future drama from the tyranny of the playwright's words: the designer and director may challenge the dominance of 'language-drama'. In 'Social Environment and Theatrical Environment: the Case of English Naturalism'[161] Raymond Williams ranges wide in the literary and fine arts, but concentrates on drama in his account of three main

[155] ed. by Ian Herbert *et al.* Pitman, and Detroit, Mich.: Gale Research. pp. xxvi + 1389. £15.
[156] ed. by Kenn Stitt *et al.* TQ Publications. pp.48. (subscription).
[157] ed. by Helen H. Palmer. Folkestone, Kent: William Dawson. pp. 653. £15.
[158] Detroit: Gale Research Company. pp. xi + 274. $18.
[159] Oxford: Phaidon. pp. vii + 160. £6.95.
[160] Provo, Utah: Brigham Young U.P. pp. xi + 212. $12.95.
[161] *English Drama: Forms and Development — Essays in Honour of Muriel Clara Bradbrook*, ed. by Marie Axton and Raymond Williams. C.U.P. pp. x + 263. £7.50.

ways in which the word 'naturalism' has been used. 'The first, and most popular, indicates a method of "accurate" or "lifelike" reproduction. The second, and historically earliest, indicates a philosophical position allied to science, natural history and materialism. The third, and most significant in the history of drama, indicates a movement in which the method of accurate production [sic] and the specific philosophical position are organically and usually consciously fused.' The discussion is crisp, many modern playwrights are referred to with shrewdness, and the various uses of the key term are handled with tact. In *Gambit* 31 there is a wide ranging discussion of 'Political Theatre in Britain Today' with contributions from Jeff Nuttall, Ken Campbell, Max Stafford-Clark, Roger Howard, John Calder, and Anton Gill.

John Arden's *To Present the Pretence* has the subtitle 'Essays on the Theatre and its Public'[162]. The first section brings together essays on playwrights of the past – Lorca, O'Casey, Ben Jonson, Brecht. There follow sections headed 'The Matter of Vietnam', 'The Matter of Ireland' and 'The Matter of Britain'. The most substantial piece, 'A Socialist Hero on the Stage', concerns the collaboration with Margaretta D'Arcy in 'dramatising the life and work of James Connolly'. This begins with a verse quotation from their play set against a corresponding quotation from the standard biography of James Connolly. The historian's claim to deal with the 'truth' depends on his scrupulous handling of evidence, and much of the present volume explores the ancient question of what the creative writer can offer against the historian. The playwright deals not in the 'real truth' but in an 'emblem' of it. The papers brought together in this volume were written over a decade and a half, and the attempts to defend his imaginative response to contemporary political issues are so tortured because he is so passionate and yet so self-critically honest. In the first phase of his career John Arden was one of those best men who, as Yeats put it, lack all conviction; and his emotional and intellectual complexity produced some of the most admirable plays of the present century. In the later sixties and in the seventies, the years covered by this volume, there has been a desperate intensity, a desperate if not well-defined sense of 'commitment'. If a frame of mind conducive to writing plays can be re-won, John Arden may yet realise his potential and stand with Shaw above all the other twentieth-century British playwrights. *Arden: Plays One*[163] contains *Serjeant Musgrave's Dance, The Workhouse Donkey, Armstrong's Last Goodnight,* and an authorial preface which ends with 'I wonder will I ever have reason to write any stage plays quite like these again . . . ?'

In 'A Thematic Approach to John Arden's *Armstrong's Last Goodnight* (*RLV*), P. Dodd offers an alternative to the usual exclusive interest in Gilnockie and Lindsay, seeing all of the characters as being deployed in an 'exploration of the value, in human and political terms, of two conflicting qualities – temperance and intemperance'.

In *The Plays of Edward Bond*[164] Tony Coult offers a thematic rather than chronological study: man in relation to the gods, to nature, to society,

---

[162] Eyre Methuen. pp.216. £5.50.
[163] Eyre Methuen. pp.350. £1.25.
[164] Eyre Methuen. pp.87. £1.95.

to other people, and man in isolation, are the themes. The discussion is energetic, defensive, and best when dealing with the plays in production. *Bond: Plays One*[165] contains *Saved, Early Morning, The Pope's Wedding* and an authorial note 'On Violence', in which the heat is considerable and the light dim.

The *Journal of Beckett Studies* continues in its second year to print articles, reviews of books, and reviews of performances. It is characterised by an unusual intelligence and sensitivity: its editor James Knowlson is to be congratulated, and the journal is necessary reading for anyone interested in modern drama.

In 'Waiting for Prospero'[166] John Northam considers *Waiting for Godot* in relation to *The Tempest*, with reference to Ibsen's *Rosmersholm* and Strindberg's *Ghost Sonata*. In 'Dimensions of Play in The Literature of Samuel Beckett' (*ArQ*) Ted L. Estess argues that the proposition 'existence is play' is 'the foundational metaphor of his entire literary cosmos . . . It is not a matter of some activities being play in Beckett's world and others not being play; it rather is a matter of seeing all activities as if they were play.' In the *JML* special number on Beckett, H. Porter Abbott offers 'A Grammar for Being Elsewere', Susan D. Brienza *'The Lost Ones:* The Reader as Searcher', Ruby Cohn 'Outward Bound Soliloquies', J. E. Dearlove '"Last Images": Samuel Beckett's Residual Fiction', Martin Esslin 'Beckett's *Rough for Radio*', S. E. Gontarski 'Crapp's First Tape: Beckett's Manuscript Revisions of *Krapp's Last Tape*', Edith Kern 'Beckett as *Homo Ludens*', Ruth Perlmutter 'Beckett's *Film* and Beckett and Film', Elizabeth Bregman Segré 'Style and Structure in Beckett's *Ping: That Something Itself*', and Mathew Winston 'Watt's First Footnote'. In *ETJ* Peyton Glass has 'Beckett: Axial Man', and Hersh Ziefman in 'The alterable Whey of Words' considers the various texts of *Waiting for Godot*. Articles on that play include Frederick Busi on 'Lucky, Luke and Samuel Beckett' (*RS*), George Martin on '"Pozzo and Lucky": A Key to *Godot*' (*ABR*), Henning Mehrert on 'Samuel Becketts Neuinzenierung als Deutungshilfe für *En attendant Godot*' (*Archiv*), and in *Notes on Contemporary Literature* Russell Sparling considers 'The Anti-Transcendental Function of Pozzo and Lucky'. In *Explicator* Joseph L. Schneider has a note comparing Godot to the Sidhe. In *CEA* Lloyd Spencer Thomas offers 'Krapp: Beckett's Aged Narcissus'. A number of the reported books on Beckett have not been seen: *Samuel Beckett* edited by Tom Bishop and Raymond Federman (Paris: Herne, 1976, pp.366), *Anatomie de Samuel Beckett,* by Peter Ehrhard (Basel: Birhauser, 1976, pp. 272), *Endspiel: Interpretation*, by Fränzi Maierhöfer (Munich: Oldenbourg, pp. 103), *Beckett/Beckett* by Vivian Mercier (New York: O.U.P., pp. 254), *Forme et signification dans le théâtre de Beckett* by Betty Rojtman (Paris: Nizet, 1976, pp.245), 'The Philosophical Significance of Beckett's *En attendant Godot*' by R. Cormier and J. L. Pollister (U. of Alabama P.).

Under the title *Der "schottische Shaw"*[167] Michael Nentwich prints his doctoral thesis on James Bridie; there is a brief biographical sketch

[165] Eyre Methuen. pp.312. £1.25.
[166] See note 161.
[167] Frankfurt am Main, Bern, Las Vegas: Peter Lang. pp. iii + 284. n.p.

and then a painstaking account of Bridie's plays. Under the title *Conference of the Birds*[168] John Heilpern gives a thoughtful and lively account of the adventures in obscure parts of Africa of Peter Brook and his troupe of actors. A welcome addition to the series Methuen's Modern Classics, Harley Granville Barker's *The Madras House*[169] is edited by Margery Morgan. The text is that of the 1911 edition and a detailed appendix lists changes made in 1925. The editor's introduction is characteristically shrewd and informative.

In *Lady Gregory: Interviews and Recollections*[170] E. H. Mikhail brings together many short pieces by George Moore, W. B. Yeats, Joseph Holloway, Walter Starkie, Sean O'Casey, Hallie Flanagan, and others with the intention of offering 'a warm anecdotal view of an important literary figure'. 'She looked', O'Casey tells us 'like an old, elegant nun of a new order, a blend of the Lord Jesus Christ and of Puck', and Yeats felt that he would have made very little of his life had it not been 'for her firmness and her care'. In 'James Joyce's *Exiles* and the Tradition of the Edwardian Problem-Play' (*MD*) Elliott M. Simon has a useful discussion of the play in the context of Joyce's interest in the 'unconventional problem-play' as essayed by Ibsen, Shaw, Pinero, Henry Arthur Jones, Synge, George Moore, Edward Martyn, and others. The play is well defended against complaints that the problems it sets are not solved — in this genre the audience is left to consider the questions.

Ronald Ayling offers 'Sean O'Casey: A Personal View with Some Letters' (*MSpr*), and 'History and Artistry in *The Plough and the Stars*' (*ArielE*). In 'Mein Freund Billy Shakespeare' (*SJW*) Manfred Pauli considers O'Casey in relation to dramatic tradition: the same writer's *Sean O'Casey: Drama, Poesie, Wirklichkeit* (Berlin: Henschel, pp.358) has not been seen. In the *Sean O'Casey Review* Bernard Benstock has 'The Plough Behind, the Stars Ahead', Christopher Murray notes 'Two More Allusions in *Cock-a-Doodle Dandy*', Mary Papke reads '*Juno and the Paycock* as a Larkinite Stage Parable', Ronald Rollins in 'O'Casey and Johnston' contrasts the different reactions to the Easter rising of 1916 in *The Plough and the Stars* and Denis Johnston's *The Scythe and the Sunset;* Bernice Shrank considers 'The Naturalism of O'Casey's Early Plays'. Bernice Shrank also offers 'Poets, Poltroons and Platitudes: A Study of Sean O'Casey's *The Shadow of a Gunman*' (*Mosaic*), and in *Éire* Naomi Pasachoff considers 'O'Casey's Not Quite Festive Comedies'.

In 'Democratic Lunacy: the Comedies of Joe Orton' (*Adam*, 1976) Leslie Smith relates the plays to the biography, deciding that the spirit of Orton's comedy, although it can be frightening as it undermines 'our sense of normality', is in the end 'conciliatory and healing'. In 'Jimmy Porter and the Gospel of Commitment' (*ArielE*) John Ditsky presents 'the notion of Jimmy Porter as an existential hero-in-the-making, a secular Christ who appears ... destined to preserve the best of Englishness by playing a redemptive part in the shaping of his country's future'. In *MQ* Brian Murphy considers 'Jimmy Porter's Past: The Logic of Rage in *Look Back in Anger*'.

---

[168] Faber. pp.317. £5.95.
[169] pp.xxxii + 160. £2.25.
[170] Macmillan. pp.xii + 113. £7.95.

Martin Esslin's *Pinter: A Study of his Plays*[171] is an expanded version
of *The Peopled Wound* (1970). With its wealth of information, its careful
and sympathetic discussion of the range of Pinter's work (now including
No Man's Land), and its judicious evaluation of his place in contemporary
drama, this book is necessary reading. Steven H. Gale's study[172] covers
the same range giving balanced accounts of opposing critical reactions
to the plays and offering his own painstaking and modest analysis of what
he sees as Pinter's main themes: Pinter 'explores the various aspects of
a question through a series of minor works and then writes a major play
which sums up his thematic conclusion. He then begins another set of
plays, which will in turn lead to another major drama.' Karl-Heinz Stoll's
Harold Pinter: Ein Beitrag zur Typologie der neuen englischen Dramas
(Düsseldorf: Bagel) has not been seen. Rudiger Imhof's *Pinter: A bibliography*[173] is a simple, useful, list of his works, of criticism, of reviews,
and even of items of newspaper gossip. The second volume of Pinter's
plays[174] in Methuen's excellent series Master Playwrights contains *The
Caretaker, The Dwarfs, The Collection, The Lover, Night School, Trouble
in the Works, The Black and White, Request Stop, Last to Go,* and *Special
Offer.* This is an admirable volume in a series which is an act of extraordinary generosity even for Methuen, a house which has been a major
public benefactor in this area of publishing for many years. In 'Quicksand in Pinterland' (*ArQ*) Charles A. Carpenter writes on the deliberate
absence of any allegorical or symbolic pattern in *The Caretaker.* In
'Temporality in Pinter's *The Dwarfs*' (*MD*) Leonard Powlick discusses
that work's indebtedness to Beckett's *Watt,* in *RHT* (1976) Jacques le
Marinel considers 'Le thème du clochard dans *En attendant Godot* et
dans *Le Gardien*' and in *Maske und Kothurn: Internationale Beiträge
zur Theater Wissenschaft* Karl-Peter Kesselring considers 'Die Kontakt-
suche des Menschen im modernen Drama exemplifiziert an Samne Becketts
Fin de partie, Harold Pinters *The Caretaker* und Edward Albee's *The Zoo
Story'.*

Stanley Weintraub contributes the excellent section on Shaw to *Anglo-
Irish Literature: A review of Research* edited for the M.L.A. by Richard
J. Finneran (1976). In *The Shaw Review* John R. Pfeiffer's 'Continuing
Checklist of Shaviana' covers books, pamphlets, articles, dissertations, and
recordings. *ShawR* also offers much of the year's work on GBS. The
September number is a special issue devoted to Shaw and Dickens: Linda
L. Herr shows in some detail how Shaw used Jaggers as a model for his
Bohun; Martin Quinn indicates 'The Dickensian Presence in *Heartbreak
House*'; Joseph Frank compares the social criticism in *Bleak House* with
Shaw's more constructive and, in *Major Barbara* if not in *Heartbreak
House,* more hopeful satire; Michael Goldberg gives an account of the
different approaches to Dickens of Shaw and G. K. Chesterton; Edgar
Rosenberg begins a list of references to Dickens in Shaw's works, to be
supplemented by a list of Dickens passages and characters referred to;

[171] Eyre Methuen. pp.273. £2.75.
[172] *Butter's Going Up: A Critical Analysis of Harold Pinter's Work.* Durham,
N.C.: Duke U.P. pp. vi + 358. $16.75.
[173] London and Los Angeles: TQ Publications. pp.64. n.p.
[174] pp.248. £0.85.

H. M. Page considers Shaw's reactions to *Little Dorrit*. The other issues of *ShawR* contain interesting articles and reviews and are necessary reading for Shaw scholars. In its much more modest way *The Independent Shavian* also offers notes of interest: there is, for example, a transcription of a 1933 conversation between Shaw and the Japanese War Minister, and *The Times* account of a 1911 Shaw lecture on 'The New Drama'.

Jean-Claude Amalric's book[175] is more comprehensive than his title suggests since it covers Shaw's whole career and takes account of criticism and scholarship to 1976. The work begins with a biographical study, and proceeds to give a vigorous and perceptive account of the wide range of Shaw's activities in and out of the theatre. The book is based on the author's 1976 Sorbonne doctoral dissertation. The elaborate and formal structure of the study, conscientiously treating every substantial aspect of the subject, is to be expected. The wealth of information and perception is beyond expectation. Naturally, the twelve items on the errata slip do not catch all of the errors in such a long study with such generous quotation in English. R. N. Roy in *George Bernard Shaw's Historical Plays*[176] writes with uniform enthusiasm for *The Man of Destiny*, *Caesar and Cleopatra*, *Saint Joan*, and *In Good King Charles's Golden Days*. One play is praised for being 'an authentic story of Joan, the Maid of France, who suffered martyrdom and glorified mankind as did Jesus Christ'. In another 'Charles is partly the Charles of history and partly a creation of Shaw. But these distortions and contraditions do not matter . . .'. Gordon N. Bergquist's *The Pen and the Sword*[177] surveys Shaw's work in an attempt to assess his ideas and reactions to war and to peace: there is a central problem in that 'Shaw is constantly accusing the public on the one hand of being politically blind, and on the other hand urging that same public to see the realities of political life'. The subject is important, but the discussion is lacklustre.

In *The Gorgon's Head*[178] William R. Brashear devotes his sixth chapter 'The Play of Will and Idea' to Shaw and Eugene O'Neill. Shaw's idiosyncratic use of Schopenhauer, Nietzsche, and Bergson is considered — 'He badly misused them, not simply because he misinterpreted them, but rather because he never grasped the real underlying purport of the crucial concepts in their philosophies. He substituted instead a surface meaning of his own. For while Shaw was facile he was not profound'. Rodelle Weintraub's *Fabian Feminist: Bernard Shaw and Women* (University Park: Pennsylvania State U.P.) brings together twenty-five essays on the subject by Shaw and various hands: it has not been available for inspection, nor has David J. Gordon's *Literary Art and the Unconscious* (Baton Rouge: Lousiana State U.P.) which has the chapter 'Two Antipuritan Puritans: Bernard Shaw and D. H. Lawrence', and nor has Robert F. Whitman's *Shaw and the Play of Ideas* (Ithaca: Cornell U.P.).

In 'Love and "Vitality" in Candida' (*MD*) Walter Lazenby analyses the play, seeing the ending as one which involves new insights for each

---

[175] *Bernard Shaw: du réformateur victorien au prophète édouardien.* Études Anglaises 67. Paris: Didier. pp.588. n.p.
[176] Macmillan. pp. x + 107. £4.95.
[177] Salzburg: Institut für Englische Sprache und Literatur. pp.xi + 211. n.p.
[178] Athens, Ga.: U. of Georgia P. pp. xi + 164. $8.

of the three main characters and denying that 'the play demands a simplistic stock response: automatic scorn for Idealists and Philistines, automatic approval for Realists', since Morell, Marchbanks, and Candida do not fit the categories neatly. In *The Pre-Raphaelite Review* Raymond S. Nelson considers 'Shaw's Pre-Raphaelite Play'. In 'Possible Sources of Shaw's *Pygmalion*' (*N&Q*) Jule Eisenbud discusses Smollett's *Peregrine Pickle* and Florence Marryat's *Out of His Reckoning*, 1879, before offering some remarks on the play from 'the standpoint of depth psychology'. Shaw's play is also discussed in 'The Liberation of Flesh from Stone: Pygmalion in Frank Wedekind's *Erdgeist*' (*GR*). In *The Tennessee Philological Bulletin* Louis Charles Stagg relates 'George Bernard Shaw and the Existentialist-Absurdist Theater', in *Modern British Literature* Alfred E. Rickert writes on 'George Bernard Shaw and the Modern Temper', and in *Arcadia* Meinhard Winkgens compares 'Shaw und Sternheim: Des Individualismus als Privatmythologie'.

Ronald Hayman's study of Tom Stoppard[179] is detailed and perceptive. The novel, the stories, the stage, television, and radio plays are discussed in chronological order. The biographical and bibliographical lists are useful, and the two interviews with Stoppard are models of the genre. This is an interesting volume in the very worthy Contemporary Playwrights Series. In *MD* Brian M. Crossley conducts 'An Investigation of Stoppard's "Hound" and "Foot"', and Lucina P. Gabbard offers 'Stoppard's *Jumpers*: A Mystery Play'. Gabrielle Scott Robinson surveys Stoppard's theatre in 'Plays without Plot' (*ETJ*), and in 'Tom Stoppard's "Artistic Failure"' (*Neophilologus*) Josef de Vos discusses *Rosenkrantz and Guildenstern are Dead*.

In 'Dualism and Paradox in the "Puritan" Plays of David Storey' (*MD*) John J. Stanton argues for a subtlety of content and form in the plays, where the naturalistic fidelity is so complete that they have been regarded by some critics as mere 'chunks of life'.

In *J. M. Synge: Interviews and Recollections*[180], E. H. Mikhail brings together thirty-two short pieces, several of which are of interest. As the Foreword remarks: 'The picture that emerges is perhaps shadowy; the witnesses are sometimes prejudiced and sometimes unreliable. Several of them seem rather to make use of Synge as a character in their own mythologies than to present him objectively.' This volume is similar to volumes on other writers from the same hand; it is an initial step towards collecting the raw material which will have to be examined critically in some future biographical study of Synge, when someone undertakes that much more onerous task. *Studies on Synge* (Ibadan U.P., pp.88) has not been available for inspection: it is reported to contain papers by Dapo Adelugba, Paul F. Botheroyd, Rene Frechet, T. F. O'Sullivan, A. W. Thomson, and S. O. Yakubu. Ann Saddlemyer's 'Synge and the Doors of Perception' appears in *Place, Personality, and the Irish Writer*, edited by Andrew Carpenter (N.Y. Barnes & Noble, pp.199). Robin Skelton considers 'The Politics of J. M. Synge' in *Massachusetts Review*, Ellen S. Spangler in *Éire* discusses *Deirdre of the Sorrows* as 'Feminine Tragedy'. In *'The Playboy of the Western World* as Antidrama' (*MD*) Bruce M. Bigley argues that the

[179] Heinemann. pp.xiv + 146. £1.95.
[180] Macmillan. pp.xiv + 138. £6.95.

implications of the play are 'antisocial, hence uncomic and undramatic in a fundamental way'.

Two articles in *Theatre Quarterly* throw light on Arnold Wesker's recent work. 'A Sense of What should Follow' is a transcript of a conversation in which Wesker discusses his method of composition with respect to *The Friends, The Old Ones, The Wedding Feast, Love Letters on Blue Paper,* and *The Merchant.* 'A Journal of *The Journalists*' is the diary Wesker kept while writing the play, in the hope that the continuous prose commentary would help him to clarify his intentions.

XVII

American Literature to 1900

DAVID JARRETT and MARY JARRETT

The Chapter is divided as follows: 1. General; 2. Poetry; 3. Prose; 4. Drama.

1. General

Bibliographies of current articles are published quarterly in *AL* and annually in the summer supplement of *AQ*. *American Literary Scholarship*[1], now edited alternately by J. Albert Robbins and James Woodress, covers work published up to the end of 1976. Harold H. Kolb Jr's *Field Guide to the Study of American Literature*[2], which is at once an introduction to American Literature and a history of American literary scholarship, provides a full section on bibliographies. Jayne K. Kribbs's *Annotated Bibliography of American Literary Periodicals, 1741-1850*[3] has a brief but useful introduction.

Two bibliographies are available for figures of general interest: one on William James[4] and one on Roger Williams[5]. John J. Teunissen and Evelyn J. Hinz write on Williams, 'one of the most radical of the colonists', in 'Roger Williams, Thomas More, and the Narragansett Utopia' (*EAL*) and Hans R. Guggisberg contributes material on his motivation in 'Religious Freedom and the History of the Christian World in Roger Williams' Thought' (*EAL*).

Bartlett Jere Whiting offers a scholarly and comprehensive collection of *Early American Proverbs and Proverbial Phrases*[6], to which he writes a genial introduction. Frank Shuffelton's excellent and unexpectedly lively biography of Thomas Hooker[7] affords a valuable background to early American literature. Shuffelton points out that, before his own, the most recent biography of Thomas Hooker was published in 1891, and that Cotton Mather's short biography included in his *Magnalia Christi Americana* was the only previous original account of Hooker's career. Two of the seven books of the 1702 *Magnalia* have now appeared in a definitive

---

[1] *American Literary Scholarship: An Annual/1976*, ed. by J. Albert Robbins. Durham, N.C.: Duke U.P. 1978. pp. xiii + 492. $17.75.

[2] *A Field Guide to the Study of American Literature*, by Harold H. Kolb Jr. Charlottesville, Va.: U.P. of Virginia. 1976. pp. xii + 136. hb $9.75, pb $4.50.

[3] *An Annotated Bibliography of American Literary Periodicals, 1741-1850*, by Jayne K. Kribbs. Boston, Mass.: G. K. Hall. pp. xvii + 285. $38.

[4] *William James: A Reference Guide*. by Ignas K. Skrupselis. Boston, Mass.: G. K. Hall. pp. xviii + 250. $18.

[5] *Roger Williams: A Reference Guide*, by Wallace Coyle. Boston, Mass.: G. K. Hall. pp. xiii + 102. $12.

[6] *Early American Proverbs and Proverbial Phrases*, by Bartlett Jere Whiting. Cambridge, Mass., and London: Belknap P., Harvard U.P. pp. lxix + 555. £14.

[7] *Thomas Hooker 1586-1647*, by Frank Shuffelton. Princeton, N.J. and Guildford, Surrey: Princeton U.P. pp. xii + 324. £13.40.

scholarly edition[8], with accompanying essays: 'The Idea of the Wilderness of the New World in the *Magnalia*' by George H. Williams, and two essays by the editor Kenneth B. Murdock, on the life and strangely contradictory personality of Cotton Mather, and on the *Magnalia* as a whole. Murdock notes that Cotton Mather seems at one point to have toyed with the idea of making the *Magnalia* primarily a record of God's 'illustrious providence', on the model of the 1684 essay by his father Increase Mather. This essay has now been reproduced in facsimile[9], with an introductory essay by James A. Levernier placing it in its historical context.

John P. McWilliams Jr in 'Fictions of Merry Mount' (*AQ*) traces the literary history of Merry Mount from William Bradford to Robert Lowell, showing how writers have found in its 'small scope and tragicomic demise a symbolic conflict of great moment for the national future'. Ursula Brumm asks (and the answer appears to be 'no') 'Did the Pilgrims Fall upon their Knees when they arrived in the New World? Art and History in the Ninth Chapter, Book One, of Bradford's *History Of Plymouth Plantation*' (*EAL*). Phyllis Jones stresses, perhaps unsurprisingly, the influence of the Bible on preaching in 'Biblical Rhetoric and the Pulpit Literature of Early New England' (*EAL*). In 'Puritan Poetics: The World, The Flesh, and God' (*EAL*) Robert Daly asserts that the Puritans' 'world-view was positive, symbolic, and therefore far more conducive to the production of poetry than the world-view hitherto imputed to them'. Jean de Beranger, in 'The Desire of Communication: Narrator and Narratee in *Letters from an American Farmer*' (*EAL*), seeks to show that students of literature have failed to place the *Letters* in the development of American fiction, and Harold Kulungian, in 'The Aestheticism of Crèvecoeur's American Farmer' (*EAL*), that Crèvecoeur and the American Farmer are not necessarily identical. There is an essay on 'Hector St John de Crèvecoeur' by A. W. Plumstead in *American Literature 1764-1789: The Revolutionary Years*[10], a major collection of scholarly articles edited by Everett Emerson. The collection also includes Everett Emerson's own contribution, 'The Cultural Context of the American Revolution', especially interesting on the role of the newspapers; 'The Patriot Pamphleteers' by Elaine K. Ginsberg, which argues the literary as well as the historical significance of the pamphlets; 'Thomas Paine' by Evelyn J. Hinz; 'The Loyalists' Reply' by Charles E. Modlin, which concludes with an account of the progress of Loyalist studies; 'The Preachers' by Robert M. Benton; 'Benjamin Franklin' by Mary E. Rucker; 'Thomas Jefferson' by Thomas Philbrick; 'Three Travelers: Carver, Bartram, and Woolman' by Patricia M. Medeiros; 'The Federalist' by Robert Bain; and 'Worried Celebrants of the American Revolution' (John Adams, Benjamin Rush, and Mercy Otis Warren) by Cecelia Tichi.

---

[8] *Magnalia Christi Americana: Books I and II,* by Cotton Mather, ed. by Kenneth B. Murdock, with Elizabeth W. Miller. Cambridge, Mass., and London: Belknap P., Harvard U.P. pp. viii + 500; 3 illustrations. £17.50.
[9] *An Essay for the Recording of Illustrious Providences,* by Increase Mather, with introd. by James A. Levernier. Delmar, N.Y.: Scholars' Facsimiles & Reprints. pp. xx + 381. $50.
[10] *American Literature 1764-1789: The Revolutionary Years,* ed. by Everett Emerson. Madison, Wisc.: U. of Wisconsin P. pp. xvi + 301. £11.25.

Pierre Marambaud discusses 'Dickinson's *Letters from a Farmer in Pennsylvania* as Political Discourse: Ideology, Imagery, and Rhetoric' (*EAL*), showing the significance of the popularity of John Dickinson's pamphlet in the Revolutionary era, and Richard Beale Davis surveys the largely unknown 'Southern Writing of the Revolutionary Period *c.* 1760–1790' (*EAL*). Robert K. Peters gives a lucid introduction to the facsimile reprint of Noah Webster's *Collection of Essays and Fugitiv Writings*[11], first published in 1790, when it sold very badly.

Two books make ambitious attempts to cross cultural boundaries: John Seelye's *Prophetic Waters: The River in Early American Life and Literature*[12] and Clive Bush's *The Dream of Reason: American Consciousness and Cultural Achievement from Independence to the Civil War*[13]. Seelye's book charts the beginnings of American culture, drawing on colonial narratives and journals and their accounts of adventure, travel, conquest, settlement, and expansion, but his main concern is with 'the narratives, histories, and poetry with which New England writers gained metaphoric mastery over the landscape, shaping it to suit the changing dimensions of their errand'. Bush draws on an even wider range of material, moving from an assessment of the European cultural legacy to an examination of the animals, birds, and landscapes themselves.

Robert B. Downs gives a brief account of the sociological significance of each of the *Books That Changed the South*[14]. His choices before 1900 are Captain John Smith's *Generall Historie of Virginia* (1624), William Byrd's *History of the Dividing Line Betwixt Virginia and North Carolina* (1841, but circulated in manuscript during Byrd's lifetime), Thomas Jefferson's *Notes on the State of Virginia* (1784–85), William Bartram's *Travels Through North and South Carolina* (1791), Mason Locke Weems's *Life of Washington the Great* (1800), the anonymous *Narrative of the Life of David Crockett* (1834), Fanny Kemble's *Journal of a Residence on a Georgian Plantation* (1863), Frederick Douglass's *Narrative of the Life of Frederick Douglass* (1845), John Caldwell Calhoun's *Disquisition on Government* (1851), Hinton Rowan Helper's *Impending Crisis of the South* (1857), Frederick Law Olmsted's *Cotton Kingdom* (1861), and Edward King's *The Great South* (1875).

Our Literary Heritage[15] by Van Wyck Brooks and Otto Bettmann runs from 1800. Lavishly illustrated, it is based on Van Wyck Brook's five-volume *Makers and Finders: a History of the Writer in America, 1800–1915*, the original text now cut down by more than five-sixths. It is simplified, but not over-simplified, as is Carla Hancock's *Seven*

---

[11] *A Collection of Essays and Fugitiv Writings*, by Noah Webster, with introd. by Robert K. Peters. Delmar, N.Y.: Scholars' Facsimiles & Reprints. pp. xi + xvi + 414. $30.

[12] *Prophetic Waters: The River in Early American Life and Literature*, by John Seelye. New York: O.U.P. pp. ix + 423; 12 illustrations. £9.75.

[13] *The Dream of Reason: American Consciousness and Cultural Achievement from Independence to the Civil War*, by Clive Bush. Edward Arnold. pp. xi + 397; 67 illustrations. £14.95.

[14] *Books That Changed the South*, by Robert B. Downs. Chapel Hill, N.C.: U. of North Carolina P. pp. xvii + 292; 8 illustrations. £6.30.

[15] *Our Literary Heritage: a Pictorial History of the Writer in America*, by Van Wyck Brooks and Otto Bettmann. New York and London: Paddington P. pp. ix 246; 502 illustrations. pb. £3.95.

Founders of American Literature[16], which is colourful, but rather archly anecdotal, and seems intended for a juvenile audience. The seven founders are Irving, Cooper, Bryant, Poe, Melville, Whitman, and Twain.

Nancy F. Cott takes her title *The Bonds of Womanhood*[17] from Sarah M. Grimke's letters to Mary Parker, commenting that 'She must have composed her phrase with care, endowing it intentionally with the double meaning that womanhood bound women together even as it bound them down'. This study, which turns to women's own private writings rather than literature, sets out to explain why an American feminist of the 1830s would have seen womanhood in this dual aspect. Bell Gale Chevigny describes her collection of Margaret Fuller's writings, *The Woman and the Myth*[18], as 'designed to trace the struggle to conceive and act out of free womanhood'. It is a large and useful anthology, and each section is prefaced by a sample of relevant writings about Margaret Fuller by her contemporaries.

2. Poetry

William J. Scheick and JoElla Doggett offer a reference guide to seventeenth-century American poetry[19], an annotated bibliography of criticism arranged chronologically and subdivided into 'Books', 'Shorter Writings', and 'Dissertations'.

In his introduction to *The Penguin Book of American Verse*[20], Geoffrey Moore states that he has 'tried to bear in mind two considerations: that of making a book which could be used as a "teaching Anthology" (i.e. one which includes generous selections from the poets normally taught in university courses) and that of making a book which would be representative, so that the full range of American poetry might be brought before the reader unfamiliar with the subject as a whole'. He has succeeded in achieving both these aims — although it is a pity that poems are not dated — while also giving some play to his own personal preferences, allotting more space to Anne Bradstreet than to Edward Taylor because 'although Taylor is intellectually more substantial, his verses make hard going for all but the most dedicated reader. Anne Bradstreet's tender humanity is nearer to my heart'.

Ann Stanford in her essay on 'Images of Women in Early American Literature', from *What Manner of Woman*[21] edited by Marlene Springer, is at her most perceptive when discussing the poetry of Anne Bradstreet, showing how her work, as well as her life, illustrates the process of immersion in a new environment. Rosamund R. Rosenmeier writes illumin-

[16] *Seven Founders of American Literature,* by Carla Hancock. Winston-Salem, N.C.: John F. Blair pp. 207; 7 illustrations. $8.95.

[17] *The Bonds of Womanhood: "Woman's Sphere" in New England, 1780-1835,* by Nancy F. Cott. New Haven, Conn. and London: Yale U.P. pp. xii + 225. £9.

[18] *The Woman and the Myth: Margaret Fuller's Life and Writings,* by Bell Gale Chevigny. Old Westbury, N.Y.: Feminist P. 1976. pp. 500. pb $6.95.

[19] *Seventeenth-Century American Poetry: A Reference Guide,* by William J. Scheick and JoElla Doggett. Boston, Mass.: G. K. Hall. pp. xix + 188. $15.

[20] *The Penguin Book of American Verse,* ed. by Geoffrey Moore. Harmondsworth, Middx.: Penguin. pp. 656. pb £1.75.

[21] *What Manner of Woman: Essays on English and American Life and Literature,* ed. by Marlene Springer. New York: New York U.P. pp. xx + 357. £12.50.

atingly on '"Divine Translation": A Contribution to the Study of Anne Bradstreet's Method in the Marriage Poems' (*EAL*).

William J. Scheick refutes the charge of disunity in '"The Inward Tacles and the Outward Traces": Edward Taylor's Elusive Transitions' (*EAL*). Thomas M. Davis discusses 'Edward Taylor's Elegies on the Mathers' (*EAL*) and Astrid Schmitt-von Mühlenfel 'John Fiske's Funeral Elegy on John Cotton' (*EAL*), placing Fiske's verse in the context of the seventeenth-century English funeral elegy.

William D. Andrews offers 'Freneau's "A Political Litany": A Note on Interpretation' (*EAL*), and an extended comparison of 'Philip Freneau and Francis Hopkinson' in *American Literature 1764-1789: The Revolutionary Years*[22] edited by Everett Emerson. This collection of essays also provides fine treatments of 'African-American Writers' (Jupiter Hammon and Phillis Wheatley) by Bernard W. Bell and of 'The Connecticut Wits' (the three major wits: John Trumbull, Timothy Dwight, and Joel Barlow) by Robert D. Arner.

Dorothy Weil in a study of Susanna Rowson[23] stresses the feminist quality of her poetry. Emily Stipes Watts in her study of *The Poetry of American Women from 1632 to 1945*[24] also discusses Susanna Rowson, together with a motley crew ranging from Anne Bradstreet to Ella Wheeler Wilcox. Emily Stipes Watts tries to view the poetry as a whole, and claims that there is a clear line of continuity running from Ann Eliza Bleecker (1752-1783) through Frances Sargent Locke Osgood (1811-1850) to Emily Dickinson.

Everett Carter defines *The American Idea*[25] as an idea of 'the possibilities of the future based upon an assumption of the goodness of man and nature', and he investigates the literary response to American optimism in the poetry of William Cullen Bryant, Longfellow, James Russell Lowell, Oliver Wendell Holmes, Emerson, Whitman, and Poe, pronouncing sadly, however, on Poe that 'Unhappily, as everything about this genius was unhappy, his poetry, the form he valued above all others, was his least successful mode'. Laurence Goldstein also discusses poetic optimism in *Ruins and Empire: The Evolution of a Theme in Augustan and Romantic Literature*[26], paying special attention among the American poets to Timothy Dwight and William Cullen Bryant.

Charles M. Lombard writes an analytical and informative introduction to Thomas Holley Chivers's *Nacoochee*[27], first published in 1837. This facsimile reprint includes Chivers's own preface, which opens: 'Poetry

[22] *American Literature 1764-1789: The Revolutionary Years*, ed. by Everett Emerson. Madison, Wisc.: U. of Wisconsin P. pp. xvi + 301. £11.25.

[23] *In Defense of Women: Susanna Rowson (1762-1824)*, by Dorothy Weil. University Park, Pa. and London: Pennsylvania State U.P. 1976. pp. 204.

[24] *The Poetry of American Women from 1632 to 1945*, by Emily Stipes Watts. Austin, Tex. and London: U. of Texas P. pp. xvi + 218. £10.50.

[25] *The American Idea: The Literary Response to American Optimism*, by Everett Carter. Chapel Hill, N.C.: U. of North Carolina P. pp. ix + 276. £11.20.

[26] *Ruins and Empire: The Evolution of a Theme in Augustan and Romantic Literature*, by Laurence Goldstein. Pittsburgh, Pa.: U. of Pittsburgh P. pp. xiv + 272. £12.50.

[27] *Nacoochee; or, The Beautiful Star, with Other Poems*, by Thomas Holley Chivers, with introd. by Charles M. Lombard. Delmar, N.Y.: Scholars' Facsimiles & Reprints. pp. xii + x + 143. $22.

is that crystal river of the soul which runs through all the avenues of life, and after purifying the affections of the heart, empties itself into the Sea of God.'

Albert J. von Frank provides a comprehensive bibliographical survey of biographical and critical works on Whittier[28]. Merrill Lewis writes 'In Praise of Whittier's "Pictures"' (*ESQ*), arguing that the distinction between Whittier's Flemish and pastoral pictures has never been made sufficiently clear.

J. Lasley Dameron, Thomas C. Carlson, John E. Reilly, and Judy Osowski contribute a 'Current Poe Bibliography' to *Poe Studies*, supplementing the previous 1975 bibliography. Robert D. Jacobs chronicles 'the development of Poe's distinctive manner' in 'The Self and the World: Poe's Early Poems' (*GaR*), and Jerome Loving in 'The Good Gray Poe: Poe's Reburial and William Douglas O'Connor's Forgotten Tribute' (*Poe Studies*) shows that O'Connor, minor poet and champion of Whitman, was almost equally an admirer of Poe. Vincent Buranelli's second edition of *Edgar Allan Poe*[29] basically follows the first edition of fifteen years ago, but the chapter on the poetry, 'Lyric Strains', has been enlarged. David Sinclair's *Edgar Allan Poe*[30] offers a chatty blend of criticism and biography: Sinclair submits that Poe must have been a diabetic. John Carl Miller's *Building Poe Biography*[31] is a far more scholarly affair – and there are three more volumes to follow. The present volume gives, with editorial commentary, the more important of the letters which the Englishman John Henry Ingram used for his biographical work on Poe, an important task since 'Ingram seldom reproduced a letter or document or manuscript exactly as he received it'.

Richard Lebeaux's *Young Man Thoreau*[32] examines the poetry as well as the prose in focusing on the period between Thoreau's graduation from Harvard in 1837 and the beginnings of the Walden experiment in 1845. Lebeaux is also keenly interested in Thoreau's early childhood, remarking regretfully that 'Of course we do not have evidence of toilet-training procedures in the Thoreau household'.

The sixth volume of Walt Whitman's *Correspondence*[33] edited by Edwin Haviland Miller updates the previous five volumes with over ninety letters and postcards that have appeared since 1969. Maurice Mendelson's *Life and Work of Walt Whitman: A Soviet View*[34] offers a few interesting

---

[28] *Whittier: A Comprehensive Annotated Bibliography*, by Albert J. von Frank. New York and London: Garland. 1976. pp. 273. $25.

[29] *Edgar Allan Poe*, by Vincent Buranelli. Boston, Mass.: (TUSAS) G. K. Hall. 2nd ed. pp. 166.

[30] *Edgar Allan Poe*, by David Sinclair. London, Melbourne, and Toronto: J. M. Dent. pp. 272; 15 illustrations. £6.95.

[31] *Building Poe Biography*, by John Carl Miller. Baton Rouge, La. and London: Louisiana State U.P. pp. xix + 269; 6 illustrations.

[32] *Young Man Thoreau*, by Richard Lebeaux. Amherst, Mass.: U. of Massachusetts P. pp. 262. £7.95.

[33] *The Correspondence of Walt Whitman: Vol VI: A Supplement with a Composite Index*, ed. by Edwin Haviland Miller. New York: New York U.P. pp. xi + 124; 6 illustrations. $19.50.

[34] *Life and Work of Walt Whitman: A Soviet View*, by Maurice Mendelson, translated from the Russian by Andrew Bromfield. Moscow: Progress Publishers. 1976. pp. 347. £2.50.

sidelights, such as the fact that 'Russian Whitman studies were begun in earnest by Turgenev', but mostly consists of bland generalities about ideals of freedom. Mutlu Konuk Blasing's *The Art of Life: Studies in American Autobiographical Literature*[35] considers 'Song of Myself' as autobiography, and places Whitman in the context of the Romantics' problems of subjectivity. Useful articles on Whitman include Erna Emminghausen Kelly's 'Whitman and Wordsworth: Childhood Experiences and the Future Poet' (*WWR*), Donald Kummings's 'The Vernacular Hero in Whitman's "Song of Myself"' (*WWR*), Michael D. Reed's 'First Person Persona and the Catalogue in "Song of Myself"' (*WWR*), Donez Xiques's 'Whitman's Catalogues and the Preface to *Leaves of Grass*' (*WWR*), Joel R. Kehler's 'A Typological Reading of "Passage to India"' (*ESQ*), and J. Thomas Chiffin's 'Give Me Faces and Streets: Walt Whitman and the City' (*WWR*). Rayburn S. Moore in 'The Literary World Gone Mad: Hayne on Whitman' (*SLJ*) recalls Paul Hamilton Hayne, writer of 'a majority report for his generation', who saw Whitman as a 'tremendous charlatan' as poet and a 'big shameless Beast' as man.

Stephen Fender's anthology *The American Long Poem: An Annotated Selection*[36] concentrates upon the Whitman tradition of the long poem in America. This characteristically American kind of poem, says Fender, has little formal outline; it is an open-ended 'assembly' rather than a 'composition'. Fender's short introduction is well-balanced and thought-provoking, stressing the importance of a millenial vision in the poetics of the American long poem. He begins by considering Emerson's essay 'The Poet' and observes that Whitman 'made himself the very poet for which Emerson was looking'. The selections from *Leaves of Grass* are prefaced by an incisive and generally factual introduction to Whitman and his work and there are also explanatory and textual notes and a short bibliography. The pieces chosen by Fender make an evocative sequence: *Starting from Paumanok, Crossing Brooklyn Ferry,* and *Passage to India.*

Kerry McSweeney's 'Melville, Dickinson, Whitman and psychoanalytic criticism' (*CritQ*) ends with the rather faint-hearted assertion that the psychoanalytic approach may prevent sympathy for the subject, while Muriel Kolinsky muses on '"Me Tarzan, You Jane?" Whitman's Attitudes toward Women from a Women's Liberation Point of View' (*WWR*). Nina Baym is decisive about this: 'Say what he will, for Whitman the sexes are fundamentally unequal. This is because women are mothers.' In the same essay, 'Portrayal of Women in American Literature, 1790–1870', from *What Manner of Woman*[37] edited by Marlene Springer, Nina Baym writes cogently of the way that Emily Dickinson's poems 'concern the experience of being female'.

Emily Dickinson is the only nineteenth-century poet discussed in Suzanne Juhasz's *Naked and Fiery Forms: Modern American Poetry*

[35] *The Art of Life: Studies in American Autobiographical Literature,* by Mutlu Konuk Blasing. Austin, Tex. and London: U. of Texas P. pp. xxviii + 193; 6 illustrations. £7.50.
[36] *The American Long Poem: an Annotated Selection,* ed. by Stephen Fender. Edward Arnold. pp. ix + 254. £3.95.
[37] *What Manner of Woman: Essays on English and American Life and Literature,* ed. by Marlene Springer. New York: New York U.P. pp. xx + 357. £12.50.

by Women, A New Tradition[38]. Suzanne Juhasz contrasts Emily Dickinson's poetry with Sylvia Plath's, and asserts that modern feminists 'need Emily Dickinson as a source of strength'. Lillian Faderman in 'Emily Dickinson's Letters to Sue Gilbert' (*MR*) argues that Dickinson's love for Sue was homosexual.

Linda J. Taylor in 'Shakespeare and Circumference: Dickinson's Hummingbird and *The Tempest*' (*ESQ*) widens the scope of 'A Route of Evanescence'. Ellen Moers in *Literary Women: The Great Writers*[39] discusses Emily Dickinson's voracious reading of contemporary women writers, and Barton Levi St Armand in 'Paradise Deferred: The Image of Heaven in the Work of Emily Dickinson and Elizabeth Stuart Phelps' (*AQ*) reveals the common ground of the poetry and *The Gates Ajar*, the Phelps best-seller of 1868.

3. Prose

There are a number of books difficult to categorise, since they cover a wide range of prose materials. For example, *What Manner of Woman*[40] edited by Marlene Springer contains an essay by Nina Baym, 'Portrayal of Women in American Literature, 1790–1870', which ranges from Charles Brockden Brown to Louisa May Alcott, passing such figures as Melville en route, to say nothing of the more cumbrously titled 'They Shall Have Faces, Minds, and (One Day) Flesh: Women in late Nineteenth-century and Early Twentieth-century American Literature' by Martha Banta. Robert B. Downs in *Books That Changed the South*[41] chooses to discuss a number of what he terms 'historical and sociological treatises in fictional form': A. B. Longstreet's *Georgia Scenes* (1835), George W. Cable's *Old Creole Days* (1879), Joel Chandler Harris's *Uncle Remus* (1880), Twain's *Life on the Mississippi* (1883), and Thomas Nelson Page's *In Ole Virginia* (1887).

The wide-ranging books which have rather more in common are *The Middle Way: Puritanism and Ideology in American Romantic Fiction*[42] by Michael T. Gilmore, *The Adventurous Muse: The Poetics of American Fiction, 1789-1900*[43] by William C. Spengemann, and *The American Idea: The Literary Response to American Optimism*[44] by Everett Carter. Gilmore's thesis is that Hawthorne, Melville, and James translated the

[38] *Naked and Fiery Forms: Modern American Poetry by Women, A New Tradition*, by Suzanne Juhasz. New York, Hagerstown, San Francisco, and London: Harper & Row 1976, pp. x + 212, pb £2.95.
[39] *Literary Women: The Great Writers*, by Ellen Moers. W. H. Allen. pp. xvi + 336; 27 illustrations. £7.50. New York: Anchor P. pp. xxiv + 496; 27 illustrations. pb $3.95.
[40] *What Manner of Woman: Essays on English and American Life and Literature*, ed. by Marlene Springer. New York: New York U.P. pp. xx + 357. £12.50.
[41] *Books That Changed the South*, by Robert B. Downs. Chapel Hill, N.C.: U. of North Carolina P. pp. xvii + 292; 8 illustrations. £6.30.
[42] *The Middle Way: Puritanism and Ideology in American Romantic Fiction*, by Michael T. Gilmore. New Brunswick, N.J.: Rutgers U.P. pp. x + 220. £7.50.
[43] *The Adventurous Muse: The Poetics of American Fiction 1789-1900*, by William C. Spengemann. New Haven, Conn. and London: Yale U.P. pp. ix + 290. £10.80.
[44] *The American Idea: The Literary Response to American Optimism*, by Everett Carter. Chapel Hill, N.C.: U. of North Carolina P. pp. ix + 276. £11.20.

world of their fiction into an aesthetic that constituted in literary terms the theological balance and equilibrium, the 'middle way', of the Puritan founders. Gilmore's book is plausible and informative, and he offers useful preliminary material on 'The Puritans' and 'Cotton Mather and Benjamin Franklin'. Spengemann, who concentrates on Hawthorne, Melville, Twain, and James, argues that the American Romantic novel emerged out of two opposing fictional poetics: one of adventure which served to portray a new world seen at its moving frontier, and one of domesticity which was designed to counter this potentially subversive vision of reality. Spengemann's scholarly work provides a wealth of background on New World exploration, and on works such as Cooper's *The Deerslayer*. Everett Carter also writes on Cooper, in his chapter on 'Progress and Primitivism in the Deerslayer Romances', and gives in addition an account of how Emerson, Thoreau, Hawthorne, Poe, Melville, Twain, Howells, and James either mirrored, replaced, or rejected American optimism.

Dorothy Weil's lively and clear study of Susanna Rowson[45] treats her as an early feminist, and argues for the sense rather than the sensibility of *Charlotte Temple:* 'The emphasis on anguish and distress in *Charlotte* is not meant to promote a cult of distress or to romanticize the suffering heroine, but to teach the young to avoid Charlotte's (and La Rue's) errors.' A. Carl Bredahl Jr in 'Transformation in *Wieland'* (*EAL*) suggests that Brockden Brown's work 'is particularly important in the development of American literature if we consider it as a study of energy, an energy traditionally denounced by society as evil'.

Martin Roth explains that his book *Comedy and America: The Lost World of Washington Irving*[46] 'grew out of an act of curiosity, a desire to understand the nature and shape of Washington Irving's American period, which culminated in *The History of New York* in 1809'. He examines, for example, 'Polite Satire', 'Political Satire', 'Domestic Humor', and 'Burlesque Comedy', and their context in American literature, remarking in the last chapter, 'The Sense of a Beginning', that 'Hawthorne's "Maypole of Merry Mount" resembles Irving's *History* more clearly than does any other single American work'. Washington Irving's *Old Christmas*[47], which first appeared in 1819–20 as part of the *Sketch Book,* now appears in a beautifully produced facsimile of the 1875 London edition, with an introduction by Andrew B. Myers placing it in the tradition of Christmas literature.

Jeffrey Steinbrink has written an acute analysis of 'Cooper's Romance of the Revolution: *Lionel Lincoln* and the Lessons of Failure' (*EAL*) and Laurence Goldstein an excellent account of the complexities of Cooper's *The Pioneers* in *Ruins and Empire*[48]. Jenni Calder examines

[45] *In Defense of Women: Susanna Rowson (1762–1824),* by Dorothy Weil. University Park, Pa. and London: Pennsylvania State U.P., 1976. pp. 204.

[46] *Comedy and America: The Lost World of Washington Irving,* by Martin Roth. Port Washington, N.Y., and London: Kennikat P. 1976. pp. xiv + 205. $12.50.

[47] *Old Christmas,* by Washington Irving, with introd. by Andrew B. Myers. Tarrytown, N.Y.: Sleepy Hollow Restorations. pp. viii + 165; 105 illustrations by Randolph Caldecott. $10.

[48] *Ruins and Empire: The Evolution of a Theme in Augustan and Romantic Literature,* by Laurence Goldstein. Pittsburgh, Pa.: U. of Pittsburgh P. pp. xiv + 272. £12.50.

Natty Bumppo's ambiguous status as American hero in *Heroes: From Byron to Guevara*[49].

The dust-jacket of H. Daniel Peck's fascinating re-appraisal of the world of Cooper's novels, *A World by Itself: The Pastoral Moment in Cooper's Fiction*[50], says that Peck 'wins the novelist away from the historical and mythic approaches that have dominated the criticism'. But this does less than justice to what Peck has contributed to Cooper criticism: his fine analysis of *The Last of the Mohicans* recognises how the novel is, 'in a profound sense . . . *about* history' and he is also concerned with the novels as enacting mythic journeys. Peck makes constant reference to the works of Gaston Bachelard and their phenomenological method, and *A World by Itself* is primarily concerned with 'The Poetics of Space'; even so, some will probably feel that Peck could have made a number of his points adequately without reference to Bachelard. When he writes of Cooper's landscape descriptions that lead to 'profound narrative stasis' or of the feminine quality of 'interiority' in Cooper, Peck's insights are reminiscent of those in Annette Kolodny's *The Lay of the Land*. Peck bases his reading of Cooper initially on the importance of sight and seeing in his work, explaining how Cooper's understanding of sight relates to his pessimistic view of human nature and to his sense of historical doom. Part II is a valuable study of the imagery that characterises Cooper's landscapes; it focuses on the contrast between the wilderness and the almost magical enclosures of Cooper's fiction and provides an interesting analysis of the neglected *The Oak Openings*. Peck is also particularly revealing on the structure and imagery of *The Last of the Mohicans*. *A World by Itself* concludes, convincingly, though perhaps surprisingly, that Cooper's deepest wish as an artist 'was to see the American landscape as organized, structured space'.

Three books on Poe have been mentioned in the Poetry section; there are a number of interesting articles about him: Mark Keller's 'Dupin in the "Rue Morgue": Another Form of Madness?' (*ArQ*), E. Miller Budick's 'The Fall of the House: A Reappraisal of Poe's Attitudes toward Life and Death' (*SLJ*), George B. von der Lippe's 'The Figure of E. T. A. Hoffmann as *Doppelganger* to Poe's Roderick Usher' (*MLN*), and from *Poe Studies* 'The Self, the Mirror, the Other: "The Fall of the House of Usher"' by Renata R. Mautner Wasserman, '"The Duc De L'Omelette" as Anti-Visionary Tale' by David H. Hirsch, 'Play and Games: An Approach to Poe's Detective Tales' by LeRoy L. Panek, 'Engraved Within the Hills: Further Perspectives on the Ending of *Pym*' by Daniel A. Wells, and 'The Word "Autorial" in Poe's Criticism: History and Implications' by Burton R. Pollin.

The thirteenth volume of Emerson's *Journals and Miscellaneous Notebooks*[51] has now come out, with an able and illuminating foreword by

[49] *Heroes: From Byron to Guevara*, by Jenni Calder. Hamish Hamilton. pp. xii + 211. £6.95.
[50] *A World by Itself: The Pastoral Moment in Cooper's Fiction*, by H. Daniel Peck. New Haven, Conn. and London: Yale U.P. pp. xiv + 213. £9.
[51] *The Journals and Miscellaneous Notebooks of Ralph Waldo Emerson, Vol. XIII, 1852–1855*, ed. by Ralph H. Orth and Alfred R. Ferguson. Cambridge, Mass.: Harvard U.P. and London: Belknap P., pp. xxi + 555; 4 illustrations. £24.50.

R. H. Orth outlining the events of Emerson's life during the period covered by the journals in this volume, from early 1852 to the summer of 1855, and summarising his views on England and the English. Barbara Packer writes on 'Uriel's Cloud: Emerson's Rhetoric' (*GaR*), and J. A. Mogat on 'Emerson's Aesthetics of Fiction' (*ESQ*).

Horace Hosmer (1830-94) was a member of the Hosmer family which settled in Concord in 1635. His letters[52] to his friend Dr S. A. Jones are valuable social records, besides affording a glimpse of Thoreau's family. Hosmer was emphatic on the influence of the parents on Thoreau: 'Henry D. Thoreau was not a superior scion upon an inferior stock, neither was he begotten by a north west wind as many have supposed.' Richard Lebeaux in *Young Man Thoreau*[53] suggests that Thoreau's father was rather weak and his mother very strong and articulate, so that Thoreau became very dependent on mother and home and his attachment to Walden was an attempt to return both to the maternal breast and the womb.

'The Economies of *Walden*' is the title of the chapter on Thoreau in Mutlu Konuk Blasing's *The Art of Life: Studies in American Autobiographical Literature*[54], but it is also the focus of three articles about him: 'Economic Metaphor Redefined: The Transcendental Capitalist at Walden' by Judith P. Saunders (*American Transcendental Quarterly*), 'Et in Arcadia Thoreau' by John O. Rees (*ESQ*), and 'Thoreau among the Classical Economists' by Herbert F. Smith (*ESQ*). Kenneth Walter Cameron extends our knowledge of Thoreau before Harvard in 'Young Thoreau and the Classics: A Review' (*ATQ*). Frederick Garber in *Thoreau's Redemptive Imagination*[55] points out that 'Thoreau's construction of experience (which is exactly parallel to that of Rousseau) placed his consciousness at the center of a concentric series of enclosures or clearings. Outside the self was Concord, and outside that was the wild and, finally, the world.' Garber writes fully about Thoreau, but concentrates on *Walden, The Maine Woods*, and 'Walking'. Robert F. Sayre in *Thoreau and the American Indians*[56] pronounces Thoreau 'nineteenth-century America's most qualified dedicated student of his red fathers and of his and their mother'. He traces Thoreau's fascination with Indian life, his attempts to learn about it and imitate it, and also some of his misconceptions about it.

Kenneth Dauber confides that he would like to think that his book, *Rediscovering Hawthorne*[57], 'is the poetics that Hawthorne might have

[52] *Remembrances of Concord and the Thoreaus: Letters of Horace Hosmer to Dr. S. A. Jones*, ed. by George Hendrick. Urbana, Chicago Ill. and London: U. of Illinois P. pp. xxvi + 157.

[53] *Young Man Thoreau*, by Richard Lebeaux. Amherst, Mass.: U. of Massachusetts P. pp. 262. £7.95.

[54] *The Art of Life: Studies in American Autobiographical Literature*, by Mutlu Konuk Blasing. Austin, Tex. and London: U. of Texas P. pp. xxviii + 193; 6 illustrations. £7.50.

[55] *Thoreau's Redemptive Imagination*, by Frederick Garber. New York: New York U.P. pp. x + 229. hb $15, pb $4.95.

[56] *Thoreau and the American Indians*, by Robert F. Sayre. Princeton, N.J.: Princeton U.P. pp. xiv + 239. £10.90.

[57] *Rediscovering Hawthorne*, by Kenneth Dauber. Princeton, N.J. and Guildford, Surrey: Princeton U.P. pp. xii + 235. £10.10.

written'. He emphasises at the conclusion of his study the conviction that the American novel 'is a self-conscious fiction, not a sterile one. It is only in self-conscious reading that we can avoid sterility ourselves.' Accordingly, he opens with a brief history of American criticism from the rediscovery of classic American literature to the present. Yet finally Dauber is far less illuminating on specific works by Hawthorne than Edgar A. Dryden in his study *Nathaniel Hawthorne: The Poetics of Enchantment*[58]. Dryden's thesis, which he perhaps slightly overworks, is that two themes persist throughout Hawthorne's writings, shaping and controlling their form and development, the themes of 'enchantment and disenchantment – enchantment as the condition generated by the lure of others and disenchantment as the discovery that the lure is deceptive and dangerous, that the experience of the other is at best fugitive and tenuous, at worst alienating and threatening'. Dryden says well that in Hawthorne's world as in Keats's 'one alternates between a world of dreams and the cold hillside of reality'.

Articles on Hawthorne include Timothy Dow Adams's 'To Prepare a Preface to Meet the Faces that you Meet: Autobiographical Rhetoric in Hawthorne's Prefaces' (*ESQ*), Frederick Newberry's 'Tradition and Disinheritance in *The Scarlet Letter*' (*ESQ*), John Gatta Jr's ' "Busy and Selfish London": The Urban Figure in Hawthorne's "Wakefield" ' (*ESQ*), and James Walter's 'A Farewell to Blithedale: Coverdale's Aborted Pastoral' (*SAQ*). *The Blithedale Romance*, as aborted utopia, is briefly treated in Melvin J. Lasky's *Utopia and Revolution*[59], and *The House of the Seven Gables* is considered in the context of the tradition of the haunted portrait in Theodore Ziolkowski's *Disenchanted Images*[60], and in a sociological and historical perspective in Morroe Berger's *Real and Imagined Worlds*[61].

At Hawthorne's death he left three unfinished manuscripts developing the theme of an American claimant to an English estate. These, with related memoranda, are now presented as Vol. XII of the Centenary Edition[62]. He also left unfinished three pieces of fiction developing the theme of immortality which with relevant writings comprise Vol. XIII[63].

Neil Schmitz in 'Tall Tale, Tall Talk: Pursuing the Lie in Jacksonian

[58] *Nathaniel Hawthorne: The Poetics of Enchantment*, by Edgar A. Dryden. Ithaca, N.Y. and London: Cornell U.P. pp. 182. £7.50.

[59] *Utopia and Revolution: On the Origins of a Metaphor, or Some Illustrations of the Problem of Political Temperament and Intellectual Climate and How Ideas, Ideals, and Ideologies Have Been Historically Related*, by Melvin J. Lasky. Chicago, Ill.: U. of Chicago P., and London: Macmillan. pp. xiii + 726. £15.

[60] *Disenchanted Images: A Literary Iconology*, by Theodore Ziolkowski. Princeton, N.J. and Guildford, Surrey: Princeton U.P. pp. ix + 273. £9.40.

[61] *Real and Imagined Worlds: The Novel and Social Science*, by Morroe Berger. Cambridge, Mass., and London: Harvard U.P. pp. viii + 303. £10.50.

[62] *The American Claimant Manuscripts: The Ancestral Footstep, Etherege, Grimshawe*, by Nathaniel Hawthorne, ed. by Edward H. Davidson, Claude M. Simpson, and L. Neal Smith. (Centenary Edition of the Works of Nathaniel Hawthorne, Vol. XII). Columbus, Ohio: Ohio State U.P. pp. xi + 657. £12.50.

[63] *The Elixir of Life Manuscripts: Septimius Felton, Septimius Norton, The Dolliver Romance*, by Nathaniel Hawthorne, ed. by Edward H. Davidson, Claude M. Simpson, and L. Neal Smith. (Centenary Edition of the Works of Nathaniel Hawthorne, Vol. XIII). Columbus, Ohio: Ohio State U.P. pp. ix + 803. £14.20.

Literature' (*AL*) examines the nature of the tall tale, concentrates on Joseph G. Baldwin's *The Flush Times of Alabama and Mississippi* and Thomas B. Thorpe's 'The Big Bear of Arkansas', and shows how Baldwin contrives an implicit distinction between tall talk and 'the Jacksonian tall tale, the lie of Jackson the Hero who smashes the monopolists and liberates the development of the West'. John C. Guilds writes on 'Simms's Use of History: Theory and Practice' (*MissQ*), while C. H. Holman in *The Immoderate Past: The Southern Writer and History*[64] treats William Gilmore Simms as 'but one of many southern novelists who used and still continue to use the Scott model for the representation of crucial events in the historical past'. Arlin Turner writes on 'George W. Cable's Use of the Past' (*MissQ*), and Calvin S. Brown catalogues literary allusions and quotations in 'Colonel Falkner As General Reader: The White Rose of Memphis' (*MissQ*).

Ellen Moers in writing on Harriet Beecher Stowe in *Literary Women*[65] opens with an account of her domestic difficulties, and Mrs Stowe herself could be eloquent on the same subject. E. B. Kirkham in his very able account of *The Building of Uncle Tom's Cabin*[66] quotes a letter to her sister-in-law describing the struggle to get her household organised, in the midst of which confusion 'comes a letter from my husband saying he is sick abed, and all but dead; don't ever expect to see his family again; wants to know how I shall manage in case I am left a widow; knows we shall get in debt and never get out; wonders at my courage; . . . warns me to be prudent, as there won't be much to live on in case of his death, etc., etc., etc. I read the letter and poke it into the stove, and proceed.' Kirkham also provides an account of the deficiencies and merits of the existing biographies in 'Harriet Beecher Stowe: Autobiography and Legend' in *Portraits of a Nineteenth-Century Family*[67] edited by Earl A. French and Diana Royce. Anthea Zeman in *Presumptuous Girls*[68] defends *Uncle Tom's Cabin* against the charge of sentimentality, and William Glasser in 'The Changing World of Harriet Beecher Stowe' from *Essays in Honour of Professor Tyrus Hillway*[69], edited by Erwin A. Sturzl, plots the changes in basic attitudes between *Uncle Tom's Cabin* and *Oldtown Folks*. Two Stowe bibliographies are available, by Jean Willoughby Ashton and Margaret Holbrook Hildreth[70].

[64] *The Immoderate Past: The Southern Writer and History*, by C. Hugh Holman. Athens, Ga.: U. of Georgia P. pp. ix + 118. £3.50.

[65] *Literary Women: The Great Writers*, by Ellen Moers. W. H. Allen. pp. xvi + 336; 27 illustrations. £7.50. New York: Anchor P. pp. xxiv + 496; 27 illustrations. pb $3.95.

[66] *The Building of Uncle Tom's Cabin*, by E. Bruce Kirkham. Knoxville, Tenn.: U. of Tennessee P. pp. x + 264; 13 illustrations. $12.95.

[67] *Portraits of a Nineteenth Century Family: A Symposium on the Beecher Family*, ed. by Earl A. French and Diana Royce. Hartford, Conn.: Stowe-Day Foundation. 1976. pp. 127; 25 illustrations. $4.95.

[68] *Presumptuous Girls: Women and Their World in the Serious Woman's Novel*, by Anthea Zeman. Weidenfeld & Nicolson. pp. 185. £5.25.

[69] *Essays in Honour of Professor Tyrus Hillway*, ed. by Erwin A. Sturzl. Salzburg: Institut für Englische Sprache und Literatur, Universität Salzburg. pp. 326.

[70] *Harriet Beecher Stowe: A Reference Guide*, by Jean Willoughby Ashton. Boston, Mass.: G. K. Hall. pp. xxiii + 168. $18. *Harriet Beecher Stowe: A Bibliography*, by Margaret Holbrook Hildreth. Hamden, Conn.: Shoe String P. 1976. $17.50.

Martha Saxton's biography of Louisa May Alcott[71] has a rather terse, choppy style, but is extremely interesting on, for example, Bronson Alcott and the family's relationship with the Transcendentalists, and the real-life dying sister who was the model for Beth in *Little Women:* 'The twenty-three-year-old woman, hairless and shrunken, looked at least forty to them.' Madeleine Stern in her introduction to *Plots and Counterplots: More Unknown Thrillers of Louisa May Alcott*[72] also investigates the relation between life and art, and notes what the heroines have in common: 'they are all extraordinary actresses, mistresses of the arts of disguise'.

Patricia Barber in *The Authority of Experience*[73] edited by Arlyn Diamond and Lee R. Edwards asks the rather startling question 'What If Bartleby Were a Woman?'. Unfortunately her essay does not live up to its promise, and she does not substantiate her claim that changing Melville's protagonist to a woman 'works to reveal an otherwise hidden erotic quality in the original'. Toshio Yagi in 'Is Ishmael, Ishmael? – An Anatomy of "Moby-Dick"' (*SELit*) admits that he is 'almost wholly lacking external evidence' for his suggestion of the late insertion of the narrator's name in *Moby-Dick*. Robert Midler considers textual history in 'The Composition of *Moby-Dick:* A Review and a Prospect' (*ESQ*). T. Walter Herbert Jr's study of '*Moby-Dick' and Calvinism*[74] shows, in a scholarly and convincing way, how Melville absorbed in his childhood the opposing theories of Unitarianism and the most conservative orthodoxy, and how he dealt creatively with the consequent spiritual conflict in *Moby-Dick*. We are reminded that in some ways *Moby-Dick* is a simple work by Brian Way's *Herman Melville: Moby Dick*[75]. Way stresses that the novel itself expresses distrust of 'certain kinds of intellectual complexity' and suggests that surface meanings be given more weight. Melville's affinity with Shakespeare is also considered here.

Maria Ujházy discusses 'Herman Melville: Social Critic' (*ZAA*), and James Duban examines 'The Spenserian Maze of Melville's *Pierre*' (*ESQ*). Two books on Melville's short fiction, *Going Under*[76] by Marvin Fisher and *Melville's Short Fiction*[77] by William B. Dillingham arrive at similar conclusions about Melville's stories of the 1850s. Marvin Fisher says that Melville 'chose to *go under* as a literary strategy, to become our first major underground writer at a time when he could not even ascertain that there existed any significant readership capable of understanding or response'. William B. Dillingham says that 'He camouflaged meanings

[71] *Louisa May: A Modern Biography of Louisa May Alcott*, by Martha Saxton. Boston, Mass.: Houghton Mifflin. pp. 428; 23 illustrations. £7.50.

[72] *Plots and Counterplots: More Unknown Thrillers of Louisa May Alcott*, ed. by Madeleine Stern. W. H. Allen pp. 315. £5.95.

[73] *The Authority of Experience: Essays in Feminist Criticism*, ed. by Arlyn Diamond and Lee R. Edwards. Amherst, Mass.: U. of Massachusetts P. pp. xiv + 304.

[74] *'Moby-Dick' and Calvinism: A World Dismantled*, by T. Walter Herbert Jr. New Brunswick, N.J.: Rutgers U.P. pp. xii + 186. £7.

[75] *Herman Melville: Moby Dick*, by Brian Way. *Studies in English Literature* No.69. Edward Arnold. pp. 64. £3.30, pb £1.65.

[76] *Going Under: Melville's Short Fiction and the American 1850s*, by Marvin Fisher. Baton Rouge, La. and London: Louisiana State U.P. pp. xii + 216. £9.35.

[77] *Melville's Short Fiction 1853–1856*, by William B. Dillingham. Athens, Ga.: U. of Georgia P. pp. 390. £9.

because concealment had already become a characteristic of his nature as a writer, because the articulation of a private vision in coded language, as it were, served the ends of both therapy and art, and because the magazines he was writing for demanded palatable art for queasy minds.'

Ludwig Rothmayr's book on Melville's novels[78] presents a definition of man's role in his works 'as caught between the forces of predestination and necessity on the one side, and chance and chaos on the other in his struggle for self-realisation and freedom'. The discussion attempts to show that 'the problem of Fate and the metaphysical determination of human life was a central key not only to Melville's novels but also to his personal problems . . . Melville thus reveals himself as a convinced determinist.' [H.C.C.]

Paul Fatout's collection, *Mark Twain Speaking*[79], despite his caveat that 'The words without the speaker put us under a handicap impossible to overcome', is immensely witty and enjoyable. Fatout's introduction provides a vivid picture of Twain's lecturing style, as well as general background on the popularity of lecturing as entertainment in the nineteenth century. *Mark Twain's 'Huckleberry Finn': Race, Class and Society*[80] by Michael Egan offers good specific examinations of Twain's language, but is far less original than Egan appears to think, as its opening sentence proves: 'For all its reputation for light and sparkle, S. L. Clemens' *Adventures of Huckleberry Finn* (1885) is one of the darkest novels in American fiction.'

Valuable articles on Twain include Guy A. Cardwell's on Twain's self-censorship and bowdlerising, 'Mark Twain: A Self-Emasculated Hero' (*ESQ*), and Arthur G. Pettit's 'Mark Twain and his Times: A Bicentennial Appreciation' (*SAQ*), which notes that 'Like other writers who followed him a half-century later, he cursed his country; and in so doing he decried a part of himself and remained the quintessential American to the end'. Thomas Asa Tenney's reference guide to Twain[81] is complete up to 1974 and also covers 1975 and 1976 in part. The intention is that this guide will be corrected, expanded, and kept up to date in an annual supplement in *American Literary Realism*.

The reference guide to Charles W. Chesnutt[82] by Curtis W. Ellison and E. W. Metcalf Jr runs from 1887 to 1975, and includes an introduction on the significance of Chesnutt for American culture. A facsimile reprint of Charles Bellamy's *An Experiment in Marriage*[83] is placed in its historical context by Joel Nydahl's introduction, as is the whole career

[78] *Der Mensch und das Schicksal in den Romanen Herman Melvilles*, by Ludwig Rothmayr. Frankfurt am Main: Peter Lang (Sprache und Literatur, Regensburger Arbeiten zur Anglistik und Amerikanistik 10). pp. 318.

[79] *Mark Twain Speaking*, ed. by Paul Fatout. Iowa City: U. of Iowa P. 1976. pp. xxxi + 688.

[80] *Mark Twain's 'Huckleberry Finn': Race, Class and Society*, by Michael Egan. (Text and Context Series). Brighton, Sussex: Sussex U.P. pp. vi + 135. hb £3.50. pb £1.75.

[81] *Mark Twain: A Reference Guide*, by Thomas Asa Tenney. Boston, Mass.: G. K. Hall. pp. xiv + 443. $45.

[82] *Charles W. Chesnutt: A Reference Guide*, by Curtis W. Ellison and E. W. Metcalf Jr. Boston, Mass.: G. K. Hall. pp. xv + 150. $15.

[83] *An Experiment in Marriage*, by Charles Bellamy, with introd. by Joel Nydahl. Delmar, N.Y.: Scholars' Facsimiles & Reprints. pp. xxviii + 286. $25.

of Sherwood Bonner, the southern woman novelist, by William L. Frank's sound and workmanlike study[84].

Friedel H. Bastein offers a history[85] of the reception of Stephen Crane's works in Germany from the 1890s to 1971. The following areas are examined: 'the role of publishing houses, periodicals, newspapers and radio as transmitters of culture, the reception by critics and scholars, and . . . the reception by the reading public'. In an initial chapter Crane's reception in America is outlined 'as a crucial determining factor for his reception in Germany' where he is now an established author and represented in school curricula. [H.C.C.]

Everett Carter gives a very full introduction to W. D. Howells's *A Hazard of New Fortunes*[86], the text of which has been established by David J. Nordloh, Don L. Cook, James P. Elliott, David Kleinman, and Robert D. Schildgen, who have also provided the notes to the text. Carter shows clearly how the novel was the product of major changes in Howell's life. Charles L. Crow and John W. Crowley in 'Psychic and Psychological Themes in Howells's "A Sleep and A Forgetting"' (*ESQ*) find Howells's story autobiographically suggestive as far as father-daughter relationships are concerned. Allen F. Stein celebrates Howells as the first American writer to explore married life in detail, analysing 'Marriage in Howells's Novels' (*AL*). Valden Madsen in 'W. D. Howells's Formal Poetics and His Appraisals of Whitman and Emily Dickinson' (*WWR*) shows how Howells could accept the greatness of Dickinson but not of Whitman.

Priscilla Allen's essay 'Old Critics and New: The Treatment of Chopin's *The Awakening*', from *The Authority of Experience*[87] edited by Arlyn Diamond and Lee R. Edwards, argues convincingly for Kate Chopin's novel as far more revolutionary than any of the critics have realised.

'Parallels: Henry James's *The Portrait of a Lady* and Nella Larsen's *Quicksand*' by Mary M. Lay (*CLAJ*) presents Helga Crane, the mulatto of Larsen's novel of 1928, 'dissatisfied, sexually confused, longing for a happiness that she can't define', as strikingly similar to Isabel Archer.

Strother B. Purdy's *The Hole in the Fabric: Science, Contemporary Literature, and Henry James*[88] is a strange, rambling mixture of things, as perhaps his title indicates. Along the way he compares *The Turn of the Screw* with Vonnegut's *Cat's Cradle*, *The Awkward Age* with Nabokov's *Lolita*, and 'The Jolly Corner' with James Blish's *Spock Must Die!*, an incident from the continuing televised saga of *Star Trek*. Shlomith Rimmon in *The Concept of Ambiguity − the Example of James*[89] concentrates on 'The Lesson of the Master', 'The Figure in the Carpet',

[84] *Sherwood Bonner (Catherine McDowell)*, by William L. Frank. Boston, Mass.: (TUSAS) G. K. Hall. 1976. pp. 158. $6.95.

[85] *Die Rezeption Stephen Cranes in Deutschland*, by Friedel H. Bastein. Frankfurt am Main: Peter Lane (Anglo-American Forum 3). pp. 361.

[86] *A Hazard of New Fortunes*, by W. D. Howells, with introd. by Everett Carter. Bloomington, Ind. and London: Indiana U.P. 1976. pp. xxix + 558. £15.

[87] *The Authority of Experience: Essays in Feminist Criticism*, ed. by Arlyn Diamond and Lee R. Edwards. Amherst, Mass.: U. of Massachusetts P. pp. xiv + 304.

[88] *The Hole in the Fabric: Science, Contemporary Literature, and Henry James*, by Strother B. Purdy. Pittsburgh, Pa.: U. of Pittsburgh P. pp. 228. $11.95.

[89] *The Concept of Ambiguity − the Example of James*, by Shlomith Rimmon. Chicago, Ill. and London: U. of Chicago P. pp. xiii + 257.

The Turn of the Screw, and *The Sacred Fount,* making rather heavy weather of rival hypotheses about James's work.

Charles R. Anderson's *Person, Place, and Thing in Henry James's Novels*[90] examines six novels in great detail: *Roderick Hudson, The American, The Portrait of a Lady, The Princess Casamassima, The Wings of the Dove,* and *The Ambassadors.* This is a stimulating study, and Anderson is particularly good on the relevance of paintings to the novels. Alan Spiegel's *Fiction and the Camera Eye*[91] includes a section on the way a scene from *What Maisie Knew* is rendered 'cinematographically', and Peter Faulkner briefly discusses James's contribution to modernism in his study of that movement[92]. Eric S. Rabkin in his consideration of *The Fantastic in Literature*[93] argues that, although perhaps 'no novelist is so unanimously accepted as a "realist" as is Henry James', James's work is really fantastic because it demands our minute attention, which is not realistic.

Theodore Ziolkowski in *Disenchanted Images*[94] places 'The Last of the Valerii' in the context of the legend of Venus and the Ring, and discusses *The Sense of the Past* in the context of a classic ghost-story formula. Elsa Nettels's excellent comparison of *James and Conrad*[95] describes their personal relationship as far as possible, and draws illuminating parallels between their works, concluding that 'The characters of James and Conrad live in a world which dooms people to intolerable alternatives' but that many of their characters 'become themselves a source of values'.

Maqbool Aziz in 'Editing James: The Question of Copy-Text' from *Editing British and American Literature, 1880-1920*[96] edited by Eric W. Domville pleads for the historical approach, even though some texts, like *The Ambassadors* and *The Wings of the Dove,* would present minor problems.

David M. Fine's *The City, The Immigrant and American Fiction, 1880-1920*[97] is in effect an expanded bibliography with plot summaries.

4. Drama

Volume VIII of *The Revels History of Drama in English*[98] treats American Drama in three sections by different authors: first, Travis

[90] *Person, Place, and Thing in Henry James's Novels,* by Charles R. Anderson. Durham, N.C.: Duke U.P. pp. ix + 308. £8.60.

[91] *Fiction and the Camera Eye: Visual Consciousness in Film and the Modern Novel,* by Alan Spiegel. Charlottesville, Va.: U.P. of Virginia. 1976. pp. xvi + 203. £7.15.

[92] *Modernism,* by Peter Faulkner. Methuen. pp. x + 86. hb £2.35, pb £1.20.

[93] *The Fantastic in Literature,* by Eric S. Rabkin. Princeton, N.J.: Princeton U.P. 1976. pp. xi + 234. £9.40.

[94] *Disenchanted Images: A Literary Iconology,* by Theodore Ziolkowski. Princeton, N.J., and Guildford, Surrey: Princeton U.P. pp. ix + 273. £9.40.

[95] *James and Conrad,* by Elsa Nettels. Athens, Ga.: U. of Georgia P. pp. xi + 289. £9.

[96] *Editing British and American Literature, 1880-1920,* ed. by Eric W. Domville. New York and London: Garland. 1976. pp. 98. $15.

[97] *The City, The Immigrant and American Fiction, 1880-1920,* by David M. Fine. Metuchen, N.J., and London: Scarecrow P. pp. x + 182.

[98] *The Revels History of Drama in English,* vol. viii *American Drama,* by Travis Bogard, Richard Moody, and Walter J. Meserve. Methuen and New York: Barnes & Noble. pp. liii + 324; 31 illustrations. hb £13, pb £8.50.

Bogard, 'The American drama: its range of Contexts'; second, Richard Moody, 'American actors, managers, producers and directors'; third, Walter J. Meserve, 'The dramatists and their plays'. There are obvious advantages in this kind of organisation, but the execution here is confusingly disparate. Travis Bogard's section, the best written of the three, is disparate enough in itself. It begins with a readably anecdotal approach to the place of actors in America, starting in the nineteenth century. Some of this material overlaps with Richard Moody's. There follows a misleadingly titled chapter on 'Art and politics' which concerns the development of the American theatre, but not politics in the usual sense of the word. Richard Moody's section begins by taking the reader back to the eighteenth century, as is the case at the start of Meserve's. There is a great deal of information in Moody's chapters, though sometimes he does little more than list actors and productions. Walter J. Meserve's portion of the book is disappointing, though the nine short sections on pre-twentieth-century American drama are more readable than his shaky remarks on later developments. The book contains a useful bibliography and a less useful Chronological Table.

The Revels *American Drama* would have benefitted from stricter editorial control. It might also have benefitted had it faced some of the problems that concern Laurence G. Avery's 'A Proposal Concerning the Study of Early American Drama' (*ETJ*). Avery complains of the 'lack of historical understanding characteristic of twentieth-century dealings with early American drama' and tries to rectify this by proposing two pragmatic, rather than mimetic, traditions that went to make up the nineteenth-century conception of the drama.

Calhoun Winton contributes an essay on 'The Theater and Drama' to *American Literature 1764-1789*[99] and he evidently feels some unease about the quality of some plays discussed. Thomas Godfrey's *The Price of Parthia*, a play of the 1760s, 'has little to recommend it', he says, while George Cocking's *The Conquest of Canada*, of the same decade, is dramatically 'a non-starter'. However, Winton has high praise for Royall Tyler's *The Contrast* (1787).

The plays of the feminist Susanna Rowson are discussed sympathetically in Dorothy Weil's *In Defense of Women*[100]. Weil shows how in a play that seems to treat primarily a patriotic theme, *Slaves of Algiers* (1794), in reality 'the courage and fortitude of woman takes precedence'.

Yvonne Shafer, in 'Black Actors in the Nineteenth Century American Theatre' (*CLAJ*), chronicles the difficulties that these actors experienced and concentrates on the careers of James Hewlett, Ira Aldridge, and Sam Lucas, three notable black actors who met with varying degrees of success. Roger A. Hall's '*Black America*: Nate Salsbury's "Afro-American Exhibition"' (*ETJ*) tells how Salsbury, the brains behind the success of Buffalo Bill's Wild West Show, followed up that success with a new spectacular in 1895. This was *Black America*, involving a cast of five hundred blacks and presenting an image of Southern black culture 'somewhat less exaggerated than the one provided in the popular minstrel show'. Such minstrel

[99] *American Literature 1764-1789: The Revolutionary Years*, ed. by Everett Emerson. Madison, Wisc.: U. of Wisconsin P. pp. xvi + 301. £11.25.
[100] *In Defense of Women: Susanna Rowson (1976-1824)*, by Dorothy Weil. University Park, Pa. and London: Pennsylvania State U.P. 1976. pp. 204.

shows figure in Stanley J. Lemons's 'Black Stereotypes as Reflected in Popular Culture, 1880–1920' (*AQ*). William Brasmer contributes an interesting essay on Buffalo Bill's Exhibition to *Western Popular Theatre*[101], a book consisting of dangerously heterogeneous materials. Brasmer reminds us 'that popular entertainment substantiates fantasies, often immoral, of a particular society. Certainly the honouring of the Indian killers in the Wild West Show distorted the reality of the Indian and contributed to the ease with which society ignored the "Indian problem"'.

[101] *Western Popular Theatre: The Proceedings of a Symposium Sponsored by the Manchester University Department of Drama*, ed. by David Mayer and Kenneth Richards. Methuen. pp. x + 277. £6.20.

XVIII

American Literature: The Twentieth Century

DAVID JARRETT and MARY JARRETT

The chapter is divided as follows: 1. General; 2. Poetry; 3. Fiction; 4. Drama.

1. General

Bibliographies of current articles are published quarterly in *AL* and annually in the summer supplement of *AQ*. Harold H. Kolb Jr's *Field Guide to the Study of American Literature*[1] is a selective bibliography of resources, and *American Literary Scholarship*[2] for 1976 summarizes work published in 1976 on individual authors, genres, and periods. *The Literary Journal in America, 1900-1950: A Guide to Information Sources*[3] by Edward E. Chielens is a guide to books and articles dealing with some hundred significant literary periodicals, and *Women in Literature: Criticism of the Seventies*[4] by Carol Fairbanks Myers is a bibliography for selected books and periodicals from January 1970 to the spring of 1975. *AQ* offers a bibliography issue on American Studies which includes 'Women's Studies/American Studies, 1970-1975' by Donna Gerstenberger and Carolyn Allen and 'The Proper Study — Autobiography in American Studies' by Robert F. Sayre.

Our Literary Heritage: A Pictorial History of the Writer in America[5] by Van Wyck Brooks and Otto Bettmann is based on the five volumes of Van Wyck Brooks's *Makers and Finders: a History of the Writer in America, 1800-1915*. The text has been reduced by more than five-sixths and is lavishly illustrated. James R. Vitelli offers a reference guide[6] to Van Wyck Brooks himself, feeling that his influence as a critic has been undervalued. The guide covers the period 1908-1974. *Milestones in American Literary History*[7] by Robert E. Spiller is a collection of writings, mostly

[1] *A Field Guide to the Study of American Literature*, by Harold H. Kolb Jr. Charlottesville, Va.: U.P. of Virginia. 1976. pp. xii + 136. $9.75. pb $4.50.
[2] *American Literary Scholarship: An Annual/1976*, ed. by J. Albert Robbins. Durham, N.C.: Duke U.P. 1978 pp. xiii + 492. $17.75.
[3] *The Literary Journal in America, 1900-1950: A Guide to Information Sources*, by Edward E. Chielens. Detroit: Gale Research. pp. viii + 186. $18.
[4] *Women in Literature: Criticism of the Seventies*, by Carol Fairbanks Myers. Metuchen, N. J.: Scarecrow P. 1976. pp. vii + 256. $10.
[5] *Our Literary Heritage: A Pictorial History of the Writer in America*, by Van Wyck Brooks and Otto Bettmann. New York and London: Paddington P. pp. ix + 246; 502 illustrations. pb £3.95.
[6] *Van Wyck Brooks: A Reference Guide*, by James R. Vitelli. Boston, Mass.: G. K. Hall. pp. xv + 108. $12.
[7] *Milestones in American Literary History*, by Robert E. Spiller, with intro. by Robert H. Walker. London and Westport, Conn.: Greenwood P. pp. xvi + 152. £8.50.

reviews, dating from 1922 to 1960, which reveal, asserts Robert H. Walker in his introduction, that 'the critical pattern of this era was not so neatly bifurcated as some like to make it: a square of Marxists on the left, a forum of New Humanists on the right, and only the author's sweet reason in between'. John Fekete in *The Critical Twilight: Explorations in the Ideology of Anglo-American Literary Theory from Eliot to McLuhan*[8] examines in detail the critical theories of John Crowe Ransom, Northrop Frye, and Marshall McLuhan.

Joseph R. Millichap covers novels and poetry in his discussion of 'Distorted Matter and Disjunctive Forms: The Grotesque as Modernist Genre' (*ArQ*), and Herbert N. Schneidau surveys 'Style and Sacrament in Modernist Writing' (*GaR*). H. Bruce Franklin in 'The Literature of the American Prison' (*MR*) examines the phenomenon of the hundreds of prisoners' and ex-prisoners' books published since the early sixties, the majority of them by 'ordinary criminals who became authors because of prison'.

Robert Chrisman in 'Blacks, Racism, and Bourgeois Culture' (*CE*) observes changing black stereotypes in American literature, television, and film. Charles Scruggs in ' "All Dressed Up But No Place to Go": The Black Writer and his Audience during the Harlem Renaissance' (*AL*) shows how, rightly, 'The central concern of the black artist was not "art" but the total culture in which his people lived'. Rebecca Chalmers Barton's *Witnesses for Freedom: Negro Americans in Autobiography*[9] is a critical comparative study ranging from Booker T. Washington's *Up From Slavery* to Richard Wright's *Black Boy*. Mutlu Konuk Blasing in *The Art of Life: Studies in American Autobiographical Literature*[10] urges that 'Only in *Black Boy*, where Wright speaks as an autobiographer, does he succeed in transcending the stereotypes of blacks as victims or criminals'. Conversely, Booker T. Washington was condemned by such figures as W. E. B. Du Bois 'for meekly submitting to injustice and committing treason against his race', as Robert B. Downs recalls in his discussion of *Up From Slavery* in *Books That Changed the South*[11]. James M. Cox places emphasis on the style of Washington's book in 'Autobiography and Washington' (*SR*), commenting on its 'air of immobility being put into slow and steady motion'. The sixth volume of *The Booker T. Washington Papers*[12], edited by Louis R. Harlan and Raymond W. Smock, has now been published. This volume includes an account of the popular reaction to Washington's dinner with Roosevelt in the White House in October 1901.

James A. Page has entries on 453 authors from colonial times to the

[8] *The Critical Twilight: Explorations in the Ideology of Anglo-American Literary Theory from Eliot to McLuhan*, by John Fekete. London and Boston, Mass.: Routledge & Kegan Paul. pp. xxviii + 300. £7.95.

[9] *Witnesses for Freedom: Negro Americans in Autobiography*, by Rebecca Chalmers Barton. Oakdale, N.Y.: Dowling College P. pp. xiii + 294. pb $6.50.

[10] *The Art of Life: Studies in American Autobiographical Literature*, by Mutlu Konuk Blasing. Austin, Tex. and London: U. of Texas P. pp. xxviii + 193; 6 illustrations. £7.50.

[11] *Books that Changed the South*, by Robert B. Downs, Chapel Hill, N.C.: U. of North Carolina P. pp. xvii + 292; 8 illustrations. £6.30.

[12] *The Booker T. Washington Papers (Vol. 6, 1901-2)*, ed. by Louis R. Harlan and Raymond W. Smock, with Barbara S. Kraft. Urbana, Chicago, Ill. and London: U. of Illinois P. pp. xxx + 661; 41 illustrations. £13.10.

present in his *Selected Black American Authors: An Illustrated Bio-Bibliography*[13]. Many of the authors included will, of course, be unfamiliar to the general reader, but Page has chosen only those who have published at least one or two books, who have already been included in other sources like anthologies and bibliographies, who, if they are poets, must have had more than one collection published, and who, if playwrights, must have published other than in anthologies. Entries consist of a bibliography of the author's work, a list of sources, biographical information, and even addresses. *Pride and Protest: Ethnic Roots in America*[14], an anthology edited by Jay Schulman, Aubrey Shatter, and Rosalie Erlich, is divided into two parts: the first, 'Third World Peoples in the U.S.A.', consists of essays, fiction, drama, and poetry written by American Indians, Asians, Blacks, Mexicans, and Puerto Ricans, while the second, 'White Ethnics', includes work by American Jews, Italians, Irish, Armenians, Greeks, and Slavs.

In *Die amerikanische Literatur der Gegenwart*[15] Hans Bungert collects sixteen previously unpublished essays on American literature after 1945. There are contributions on recent trends in the fields of drama, film, experimental theatre, poetry, the novel, the short story, the reception of modern American literature in West Germany, and on new developments in American literary criticism. Originally published in 1963, Schirmer and Esch's useful *Short History of English and American Literature*[16] has been revised, brought up to date, and re-issued this year. Angelika Schmitt-Kaufhold writes[17] on the reception of North American literature in German-speaking countries (including the DDR) after 1945. The book's first part proceeds thematically, looking in turn at the critical reaction to works on subjects like 'The Color Problem', 'The American Jew', 'The American Dream', 'The Deep South', etc. The second part divides according to genres — the short story, the novel, drama, and poetry, pointing to a marked critical preference for short stories and the novel, and a relative neglect of poetry. In a final section the author details critics' attempts to establish links between American and European authors and to estimate the influence of American literature on German-speaking writers. Alexander Ritter has brought together a collection of essays[18] in German and English on the image of America in German literature. An introductory article by Hans Galinsky discusses the problems and tasks of research in the field both for the past and the present. The remaining twenty-eight contributions were written between 1945 and 1976 and analyse the image of America in the work of a wide range of authors — among the most important are Herder, Goethe, Novalis,

[13] *Selected Black American Authors: An Illustrated Bio-Bibliography*, compiled by James A. Page. Boston, Mass.: G. K. Hall. pp. xv + 398. 285 illustrations. $30.

[14] *Pride and Protest: Ethnic Roots in America*, ed. by Jay Schulman, Aubrey Shatter, and Rosalie Erlich. New York: Dell. pp. 349. pb $2.50.

[15] *Die amerikanische Literatur der Gegenwart. Aspekte und Tendenzen*, ed. by Hans Bungert. Stuttgart: Reclam. pp. 347. DM 32.80.

[16] *Kurze Geschichte der englischen und amerikanischen Literatur*, by Walter F. Schirmer and Arno Esch. Tubingen: Niemeyer. pp. xii + 399. DM 38.

[17] *Nordamerikanische Literatur im deutschen Sprachraum nach 1945*, by Angelika Schmitt-Kaufhold. Frankfurt am Main: Peter Lang. pp. 375.

[18] *Deutschlands literarisches Amerikabild*, ed. by Alexander Ritter. Hildesheim: Olms Verlag. pp. 615. DM 49.50.

Heine, Fontane, Hauptmann, Wedekind, Thomas Mann, Brecht, Max
Frisch, and Wolfgang Koeppen. There is a concluding essay by Manfred
Durzak on the treatment of America in very recent German fiction
(Handke, H. Heckmann, Uwe Johnson) and the editor has compiled
a bibliography covering the years 1945–1976. [H.C.C.]

2. Poetry

Geoffrey Moore's selection for *The Penguin Book of American Verse*[19]
includes 101 poets born between 1612 and 1943. This is a considerable
range, but inevitably every reader is going to regret the omission of one
writer or another; for example, Hilda Doolittle, Kenneth Patchen, Michael
McClure, and Denise Levertov are not represented in the twentieth century.
Moore's introduction is concise and undogmatic and his conclusion that
perhaps English poetic language has not been Americanised enough, which
is contrary to popular opinion, will bear some thinking about.

The American Long Poem: An Annotated Selection[20] edited by
Stephen Fender sets itself some problems too, the most obvious of which
is that an anthology of long poems which is not much more than 250
pages long cannot contain many complete long poems. But Fender's
choice of poems and extracts is judicious and each is well introduced
and annotated. *The Waste Land* he regards as the 'ghost' at the feast,
recognising its central importance as an American long poem, but feeling
that annotated texts of it are easily available elsewhere. The work of
Charles Olson is not represented because there was not room for it. The
twentieth-century poems, which make up most of the volume, are: Hart
Crane, *The Bridge*; Ezra Pound, *Cantos 31, 37, 38, 39;* Wallace Stevens,
Notes toward a Supreme Fiction; William Carlos Williams, *Paterson*,
Book IV. Fender's introduction justifies his concentration on long poems
of the Whitman tradition and develops the idea of the importance of
millennial vision to the poetics of the American long poem. He says that
Stevens is the 'most completely millennial' poet in the collection and
provides a good analysis of 'The Comedian as the Letter C' to support his
view.

That American women poets have been more concerned with 'international' or 'universal' themes is one of the conclusions of Emily Stipes
Watts's *The Poetry of American Women from 1632 to 1945*[21]. Watts
also discusses the prosodic innovations of American women poets and
concludes that it is time we began to understand the 'complex interrelationship between male and female poets of America'. The twentieth-
century poets on whom she concentrates are Hilda Doolittle, Amy Lowell,
Adelaide Crapsey, Marianne Moore, Laura Riding, Edna St Vincent Millay,
Elinor Wylie, and Muriel Rukeyser. Susan Sutton Smith has edited *The
Complete Poems and Collected Letters*[22] of Adelaide Crapsey, including

[19] *The Penguin Book of American Verse*, ed. by Geoffrey Moore. Harmonds-
worth, Middx.: Penguin. pp. 656. pb £1.75.
    [20] *The American Long Poem: An Annotated Selection*, ed. by Stephen Fender.
Edward Arnold. pp. ix + 254. £8.95, pb £3.95.
    [21] *The Poetry of American Women from 1632 to 1945*, by Emily Stipes Watts.
Austin, Tex. and London: U. of Texas P. pp. xiv + 218. £10.50.
    [22] *The Complete Poems and Collected Letters*, by Adelaide Crapsey, ed. by
Susan Sutton Smith. Albany, N.Y.: State U. of New York P. pp. vii + 288; 11 illustra-
tions. $20.

thirty-nine poems and sixty-nine letters not previously published. Smith tells us something of Crapsey's life, of previous criticism of her poetry, and attempts a critical revaluation of her work, claiming that her poetic development was not so isolated as it might appear. *Time's Unfading Garden*[23] by J. Lee Greene does not assert that its subject, the black southern poet Anne Spencer, is 'a major or even grossly neglected minor American poet'; but Greene makes a case for her significance. Suzanne Juhasz, in *Naked and Fiery Forms: Modern American Poetry by Women: A New Tradition*[24], offers a feminist view of her subject that is both forceful and critically subtle. Among twentieth-century poets she discusses the work of Marianne Moore, Denise Levertov, Sylvia Plath, Anne Sexton, Gwendolyn Brooks, Nikki Giovanni, Alta, and Adrienne Rich. Claire Healey has recorded a stimulating and revealing interview with Diane Wakoski (*ConL*), while Marilyn R. Farwell, in 'Adrienne Rich and an Organic Feminist Criticism' (*CE*), claims that Rich's essays embody a coherent feminist theory on which her literary criticism is based.

Of particular interest is Ellen Williams's well-researched *Harriet Monroe and the Poetry Renaissance: The First Ten Years of 'Poetry', 1912-22*[25]. It takes a little time to adjust to the fact that Williams is going to offer nothing about Harriet Monroe and her life that does not bear directly upon *Poetry*, but this is probably the most fascinating part of the story as well as the best tribute to Harriet Monroe. The book allows us to see poetry in terms of the market-place, well-known poets in unfamiliar contexts, less well-known poets who were in the running with those who have proved more enduring, literary fashions, intrigues, quarrels, even hoaxes, and, of course, Harriet Monroe's own passionate commitment to the promotion of poetry. This commitment did not waver, though *Poetry* suffered from problems of identity, which is hardly surprising in view of the personalities of the poets who were closely involved with the magazine. Pound, maddening and energetic as ever, figures prominently in Ellen Williams's book. *Harriet Monroe and the Poetry Renaissance* will be of great value to students of the period.

Geoffrey Thurley's *The American Moment: American Poetry in the Mid-Century*[26] begins promisingly with an introduction on the provincialism of much American poetry before the mid-twentieth century. Even here, however, there is a hint that what purports to be neutral sociological observation is, in fact, value judgement; one senses that Thurley simply believes that Tennyson is a much better poet than Whitman. Unfortunately this hint is confirmed during the course of the book, which is markedly partisan and often cantankerous. We are told that Ted Hughes is a better poet than Richard Wilbur, that John Berryman fails where Gerard Manley Hopkins succeeds, that Robert Lowell lacks

[23] *Time's Unfading Garden: Anne Spencer's Life and Poetry*, by J. Lee Greene. Baton Rouge, La. and London: Louisiana State U.P. pp. ix + 204; 6 illustrations.
[24] *Naked and Fiery Forms; Modern American Poetry by Women: A New Tradition*, by Suzanne Juhasz. New York and London: Harper and Row, 1976. pp. x + 212. pb $3.95.
[25] *Harriet Monroe and the Poetry Renaissance: The First Ten Years of 'Poetry', 1912-22*, by Ellen Williams. Urbana, Chicago, Ill. and London, U. of Illinois P. pp. xiv + 312. £6.75.
[26] *The American Moment: American Poetry in the Mid-Century*, by Geoffrey Thurley. Edward Arnold. pp. viii + 249. £11.75.

the gifts of Philip Larkin or W. H. Auden, that Theodore Roethke is inferior to Eliot. Thurley's dismissal of American 'confessional' poets is extravagant and shrill and, though he can provide sound analyses of individual poems, in this context his criticism becomes unreliable: he misreads Berryman's 'New Year's Eve', for example, and his assault on Lowell's 'The Quaker Graveyard in Nantucket' is a misdirection of critical skills. Thurley does not just object to the Freudianism of poets like Berryman, Lowell, Sexton, and Plath; he dismisses Freud himself. William Carlos Williams is presented primarily as a bad influence and Charles Olson as a slack and inconsistent poet and critic. The rigidity and fierceness of Thurley's approving and disapproving prevent *The American Moment* from giving a convincing account of an American tradition in poetry or of the discovery of an American poetic voice.

Where Geoffrey Thurley is angered by what he sees as the preoccupation with self of many twentieth-century American poets, Karl Malkoff, in *Escape from the Self: A Study in Contemporary Poetry and Poetics*[27], argues that many of these poets are concerned to abandon 'the conscious, rational self as the inevitable perspective from which reality must be viewed'. The traditions of both Objectism and Confessional poetry, he says, have sought to abandon such a self, the former in a way that can be paralleled usefully with the thought of Marshall McLuhan and the latter with that of Norman O. Brown, two contemporary 'prophets of liberation'. Malkoff's case is often interestingly argued, though sometimes his analysis of individual poems or parts of poems is not as revealing as it might be. There is something too flat and familiar in concluding about Pound's *Cantos:* 'In the end, the poem is about itself, about its own creation'. Malkoff traces the movement from Imagism to Objectivism to Projectivism, which Olson sums up in the term Objectism, and tells how Williams 'pinpoints the movement's basis, a new relationship between the self and the world', while Olson 'explicitly asserts a new version of the self, one that plays down the traditional role of consciousness'. Confessionals, like Lowell, Plath, and Berryman, have tried to escape from the traditional self by eroding the boundaries between conscious and unconscious, but Malkoff speculates that Lowell's retreat from a non-rational extreme in *History* might signal a 'widespread rejection of the search — in its extremest form — for the alternative to the ego-position'.

Like Thurley, Eric Homberger, in *The Art of the Real: Poetry in England and America since 1939*,[28] is concerned with English and American poetic relations, though, happily, Homberger's book is not marred by narrow value-judgements. It deliberately ignores 'ethnopoetics' and acknowledges that there are some poetic traditions 'which do not easily cross the Atlantic', but Homberger says, 'the Americans and the English have been living out of each other's cultural pocket for a long time'. The book is divided into three main sections: 1. The 1940s, 2. The 1950s,

[27] *Escape from the Self: A Study in Contemporary American Poetry And Poetics,* by Karl Malkoff. New York: Columbia U.P. pp. xiv + 181. £8.35.
[28] *The Art of the Real: Poetry in England and America since 1939,* by Eric Homberger. London and Toronto: Dent; Totowa, N.J.: Rowman & Littlefield. pp. x + 246. £5.95.

3. The 1960s and 1970s, of which the second is the longest. Each chapter is prefaced by an often witty summary of contents; for example, 'William Carlos Williams takes the measure of American life in *Paterson*; but Charles Olson wasn't impressed', which is typical of Homberger's tone and approach in general. Homberger has also assembled useful selected chronologies as well as a bibliography which includes works that are not primarily about poetry but which convey something of the 'wider social and historical ambience'.

Chapter I is dominated by English poets, including Auden, and the American who receives most attention is Randall Jarrell. Homberger deals with his wartime sense of engagement with contemporary events and his loss of 'contemporaneity' after the war. In chapter II we are given something of an historical/sociological context for poetic formalism and the revolt against it. Homberger does not have many good words for Charles Olson, though he insists on the importance of Williams as 'an intellectual, an advanced thinker, and a man of scientific training'. This chapter also contains some sensitive analysis of poems by Robert Lowell and Sylvia Plath. Chapter III presents a contrast between Lowell and Snyder. Homberger concludes that 'poetry in England and America shares the numbness that has given the 1970s its insubstantial, styleless quality'. *The Art of the Real* is a spirited piece of writing, approaching an overview of poetic tendencies and developments in Britain and the U.S. in post-war years; it is not based on any special theory of poetic relations between the two countries and one is probably justified in taking or leaving the theory of modern art implicit in Homberger's title.

Richard Poirier's *Robert Frost: The Work of Knowing*[29] is a first-rate reading and placing of Frost's poetry, which continues the work of clearing away modernist or academic uncertainties about how to evaluate this wily, deceptive, and, most worryingly, enormously popular poet. Poirier does not ignore Frost's shortcomings — he acknowledges, for example, that Frost's desire to be 'genteel' was a disadvantage, that he was blind to social systems, that his work could be smug — but he also demonstrates how Frost's poetry rewards close, sophisticated critical reading that attends to verbal subtlety, to psychological implication, and to sociological setting. Poirier writes illuminatingly on the relations between sex, language, and the making of a poem in Frost, and when he asserts that Frost, in writing poems about work, is really writing about the work of writing poems, the insight has the appearance of freshness, like much in this book. Frost is presented as a visionary poet of nature by virtue of his scenes of 'negative designation', seeming to reassure his readers on the surface that he is not a visionary. The extensive analysis of images in Frost relating to home and 'extra-vagance' is a particularly valuable part of the book and it usefully underpins the fifth chapter, in which the language and themes of Frost's poety are seen in political context. Perhaps the basis of Poirier's approach to Frost is the poet's claim that his poems have 'a lot of literary criticism in them — *in them*'.

Poirier's essay 'Soundings for Home: Frost's Poetry of Extravagance and Return' (*GR*) forms part of *Robert Frost: The Work of Knowing*.

[29] *Robert Frost: The Work of Knowing*, by Richard Poirier. New York: O.U.P. pp. xvii + 322. $11.95.

Because of the problems posed by Frost and his work for critics and scholars over a long period, *Robert Frost: The Critical Reception*[30], edited by Linda Welsheimer Wagner, is of special interest and value. The book focuses on American criticism, though some British reviews are included. The introduction gives Frost's publishing history and a summary of the development of his critical reputation. Some reminiscences concerning Frost in Miami are included in *The Carrell: The Journal of the Friends of the University of Miami Library*.

Louis D. Rubin Jr.'s 'Not to Forget Carl Sandburg . . .' (*SR*) is an affectionate, not altogether sanguine expression of hope that Sandburg's reputation will be favourably reappraised.

Harold Bloom has produced another critical *tour de force* with *Wallace Stevens: The Poems of Our Climate*[31]. Like Poirier he can illuminate and sometimes dazzle with his analyses of individual poems and, happily, there are many of these in *The Poems of Our Climate*. But Bloom's book is not as accessible as Poirier's because he has developed his own critical language. The book begins with a 'Gnostic apothegm', and to understand Bloom's theory of poetic 'crossing', one must learn of 'Kabbalistic rhetorical theory, as formulated particularly by Cordovero in the figurations he called *behinot'*. This very clever book seems enamoured of its own cleverness. However, when Bloom analyses familiar poems like 'Sunday Morning' (Chapter II), 'The Man Whose Pharynx Was Bad', 'The Snow Man', 'Tea at the Palaz of Hoon' (Chapter III), 'The Comedian as the Letter C' (Chapter IV), or 'The Idea of Order at Key West' (Chapter V) he can do so brilliantly, recognising their complexity in terms of tradition and literary influence, placing them in the development of Stevens's poetic career and crises, and registering the significance of linguistic subtleties and felicities.

Susan B. Weston's *Wallace Stevens: An Introduction to the Poetry*[32] is a more straightforward book which deliberately keeps to a minimum references to other poets and philosophers. This is to be welcomed in as far as it concentrates attention upon the poetry itself and that, after initial remarks on 'Continuity and Change', 'The Supreme Fiction', and 'The Poet', is what Susan Weston does. It is curious, however, that when one has read her paraphrase of Crispin's progress in 'The Comedian as the Letter C' one is still left wondering about the point of the poem, whereas Harold Bloom's account of the 'The Comedian' — demonstrating how it is almost a parody of the High-Romantic quest poem, a poem about 'the anxiety of influence', about Crispin becoming the Emersonian Self — effectively imparts a sense of understanding. The ideal critic of Wallace Stevens would perhaps lie somewhere between Susan Weston and Harold Bloom.

James Rother's 'The Tempering of *Harmonium:* The Last Years of Wallace Stevens's Apprenticeship' (*ArQ*) gives an account of Stevens's

[30] *Robert Frost: The Critical Reception*, ed. by Linda Welsheimer Wagner. New York: Burt Franklin. pp. xxv + 280; 14 illustrations. $8.95.
[31] *Wallace Stevens: The Poems of Our Climate*, by Harold Bloom. Ithaca, N.Y. and London: Cornell U.P. pp. viii + 413. £12.
[32] *Wallace Stevens: An Introduction to the Poetry*, by Susan B. Weston. New York: Columbia U.P. pp. xix + 151. $13.70.

development from *fin-de-siecle* influences to his own 'spare, confident, and imagistically quite striking style'; it also contains a significant amount of analysis of individual poems. David Howard's 'Wallace Stevens and Politics' (*RMS*) is an admirably thought-provoking account of Stevens's preoccupation with force, violence, and war; it is a useful antidote to some of the criticism that concentrates on Stevens the 'philosophical' poet.

Lucile F. Aly's *John G. Nierhardt*[33] is a lively, anecdotal, almost gushing account of the poet. It concentrates on Nierhardt's courage and his faith in mankind. Aly believes that 'Nierhardt points something of a moral' in that he has always retained an audience even when unsupported by critics and publishers.

The relation between *Paterson* and *Finnegans Wake* is explored by Stephen Tapscott in 'Paterson A'Bloom: Williams, Joyce, and the Virtue of "Abcedmindedness"' (*ArQ*). Williams, says Tapscott, learns from Joyce to have 'faith in the objective power of the word'. Surface resemblances between the two works involve images of rivers and giants, tree/woman and flower/woman motifs, themes of paternity and spiritual inheritance, and the use of different styles of writing in a single section. More important is that 'both . . . move behind language to its essential structures'.

The work of explicating Pound's *Cantos* is carried on in James J. Wilhelm's *The Later Cantos of Ezra Pound*[34], some of which, like the *Rock-Drill* and *Thrones* Cantos, have not received a great deal of critical attention. Naturally this is a formidable task, for the critic must gloss, link, and interpret a heterogenous array of materials that must sometimes look like fragments. And, indeed, Wilhelm does have to pause on occasion and exclaim 'The reader might well ask why all these references?' and the chapter on Canto 94 inevitably slides into being a summary of the history with which the Canto teems. Then, in considering Canto 101, Wilhelm becomes so involved with the losers with which the poem deals that he seems to confuse them and the problems they raise with the question of whether the Canto has a coherent literary form. Generally, however, this is an admirable guide to the later Cantos, particularly in its explanations of what the troubadours meant to Pound, of the figure of Dante as a cohering voice in the Cantos, and of how Byzantium, 'the sacred symbol of Yeats', comes to be the epitome of the 'well-run metropolis' for Pound.

In *Ezra Pound and Music: The Complete Criticism*[35] R. Murray Schafer has edited and commented on the considerable volume of Pound's music criticism, including concert reviews, the columns written for *The New Age* between 1917 and 1921, and the text of his *Antheil and the Treatise on Harmony* as well as writings on music from other sources, like letters. This collection demonstrates the importance of Pound's assertion 'Poets who will not study music are defective'. Schafer's Introduction offers a substantial discussion of the influence of music on Pound's literary work and

[33] *John G. Nierhardt: A Critical Biography,* by Lucile F. Aly Amsterdam: Rodopi. pp. 307.
[34] *The Later Cantos of Ezra Pound,* by James J. Wilhelm. New York: Walker & Co. pp. xvii + 221. £9.90.
[35] *Ezra Pound and Music: The Complete Criticism,* ed. by R. Murray Schafer. Faber. pp. xiii + 530. £25.

he includes an Appendix which is a 'Glossary of Important Musical Personalities'. The Introduction suggests that we can best understand the Cantos
by a musical analogy, seeing the canto form as akin to that of the fugue.
This book has been interestingly reviewed at some length by Samuel
Lipman (*TLS* April 1978), who is able to comment expertly on Pound's
musical prejudices and insufficiencies. But music was important enough
to Pound for Schafer to promise a second volume in which Pound's own
music is to be examined.

George Fraser's *Essays on Twentieth-Century Poetry*[36] reprints his
1950 essay 'Pound: Masks, Myth, Man' which is still relevant, lively, and
useful. A good discussion of *Hugh Selwyn Mauberley* is included in Peter
Faulkner's *Modernism*[36a], while a biographical note on Pound is provided
by Barbara Scott Jordan in 'Viola Jordan and Ezra Pound: Some Notes on
their Friendship' (*YULG*).

Pamela White Hadas's *Marianne Moore*[37] is an affectionate tribute to
the poet. The book contains a certain amount of biography, but it consists mainly of a commentary on the poems in which quotations from the
poetry are applied to Marianne Moore herself. It is written with delicacy,
intricacy, and subtlety, though the reader does not often get the sense
of anything explained. Craig S. Abbott's *Marianne Moore: A Descriptive
Bibliography*[38] supersedes the only previous bibliography of Moore's
work. Margaret Newlin, in '"Unhelpful Hymen!"': Marianne Moore and
Hilda Doolittle' (*EIC*), begins with a defence of the idea of a woman as
poet and goes on to consider the difficulty of reconciling love and poetry
in relation to the lives of Moore and H.D.

Edward Germain's Introduction to *Shadows of the Sun: The Diaries
of Harry Crosby*[39] concentrates on Crosby's bizarre suicide in 1929.
Judith Nierman gives a short introduction on Millay in *Edna St. Vincent
Millay: A Reference Guide*[40]. The book which contains criticism, reviews,
and comments on Millay published between 1918 and 1973, attempts
to be as inclusive as possible and lists a number of items not previously
mentioned in bibliographical guides.

The Winter issue of *MissQ* is devoted to the work of John Crowe
Ransom. It contains seven essays on Ransom's poetry and his critical
and 'religious' thought as well as a checklist of relevant works 1967–
1976. William Pratt traces the development of the fourteen versions of
the poem that became 'The Vanity of the Bright Boys', while Robert
Buffington emphasises that Ransom revised his poems so meticulously
because of his sensitivity to criticism and because he 'was conscious
of the literary figure he cut'. Thomas Daniel Young and Marcia McDonald

---

[36] *Essays on Twentieth-Century Poets*, by George Fraser. Leicester: Leicester
U.P. pp. 255. £3.95.

[36a] *Modernism*, by Peter Faulkner. Methuen. pp. x + 86. £2.35; pb £1.20.

[37] *Marianne Moore: Poet of Affection*, by Pamela White Hadas. Syracuse U.P.
pp. xii + 243. $15.

[38] *Marianne Moore: A Descriptive Bibliography*, by Craig S. Abbott. Pittsburgh,
Pa. and London: U. of Pittsburgh P. pp. xiii + 265; 60 illustrations. $20.

[39] *Shadows of the Sun: The Diaries of Harry Crosby*, ed. by Edward Germain.
Santa Barbara, Calif.: Black Sparrow P. pp. 304; 35 illustrations. $14, pb. $5.

[40] *Edna St. Vincent Millay: A Reference Guide*, by Judith Nierman. Boston,
Mass.: G. K. Hall. pp. xiii + 191. $16.

concern themselves with his critical theories and techniques, and Eugenie Lambert Hausner and Wayne A. Knoll suggest that Ransom's concern for aesthetic value is akin to a religious sense. W. Potter Woodbery (*SLJ*) writes about Ransom's resurrection of the love myth of Provence in 'The Equilibrists'.

Samuel Hazo's biographical and critical account of Hart Crane, *Smithereened Apart: A Critique of Hart Crane*[41], first published in 1963, has been reprinted with an updated bibliography. Denis Donoghue's introduction to *Poems of R. P. Blackmur*[42] is a subtle and perceptive essay which concerns both Blackmur's poetry and his criticism. Richard K. Barksdale's *Langston Hughes: The Poet and His Critics*[43] is an assessment of critical responses to the poetry of Hughes over forty-seven years. Each chapter begins with an introduction to the poetry and ends with a consideration of the various critical judgements that have been presented in the main body of the chapter. The introduction to *Theodore Roethke's Career: An Annotated Bibliography*[44] by Keith R. Moul is lively, if somewhat overblown. It is a reliable guide up to about 1974. Also lively, neat, and pleasant is John Haffenden's introduction[44a] to Berryman's *Henry's Fate*, though it is more of a personal tribute than a critical appraisal.

James Atlas's *Delmore Schwartz: The Life of an American Poet*[45] is a fine and substantial biography that has already received a lot of deserved favourable notice. Schwartz's story of early success and high ambition followed by sad decline offers, of course, a great opportunity for a biographer and Atlas has done more than justice to it. He not only gives a painfully involving rendering of Schwartz, but also brings to life the literary and academic world in which he moved. It may be that Schwartz's career is so fascinating because of its failure and it is doubtful that this excellent biography will rescue his reputation as a poet; when Atlas talks of the inventiveness of Schwartz's prose, or of 'In the Naked Bed' as 'an astonishing poem', one cannot help feeling that he is being very generous. The first selection of Schwartz's poems to appear in England, *What is to be Given*[46], gives readers a chance to assess his gifts as a poet, and Carcanet Press intend to follow this volume with some of Schwartz's prose writings.

Frank O'Hara: Poet Among Painters[47] by Marjorie Perloff is an ap-

[41] *Smithereened Apart: A Critique of Hart Crane*, by Samuel Hazo. Athens, Ohio: Ohio U.P. pp. x + 152. $9, pb $3.50.

[42] *Poems of R. P. Blackmur*, introd. by Denis Donoghue. Princeton, N.J.: Princeton U.P. pp. xxix + 153. £9.40, pb £2.90.

[43] *Langston Hughes: The Poet and His Critics*, by Richard K. Barksdale. Chicago, Ill.: American Library Association. pp. xii + 155. £10.50.

[44] *Theodore Roethke's Career: An Annotated Bibliography*, by Keith R. Moul. Boston, Mass.: G. K. Hall. pp. xxi + 254. $20.

[44a] *Henry's Fate & Other Poems, 1967-1972*, by John Berryman, introd. by John Haffenden, New York: Farrar, Straus, & Giroux, and London: Faber. pp. xviii + 94. £2.75.

[45] *Delmore Schwartz: The Life of an American Poet*, by James Atlas. New York: Farrar, Strauss, & Giroux. pp. xiii + 417. £8.25.

[46] *What is to be Given: Selected Poems*, by Delmore Schwartz, intro. by Douglas Dunn. Manchester: Carcanet New P. 1976. pp.xix + 75. £2.90.

[47] *Frank O'Hara: Poet Among Painters*, by Marjorie Perloff. New York: George Braziller. pp. xv + 234. $12.50.

preciative, almost loving account of O'Hara's literary career. As is often the case with those who write about O'Hara, Perloff finds it hard to detach the poetry from the man and perhaps most readers will not wish it otherwise. Mutlu Konuk Blasing, in *The Art of Life: Studies in American Autobiographical Literature*[48], places O'Hara in the American tradition of 'personal poetry that extends back through William Carlos Williams to Walt Whitman'. Two collections of O'Hara's work have also been published this year, both edited and introduced by Donald Allen: they are *Early Writing*[49] and *Poems Retrieved*[50].

David Holbrook's *Lost Bearings in English Poetry*[51] pays some attention to American poetry too. For example, he includes quite a full analysis of Robert Lowell's 'For the Union Dead', of which he concludes that Lowell 'has wrung out of [his] paralysis a marvellously poised and insightful poem'. Holbrook is vexed about the problem of moving forward from such a poem. Jack Branscomb, in 'Robert Lowell's Painters: Two Sources' (*ELN*), notes that the sonnets 'Rembrandt' and 'For Elizabeth Bishop 4' from *History* both base their comments about painting on the written word rather than directly on the paintings in question. Lowell's use of the dramatic monologue is discussed by Alan Sinfield in *Dramatic Monologue*[52]. *The Advantage of Lyric*[53] by Barbara Hardy reprints a slightly revised version of her excellent 'The Poetry of Sylvia Plath'. The chapter is wide in scope, but gives particular attention to 'Nick and the Candlestick'.

Allen Ginsberg's *Journals: Early Fifties, Early Sixties*[54], edited by Gordon Ball, is made up of edited transcriptions from eighteen notebooks ranging, with many gaps, from March 1952 to February 1962. Ball thinks highly of Ginsberg's prose style in the *Journals* and he detects the influence of Jack Kerouac, Lucien Carr, and Hart Crane. It is interesting that Ginsberg has not been in the habit of lifting poems from his journals for inclusion in his books of poetry; the journal poems 'have a life of their own', which is perhaps just as well in the case of doggerel. The *Journals* are accurately described by Ball as a 'selection of minute irregular observations, dream confusions, self-anxieties and revelations, X-rays of consciousness, household talk and kitchen conversations, illuminations, bedside notes, elegies, proclamations and celebrations, meetings and departures of many years ago'.

Ingegerd Friberg's *Moving Inward: A Study of Robert Bly's Poetry*[55]

[48] *The Art of Life: Studies in American Autobiographical Literature*, by Mutlu Konuk Blasing. Austin, Texas and London: U. of Texas P. pp. xxviii + 193; 6 illustrations. £7.50.

[49] *Early Writing*, by Frank O'Hara, ed. by Donald Allen. Bolinas, Calif.: Grey Fox P. pp. ix + 163. pb $4.

[50] *Poems Retrieved*, Frank O'Hara, ed. by Donald Allen. Bolinas, Calif.: Grey Fox P. pp. xvi + 242. pb $5.

[51] *Lost Bearings in English Poetry*, by David Holbrook. Vision P. pp. 255. £5.80.

[52] *Dramatic Monologue*, by Alan Sinfield. Methuen. New York: Barnes & Noble. pp. ix + 85. £2.50, £1.40.

[53] *The Advantage of Lyric: Essays on Feeling in Poetry*, by Barbara Hardy. Athlone P. pp. 142.

[54] *Journals: Early Fifties, Early Sixties*, by Allen Ginsberg, ed. by Gordon Ball. New York: Grove P. pp. xxx + 302; 52 illustrations.

[55] *Moving Inward: A Study of Robert Bly's Poetry*, by Ingegerd Friberg. Goteborg: Acta Universitatis Gothoburgensis. pp. ii + 225. Sw. Cr. 60.

gives a biographical introduction to Bly's work, emphasizing his Minnesota background, an account of Bly criticism, and of Bly's poetic theory. Friberg tries to place Bly's stress on the image in a very extensive American tradition. Bob Steuding's *Gary Snyder*[56] also combines some biography with critical material and, though Steuding writes about many influences on Snyder's work, he believes that 'Snyder's work will be remembered in its own right as the example of a new direction taken in American literature'.

'It is almost impossible to overestimate the influence of the "New Internationalism" on American poetry,' says Ira Sadoff in 'A Chronicle of Recent Poetry' (*AR*). Sadoff deals in particular with the importance of *Another Republic*, an anthology of translations edited by Charles Simic and Mark Strand, and of recent volumes by Cesare Pavese, Philip Levine, William Heyen, Tess Gallagher, David St John, and William Keens.

3. Fiction

Ian Reid in his slender volume on *The Short Story*[57] writes tersely on some aspects of American fiction. David Fine's *The City, The Immigrant and American Fiction, 1880-1920*[58] is in effect an expanded bibliography with plot summaries, which serves to illustrate that in the twentieth century, 'Urban loneliness, alienation, isolation . . . have become the standard themes. In the modern setting the victim or marginal figure has become the central, symbolic figure'.

There are a number of general studies of the novel which include some examination of the American novel. *The Novel Today: Contemporary Writers on Modern Fiction*[59] edited by Malcolm Bradbury is a selection of reprinted pieces, among which are 'Some Notes on Recent American Fiction' by Saul Bellow (1963) and 'Writing American Fiction' by Philip Roth (1975). David Lodge's excellent *The Modes of Modern Writing*[60] examines, for example, the influence of Gertrude Stein on Hemingway, analyses Kurt Vonnegut's 'apparently artless improvised mixing of modes', and shows how 'In their play with the ideas of illusion, authorship and literary convention . . . Nabokov and Salinger maintain a precarious poise. Their narratives wobble on the edge of the aesthetic, but never quite fall off.' Lodge is particularly acute in his assessment of the ultimate effect of William Burroughs's 'fluid, fragmentary style of verbal montage' in *The Naked Lunch*.

Jerome Klinkowitz in his very wide-ranging but rather fragmentary study of contemporary fiction, *The Life of Fiction*[61], urges the merits

[56] *Gary Snyder*, by Bob Steuding. TUSAS. Boston, Mass. G. K. Hall. 1976. pp. 189. $7.95.
[57] *The Short Story*, by Ian Reid. Methuen. New York: Barnes & Noble. pp. ix + 76. £2.50. pb £1.40.
[58] *The City, The Immigrant and American Fiction, 1880-1920*, by David M. Fine. Metuchen, N.J., and London: Scarecrow P. pp. x + 182.
[59] *The Novel Today: Contemporary Writers on Modern Fiction*, ed. by Malcolm Bradbury. Manchester: Manchester U.P.; Totowa, N.J.: Rowman & Littlefield. £4.95.
[60] *The Modes of Modern Writing: Metaphor, Metonymy, and the Typology of Modern Literature*, by David Lodge. Ithaca, N.Y.: Cornell U.P. pp. xvi + 279. £9.50.
[61] *The Life of Fiction*, by Jerome Klinkowitz, with graphics by Roy R. Behrens. Urbana, Chicago, Ill. and London: U. of Illinois P. pp. 156. £9.95.

of literature which 'restores the act of reading to its original pleasure status: not as an academic exercise, but as a valid equivalent for the films and television and art and music which come into our lives'. Klinkowitz is at his best in discussing the autobiographical impulses in Kurt Vonnegut. Morroe Berger's *Real and Imagined Worlds: The Novel and Social Science*[62] is primarily an investigation of the use of fiction to popularise ideas about personal behaviour and social institutions. Berger is interested, therefore, in such diverse topics as Edith Wharton's handling of sexuality and Norman Mailer's efforts to combine journalism, history, and the novel in *The Armies of the Night;* he pays close attention to the work of T. S. Stribling, particularly his novel *Birthright* (1922), 'a hodgepodge of nineteenth century extensions of Darwinism to social life, biological determination, populism, and twentieth century liberation of a sort'. Keith M. May's *Out of the Maelstrom: Psychology and the Novel in the Twentieth Century*[63] includes an assessment of existentialist thought in Hemingway, Mailer, Salinger, Updike, and Bellow. May asserts, for example, that Salinger's Holden Caulfield is 'stuck in the first stage of existentialist progress, the stage of rejection', but that 'By the time of *Franny and Zooey* (1961) Salinger had progressed from this phase of rejection to a phase of affirmation.' He feels, too, that Harry Angstrom in Updike's *Rabbit, Run,* as 'a man in pursuit of utter perfection . . . is of saintly disposition: he "runs" from one activity to another looking for whatever is without blemish or limitedness'. May concludes his analysis by fixing on Saul Bellow as the most consistent and successful existentialist writer.

The current *Writers at Work: The 'Paris Review' Interviews*[64] edited by George Plimpton contains interviews with Dos Passos, Nabokov, Steinbeck, Eudora Welty, Kerouac, and Updike — all illuminating, but particularly the last-named.

What Manner of Woman: Essays on English and American Life and Literature[65] edited by Marlene Springer has an essay by James W. Tuttleton on '"Combat in the Erogenous Zone": Women in the American Novel between the Two World Wars' which comments on the image of women in Fitzgerald, Hemingway, and Faulkner: Fitzgerald's heroines reflect a liberated Midwestern social type, as well as expressing deep fantasies about beautiful, emotionally inaccessible, wealthy, and socially desirable women; the characterisation of Hemingway's women suggests that he was profoundly disturbed about male and female sexuality; Faulkner celebrates the enduring spiritual strength of women. Rather more original, but similarly very competent, are two more essays from *What Manner of Woman:* 'Second-class Citizenship: The Status of Women in Contemporary American Fiction' by Martha Masington and Charles G. Masington, and '"Free in Fact and at Last": The Image of the Black

[62] *Real and Imagined Worlds: The Novel and Social Science,* by Morroe Berger. Cambridge, Mass., and London: Harvard U.P. pp. viii + 303. £10.50.

[63] *Out of the Maelstrom: Psychology and the Novel in the Twentieth Century,* by Keith M. May. Paul Elek. pp. xvi + 135. £5.50.

[64] *Writers at Work: The 'Paris Review' Interviews (Fourth Series),* ed. by George Plimpton, with intro. by Wilfrid Sheed. Secker & Warburg. pp. xv + 459. £6.50.

[65] *What Manner of Woman: Essays on English and American Life and Literature,* ed. by Marlene Springer. New York: New York U.P. pp. xx + 357. £12.50.

Woman in Black American Fiction' by Elizabeth Schultz. The Masingtons are gloomy about the majority of contemporary novelists, but single out for praise Marge Piercy, Joan Didion, and Joyce Carol Oates. Elizabeth Schultz concludes that it is the older black woman who is most likely to achieve satisfactory treatment in black American fiction. Anthea Zeman's *Presumptuous Girls: Women and Their World in the Serious Woman's Novel*[66] includes discussion of Edith Wharton, Hannah Green, Alison Lurie, Sylvia Plath, and Sue Kaufman. It is an intelligent and well organised book, bringing the authors together in a deft, lighthearted way, but its weakness is a lack of real literary criticism.

Seven American Women Writers of the Twentieth Century[67] is a collection of reprinted essays on women writers, 'which were published', says Maureen Howard severely in her introduction, 'not because the writers are women but because they are literary figures worthy of our study'. The seven essays, which are without exception stimulating and lively, are 'Ellen Glasgow' by Louis Auchincloss; 'Willa Cather' by Dorothy Van Ghent; 'Katherine Anne Porter' by Ray B. West Jr; 'Eudora Welty' by J. A. Bryant Jr, 'Mary McCarthy' by Irvin Stock; 'Carson McCullers' by Laurence Graver, and 'Flannery O'Connor' by Stanley Edgar Hyman. Ellen Moers's *Literary Women: The Great Writers*[68] is not arranged by authors, but her very useful study makes reference to the writing of Willa Cather, Gertrude Stein, Carson McCullers, and Sylvia Plath, among others.

Miles Donald's *The American Novel in the Twentieth Century*[69] fills a surprising gap. His account is always readable and witty — especially valuable in a survey of this kind. There are chapters on 'The Traditional Novel', focusing on Fitzgerald, Hemingway, Wolfe, Dos Passos, and Steinbeck; 'The Fate of the Traditional Novel', with the perhaps unexpected coupling of Faulkner and Updike; 'Fantasy', dealing with Miller, Burroughs, Kerouac, and Nabokov; 'The Minorities', which considers black fiction and the Jewish-American novel; and 'Popular Fiction', which surveys the fields of science fiction and detective fiction. Donald writes interestingly on the social context of many of the novelists under consideration, and his section on Nabokov has special flair. He expresses forthrightly his preferences and reservations: this is an idiosyncratic but critically tough book.

Frank McConnell chooses *Four Postwar American Novelists: Bellow, Mailer, Barth, and Pynchon*[70] 'not only because of their individual brilliance, but because, among them, they appear to signal something like a

[66] *Presumptuous Girls: Women and Their World in the Serious Woman's Novel*, by Anthea Zeman. Weidenfeld & Nicolson. pp. 185. £5.25.
[67] *Seven American Women Writers of the Twentieth Century: An Introduction*, ed. by Maureen Howard. Minneapolis, Minn.: U. of Minnesota P. pp. 380. £10.90.
[68] *Literary Women: The Great Writers*, by Ellen Moers. W. H. Allen. pp. xvi + 336; 27 illustrations. £7.50. New York: Anchor P. pp. xxiv + 496; 27 illustrations. pb $3.95.
[69] *The American Novel in the Twentieth Century*, by Miles Donald. Newton Abbot, London, and Vancouver: David & Charles. New York: Barnes & Noble. pp. 215. £6.95.
[70] *Four Postwar American Novelists: Bellow, Mailer, Barth, and Pynchon*, by Frank D. McConnell. Chicago, Ill. and London: U. of Chicago P. pp. xxix + 206. £10.50.

renaissance in American fiction'. In his chapter on 'Saul Bellow and the terms of our contract' McConnell deals at length with Bellow's reputation, and writes cogently of the relationship between *Humboldt's Gift* and Berryman's *Dream Songs*. The chapter on 'Norman Mailer and the cutting edge of style' is good on Mailer's presentation of his public self, and on 'the nervous, run-on confession, the blustering vulgarity and deep insecurity, the acute culture and genius for metaphor which characterize Mailer's distinctive talent'; the remaining chapters on John Barth and Thomas Pynchon are less forceful, although McConnell is perceptive about the narrowness of Barth's world. Macel D. Ezell's *Unequivocal Americanism: Right-Wing Novels in the Cold War Era*[71] supplies plot summaries of what are, largely, very little-known works: 'Understandably, critical and market appeal of most of the books remain marginal', remarks Ezell.

Paul A. Carter's book *The Creation of Tomorrow: Fifty Years of Magazine Science Fiction*[72] is proof of its own opening sentence: 'Science fiction in recent years has suffered a fall into respectability.' This is also demonstrated by *Many Futures, Many Worlds: Theme and Form in Science Fiction*[73], a collection of essays on the genre edited by Thomas D. Clareson. The fourteen essays are almost as varied as the field which they survey, but nearly all would agree that, in the words of Thomas L. Wymer, 'Science fiction reveals that popular literature need not be inferior, that it can function as the means by which a culture critically explores and creates its own values and consciousness'. Among the subjects treated are the use of science in science fiction, the place of women in the genre, revivals of ancient mythologies, and science fiction as fictive history. Joseph D. Olander and Martin Harry Greenberg, in *Isaac Asimov*[74], have collected nine varied essays on this prolific author; Asimov himself has contributed his own 'Guide to Asimov'. There are essays on Asimov's fiction as an agent in accustoming readers to social change, on his use of mystery elements in science fiction, on his handling of technical metaphors, on his art of characterisation, and on his use of computers and robots. The *Foundation* novels have an essay to themselves.

Phyllis Rauch Klotman's *Another Man Gone: The Black Runner in Contemporary Afro-American Literature*[75] ranges from Ralph Ellison's *Invisible Man* of 1952 to Barry Beckham's *Runner Mack* (1972). It is a useful account of the fiction, but suffers from the laborious identification of the 'runner' (a term which becomes progressively looser) in each work. Marion Berghahn's *Images of Africa in Black American Literature*[76]

[71] *Unequivocal Americanism: Right-Wing Novels in the Cold War Era*, by Macel D. Ezell. Metuchen, N.J.: Scarecrow P. pp. viii + 152. $6.50.
[72] *The Creation of Tomorrow: Fifty Years of Magazine Science Fiction*, by Paul A. Carter. New York: Columbia U.P. pp. x + 318; 15 illustrations.
[73] *Many Futures, Many Worlds: Theme and Form in Science Fiction*, ed. by Thomas D. Clareson, Kent, Ohio: Kent State U.P. pp. ix + 303.
[74] *Isaac Asimov*, ed. by Joseph D. Olander and Martin Harry Greenberg. Edinburgh: Paul Harris. pp. 247. £6.
[75] *Another Man Gone: The Black Runner in Contemporary Afro-American Literature*, by Phyllis Rauch Klotman. Port Washington, N. Y. and London: Kennikat P. pp. 160. $9.95.
[76] *Images of Africa in Black American Literature*, by Marion Berghahn. Macmillan. pp. ix + 230. £8.95.

includes sections on Richard Wright, Ralph Ellison, and James Baldwin, but gets no further forward in time; obviously the book seems somewhat dated as a result. There are some eccentricities of style and presentation too; for example, Jean Toomer, Claude McKay, and Countee Cullen are never given first names by Berghahn, and the Harlem Renaissance is characterised as 'literary Garveyism' a long time before we are told anything about Garvey. The novels of W. E. B. Dubois are discussed unsympathetically.

Floyd C. Watkins's *In Time and Place: Some Origins of American Fiction*[77] copes with what he himself describes as 'a strange assortment' of novels: Steinbeck's *The Grapes of Wrath*, Margaret Mitchell's *Gone with the Wind*, Styron's *The Confessions of Nat Turner*, Willa Cather's *My Antonia* and *Death Comes for the Archbishop*, Scott Momaday's *House Made of Dawn*, Faulkner's *As I Lay Dying*, and Lewis's *Main Street*. But Watkins's interest is in the author's use of cultural materials, and therefore a diversity of literature suits his aim. He is especially interested in the accuracy, or lack of it, achieved by his authors, but he is also genuinely critical of their art.

Richard Gray's *The Literature of Memory: Modern Writers of the American South*[78] is an ambitious, full, and generally convincing treatment of the southern tradition, which concentrates upon prose fiction. Gray provides the background which demonstrates the importance of the figures of the 'good farmer' and the 'aristocratic planter' in the Southern consciousness and he traces the ways in which these almost mythic figures are used in the complex relation between the Southern writer and his environment. Gray dwells at length on the relation between literature, history, and society, and he is alive to the difficulty as well as the fascination of such an approach; at times his style becomes apologetically over-complex when he confronts problems in this area. Faulkner is presented as the pre-eminent writer in *The Literature of Memory*, though, in fact, the chapter on the Yoknapatawpha novels is sound, but not particularly original. More revealing are the accounts of the Nashville Agrarians, Erskine Caldwell, Eudora Welty, Katherine Anne Porter, Carson McCullers, Flannery O'Connor, and William Styron. Gray is rather hard on Tennessee Williams and Truman Capote and he draws attention to the limitations of James Dickey, suggesting that a good deal of Southern writing of the present is characterized by 'moral laziness'. But, having elevated the work of McCullers and O'Connor, he has quite high praise for William Styron's *The Confessions of Nat Turner*, which, he says, 'represents a deliberate attempt to explain history'. Gray's notes and bibliography are usefully full and *The Literature of Memory* will be of considerable interest not just to those interested in Southern writing, but to anyone who is concerned with the relation between literature and society.

There are several articles which complement *The Literature of Memory*. Thomas Daniel Young, in 'Allen Tate's Double Focus: The Past in the

---

[77] *In Time and Place: Some Origins of American Fiction*, by Floyd C. Watkins. Athens, Ga.: U. of Georgia P. pp. xiii + 250; 9 illustrations. $10.50.
[78] *The Literature of Memory: Modern Writers of the American South*, by Richard Gray. Edward Arnold. pp. xi + 337. £12.50.

Present' (*MissQ*), shows how Tate's myth of the antebellum South differs from Faulkner's and attempts to define his vision of a vital, permanent social order. Eudora Welty's historicism is considered by Albert B. Devlin (*MissQ*) and the same volume contains an interview with William Styron. The metaphysical complexity of the metaphors of James Agee's work is the subject of Jonathan Morse's 'James Agee, Southern Literature, and the Domain of Metaphor' (*SAQ*).

C. Hugh Holman in *The Immoderate Past: The Southern Writer and History*[79] speaks of the special characteristics of Southern writing: 'its concreteness, its specificity, its Aristotelian rather than Platonic quality, its urgent sense of time, and its deep respect for tradition'. In his consideration of Ellen Glasgow's *The Sheltered Life*, Faulkner's *Light in August* and *Absalom, Absalom!*, Robert Penn Warren's *All the King's Men, World Enough and Time, Brother to Dragons*, and *Band of Angels*, and William Styron's *The Confessions of Nat Turner*, Holman concludes that the Southern writer is consistently distrustful of treating the individual outside the context of time and society.

Hamlin Garland appears in rather strange company in *Henry Blake Fuller and Hamlin Garland: A Reference Guide*[80], although Charles L. P. Silet gives plausible reasons for this in his introduction.

Elizabeth Janeway writes an afterword to David Graham Phillips's *Susan Lenox*[81], first published 1917, analysing Phillips's art and concluding that, 'He wasn't a master, but I think he was entitled to repeat Isherwood's description of his own role in Berlin of the early Thirties: "I am a camera."' Thomas H. Landess is similarly a little defensive in his study *Julia Peterkin*[82], conceding that 'At the moment Mrs. Peterkin is all but forgotten; and her fiction, when it is discussed at all, is usually dismissed as either malicious or trivial.' However, he argues for her technical skill, and makes various valid comparisons between her work and Faulkner's.

Modern Fiction Studies offers a special issue on Dreiser. Jack Salzman, the guest editor, gives a selected checklist of Dreiser criticism, and an essay by Robert Forrey, 'Theodore Dreiser: Oedipus Redivivus', applies French Freudian structuralist method to Dreiser. Other essays include Lester H. Cohen's 'Locating One's Self: The Problematics of Dreiser's Social World', which uses as a starting-point Dreiser's essay 'A Counsel to Perfection', and applies it to his protagonists; Frederic Rusch's 'Dreiser's Other Tragedy' on *The Hand of the Potter*, a play written in 1916; Max Westbrook's 'Dreiser's Defense of Carrie Meeber'; 'Carrie's Sisters: The Popular Prototypes for Dreiser's Heroine' by Cathy N. Davidson and Arnold E. Davidson, which sets *Sister Carrie* in the context of popular contemporary literature; John O'Neill's 'The Disproportion of Sad-

[79] *The Immoderate Past: The Southern Writer and History*, by C. Hugh Holman. Athens, Ga.: U. of Georgia P. pp. ix + 118. £3.50.

[80] *Henry Blake Fuller and Hamlin Garland: A Reference Guide*, by Charles L. P. Silet. Boston, Mass.: G. K. Hall. pp. xiii + 148. $14.

[81] *Susan Lenox: Her Fall and Rise*, by David Graham Phillips, with afterword by Elizabeth Janeway. Carbondale and Edwardsville Ill.: Southern Illinois U. P.; London and Amsterdam: Feffer & Simons. pp. xx + 490.

[82] *Julia Peterkin*, by Thomas H. Landess. TUSAS. Boston, Mass.: G. K. Hall. 1976. pp. 160. $7.50.

THE TWENTIETH CENTURY 467

ness: Dreiser's *The Financier* and *The Titan*'; and Paul A. Orlov's 'The Subversion of the Self: Anti-Naturalistic Crux in *An American Tragedy*'. Wieslaw Furmanczyk writes on Dreiser's materialistic outlook in 'Theodore Dreiser's Views on Religion in the Light of His Philosophical Papers' (*ZAA*). Philip L. Gerber provides a reference guide to *Plots and Characters in the Fiction of Theodore Dreiser*[83], with a preface outlining the nature of Dreiser's art. Rolf Lunden provides a description of Dreiser's 1926 trip to Scandinavia, with some account of his Scandinavian reputation, in *Dreiser Looks at Scandinavia*[84].

Reference guides are available for Jack London[85] and Sherwood Anderson[86]. Of the two for Sherwood Anderson, that by Douglas G. Rogers concentrates on English and American criticism, while that by Ray Lewis White also provides extensive commentary on Anderson in other languages. Martha M. Park asks 'How Far From Emerson's Man of One Idea to Anderson's Grotesques?' (*CLAJ*), suggesting that Anderson, consciously or not, echoed Emersonian ideas and sometimes even his phraseology. David Stouck argues convincingly for '*Winesburg, Ohio* As a dance of Death' (*AL*).

Cynthia Griffin Wolff has written a major critical biography of Edith Wharton: *A Feast of Words: The Triumph of Edith Wharton*[87]. This study, illustrated by curiously haunting photographs, examines in particular the emotional problems that dominated Edith Wharton's life and earlier fiction. Cynthia Griffin Wolff feels that Edith Wharton's repression of sexual ignorance and fear 'was for years to cripple her as a woman and as an artist', and points out how striking it is that *Summer,* 'the most genuinely erotic novel that Wharton ever published concludes with a young girl marrying her "father"; the one piece of explicitly sexual fiction that she left is a description of an incestuous relationship between father and daughter'. Wolff reproduces the latter piece of fiction – the 'unpublishable fragment of Beatrice Palmato', as Edith Wharton herself called it. *A Feast of Words* examines the full range of Wharton's work very closely and critically; it seems unlikely that this study will be superseded for some time to come. Theodore Ziolkowski in *Disenchanted Images*[88] offers an interesting discussion of Wharton's conflation of two of her obsessions, art and ghosts, in her story 'The Moving Finger'.

Wendy Steiner's article 'Gertrude Stein in Manuscript' (*YULG*) explains some wilful obscurities 'of this frustrating writer'. *Dear Sammy: Letters*

[83] *Plots and Characters in the Fiction of Theodore Dreiser,* by Philip L. Gerber. Hamden, Conn.: Archon Books and Folkestone, Kent.: Dawson. pp. xxi + 153. $12.50.
[84] *Dreiser Looks at Scandinavia,* by Rolf Lunden. Stockholm: Almqvist & Wiksell. pp. 143.
[85] *Jack London: A Reference Guide,* by Joan R. Sherman. Boston, Mass.: G. K. Hall. pp. xxviii + 323. $22.
[86] *Sherwood Anderson: A Selective, Annotated Bibliography,* by Douglas G. Rogers. Metuchen, N.J.: Scarecrow P. 1976. pp. vi + 157. $6. *Sherwood Anderson: A Reference Guide,* by Ray Lewis White. Boston, Mass.: G. K. Hall. pp. xi + 430. $25.
[87] *A Feast of Words: The Triumph of Edith Wharton,* by Cynthia Griffin Wolff. New York: O.U.P. pp. viii + 453; 12 illustrations. £9.15.
[88] *Disenchanted Images: A Literary Iconology,* by Theodore Ziolkowski. Princeton, N.J., and Guildford, Surrey.: Princeton U.P. pp. ix + 273. £9.40.

from Gertrude Stein and Alice B. Toklas[89] edited with a memoir by Samuel M. Steward is an unrevealing collection. Steward is endearingly delighted by his contact with the great, but one feels that he must have been a trying guest for Stein and Toklas, with his 'complicated allergies' to food.

Julius Rowan Raper argues that greater critical significance should be attached to the psychological insight of some of Ellen Glasgow's short fiction in 'Invisible Things: The Short Stories of Ellen Glasgow' (*SLJ*).

Thomas Wolfe Undergraduate[90] by Richard Walser offers a meticulous and minute coverage of Wolfe's career at the University of North Carolina. It is rather over-dramatic in style, especially as nothing crucial about either Wolfe's art or personality emerges. Floyd C. Watkins gives a full and competent account of Asheville and what Wolfe was able to make of it in his fiction in 'Thomas Wolfe and Asheville Again and Again and Again' (*SLJ*), and C. Hugh Holman treats Wolfe's explorations of America after Asheville in 'Thomas Wolfe and America' (*SLJ*). John S. Phillipson provides a reference guide[91] — not an exhaustive guide, since Phillipson has, as a matter of principle, generally omitted reviews unless they were also critiques.

Ring[92], Jonathan Yardley's biography of Ring Lardner, supplies a comprehensive background to the baseball journalism. Yardley pleads for more, and better, critical attention to be paid to Lardner's stories, and examines their techniques, but what is most powerfully conveyed is the warmth of the human being; Yardley ends with the tribute from Scott Fitzgerald which ends: 'Ring made no enemies, because he was kind, and to millions he gave release and delight'.

Philip A. Shreffler's *H. P. Lovecraft Companion*[93] ends rather differently: 'And it is undoubtedly safe to presume that although Lovecraft himself has passed from this world, the demons he brought forth will live long after him.' Shreffler's immensely enthusiastic but not very well written book covers Lovecraft's literary theory, his plots and sources, and the full range of his characters and monsters; it includes an appendix on the Order of the Golden Dawn.

Louis F. Kannenstine's serious and scholarly study *The Art of Djuna Barnes: Duality and Damnation*[94] deprecates the fact that Djuna Barnes is generally known only for *Nightwood*, her experimental novel of 1936. Kannenstine traces evolving themes and techniques throughout her work; his sub-title expresses his conviction that Djuna Barnes' central concern is with characters caught between two modes of existence in the 'halt position of the damned'.

[89] *Dear Sammy: Letters from Gertrude Stein and Alice B. Toklas*, ed. with a memoir by Samuel M. Steward. Boston, Mass.: Houghton Mifflin. pp. x + 260; 27 illustrations.

[90] *Thomas Wolfe Undergraduate*, by Richard Walser. Durham, N. C.: Duke U. P. pp. ix + 166; 13 illustrations. $8.75.

[91] *Thomas Wolfe: A Reference Guide*, by John S. Phillipson. Boston, Mass.: G. K. Hall. pp. xiii + 218. $18.

[92] *Ring: A Biography of Ring Lardner*, by Jonathan Yardley. New York: Random House. pp. 415. $12.95.

[93] *The H. P. Lovecraft Companion*, by Philip A. Shreffler. London and Westport, Conn.: Greenwood P. pp. xvi + 198; 24 illustrations. £9.95.

[94] *The Art of Djuna Barnes: Duality and Damnation*, by Louis F. Kannenstine. New York: New York U. P. pp. xviii + 194.

Ann Douglas in 'Studs Lonigan and the Failure of History in Mass Society: A Study in Claustrophobia' (AQ) refutes the received opinion that James T. Farrell wrote nothing important after Studs Lonigan and argues that 'Perhaps the central reason for Farrell's neglect is that he has confronted a problem modern America has determined to evade: our sense of history predicates a vision of Anglo-Saxon progress and expansion which our intellect no longer supports.'

Ray Lewis has more than doubled the known body of review-commentary on West, as he reports in 'Nathanael West: Additional Reviews of his Work, 1933-57' (YULG).

Robert W. Schneider in Novelist to a Generation: The Life and Thought of Winston Churchill[95] reminds us of a man who wrote ten popular novels, and who was for two decades 'looked upon as one of America's foremost novelists'. Churchill, incidentally, early established an unchanging relationship of quiet hostility to the British Prime Minister.

Kenneth Eble's F. Scott Fitzgerald[96], first published in 1963, has been issued in a revised edition, the main revision being the incorporation of recent Fitzgerald criticism. In a new preface, Eble predicts that Fitzgerald's work will be seen more and more as the novel of manners and less and less as produced by 'the arch representative of the Jazz Age': this is, however, exactly how it is seen by Paula S. Fass in her mainly sociological survey The Damned and the Beautiful: American Youth in the 1920s[97]. The title of John O'Hara's "An Artist Is His Own Fault"[98], a collection of short journalistic pieces, is taken from his new title for a 1945 intro-duction to Fitzgerald's work. This, with other fragments of reminiscence, is easily the most interesting section of the book. Edmund Wilson's Letters on Literature and Politics 1912-1972[99] include his fascinating letters 'On Editing F. Scott Fitzgerald' (1941-44); it is precisely this editing which comes under very heavy attack in Matthew J. Bruccoli's "The Last of the Novelists": F. Scott Fitzgerald and The Last Tycoon[100]. Bruccoli claim that Wilson's editing of The Last Tycoon was vitiated by two factors: the nature of the job that Scribner expected – that is, a reading text for a popular audience, and Wilson's feelings of superiority to Fitzgerald, 'whom he had patronized for more than twenty years'. Besides fulmin-ating against Wilson, Bruccoli provides a very full background on the models for the characters, and Fitzgerald's ultimate intentions. Fitzgerald's own general notes include this touching declaration of faith in himself:

[95] Novelist to a Generation: The Life and Thought of Winston Churchill, by Robert W. Schneider. Bowling Green, Ohio: Bowling Green U. Popular P. 1976. pp. xvi + 333.
[96] F. Scott Fitzgerald, by Kenneth Eble. TUSAS. Boston, Mass.: G. K. Hall. (rev. ed.) pp. 187.
[97] The Damned and the Beautiful: American Youth in the 1920s, by Paula S. Fass. New York: O.U.P. pp. xii + 497. $15.95.
[98] "An Artist Is His Own Fault", by John O'Hara, ed. by Matthew J. Bruccoli. Carbondale and Edwardsville, Ill.: Southern Illinois U. P.: London and Amsterdam: Feffer & Simons. pp. xv + 226. $8.95.
[99] Letters on Literature and Politics 1912-1972, by Edmund Wilson, ed. by Elena Wilson, with introd. by Daniel Aaron and foreword by Leon Edel. Routledge & Kegan Paul. pp. xxxviii + 768. £12.50.
[100] "The Last of the Novelists": F. Scott Fitzgerald and The Last Tycoon, by Matthew J. Bruccoli. Carondale and Edwardsville, Ill.: Southern Illinois U. P.; London and Amsterdam: Feffer & Simons. pp. 163; 9 illustrations.

'I want to write scenes that are frightening and inimitable. I don't want to be intelligible to my contemporaries as Ernest who as Gertrude Stein said, is bound for the Museums. I am sure I am far enough ahead to have some small immortality if I can keep well.'

Ernest, whether ultimately bound for the Museums or not, is still receiving a generous amount of critical attention. Linda Welsheimer Wagner, in her introduction to *Ernest Hemingway: A Reference Guide*[101], which goes up to 1975, points out that since 1924 criticism of Hemingway's writing has never diminished. Robert O. Stephens offers an extensive anthology of this criticism in *Ernest Hemingway: The Critical Reception*[102], which moves through all the works in turn, and includes a general introduction which summarizes major critical trends.

Arizona Quarterly devoted its summer issue to articles on Hemingway: Gerry Brenner's study of the novel's 'paradoxical vulgarity' in 'Hemingway's "Vulgar Ethic": Revaluating *The Sun Also Rises*'; J. M. Ferguson Jr's 'Hemingway's Man of the World'; Robert E. Fleming's 'Hemingway's Treatment of Suicide: "Fathers and Sons" and *For Whom the Bell Tolls*', which sees the novel as 'Hemingway's attempt to purge himself, through his art, of the debilitating psychological effects of his father's suicide'; Stuart L. Burns's 'Scrambling the Unscrambleable: *The Nick Adams Stories*', which asserts that Nick cannot be regarded as a consistent character; William E. Meyer Jr's 'Hemingway's Novels: The Shift in Orthodoxy and Symbolism', which shows how Hemingway's religious convictions changed over the course of three wars; David Morgan Zehr's 'Paris and the Expatriate Mystique: Hemingway's *The Sun Also Rises*'; Herman Nibbelink's 'The Meaning of Nature in *For Whom the Bell Tolls*'; Amberys R. Whittle's 'A Reading of Hemingway's "The Gambler, The Nun, and the Radio"', which interprets the story as a parable; and Sister Mary Kathryn Grant's 'The Search for Celebration in *The Sun Also Rises* and *The Great Gatsby*', which traces dance motifs in each.

Eric S. Rabkin takes a sympathetic view of the love story in *A Farewell to Arms* in his study of *The Fantastic in Literature*[103], seeing it as a conflict between fantasy and reality, but Judith Fetterley in her essay '*A Farewell to Arms*: Ernest Hemingway's "Resentful Cryptogram"' from *The Authority of Experience*[104] compares it with Erich Segal's *Love Story* in that 'Both stories are characterised by a disparity between what is overtly stated and what is covertly expressed. Both ask the reader to believe in the perfection of a love whose substance seems woefully inadequate and whose signature is death'. John Orr in *Tragic Realism and Modern Society*[105] compares *For Whom the Bell Tolls* with André

[101] *Ernest Hemingway: A Reference Guide*, by Linda Welsheimer Wagner. Boston, Mass.: G. K. Hall. pp. xix + 363. $22.

[102] *Ernest Hemingway: The Critical Reception*, ed. by Robert O. Stephens. New York: Burt Franklin. pp. xli + 502. pb $9.95.

[103] *The Fantastic in Literature*, by Eric S. Rabkin. Princeton, N. J.: Princeton U. P. 1976. pp. xi + 234. £9.40.

[104] *The Authority of Experience: Essays in Feminist Criticism*, ed. by Arlyn Diamond and Lee R. Edwards. Amherst, Mass.: U. of Massachusetts P. pp. xiv + 304.

[105] *Tragic Realism and Modern Society: Studies in the Sociology of the Modern Novel*, by John Orr. London and Basingstoke: Macmillan. pp. x + 198. £7.95.

Malraux's *Days of Hope*, commenting favourably on Hemingway's dialogue but unfavourably on the character of Robert Jordan. David M. Wyatt in 'Hemingway's Uncanny Beginnings' (*GaR*) declares that 'Hemingway has a hard time imagining beginnings but an easy time inventing ends'.

Floyd C. Watkins surveys recent Faulkner criticism in 'Through a glass Darkly: Recent Faulkner Studies' (*SR*). Philip Momberger offers in *SLJ* 'A Reading of Faulkner's "The Hill"', an apprentice piece already featuring an estranged hero. Cleanth Brooks writes of Faulkner as chivalric lover in 'The Image of Helen Baird in Faulkner's early Poetry and Fiction' (*SR*), dealing with Faulkner's unsuccessful courtship of Helen Baird, who thought of him as 'one of her screwballs' and 'a fuzzy little animal'. Brooks also writes of the early Faulkner in 'Faulkner's Mosquitoes' (*GaR*). *Mississippi Quarterly* offers a special Faulkner issue, which includes Boyd Davis writing on Faulkner's garden imagery in 'Caddy Compson's Eden', Linda Kauffman on 'The Madam and the Midwife: Reba Rivers and Sairey Gamp', Kathryn A. Chittick on Faulkner's use of sacred stories in 'The Fables in William Faulkner's *A Fable*', and James B. Meriwether's guide for students and scholars, 'The Books of William Faulkner'. Adrienne Bond writes on *A Fable* and 'Notes on a Horsethief' in 'Eneas Africanus and Faulkner's Fabulous Racehorse' (*SLJ*), and Joan D. Winslow, very perceptively, on 'Language and Destruction in Faulkner's "Dry September"' (*CLAJ*).

'The most splendid failure' is Faulkner's own description of *The Sound and the Fury*, of which André Bleikasten provides an enthusiastic and convincing account[106]. He is especially good on the selfishness of Benjy's love for Caddy, with its incestuous implications, the elusiveness of the figure of Caddy, and Christian tradition in *The Sound and the Fury*. He also provides a perceptive summary of the early work — what he calls 'Faulkner before Faulkner'. Joanne V. Creighton examines Faulkner's process of revision and composition when he incorporated short stories into longer works in *William Faulkner's Craft of Revision: The Snopes Trilogy, "The Unvanquished" and "Go Down, Moses"*[107]. She is able to formulate four general observations about Faulkner's craft of revision: that he is impressively flexible; that he almost always moves from simplicity to complexity, and from the comic to the serious; that he characteristically retains the narrative frame in which the original stories were cast; and that his descriptive details grow more profuse but his style more precise.

The South and Faulkner's Yoknapatawpha[108] is a selection of speeches and discussions from the 1976 Faulkner conference at the University of Mississippi. It includes Daniel Aaron's examination of myths and preju-

---

[106] *The Most Splendid Failure: Faulkner's 'The Sound and the Fury'*, by André Bleikasten. Bloomington, Ind. and London: Indiana U. P. 1976. pp. xi + 275. £5.35.
[107] *William Faulkner's Craft of Revision: The Snopes Trilogy, "The Unvanquished" and "Go Down, Moses"*, by Joanne V. Creighton. Detroit, Mich.: Wayne State U. P. pp. 182.
[108] *The South and Faulkner's Yoknapatawpha: The Actual and the Apocryphal*, ed. by Evans Harrington and Ann J. Abadie. Jackson, Miss.: U. P. of Mississippi. pp. xii + 212.

dices in 'The South in American History', Michael Millgate's genial 'Faulkner and History', 'Faulkner's Depiction of the Planter Aristocracy' by Shelby Foote (who knew Faulkner, and regards this as a non-subject), and 'Faulkner and Slavery' by Darwin T. Turner, who claims that Faulkner 'perpetuated antebellum myths'. It also includes a comparison of Fenimore Cooper and Faulkner in 'Nature's Legacy to William Faulkner' by John Pilkington, a tribute to Faulkner as feminist in 'Faulkner and (Southern) Women' by Linda Welsheimer Wagner, and, most impressively, 'Scarlett O'Hara and the Two Quentin Compsons' by Louis D. Rubin Jr.

A Loving Gentleman: The Love Story of William Faulkner and Meta Carpenter[109] by Meta Carpenter Wilde and Orin Borsten is occasionally stilted, but unexpectedly absorbing. Meta Carpenter Wilde explains how Faulkner fitted into the whole context of her life, and how, for example, the writing of *The Wild Palms* became her 'rival'. She is not mentioned at all in Joseph Blotner's very full selection of Faulkner's letters[110], except for a request that *The Wild Palms* should be sent her, under her married name, but Faulkner recalls in a letter to Joan Williams of August 1952 'how I wrote THE WILD PALMS in order to try to stave off what I thought was heart-break too'. The letters, which run from 1918 to 1962, give us some indication of Faulkner's process of composition, besides revealing the usual writer's lack of money: 'I dont seem to know my own strength with a pen and a check book' writes Faulkner ruefully to Robert J. Haas in March 1949. One of the most interesting passages in the letters is Faulkner's assessment of himself in April, 1953. Writing to Joan Williams, he says, 'And now I realise for the first time what an amazing gift I had: uneducated in every formal sense, without even very literate, let alone literary, companions, yet to have made the things I made. I dont know where it came from. I dont know why God or gods or whoever it was, selected me to be the vessel. Believe me, this is not humility, false modesty: it is simply amazement. I wonder if you have ever had that thought about the work and the country man whom you know as Bill Faulkner — what little connection there seems to be between them.'

James B. Lloyd offers a specialised Faulkner checklist[111], and Bruce F. Kawin a serious consideration of Faulkner's film work[112], which includes a close examination of two screenplays, *Revolt in the Earth* (an adaptation of *Absalom, Absalom!*) and the unknown original horror film *Dreadful Hollow*.

Stephen Pendo in *Raymond Chandler on Screen: His Novels into Film*[113] discusses the six novels which have been filmed, and the seven films (there being two film versions of *Farewell, My Lovely*). He starts

[109] *A Loving Gentleman: The Love Story of William Faulkner and Meta Carpenter*, by Meta Carpenter Wilde and Orin Borsten. New York: Simon & Schuster. 1976. pp. 334; 36 illustrations. $9.95.

[110] *Selected Letters of William Faulkner*, ed. by Joseph Blotner. New York: Random House. pp. xvii + 488. £15.

[111] *The Oxford "Eagle", 1900-1962: An Annotated Checklist of Material on William Faulkner and the History of Lafayette County*, by James B. Lloyd. Oxford, Miss.: *Miss Q*. pp. 58.

[112] *Faulkner and Film*, by Bruce F. Kawin. New York: Frederick Ungar. pp. xiii + 194; 12 illustrations.

[113] *Raymond Chandler on Screen: His Novels Into Film*, by Stephen Pendo. Metuchen, N. J.: Scarecrow P. 1976. pp. xv + 240; 40 illustrations. $10.

with a short history of the detective both in film and literature, which he relates to the character of Marlowe; Jenni Calder in *Heroes*[114] examines the hero in Chandler, Dashiell Hammett, and Ross Macdonald, and relates him to the frontier hero. Frank MacShane has written a very brief introduction to *The Notebooks of Raymond Chandler*[115], stressing Chandler's professionalism. *The World of Raymond Chandler*[116] edited by Miriam Gross is a mixture of criticism and personal reminiscence. The best pieces are 'Omnes Me Impune Lacessunt' by Russell Davies, about the 'struggle between soul-baring and reticence in Raymond Chandler's mind', 'On the Fourth Floor of Paramount', a very amusing interview with Billy Wilder by Ivan Moffat, and 'Marlowe, Men and Women' by Michael Mason, about the feminine domesticity of Marlowe's nature.

A. Grove Day's study of *James Michener*[117], first published in 1964, has now been revised, and a bibliography has been added. *Wallace Stegner*[118] by Forrest G. Robinson and Margaret G. Robinson is the first full-length book on Stegner. It includes much plot summary, examines the fiction carefully and chronologically, and concludes with a comparison with Mark Twain.

Flannery O'Connor and Caroline Gordon: A Reference Guide[119] is in two separate parts. The section on Flannery O'Connor is by Robert E. Golden and goes up to 1976. The section on Caroline Gordon is by Mary C. Sullivan and goes up to 1975. Joan Givner writes of a twenty-page letter from Katherine Anne Porter to Caroline Gordon as 'The Genesis of *Ship of Fools*' (*SLJ*).

Virginia Spencer Carr's *The Lonely Hunter: A Biography of Carson McCullers*[120] is a meticulous, indeed over-meticulous work — as the immensely long list of acknowledgements shows. Carson McCullers's slightest conversation has been recorded; but this has no pretensions to being a critical biography, although Virginia Spencer Carr does let slip damaging admissions such as, 'To her, Edith Sitwell was the greatest poet on earth'. Nancy B. Rich takes seriously the notion of politics as a motivating factor in McCullers in 'The "Ironic Parable of Fascism" in *The Heart is a Lonely Hunter*' (*SLJ*).

Ralph Reckley in 'The Use of the Doppelganger or Double in Chester Himes' *Lonely Crusade*' shows how Himes uses doubles throughout the novel to convey his ideas about the emasculation of the black male.

[114] *Heroes: From Byron to Guevara*, by Jenni Calder. Hamish Hamilton. pp. xii + 211. £6.95.

[115] *The Notebooks of Raymond Chandler and English Summer, A Gothic Romance*, by Raymond Chandler, ed. by Frank MacShane. New York: Ecco P. 1976. pp. 113; 10 illustrations.

[116] *The World of Raymond Chandler*, ed. by Miriam Gross. Weidenfeld & Nicholson. pp. 190; 50 illustrations. £5.95.

[117] *James Michener*, by A. Grove Day. TUSAS. Boston, Mass.: G. K. Hall, (rev. ed.) pp. 195.

[118] *Wallace Stegner*, by Forrest G. Robinson and Margaret G. Robinson. TUSAS. Boston, Mass.: G. K. Hall. pp. 188.

[119] *Flannery O'Connor and Caroline Gordon: A Reference Guide*, by Robert E. Golden and Mary C. Sullivan. Boston, Mass.: G. K. Hall. pp. v + 342. $22.

[120] *The Lonely Hunter: A Biography of Carson McCullers*, by Virginia Spencer Carr. Peter Owen. pp. xix + 598; 27 illustrations. £8.50.

Michael Harper and Robert B. Stepto record 'Study and Experience, an Interview with Ralph Ellison' (*MR*).

Though the work of Wright Morris has never achieved widespread popular success, *Conversations with Wright Morris: Critical Reviews and Responses*[121], edited by Robert E. Knoll, underlines why he has long been accorded critical respect. The book is the product of 'a semester-long celebration of Wright Morris' at the University of Nebraska and it consists of papers delivered at the University in 1975 and of conversations between Morris and various critics; it also contains a portfolio of Morris's own evocative photographs and a bibliography of works by and about Wright Morris. John W. Aldridge and Wayne C. Booth, in their essays and interviews, focus on Morris as part of a specifically American tradition, with Aldridge concentrating on the various possibilities open to the contemporary novelist and Booth on form in Wright's work. David Madden's conversation with Morris concerns style and Morris's own essay is on the importance of memory to the writer.

Robert B. Stepto offers a discussion of 'Richard Wright and Afro-American Literary Tradition' (*MR*).

James Baldwin: A Critical Evaluation[122] edited by Therman B. O'Daniel is an important collection of essays. 'James Baldwin: The Political Anatomy of Space' by Donald B. Gibson considers Baldwin as liberal Democrat. 'Baldwin and the Problem of Being' by George E. Kent concludes by suggesting that Baldwin can and should take more artistic risks. Shirley S. Allen considers 'The Ironic Voice in Baldwin's *Go Tell It On The Mountain*' and Eugenia W. Collier 'The Phrase Unbearably Repeated' (*Do you love me?*) in *Another Country*. 'Baldwin Beside Himself: A Study in Modern Phallicism' by John S. Lash is somewhat woolly. Jacqueline E. Orsagh in 'Baldwin's Female Characters: A Step Forward?' finds Baldwin's women 'believable', and William Edward Farrison in 'If Baldwin's Train Has Not Gone' objects to Baldwin's vulgarity of language. Nick Aaron Ford, Hobart Jarrett, A. Russell Brooks, and Eugenia W. Collier consider Baldwin as essayist. Harry L. Jones writes, not entirely approvingly, on 'Style, Form, and Content in the Short Fiction of James Baldwin', and 'Previous Condition', 'This Morning, This Evening, So Soon', 'Sonny's Blues' and 'Going to Meet the Man' are discussed by, respectively, Sam Bluefarb, John V. Hagopian, John M. Reilly, and Arthenia Bates Millican.

Luc Gaffié's study *Jack Kerouac: The New Picaroon*[123] describes Kerouac's work as 'a landmark in the history of Modern American Literature', but makes little attempt to explain this. The style is stilted — Gaffié remarks carefully that 'Irregular households are common in *On the Road*. Lucile, a stevedore's wife, lives with Sal; Dean, Mary Lou's husband, lives with Camille. The narrator appears to have a great number of female friends'. To quote Gaffié himself on Kerouac: 'Some pages are indeed toilsome reading'.

[121] *Conversations with Wright Morris: Critical Views and Responses*, ed. by Robert E. Knoll. Lincoln, Neb., and London: U. of Nebraska P. pp. xiv + 211. pb £3.

[122] *James Baldwin: A Critical Evaluation*, ed. by Therman B. O'Daniel. Washington, D.C.: Howard U. P. pp. xiii + 273.

[123] *Jack Kerouac: The New Picaroon*, by Luc Gaffié. New York: Postillion P. pp. 65.

The 'myth' of Henry Miller is exploded by Henning Schmidt in an irreverent study of Miller and his critics[124]. His tendency to overestimate his own significance and his need for self-aggrandisement are seen as typical of a specifically American institutionalised individualism. [H.C.C.]

Eric Mottram's energetic and scholarly study of William Burroughs[125] uses all possible source materials in defining and praising Burroughs's art. Mottram follows Burroughs's developing and consistent themes, identifies literary allusions, and investigates, for example, 'puritanical obsession' in *The Ticket That Exploded*.

Gerald Rosen in 'A Retrospective Look at *The Catcher in the Rye*' (*AQ*) assesses the importance to Salinger of Eastern thought and Zen Buddhism.

G. M. Hyde in *Vladimir Nabokov: America's Russian Novelist*[126] discusses the importance to Nabokov of Gogol, Pushkin, Dostoevsky, Tolstoy, and Turgenev. Hyde's important and useful study also examines the role of chess strategy in Nabokov's fiction, and discusses the creativity of his use of language — as does Robert T. Levine in '*Lolita* and the Originality of Style' (*ELWIU*). Jane Grayson's book *Nabokov Translated*[127] describes Nabokov's part in the translation of his own work, outlines his theory of translation, and examines the alterations which Nabokov makes when translating and reworking his fiction and auto-biography: successive versions are analysed for development in narrative technique, structure, characterisation, and style. Especially useful is Jane Grayson's study of the translations for the light they shed on Nabokov's distinctive features of style in English. Strother B. Purdy in *The Hole in the Fabric: Science, Contemporary Literature, and Henry James*[128] presents an extended comparison of *Lolita* with James's *The Awkward Age*. Purdy also compares *Pale Fire* with James's 'The Jolly Corner' and *Ada* with James's *The Sense of the Past*. He feels that *Ada*'s main weaknesses are 'a projection of sentimentalized preindustrial society and a hero who ought to be, but is not, a parody of the romantic-erotic excesses of third-rate Victorian fiction'.

Eugene M. Longen in 'Dickey's *Deliverance*: Sex and the Great Outdoors' (*SLJ*) writes of the fundamental importance of sex in Dickey's novel and the kinds of deliverance associated with it.

Reference guides are available for Louis Auchincloss[129] (going up to 1976) and for Robert Penn Warren[130] (going up to 1975, but recording writings by Robert Penn Warren up to 1977). Peter Stitt presents 'An Interview with Robert Penn Warren' (*SR*) in which Warren talks about

[124] *Der Mythos Henry Miller*, by Henning Schmidt. Heidelberg: Carl Winter (Anglistische Forschungen 118) pp. 277.

[125] *William Burroughs: The Algebra of Need*, by Eric Mottram. Marion Boyars. pp. 282. £6.95. pb £2.95.

[126] *Vladimir Nabokov: America's Russian Novelist*, by G. M. Hyde. Marion Boyars. pp. 230. £6.95.

[127] *Nabokov Translated: A Comparison of Nabokov's Russian and English Prose*, by Jane Grayson. Oxford: O. U. P. pp. xi + 257. £9.50.

[128] *The Hole in the Fabric: Science, Contemporary Literature, and Henry James*, by Strother B. Purdy. Pittsburgh, Pa.: U. of Pittsburgh P. pp. 228. $11.95.

[129] *Louis Auchincloss and His Critics: A Bibliographical Record*, by Jackson R. Bryer. Boston, Mass.: G. K. Hall. pp. xiv + 261. $18.

[130] *Robert Penn Warren: A Reference Guide*, by Neil Nakadate. Boston, Mass.: G. K. Hall. pp. xxii + 396. $30.

his early life, writing, teaching, and editing. J. E. Vacha considers *All the King's Men* in 'It Could Happen Here: The Rise of the Political Scenario Novel' *(AQ)*.

James L. W. West III's descriptive bibliography of William Styron[131] includes an introduction giving some account of Styron's career. Marianne Nault provides the first fully annotated comprehensive listing of Saul Bellow's works and criticism[132]; Everett Carter in *The American Idea; The Literary Response to American Optimism*[133] presents a section on 'Optimism in the Twentieth Century: Saul Bellow' which examines *Henderson the Rain King* as Bellow's use of 'a romantic mode to defend a commonsense realism, a realism that is an Emersonian affirmation of the actual world'.

J. Michael Lennon writes on Mailer's dangerous but generally fruitful relationship with the media in 'Mailer's Sarcophagus: The Artist, The Media, and the "Wad"' *(MFS)*. Pierre Michel writes on Roth's decline in 'What Price Misanthropy? Philip Roth's Fiction' *(ES)*.

William B. Wahl's 'Updike's World and *Couples*' from *Essays in Honour of Professor Tyrus Hillway*[134] views the novel with hostility and, finally, with grudging admiration.

Daniel V. Fraustino's archly titled '*The Country Wife* comes to *The End of the Road:* Wycherley bewitches Barth' *(ArQ)* treats *The Country Wife* as 'source for character, plot, imagery, and theme' in *The End of the Road*. Evelyn Glaser-Wohrer's painstaking and rather humourless study of Barth[135] includes two interviews with him in November 1975, and attempts to summarise his ethics, metaphysics, and aesthetics. Thomas P. Walsh and Cameron Northouse have produced *John Barth, Jerzy Kosinski, and Thomas Pynchon: A Reference Guide*[136], which covers writings about Barth from 1956 to 1973, writings about Kosinski from 1960 to 1973, and writings about Pynchon from 1963 to 1975.

Joseph Fahy considers 'Thomas Pynchon's *V* and Mythology' *(Crit)*. Robert Merrill analyses what he considers a neglected work in 'The Form and Meaning of Pynchon's *The Crying of Lot 49*' *(ArielE)* and David Cowart discusses 'Pynchon's *The Crying of Lot 49* and the Paintings of Remedios Varo' *(Crit)*. Speer Morgan sets Pynchon in the tradition of Sterne in '*Gravity's Rainbow*: What's the Big Idea?' *(MFS)*, Lawrence C. Wolfley declares Pynchon's debt to psychoanalytic criticism in 'Repression's Rainbow: The Presence of Norman O. Brown in Pynchon's Big

[131] *William Styron: A Descriptive Bibliography*, by James L. W. West III. Boston, Mass.: G. K. Hall. pp. xxxvii + 252. $30.
[132] *Saul Bellow: His Works and His Critics: An Annotated International Bibliography*, by Marianne Nault. New York and London: Garland. pp. xix + 191. $18.
[133] *The American Idea: The Literary Response to American Optimism*, by Everett Carter. Chapel Hill, N. J.: U. of North Carolina P. pp. ix + 276. £11.30.
[134] *Essays in Honour of Professor Tyrus Hillway*, ed. by Erwin A. Sturzl. Salzburg: Institut für Englische Sprache und Literatur, Universität Salzburg. pp. 326.
[135] *An Analysis of John Barth's 'Weltanschauung': His View of Life and Literature*, by Evelyn Glaser-Wohrer. Salzburg: Institut für Englische Sprache und Literatur, Universitat Salzburg. pp. 282.
[136] *John Barth, Jerzy Kosinski, and Thomas Pynchon: A Reference Guide*, by Thomas P. Walsh and Cameron Northouse. Boston, Mass.: G. K. Hall. pp. xii + 145. $15.

Novel' (*PMLA*), and Mark R. Siegl stresses the big novel's ambiguities and complexities in 'Creative Paranoia: Understanding the System of *Gravity's Rainbow*' (*Crit*).

4. Drama

Floyd Eddleman's second supplement to *American Drama Criticism*[137] enlarges and brings up to date the previous supplement, and the bibliography is now carried forward to January 1975. Some general remarks on the confusingly disparate organisation of the eighth volume of *The Revels History of Drama in English*[138], treating American Drama, have been made in our Chapter XVII. Travis Bogard's third chapter attempts, by citing examples of dramatists responding to the land, to examine twentieth-century American drama which serves 'as a central reflector of the dominant cultural drives of the nation'. His last chapter, misleadingly titled 'O'Neill versus Shaw', draws parallels between the work of Shaw and O'Neill. O'Neill is treated again in Walter J. Meserve's chapter 'Arrival of a master playwright, Eugene O'Neill'. Bogard provides an analysis of Albee's *Zoo Story* in 'The central reflector' and the same play is cryptically analyzed in Meserve's strikingly mistitled 'Contemporary trends in American drama'. It is also uneconomic to waste space, which could be devoted to expanding the bibliography, in dealing with the work of John Howard Lawson in 'The central reflector' and again in Meserve's 'Distinct approaches for the modern dramatist after 1900'. Meserve's 'Contemporary trends' provides brief and often unclear accounts of some themes handled by individual playwrights. This chapter, with its reference to 'pretenders to scholarship' and 'so-called absurdists', has a suspicious ring of philistinism. The indexing of *American Drama* is somewhat haphazard. Imamu Baraka, Julian Beck, Joseph Chaikin, Joseph Hiller, the Living Theatre, Judith Malina, La Mama Experimental Theatre Club, and the Open Theatre all deserve to be indexed.

The Best Plays of 1976-1977[139], edited by Otis L. Guernsey, is concerned specifically with performances and not all the plays are American. It includes listings of all New York performances, details of aspects of production, awards, and actors. The editor gives extracts from what he considers to have been the ten best plays of the period and there is a directory of professional regional theatres.

Eberhard Bruning, in 'Relations between Progressive American and German Drama in the Twenties and Thirties' (*ZAA*), claims that the influence of the Weimar Republic's progressive theatre was more considerable in America than has been thought. Harry Goldman's 'When Social Significance came to Broadway: "Pins and Needles" in Production' (*ThQ*), is an interesting account of the satirical review of 1937 which managed

[137] *American Drama Criticism: Supplement II*, by Floyd Eugene Eddleman. Hamden, Conn.: Shoe String P., 1976. pp. v + 217. $9.
[138] *The Revels History of Drama in English*, vol. viii, *American Drama*. Methuen, and New York: Barnes & Noble. pp. liii + 324; 31 illustrations. £13.
[139] *The Best Plays of 1976-1977*, ed. by Otis L. Guernsey Jr. New York and Toronto: Dodd, Mead. pp. xi + 483; 106 illustrations. $17.95.

to offend both the Daughters of the American Revolution and the Communist Party. *Pins and Needles* was produced by Labor Stage Inc, part of the International Ladies Garment Workers' Union, and it ran for a record time on Broadway; a private performance was even given at the White House, though black actors were dropped from the cast on that occasion.

The little-known early plays of Djuna Barnes are examined by Louis F. Kannenstine in *The Art of Djuna Barnes*[140], though the focus of the examination is determined by what Kannenstine has to say about the later, better-known *Antiphon*, which is presented as Barnes's 'most compact and definitive work'.

William Klink has produced *Maxwell Anderson and S. N. Behrman: A Reference Guide*[141] in the belief that his subjects are two of America's greatest playwrights, 'ranking below only Eugene O'Neill in achievement'. On Anderson's work the guide reaches only up to 1970, while on Behrman's we are brought up to 1973. Maxwell Anderson's career and plays are discussed in a study by Alfred S. Shivers; his *Maxwell Anderson*[142] treats twenty-five plays in order to give a representative sample of Anderson's work as well as to direct attention to outstanding plays. A. P. Hinchliffe, in *Modern Verse Drama*[143], points out that one of the ways in which the writer of verse drama can overcome the problem of the artifice of his medium is to escape, like Maxwell Anderson, into a remote domestic situation; but Hinchliffe believes that it is unkind to pin the label 'historical dramatist' on Anderson despite his persistent production of poetic, romantic tragedies. The verse drama of Cummings, Stevens, Williams, MacLeish, Eberhart, and Lowell, Hinchliffe regards as essentially 'coterie theatre'. G. L. Evans goes so far as to say that the 'American theatre has been . . . almost wholly bereft of any body of verse drama'. His *The Language of Modern Drama*[144] includes a chapter on O'Neill, Miller, Williams, and Albee, in which there is an interesting discussion of the successes and failures of the language of *Death of a Salesman*. Evans also shows how Tennessee Williams is searching for 'a form of communication which will have the effect of poetry without losing the immediacy of naturalistic prose'. Albee is said to be the 'most brilliantly effective user of the American language in drama'.

Ingrid Rogers, in *Tennessee Williams: A Moralist's Answer to the Perils of Life*[145], deals with a good deal of criticism on Williams and discusses the plays in order, but the book as a whole is somewhat plodding. *Tennessee Williams and Film*[146], by Maurice Yacowar, begins by pointing out how important the cinema has been to Williams since his child-

[140] *The Art of Djuna Barnes: Duality and Damnation*, by Louis F. Kannenstine. New York: New York U. P. pp. xviii + 194.
[141] *Maxwell Anderson and S. N. Behrman: A Reference Guide*, by William Klink. Boston, Mass.: G. K. Hall. pp. xii + 103. $12.
[142] *Maxwell Anderson*, by Alfred S. Shivers. TUSAS. Boston, Mass.: G. K. Hall. 1976. pp. 176. $7.50.
[143] *Modern Verse Drama*, by Arnold P. Hinchliffe. Methuen. pp. 80 £1.20.
[144] *The Language of Modern Drama*, by Gareth Lloyd Evans. Dent, and Totowa, N. J.: Rowman & Littlefield. pp. xx + 252. £6.50.
[145] *Tennessee Williams: A Moralist's Answer to the Perils of Life*, by Ingrid Rogers. Frankfurt: Peter Lang, 1976. pp. ix + 267.
[146] *Tennessee Williams and Film*, by Maurice Yacowar. New York: Frederick Ungar. pp. viii + 168; 9 illustrations.

hood and concludes, after discussing individual film versions of his plays, that the drama has 'weathered' filming rather well. The critical process as developed from the point of view of a director is the focus of N. Joseph Calarco's 'Production as Criticism: Miller's *The Crucible*' (*ETJ*). Calarco writes about a production of the play that ran for two seasons at Wayne State University.

James Baldwin has had only two plays professionally produced and published, but his dramatic output and potential is considered in *James Baldwin: A Critical Evaluation*[147], edited by Therman B. O'Daniel. Carlton W. Molette feels that Baldwin could become a much better playwright if he were to write more drama, but he adds that Baldwin cannot be blamed for not extending his skills in this area considering the present system of producing plays in America. Darwin T. Turner comes to a similar conclusion after examining *Blues for Mister Charlie* and *The Amen Corner* as reflections of 'two divergent positions of contemporary black dramatists'. The *Amen Corner*, he says, is art, whereas '*Blues for Mister Charlie* earned sensation and money for Baldwin'. 'Images of Black Women in Plays by Black Playwrights' (*CLAJ*), by Jeanne-Marie A. Miller, discusses plays by Alice Childress, Lorraine Hansberry, J. E. Franklin, Ron Milner, Ed Bullins, Imamu Baraka, and Adrienne Kennedy. Miller concludes that most of their plays present positive images of women.

Barnet Kellman, in 'David Rabe's "The Orphan": a Peripatetic Work in Progress' (*ThQ*), gives a director's account of the various and developing productions of *The Orphan* and of 'the creative process through which this reworking of Aeschylus' *Oresteia* was linked with the 'seventies through the analogous horrors of My Lai and the Manson murders'. Another casebook of the evolution of a production is Theodore Shank's 'The San Francisco Mime Troupe's Production of "False Promises" ' (*ThQ*). John Rees Moore's 'Perspectives on Modern Drama' (*SR*) is a review-article citing a lot of recent drama criticism and dealing with various tendencies in modern drama and in its reviewing and criticism.

---

[147] *James Baldwin: A Critical Evaluation*, ed. by Therman B. O'Daniel. Washington, D.C.: Howard U. P. pp. xiii + 273.

Index I. Critics

Index II. Authors and Subjects Treated